D1417611

Perceptual and Learning Disabilities in Children

Perceptual and Learning

VOLUME 2

EDITED BY

AND

Disabilities in Children

RESEARCH AND THEORY

William M. Cruickshank, Ph.D.
University of Michigan

Daniel P. Hallahan, Ph.D.
University of Virginia

SYRACUSE UNIVERSITY PRESS 1975

Syracuse, New York 13210

FIRST EDITION

Library of Congress Cataloging in Publication Data
Cruickshank, William M., 1915–
Perceptual and learning disabilities in children.

Includes bibliographies and indexes.
CONTENTS: v. 1. Psychoeducational practices.—v. 2. Research and theory.
1. Learning disabilities. 2. Perception, Disorders of. I. Hallahan, Daniel P., 1944– joint author. II. Title. [DNLM: 1. Education, Special. 2. Learning disorders. 3. Perceptual disorders—In infancy and childhood. 4. Psychology, Educational. LC4661 C955p]
LC4704.C78 371.9′2 74-24303
ISBN 0-8156-2165-5 (v.1)
ISBN 0-8156-2166-3 (v.2)

Manufactured in the United States of America

Preface

The amount of literature that has appeared in the past thirty years directly or indirectly related to children with perceptual and specific learning disabilities is voluminous. In an earlier publication (D. P. Hallahan and W. M. Cruickshank, *Psychoeducational Foundations of Learning Disabilities,* Prentice-Hall, 1973) an attempt was made to bring the psychological and educational literature into historical perspective. It became apparent that the problem was significantly greater than anticipated and that a still more inclusive publication was needed.

Since the appearance of the term "learning disability" in 1963, a degree of heterogeneity has developed regarding the definition of the term which has served to produce confusion in the field as a whole and to result in poor programming for children needing services. Recently, in connection with a national study, a committee (whose membership consisted of Dr. Joseph Wepman, University of Chicago; Dr. Charles Strother, University of Washington; Dr. Cynthia Deutsch, New York University; Dr. Anne Morency, University of Chicago; and Dr. William Cruickshank, University of Michigan) submitted a report which directed attention to a definition of this problem based upon perceptual problems of a neurological origin. There is little question but that originally the concepts held about a problem in children, later designated as "learning disability," were based on a similar orientation. Only since 1963 has the term been extended to include remedial reading concepts, remedial arithmetic problems, emotional disturbances, and a great variety of more esoteric problems. The imprecise use of the term has created communication difficulties among professional people, parents, and legislators.

The two volumes included in this publication—Volume 1, *Psychoeducational Practices,* and Volume 2, *Research and Theory*—contain writings from physicians, psychologists, nutritionists, audiologists, speech pathologists, and educators, among others, and an attempt has been made to broaden the base initiated by the Hallahan and Cruickshank volume noted above. Each of the contributors to the present volumes has essentially viewed the assignment from the point of view of the emerging definition of the problem. Children who have experienced a prenatal, perinatal, or postnatal impact on the central nervous system, whether specially diagnosed or assumed, present highly individualized characteristics of perceptual disturbance. It is assumed by a growing number of persons that environmental and nutritional deprivations likewise produce behavior and perceptual characteristics which are like or closely approximate those of children who have a known specific neurological disturbance. The direct relationship on the neurological and perceptual systems is still subject to investigation, but the issue is significantly joined so that in these volumes chapters on these two areas have been included.

We believe these books are appropriate for courses in learning disabilities, other areas of special education, developmental pediatrics, and abnormal child development. The classroom teacher, too, should find practical teaching suggestions as well as a solid research and theoretical foundation for these techniques.

These two volumes continue the effort, begun as early as 1966 on the part of one of the editors, to provide professional up-dating for those who rear and work with children who have perceptual and specific learning disabilities. This effort will undoubtedly have to continue for many years in the future, for the problem is not yet satisfactorily defined, nor is it in any sense thoroughly researched. The reader will note areas which still need to be reviewed in relation to the central issue of the books. Research in such areas as physiology, ophthalmology, otology, reaction to color, and exploratory research in gustation, olfaction, the tactual modality, and response to thermal change and relative humidity need to be included in future publications. It is hoped, however, that in bringing together the material included here we have assisted the reader in reaching a more realistic understanding of what perceptual and learning disabilities in children really are.

Fall 1974

WILLIAM M. CRUICKSHANK
DANIEL P. HALLAHAN

Contents

List of Figures

List of Tables

Perceptual and Learning Disabilities in Children

Editors' note: Dr. Joaquín Cravioto and Ms. Elsa DeLicardie have, through their research, brought to the scientific community the realization that environmental and nutritional deprivation are significant factors in the production of learning problems. Their research in a variety of places around the globe has begun to extend the parameters of the impact of nutritional deprivation to include neurological and psychological functioning. This chapter presents the major results of their many years of research into nutritional and environmental deprivation. The potential of field-based research is highlighted in this chapter. Cravioto and DeLicardie have successfully performed the arduous task of obtaining research data to verify the dire need for social reform. Their chapter points to the rewards gained from systematic, scientific exploration of a problem facing millions of individuals.

Joaquín Cravioto, M.D., M.P.H., D.Sc., is Chairman of the Scientific Research Division, Chief of the Nutrition Services, and Head of the Group for Research on the Relation Among Nutrition, Environment, and Mental Development and Learning, Hospital del Niño, Mexican Institution for Child Care (IMAN). He is Professor of Pediatrics at the National University of Mexico. Dr. Cravioto was formerly Chief of the Teaching Division Hospital Infantil de Mexico and Professor of Nutrition School of Public Health, Ministry of Health and Welfare of Mexico. He is a fellow of the Society for Pediatric Research (USA), fellow of the American Institute of Nutrition, a full member of the National Academy of Medicine (Mexico), and of the Protein Advisory Group of the United Nations System. Dr. Cravioto has done research on the clinical, biochemical, and social aspects of infantile malnutrition with particular reference to the study of the late consequences of early malnutrition.

Elsa R. DeLicardie B.A., M.Sc., is Chief of the Research and Training Rural Center of the Mexican Institution for Child Care (IMAN), Senior Investigator of the Group for Research on the Relation Among Nutrition, Environment and Mental Development and Learning, Hospital del Niño IMAN. Associate Professor of Growth and Development, Graduate School of Pediatric Nursing, IMAN, she was formerly Assistant Professor of Statistics in Psychology and Assistant Professor of Experimental Psychology at the University of San Carlos, Guatemala. She is Associate Professor, Postgraduate Training in Pediatrics, National University of Mexico at the Children's Hospital, and a member of the Mexican Society for Pediatric Research, a founding member of the Association of Perinatology of Mexico, and a Full Member of the College of Humanities of the San Carlos University of Guatemala, Central America. Ms. DeLicardie has done research on the short- and long-term effects of infantile malnutrition, on the effects of social class on learning, and on the mental development of rural infants and children in preindustrial societies.

1

Environmental and Learning Deprivation in Children with Learning Disabilities

JOAQUÍN CRAVIOTO AND ELSA R. DELICARDIE

The second-half of the twentieth century has witnessed an increasing degree of concern both with the health of peoples and with the requirements of national development and public policy. This in turn has led to the consideration of "unfavorable environment" as an important factor in the life of an individual from the time of gestation to the time of his or her acceptance of full responsibility as a socially functioning adult. As the growth of a society becomes more dependent on industrial- and science-oriented technologies, and to the degree to which social and economic status is identified with scholastic achievement, intellectual performance and learning come more to the forefront of public and scientific concern. The loud voice and political weight of minority groups in the affluent countries and the awareness of the conditions under which the majority of the world's population live today have helped to maintain the interest of scientists in the search for the reasons behind the well-documented differences in achievement and behavior between individuals living in privileged and underprivileged conditions.

Among the many factors that comprise the child's environment, nutrition was recognized as important for the adequate growth and development of infants and children even before child care became a scientific discipline. Perhaps the greatest impetus to the study of the relation of nutrition to health and to human development was given by the work of Sir John Boyd Orr who, in his classic book "Food, Health and Income" (1936), analyzed the relation among nutrition, development, and health performance in the population of an advanced industrial country. Twenty-three years later Leitch (1959) introduced the genetic dimension into the picture and pointed out that both in industrial and preindustrial countries or between social classes in any country there was always a gradient with wealth

The authors' research has been supported in part by the Nutrition Foundation Inc., the Foundation for Child Development (formerly Association for the Aid of Crippled Children), the Foundation von Monell, and the van Ameringen Foundation.

in quantity and quality of diet associated with parallel gradients in rate of growth and adult stature, physical performance, mental ability and resistance to disease.

The scientific endeavor in the field of nutrition and mental development and learning has progressed from mere descriptive studies on differences in performance between well-nourished and malnourished individuals to attempts at identifying the role of the nutritional variable *vis à vis* other variables that almost always are present in the environments in which malnutrition occurs.

Learning to learn seems to be an ability particularly evolved in the human organism. This ability is manifested in the child by the emergence of so-called learning strategies which in a simplistic form could be described as composed of a series of subroutines or modules, and of the rules that determine the adequacy of their combinations. Attention to differences in learning strategies as a function of social class has brought a new qualitative dimension to the studies on environmental influences on mental development, which with few exceptions have dealt largely with the magnitude of the difference rather than with the style of behavior. In this same category can be placed a few studies concerned with the qualitative aspects of behavior shown by children reared in different environments.

In this paper we have attempted a review of selected investigations which in our opinion represent the current status of research in the area of environmental and nutrition factors involved in learning disability.

The term "learning disabled" is given to children who fail to learn in circumstances under which most children of the same culture ordinarily learn, *learning* being defined as "any lasting change in behavior that is not the result of fatigue or disease" (Nathan 1963). In the field of psychology there is no longer a discussion of the genetic or environmental nature of performance and behavior. It is widely accepted that inheritance and environment are interdependent factors whose interactive role determines the level of performance and achievement. At each stage of development the human organism is the product of his or her genetic endowment and environmental past history. The environment of the present provides the immediate stimuli which determine the specific behavior exhibited by the individual at each time in life. In this manner, any individual characteristic is the result of the combined influences of environmental and genetic conditions. This concept does not imply that a specific difference among groups or among individuals cannot be explained as solely due to either genetic or environmental factors. It has been stated (Throne 1970, 1972) that even the radical behaviorists agree that organismic variables, genetic or acquired, do contribute to behavior since environment does not act in a vacuum; it requires a responding organism in terms of whose effects the effectiveness of the environment is expressed. At present, it can be accepted that heredity and environment do not interact as additive combinations. The quantitative effect of either is dependent on the contribution given by the other factor. Thus, the contribution of heredity to the variance of a certain trait or characteristic is not a constant but a variable whose magnitude depends on the environment in which the individual is located. Similarly, under different genetic conditions the same environment would contribute in different proportions. The fundamental research question at present deals with the ways through which heredity and environment influence learning and behavior, not with the quantitative contribution made by each. This shift in the investigation of the issue is important because it opens the possibility of changes in the behavior and learning of the individual through the manipulation of the environmental and genetic variables either alone or in specific combinations at specific times during the individual's development. In more practical terms, this is the view of radical behaviorists when they claim that children with learning disabilities or mentally retarded, brain-damaged, cerebral palsied, and in general handicapped children respond more successfully under extraordinary environmental conditions. It is this need for extraordinary environments that, at least responsively, is all that distinguishes them from normal children. Given those special environments handicapped children would function more successfully, whatever their organismic statuses (Throne 1973).

If *intelligence* is operationally defined as the process through which the child learns the use of the tools of this culture in order to know and manipulate the environment, it is easy to accept that at each stage of development intelligence will be directly associated with both the genetic endowment of the individual and the several environments in which the child has lived so far. Different environments would affect differently the development of intelligence and the relative proportions of genetic and environmental variances in intelligence test scores.

Preindustrial societies, which hold more than two-thirds of the world's population, are characterized by the presence of a large sector of the population having little or no systematic access to modern technology and scientific thinking. Such low social and economic segments differ from the remainder in a host of other variables. They tend to have poorer housing, higher morbidity and mortality, lower levels of formal education, greater degrees of attachment to outmoded and inadequate patterns of child care, and in general to live in circumstances which are less conducive to the development of technologic and educational competence (Cravioto 1958, 1967). Among these segments of society cognition is seldom identified as an active powerful tool of individual achievement. This is most often seen during infancy and the preschool years. In the presence of low purchasing power, resulting directly from the lack of modern technology and factual information, parents are preoccupied with the more pressing needs of life. Problems related to housing, sufficient food, employment, transportation, disease, physical energy, family conflict, and economic and physical safety take the highest priority. Under this load, frequently neglected are activities of the infant and preschool child in manipulating and exploring his physical environment and in being introduced through play to auditory, visual, and tactile stimuli that constitute the precursors of symbols. Seldom is there time for the adult to play with, talk, or read to a child. In many of these families there is a lack of awareness of the importance of these activities for the child's development.

Since the factors cited are present in various degrees in different communities, and also vary within families in the same community, it is possible to identify several patterns of life style, nutrition, health, and child care among the underprivileged members of the society. The study of child development, behavior, and learning across the gradient of disadvantage has permitted the assessment of the effects of environment and genetics on intelligence and learning.

Taking race and social class as the environmental variables, Scarr-Salapatek (1971) has outlined important concepts and methods in the study of individual and group variation and has described a new study of genetic and environmental variances in aptitude scores in black and white and advantaged and disadvantaged populations. Two major competing hypotheses for the prediction of the relation among social class, race, and intelligence test scores (IQ) have been advanced: the environmental-disadvantage

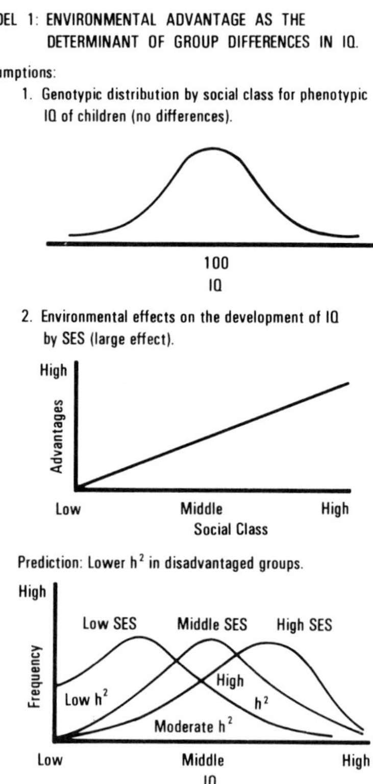
MODEL 1: ENVIRONMENTAL ADVANTAGE AS THE DETERMINANT OF GROUP DIFFERENCES IN IQ.
Assumptions:
1. Genotypic distribution by social class for phenotypic IQ of children (no differences).
100
IQ
2. Environmental effects on the development of IQ by SES (large effect).
High
Advantages
Low
Middle
High
Social Class
Prediction: Lower h² in disadvantaged groups.
High
Frequency
Low SES
Middle SES
High SES
Low h²
High h²
Moderate h²
Low
Middle
High
IQ

Figure 1.1. Environmental disadvantage, Model 1. h^2 is heritability for twins; SES is socioeconomic status. *From Cravioto* et al. Science *174* (*1971*):*1285*.

hypothesis and the genotype-distribution hypothesis. Both hypotheses make differential predictions about the proportions of genetic and environmental variance in IQ within lower and higher social class groups.

The environmental-disadvantage hypothesis assumes that lower-class whites and most blacks, at least in the USA, live under conditions suppressive for the development of IQ. Defining "suppressive environments" as those which neither permit nor evoke the development of a genetic characteristic, the disadvantage hypothesis predicts that IQ scores within advantaged groups will show larger proportions of genetic variance and smaller proportions of environmental variance than IQ scores for disadvantaged groups.

The genotype-distribution hypothesis assumes that social-class differences in IQ are mainly genetic in origin and are a consequence of the high heritability of IQ throughout the population, assortative mating for IQ, and a small contribution stemming from the educational advantages that brighter parents may provide for their brighter children. According to this hypothesis environmental differences between groups are seen as insignificant in determining total phenotypic variance in intelligence test scores. The prediction derived from the hypothesis is that the proportion of genetic variance in IQ scores will be equally high for all social-class groups and for all races.

Figures 1.1 and 1.2, taken from Scarr-Salapatek, illustrate the two hypothesis as they apply to social class. In Model 1, the assumption is one of equal distribution of genotypes across social classes. In Model 2, there are assumed to be unequal distributions of genotypes for IQ, the lower class having proportionally more genotypes for low IQ, and the upper social class having proportionally more genotypes for high IQ. The effects of environment would be minimal in Model 2 and strong in Model 1. In this latter model environmental factors are predicted to reduce the mean and the heritability of IQ in the lower social-class groups and raise both in the higher social groups. Model 2 predicts that regardless of the quality of the environments and regardless of mean scores, equally high heritabilities will be present in all social-class groups.

Accepting that the black group contains a larger proportion of disadvantaged children, the environmental-disadvantage hypothesis must predict a smaller proportion of genetic variance to account for differences in phenotypic IQ among blacks than among whites as whole populations. On the other hand, since the genotypic-distribution hypothesis predicts no difference in the proportion of genetic variance for social-class groups within the races, it should come as a corollary that blacks and whites should have the same proportions of genetic variance.

In order to test the hypotheses, all twins attending the public schools of Philadelphia, Pennsylvania, in April 1968 were identified. The total number of twins included 493 opposite-sex pairs and 1,028 same-sex pairs. The racial distribution of these twins was 36 percent white and 59 percent black. After losses for several reasons 635 black and 357 white pairs were studied. Census tract information from 1960 was used to assign pairs to relatively

MODEL 2: GENETIC DIFFERENCES AS THE PRIMARY DETERMINANT OF GROUP DIFFERENCES IN IQ.

Assumptions:

1. Genotypic distribution by social class for phenotypic IQ of children (differences).

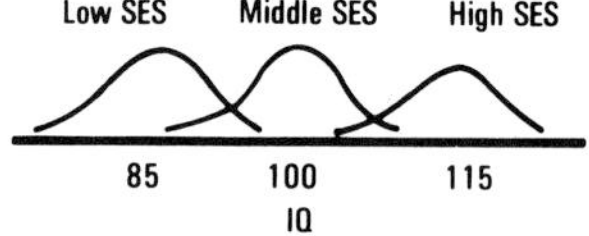

2. Environmental effects on the development of IQ by SES (small effect).

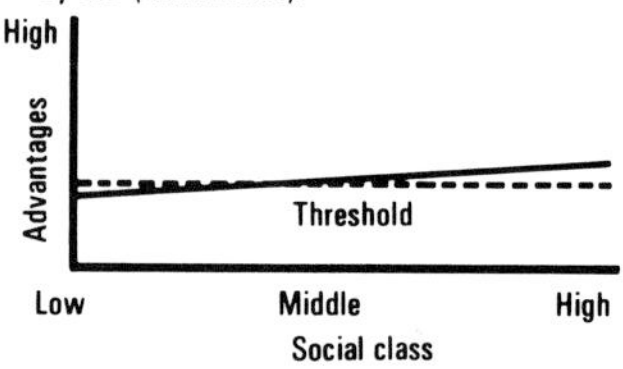

Prediction: Equal h^2 in all groups.

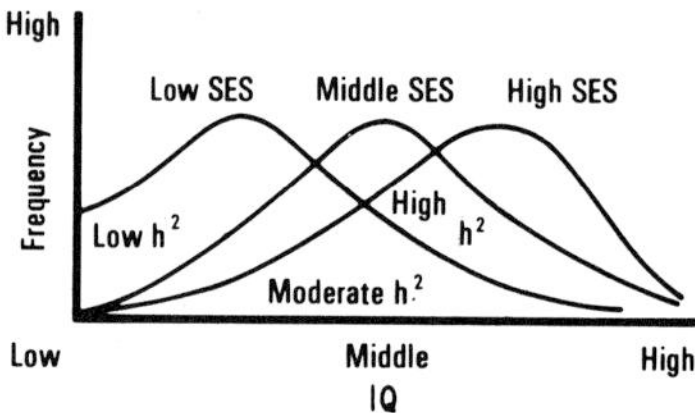

Figure 1.2. Genetic differences, Model 2. h^2 is heritability for twins; SES is socioeconomic status. *From Cravioto* et al. Science *174* (*1971*):*1285.*

advantaged and disadvantaged groups. Social-class assignment was made by establishing a median level of income and educational characteristics for the total number of census tracts from which the twin sample was drawn, regardless of race. Cross-tabulations of above- and below-median levels of income and education provided three groups: one below the census tract medians for both income and education; one above the medians in both; and a third above in one and below in the other. On this basis, the three groups were designated as below median, above median, and middle status. Aptitude and achievement tests were obtained in a total of 319 black and 163 white pairs. The Iowa Test of Basic Skills was used to measure scholastic achievement. The vocabulary, reading, language total, arithmetic total, and composite scores were obtained. Aptitude tests included in all cases two subtests, a verbal and a nonverbal or numerical, besides a total score.

By means of statistical techniques estimates of heritability were calculated. Once the heritability of a trait was known, the total variance could be apportioned into four major components: within-family genetic variance, within-family environmental variance, between-family genetic variance, and

Table 1.1
Percentages of Variance in Nonverbal Aptitude Scores for Opposite-Sex Twins by Race and Social Class

Source	Disadvantaged			Advantaged		
	Between Family	Within Family	Total	Between Family	Within Family	Total
			Black			
Genetic	*	*	*	35.4	29.0	64.4
Environmental	52.3	47.7	*	8.3	27.3	35.6
Total	52.3	47.7	*	43.7	56.3	100.0
			White			
Genetic	*	*	*	2.3	1.9	4.2
Environmental	61.9	38.1	*	60.2	35.6	95.8
Total	61.9	38.1	*	62.5	37.5	100.0

*Cannot be estimated.

Source: *Science* 174(1971):1,285.

between-family environmental variance. It may be of interest to remember that the heritability of a trait is an expression of the ratio of the total genetic variance to total phenotypic variance.

As can be seen in Tables 1.1 and 1.2, taken as examples of the main findings, the percentage of total variance attributable to environmental sources was always lower in the advantaged groups of both blacks and whites. In most cases genetic variance could not be estimated for the aptitude scores of lower-class children. Although in both advantaged and disadvantaged children, there were approximately equal variances between and within families, there was a tendency for the between-variance to be somewhat larger. The analysis of variance demonstrated that advantaged and disadvantaged children differed mainly in the proportion of variance in aptitude scores that could be attributed to environmental sources. Analysis

Table 1.2
Percentages of Variance in Total Aptitude for Opposite-Sex Twins by Race and Social Class

Source	Disadvantaged			Advantaged		
	Between Family	Within Family	Total	Between Family	Within Family	Total
			Black			
Genetic	*	*	*	14.3	11.7	26.0
Environmental	59.9	40.1	*	42.7	31.3	74.0
Total	59.9	40.1	*	57.0	43.0	100.0
			White			
Genetic	*	*	*	21.5	17.5	39.0
Environmental	63.1	36.9	*	43.5	17.5	61.0
Total	63.1	36.9	*	65.0	35.0	100.0

*Cannot be estimated.

Source: *Science* 174(1971):1,285.

of the data separately for same-sex pairs gave correlations of the same order of magnitude. Thus, it could be concluded that the lower mean scores of disadvantaged children, regardless of race, were explained in a large part by the lower genetic variance in their scores.

An analysis of the data separating the children according to their level of aptitude demonstrated that siblings below the aptitude mean had consistently lower correlations between their scores than did siblings above the mean in aptitude scores. The lower correlations between siblings with lower scores were not a function of social class, but of smaller between-pair variances. The findings are consistent with the idea that children with lower IQs are less susceptible to environmental differences between families than are children with higher IQs.

The main results of Scarr-Salapatek's study reveal that the mean intelligence test scores and the percentage of genetic variance of children developing in unfavorable environments are mainly a function of the rearing condition of the population. In other words, the study confirms the view that given a better environment disadvantaged children will have higher mean scores and higher genetic variance. The opportunity of having these children reach their genetic potential could thus be achieved.

As the field is moving away from the controversy of genetics versus environment as the explanation for the differences found between children of high and low social class, interest has centered more and more around the realization that the whole life of an individual is a continuous process of solving the problems of transaction between the organism and the environment. Therefore, from gestation, the human is viewed as a learner, as an individual selectively responding to stimuli, and as a developer of patterns of response that will influence behavior in later periods of life. It is the study of these mechanisms of interchange between the individual and the environment that have motivated research workers to address themselves to the question of how sociocultural experience is translated into cognitive behavior and academic achievement. One way of approaching the problem is through the conceptualization of the social-class construct as an array of clearly identifiable experiences and patterns of experiences that may be systematically examined in relation to their possible effects on the formation of the cognitive makeup of the child along his or her different stages of development. The question could be thus paraphrased: what, operationally, is environmental deprivation, and how does it act to modulate and depress the genetic potential of the individual's mentation?

In trying to investigate this issue research workers have used two main strategies—comprehensive multifactoral studies, and experimental or clinical observation studies that focus on specific individual factors. The first strategy is based on the concept that a complex interaction of biologic, psychologic, and sociocultural factors may be involved in the etiology of psychosocial maladaptation; therefore, if a large number of children with that condition are studied relative to a large number of variables it will be possible to determine the role played by each variable in the sample population of affected children. The principal merit of this approach is that it allows for a degree of generalization to the broad population of children from which the study sample was drawn. The limitation of this type of study is the frequent lack of specificity in defining a particular facet of the problem under consideration. The second methodological approach focuses more specifically on the variables being studied. Selection of population sample is done on the basis of specifically defined etiological factors, or groups of children with specific outcomes are studied relative to a specific variable considered as important by the researcher. This second strategy can provide a large body of information about either the specific population studied or the specific variable investigated. It also offers the possibility of identifying deviant children early in life by focusing detection on populations most at risk for developing those disorders. The main limitation of this approach is that the more specific the population studied, and the more specific the variable selected, the more limited the generalizations that can be made with respect to the broad population of children under consideration (Walzer 1973).

In dealing with the so-called lower achievement or in general lower scores or non-normal behavior, it is extremely important to recognize the context in which these categorizations are made. In the words of Rafferty (1973):

> Every individual behavior event is simultaneously a social event in some multi-individual system such as a family, classroom, school, neighborhood, ethnic group, or social class. The behavior is scrutinized as a social event and a value placed on it, but a value relative to the social system doing the evaluation. Quite probably that value would be different in a different social system. This type of situation leaves the normalcy or deviancy of a behavior to be determined by a political process and opens the way for the oppression of people by other people who have the political power, however derived, to specify deviancy and its treatment.

In order to explain the differences in cognitive functioning found between socioeconomic levels, one of the earliest hypotheses proposed that the tasks employed in those studies have often been measures of academic ability and have typically involved materials and procedures not familiar to most lower-class children. According to this hypothesis it was not possible to determine whether differences in performance were derived from differences in familiarity with the task materials or in the level of cognition. Odom (1967) tested this hypothesis in a study using a three-choice discrimination task in which one of the choices was partially rewarded while the remaining two were never rewarded. Children five, six, and ten years old were adscribed to low or median social-class according to their family score on the Minnesota Scale of Parental Occupations (Goodenough and Anderson 1954). According to the author there was no reason to believe that the children from any socioeconomic level were familiar with the procedures involved in the testing situation.

The three-choice discrimination task was selected because a previous study of Weir (1964) had shown that the kind of strategies used by individuals from three to twenty years of age, belonging to the middle- and upper-middle social class, were typical of different age groups. Thus, a strategy which involved selection of the relevant stimulus regardless of outcome, win-stay or lose-stay strategy was most frequently observed in the three- and five-year-old group. Children from seven to eleven years of age used a type of searching strategy involving left-middle-right, and right-middle-left pattern responses. Since pattern responses were considered as indicators of hypothesis testing, the searching strategy was accepted to reflect a higher level of cognitive development than the strategy of win-stay or lose-stay, which was assumed to reflect a maximization strategy and an inability on the part of the younger group to form more complex task-related hypotheses.

The results confirmed that as age increased the strategies thought to reflect higher cognitive processes also increased. Similarly, as socioeconomic level increased, higher-order strategies also increased. Another important finding in Odom's study was the lack of correlation between the IQ scores, derived from the California Test of Mental Maturity or the Lorge-Thorndike Intelligence Test, and the performance measures in any of the four older age and socioeconomic groups. The lack of correlation between a qualitative feature of development, such as problem-solving strategies, and a quantitative measure of intelligence has been corroborated in other studies dealing with concept formation and IQ (Bresnahan and Shapiro 1972).

Odom's results lead to the rejection of unfamiliarity with materials and/or testing procedures as the explanation for differences in performance levels between children varying in social class. Thus, a confirmation of actual differences in measures of performance among children living in different environments should be accepted.

Since the social-class construct is too vague a term, research workers have attempted to define in a more specific way some of the relevant elements in the environment associated with identifiable patterns of behavior. Jacobson *et al.* (1971) for example, have shown that systematic modifications, either cognitive or motivational, change the performance level of children of a homogeneous social class. A marked increase in intelligence scores was observed in low socioeconomic-class children as a result of a systematic modification of factors related to cognition. When motivational factors of a social nature were introduced, change in intelligence level was observed only in those children whose initial IQs were around the mean value. It seems of importance to point out that in low-class children a period of systematic experiential activities with a duration of only twenty hours was sufficient to change significantly the intelligence scores derived from the Stanford-Binet Test.

A somewhat similar approach was utilized by Beckwith (1971), who, analyzing the environment of twenty-four children adopted by middle-class families, found that the frequency of opportunities that the child had for exploring his or her home, the degree of contact with other adults besides the mother, and the quantity of verbal communication between mother and child were the factors more strongly correlated with the intelligence scores derived from the Catell Test and with the performance of motor ability as measured by the Gesell technique.

One of the most impressive studies on the relation between quality of environment and performance is the study of Skeels (1966), who was able to follow up a group of twenty-five children from age twelve months until adulthood. Thirteen children who were mentally retarded were transferred at the age of eighteen months to an institution where the relation between mother surrogate and children was considered good. Eleven of these thirteen children were later placed in substitute homes. The other twelve children from the original twenty-five had a mean twenty-two points above the mean of the IQ of the mentally retarded group. This comparison group remained during a long period of time in an orphanage whose environment was not stimulating at all. It is appropriate to state that this comparison group was not a control group in the sense of an experimental design; according to Skeels it was just not possible to modify the environment of this group.

After two years of living in these contrasting environments the group with a better environment showed a mean increment of 28.5 points in intellectual quotient while the group of children with a poor environment showed a mean loss of 26.2 points in intellectual score.

After a lapse of twenty-one years it was possible to locate all cases. Both groups had maintained divergent patterns of intellectual competence. None of the thirteen children whose environment was modified at an earlier age were living in institutions. As a contrast, of the twelve children in the group with a poor environment one had remained in an institution for mentally retarded children until the age of adolescence, when the child died. Three other children were in institutions for mentally retarded, and a fourth was a patient in a hospital for mental disorders. The educational level of both groups of children also was markedly different. The group without modification of the environment at an early age had a mean scholarity of three grades while the group with environmental modification had a median of scholarity equivalent to twelve grades. Four of these individuals had one or more years of college studies, and one was a college graduate. The occupation of the group which changed its environment was at a level entirely similar to that of the general population of the USA according to the census data of 1960. As a contrast the individuals who could not change their environment were either interns of institutions or were employed as servants.

Because the study of Skeels has a number of methodological faults, his results cannot be taken literally, but it certainly shows that at least some children considered as mentally retarded at a very early age can perform as normal adults if they are transferred early in life to a better environment.

It might be of interest to mention here that Kagan (1969) has proposed that the genetic endowment of the individual does not produce a specific level of mental ability but rather what it gives is a range within which the reaching of the superior or inferior level will be determined by the environmental experiences that the child will have during his life. This notion could explain why even middle-class children exhibit a marked degree of plasticity in their behavioral development. A reinforcement for this point of view is given by studies that have demonstrated a direct relation between maternal characteristics or infant's personality and level of mental performance in normal children (Honzik 1957; Moss and Kagan 1958; Stern *et al.* 1969).

In the search for differences and similarities that may be attributed to social-class membership, the need for taking into account some features of the microenvironment of life style, in order to form subgroups out of the classical classification through occupation, education, and income, is becoming more and more apparent.

Adler (1973), in a sort of exploratory investigation, has studied the relationship between articulatory deviancies and social-class membership, extending the usual criteria of social-class as measured by education and occupation with the inclusion of a socio-psychological appraisal of the home environment, particularly the presence or absence of a father figure, the stability of the environment, and the chronicity of welfare aid, in an attempt to separate the lower-social class into two subgroups: the upper-lower and the lower-lower. Articulation test scores of a group of socially different children receiving speech therapy in public schools were chosen at random for the study. The incorrect responses to items 19–43 on the Templin-Darley Articulation Test, previously administered by ten speech correctionists employed in the school system, were related to the children's social-class membership. To test for interaction between social class and race two different ethnic groups, black and white, were included in the comparisons.

After confirming Winitz's (1969) findings of a higher number of articulatory errors in the lower social-class children, and Templin's (1957) report that poor children have an elevated frequency of omissions and substitutions of consonants in all positions, Adler's data showed differences according to race and socioeconomic status. The main value of this work is the clear demonstration of the race–social-class interaction, with the circumstance that if the microenvironment is not taken into consideration the socioeconomic differences tend to disappear. Thus for example, the analysis of the percentage of incorrect replies to phonemes according to race and social class showed that for both black and white the percent of voiced and unvoiced *th* deviancies was high regardless of social-class differences. On the other hand, the frequency of incorrectly pronounced *r* was much higher in the white than in the black children. Sibilants showed still a different pattern, being more frequently differentially articulated by lower–lower-class white children as compared to upper–lower-class white children. The small number of children included in the study, particularly in the black group, prevents any conclusion to be forwarded, but the study points toward the importance of a proper classification that should take into account both culture as represented by the ethnic group and social class at both the macro- and microenvironmental levels.

Perhaps the greatest advance in our knowledge of the role played by social class in learning has come from the studies of Jean L. Bresnahan and Martin M. Shapiro and co-workers (1972). These investigators have approached the study of behavioral differences between social classes asking themselves what are the necessary or sufficient environmental conditions for the establishment of identifiable patterns of behavior. To answer this question children classified as belonging to the higher or lower social class, on the basis of occupation, income, and education of their parents, were trained to select one of two stimuli on the basis of size or on the basis of number. It was postulated that the discrepancy in the performance of the two groups would be reduced if reinforcers and tasks appropriate to the lower group were utilized. Therefore, the stimuli and apparatus were chosen or constructed with the intent of maximizing performance for the lower group, and tasks and incentives were manipulated in order to investigate the kind of situations which will produce equal or differential success between higher- and lower-class groups.

Defining "concept formation" as the acquisition of common responses to dissimilar stimuli, children were tested for the concepts of size and number. It was considered that size is a concept that all children learn by themselves at a very early age. Number, on the other hand, is a concept more dependent on specific teaching by others, or at least more related to previous training. For the experimental tasks buttons were used as stimuli. The selection was made on the basis of familiarity of the children with the object and use of actual objects, not of pictorial representations or small facsimiles that might have given upper-class children certain advantages. The size and number tasks differed in difficulty in another important aspect which is related to the functional conceptual classification. From infancy, size is a relevant and pervasive dimension for all children. It is a variable which they encounter in countless ways. Even more specifically, the attribute of "bigness" itself comes to have positive value for the child. Since in the case of buttons, size can be considered the most obvious and most functional dimension, it was expected that the task of choosing the larger of two different sizes of buttons would be extremely easy. Choosing the button with the greater number of holes, however, has very little relevance to experience in an ordinary environment since the utility of number of holes with respect to the usual function of buttons is trivial. When contrasted with the dimensions of size and color, the number of holes is a rather obscure dimension.

The incentives included in the testing with the idea they would result in different levels of performance were knowledge of results only, knowledge of results plus social reinforcement, and knowledge of results plus social reinforcement plus a tangible reward. Ninety-eight first-grade girls were used in the study. The Peabody Picture Vocabulary Test was administered in the experiment room. Immediately after completion of the intelligence test, the concept-acquisition experiments were conducted in a game-like situation.

The first finding of interest was that although there was a significant difference in the mean IQ of the two social classes, correlations and partial correlations between IQ and the concept-formation tasks yielded insignificant results in all cases.

The acquisition curves showed that size was significantly easier than number as a task. On the number task the higher-class group made fewer errors, and on the size task the lower-class group made fewer errors. This reversal was reflected in a 0.06 probability of interaction between socioeconomic status and task.

Since the lower-class group performed better on the size problem, the question arose as to whether this group was using size differences in their attempt to solve the number problems. The design of the experiment permitted the analysis of trials in which size and number were correlated and of trials in which size and number were uncorrelated. The results showed that the lower-class children maintained a partially successful size hypothesis on the number problem.

It is generally considered that on a concept-formation problem the subject selects a hypothesis and retains it until he or she makes an incorrect response, at which time the subject rejects the hypothesis and samples a new one. If the hypothesis produces the correct response the subject stays with it. If the hypothesis produces an incorrect response, the subject shifts to a new hypothesis. This strategy is known as "win-stay, lose-shift." The lower-class children did not display this win-stay, lose-shift behavior, but continued to perseverate on a partially reinforced hypothesis. On the number task the size hypothesis produced approximately 75 percent reinforcement, and the lower-class child persisted with the size hypothesis despite the fact that a number hypothesis would have been reinforced 100 percent of the time. As a contrast, young higher-class children adopted a win-stay, lose-shift strategy which ultimately resulted in nearly perfect performance even when the 100 percent reinforced hypothesis corresponded to a dimension low in their hierarchy.

Bresnahan continued the investigation, reasoning that if the lower performance of lower-class children was a consequence of their inconsistent reinforcement histories, the introduction of chaotic reinforcement into the histories of higher-class children would lead to a comparable decrement in their performance (Bresnahan and Blum 1971).

Thirty boys and thirty girls with a mean age of seven years served as experimental subjects, one half of the children being from a high socioeconomic level and one half from a low level. The experiment showed that the introduction of random reinforcement produced typically lower-class behavior in higher-class subjects. It could be shown that this result was not a simple consequence of all concept acquisition degenerating to a chance level. As may be seen in Figure 1.3, both number of errors and trials to criterion reveal that the performance of the higher-class children progressively approaches and ultimately equals the ineffectual lower-class performance. The data strongly support the hypothesis that the difference in performance

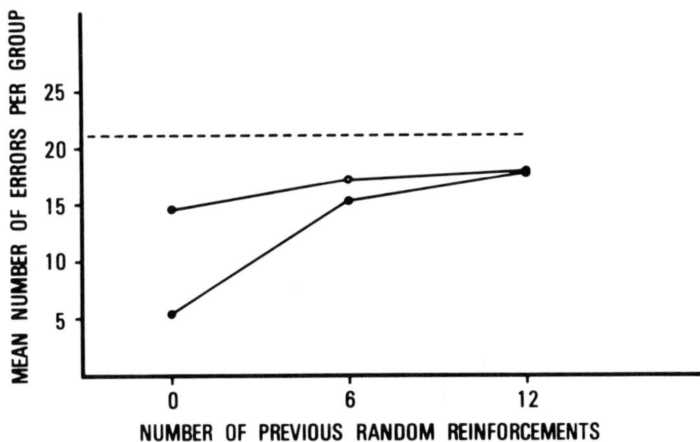

Figure 1.3. Learning strategies in children of different social class. *From Bresnahan* et al. *(1972)*.

level is a function of the reinforcement history, lower performance being associated with chaotic or inconsistent reinforcement histories.

Since, on the one hand, lower-class children did not shift from a partially reinforced hypothesis which was high in their hierarchy, and on the other hand higher-class children after random reinforcement exhibited inferior concept acquisition similar to that displayed by lower-class subjects, Bresnahan proceeded to investigate the conditions under which children would or would not shift from a nonconfirmed hypothesis as a function of the degree of original learning and the frequency of nonconfirmation.

Forty-five boys and forty-five girls, randomly sampled from schools which had been identified as being located in areas neither predominantly high nor predominantly low socioeconomically, were individually tested in a mobile laboratory parked outside each school. The task employed simply consisted of selecting one of two keys. On each trial a red and a green light were presented, the position of the lights being an irrelevant dimension. The child was shown the two lights and instructed to press one of the keys. If the child made the correct response, a trinket was presented by a universal feeder. The trinkets won by the child were always within the child's range of vision, and the child was told that after completion of the game being played the child would be allowed to keep the trinkets.

The experiment was divided in two parts. In the first part, the children received trinkets for every and all correct responses until a criterion run was completed. For one third of the subjects, the criterion run was defined as six correct responses in succession; for the second one third, criterion was twelve correct responses; and for the remainder third, criterion was eighteen responses. Once the criterion run was achieved partial reinforcement of the correct response was introduced with no indication to the child. The partial reinforcement was 90 percent for one third of the children, 80 percent for another one third, and 70 percent for the last one third. The partial response schedules were run for sixty trials.

The results clearly showed that the number of trials required to reach criterion, i.e., the degree of previous training, and the percentage of partial reinforcement both significantly influenced the number of errors committed by the children. The longer the criterion run before shifting to the partial reinforcement schedule the less the number of errors. In other words, the more previous training to reach criterion, the less likely was the child to shift after a nonconfirmation. When the number of nonconfirmations became significantly high there was an increased tendency for the children to shift from their previous reinforcement hypothesis. The subjects thus continue to conform to the general strategy of win-stay, lose-shift.

Taking together the series of experiments it becomes apparent that lower-class children do not adopt the win-stay, lose-shift strategy displayed by higher-class children and adults. This failure to display the win-stay, lose-shift strategy may be the result of a chaotic reinforcement history, plus a high degree of overlearning, and the perseverance on an incorrect hypothesis which may enable the child to obtain a reinforcement level higher than the level to which he or she is accustomed. The net result is that lower-class children are not only slow in learning new solutions but are also slow in giving up old solutions.

Another strategy in trying to determine the origin of performance differences found in ethnically and socially differentiated school children was used by Hertzig and associates (1968), who, rather than focusing on achievement, have been concerned with the behavioral style exhibited by preschool children as a response to a cognitive demand. In a study of two groups of children with differential educational expectancies they have compared and contrasted the responsiveness to cognitive demands in three-year-old children from Puerto Rican, working-class families living in New York City with the responsiveness to identical demands in similarly aged native-born middle-class children whose parents are businesspeople and professionals. Both groups of children and their families have been followed from the child's early infancy onward as a part of a research on behavioral development (Thomas *et al.* 1963).

At the age of three years intelligence was estimated, and the behavioral responses of the children to cognitive demands associated with such evaluation were independently assessed. The middle-class children included fifty-eight boys and fifty-eight girls. The Puerto Rican sample had twenty-seven boys and thirty-three girls. Both groups of children were comparable with respect to family stability and were large enough to allow comparisons of behavioral style after matching for general level of intelligence.

The behavioral information on response style to cognitive demands was obtained by observing the behavior and recording the child's verbalizations in the course of the administration of the Stanford-Binet Intelligence Test, Form L. At the time each child was being examined, a detailed protocol of the child's behavior and verbalizations was recorded by an independent observer. This observer was seated in a corner of the examination room before the entrance of the tester and the child, and in no way participated in the intelligence testing procedure. The tester followed the standard procedure for the administration of the Stanford-Binet. The observer kept a consecutive written record of the behavior of the child during the examination session. This record was kept in terms of the explicit responses made to each one of the specific demands made for cognitive functioning on the test. The observer simply described the child's overt behavior when confronted with a task. At no point was the observer concerned with whether or not the child's response was correct. Independently of its correctness, a complete account was made of all observable behavior and speech. A particular effort was made to obtain a verbatim account of the child's verbalizations.

For the analysis Hertzig *et al.* devised a method for classifying the behavioral styles based on the objective possibilities of response to a cognitive demand. The schematic representation of the method corresponds to a logic tree (Figure 1.4). When confronted with a demand, a child is given the choice of either working or not working. This initial bifurcation could be expressed through either verbalization or action. If the choice was to work, whether verbally or nonverbally, the response could be delimited and restricted to the defined requirements of the task or could extend beyond these limits in the form of spontaneous associations or other extensions expressed in action or speech. If the initial decision made by the child was not to work, this could be expressed either verbally or nonverbally as well, and

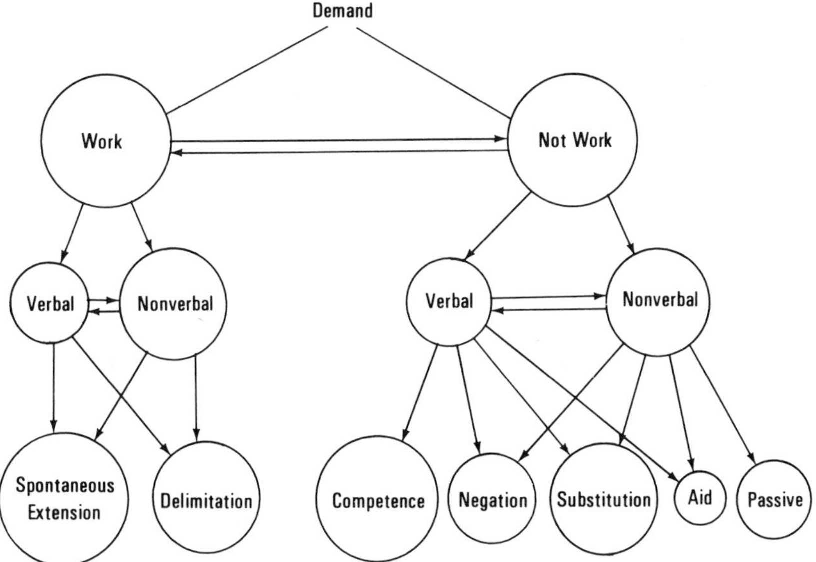

Figure 1.4. Response styles to cognitive demands. *From Hertzig* et al. *(1968).*

take the form of simple negation, rationalizations or competence, substitutive verbalizations or actions, requests for assistance, or passive nonparticipation. Clearly, the child's initial response could either be continued or altered in response to the reiteration of demand by the examiner. Thus, initial work responses could be followed by refusals to work, verbal responses by action, or by any other pattern or redundancy or change. The scheme of analysis, therefore, made it possible to classify initial responses and to engage in a sequential analysis of response chains. The categories, in terms of which response styles to demands for cognitive functioning were classified, were thus objective generalizations about observed behavior. They were not, nor were they intended to be, inferences about the underlying reasons for the expression of the observed behavioral patterns.

The results clearly demonstrated marked differences in the behavioral styles of U.S. middle-class and Puerto Rican working-class preschool children. The middle-class children characteristically responded to demands for cognitive functioning by making a greater proportion of work responses than the Puerto Rican children. One of the greatest differences between the two groups was the tendency of the middle-class children to respond to the cognitive demands by verbalization much more frequently than by action or gesture. The increased verbalization of the middle-class children occurred for both work and not-work responses.

In addition to differences in the overall amount of verbalization, differences also existed in the kinds of verbalizations made when the children had not-work responses. Thus, while in the middle-class children the most frequent kind of verbal not-work response was an ability-related rationalization of competence, in the Puerto Rican group the style corresponded to an irrelevant substitution.

The behavioral styles of the two groups were influenced by the nature of the task demands, with the middle-class children making work responses with equal frequency when confronted with either a verbal or a performance demand, and the Puerto Rican children making work responses more frequently to tasks requiring motoric action than to tasks requiring verbal responses.

Hertzig *et al.* also reported that their Puerto Rican children had frequent verbal exchanges before, during, and after the testing session. However, these children differed significantly from the middle-class children with respect to the ways in which language was used in responding to demands for cognitive functioning. These differences emphasize the view of a distinction between the possession of language and the use of the language. In other words, children whose spontaneous speech may show a high level of formal organization, as measured by mean sentence length and complexity and maturity of sentence structure, may still be unable to use this tool in the solution of cognitive tasks.

Since Hertzig's study is a longitudinal one in which a large series of factors previously considered as potential sources of differences in abilities between ethnic groups or social classes have been included, it was possible to test for significant associations between those factors and behavior style.

The differences in behavior styles between American middle-class and Puerto Rican working-class children could not be explained on the basis of family size, overcrowding in the home, substandard housing, or instability of place of dwelling. Nor was there a significant association of style of response to cognitive demand and instability of family organization, lack of maternal care, use of unfamiliar language during the examination, and lack of acquaintance with the examiner.

Of particular importance are the absence of relations between behavior style and intellectual level and education of poor quality in inferior schools. When differences in performance level on the Stanford-Binet were controlled, the stylistic differences between the two groups of children were sustained. Consequently, the observed differences in response could not be explained by differences in intellectual level. However, the effect of IQ on the pattern of response in the two groups was not identical. In the middle-class group, children with lower or higher IQ did not show marked differences in behavioral style. As a contrast, in the Puerto Rican group, the children with the lower levels of intellectual performance had a tendency to respond more exaggeratedly in the style that characterized their group as a whole.

The differences found between the middle-class and the Puerto Rican children could not be attributed to the effects of poor schools and disinterested or unskilled teachers, since the children studied were three years old and almost all below school-entrance and nursery-school age. The findings of the study, therefore, support the view that differences in behavior between middle-class and Puerto Rican children develop long before exposure to formal learning in school or experience in nursery school.

With the data presented by Hertzig *et al.* it is not possible to assess the separate influence of ethnicity and social class since both groups of children included in the study differed in ethnicity as well as in social class. We have explored this aspect by examining the responses to cognitive demands that are made by an ethnically homogeneous but socially differentiated group of children in their first school year. This investigation, carried out by Guadalupe Lugo (1971), included one hundred Mexican children six years of age attending public and private schools in Mexico City.

The social-class status of all children was defined on a scale which assessed four aspects of social circumstance: per-capita income, occupation of head of household, housing conditions, and mother's formal education. Each of these characteristics was distributed on a five-point scale, each point having unit value. The lowest level in each scale was represented by a score of five and the highest level by a score of one. Illustratively, on the occupational scale a score of five would be given for domestic work, unskilled labor, or unemployment. A score of one was given if the father had a profession or a moderate-to-large business or if he occupied an executive and supervisory position. A mother received an educational score of one if she had attended university, and a score of five if she had less than three years of formal schooling. The other scales were similarly distributed. A child's social status was defined by the sum of the scores on the four scales. A score of twenty represented the lowest aggregate social level and a score of four the highest. Analysis of the social-status data indicated that children with scores of four to eight were clearly in the upper middle class. Those with scores of nine through fifteen in the middle middle and upper working class, and those children with scores of sixteen to twenty were in the lower working class. Of the hundred children studied, thirty-seven were in the highest social group, twenty-six in the middle grouping, and thirty-seven in the lowest social group.

The Terman-Merrill version of the Stanford-Binet Test of Intelligence, Form L-M, was individually administered to every child. The tasks of this test were used to obtain behavioral information to a standardly presented set of cognitive demands. The procedures for administering the intelligence test, recording of the behavior protocol, and analyzing of the responses were those described by Hertzig *et al.* (1968).

The frequency of both work and not-work responses differed systematically by social class. Upper-class children made larger numbers of work responses and smaller numbers of not-work responses than did children in the other two social groupings. Work responses were least frequent and not-work responses most frequent in the lowest-class children. The middle socioeconomic group was intermediate in its frequency level on both types of response. Difference between groups in the frequency of work responses is significant at less than the 0.001 level of confidence. The difference in the direction of frequencies with which not-work responses were made approaches but does not reach significance at the 0.05 level.

Since the absolute response numbers differ for the different social groups a direct consideration of the frequency of responses of different types could not be made between groups. To make such a comparison it would have been necessary to consider the relative frequency of the different types of response using the absolute response number as the denominator.

Children in the different social classes differed from one another in a number of aspects of response to demands for cognitive work. Upper-class children made a significantly higher proportion of work responses than did either the middle- or lower-class children. Very few spontaneous extensions characterized the responses of children in any of the social groupings. An analysis of the limited responses indicated that these were significantly more frequently verbal in the upper-class children than in either the lower- or middle-class groups.

When children did not work on an item, the manner in which such work refusal was expressed was significantly different in upper-class and lower-class children. Upper-class children tended to express a significantly greater proportion of their not-work responses in terms of competence rationalizations than did the lower-class children. In contrast, lower-class children expressed significantly more substitutive behaviors than did either the upper- or middle-class children.

No significant differences were found in the proportions of responses expressed as verbal negatives, passive not-work behaviors, or request for aid in the different social groups. As would have been expected from the very high proportion of limited responses in all groups, no significant differences with respect to any of the aspects of spontaneous extension were obtained.

It would of course be expected that IQ levels of children in the different social-class groupings would be significantly different. None of the upper-class children had IQs below 91 and none of the lower-class children had an IQ higher than 120. In contrast, twelve of the lower-class children and eight of the middle-class children had IQs below 91 with two middle-class children having an IQ above 120.

Since style of response to cognitive demand may be influenced by IQ level, the differences between the total groups could have derived from this factor rather than from social-class differences in styles of response as such. The data was therefore reexamined, taking only those children with IQs between 91 and 120. All of the trends of difference that were found between upper and lower social-class groupings were sustained, but the absolute size of differences was reduced. Upper-class children responded with a significantly higher proportion of work rather than not-work responses than did lower-class children. All groups once again tended to make limited responses to demands. However, within these limited responses the upper-class children responded verbally significantly more frequently than did the lower-class children. Differential styles of not-work responses were also sustained, with lower-class children continuing to make a greater proportion of substitutive responses than either upper or middle-class children.

Differences in the frequency with which not-work responses were expressed as competence rationalizations continued to obtain between the upper- and middle-class versus the lower-class children, with both upper social groupings making a higher proportion of competence rationalizations. These differences, however, just failed to meet a 5 percent level of confidence.

The findings indicate that certain of the differences that Hertzig *et al.* (1968) found as to characteristic responses to cognitive demands in middle-class Native American and Puerto Rican working-class children at three years of age are present in Mexican children of different socioeconomic levels at six years of age. In both sets of groups studied children in the higher socioeconomic group characteristically responded to demands to cognitive function by making a greater proportion of work as contrasted with not-work responses. In both groups, too, a greater proportion of work responses were verbally expressed in the children of higher social status. Styles in which children made not-work responses were also similar in the two studies, with children of higher social status expressing a greater proportion of their not-work responses in terms of competence rationalizations and children of lower social status tending to engage in substitutive not-work responses with significantly higher frequency.

These differences in style between upper- and lower-class groupings are not a function of differences in intellectual level of the groupings. When a common IQ range is established, differences in response style are persistent across the socioeconomic levels. Though absolute values of difference change, the direction of difference is sustained.

An interesting difference between the findings in Mexican children and Hertzig's findings for younger children is the absence in the Mexican groups of a social-class gradient with respect to spontaneous extension of work responses. In the study of middle-class U.S. and Puerto Rican working-class children it was found that the middle-class group more frequently tended to make spontaneous remarks extending their work responses. Thus, middle-class children, when given a bead-stringing task, would complete the task and say such things as: "I can wear this"; "I have beads at home"; "My mamma has a necklace." The Puerto Rican working-class children in contrast tended much more frequently to complete the task and merely to wait for the next problem posed by the examiner without engaging in any spontaneous extension responses. Among the Mexican children of all social classes responses tended to be limited to the explicits of the tasks presented. Thus, in the groups of common IQ range, approximately 99 percent of all work responses made by children in all social classes were delimited with no social-class gradient manifested. This difference between the findings of the two studies may reflect differences between the cultures with respect to the degree to which children have learned to restrict their responses to the demand made or to go beyond the explicits of the demand. Alternatively, it is possible that the differences reflect changes with age and that spontaneous extension is an attribute of the functioning of children of preschool rather than of school age. A consideration of this alternative would of course require a comparison of like-aged children in the two cultures.

It is clear from the data that the differences which were previously found to characterize children who differed both in ethnicity and in social class are ones which characterize children of common ethnicity but different socioeconomic levels. The differences in behavioral response to demands for cognitive work are therefore most parsimoniously viewed as reflecting social class rather than ethnic variables. It also appears from the data that differences in response styles to cognitive demands which typified socially differentiated groups of three-year-old children in one culture continue in the main to be associated with social differences in older children in a different culture. It would be interesting to know whether the children in the two groups studied by Hertzig *et al.* continued to differ at six years of age. However, our finding of these differences in six-year-old children would suggest that the social-class differences in response style are persistent to that age level. This would suggest that earlier-acquired patterns of response to cognitive demands do persist when social circumstances remain relatively stable.

To what extent are the findings of differences in response styles to cognitive demands across social classes remanifestations of social-class differences that have already been described, and to what extent do they reflect additional elements of functional differences among social classes? Numerous studies have indicated that verbalization, and in particular the ease with which language expression occurs in relation to cognitive tasks, differs between social classes. Our finding of a greater proportion of the limited responses being verbal in the upper as compared with the lower social-class children is in accord with these findings and in fact could be anticipated. The same ease of anticipation does not obtain for the other differences noted. The degree to which children respond to cognitive demands by work rather than by its opposite can in part be considered to reflect the fact that verbal functioning not infrequently is involved in responding. However, such a pattern was not restricted to verbal tasks and involved responses to demands for nonverbal performances as well. Similarly, the tendency for lower-class children to use substitution as a characteristic way to express their not-work responses cannot readily be embraced by differences in verbal facility across the two groups. Most frequently these requests for engaging in substitutive behavior were expressed verbally. Competence rationalization was expressed significantly more frequently as a reason for not working at a task in the upper-class children. Such expressions reflect a recognition of the relation between developmental level and instruction to task competence rather than the presence of verbal facility alone. Both upper- and lower-class children verbalized their refusals to work. For one group, however, this verbalization takes the form of expressions with relation to prior training, age, and experience whereas in the other it takes the form of verbalizations requesting withdrawal from the demand situation and the substitution of other activities in place of it.

There is good reason to believe that these differences in response style may have important implications for formal educational success. The child with a given intellectual level who makes work responses significantly more frequently to demands for cognitive work, who reacts to difficulties in terms of evaluating his or her performance against acquired competence and training, is more likely to function well in an educational setting than is the child who makes a higher frequency of not-work responses and who, when confronted with difficulties, seeks substitutive behaviors.

Although the phenomena of social-class differences in response styles and their potential contribution to educational course are clear, the sources for such differences in the child's background and development remain obscure. Hertzig *et al.* have on anecdotal grounds related the difference that they have observed to aspects of parental care, and particularly to differences by social class in the styles with which children have been instructed both in play and in the acquisition of normal age-specific competences and skills. Observations suggest that whereas play is for play's sake in the lower social classes, play is for learning both concepts and skills in the upper social-class groupings. Moreover, they indicate that the teaching of skills accompanied by verbalization characterizes the upper social-class groupings, while globally more action-oriented instruction is characteristic of the lower social class. Such anecdotal observations and inferences have tended to receive support from the work of Hess and Shipman (1965) on styles of cooperative work of pairs of lower- and middle-class mother and children.

Whether or not these factors in fact underlay the social-class differences in styles of response to cognitive demands still remains to be tested. In our own setting anecdotal impression is not in agreement with the descriptions from United States culture. This disagreement can at present merely be stated. Future research will be required to indicate whether these factors are in fact the relevant ones in either cultural setting.

Notwithstanding our inability to account for the differences in styles of response to cognitive demands in six-year-old children from different social classes, the phenomenon of difference is clear and of sufficient potential importance for functioning to warrant a detailed consideration of its possible consequences.

If the patterns of style of response to cognitive demands continue to define the developmental course of the groups of children involved in the respective studies, it is apparent that the likelihood for school failure and underachievement will be high for the Puerto Rican and for the low social-class Mexican children. The tendency of these groups to make fewer work responses when confronted with a demand, and the almost total lack of responses with spontaneous extension, may easily be interpreted in terms of low motivation in the child. Teachers, trained in a typically middle-class context, may judge these children to be disinterested, unwilling to learn, and inattentive. Other features characteristic of the behavior style of the low social-class children, such as passive nonresponsiveness, may readily be viewed as resistence, disobedience, surliness, and in general as a negative attitude on the part of the child. A similar interpretation is likely to be given to the high frequency of irrelevant verbal substitutive responses. The total picture may result in the teacher's inferring that the child's behavior reflects immaturity or negative attitudes toward learning rather than a behavioral style characteristic of a socially differentiated group. The net result may be a lack of awareness on the part of the teacher of the need for finding a way to alter the pattern of response or the need in changing the form of presenting the demands in a manner more congruent to the characteristic style of these children.

Since differences in style of response are established at a very early age, and apparently they persist to later ages, it seems that mere exposure to supplementary educational opportunities may be an insufficient procedure to modify function significantly. It seems imperative to find the factors relevant to the emergence of particular behavioral styles of response in order to expose the lower-class subjects, at a very early age, to the influence of those conditions with the aim of having them respond in a manner that will resemble more closely the style of the middle-class children. This approach of course assumes that the middle-class style is the most desirable and the best for the future makeup of the human society.

The work of Hertzig and co-workers opens the possibility of identifying groups of children who, due to ethnicity or social-class factors, have different styles of behavior when presented with cognitive demands. Methods of instruction appropriate to their particular response styles could be developed and educational success thus enhanced.

MALNUTRITION AND LEARNING

Although concern with nutrition in child development is not new, and one of the basic concepts in child health has always been that ingestion of a diet adequate in quantity and quality is an essential prerequisite for optimal growth and development of infants and children, it is only recently that systematic research has been focused on the possibility that malnutrition in early life may contribute to suboptimal functioning and learning disabilities in later life.

At the individual level, protein-calorie malnutrition is the name of a clinical syndrome present in infants and children as a consequence of a deficient intake and/or utilization of foods of animal origin accompanied of variable intakes of rich carbohydrate foods. The terms "kwashiorkor" and "marasmus" correspond to two extreme clinical expressions of the syndrome whose presence is conditioned by a series of factors which include: age of the child, age of weaning, time of introduction of supplementary foods to breast milk, caloric density and protein concentration of the supplements actually ingested by the child, and frequency and severity of infectious episodes during weaning. Protein-calorie malnutrition is more frequently observed in young weaned children who are on marginal diets when an intercurrent gastrointestinal disturbance or a disease accompanied with high fever is present. In general, the full-blown picture of kwashiokor appears only if the intercurrent process suddenly increases the child's needs for protein or if protein is not fully utilized due to insufficient calorie intake.

Although the proximal causal factors may vary, the syndrome is associated with the same basic characteristics of clinical and biochemical pathology in all countries. The regional variations observed are generally due to the presence of other nutritional deficiencies prevalent in the area, to the pattern of weaning, and to the infectious pathology characteristic of the region.

The interpretation of the role of malnutrition in the production of disorders of mental development and learning is complicated by the presence of a great number of variables that are in themselves capable of producing those disabilities. Evaluation of a truly causal relationship is a rather difficult task because malnutrition is an ecologic outcome. To illustrate some of the interrelations among biological, social, cultural, and economic factors that produce or accompany human malnutrition in infancy, we have constructed a series of flow diagrams with the data obtained from the study of several communities in Mexico, Central and South America, and Africa (Cravioto 1967). In Figure 1.5, it may be seen that in a

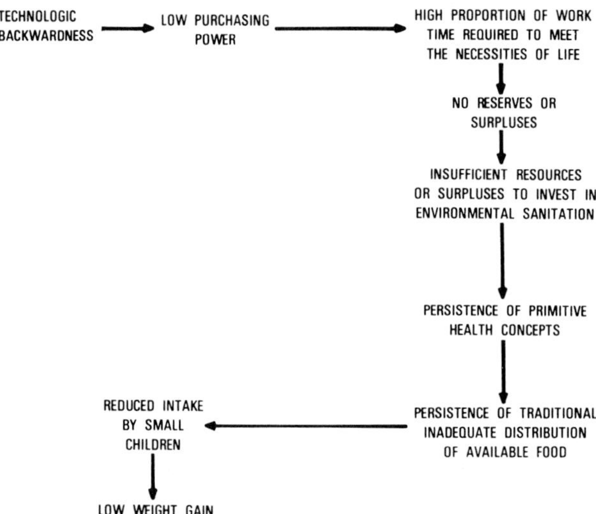

Figure 1.5. Interrelation among biosocial factors and low weight gain. *From Turk et al. (1967).*

society where the systematic application of modern technology is minimal or absent a sector of the population would have a low purchasing power as a result of a limited income. Since the total income (measured as the rate of conversion of energy into consumption goods) is barely enough to cope with the minimal necessities of life, lack of surplus of reserves will limit invest-

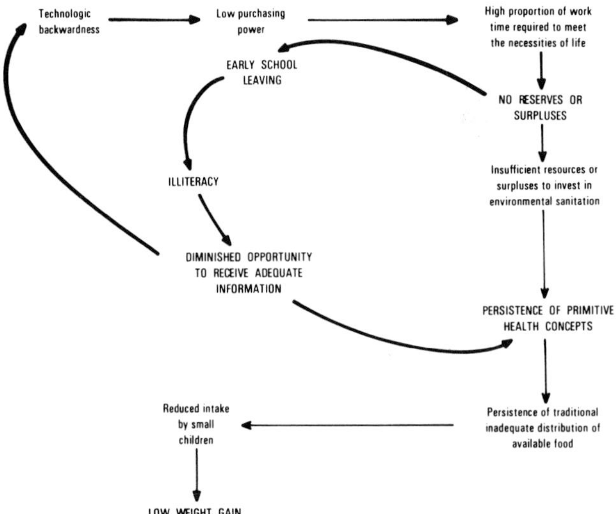

Figure 1.6. Interrelation among biosocial factors and low weight gain. *From Turk* et al. (*1967*).

ment in environmental sanitation; this in turn will maintain, in the group, traditional concepts on health and disease. This prescientific conception of the role of food in the production of disease (Cravioto 1962; Rosales *et al.* 1964) is one of the main determinants of the pattern of distribution of available food within the family according to age, and gives as a net result a reduction in the type and amounts of food that the infant is allowed to consume. This ultimate step would then be responsible for malnutrition, expressed in the diagram as low weight gain.

A second pathway (Figure 1.6) initiated with the lack of surpluses proceeds to pressures for early school leaving as an attempt to increase the purchasing power of the family unit. The consequence of this early school dropout would be illiteracy or at least a diminished opportunity for receiving adequate information; this establishes a feedback mechanism for technological backwardness, and for the persistence of primitive concepts on health and disease. Alternatively (Figure 1.7), early school dropout would result in society giving adulthood status and role to a group of individuals at an earlier age than would be the case had they remained as pupils. This early adulthood situation leads to an increased probability of marrying at a younger age and to an equally uneducated spouse, thus multiplying the risks for inadequate child care, illness, and malnutrition.

Another pathway (Figure 1.8) has at least two different starting points. One could be considered as a branching at the level of the persistence of primitive conceptions of health and disease which results in insufficient awareness of the hygienic requirements of the child. This, through a chain of unsanitary conditions in the community and in the home, would lead to poor cleanliness of the mother and to a higher frequency of infectious

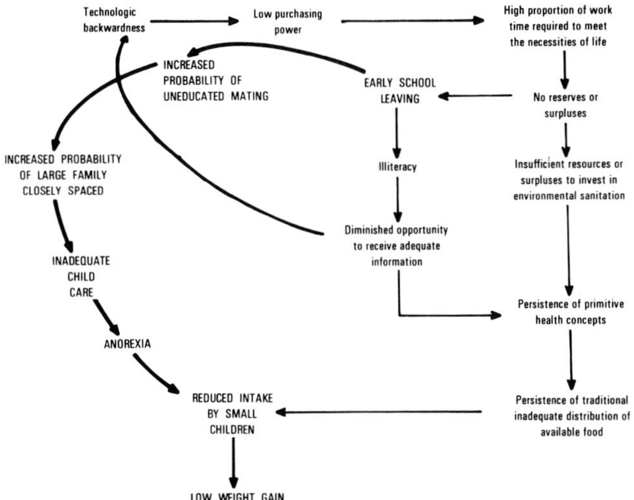

Figure 1.7. Interrelation among biosocial factors and low weight gain. *From Turk* et al. (*1967*).

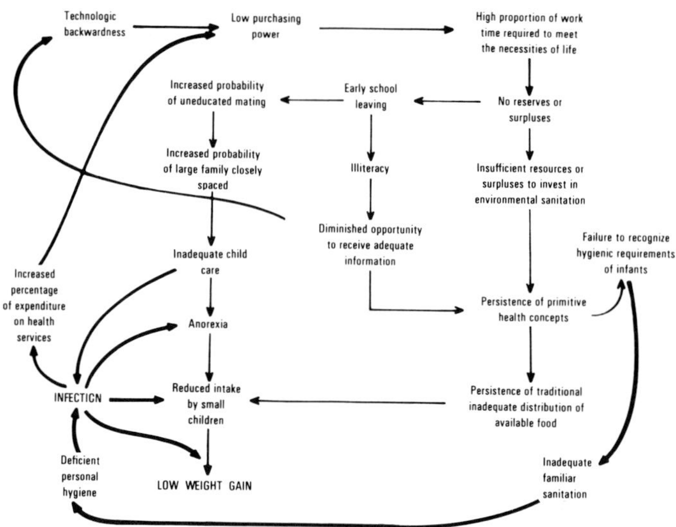

Figure 1.8. Interrelation among biosocial factors and low weight gain. *From Turk* et al. (*1967*).

processes in the child, which directly or indirectly produce malnutrition. The other starting point is in fact the link between inadequate child care in the large uneducated family and the poor personal hygiene cycle just described. The increased morbidity would increase expenditures on health services, thus acting as a feedback mechanism for the low purchasing power.

It is of course apparent that other pathways may be identified, all of them resulting in a reinforcement of opportunities for the persistence of a way of life whose main characteristic is preindustrialization, represented in a deficient application of modern knowledge, with economic and social disadvantage as the main outcome.

Within the context of nutrition and mental development, even food should be viewed in at least three dimensions. The first, the physiological dimension, has as a unit of measurement, the nutrient, whose function is to provide chemical substances to the organism for growth, maintenance, and regulation. The second, the psychophysical dimension, is measured by the foodstuff which, through its organoleptic properties, provides the organism with a variety of sensory stimuli through consistency, color, aroma, flavor, temperature, etc. In this dimension the same foodstuff, prepared in two different culinary ways but having the same nutrient content, will in fact evoke response as if to two different foods. The third, or psychosocial, dimension is developed during mealtime. Its functions, on the one hand, are to aid in symbol formation through the value attached to it in aspects such as reward or punishment, as an experience attached to gratifying or not gratifying a person, as a characteristic of the ethnic or social group, and so on.

On the other hand, the mealtime provides opportunities to demonstrate and practice the role and status of individuals within the family and within the community. Who is served first? Who takes the place of honor at the table? Who receives the choice portion of the food served? Who moderates conversation at the table? These are some of the ways in which this food dimension is expressed.

The complexities of assessing the contribution that malnutrition may make *per se* on mental development are increased by factors such as the time of life at which malnutrition is experienced, its severity and duration, and the time that must elapse between the episode of malnutrition and the dates at which more sensitive and meaningful evaluations of its consequences for adaptive functioning and learning may take place.

In this section we will selectively review research in the area of malnutrition, mental development, and learning in human infants and children, with emphasis on our own studies.

Effects on Sensorimotor Functioning

The available data both in human infants and growing animals indicating that severe malnutrition affects the normal pattern of biochemical maturation (Cravioto 1962; Ramos-Galván and Cravioto 1958; Waterlow *et al.* 1960) and produces physical growth retardation which for some organic structures seems to be permanent (Jackson and Stewart 1920; McCance 1962) led us in 1958 to consider as highly improbable that the central nervous system could not participate in this general retardation of growth and development. Accordingly, it was hypothesized that the effect of severe malnutrition on the mental performance of human infants would vary as a function of the period of life at which malnutrition was experienced.

Twenty infants hospitalized for severe protein-calorie malnutrition were examined with the Gesell Infant Test every two weeks during treatment and rehabilitation. The follow-up period lasted as long as six months for some children. On the first examination, administered just after the acute electrolyte disturbance or infectious processes, or both, had been treated, all infants were well below age norms on all four spheres of the Gesell Test—motor, adaptive, language, and social-personal—with Developmental Quotients mainly below 60.

During rehabilitation the performance of fourteen children who had been admitted for treatment between fifteen and forty-two months of age showed considerable improvement in Gesell performance, Developmental Quotients coming progressively closer to age expectation. However, the developmental deficit shown on admission by the six infants admitted between three and six months of age, whose weight retardation was so severe that weight on admission was almost equal to birth weight, was still present after nutritional rehabilitation. In other words, these latter infants showed virtually no recovery of their developmental deficit. In the older children not all spheres of behavior exhibited the same speed of recovery. Communication and language, which in general was the area most affected, showed the slowest rate of return toward normal age expectancy. When the serial data for each child were plotted against days after admission it was seen that mental performance varied in direct relation to age on admission. The older the group the greater the value of the slope. The slopes were sufficiently steep and progress in the first weeks of nutritional rehabilitation was so rapid that it appeared unlikely that the differences between initial test performance and level of functioning at the end of the observation period could be just the result of the extra care that the children received in the ward (Cravioto and Robles 1963).

These findings have been confirmed by Pollitt and Granoff (1968) in Peru, Barrera-Moncada (1963) in Venezuela, Chase and Martin (1970) in the USA, Stoch and Smythe (1963) in South Africa, Bothe-Antoun, Babayan, and Harfouche (1968) and Yatkin and McLaren (1970) in Lebanon, and Marcondes, Lefevre, and Machado (1969) in Brazil.

Pollitt and Granoff contrasted the levels of performance on the Bayley Infant Scales for Mental and Motor Development of a group of previously marasmic infants, all below two years of age at the time of the study, with performance obtained in a group of siblings of similar age who had no unusual medical history and whose weights, heights, and head circumferences were within normal limits. It was found that, while the siblings were developing according to age expectations, seventeen of the nineteen children who recovered from marasmus had severe mental and motor retardation. Monckeberg (1968), working with Chilean marasmic infants, had independently arrived at the same conclusion. He also stated that children with poor nutritional conditions show a less than normal head circumference for their age, and a significant correlation between deficit of cranial growth and mental performance was seen in his patients. This relationship ceased to be significant when cranial growth was within normal limits.

Kardonsky and associates (1971) also found evidence of reduced mental functioning in Chilean preschool children hospitalized for severe malnutrition in the first year of life. When these infants were reexamined at three to four years of age their mean IQ was 73. These authors have reported a marked increase in performance level for the period five to six years. Taking weight deficit as a criterion of the time in life at which malnutrition was apparent, those children whose malnutrition occurred earlier, and whose recovery was more rapid, tended to present less marked IQ deficits. Reduced exploratory activity was a constant feature of the behavior in their malnourished infants. This finding is in agreement with all the published descriptions of behavior carried out in malnourished children. Since the classical descriptions of Meneghello (1949) and Clark (1951) to the more recent and semiquantitative observations of Chávez (1973) passing through those of Autret and Behar (1954) and Gómez *et al.* (1954) reduced exploration of the environment probably constitutes the single most common behavioral feature. The condition becomes so marked in the severely malnourished child that renewal of interest in his surroundings is considered by clinicians as one of the most reliable signs of improvement. "The child who smiles is well on the way to recovery."

It would, of course, be ingenuous to view the observed apathy as the simple and direct result of malnutrition. If one uses Wilson's (1964) attempt to distinguish four categories of apathy (primarily physiological, primarily psychological, apathy at the community level, and apathy as a characteristic of a regional culture), the apathy of the protein-calorie deficient child can most profitably be viewed as a mixed type. Nutritional deprivation *per se* can and does contribute to apathy and unresponsiveness as in the case in experimental animals fed on low-protein, high-carbohydrate diets (Platt, Heard, and Steward 1964). However, when noted clinically such behavior is never separable from possible sequelae to emotional deprivation and loss which may be produced by the separation which accompanies hospitalization. It has been repeatedly stated that in most communities where malnutrition is highly prevalent the mother-child relationship prior to weaning is very close and frequently includes the mother taking the nursling with her everywhere she goes. This fact, when considered together with the observations made by Geber and Dean (1956) that recovery is more rapid among infants whose mothers show the greatest interest and solicitude, has been interpreted as suggesting that separation from the mother may make an important contribution to the behavioral disturbance. In any event, the behavior of the malnourished infant strikingly resembles that described by Bowlby (1960) in the fifteen-to-twenty-month-old healthy child who has been abruptly separated from his mother by hospitalization.

In considering psychological features of severe malnutrition it is important to note that in a high proportion of cases the disorder is closely associated in time with weaning. In preindustrial societies the frequent absence of effective and continued mothering as reflected in the absence of a stable surrogate and repeated "randomized" change in the persons responsible for the care of the weaned child may also play a part in the production of apathy in those communities in which this is a common practice. Such a complication is particularly likely at the time the mother shows the evident signs of a next pregnancy (Cravioto, unpublished). However, despite the influence on behavior of these non-nutritional general factors, as Meneghello has pointed out, the psychological changes in malnutrition are not simply a response to hospitalization or to general maternal deprivation, since they are present even if the child remains at home and is most affectionately cared for by a devoted, if nutritionally misguided, mother.

Independently of whether the cause of apathy is simple or multiple, it is clear that during the development of chronic malnutrition from the mild-moderate to the severe, failure to respond appropriately to significant stimuli is reflected in a progressive withdrawal from the environment, and by progressive behavioral regression. At the very least such changes produce a period of experiential reduction. It is therefore possible that, although the physical signs of bodily wasting are perhaps more dramatic, the behavioral changes may have greater developmental importance in the long run because of their potential for interferring with the course of cognitive growth, and eventually acting as a feedback for malnutrition (Pollitt 1973).

Yatkin and McLaren's study using the Griffiths Developmental Scale yielded essentially similar results to those obtained by the Latin American research workers. At the time of hospitalization, when the marasmic children were between 2.5 to 16 months of age, their average developmental quotient was approximately 50. During rehabilitation there was a steady improvement in performance which after four months reached values between 70 and 75. In an attempt to assess the effect of added stimulation during initial recovery Yatkin and McLaren divided the group of marasmic children in two subgroups paired for sex and age. One of these groups was provided with stimulating environment consisting of a colorful ward with pictures, toys, and music, where nurses deliberatedly played with and sang to the children and established a warm nurse-child relationship. The other group did not receive this stimulation. It remained in a place with similar dimensions but not colorful and without toys, music, and extra attention from the nursing staff. Both groups of children received the same medical and dietary treatment. There was no initial difference in Developmental Quotients between the groups. Nutritional rehabilitation was accompanied by increases in mental performance in both groups in an almost parallel form. Only toward the end of the four-month observation period did the stimulated group show significantly higher quotients due mainly to a drop in the mean performance of the nonstimulated group. Nonetheless, at the end of four months of nutrition rehabilitation in the presence of physical recovery both groups of children remained below the values expected for their age, with the interesting finding that the greater deficit was present, as was the case in the Mexican children, in the area of language and communication.

In the United States, Chase and Martin have reported a study on the influence of duration of early malnutrition on later mental functioning. Nineteen children, hospitalized at less than one year of age with primary diagnosis of generalized undernutrition, were compared three and a half years after discharge with a control group matched for birth date, weight, sex, race, and socioeconomic status. Mean Developmental Quotient (Yale Revised Developmental Examination) for the control group was 99.4 as compared to a mean of 82 for the rehabilitated children. The index cases were lower in all areas of the developmental quotient, but they were particularly low in language. Children admitted to the hospital with severe malnutrition lasting longer than the first four months of life were most severely impaired on follow-up. Performance in all areas of development tested was significantly lower than performance exhibited by children admitted with malnutrition before the age of four months. The development of the children with shorter duration of malnutrition did not differ from that found in the control group when examined a mean of three and a half years later. At this time all the index cases admitted in the first four months of life had

Developmental Quotients above 80, whereas nine of ten children suffering from malnutrition for periods longer than the first four months of life had Developmental Quotients below 80. This lower performance was evident even in children who after discharge from the hospital were placed in a bountiful stimulating home environment. It should be mentioned that the infants in this investigation, who were hospitalized for sixteen days on the average, were not as severely malnourished as most infants included in the Chilean, the Peruvian, and the Mexican studies.

Turning away from general measures of mental development, Brockman and Ricciuti (1971) examined a more specific cognitive function—categorization behavior—in relation to malnutrition in twenty severe marasmic children aged 11.8 to 43.5 months, and in nineteen control children matched for age and sex, without a history of malnutrition and with heights above the tenth percentile of the Boston norms. Using simple sorting tasks to assess categorizing behavior, it was found that the total test scores of the malnourished children were significantly lower than those obtained in the control children. On retest after twelve weeks of treatment the malnourished children showed no significant increase in scores. Analysis of the ten individual sort task differences disclosed not only lower scores for the malnourished among task differences. Children with a longer period of nutritional treatment, with greater gains in body length and head circumference, and with high medical ratings of nutritional recovery, tended to perform better on the cognitive tasks.

From all the above-mentioned data it is clear that even after a period of several months children who have been successfully treated for severe malnutrition and are considered as cured, whether they have received extra stimulation or not during hospitalization, still show developmental lags not only in motor behavior but in several other areas, including hearing and speech, social-personal behavior, problem-solving ability, eye-hand coordination, and categorizing skills.

The data of Chase and Martin showing that the infants who apparently were malnourished for no longer than the first four months of life were less retarded in physical growth and in mental development than infants who presumably had been malnourished for a longer period of time in early life are in agreement with the report of DeLicardie *et al.* (1971) who found that a group of infants who, for no apparent reason, had a body weight at fifteen days of life below their birth weight, continued to weigh less than their matched controls throughout the first year and to lag behind them in total body length, head circumference, chest circumference, arm circumference, and skin-fold thickness. The lag in somatic growth appears to be unaccompanied by a lag in behavioral development as defined by repeated Gesell testing at monthly intervals. Motor, adaptive, and language development in the weight-loss group is indistinguishable from that of the controls at all ages studied. Thus, initial weight loss followed by a normal rate-of-growth increment does not appear to have significant consequences for behavioral development during the first year of life.

It must be clearly stated that even if all the studies reviewed show an association between the antecedent of malnutrition and mental performance on the child, this in no way represents a causal relationship. Up to the present it is not yet known if postnatal malnutrition is the primary determinant of suboptimal mental functioning, or how it may interact with other factors in the micro- and macroenvironment in producing such effects.

Effects on Performance at School Age

Intelligence Test Performance

Two main research strategies have been used to explore the consequences of early severe malnutrition for intellectual development at school age. The first one compares the IQ of children with documented past histories of severe malnutrition with the IQ of children belonging to the same community but without antecedents of severe malnutrition. Since all research workers have been aware that severely malnourished children live in environments conducive in many ways to lower intellectual performance, they have tried to match index cases with control children for those variables considered of primary importance. The other strategy involves the use of siblings as controls. The assumption here is that siblings will minimize the majority of the demographic or macroenvironmental factors, leaving those related to the specific microenvironment of each child within his or her own family to be accounted for in another way or study.

We will review six studies employing the first strategy and two studies that have used siblings as controls. In total these reports deal with children living in quite different cultural settings, with geographical representations for Europe (Yugoslavia), Asia (India, Indonesia, and the Philippines), Africa (Uganda), the Caribbean (Jamaica), and Latin America (El Salvador and Mexico).

The first study, conducted by Cabak and Najdavic (1965) is a report on the follow-up of thirty-nine Serbian children who had been admitted into a hospital for treatment of severe malnutrition when they were between four and twenty-four months of age. IQ level was assessed at the time the children were between seven and fourteen years old, using the Stepanovic adaptation of the Binet-Simon Scale. The mean IQ in the survivors of malnutrition was 88, which is significantly lower than the mean of 93 found in a group of similar-aged normal children of unskilled workers. This difference is more meaningful when one considers that one third of the children rehabilitated from malnutrition were of a better socioeconomic condition than the controls. Taking occupation as an indicator of social class, the fathers of one third of the previously malnourished children were either professionals or army officers; the rest of the fathers in this group were skilled or unskilled workers. All the fathers in the control group were unskilled workers. Not only was mean IQ lower in the survivors of malnutrition, IQ distribution showed that not a single child in the malnourished group had IQ greater than 110. As a contrast, one half of these children had IQs below 90, with six of them not scoring above 70. These frequencies are in contrast with those found in the general population of Serbian children, in which 32 percent had IQ scores above 110, and only 2.5 percent scored below 70.

The weight deficit at the time of admission into the hospital and the IQ at school age showed a significant association. The more the actual weight differed from the expected for age and sex the lower the IQ score. In other words, intensity and duration of malnutrition in early life appeared to be related to magnitude of intellectual deficit after rehabilitation.

The second study was done in Indonesia by Liang *et al.* (1967) in a group of sixty-four children five to twelve years old whose nutritional status at the age of two to four years was known. Thirty-one children had suffered severe malnutrition in the preschool-age period, with twelve of the patients showing typical signs of vitamin A deficiency. Three to ten years after rehabilitation, when the children were tested with the Goodenough and Wechsler techniques, the children who had been previously malnourished and who had shown signs of vitamin A deficiency in the preschool years had significantly lower intelligence scores than the children who were regarded as non-malnourished during the two to four year age period. The IQ derived from the total Wechsler Scale were 77 ± 2.3 and 68 ± 2.7 respectively for thirty-three children considered as well nourished in the preschool period, and for twelve children who at that time were diagnosed as malnourished and showing vitamin A deficiency. The group of nineteen school-age children whose diagnosis at the preschool age was malnutrition without vitamin A deficiency had a mean IQ of 73 ± 3.3. The difference between normal and malnourished, with or without vitamin A deficiency, is significant at the 0.01 level of confidence. According to the authors, both the intellectual development and the physical size of the school-age children could be predicted with a high degree of accuracy on the basis of their nutritional status during the preschool years.

The third study was conducted in the area of Andhra Pradesh, India, by Champakam, Srikantia, and Gopalan (1968). These authors decided to construct their own intelligence tests in view of the wide cultural differences, regional-linguistic variations, and differences in levels of literacy and education between their subjects and the subjects included in the samples on which standardization has been carried out in India. The battery of intelligence tests developed was based on a point scale devised for subjects ranging in age from eight to eleven years. The test items were chosen so as to explore different functions—reasoning, organization of knowledge, memory, and several perceptual processes. Most of the tests have as their basis the actual manipulation of varied concrete materials by the subjects. Some of the tasks included object assembly, block design, memory of digits and objects, comprehension, and picture arrangement. The population chosen for standardizing the test battery belonged to the same cultural and socio-economic class from which the cases of malnutrition admitted into the hospital were derived.

Nineteen children who had been treated for severe clinical malnutrition of the kwashiorkor type when they were between eighteen and thirty-six months of age were individually tested for intelligence performance when they were between eight and eleven years of age. Each rehabilitated child was matched for age, sex, religion, caste, socioeconomic status, family size, birth order, and educational background of the parents, with three children from the same locality and the same school where the index cases were found. It was also ensured that the control children corresponding to a given index case also were placed in the same class in the school. It was considered that matching for school grade might be a factor that could hide the presence of actual differences between well-nourished and rehabilitated children; but, on the other hand, if differences could be shown under these conditions their significance would be automatically increased.

The results showed a significant difference between the performance of the control and the index subjects with regard to the intelligence tests. The difference was more marked in the younger age group and tended to diminish in the older age group. The mean performance of the index cases, expressed as a percentage of the control subjects was 31.30, 54.45, and 52.44, respectively, for age groups eight to nine, nine to ten, and ten to eleven years. When the total intelligence scale was split into its four main components—memory, perceptual ability, abstract ability, and verbal ability—the differences between the groups were sustained in all four abilities. Very seldom was an overlapping of values observed between the low scores of the previously malnourished children and the relatively much higher values of the controls.

Guthrie, Guthrie, and Tayag (1969) approached the study of nutrition and intellectual development in a slightly different way. They chose a sample of school-age children from a relatively homogeneous socioeconomic and environmental background, with the idea of minimizing the extent to which differences in performance could be attributed to other factors such as impoverished intellectual environment, social deprivation, and minimal motivation. These factors were actually found to vary little from family to family in the sample.

A nonverbal intelligence test standardized for use in Philippine children was administered to 413 children attending an elementary school in a rural village in the Philippines. Correlations between total body height and intelligence scores indicated that taller children at any age performed better on the intelligence test than the shorter children. Since Guthrie and associates have shown that the correlation between height and intellectual development is essentially zero among urban Philippine populations, the positive and significant correlations found in the sample of children exhibiting marked deficiencies in height in comparison with children from urban public schools is taken as a suggestion that malnutrition may be at least partly responsible for the lower levels of intellectual performance characteristic of the shorter rural children.

From a total of ninety cases of marasmus admitted to the Rosales Hospital of El Salvador, Central America, during the years 1958–60, Guillen-Alvarez (1971) was able to locate fourteen cases who had suffered the disease at ages between three to nineteen months. Psychological test performance of the survivors aged ten to twelve years old was compared with the performance of a group of twenty-five rural children of similar age and socioeconomic condition who did not have antecedents of severe malnutrition. IQs were obtained from a battery of tests which included: Raven Progressive Matrices, Koch Test, and Goodenough Test.

The results of the psychometric evaluation showed significant differences in intellectual performance between the survivors of marasmus and the control children. Thus, while three of the twenty-five controls had IQs below 70, twelve of the fourteen nutritionally rehabilitated children scored that low. At the other end of the scale, while fourteen out of the twenty-five controls had IQs at or above 91, only one child with antecedents of marasmus reached that level.

The sixth study was conducted in Uganda, Africa, by Hoorweg and Stanfield (1972) in a group of eighty children aged eleven to seventeen years. Sixty of the eighty subjects were survivors of clinical severe malnutrition (a combination of kwashiorkor and marasmus) suffered before twenty-seven months of age. The other twenty children had no antecedents (clinical and anthropometric) of severe malnutrition. To test the hypothesis that the effects of malnutrition are greater the more severe the illness and the younger the age of the affected child, the subjects to be examined were selected, from all the records of patients and normal children kept and carefully preserved in a rural clinic near Kampala, in such a way as to give three groups of twenty former patients each, who had been treated for severe malnutrition at different ages, and a group of twenty controls. Group 1 consisted of former patients who had been treated before sixteen months of age (average admission age, 12.6 months). Group 2 consisted of former patients who had been admitted between the ages of sixteen and twenty-one months (average 24.1 months). Group 3 consisted of children between twenty-two and twenty-seven months.

Severity of malnutrition was scored according to: (1) overall clinical impression made and recorded at the actual time of discharge from hospital; (2) weight on admission as a percentage of expected mean for age in the same ethnic group (Baganda); (3) the amount of edema; (4) skin changes; and (5) the total serum protein level. Although severity of malnutrition was not taken into account in matching, the average severity scores of the three malnourished groups did not differ.

The controls were children with a recorded follow-up of at least two years beginning in the first year of life and a weight curve that did not fall below the Boston tenth percentile during the recorded period. For both control and index cases, children who had had any possible acute brain insult such as convulsions or severe respiratory infection with anoxia were excluded, as were those with long-term chronic infections such as tuberculosis.

All four groups of Baganda children were matched, as nearly as possible, on the variables of age; sex (eleven boys and nine girls in each group); child's educational level; guardians' education; guardians' occupation; quality of house; and presence of radio, bicycle, and dining table.

Psychological test performance was assessed in terms of general intelligence (Raven Coloured Matrices), verbal abilities (arithmetic test of the Wechsler Intelligence Scale for Children, and a vocabulary test of Luganda words and idioms); spatial and perceptual abilities (Block Design subtest of the Wechsler Adult Intelligence Scale and Porteus mazes); visual memory (Graham and Kendall's Memory for Designs); short-term memory (Knox Cubes). Learning and incidental learning was examined by instructing subjects to memorize associations between six animals and six colors, each color presented on two shapes; motor development assessment was measured by the Lincoln-Oseretsky Scale.

Five of the ten psychological tests revealed significantly better performance in the control group as compared with the three mal-nourished groups taken together. These were the Raven Matrices as a measure of general intelligence, the Block Design Test, Memory for Designs, incidental learning, and the dexterity part of the Lincoln-Oseretsky Motor Development Scale. No difference was found on verbal abilities, a maze test, and a short-term memory test.

When the performance was compared of the survivors of malnutrition suffered at different ages, significant differences were found in Memory for Designs on which group 3 did better than groups 1 and 2, and in the learning task (first trial) on which group 2 did better than group 1. In two other tests, incidental learning and Knox Cubes, the differences as a function of age at which malnutrition occurred reached a significant level of confidence of 0.10. It seems important to remark that these four tests are all concerned with different aspects of memory and learning. The findings are then in the expected direction in which those who suffered younger do more poorly.

Unfortunately, a test for the hypothesis of severity could not be done since the survivors of malnutrition did not differ in the severity score, there were no differences in anthropometric measurements at the age of testing, and duration of malnutrition before admission for treatment was unknown.

Two studies on the effect of early malnutrition on intellectual performance using the sibling strategy will be reviewed. In the first one, conducted in Mexico (Birch et al. 1971), measured intelligence at school age was compared in thirty seven survivors of severe malnutrition and in thirty seven of their siblings closest in age. The malnourished children all had been hospitalized for severe chronic malnutrition of the kwashiorkor type when they were between six and thirty months of age. No cases of marasmus were included, and the group was relatively homogeneous both for severity of illness and for type. All children had been discharged to the family following nutritional rehabilitation. The average time of hospitalization was six weeks, with a range of from one to two months. During the hospital stay children were visited by their mothers for a three- to four-hour period every other day. The ratio of nursing staff to children was high, with one nurse available for every three children. Care in hospital in general was good and considerate, but no special stimulation procedures were applied.

No detailed data were available with respect to the quality of the diets received by the children after their discharge from the hospital. Although it would be appropriate to assume from knowledge of the social circumstances in which the children lived that such diets were suboptimal, in no cases were any of the children ever readmitted to any hospital for severe malnutrition.

At follow-up the children were between five and thirteen years of age. In all cases intellectual evaluation was carried out at least three years after discharge from the hospital. To make follow-up practicable, the cases selected were restricted to children living in the vicinity of Mexico City. To obtain the sample the archives of the Department of Pediatrics were searched to produce a consecutive series of cases of severe malnutrition at appropriate ages at admission, follow-up, and residence. Fifty-one cases were identified and searched for in the community. Forty-two children were located, and thirty-seven of these had a sibling whose age was within three years of the index case and a family willing to take part in the follow-up. The child chosen as the control was the one in the surviving subship nearest in age to the index case and without any prior history of an incident of severe malnutrition. The age distributions of the index cases and of the sibling controls were very similar. This was the consequence of the sibling closest in age tending to be randomly older or younger than the index case. Sex distribution was somewhat divergent with relatively more females in the control cases. Difference in sex ratio, however, was not significant (chi-square $= 1.95; p > 0.10$).

At follow-up each child was individually examined to determine intellectual level. The test used was the Wechsler Intelligence Scale for Children (WISC) in its Spanish adaptation. Although it was recognized that this test lacks sensitivity for the youngest children studied, it was judged desirable to use it for all children rather than to substitute a different and probably noncomparable test for the youngest age group.

Full scale WISC IQ of the index cases (sexes combined) was 68.5 and of the controls 81.5. Verbal and performance differences were of similar magnitude and in the same direction. All mean IQ differences were significant at less than the 5 percent level of confidence. If an IQ score of below 70 is considered a customary cut-off point for the definition of mental retardation then twice as many of the previously malnourished children as their siblings functioned below this level; eighteen malnourished, compared with nine of the control subjects, had an IQ below 70. Moreover, of those with a low IQ, ten of the index cases were below 60, contrasted with only two of the control subjects. At the other extreme of the distribution, in the conventionally normal range, the reverse picture obtains: ten of the control subjects compared with four of the index cases had an IQ of 90 or higher. Differences in age between the survivors of malnutrition and their siblings did not affect the differences in intellectual test performance between the two groups. No significant sex difference in IQ was found among the rehabilitated children. The mean full scale IQ for boys and girls, respectively, was 70.7 ± 14.08 and 68.6 ± 13.83. In the siblings there was a significant difference between the sexes, with the boys having significantly higher full scale and verbal IQ than the girls. When comparisons between index cases and siblings were done separately by sex, it was found that the previously malnourished boys differed from the control boys significantly, with control subjects having a full scale IQ approximately twelve points higher than the survivors of severe malnutrition. Although control girls also had somewhat higher IQ than girls who were previously malnourished, the size of the difference was insufficient to result in statistical significance. This pattern of findings was entirely the result of the depressed level of IQ in the girls in the control group. No reasons for this depression could be found in differing educational experience since there were no sex differences in school attendance. A depressed level of IQ in girls relative to boys, however, has been repeatedly found in children of school age in the social groups considered and probably derives from the far lower social value attached to girls in this particular subculture (Cravioto, Lindoro, and Birch 1971).

Our finding of sex differences in the degree to which index cases and controls differed poses a difficult issue for interpretation. It may be argued that a bout of severe malnutrition has greater effects on boys than on girls because of genetic differences between the sexes in their abilities to withstand the negative effects of stress. Such an interpretation, however, is difficult to defend in view of the significantly lower IQ of control females over control males. This finding, together with the fact that male and female index cases had comparable levels of IQ, suggests that females were more significantly disadvantaged within the families on a long-term basis whether or not they have had an acute episode of severe malnutrition and hospitalization. Such an inference is in accord with the value systems of the social group to which the families belong and in accord with findings on Puerto Rican children in New York (Lesser, Fifer, and Clark 1965).

The use of siblings as control subjects has certain implications for the interpretation of findings. Such controls are of course advantageous in that the children who are compared come from the same families and share a common experiential ambience. Demographic data, however, strongly suggest that having a child hospitalized for severe malnutrition in fact identifies a family in which all children are at risk for significant subnutrition on a chronic basis. Therefore, the cases and controls are similar in sharing a common exposure to subnutrition on a lifelong basis and differ only in that the cases have a superimposed episode of acute exacerbation. As a result, growth achievements may be similar in patients and siblings, and developmental differences minimized. Consequently, the comparison of sibs and patients does not provide a full picture of the overall effects of nutritional inadequacy on development. Rather, it indicates the additional consequence for maldevelopment which may attach to an acute episode of severe malnutrition. One would, therefore, expect intellectual level in the entire subship to be depressed, a view supported by our findings. Therefore, a significant difference in IQ between children hospitalized in early childhood with a bout of severe malnutrition and their siblings is especially convincing evidence of the negative contribution which an episode of kwashiorkor with hospitalization makes to mental development. The use of siblings as controls also means that the children compared have shared a generally disadvantageous social and family environment which in itself can contribute to the depression of intellectual level. This factor, too, should result in the minimizing of differences between controls and cases and provides further support to the significance of the influence of the acute episode of severe malnutrition on cognitive competence.

Hertzig, Birch, Richardson, and Tizard (1972) in examining our study on siblings and survivors of severe malnutrition, have considered that our conclusions are limited by the facts that the sample studied was relatively small, the sibs not of the same sex, and that no general population comparison group was concomitantly examined. They also point out that in conducting a sibling-comparison study, differences in certain characteristics of the siblings to be compared must be considered in the analysis of findings. Among these differences age and ordinal position are singled out since both may affect child-rearing practices as well as intellectual outcome. These authors have also rightly questioned our suggestion that children who had suffered severe chronic malnutrition in the first year of life may have more serious consequences than children who experienced the disorder at a later time in life, the main argument in favor of their opinion being the lack of follow-up of our patients after discharge from the hospital. They have also indicated that since interference with brain development would be reflected in altered IQ, a first step in exploring this issue is the determination of the degree to which intellectual functioning at school age is differentially depressed in children who have experienced severe clinical malnutrition at different ages in the first years of life.

In view of those considerations they decided to conduct a study concerned with two issues:

1. The degree to which children malnourished before two years of age differ from their sibs and classmates in intellectual competence at school age.

2. The degree to which malnutrition at different times during the first two years of life is differentially associated with intellectual outcome at school age.

Intellectual functioning (WISC) at school age was studied in seventy-four Jamaican boys who had suffered from severe malnutrition before the age of two years. In all cases detailed clinical and metabolic records were available. The three main clinic types of severe malnutrition—kwashiorkor, marasmus, and marasmic-kwashiorkor—were represented. Children on the average were hospitalized for a period of eight weeks. In general, follow-up visits in the homes were conducted for two years following discharge. At time of the study the children were five years, eleven months through ten years of age. This age range was selected in order to be far enough removed from the time of acute illness, and for the children to be at an age where intelligence testing has predictive validity for later life.

Two control groups were included in the study, the first one composed of male siblings from the previously malnourished children. For a sibling to be included in this control group he had to be male of course, between six and twelve years of age, nearest in age to his malnourished brother, and without a history of severe clinical malnutrition. In view of the patterns of family composition in Jamaica, a sibling was defined as a child having the same biologic mother as the index case and having shared a home residence with the previously malnourished child for most of his life. Only thirty-eight of such siblings were identified and studied. Because of the selection criteria used, the siblings were somewhat older than the survivors of severe malnutrition.

The second control group was made up of classmates or neighbors of the index cases. For index children attending school, two male classmates closest in age to the index case were selected. If the first comparison child was not available for examination, the second comparison was used. Some of the index boys, though of school age, were not going to school. For these cases, a comparison case was chosen by finding the nearest neighboring child who was not a relative and who was of an age within six months of the index case. For some index cases at small schools no classmate was within six months of age. For these cases neighbor children were also used as comparisons. Of the seventy-four comparison cases, sixty-three were classmates and eleven were yardmates who met all criteria of selection. As would be expected from the method of selecting comparison children, index and comparison children lived in the same general neighborhood from which the school drew its pupils. In three cases comparison children could not be brought in for study. This resulted in seventy-one pairs of index and comparison children.

Each child's intellectual level was individually evaluated by means of the WISC. All children were examined without the examiners being aware of the group to which the child belonged.

A comparison of the Full Scale, Verbal, and Performance IQ in the three groups showed that survivors of severe malnutrition had all IQ measures at significantly lower levels than the control groups, with siblings placed at an intermediate position and classmates and neighbors having the highest scores. When the intellectual quotients of survivors and siblings were compared, only Full Scale IQ and Verbal IQ were significantly different. Performance IQ, although slightly higher in the sibling group, was not statistically different from the mean obtained in the survivors. Contrariwise, Performance IQ was the only significant measure different between siblings and the control group of mates. In interpreting the data it is of importance to note that no age trend for IQ was found in the study groups, nor was ordinal position of sibs responsible for the differences obtained.

Since the WISC test has a floor value of forty-six points for the Full Scale and the Verbal Scale, and of forty-four points for the Performance Scale, it is apparent that even if a child were always wrong, his minimal IQ would be the floor value. With this in mind, Hertzig *et al.* compared the number of survivors of severe malnutrition and of control children who scored at this low level. Twenty-three percent of the survivors against 7 percent of the controls were at the floor level for the Full Scale IQ. This difference is significant at the 0.01 level of statistical confidence. Similar results were obtained for the Performance Scale with no significant difference in the Verbal Scale. This analysis clearly shows the very low levels of IQ present in the survivors of severe malnutrition and points out the lack of representativeness of the median IQ values.

In relation to the question of age at which severe malnutrition occurs and severity of intellectual impairment, Hertzig *et al.* decided to approach the issue through a correlation between age of hospitalization of the child for treatment and IQ at school age. Accordingly, they divided their group of survivors of malnutrition into three sub-groups whose ages on admission were below eight months for subgroup 1, between eight and twelve months for subgroup 2, and between thirteen and twenty-four months for the third subgroup. An analysis of variance of IQ levels showed that the means for the subgroups were not statistically different at the 0.05 level of confidence. The authors' conclusion is that no systematic differences in intellectual outcome at school age attached to severe malnutrition experienced at different ages during the first two years of life.

It is unfortunate that Hertzig *et al.* fell in the trap of considering time of appearance of a malnourished child for treatment as equivalent to time at which malnutrition is experienced. In almost all societies where malnutrition is highly prevalent children are not taken to the hospital because of malnutrition *per se;* the reason for seeking treatment is the presence of an added infection producing an emergency situation superimposed on a chronic condition generally not recognized by the child's caretaker. Acute electrolyte disturbances due to an especially severe bout of diarrhea and bronchopneumonia are among the most common type of intercurrent problems that force the parents to take the child to the hospital. Accordingly, age of admission is not a measure of the time at which malnutrition is experienced but rather of the time at which "something" called the attention of the caretaker. Moreover, in the particular case of the kwashiorkor type of the nutritional deprivation it should be remembered that the characteristic edema is rarely noticed by the parents unless it appears suddenly. It can be easily shown that after the edema disappears during the recovery period body weight and body height give clear indications of the chronicity of the nutritional deprivation. Perhaps a better measure of time of appearance of severe malnutrition would be the difference in body height between the children. One could hypothesize that the greater the difference between actual height and expected height for age on admission may show differences in both height and performance at school age. A combination of time of occurrence of malnutrition and severity could then be tested. Since Hertzig's data show very clearly that mean differences in IQ between survivors of malnutrition and the comparison groups are obscured by the significant number of survivors who score at the floor level of the WISC, it might be convenient to test for differences in outcome as related to time, duration, and severity of chronic malnutrition with non-parametric techniques since in fact IQ values in survivors do not conform to an interval scale.

The results of all the eight reported studies show that the environment in which children at risk of malnutrition live is highly negative in its effects on mental development. Irrespective of the presence or absence of a previous admission to a hospital because of severe malnutrition, children developing in this milieu have a high probability of showing poor performance on intelligence testing. The presence of a superimposed episode of malnutrition occurring early in life and of enough severity to force the child into a hospital increases the change of scoring at values even lower than those characteristic of the poor environment.

It must be emphasized that the finding of an association between early malnutrition and lower mental development is by no means evidence that the insufficient intake of nutrients and calories *per se* affects intellectual competence and learning in man.

Neurointegrative Functioning

To explore the effects of malnutrition on neurointegrative development it was decided to carry out a cross-sectional study of intersensory functioning in the total population of primary school children in a village in which detailed prior information indicated the presence of a significant prevalence level of serious acute or prolonged malnutrition during infancy and the preschool years (Cravioto, DeLicardie, and Birch 1966). For purposes of the investigation malnutrition was defined retrospectively on the basis of height for age in all children ranging in age from six to eleven years. When the child showed a significant diminution of stature with respect to his age mates in the total village population of children, he was assumed to have an increased likelihood of having been at earlier risk of malnutrition. On this basis, at each age level, a group of children representing the lowest 25 percent of the height distribution was identified and designated as the group having the greatest likelihood of having been at earlier nutritional risk. The functioning of this group was compared with that of the children in the village who were in the tallest quartile for age and so, assuming all other factors to be equal, representing those with the least likelihood of having experienced a significant degree of malnution earlier in life. In this way groups of children with common ethnic background were identified and represented the upper and lower quartiles by height of individuals in the age groups studied.

Clearly, at least three important variables must be controlled for when height for age is used as an index of prior nutritional risk. The first is related to parental stature and thus to familial factors affecting height. Since height at school age may reflect not only the individual's nutritional background but also his parental endowment, it was necessary in designing the study to obtain anthropometric information on parents as well as on children in order to control for this variable.

A second consideration was that low stature during the years studied may represent a general maturational lag in the course of which both height and intersensory functioning may both be subnormal. To control for this possibility it was necessary to study a second sample of children of the same ages who exhibited equivalent differences in height but who had little or no likelihood of ever having been at nutritional risk.

Finally, since no integrative capacity is unaffected by environmental influences, comparative information on the social, economic, and educational status of the families from which the children derived had to be obtained.

The indicator of neurointegrative development selected for study was intersensory organization. This was done for two reasons. In the first place a considerable body of evidence both in comparative psychology (Maier and Schneirla 1935; Birch 1954) and evolutionary physiology (Voronin and Guselnikov 1963) has accumulated, suggesting that the emergence of complex adaptive capacities was underlain by the growth of increasing liaison and interdependence among the separate sense systems. Sherrington (1951) in considering this process, has gone so far as to argue that "the naive would have expected evolution in its course to have supplied us with more various sense organs for ampler perception of the world. . . . The policy had rather been to bring by the nervous system the so-called 'five' into closer touch with one another. . . . A central clearing house of sense has grown up. . . . Not new senses, but better liaison between old senses is what the developing nervous system had in this respect stood for." In addition, a variety of studies (Birch and Bitterman 1949, 1951) indicated that the basic mechanisms involved in primary learning (i.e., the formation of conditioned reflexes) was probably the effective establishment and patterning of intersensory organization.

The second reason for using intersensory competence as an indicator of neurointegrative development stems from the fact that Birch and Lefford (1964) had shown that adequacy of intersensory interrelations improved as a clearly defined growth function in normal children between the ages of six to twelve years. In school children, comparable in age with the ones we were planning to study, they found that the interrelations among three sense systems—touch, vision, and kinesthesis—improved in an age-specific manner and resulted in developmental curves that were as regular as those for skeletal growth.

The design of the study was based on the view that it was feasible to conduct a comparative study of neurointegrative functioning in school-age children in whom extremes of difference in height at school ages were to be used as an index of preschool nutritional adequacy. Since height as such may with equal readiness be an indicator of maturation or constitution as of antecedent malnutrition, height as such had to be controlled for by studying a comparison sample of children who differed in stature but among whom it was most improbable that the shortest children had been subjected to nutritional stress. It was therefore decided to replicate the rural study on an upper-class urban sample of school children who were most unlikely to have been at nutritional risk and whose variations in height would be unrelated to either primary or secondary malnutrition. The rural-community study was ecologic in its organization and sought to relate growth achievements as well as intersensory development to the social, economic, educational, and physical characteristics of the families from which the children derived. In this connection the findings obtained through studying the urban group could be treated not only with respect to the problem of stature but also as a device for teasing out the relations between growth and function in a socially differentiated rural group by comparing it with a socially and economically homogenous urban group in which height differences existed but could not be related to conditions of nutrition, health, or social standing.

The standing height of all the children aged six to eleven was measured by two pediatricians previously trained in standardized procedures. All the measurements were then arranged in decreasing order of magnitude. Quartiles were calculated for each age and sex. All the children who fell in the upper- and lower-height quartiles were selected to be tested for intersensory development.

The comparison group of school age children were all students at a private school whose pupils were drawn from upper–middle-class and upper-class families. Family income was uniformly high, and educational background of the parents in all cases was beyond the secondary school level.

The method used for studying intersensory integration was that developed and described by Birch and Lefford (1964). Equivalence relationships among the visual, haptic, and kinesthetic sense modalities were explored for geometric-form recognition. The term "haptic" is used here for the complex sensory input obtained by active manual exploration of a test object. Such exploration involves tactile, kinesthetic, and surface-movement sensations from the subjects' fingers and hand, such as are obtained in manipulating an object. The kinesthetic sense, in this study, refers to the sensory inputs obtained through passive arm movement. In the current investigation such a motion entailed sensory input from the wrist, elbow, and shoulder joints and from the arm and shoulder musculature as its principal components.

To study intersensory equivalence in the perception of geometric forms, a paired comparison technique was utilized. A form presented to one sensory system was compared with forms presented in another sensory system. Thus, a visually presented standard was compared with a series of forms presented haptically or kinesthetically. Similarly, a haptically presented standard was compared with a kinesthetically presented series. On the basis of such examination the existence of cross-modality equivalences and nonequivalences between the visual and hapatic sensory systems, between the visual and the kinesthetic sensory systems, and between the haptic and kinesthetic sensory systems could be determined.

The physical growth achievements at each age level of the most stunted and the most fully grown 25 percent of the rural children are summarized in Table 1.3. It may be noted from this table that in the rural community at

Table 1.3
Mean and Range of Height in Centimeters of Rural School-Age Children at Extremes of Difference in Stature

Age (yr)	6	7	8	9	10	11
Lower quartile for height	98	106	108	113	114	119
Range	96–99.5	101–108	99–110	107–116.5	109–116.5	113–123
Upper quartile for height	107	113	119	124	127	134
Range	105–113	111.5–118	116–122	122–126	124–133	131–138

each year of age the children in the lower quartile and the upper quartile represented extremes of growth achievement.

When the intersensory performances of the children in the upper quartile of growth achievement are contrasted with those made by the children in the lower-height quartile, differences in intersensory integrative skills are manifested for all three combinations of intersensory integration studied. These differences are particularly clear over the whole age span for the errors of nonequivalence that were made when children misjudged identical forms presented across two modalities.

Differences in the number of errors of equivalence made by the two

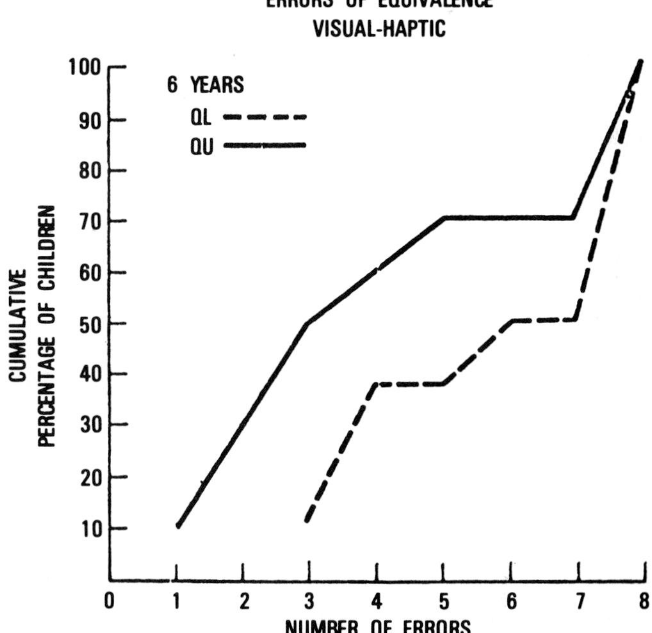

Figure 1.9. Proportions of tall and short six-year-old rural children making errors of equivalence in visual-haptic judgment. QL = Lower Quartile; QU = Upper Quartile. *From Cravioto* et al. (*1966*).

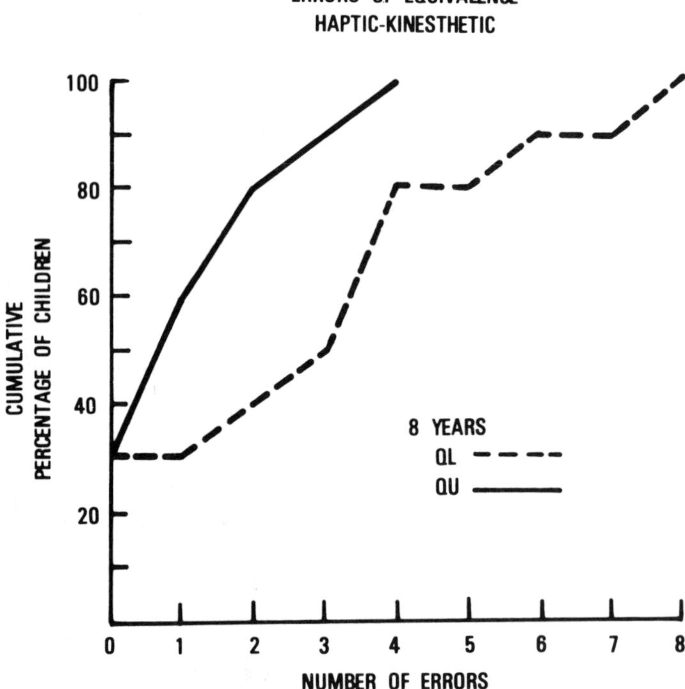

Figure 1.10. Proportions of tall and short eight-year-old rural children making errors of equivalence in haptic-kinesthetic judgment. *From Cravioto* et al. (*1966*).

height groups in judging nonidentical forms also tended to favor the taller group of children. This difference was most notable in the performance of the youngest groups of children, the six-year olds. Figures 1.9, 1.10, and 1.11 present the data on the cumulative percentage of six-year-old children in the two height groups who made errors of equivalence and clearly indicate the lag in development of intersensory competence that was present in the shorter children during the first school year.

As may be seen from Table 1.4 the upper and lower height quartiles of the upper social class also represented extremes of growth achievement. The mean difference in height across ages for the tallest and shortest urban children was 15.5 cm., a value which was absolutely larger than that obtained between upper and lower quartiles in the rural population studied. Moreover, as may be noted by comparing the data in Table 1.3 with those in Table 1.4, the shortest urban children were comparable in height to the tallest group in the rural sample.

The general form of curves for age-specific performances in the urban children resembles that obtained for the rural children, the only difference is of a quantitative nature; urban children being significantly more advanced in their intersensory integrative ability. In Figures 1.12 and 1.13 it can be seen

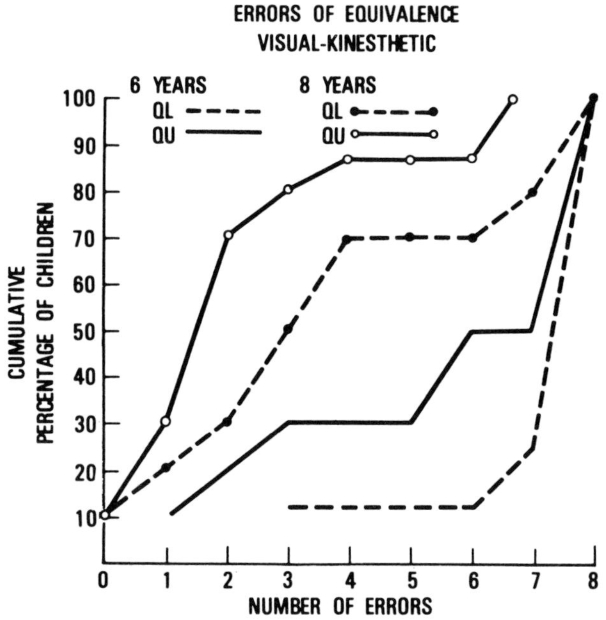

Figure 1.11. Proportions of tall and short six and eight-year-old rural children making errors of equivalence in visual-kinesthetic judgment. *From Cravioto* et al. (*1966*).

that the developmental course of visual-kinesthetic and haptic-kinesthetic integration is identical for the two groups and a simple modification of constants would clearly result in the super-imposition of the age-specific error curves.

For neither errors of equivalence or nonequivalence nor for any pair of sense modalities did difference in height in this upper social stratum find a reflection in differences in the adequacy of intersensory integration. It appeared, therefore, that differences in height as such, when they occurred in children who were not at risk of nutritional deprivation, did not result in differences in the rate of intersensory development or in the level of in-

Table 1.4

Mean and Range of Height in Centimeters of the Groups of School-Age Children of an Urban Upper Social Class Tested for Intersensory Organization

Age (yr)	6	7	8	9	10	11
Lower quartile						
for height	111	115	121	130	130	135
Range	106–115.5	110–118	119–123	125.5–133	127–132	132.5–137.5
Upper quartile						
for height	126	130	137	141	147	156
Range	124.5–129	128.5–135	132.5–141	137–147	145–150	155–157

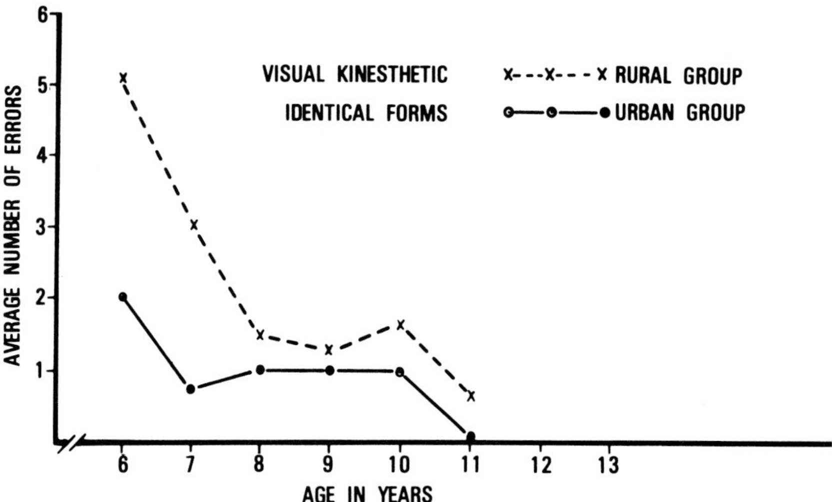

Figure 1.12. Comparison of the age-specific error curves for visual-kinesthetic intersensory organization of rural children and upper social-class urban children. *From Cravioto* et al. (*1966*).

tersensory competence that was achieved at a given age. This lack of difference is illustrated by Figure 1.14, in which the visual-kinesthetic error performance by age of the two height extremes of the upper social class urban group are plotted. Similar overlapping between the two height groups occurred for the other intersensory integrations studied.

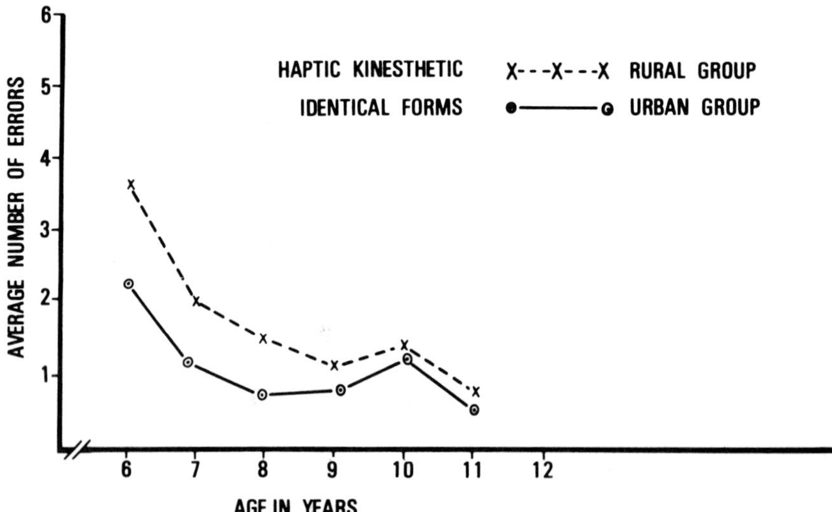

Figure 1.13. Comparison of the age-specific error curves for haptic-kinesthetic intersensory organization of rural children and upper social-class urban children. *From Carvioto* et al. (*1966*).

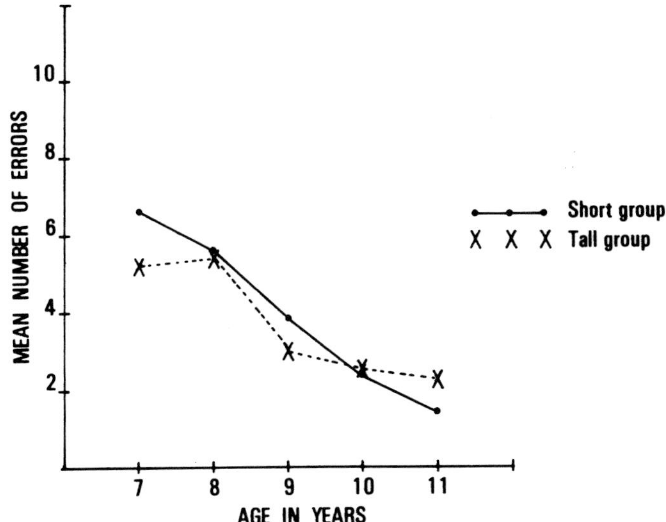

Figure 1.14. Comparative performance of tall and short urban children in judgments of nonequivalence in kinesthetic-visual modalities. *From Cravioto,* Czechoslovak Academy of Sciences *1 (1967b):57.*

Two types of analysis were made of the available familial and environmental background information. The first of these was concerned with identifying factors which contributed to growth achievement. On the basis of the information collected, it was possible to analyze the relation of height at a given age to height of the parents, to the family's economic status, to housing conditions, and to parental education level. Each of these will be considered in turn.

There was a tendency for the fathers of the taller children in the rural sample to be taller than the fathers of the children in the lowest quartile, with the mean difference in paternal height across ages 4.3 cm. However, this difference failed to meet an acceptable criterion of statistical significance. The mean heights of the mothers of the rural children in the upper and lower height quartiles were also insignificantly different from one another. Thus, parental height in the group did not appear to be significantly related to the height of the children. The height of the fathers of the upper social-class urban children appears to be more significantly related to the height of the child. The mean difference in paternal height across ages was 8.8 cm and is statistically significant (p. less than 0.05 one tail). Maternal height however, showed no systematic relation to height of offspring.

In the rural community studied, neither income per capita nor the proportion of total expenditure devoted to food bore any systematic relation to the height of the children.

Although there was a tendency for the shorter rural children to live in families having somewhat superior housing conditions, the difference was not significant at the 0.05 level of statistical confidence. Similarly, the relation of personal cleanliness of either parents or child to height of child was not statistically significant.

The only strong positive association found between background circumstances and the child's height was between height of child and educational level of the mother. When the educational level was below the median for the sample of mothers studied, the likelihood was greater that her child would be short. Conversely, if her educational level was above the population median there was a strong likelihood that her child would be in the taller segment of the population. It is of interest that no significant association was obtained between the father's educational status and the child's height.

Since the height of the father in the urban group had been found to be ralated to the height of the child, it was decided to examine whether the father's height made any significant contribution to the child's intersensory performance. To carry out this analysis fathers were grouped in accordance with whether their heights were above or below the median for the sample, and the relation of the father's group position to the intersensory performance of the children was plotted.

No significant association was found between the height of the fathers and the level of intersensory competence achieved by the child.

A replication of this study in a different cultural setting gave essentially the same results (Cravioto and Birch 1967).

Trying to extend our inquiry to other types of cross-modal integration, a study of auditory visual equivalence was carried out in the school children of a Mexican rural area where malnutrition in early life is highly prevalent (Cravioto, Gaona-Espinosa, and Birch 1967).

All children aged seven through twelve were weighed and measured by a pediatrician especially trained in somatic measurement, and on the basis of height two groups were identified, one representing the upper 25 percent of the height group for each age and sex and the other the lowest 25 percent. This resulted in a total group of 296 children, 141 boys and 155 girls.

The children's ability to integrate auditory and visual stimuli was individually studied by a method of equivalence (Birch and Belmont 1964). The children were asked to identify visual dot patterns corresponding to rhythmic auditory patterns. The task therefore explored the ability to equate a temporally structured set of auditory stimuli with a spatially distributed set of visual ones. Sounds were tapped with a 1/2-second pause between taps for short intervals and a 1-second pause for long intervals. The corresponding visual patterns from which the specific selections were to be made were presented immediately after the completion of the auditory stimulation. Each set of visual stimuli was presented on separate 5 × 8 inch cards, and on any exposure only the specific set of visual dot patterns appropriate to the given auditory presentation was viewed.

Figure 1.15 shows that for the children as a whole the ability to in-

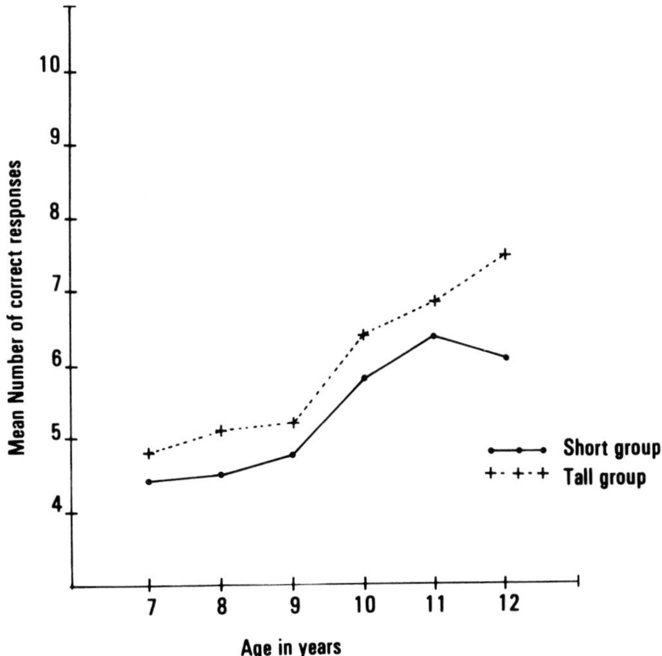

Figure 1.15. Auditory-visual integrative ability of rural children differing in height. *From Cravioto* et al. (*1967d*).

tegrate auditory and visual information over the age span considered. The most rapid improvement occurred between the ages of nine and eleven years. The relative ability of the short and tall children to integrate auditory and visual information over the age span may be seen in Figure 1.15. Both groups show improvement with age, with the greatest rate of improvement occurring between the ages of nine and eleven. However, at each age level the mean performance of the taller group is higher than that of the shorter. This difference is most striking at age twelve, when the shorter group has a mean score of 6.1 correct responses in contrast to 7.5 correct responses for the taller children.

A more detailed view of the differences in performance in the two groups may be obtained from the cumulative-frequency percentage curves presented in Figure 1.16 and 1.17. These data suggest that not only are the mean values for the two groups different, but that these do not reflect a small number of extreme cases. Rather, they characterize general differences in the groups as a whole. By age twelve, 42 percent of the taller children were making eight or more correct judgments, with 30 percent achieving a perfect score of 10. In contrast, only 9 percent of the shorter children in this age group achieved scores of eight or greater, with none making a perfect score.

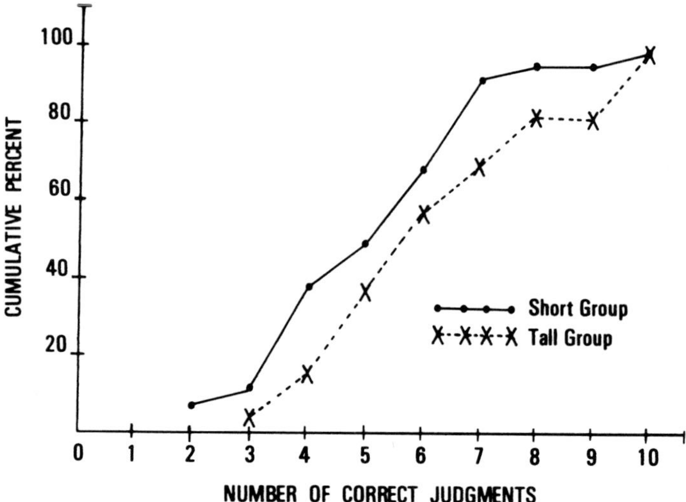

Figure 1.16. Auditory-visual integration in rural children (ten years old). *From Cravioto* et al. (*1967d*).

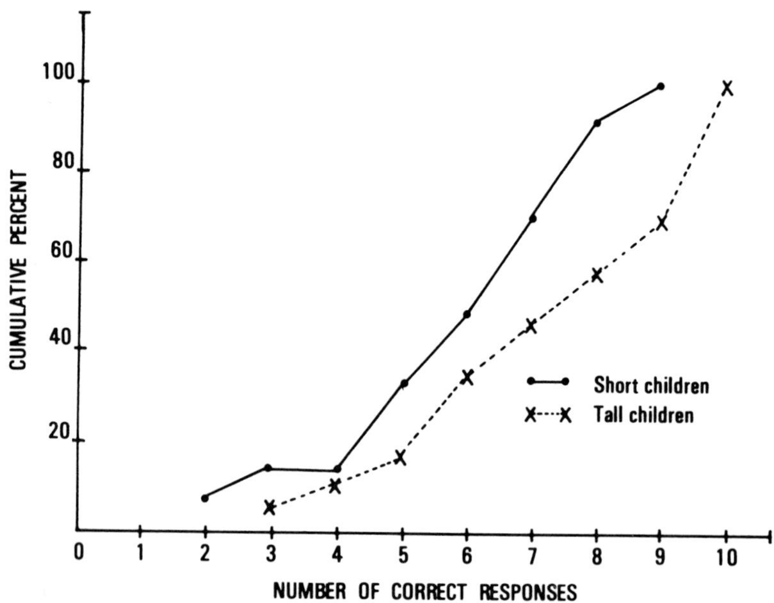

Figure 1.17. Auditory-visual integration in rural children (twelve years old). *From Cravioto* et al. (*1967d*).

Two facts clearly emerge from the results presented. For these rural children a difference in height is accompanied by a difference in intersensory integrative ability. For the upper social-class urban sample, differences in height are not associated with differences in intersensory integrative competence. Therefore, height as such cannot be considered as a determinant of intersensory integrative organization unless such differences in height occurred under circumstances in which the height differential developed from causes which affect intersensory integrative organization.

Differences in growth in the rural children are most likely to have derived from a failure to have received appropriate amounts and kinds of food (primary malnutrition), or to have been the product of infectious disease or parasitic infestations which have secondarily interfered with the individual's nutritional state either directly by increasing tissue catabolism without a compensatory increase in food intake, or indirectly through anorexia or social custom, in accordance with which greatly reduced food consumption is deemed therapeutic in preschool children during illness and convalescence (Wilson, Bressani, and Scrimshaw 1961; Cravioto 1958). When group differences in height do not derive from such a background set of risks, short stature is most likely to reflect familial differences in stature and therefore to be unassociated with disturbances in growth deriving from malnutrition. Such a view is supported by the strong relation of paternal height to height of the offspring in the upper social-class urban group and the presence of a weak association in the rural population.

Whether the inadequacy in intersensory integrative performance in the rural children represents a reflection of malnutrition, or whether both poor integration and growth differences are associated with more general subcultural differences, which, in an underlying way may have contributed independently to differences in growth and to differences in intersensory functioning, is a question that cannot be answered with the design employed in the investigation. However, one can speculate that if social impoverishment, including inadequate opportunity for learning, were the primary interference contributing independently to low stature and to poor intersensory development, a significant association would have been found between low stature and the various social factors that have been implicated as contributors to poor psychological development, such as family income, proportion of income spent on food, housing conditions, and personal cleanliness. It is against this hypothesis that none of these variables were significantly associated with body height in the rural children. The only significant association with a sociocultural factor was the correlation with the mother's educational level.

The positive relation of the mother's education to intersensory adequacy must be considered in association with the distribution of responsibility within the household, and particularly with the relation of the mother to child care and child health. It is important to remember, in this respect, that in this, as in many other rural societies in Latin America, the closeness of the child to his mother during the first years of life is not confined to physical contact, but that rules and practices of health and care in the household belong to the women's world. There is, therefore, a strong posibility that the better-educated female will rely less on traditional methods of feeding and child care, which are a direct cause of reduced intake of nutrients in health and disease particularly in early life. On the other hand, it is also possible that a better-educated mother would function as a more efficient primary socializing agent, and in this way may exert a stronger positive influence on the mental development of her infant. In support of this idea Bayley (1954) has reported a strong association between the IQs of mothers and children. Similar data have been presented by Kagan and Moss (1959).

Considering that, independently of the mechanism involved, the children who showed poor growth also showed delayed development in intersensory functioning, it seems important to discuss the possible significance of the developmental lag to more complex behavioral functioning. Two significant features of learning will be considered: conditioned-reflex formation and the acquisition of certain academic skills.

In most conditioning situations, what is demanded is the integration of two stimuli each belonging to a different sensory modality. For example, in classical salivary conditioning or in conditioning of leg withdrawal, a taste or a touch stimulus is being linked to an auditory or a visual one. The establishment of equivalences between them is thus required. If interrelations among the sensory modalities are inadequate, conditioning may be either delayed or ineffective. Therefore, if intersensory integration fails to occur at normal age-specific points, a risk of inadequate primary learning at normal age-specific points, a risk of inadequate primary learning at each level can be created.

Alekseeva and Kaplanskaya-Raiskaya (1960) have found that protein deficiency often alters conditioned responses in young children. The capacity to elaborate new, conditioned reflexes is said to be affected first, but even previously well-established reflex responses may be depressed or abolished.

Birch and Lefford (unpublished) have reported that visual-motor control in design copying is dependent on visual-kinesthetic intersensory adequacy. If it is recognized that, as Baldwin (1897) has pointed out, such visual-motor control is essential for learning to write, it becomes apparent that inadequacy in visual-kinesthetic organization can interfere with the primary educational skill of learning to write.

The less adequate development of auditory-visual integration in children exposed to serious nutritional risk has a twofold implication. In the first place, it gives one more argument to the suggestion that the findings of neurological changes present in animals experimentally fed on grossly deficient diets may have their counter-part in human populations socially subjected to significant degrees of malnutrition.

The second implication is directly related to the functional significance of such neuro-integrative lag. Learning to read as an educational task requires the ability to transform temporally distributed auditory patterns into spatially distributed visual ones. Accordingly, if it is accepted that for the beginning reader reading is largely concerned with learning to recognize the symbols which represent spoken words (Harris 1946), a primary disturbance in the ability to integrate stimuli from the two critical sense modalities—hearing and vision—may increase the risk of becoming a poor reader.

The available evidence thus indicates that inadequacies in intersensory development place the child at risk of failing in his preschool years to establish a normal background of conditioning and of failing in his school years to profit from his exposure to education.

The data interpreted in this way will lead to the prediction that the shorter children whose height is a reflection of their earlier and sometimes continuing malnutrition are educationally at risk for school failure stemming from an incapacity to master primary school subjects. If this prediction is substantiated as field observations suggest, early malnutrition from either primary or secondary sources may be the starting point of a developmental path characterized by neuro-integrative inadequacy, school failure, and subsequent subnormal adaptive functioning.

It has been rightly argued that differences in height for age as an indication of past severe malnutrition are inferences not fully justified since a wide range of variables other than nutritional ones may differentiate the families of tall children from those of short ones (Pollitt and Ricciuti 1969). Therefore, one must have more direct evidence of malnutrition as an actual antecedent in the life of the children assessed in later life.

With those considerations in mind, and trying further to assess the performance of school-age children who experienced severe malnutrition early in life, we conducted a series of investigations comparing the performance of survivors of severe malnutrition suffered before the age of thirty months with the performance obtained in a group of their siblings who had never experienced a bout of severe malnutrition. It was assumed that selecting a comparable group from within the sibship to which the survivor of malnutrition belongs is probably a good device, in a cross-sectional study, to cancel out many of the familial and social circumstances which in themselves may be conducive to impaired development. By selecting the closest sibling in age as a control, differences in many variables such as ordinality, social-familial circumstances, economic status, and age of parents may be minimized. Of course microenvironmental variables, particularly those related to parent-child interaction, and sibling-index interaction cannot be controlled through this method of study.

Mental performance on a variety of tests related to basic learning mechanisms was evaluated in index cases and siblings in a series of sessions, meanwhile maintaining high motivation during the administration of the stimuli.

In a first study (Cravioto 1971), the developmental course of auditory-visual equivalence was studied in thirty-nine index cases and in thirty-nine

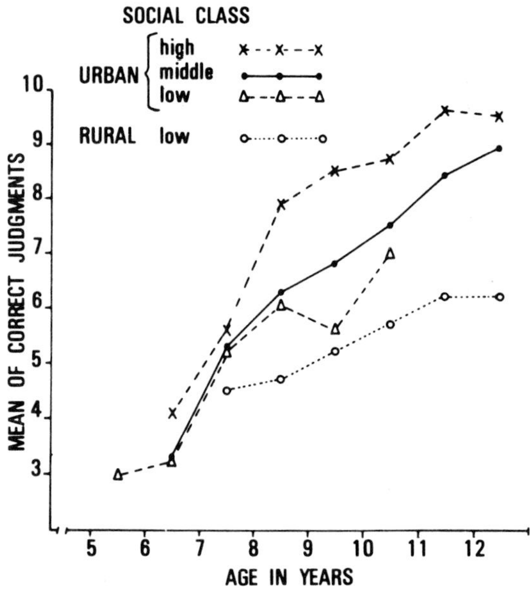

Figure 1.18. Auditory-visual integration as a function of age and social class. *From Cravioto* et al. (*1969b*).

siblings. The results obtained in the siblings are presented in Figure 1.18. The siblings represented in the illustration as the low-urban social class have scores below those corresponding to children of the same age but of a better socioeconomic condition. The improvement in auditory-visual competence with age is obvious for all social classes and for urban and rural environments. The difference in performance is given by the slope of the lines relating achievement score to age.

When the performance age by age of siblings and index cases is contrasted (Figure 1.19), it becomes apparent that the children recovered from severe malnutrition are well below their siblings in auditory-visual competence. Thus, children who had suffered severe malnutrition scored well below the expected values for their social class. To illustrate that this difference in ability is not due to a few extreme cases affecting the mean value of the group, Figure 1.20 compares the cumulative percentage of seven-year-old children in the series. The lag in development of auditory-visual competence of the index cases is evident.

In a second study (Cravioto *et al.* 1969) the visual-kinesthetic intersensory integration, an ability closely related to learning to write, was explored by a method of equivalence in the perception of geometric forms. In this test, kinesthetic information is provided by placing the child's preferred arm behind a screen and, with the arm out of sight, passively moving it through a path describing a geometric form.

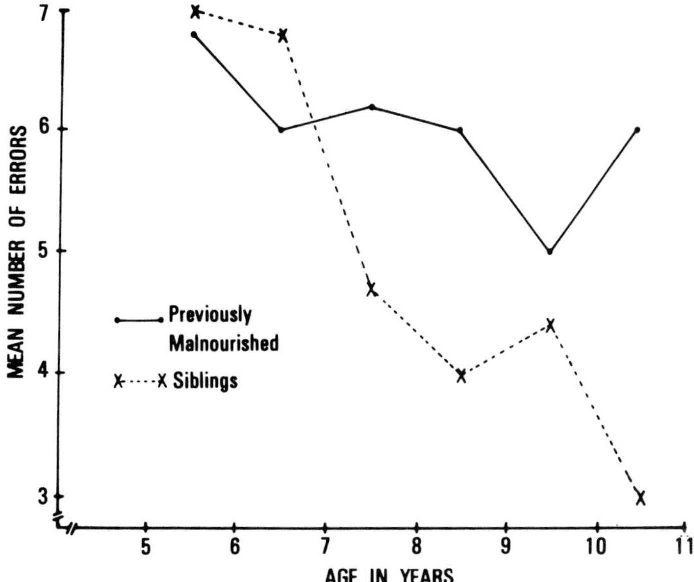

Figure 1.19. Auditory-visual integration in previously malnourished children and their siblings. *From Cravioto* et al. (*1969b*).

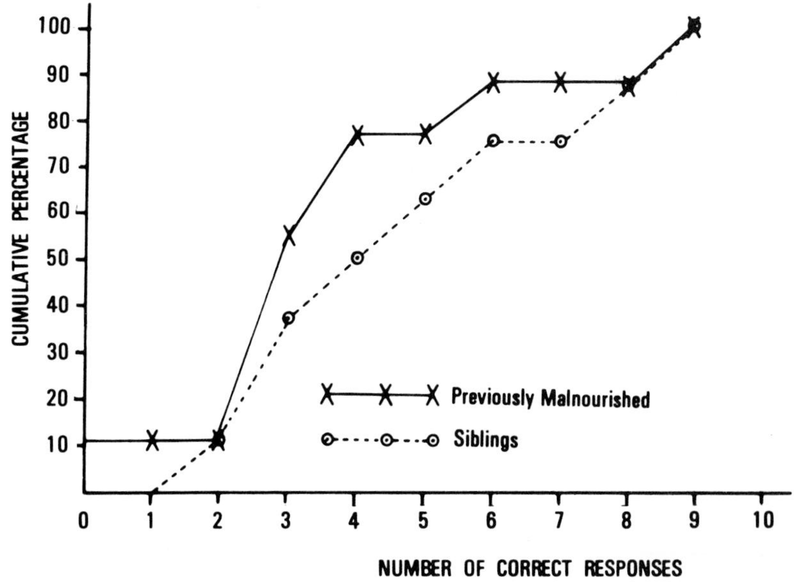

Figure 1.20. Auditory-visual integration at age seven years of severely malnourished infants and their siblings. *From Cravioto* et al. (*1969b*).

It was evident that age by age the children recovered from severe early malnutrition had significantly lower performance levels than their siblings. Figures 1.21 through 1.23 illustrate the proportion of index cases and siblings making different number of errors in the identification of either identical or nonidentical geometric forms at ages five to seven. It may be seen that significant differences in accuracy of judgment always are in favor of the siblings.

Champakam, Srikantia, and Gopalan (1968) have explored the visual-kinesthetic level of competence in a group of nineteen survivors of severe malnutrition. Their results are in complete agreement with our own findings. The mean number of errors, either of equivalence or nonequivalence, in the survivors of severe malnutrition are almost twice the number of errors made by the matched controls.

The data from the siblings in our study and from the matched controls

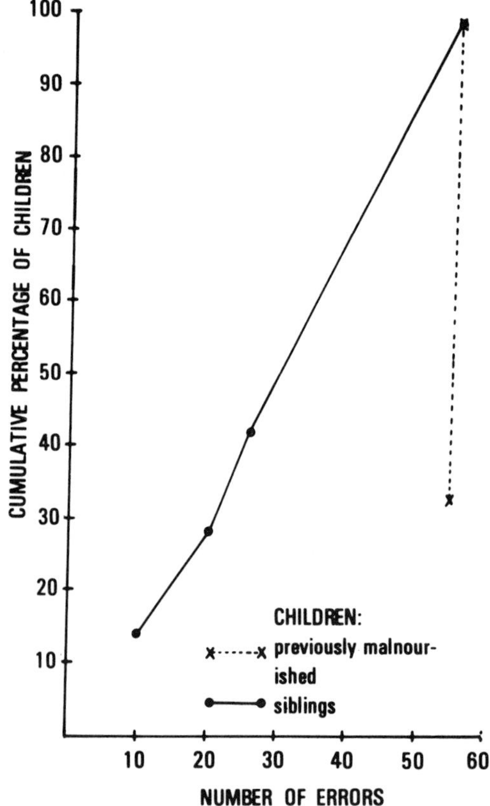

Figure 1.21. Errors in judgment of nonidentical forms in visual-kinesthetic modalities at five years of age. *From Cravioto* et al. (*1969b*).

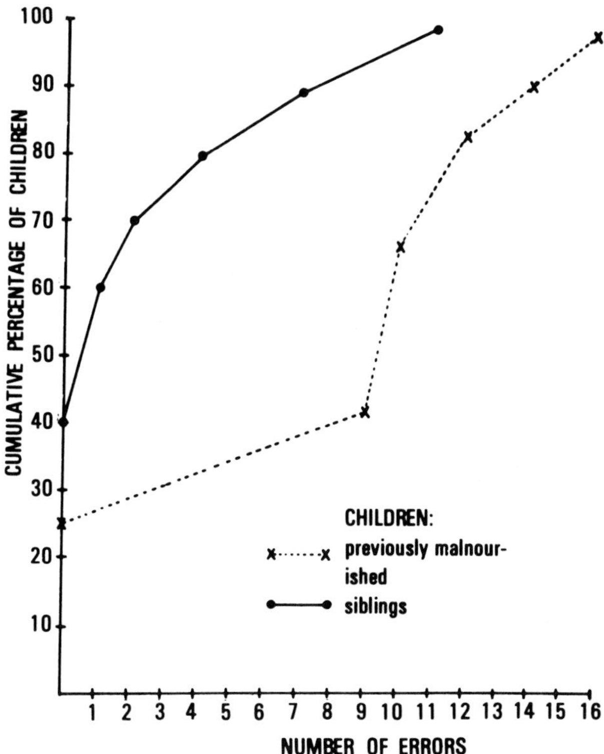

Figure 1.22. Errors of judgment of identical forms in visual-kinesthetic modalities at six years of age. *From Cravioto* et al. (*1969b*).

of Champakam's group show that the lag in a mechanism basic for learning to write present in the children rehabilitated from early severe malnutrition is greater than the lag which could be expected as an effect merely of the low social class.

Temporal Information Processing and Auditory-Visual Integration

In previous studies we have been concerned with the effects of antecedent conditions of nutritional inadequacy as well as other aspects of environmental disadvantage on the ability of children to process afferent information. In the main these studies have focused on the child's ability to integrate information across sensory systems and to treat objectively identical signals presented in different sense modalities as equivalent. These studies have indicated that intersensory judgment is impaired in the children at high risk of exposure to nutritional stress, with such children significantly inferior in their performances to children in the same subculture not so exposed.

Clearly, the ability to make intersensory judgments of equivalence and

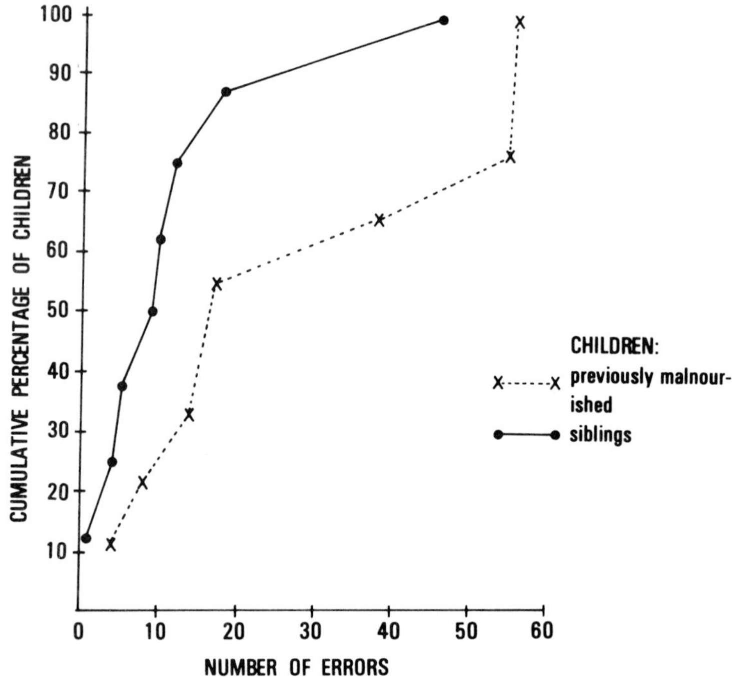

Figure 1.23. Errors in judgment of nonidentical forms in visual-kinesthetic modalities at seven years of age. *From Cravioto* et al. (*1969b*).

nonequivalence depends, at least in part, upon differentiation within each of the sense systems across which the stimuli are to be compared. In one of the intersensory integrated tasks we have employed auditory-visual integration, where a temporally distributed auditory stimulus pattern had to be related to a spatially distributed visual one. Competence in making such integrations of necessity depends upon the ability to process temporally distributed information, and to treat such a temporal distribution as the equivalent of a spatial distribution. It was therefore possible that incompetence in intersensory integration between the auditory and visual modalities was underlain by an intrasensory defect, namely the inability to process temporally distributed sequences.

As a first step in examining this possibility it appeared desirable to study the developmental course for processing temporally distributed information within separate sense modalities, and to explore the relation of this aspect of development to the emergence of intersensory integrative ability (Cravioto and DeLicardie 1974).

The children studied were healthy school children from seven through eleven years of age living in a rural Mexican community. None of the children had either in the past or in the present period been exposed to severe degrees of nutritional disease, and in general they derived from the best-functioning families in the community. All had regular histories of school attendance and were in the appropriate grade placement for chronologic age. The growth achievements of these children were superior to those of children of the same age in the community in general, with heights at both eight and eleven years of age being on the average 5 centimeters greater in the children studied. These mean differences are significant at less than 0.01 level of confidence.

Sixteen of the children were seven years of age, and twenty were studied at successive-year level from eight through eleven years of age. Sex distribution was about equal in each age group.

The ability to judge temporally patterned auditory and visual and tactile stimuli was studied in all children by a method of successive paired comparison. The standard pattern was always presented first and the child was asked to judge whether the second pattern was the same or not the same as the standard. All comparisons were unimodal with visual standards compared to visual variables, tactile with tactile, and auditory standards with variables in that modality.

The visual stimuli were flashes of light of equal duration projected on a single locus in space. The auditory stimuli were clicks emanating from a constant spatial source out of sight of the subject. The visual stimuli were generated by a silent flashlight and the auditory stimuli by a gun click. Both stimulus sources were manually operated. Off phases were constant between types of stimuli, and care was taken to insure consistency in the duration of on and off phases in the stimulus sequences presented in the two modalities by gearing stimulation to a sweep second hand. The flashlight was turned on and off as rapidly as possible to ensure comparability of on phase with the click.

It was possible that manual presentation of the stimuli, despite these precautions, could have contributed to systematic differences in the findings because of the inadvertent expression of experimenter bias. To check for this, a small sample of similarly aged children was selected for the same social group and tested under mechanically controlled conditions of stimulus presentation. The visual stimuli were presented as a film strip and the auditory stimuli from a prepared tape. The findings at each age level were at near perfect agreement with those that obtained under the conditions of manual presentation of the stimuli.

Tactile intrasensory discrimination was examined for the same stimulus patterns. The child was blindfolded and the examiner placed the child's preferred hand on a plaque containing raised coins of equal size. The examiner moved the child's hand across the plaque at a uniform rate from left to right. The spatial distribution of the coins was such as to result in the same time intervals between successive stimulations under conditions of uniform movement as those which obtained for the visual and auditory stimuli.

The same stimulus patterns were used in all modalities. In order to guarantee that differences in competence within the separate modalities were not pattern specific, three series of ten pairs were set up, each differing from the other in the specific stimulus patterns to be judged. Within each series one half of the paired presentations were of identities and one half were not. The same random sequence for matched and unmatched pairs was used for the presentations in each series.

Judgments were recorded as correct or incorrect for each pair, resulting in a maximum score of 10 for any series. Evasive or "I don't know" responses were recorded as errors.

The testing procedure was as follows: The examiner explained that she and the child were going to play a "looking" and a "listening" game. She then showed the subject a box of rewards and an abacus with four rows of beads and indicated that one row would be used for scoring the looking game, another one for scoring the listening game, and a third one for scoring the "blind game." The child was told that once the beads were completely moved to the "finish" side, the child could pick a prize from the prize box, one for each row of beads.

The examiner then showed the child a matched and an unmatched pair of stimuli in each of the modalities and said: "In this game I flash [click, touch] two sets of flashes [clicks, touches]. They are sometimes the same [examiner demonstrates] and sometimes not the same [examiner demonstrates]. It is your job to look [listen, feel] very carefully and tell me if they are the same or if they are not the same. See [hear, touch] this [examiner presents standard], and now [examiner presents comparison] are they the same or not the same?" After this last demonstration trial, the subject was reminded that he was going to see or hear two sets of clicks, touch two groups, or see two sets of blinks, and that he would hear the examiner say, "See [hear, touch] *this*" before the first of the pairs, "and now" before the second. The child was instructed to respond with "same" or "not same" after the second sequence had been presented. All children were individually tested by the same examiner in a single session.

The children's ability to integrate auditory and visual stimuli was individually studied by the method of equivalence of Birch and Belmont (1964).

The order of presentation of tasks was the same for all children. They were first given the auditory-visual task. This was followed by a rest period, after which they received the visual, tactile, and auditory tasks. To control for practice effects a separate group of similarly aged children was studied. The findings indicated no significant degrees of influence attaching to the order of presentation.

A clear improvement in competence in making intrasensory judgments of sequential patterns occurs with age. Seven-year-old children, as may be seen from Figure 1.24, perform at a mean level which is insiginificantly different from chance expectancy.

The most rapid improvement occurs in the age span of eight through ten years. In this period competence improves and tends to reach an asymptote. The earliest and most rapid development of competence occurs

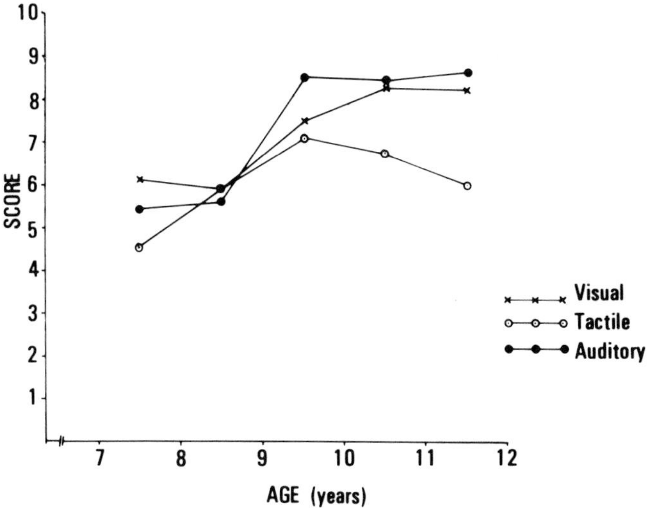

Figure 1.24. Mean competence levels in intrasensory judgments. *From Cravioto* et al. (*1974*).

in the auditory modality, with children reaching the mean asymptote for competence by nine years of age. A similar level is achieved for visual intrasensory judgments by ten years of age. Tactile competence lags behind competence in the other two modalities. It reaches a peak at nine years of age and thereafter exhibits no further improvement. At maximal levels auditory and visual competence are significantly superior to tactile. An analysis of variance (Table 1.5) by age and modality indicates a highly significant age trend, as well as a significant difference among modalities in age-specific course of development. This latter difference is most probably contributed largely by the difference between the tactile and the other senses.

The developmental course of competence in the critical age period is

Table 1.5
Analysis of Variance by Age and Sense Mode

Source	Degrees of Freedom	Sum of Squares	Mean Square	F
Between Modalities	2	93.97	46.98	5.25*
Between Ages	4	325.37	81.34	9.09†
Interaction	8	71.55	8.94	3.74‡
Between duplicates	273	653.73	2.39	
Total	287	1144.62		

*p 0.05
†p 0.01
‡p 0.001

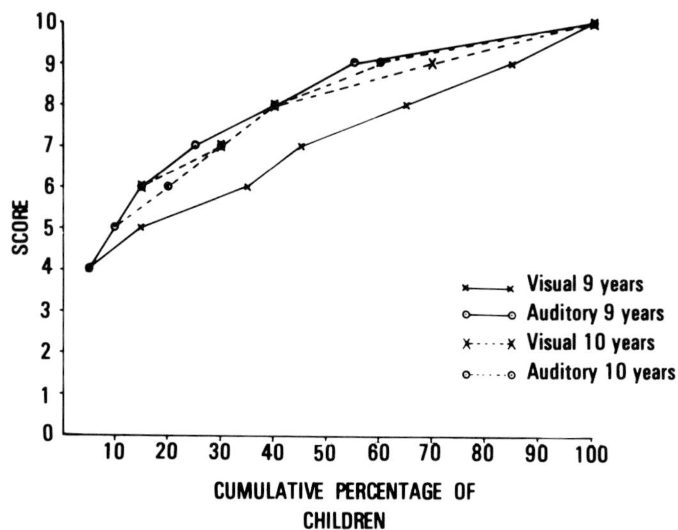

Figure 1.25. Auditory and visual discrimination at ages nine and ten years. *From Cravioto* et al. *(1974)*.

illustrated by the cumulative frequency percentage scores for auditory and visual discrimination at ages nine and ten shown in Figure 1.25. As may be seen from these data, auditory competence speeds forward rapidly at nine years and does not improve significantly thereafter. Visual competence improves more slowly and, though significantly inferior to auditory competence at nine years, continues to improve and to reach equivalent levels at ten years of age.

An analysis of the data by sex indicated no significant trends of difference by sex over the age span studied.

The developmental course for auditory-visual integrative competence is graphically expressed in Figure 1.26. Mean performance is at a chance level in children seven and eight years of age. Competence improves markedly between eight and nine years with mean values reaching an asymptote at that age. An analysis of variance indicates a significant slope of improvement competence over the age span studied.

The age-specific course of improvement in intrasensory and intersensory integrative competences are markedly similar as manifested by the parallel course of development. Both types of competence improve more rapidly between eight and ten years and reach an asymptote thereafter. This coincidence could represent either interdependencies in development or parallelism in age-specific course among otherwise independent developmental processes. If the competencies are dependent it would be expected that each would correlate highly with the other when individual performances are considered. To test this possibility, visual, auditory, and

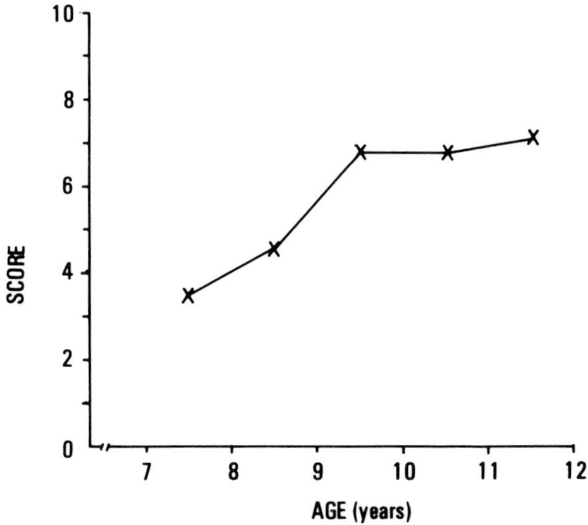

Figure 1.26. Mean number of auditory-visual correct integrations. *From Cravioto* et al. (*1974*).

combined visual and auditory competencies were correlated with auditory-visual integrative scores in the ages having the most explicit manifestations of continuing development, eight and nine years. As may be seen from the data in Table 1.6, the intercorrelations of intra- and intersensory competencies in eight- and nine-year-old children are all low and statistically insignificant. These findings suggest that competence in making intrasensory judgments is a poor predictor of competence in making judgments across modalities, at least in the visual and auditory modalities studied.

Since the group curves for the development of competence in intrasensory processing are similar, and because the age period in which such processing improves is common for the different modalities, it is tempting to speculate that some single underlying process contributes to improvement in judgments in all the sense systems studied. The data

Table 1.6
Intercorrelations of Intra- and Intersensory Competencies in Eight- and Nine-Year-Old Children

Variables	r (8 years)	r (9 years)
Auditory-Visual vs. Visual N = 20	0.16	0.28
Auditory-Visual vs. Auditory N = 20	−0.27	0.06
Auditory-Visual vs. Auditory and Visual Combined N = 20	−0.09	0.20

however, do not support such speculation and indicate that no significant correlations are to be found between competencies in the separate sense systems at any age. It appears therefore, that different processes underlie the development of competence in different modalities and that competence in one modality does not predict competence in the others.

A similar set of considerations may be applied to the relation of the ability to process temporally distributed information within and between the auditory and visual modalities. Here again, one is confronted with a similarity in developmental curve and a coincidence of the age-specific course of the elaboration of skill. However, no systematic association obtains between the abilities of individuals to process intersensory and intrasensory information. Although the processing of intrasensory information is a necessary prerequisite for intersensory processing, the level of competence in intrasensory processing has no predictive value for levels of competence in intersensory integration. It appears most likely that a certain level of intrasensory competence is a threshold value for intersensory integrations which in their turn reflect a different developmental process.

The findings indicate that a failure to meet or to achieve a threshold value for intrasensory processing may underlie incompetence in intersensory integration. It would therefore be desirable to estimate intrasensory organization in any studies of the effects of conditions of deprivation on the development of neurointegrative capacities.

Visual Perception

There is a tendency to view the human organism as an agent that processes information. Humans live primarily in a visual world, and, logically, we expect more elaboration and more uses of visual information than we do of information from other sense modalities. In this sense, reading and writing have become primary tools in our society.

Learning to read has an essential prerequisite: the ability to distinguish simple visually presented figures. However, the ability to make gross discriminations among visually perceived figures (form recognition), although it is a necessary component ability, does not constitute a sufficient refinement of perceptual skill for a task such as reading. In addition to making gross discriminations, if a child is to learn to read he or she must also respond to more differentiated aspects of the figural percept such as angular properties and spatial orientation (form analysis).

The child's failure to respond to the spatial orientation of a visual form can result in his confusing a number of letters in the roman alphabet which are identical in form but distinguishable by their spatial positioning. Letters such as *b*, *p*, *d*, and *q*, or *N*, *Z*, *W*, and *M*, all represent equivalent shapes, with the distinction among them depending upon the child's ability to respond simultaneously to shape and to orientation in visual space.

The above-mentioned considerations led us to examine the level of competence in visual perception of forms in our children recovered from early severe malnutrition as a means of assessing their readiness to learn to read. A visual-discrimination task developed by Birch and Lefford (1964) was administered to both rehabilitated children and siblings. The task provides information on gross-discrimination ability (form recognition) and on response to spatial position and to differences in angular symmetry (form analysis).

The performance of both groups on the recognition of geometric two-dimensional forms showed that as age increased from five to ten years the mean number of errors committed progressively diminished. Again the performance level, although low for both groups of children, was significantly lower for the previously malnourished children until age nine, when both siblings and recovered children achieved similar levels of performance (Figure 1.27).

When the children were tested for their ability to analyze geometric forms, the mean number of errors committed also decreased as age advanced (Figure 1.28). A sharp difference was found again to be in favor of the siblings.

It is apparent that children who survive a severe episode of malnutrition early in life are handicapped in developing skill in reading and are less able to profit from the cumulative knowledge available to the human species in general and to their socioeconomic group in particular. Their readiness is even lower than the low readiness characteristic of their low social class. It

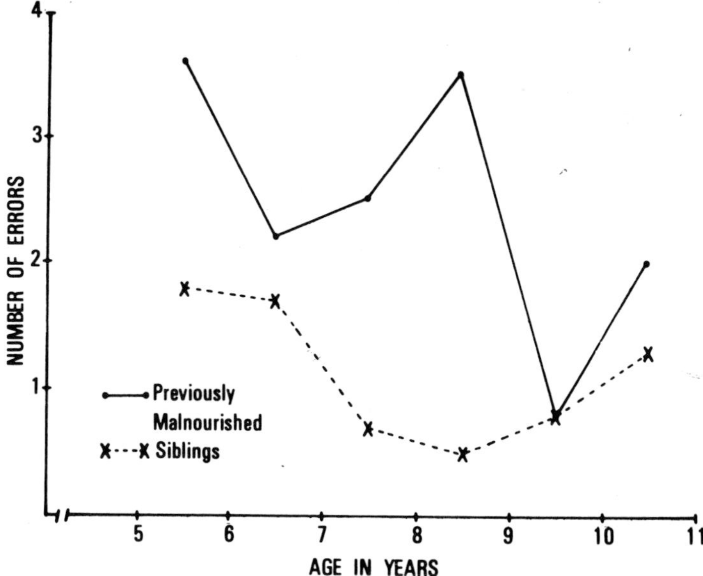

Figure 1.27. Mean number of errors made in form recognition by previously malnourished children and their siblings. *From Cravioto* et al. (*1969b*).

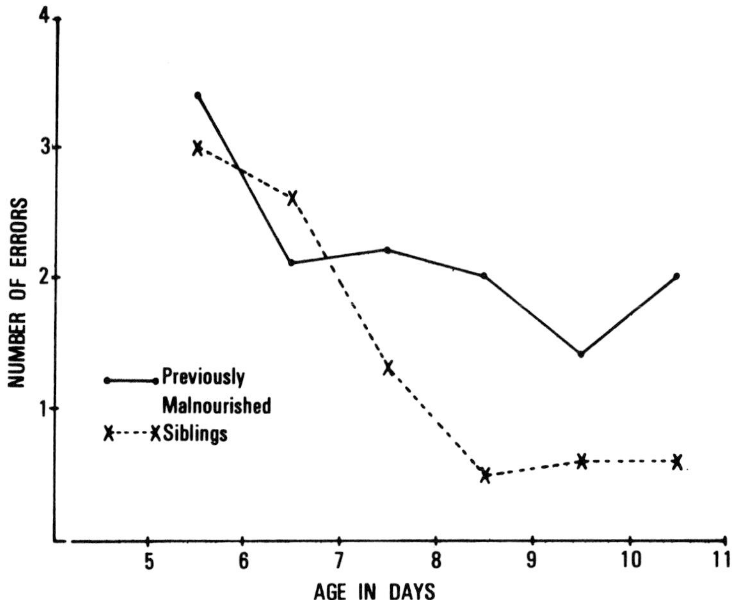

Figure 1.28. Analysis of forms. Mean number of errors in analysis of triangle made by malnourished children and their siblings. *From Cravioto* et al. (*1969b*).

seems of interest in this context that children with mental subnormalities are incapable of making a discrimination requiring that they: (1) respond selectively to aspects of the whole figure, (2) take into account spatial orientation with respect to a coordinate system, (3) separate complex visual wholes into their component subwholes, or (4) reconstruct a pattern from its elements. Survivors of early severe malnutrition display a similar behavior in these aspects of learning.

Language Development

Since March 1966 we have been engaged in an ecologic study of a cohort of children born in a community where preschool malnutrition is highly prevalent and where other factors related to the life of the children have variations of sufficient range to permit associative analyses to be carried out.

In brief, the project is the study of a total one-year cohort of children, all born in a rural village between March 1, 1966, and February 28, 1967. The children and their families have been closely observed from the nutritional, pediatric, socioeconomic, and developmental points of view in a coordinated manner, with great attention to detail, and so far as feasible using validated research instruments. A good number of the instruments were devised and tested by the project staff during the ten years before the start of the cohort's induction (Cravioto *et al.* 1969).

The objective of the study is to analyze the relationship between the conditions surrounding care of the child, especially as they affect nutrition, and the course of the child's physical growth, mental development, and learning.

The children first brought into the study during the prenatal period have been followed for five years and will continue to be observed until they have completed their first seven years, the earliest time at which certain crucial mental examinations can be meaningfully applied. At that time the children can all be assessed in the relatively uniform environment of a primary school.

While the particular focus of the project is on the relationship between nutrition and mental development, by the nature of both variables the design is that of an ecologic study of young children in their family and social environments.

Through the use of the ecologic method we plan to analyze: (1) the influence of social, economic, and familial conditions on the development of malnutrition; (2) the effect of malnutrition on physical growth, mental development, and learning; and (3) the interaction of nutritional factors with infectious disease, family circumstances, and social circumstances on the processes of growth and development.

During the first five years of life of the cohort out of the 334 children inducted, twenty-two developed severe clinical malnutrition. Such cases occurred despite the fact that all children in the cohort studied were examined on a biweekly basis, growth failures identified, infectious illness treated, and the parents given advice (which they did not follow) on the appropriate feeding and management of the child.

The occurrence of severe malnutrition under such circumstances makes possible a prospective analysis of the ecology of severe clinical malnutrition and makes less difficult the interpretation of its relation to physical and mental development. Among the many aspects that can be studied under these circumstances, one that has attracted our attention is the development of language and communication prior, during, and after the episode of severe malnutrition. In our first attempt we have compared language development and appearance of bipolar concepts in the group of malnourished children in comparison with a control group of children selected from the same birth cohort who were never diagnosed as severely malnourished and who were matched, case by case at birth for sex, gestational age, season of birth, body weight, body length, and performance on the Gesell Test (Cravioto and DeLicardie 1972).

The severely malnourished children were fourteen girls and eight boys whose age at the time of the diagnoses ranged from four to fifty-three months, with a single infant below one year of age, nine cases between one and two years, eight cases between two and three years of age, three patients with ages between three and four years, and one case diagnosed at fifty-three months of age.

Fifteen of the twenty-two patients corresponded to the kwashiorkor type; the other seven cases were of the marasmic variety. The proportion of marasmus in females and males was 4:3, while the number of females with kwashiorkor was twice the number for boys.

Ten children, six with kwashiorkor and four with marasmus, were treated at home, while nine children with kwashiorkor and three with marasmus were treated in a pediatric hospital. No deaths occurred in this latter group while three of the ten children treated at home died. Of these, two were of the kwashiorkor and one of the marasmic clinical type. Ages of these three at the time of diagnoses were twelve, fourteen, and twenty-two months. In all three patients death occurred within a period of fifteen to sixty days after diagnosis. Of the nineteen survivors one child emigrated from the village after his discharge from the hospital, leaving a total of eighteen cases for study.

Before presenting the results obtained it seems convenient to describe in some detail the familial and social characteristics of both the malnourished and the control children, in order to have an idea of their similarities and differences.

Family Structure

Family size was not different in children with and without severe malnutrition. The number of members in the families having a severely malnourished child was 7.4 ± 3. This number is not statistically different from 7.2 ± 2.8 obtained for the families of the matched comparison group. Although the ordinality of the malnourished child was slightly less than the corresponding ordinality for the child's matched control, the difference between the means did not reach the 5 percent limit of confidence. Similarly, the closest older sibling of the malnourished child was a bit younger than the sibling of the paired non-severely malnourished child; however, once again, the difference was not statistically significant. Finally, the proportion of nuclear families to extended families was practically the same in both groups of children.

Biological Characteristics of Parents

With respect to the biological characteristics of the parents, age, height, and weight of neither parent could discriminate between families with or without severely malnourished children. The number of pregnancies also failed to separate families of malnourished children from families of the matched controls.

Family Economics

There was no difference in main sources of income among the families of the malnourished and the comparison children. The proportion of agricultural to nonagricultural workers was the same. Even within the agricultural workers twelve families in each group derived their income as day-laborers and the thirteenth family as a land-renter. The fathers of the other six families in the control group were either workers or artisans. Among the malnourished group four fathers were workers or artisans, one was a small business owner, and one a public accountant.

Even though the mean annual income per capita appeared to be a little higher in the families of the control group, the difference corresponded to 2.5 American cents per person per day.

The percentage of total expenditures devoted to food procurement is considered as a good indicator of level of living. The greater the percentage spent on food the less purchasing power left for all other necessary expenditures such as clothing, housing, education, and health. Consequently, the greater the percentage spent on food the lower the level of family living. In the case of the families without severely malnourished children the mean percentage of total expenditures spent on food was 44.3 ± 16.3. The corresponding figure for the families with malnourished children was 45.7 ± 15.2. The mean difference is not statistically significant at the 0.10 level of confidence.

Sanitary facilities of the households, taken as an indication of economic investment, were substandard in both the severely malnourished and the comparison group. The percentage scores based upon the objective assessment of conditions and facilities for sanitation were 28 ± 17 for the homes of the malnourished children, and 31 ± 20 for the homes of the control children. The numerical difference is not enough to be statistically significant at the 0.05 level of confidence.

Sociocultural Conditions

The mean scores for personal cleanliness of the mothers of the malnourished and control groups were respectively 61 ± 20 and 68 ± 19. For the fathers the corresponding mean scores were 62 ± 16 and 61 ± 19. The differences in both sets fail to reach a level of significance of 0.05. Intergenerational change in formal education was slightly higher in the group of control children. The average change in schooling was equivalent to 1.5 ± 3.3 grades in the control group, and 1.07 ± 1.8 grades in the malnourished group, the difference being nonsignificant. Similarly, the proportion of illiterate to literate mothers was about equal in both groups of children.

Contact of the parents with mass information media was assessed through regular radio listening. The number of fathers who listen regularly to the radio was the same in both malnourished and control groups. The case for the mothers was different. There were almost equal number of listeners and not listeners in the malnourished group while the number of listeners in the matched controls was more than three times the number of not listeners. The difference in proportions is significant at the 5 percent level of confidence.

In summary, of all the features of the macroenvironment considered, the only differential between severely malnourished children and controls, matched at birth for gestational age, body weight, and total body length, was the mother's contact with the world outside the village through regular radio listening. None of the other characteristics of the parents (biologic, social, or cultural) or familial circumstances—including income per capita, main source of income, and family size—were significantly associated with the presence or absence of severely malnourished children.

Home Stimulation

To assess in a global way the child's microenvironment, the Inventory of Home Stimulation devised by Caldwell (1967) to sample certain aspects of the quantity and, in some ways, the quality of social, emotional, and cognitive stimulation available to a young child within his home, was recorded and scored at six-month intervals during the first three years of life of the cohort, and annually thereafter. Two forms of the inventory were used, one adequate for infants up to three years of age and the other one suitable for children three to six years old. The psychologist who scored the inventory was not aware of the nutritional status of the children.

Table 1.7 shows the mean scores for total home stimulation in both the malnourished and the matched control groups. At all ages but age eighteen months, there was a significant difference favorable to the children who never experienced severe malnutrition. It is important to notice that even at six months of age, when only one child in the malnourished group was actually severely malnourished, the scores of his group are below those of the control group. Table 1.8 shows that at six months of age on a range of 27 to 41 scoring points in home stimulation, one of every four malnourished children had 30 or less points, and none scored higher than 36 points. As a contrast, none of the control children had homes with a score of less than 32 points, and at least one of every four homes scored above 36 points. Similarly, at fifty-eight months of age in a range of scores from 55 to 124, almost one half of the survivors from severe malnutrition had homes with scores below 104 points, with one fourth of the homes not reaching more than 84 points. On the other hand, the homes of the control children had a

Table 1.7
Mean Values of Total Home Stimulation for
Severely Malnourished Children and Controls

Chronological Age (months)	Home Stimulation (Mean and Standard Deviation): Severely Malnourished Children	Control Children	"d" test
6	32.37 ± 2.57	35.35 ± 4.71	3.46*
12	36.41 ± 3.44	39.83 ± 4.71	2.47†
18	39.68 ± 4.89	42.43 ± 4.01	1.78
24	39.43 ± 4.81	44.16 ± 6.26	2.48†
26	39.46 ± 4.98	44.33 ± 5.69	2.51†
31	40.66 ± 7.22	45.86 ± 6.68	2.05†
34	44.40 ± 5.31	48.20 ± 5.12	2.00†
38	44.40 ± 5.31	48.20 ± 5.12	2.00†
46	88.53 ± 16.77	101.40 ± 10.62	2.51†
52	90.35 ± 11.83	102.80 ± 11.36	2.88†
58	97.71 ± 16.98	109.86 ± 6.38	2.52†

*Significant at 0.01
†Significant at 0.05

Table 1.8
Proportion of Malnourished Children and Controls at Six Months of Age Showing Different Total Scores in Home Stimulation

Home Stimulation Score	Cumulative Proportion of Children with Severe Malnutrition	
	Present or Future	Absent
27	0.06	
28	0.06	
29	0.12	
30	0.25	
31	0.31	
32	0.56	0.12
33	0.62	0.17
34	0.75	0.41
35	0.87	0.65
36	1.00	0.70
37		0.76
38		0.94
39		0.94
40		0.94
41		1.00

minimum of 100 points, with almost one half of them scoring above 110 level (Table 1.9).

During the first three years of life language development was evaluated by means of a technique similar to the Gesell. Language level was estimated in days equivalent. As may be seen in Table 1.10 and Figure 1.29, mean language development as measured by the Gesell method is very similar in index patients and controls during the first year of life when only one case of severe malnutrition had been diagnosed. As time elapsed and more children came down with severe malnutrition, a difference in language performance favorable to the matched controls became evident. The difference was more pronounced at each successive age tested.

Not only were mean values significantly lower in the index cases, the distribution of individual scores was also markedly different from that obtained in the control group. Thus, for example (Table 1.11), while none of the children in the control group at three years of age had a language score below 660 days equivalent, almost one half of the malnourished group had scores below this level. At the other end of the distribution no child in the malnourished group had language performance above the 960 days equivalent while more than one half of the control children scored in the range of 1021 to 1080 days, corresponding to the ideal score.

It is thus apparent that at three years of age the language behavior of the malnourished group and of the control group, matched at birth for size and performance, are markedly different, with almost one half of the malnourished children one year or more behind the controls.

Table 1.9
Proportion of Survivors of Severe Clinical Malnutrition and Controls at Fifty-Eight Months of Age Showing Different Total Scores in Home Stimulation

Home Stimulation Score	Cumulative Proportion of Children with or without Antecedents of Severe Malnutrition	
	With	Without
55–59	0.07	
60–64	0.07	
65–69	0.07	
70–74	0.07	
75–79	0.14	
80–84	0.21	
85–89	0.21	
90–94	0.28	
95–99	0.36	
100–104	0.57	0.20
105–109	0.71	0.53
110–114	0.93	0.73
115–119	1.00	0.93
120–124		1.00

Concept development and particularly the emergence of verbal concepts have long been viewed as a basic factor in the development of human intelligence. The emergence of the conception of opposites and with it bipolar labelling represents an early and readily measured aspect of the development of concepts in young children. As a consequence of their concern with improving the school performance of disadvantaged children, Francis H. Palmer and his colleagues at the Institute for Child Development and Experimental Education of the City University of New York formed the view that the development of a progressively more difficult series of bipolar concepts could be used for the systematic training and enrichment of language experience. Accordingly, as part of their studies on the effects of intervention programs started at age two, they developed a test covering both "poles" of twenty-three concepts (e.g., big-little, long-short, in-out) in two different situations. Most of the items included require the child to select an object representing a given pole from two objects differing only with respect to their position on one of the concepts' continua. The items are grouped into two forms so that each form contains items covering both poles of each concept. The forms differ only with respect to the setting in which the concepts are placed. The score derived from the test provides a measure of the child's knowledge of various categories that are commonly used in organizing sensory experience.

Although Palmer and his associates have not viewed the series of bipolar concepts that were developed to be a language test, it is implicit in their protocols that the progressively more difficult training series could

Table 1.10
Language Development Scores of Severely Malnourished Children and Matched Controls (Days Equivalence)

Age (days)	Birth	180	360	540	720	900	1080
Past or Present							
Severe Malnutrition	27 ± 3.2	167 ± 14.4	289 ± 47.2	385 ± 86.0	467 ± 102.7	534 ± 103.0	657 ± 119.5
Controls	28 ± 1	177 ± 21.2	334 ± 55.4	490 ± 73.3	633 ± 93.4	785 ± 143.1	947 ± 135.2
"t" test	1.37	1.69	2.69*	3.90*	4.80*	5.80*	6.53*

*Significant at less than 0.01

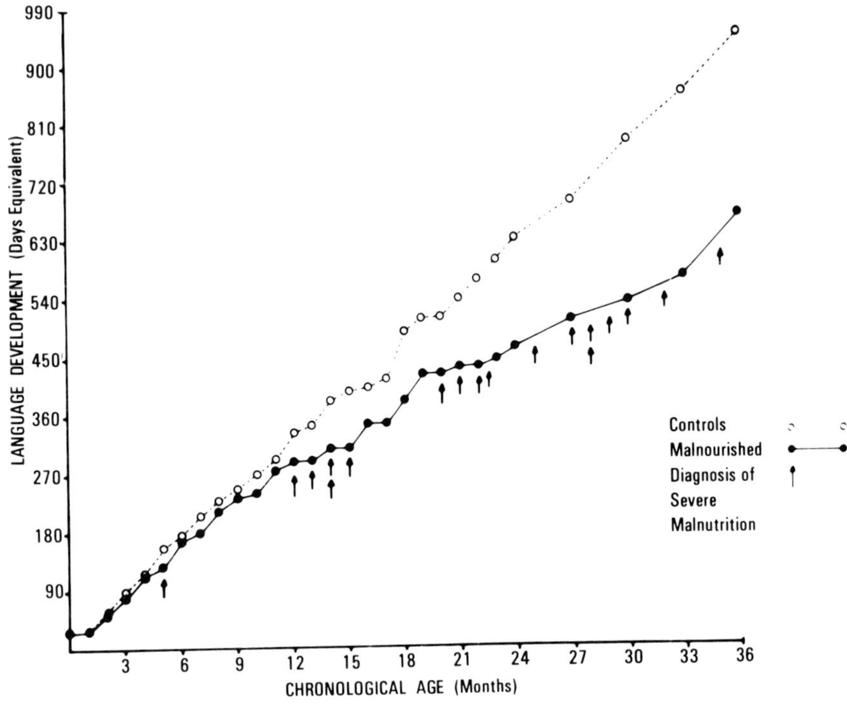

Figure 1.29. Mean language development as a function of age in severely malnourished children and matched controls. *From Cravioto* et al. (*1972*).

Table 1.11
Proportions of Malnourished Children and Matched Controls Showing Different Language Performance at Thirty-Six Months of Age (Land of the White Dust)

Language Performance (Days Equivalent)	Cumulative Proportion of Children: Malnourished (Past or Present)	Controls
480	0.06	
481–540	0.20	
541–600	0.33	
601–660	0.46	
661–720	0.80	0.05
721–780	0.80	0.16
781–840	0.93	0.26
841–900	0.93	0.26
901–960	1.00	0.42
961–1020		0.42
1021–1080		1.00

indeed be used in itself without training as a measure for assessing the natural acquisition of bipolar concepts in young children. To test this hypothesis, we administered twenty-two of the twenty-three concepts selected by Palmer as a repeated test of bipolar concept acquisition at ages twenty-six, thirty-one, thirty-four, and thirty-eight months to a total cohort of children living in a preindustrial society. All items were presented to the 229 children at all ages independently of the number of successes or failures. In all instances the order of presentation was the same. Data obtained at the successive ages tested clearly demonstrated a developmental course of competence in response to tasks involving the utilization of bipolar concepts.

Having demonstrated a developmental course in bipolar concept acquisition, we decided to analyze the patterns of development of this function in the malnourished children and in the controls. Since examinations had been conducted at twenty-six, thirty-one, thirty-four, thirty-eight, forty-six, fifty-two, and fifty-eight months of age, it was possible to analyze the competence patterns both at the time some of the children were experiencing severe malnutrition and after they had been nutritionally rehabilitated.

The competence in bipolar-concept acquisition in children with past or present severe malnutrition and matched controls at successive ages is presented in Table 1.12 and illustrated in Figure 1.30. As may be seen, the mean number of bipolar concepts present in the index children is significantly lower than the mean number of concepts shown by the control group. The differences at all ages but age thirty-one months are statistically significant.

Mean increments for the age periods considered are presented in Table 1.13. It may be noticed that between ages twenty-six and thirty-eight months, a time at which the last cases of severe malnutrition occurred, increments in the control group are far greater than those exhibited by the

Table 1.12
Mean Number of Bipolar Concepts as a Function of Age in Malnourished Children and Controls

Age (months)	Number of Bipolar Concepts in Children: Malnourished	Matched Controls	"d" Test
26	1.61 ± 1.26	3.54 ± 2.11	2.68*
31	3.92 ± 2.65	5.46 ± 2.96	1.42
34	4.85 ± 3.15	8.92 ± 3.26	3.36†
38	6.07 ± 2.94	13.42 ± 3.56	5.97†
46	12.16 ± 4.13	16.92 ± 3.26	3.23†
52	15.35 ± 3.05	18.42 ± 3.29	2.57*
58	17.21 ± 2.60	20.07 ± 1.38	3.66†

*Significant at 0.05
†Significant at 0.01

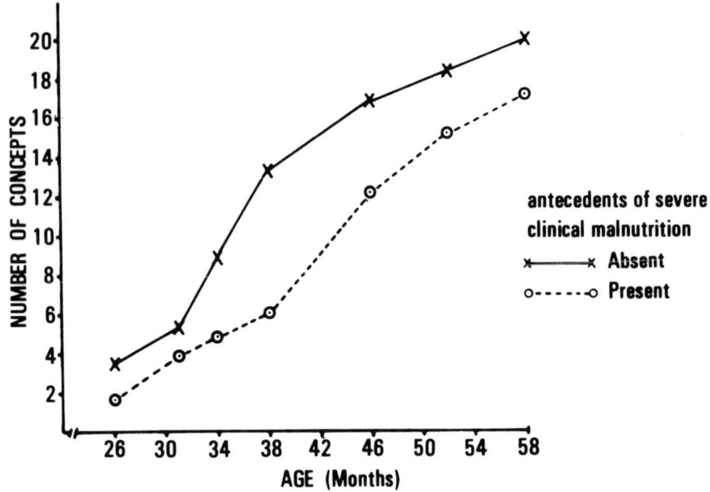

Figure 1.30. Number of bipolar language concepts present in children with and without antecedents of severe clinical malnutrition. *From Cravioto* et al. (*1972*).

malnourished group. During rehabilitation the survivors of severe malnutrition had an increment twice as big as that of controls; unfortunately, at successive ages the increments tend to be lower, with not enough time for the malnourished group to catch up. It is important to remember that after forty months all the children included in the malnourished group actually represent cases rehabilitated from severe clinical malnutrition, i.e., survivors considered as cured of the disease. It may be noted in this respect that the mean value found in the index cases at forty-six months of age is almost twice the value obtained at thirty-eight months. Nonetheless, the increment is not enough to bring the index children to the value shown by the controls. In other words, the lag in language development found in severely

Table 1.13
Mean Increment in Bipolar Concepts in Children with Past or Present Malnutrition and Controls

Age Interval (months)	Increment in Number of Concepts in Children with Malnutrition	
	Past or Present	Absent
26–31	2.31	1.92
31–34	0.93	3.46
34–38	1.22	4.50
38–46	6.09	3.50
46–52	3.19	1.50
52–58	1.86	1.65

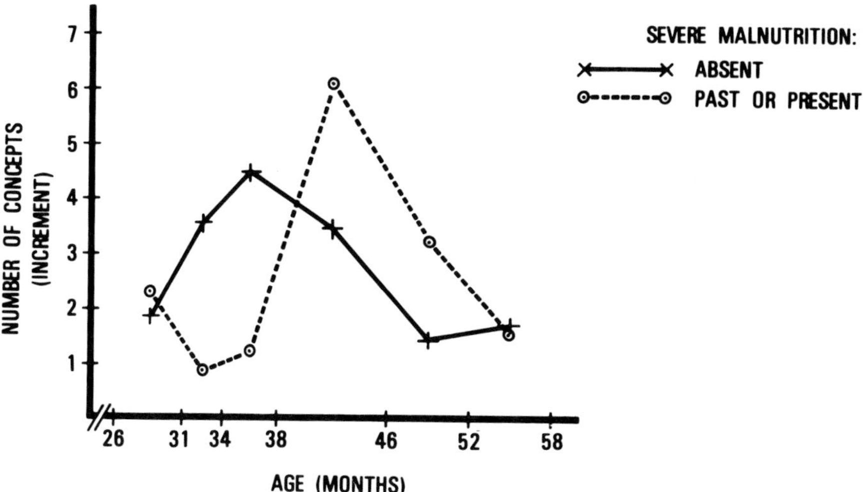

Figure 1.31. Mean increment in bipolar concepts. *From Cravioto* et al. (*1972*).

malnourished children continued to be present after clinical recovery had taken place (Figure 1.31).

To illustrate that not only are the mean number of concepts different in malnourished and control children, Tables 1.14 and 1.15 show the cumulative proportions of children in both groups exhibiting different numbers of concepts. At twenty-six months it may be seen that while almost one half of control children have five or six concepts, none of the malnourished subjects had reached this level of performance. On the other hand one out of every three malnourished children had a maximum of one concept, while seven out of ten controls are at the level of two or more concepts. Even when the malnourished children are rehabilitated, their lag behind the controls continues. Table 1.15 shows that four out of ten survivors of severe

Table 1.14

Proportion of Malnourished and Control Children Showing Different Number of Bipolar Concepts at Twenty-Six Months of Age

Number of Concepts	Cumulative Proportion of Children	
	Malnourished	Controls
0	0.29	0.00
1	0.36	0.25
2	0.64	0.42
3	0.93	0.58
4	1.00	0.58
5		0.75
6		1.00

Table 1.15
Proportion of Children With and Without Antecedents of Severe Malnutrition Showing Different Number of Bipolar Concepts at Fifty-Eight Months of Age

Number of Concepts	Cumulative Proportion of Children with Antecedents of Severe Malnutrition	
	Present	Absent
12	0.07	
13	0.07	
14	0.21	
15	0.28	
16	0.36	
17	0.43	
18	0.57	0.20
19	0.78	0.40
20	1.00	0.67
21		0.80
22		1.00

malnutrition had no more than seventeen concepts at fifty-eight months of age, a time at which all the controls showed at least eighteen concepts. Similarly, none of the previously malnourished children had more than twenty concepts, while two out of every ten controls are above this level.

In trying to evaluate the role of malnutrition on language competence, one must remember that malnourished children and controls differed not only in nutritional status but also in home stimulation scores. Thus, since on the one hand the presence of severe malnutrition was significantly associated with lack of home stimulation, and on the other hand survivors of severe malnutrition showed a significant lag in language bipolar-concept formation, it seemed logical to investigate the interrelations among these three factors in order to estimate their possible role. As a first approach to this issue a technique of partial correlation was used to look at the degree of association between two variables "holding constant" the influence of the third variable. Since the number of cases of malnutrition was rather small, we decided to test for interrelations in the total birth cohort.

The coefficients of correlation product times moment among home stimulation scores, total body height, and number of bipolar concepts present at forty-six months of age in the total cohort (229 children) were:

Home stimulation score and number of bipolar concepts = 0.20

Home stimulation score and total body height = 0.23

Total body height and number of bipolar concepts = 0.26

When the relation between home stimulation and number of bipolar concepts was partialed out for body height, the coefficient of correlation dropped from 0.20 to 0.15. When the relation between body height and number of bipolar concepts was partialed out for home stimulation, the coefficient changed from 0.26 to 0.23. Finally, when the number of bipolar concepts was "held constant," the coefficient of correlation between home stimulation and body height changed from 0.23 to 0.19. These results suggest that the association between home stimulation and number of bipolar concepts is mediated to a good extent through body height, which in turn holds a significant degree of association with the number of bipolar concepts independently—to a large extent—of home stimulation. Within the limits of the probabilities given by the magnitude of the coefficients, home stimulation contributes relatively more to body height than to number of bipolar concepts, while body height contributes more than home stimulation to the variance of bipolar concepts.

Behavioral Response to Cognitive Demands

It has been suggested that the behavioral style that seems to characterize preschool lower-class children may have serious negative consequences for later education unless modes of instruction and conditions for learning take into account that this pattern differs from that obtained in middle-class children (Hertzig *et al.* 1968). Since malnutrition is one among the complex of factors embraced by social class, we decided to explore the modification that an episode of severe malnutrition might make on the behavioral style of lower-class children, in order to assess if the risk for learning disability of the survivors would be equal to the risk of their classmates of lower social strata. The study aimed at extending our understanding of factors contributing to differences in performance in survivors of severe malnutrition, by comparing the responsiveness to cognitive demands of five-year-old survivors with the responsiveness to identical demands in similarly aged children belonging to the same birth cohort who have not suffered severe malnutrition, and who are either equal or superior in intellectual performance (DeLicardie and Cravioto 1973).

The strategy for the analysis of behavioral styles focused on the comparison of responsiveness to cognitive demands observed in the fourteen survivors who developed severe protein-calorie malnutrition before thirty-eight months of age (see previous section on language development), and in two groups of children selected from the same birth cohort who were never diagnosed as severely malnourished and who were matched, case by case, with the survivors. One group was matched at birth for sex, gestational age, season of birth, body weight, total body length, and organization of the central nervous system as determined by the Gesell method. The second comparison group included fourteen children, full-term and healthy at delivery, who were matched for sex and IQ (WPPSI) at five years of age with the survivors of severe malnutrition (Table 1.16).

One of the main obstacles in the interpretation of findings obtained in studies of malnourished children results from the scarcity of pertinent data relative to the child's environment and the child himself before the episode of severe malnutrition and often during the intervening period between his discharge as a rehabilitated patient and the time at which he is reexamined looking for sequelae of malnutrition. Because of the manner in which the

Table 1.16
Total Intellectual Quotients (WPPSI)
Obtained in Survivors of Clinical Severe Malnutrition
and Control Children at Five Years of Age

	Number of Children		
IQ Total Score	Survivors of Malnutrition	Controls for Sex and IQ	Controls Matched at Birth
60–64	1	2	
65–69	2	2	
70–74	5	4	
75–79	2	2	1
80–84	3	3	2
85–89	1	1	5
90–94			2
95–99			3
100–104			0
105–109			0
110–114			1

samples of survivors and controls have been identified, the present study considerably reduces the complexities of interpretation since all children included have been followed longitudinally from birth onwards, and contemporaneously acquired background information is available for each child.

Broadly considered, the variables included as a part of the child's environment were of four kinds, relating first to the family structure and the sociocultural characteristics of the parents; second, to objective circumstances of life such as sources of family income, income per capita, and sanitary facilities of the home; third, to the home stimulation available to the child. It is apparent that certain biological characteristics of the parents such as age, weight, height, and mother's parity are in fact modulated by social circumstances; therefore, in this contest they also belong to the child's environment, as a fourth kind of variable.

With the exception of the proportion of illiterate mothers and the proportion of mothers who regularly listened to the radio, none of the other features of the sociocultural background, family structure, family economics, biological characteristics of the parents, and total scores in home stimulation were significantly different in the survivors of clinical severe malnutrition and in the controls matched for sex and IQ. On the other hand, IQ scores and home stimulation scores, together with proportion of mothers who regularly listen to the radio, were the distinctive features between survivors and controls matched at birth.

At the age of five years, intelligence was estimated and the behavioral responses of the children were independently recorded, all this as a part of a longitudinal study of growth and development of rural children in central Mexico. All children were individually examined using an adapted version of the Wechsler Preschool Primary Scale of Intelligence (WPPSI). The tasks of this test were used to obtain behavioral information on response style to a standardly presented set of cognitive demands. During the administration of the test a detailed protocol of the child's behavior and verbalizations was recorded by an independent observer. The tester followed the standard procedures for the WPPSI administration. The observer kept a consecutive written record of the behavior of the child during the examination session. This record was kept in terms of the explicit responses made to each of the specific demands made for cognitive functioning on the test.

Analysis of response styles followed the logic tree developed by Hertzig *et al.* (1968). Scoring reliability was determined by the method of score-rescore. Spearman rank-order correlations were calculated for score-rescore done by the same person, and also for score-rescore done by two independent persons. The corresponding coefficients for two fifteen-protocol series were 0.95 and 0.97 for the same psychologist, and 0.93 and 0.97 when two psychologists independently scored the same protocols. Divergences were present only in judging spontaneous extensions and responses of competence.

To evaluate differences between survivors and controls the behavioral style of each child was characterized, the proportion of responses in each category were calculated, and with the individual values and the means for each group analyses of variance were performed.

The mean proportions for work as a style of response were 0.73, 0.78, and 0.86, respectively, for survivors of severe malnutrition, controls matched for IQ and sex, and controls matched at birth. The differences among these proportions were not statistically significant ($F = 1.88$; $p > 0.05$).

When children were judged as to their proportions of total verbal responses (work plus not-work responses) the survivors and the controls matched for IQ and sex gave similar mean values, 0.63 for survivors and 0.67 for controls. These mean values are statistically lower than the mean value of 0.81 found in the children who served as controls for size and performance at birth ($F = 5.03$; $p < 0.05$). Both, the survivors of severe malnutrition and their controls for IQ and sex, had significantly lower proportions of total responses expressed verbally as work responses than the proportions exhibited by the children in the group of controls at birth ($F = 4.51$; $p < 0.05$). The proportions of nonverbal work responses were similar among the children in the three groups.

When the responses were styled as not-work nonverbal the survivors showed significantly higher proportions than the control children matched at birth. No difference was obtained between survivors and controls matched for IQ and sex. Finally, although the great majority of children in all three groups expressed their not-work nonverbal responses in a passive style, the survivors and the controls matched for IQ and sex exhibited a significantly higher proportion of unresponsiveness than the controls matched at birth ($F = 6.26$; $p < 0.05$). None of the other styles of verbal or nonverbal not-work responses gave significant differences among the children in the three groups.

Since the logic classification of styles is done mainly through a series of dichotomies, another way of exploring the problem of identifying individual differences in the responsiveness to cognitive demands consisted in ascribing a child to a particular style when his proportion of responses of that style was equal to or greater than 0.75. Table 1.17 presents the results obtained when that criterion was applied to the children in the three groups. It is apparent that while survivors of clinical severe malnutrition and controls matched for IQ and sex had similar styles of response, the children in the group of controls matched at birth showed a different style. Verbal behavior predominated among this latter group, and the two children who were classified as of the not-work type had verbal competence as their main style of response. Conversely, among the survivors and the controls matched for IQ and sex, almost all the not-work children were of the not-work–nonverbal type, unresponsiveness being the typical behavior of these not-work children.

The main findings of the study seem to indicate that survivors of clinical severe malnutrition responded to cognitive demands in a manner significantly different than did children from the same birth cohort who have not suffered from severe malnutrition and who were matched with the survivors for body size and performance on the Gesell test at birth. On the other hand, the pattern of behavioral responsiveness of survivors did not differ from the pattern observed in children without antecedents of severe malnutrition matched with the survivors for sex and intellectual performance at five years of age.

In the presence of these findings, one might tend to consider that the differences in patterns of response between the controls matched at birth and the survivors of severe malnutrition could be explained on the basis of differences in intellectual performance. The observation of similar be-

Table 1.17
Distribution of Children According to
Main Style of Response to Cognitive Demands

Style of Response	Survivors	Controls Matched for IQ and Sex	Controls Matched at Birth
Work	8/14	10/14	12/14
Not-Work	6/14	4/14	2/14
Work Verbal	5/8	8/10	9/12
Work Nonverbal	3/8	2/10	3/12
Not-Work Verbal	0/6	0/4	2/2
Competence	—	—	2/2
Not-Work Nonverbal	6/6	4/4	—
Passivity	6/6	4/4	—

havioral patterns in children with and without antecedents of severe malnutrition but with equal low intellectual performance would be in favor of this explanation. Moreover, Hertzig *et al.* (1968), in their study of middle-class American and working-class Puerto Rican children, found that differences in IQ affected the proportion of demands that was met by a work response, the proportion of total responses that were verbally expressed, and the style of verbal not-work. However, the difference in styles observed between middle-class and Puerto Rican children persisted at all IQ levels. Lugo (1971) in her study of urban Mexican children of three different social classes, also found a quantitative difference in responsiveness as a function of IQ level, but the differences in response style persisted across the socioeconomic levels in the presence of a common IQ range. Accordingly, one cannot accept differences in IQ as the reason for differences in behavioral patterns of response.

Since home-stimulation scores were significantly higher in the controls matched at birth, with similar low scores in both survivors and controls matched for IQ and sex, it is possible that the difference in available stimulation may significantly contribute to the development of dissimilar patterns of responsiveness, particularly in regard to amount and type of verbalizations. The difference in these aspects of behavior between the groups of survivors and controls is very striking. Controls at birth are not only more verbal, but even when they give not-work verbal responses these are mainly expressed in terms of competence rationalizations. The survivors and controls matched for sex and IQ, i.e., the children with persistent low scores in home stimulation, have less verbal expressions, and their verbal not-work responses are styled as requests for aid.

Trying to separate the effects of stimuli deprivation from those which could be due to malnutrition, survivors and controls with equal scores in total home stimulation were identified in order to compare their styles of response. Ten controls for IQ and sex, seven survivors, and six controls matched at birth met this requirement.

There was no difference among the three groups of children in the mean number of total responses, in the proportion of work responses, in the proportion of total responses verbally expressed, and in the styles of nonverbal non-work responses. On the other hand, the proportion of verbal not-work responses observed in controls matched at birth (0.87) was almost three times the proportion found in either survivors (0.30) or controls matched for IQ and sex (0.26). The difference between controls matched at birth and the other two groups is significant at the level of confidence of 0.001.

When the styles of verbal not-work responses were compared, it was observed that the three groups were markedly different (Figure 1.32). Controls matched at birth expressed their verbal not-work responses in terms of rationalizations of competence; survivors expressed their responses mainly as request for aid, and controls matched for IQ and sex had similar proportions of styles of competence, requests for aid, and substitution.

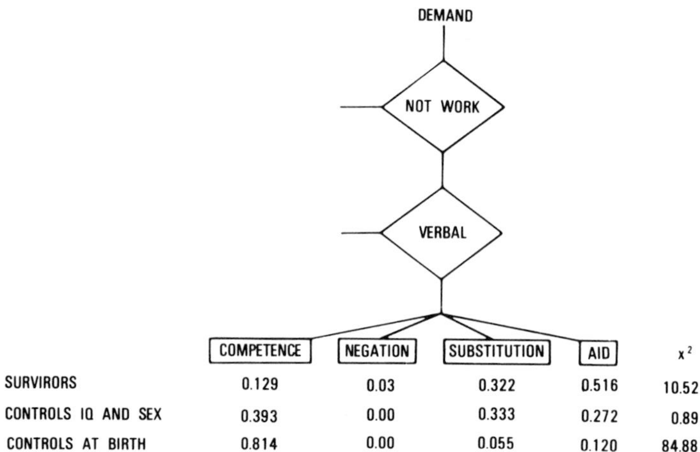

Figure 1.32. Proportion of each style of not-work verbal responses in survivors of severe clinical malnutrition and controls having equal home stimulation scores. *From DeLicardie* et al. *(1973)*.

Finally, the proportion of total responses classified as nonverbal not-work responses is markedly lower in controls matched at birth (0.01) when compared with either survivors (0.18) or controls matched for IQ and sex (0.14). These differences are more significant since the number of total responses had exactly the opposite trend.

The differences observed between survivors of severe malnutrition and controls with equal scores of home stimulation seem to indicate that besides the effect of stimuli deprivation on the styles of response, the antecedent of clinical severe malnutrition appears to be another influential factor.

The finding of unresponsiveness as a characteristic style in children who with or without antecedents of severe malnutrition have as a common background factor a low level of home stimulation leads one to consider that regardless of a physiological component that may be present when the children were malnourished, the passive behavior of survivors of severe malnutrition is probably linked to stimuli deprivation.

It has been suggested by Canosa, Solomon, and Klein (1973) that differences in performance between well-nourished and malnourished children may be due to a lower ability of the malnourished subjects to attend to or concentrate on the given task. However, since these children have a high frequency of passive responses when confronted with a demand, failure to perform efficiently could be a consequence of this style of behavior. For example, any task requiring systematic scanning or elaboration of information by progressively more complicated steps requires the child to engage actively in the pursuit of an answer. Unresponsiveness as a style of behavior may lead to a quick answer without regard for its accuracy. Similarly, children with passive patterns of behavior may give low scores on tasks that are penalized for time.

Mechanisms of Action of Malnutrition

In attempting to explain the mechanism of action of malnutrition on intellectual competence and learning, at least two possibilities can be entertained. The simplest hypothesis would be that nutrient deficiency directly affects intellect by producing central nervous system damage. In favor of this explanation it is relevant to remember that increase of cell cytoplasm with extension of axons and dendrites (one of the processes associated with the growth of the brain in early life) is largely a process of protein synthesis. From the microspectrographic investigation of the regenerating nerve fibers it has been estimated that protein substance increases more than 200 times as the apolar neuroblast matures into the young anterior horn cell. In experimental animals specific amino acid deficiencies can cause structural and functional lesions of the central nervous system (Scott 1964). In mice, inhibition of protein synthesis in the brain produced by puromycin is accompanied by loss of memory (Flexner *et al.* 1962). Delays in myelination and reduction in cell number and in cell distribution in the brain caused by interference with adequate nutrition in early age have been amply documented (Dobing 1968; Winick and Rosso 1969; Chase, Dorsey, and McKhann 1967). Preliminary findings of reduction in brain size and even in cell number in children who died with severe malnutrition have been reported from Mexico (Ambrosius 1961), Uganda (Brown 1965), and Chile (Winick 1969).

The second hypothesis considers that malnutrition in human infants may contribute to intellectual inadequacy through at least three possible indirect mechanisms:

1. *Loss of learning time.* Since the child was less responsive to the environment when malnourished, at the very least the child had less time in which to learn and had lost a certain number of months of experience. On the simplest basis, therefore, the child would be expected to show some developmental lags.

2. *Interference with learning during critical periods of development.* Learning is by no means a simply cumulative process. A considerable body of evidence exists indicating that interference with the learning process at specific times during its course may result in disturbances in function that are both profound and of long-term significance. Such disturbance is not merely a function of the length of time the organism is deprived of the opportunities for learning. Rather, what appears to be important is the correlation of the experiential opportunity with a given stage of development, the so-called critical periods of learning. It is possible that exposure to malnutrition at particular ages may in fact interfere with development at critical points in the child's growth course and so provide either abnormalities in the sequential emergence of competence or a redirection of the developmental course in undesired directions.

3. *Motivation and personality changes.* It should be recognized that the mother's response to the infant is to a considerable degree a function of the child's own characteristics of reactivity. One of the first effects of malnutrition is a reduction in the child's responsiveness to stimulation and the

emergence of various degrees of apathy. Apathetic behavior in its turn can function to reduce the value of the child as a stimulus and to diminish the adult's responsiveness to the child. Thus, apathy can provoke apathy and so contribute to a cumulative pattern of reduced adult-child interaction. If this occurs it can have consequences for stimulation, for learning, for maturation, and for interpersonal relations, the end result being significant backwardness in performance on later more complex learning tasks. It has been reported in experimental animals that small but statistically significant differences in the size of the cerebral cortex can be obtained by manipulation of the stimulatory aspects of the environment (Diamond *et al.* 1966). Recently (Castilla-Serna, Cravioto, and Cravioto 1973) we have reported the synergistic effects of malnutrition and stimuli deprivation on the biochemical structure of the brain, confirming and extending the findings of Levitsky and Barnes (1972) on the effects of nutrition and isolation on animal behavior.

Barnes and his group, on the basis of their results from a long series of animal experiments (Barnes 1968; Barnes, Moore, and Pond 1970; Frankova and Barnes 1968; Levitsky and Barnes 1973), prefer to speak of the interaction between malnutrition and environmental stimulation. The similarity of the biochemical changes produced in the brain by nutrition or by stimulation have led them to consider that the physiological mechanisms which may be responsible for the long-term effects of early stimulation may not be operative if a concurrent state of malnutrition is present during a critical period of development. Malnutrition may thus change the experience or perception of the environment by physiologically rendering the animal less capable of receiving or integrating, or both, information about the environment. These authors have also considered that even in the absence of biochemical alterations of the brain, malnutrition may elicit behavior that is incompatible with the incorporation of environmental information necessary for optimum cognitive development. Behavior primarily food-oriented and behavior expressed as apathy and social withdrawal are two examples of the kind of behaviors exhibited with a very high frequency by malnourished subjects.

Klein and his associates (1972) have also been concerned with the task of sorting out the possible effects that malnutrition may have on mental development from the effects which may be due to the impoverished environment which generally accompanies or produces malnutrition. In a study of a group of three-to-seven-year-old mild to severely malnourished children, height and head circumference were taken as indicators of nutritional status. Quality of house, father's occupation, mother's dress, mother's hygienic practices, task instruction, and social contacts were the estimates of sociocultural status, and language, memory, and perception were the dependent cognitive measures. The main question asked was if physical growth variables would predict cognitive development and functioning after the variance attributable to sociocultural variables had been acknowledged. The results showed that the growth measures do increase the level of prediction of cognitive function over and above the prediction level given by the sociocultural indicators. The proportion of variance that height and head circumference contribute uniquely to the variation in cognition was not the same for all the measures of cognition included in the study. Thus, while the proportion contributed to language development was of only 0.20 for boys and 0.30 for girls, the proportion of explained variance in perception accounted for the physical growth measures was 0.92 for girls and 0.80 for boys. In the case of memory the proportions contributed by physical growth and sociocultural factors were about equal, with no significant difference between the sexes.

It is important to bear in mind that the results obtained by Klein apply to children whose malnutrition ranged from mild to severe, with the vast majority of them in the mild to moderate category. In other words, it seems that a lower performance, particularly in certain areas of cognition, is not contingent on the presence of severe malnutrition. Mild-moderate malnutrition is sufficient to interfere with normal mental development.

In attempting to understand how cognitive development is affected by severe malnutrition during the first year of life, Klein, starting with the clinical observation that the reduced attentiveness and responsiveness to the environment characteristic of the severely malnourished child tends to persist after nutrition rehabilitation, has proceeded to study attention in children recovered from severe malnutrition using both physiologic and behavioral indicators.

Accepting the hypothesis of Sokolov (1963) that a novel stimulus produces an orienting response which tends to disappear with repeated presentations of the stimulus (habituation) because the organism is capable of coding it and producing a neural model which contains the information necessary to recognize the stimulus, a comparative study of habituation in eight fourteen-month-old infants rehabilitated of severe malnutrition and in eight well-nourished control children was carried out. Heart frequency deceleration in response to trials of pure tones alternatively of 750 and 400 Hz, at a constant intensity of 65 decibels and five-second duration, were employed as dependent and independent variables, respectively, on the basis that heart deceleration, which is a component of the orienting reflex, is a widely used measure of attention.

Although both malnourished and well-nourished infants had similar basal heart frequencies, and both groups showed evidence of habituation, there was a marked difference in the immediate response of the infants to the initial presentation of each pure tone. The well-nourished infants showed substantial heart rate deceleration to the onset of the pure tone as well as to the change in frequency of the tone. In contrast, the infants rehabilitated from malnutrition showed a time lag between the initial presentation of a pure tone and a substantial heart rate deceleration. In other words, while both groups of infants habituated to the pure tone and recognized the changes in frequency, this recognition process occurred on the first trial for the well-nourished group and was delayed by several trials in the group of previously malnourished infants. It appears as if the antecedent of severe malnutrition is causing the infant to require a longer presentation time to respond to, and presumably to process, both a novel stimulus and change in a relevant characteristic of that stimulus.

Reduced levels of attention to novel stimuli during infancy may have important consequences for later intellectual competence, since much of the early intellectual development proceeds by attention to and incorporation of novel sensory and motor stimuli. It is thus conceivable that severe chronic malnutrition suffered in early life may alter the normal course of early cognitive development by limiting the amount of effective interaction between the sensory-motor abilities of the infant and his environment.

A third study done by Klein (1972) and co-workers seems to support the hypothesis of reduced levels of attention as an important mediating mechanism in the poor mental performance of malnourished children. In this study, performance level on each of eleven psychological tasks obtained in seventeen previously malnourished children five to six years old was compared with the level obtained in a group of eleven well-nourished children of similar age. Main differences between the groups were found on those tasks which demanded a high level of attentional involvement, particularly in tests where stimuli are presented for only short periods of time. Well-nourished children systematically showed higher scores than did the previously malnourished children. In the test in which the stimuli were available for a longer time, the difference between well-nourished and malnourished groups tended to disappear. Considering that the better performance of the well-nourished group was obtained only when attentional demands on the child were increased, it seems possible to conclude that attentional processes may be one of the mechanisms responsible for the lower performance observed in malnutrition.

A strong support for Klein's hypothesis of reduced attention as a mediator of poor performance in malnutrition has come from the masterly series of experiments carried out by Zimmermann *et al.* (1973) in developing monkeys.

Considering that in animal behavior the area of learning offers the best chances of analogy to human mental development, performance level in a total of 10 learning tasks was studied in malnourished and control monkeys using the Wisconsin General Test apparatus. Five out of the ten tasks—discrimination learning, reversal learning, delayed response, learning set problems, and memory—did not differentiate between animals raised on low- or high-protein diets. On the other hand, the low-protein raised animals showed a systematic lower performance in the following tasks: patterned object-reversal learning, central stimulus-reversal learning, conditional-discrimination learning, embedded-figures discrimination, and patterned strings, crossed pattern. It is apparent that those tasks that required attentional or observing behaviors were the only ones in which the malnourished monkeys showed inferior performance with respect to the control animals.

In the other tasks where object discrimination does not require detailed attention, well-nourished and malnourished subjects exhibited similar levels of performance. Thus it appears as if animals suffering from protein-calorie malnutrition fail to develop the supporting behaviors that lead to the successful solution of problems that require attention.

School Performance and Achievement

Independently of whether or not insufficient nutrient intake *per se* may cause subnormal mental performance, it is evident that children who have experienced moderate or severe forms of malnutrition show alterations in intellectual performance and learning ability which clearly place them at a higher risk of failure to profit from school exposure.

Recently, Richardson, Birch, and Hertzig (1973) have examined school performance in survivors of severe malnutrition. Measures of reading, spelling and arithmetic, and teacher's assessment of school performance and level of intellectual function were obtained in sixty-two school-age children who had a documented episode of severe protein-calorie malnutrition before the age of two years, thirty-one siblings, sixty-two classmates, and six yardmates matched to the six survivors of malnutrition who were not attending school. The results showed that survivors of severe malnutrition and siblings did less well than their classmates on formal tests of reading, spelling, and arithmetic, with no difference between survivors and siblings. In addition, teachers judged the survivors as having "a poorer overall level of performance, poor mastery of school subjects, and more frequent manifestations of special problems in classwork." Siblings and classmates did not differ on teachers' evaluation of school functioning. The similarity of survivors and siblings on school achievement suggests that common elements in macro- and microenvironmental conditions may be responsible for their lower cognitive development. However, when median grades across school subjects were obtained the survivors had a significantly lower median grade than their classmates, with no significant difference between siblings and classmates.

Given the high correlations between kinesthetic-visual integration and learning to write and between auditory-visual integration and learning to read, it is not difficult to visualize the handicap that children retarded in their neurointegrative organization will have in the acquisition of these basic academic skills. The child who lags in the performance of basic mechanisms related to fundamental skills such as reading and writing will be ill-prepared for the learning tasks required of him or her on entering school. If the child is behind on entering, the child may never have an opportunity to match the performance of his or her mates. If the initial impression is of a child who cannot fully benefit from the learning experiences provided by the school the behavior of the child's teachers will reflect their expectations of the child's performance below par, thus reinforcing the probability of inadequate performance. Moreover, if the style of response when confronted with a demand is different in the survivor of malnutrition than the style of his or her mates, the child may be misinterpreted by the teacher as lazy, resistant, and unattentive. The implications of this label are too well known to deserve any further comment.

In a preindustrial society where staying in school imposes a real sacrifice to the parents and other members of the household, the demand for leaving school to contribute to the familial purchasing power may be a social mechanism which prevents the child from being classed as backward, giving the child instead the role of a victim whose sacrifice is necessary, almost indispensable, for the survival of the family group. It is conceivable that through this mechanism the self-esteem of these individuals may be sustained, since the self-concept, i.e., the individual as he is known to himself, is the resultant of the reactions that other persons have to the child's behaviors and of the expectations that those others hold about the ways in which the child will behave. To remain in school could lead to a series of failures which will create a negative self-image which in turn will produce a self-concept in which the individual will have to define himself as incompetent. To abandon school, on the other hand, is to conform to the expected pattern of behavior, to take the role and status of a victim, avoiding without trying a series of continuous failures. Motivation to complete a fairly good number of school years, the national norm, for example, would be markedly reduced under these circumstances.

One of the main differences between learning in humans and learning in other animal species is that only humans have the ability to receive and transmit newly acquired knowledge to the younger members of the species. In this manner humans avoid the need of experimenting with actual noxious agents and environments. Through the use of the oral and written language knowledge is acquired without the learner having to engage personally in actual trial and error during the process.

It is apparent that children who survive a severe episode of malnutrition of sufficient duration early in life are handicapped in learning some of the more fundamental academic skills and are therefore less able to profit from the cumulative knowledge available to the human species in general, and to their socioeconomic group in particular.

References

Adler, S. "Articulatory Deviances and Social-Class Membership." *Journal of Learning Disabilities* 6(1973):650.

Alekseeva, I. A., and Kaplanskaya-Raiskaya, S. I. "Effects of Methionine on Higher Nervous Activity in Protein-Deficient Rats." *Voprosy Pitaniya* [Questions of Nutrition] 19(1960):44.

Ambrosius, K. "El Comportamiento del Peso de Algunos Órganos en Niños con Desnutrición de Tercer Grado." *Boletin Médical Hospital Infantil (Méx)* 18(1961):47.

Autret, M., and Behar, M. *Síndrome Pluricarencial Infantil (Kwashiorkor) and its Prevention in Central America.* FAO Nutrition Series No. 13, Rome, Italy, 1954.

Baldwin, J. M. *Mental Development in the Child and the Race.* New York: Macmillan, 1897.

Barnes, R. H. "Behavioral Changes Caused by Malnutrition in the Rat and the Pig." In *Envi-*

ronmental Influences, edited by Glass. New York: Rockefeller University Press and Russell Sage Foundation, 1968.

———; Moore, A. V.; and Pond, W. G. "Behavioral Abnormalities in Young Adult Pigs caused by Malnutrition in Early Life." *Journal of Nutrition* 100(1970):149.

Barrera-Moncada, G. *Estudios Sobre el Crecimiento y Desarrollo Psicológico del Síndrome Pluricarencial (Kwashiorkor).* Caracas: Grafos, 1963.

Bayley, N. "Some Increasing Parent-Child Similarities During the Growth of Children." *Journal of Educational Psychology* 45(1954):1.

Beckwith, L. "Relationships Between Attributes of Mothers and their Infants' I.Q. Scores." *Child Development* 42(1971):1083.

Birch, H. G. "Comparative Psychology." In *Areas of Psychology,* edited by F. Marcuse. New York: Harper, 1954.

———, and Belmont, L. "Auditory-Visual Integration in Normal and Retarded Readers." *American Journal of Orthopsychiatry* 34(1964):852.

———, and Bitterman, M. E. "Reinforcement and Learning: The Process of Sensory Integration." *Psychological Review* 56(1949):292.

———, and Bitterman, M. E. "Sensory Integration and Cognitive Theory." *Psychological Review* 58(1951):355.

———, and Lefford, A. "Two Strategies for Studying Perception in 'Brain-damaged' Children." In *Brain Damage in Children: Biological and Social Aspects,* edited by H. G. Birch. Baltimore: Williams and Wilkins, 1964.

———, and Lefford, A. "Intersensory Organization and Voluntary Motor Control." Unpublished Manuscript.

———, Piñeiro, C.; Alcalde, E.; Toca, T.; and Cravioto, J. "Relation of Kwashiorkor in Early Childhood and Intelligence at School Age." *Pediatric Research* 5(1971):579.

Botha-Antoun, E.; Babayan, S.; and Harfouche, J. "Intellectual Development Relating to Nutritional Status." *Journal of Tropical Pediatrics* 14(1968):112.

Bowlby, J. "Separation Anxiety." *International Journal of Psychoanalysis* 41(1960):89.

Bresnahan, J. L., and Blum, W. L. "Chaotic Reinforcement: A Socioeconomic Leveler." *Developmental Psychology* 4(1971):89.

———, and Shapiro, M. M. "Learning Strategies in Children from Different Socioeconomic Levels." *Advances in Child Development and Behavior,* edited by H. W. Reese 7(1972):32.

Brockman, L. M., and Ricciuti, H. N. "Severe Protein-Calorie Malnutrition in Infancy and Childhood." *Developmental Psychology* 4(1971):312.

Brown, R. E. "Decreased Brain Weight in Malnutrition and its Implications." *East African Medical Journal* 42(1965):584.

Cabak, V., and Najdavic, R. "Effect of Undernutrition in Early Life on Physical and Mental Development." *Archives of Diseases in Childhood* 40(1965):532.

Caldwell, B. M. "Descriptive Evaluations of Child Development and of Developmental Settings." *Pediatrics* 40(1967):46.

Canosa, C. A.; Solomon, R. L.; and Klein, R. E. "The Intervention Approach: The Guatemalan Study." In *Nutrition, Growth and Development of the North American Indian Children,* edited by W. M. Moore, M. M. Silver, and M. S. Read. Washington, D.C.: USGPO, 1973, Publication No. NIH 72.

Castilla-Serna; Cravioto, L. A.; and Cravioto, J. "Interacción de la Estimulación y la Nutrición Sobre el Desarrollo Bioquímico del Sistema Nervioso Central (Informe Preliminar)." Proc. XXXVII Meeting Mexican Pediatric Society, San José Vista Hermosa, Mor., México, December 7–8, 1973.

Champakam, S.; Srikantia, S. G.; and Gopalan, C. "Kwashiorkor and Mental Development." *American Journal of Clinical Nutrition* 21(1968):844.

Chase, P. H.; Dorsey, J.; and McKhann, G. M. "The Effect of Malnutrition on the Synthesis of Myelin Lipid." *Pediatrics* 40(1967):551.

______, and Martin, H. P. "Undernutrition and Child Development." *New England Journal of Medicine* 282(1970):933.

Chávez, A.; Martínez, C.; and Yascine, T. "The Importance of Nutrition and Stimulation on Child Mental and Social Development." In *Early Malnutrition and Mental Development*, XII Symposium of the Swedish Nutrition Foundation, Saltsjobaden (Stockholm), Sweden, August 20–23, 1973.

Clark, M. "Kwashiorkor." *East African Medical Journal* 28(1951):299.

Cravioto, J. "Consideraciones Epidemiológicas y Bases para la Formulación de un Programa de Prevención de la Desnutrición." *Boletin Medical Hospital Infantil (Méx)* 15(1958):925.

______. "Appraisal of the Effect of Nutrition on Biochemical Maturation." *American Journal of Clinical Nutrition* 11(1962):484.

______. "Nutritional Problems in Rural Areas" In Turk and Crowder, *Rural Development in Tropical Latin America.* Ithaca, N.Y.: New York State College of Agriculture, 1967*a*.

______. *Czechoslovak Academy of Sciences* 1(1967*b*):57.

______; Birch, H. G; and Delicardie, E. R. "Influencia de la Desnutrición Sobre la Capacidad de aprendizaje del niño Escolar." *Boletin Médical Hospital Infantil (Méx)* 24(1967*c*):217.

______. "Infant Malnutrition and Later Learning." In *Progress in Human Nutrition*, edited by S. Margen and N. L. Wilson. Vol. 1, 1971.

______. "Patterns of Child Care during the Preschool Years in Rural Communities." Unpublished Manuscript.

______; Gaona-Espinosa, C.; and Birch, H. G. "Early Malnutrition and Auditory-Visual Integration in School-Age Children." *Journal of Special Education* 2(1967*d*):75.

______; Birch, H. G.; DeLicardie, E. R.; and Rosales, L. "The Ecology of Infant Weight Gain in a Preindustrial Society." *Acta Paediatrica Scandinavica* 56(1967):71.

______; Birch, H. G.; DeLicardie, E. R.; Rosales, L.; and Vega, L. "The Ecology of Growth and Development in a Mexican Preindustrial Community. 1. Methods and Findings from Birth to One Month of Age." *Monographs of the Society for Research in Child Development* 34(1969*a*):129.

______; DeLicardie, E. R.; Piñero, C.; and Alcalde, E. "Neurointegrative Development and Intelligence in School Children Recovered from Malnutrition in Infancy." Paper read before the Seminar on Effects of Malnutrition on Growth and Development, Golden Jubileum Nutrition Research Laboratories of India, Hyderabad, India, 1969*b*.

______, and DeLicardie, E. R. "Environmental Correlates of Severe Clinical Malnutrition and Language Development in Survivors from Kwashiorkor or Marasmus." In *Nutrition, The Nervous System and Behavior.* Washington, D.C.: Panamerican Health Organization, Scientific Publication No. 251, 1972.

______, and DeLicardie, E. R. "The Development of Temporal Information Processing and Auditory-Visual Integration." Proceedings of the 38th Reunion of the Mexican Society for Pediatric Research, San Miguel Regla, Mexico, June 7–8, 1974.

______; DeLicardie, E. R; and Birch, H. G. "Nutrition, Growth and Neurointegrative Development: An Experimental and Ecologic Study." *Pediatrics* 38(1966):319.

______; Lindoro, M.; and Birch, H. G. "Sex Differences in I.Q. Pattern of Children with Congenital Heart Defects." *Science* 174(1971):1042.

______; Rivera, L.; Pérez-Navarrete, J. L.; González, J.; Vilchis, A.; Arrietz, R.; and Santibáñez, E. "The Popular Concept of Communicable Disease." *Boletin de la Oficicina Sanitaria Panamericana* 53(1962):136.

______, and Robles, B. "The Influence of Protein-Calorie Malnutrition on Psychological Test Behavior." In First Symposium of the Swedish Nutrition Foundation. *Mild-Moderate Forms of Protein-Calorie Malnutrition.* Uppsala: Almquist and Wiksells, 1963.

DeLicardie, E. R., and Cravioto, J. "Behavioral Responsiveness of Survivors of Clinical Severe Malnutrition to Cognitive Demands." In *Early Malnutrition and Mental Development.* Twelfth Symposium of the Swedish Nutrition Foundation. Stockholm, Sweden, August 20–22, 1973.

______; Vega, L.; Birch, H. G.; and Cravioto, J. "The Effect of Weight Loss from Birth to Fifteen Days on Growth and Development in the First Year." *Biology of the Neonate* 17(1971):249.

Diamond, M. C.; Law, F.; Rhodes, H.; Lindner, B.; Rosenzweig, M. R.; Krech, D.; and Bennett, E. L. "Increases in Cortical Depth and Glia Number in Rats Subjected to Enriched Environment." *Journal of Comparative Neurology* 128(1966):117.

Dobing, J. "Vulnerable Periods in Developing Brain." In *Applied Neurochemistry,* edited by Davidson and Dobingo. Oxford: Blackwell Scientific Publications, 1968.

Flexner, L. B.; Stellar, E.; de la Haba, G.; and Roberts, R. B. "Inhibition of Protein Synthesis in Brain and Learning and Memory Following Puromycin." *Journal of Neurochemistry* 5(1962):595.

Frankova, S., and Barnes, R. H. "Effect of Malnutrition in Early Life on Avoidance Conditioning and Behavior of Adult Rats." *Journal of Nutrition* 96(1968):485.

Geber, M., and Dean, R. F. A. "The Psychological Changes Accompanying Kwashiorkor." *Courrier* 6(1956):3.

Gómez, F.; Velasco-Alzaga, J.; Ramos-Galván, R.; Cravioto, J.; and Frenk, S. "Estudios sobre el niño desnutrido XVII-Manifestaciones psicológicas (Comunicación preliminar)." *Boletin Mêdical Hospital Infantil (Mêx.)* 11(1954):631.

Goodenough, F. L., and Anderson, J. E. *Minnesota Scale of Parental Occupations.* Rev. ed. Minneapolis: Institute of Child Development, 1954.

Guillen-Alvarez, G. "Influence of Severe Marasmic Malnutrition in Early Infancy on Mental Development at School Age." Proceedings of the Twelfth International Congress of Pediatrics, Vienna, Austria, August 29–September 4, 1971. *Wiener Medizinischen Akademie* (1971).

Guthrie, H. A.; Guthrie, G. M.; and Tayag, A. "Nutritional Status and Intellectual Performance in a Rural Philippine Community," *Philippine Journal of Nutrition* 22(1969):2.

Harris, A. J. *How to Increase Reading Ability.* 2nd ed. New York: Longmans Green, 1946.

Hertzig, M. E.; Birch, H. G.; Richardson, S. A.; Tizard, J. "Intellectual Levels of School Age Children Severely Malnourished During the First Two Years of Life." *Pediatrics* 49(1972):814.

______; Birch, H. G.; Thomas, A.; and Arán-Méndez, O. "Class and Ethnic Differences in the Responsiveness of Preschool Children to Cognitive Demands." *Monographs of the Society for Research in Child Development.* 33(1968):Serial No. 117.

Hess, R., and Shipman, V. C. "Early Experience and the Socialization of Cognitive Modes in Children." *Child Development* 36(1965):869.

Honzik, M. P. "Environmental Correlates of Mental Growth." *Child Development* 28(1957):215.

Hoorweg, J., and Stanfield, P. "The Influence of Malnutrition on Psychologic and Neurologic Development: Preliminary Communications." In *Nutrition, The Nervous System and Behavior.* Panamerican Health Organization, Scientific Publication No. 251, 1972.

Jackson, C. M., and Steward, C. A. "The Effects of Inanition in the Young upon the Ultimate Size of the Body and of the Various Organs in the Albino Rat." *Journal of Experimental Zoology* 30(1920):97.

Jacobson, L. I.; Berger, S.; Bergman, R. L.; Millham, J.; and Greeson, L. E. "Effects of Age, Sex, Systematic Conceptual Learning, Acquisition of Learning Sets and Programmed Social Interaction on the Intellectual and Conceptual Development of Preschool Children from Poverty Backgrounds." *Child Development* 42(1971):1399.

Kagan, J. "Inadequate Evidence and Illogical Conclusions." *Harvard Education Review* 39(1969):274.

———, and Moss, H. A. "Parental Correlates of Child's I.Q. and Height: A Cross-Validation of the Berkeley Growth Study Results." *Child Development* 30(1959):325.

Kardonsky, V.; Alvarado, M.; Undurraga, O.; Manterola, A.; and Segure, T. "Desarrollo Intelectual y Físico en el Niño Desnutrido." Unpublished manuscript. Santiago: University of Chile, Department of Psychology, 1971.

Klein, R. E.; Lester, B. M.; Yarbrough, C.; and Habitch, J. P. "On Malnutrition and Mental Development: Some Preliminary Findings." Proceedings of the Ninth International Congress of Nutrition. Mexico City, Mexico, September 2–9, 1972.

Leitch, I. "Growth, Heredity and Nutrition." *Eugenics Review* 51(1959):155.

Lesser, G. S.; Fifer, G.; and Clark, D. H. "Mental Abilities of Children from Different Social Class and Cultural Groups." *Monographs of the Society for Research in Child Development* 30(1965):4.

Levitsky, D. A., and Barnes, R. H. "Nutritional and Environmental Interactions in the Behavioral Development of the Rat: Long-Term Effects." *Science* 176(1972):68.

———, and Barnes, R. H. "Malnutrition and Animal Behavior." In *Nutrition, Development and Social Behavior,* edited by D. J. Kalleen. Washington, D.C.: USGPO, 1973, Pub. No. NIH 73-242.

Liang, P. H.; Hie, T. T.; Jan, O. H.; and Giok, L. T. "Evaluation of Mental Development in Relation to Nutrition." *American Journal of Clinical Nutrition* 20(1967):1290.

Lugo, G. "Influencia de Clase Social Sobre el Estilo de Respuesta Ante una Demanda Cognoscitiva." Tesis, Facultad de Filosfía y Letras, UNAM, México, D.F., 1971.

Maier, N. R. F., and Schneirla, T. C. *Principles of Animal Behavior.* New York: McGraw-Hill, 1935.

Marcondes, E.; Lefevre, A. B.; and Machado, D. V. "Desenvolvimiento Neuropsicomotor da Crianca Desnutrida." *Revista Brasileira de Psiquiatría* 3(1969):173.

McCance, R. A. "Food, Growth and Time." *Lancet* (1962):671.

Meneghello, J. *Desnutrición en el lactante mayor (distrofia policarencial).* Santiago, Chile: Central de Publicaciones, 1949.

Monckeberg, F. "Effect of Early Marasmic Malnutrition on Subsequent Physical and Psychological Development." In *Malnutrition, Learning and Behavior,* edited by N. E. Scrimshaw and J. E. Gordon. Cambridge, Mass.: MIT Press, 1968.

Moss, H. A., and Kagan, J. "Maternal Influence on I.Q. Scores." *Psychological Reports* 4(1958):655.

Nathan, P. *The Nervous System,* Philadelphia: Lippincott, 1969.

Odom, R. D. "Problem-Solving Strategies as a Function of Age and Socioeconomic Level." *Child Development* 38(1967):747.

Orr, J. B. *Food, Health and Income.* London: Macmillan, 1936.

Platt, B. S.; Heard, C. R. C.; and Steward, R. J. C. "Experimental Protein-Calorie Deficiency." In *Mammalian Protein Metabolism,* edited by Munro and Allison. New York: Academic Press, 1964.

Pollitt, E. "Behavior of Infant in Causation of Nutritional Marasmus." *American Journal of Clinical Nutrition* 26(1973):264.

———, and Granoff, D. "Mental and Motor Development of Peruvian Children Treated for Severe Malnutrition." *Revista Interamerica Psicologiga* 1(1968):93.

———, and Ricciuti, H. N. "Biological and Social Correlates of Stature among Children Living in the Slums of Lima, Peru." *American Journal of Orthopsychiatry* 39(1969):735.

Rafferty, F. T. "Functional Learning Disorders." *Pediatric Clinics of North America* 20(1973):653.

Ramos-Galván, R., and Cravioto, J. "La desnutrición en el niño. Concepto y ensayo de sistematización." *Boletin Médical Hospital Infantil (Méx.)* 15(1958):763.

Richardson, S. A.; Birch, H. G.; and Hertzig, M. E. "School Performance of Children who were Severely Malnourished in Infancy." *American Journal of Mental Deficiency* 77(1973):623.

Rosales, L.; Quintanilla, C. L.; and Cravioto, J. "Operación Nimiquipalg III-Epidemiologiá popular de las enfermedades prevalentes en el medio rural de Guatemala." *Guatemala Pediatrica* 4(1964):59.

Scarr-Salapatek, S. "Race, Social Class, and I.Q." *Science* 174(1971):1285.

Scott, E. B. "Histopathology of Aminoacid Deficiencies. VII. Valine." *Journal of Experimental Molecular Pathology* 3(1964):10.

Sherrington, C. S. *Man on his Nature.* London: Cambridge University Press, 1951.

Skeels, H. M. "Adult Status of Children with Contrasting Early Life Experience." *Monographs of the Society for Research in Child Development* 31(1966):Serial No. 105.

Sokolov, E. N. *Perception and the Conditioned Reflex.* New York: Macmillan, 1963.

Stern, G.; Caldwell, B. M.; Hersher, L.; Lipton, E.; and Richmond, J. B. "A Factor Analytic Study of the Mother-Infant Dyad." *Child Development* 40(1969):163.

Stoch, M. B., and Smythe, P. M. "Does Undernutrition during Infancy Inhibit Brain Growth and Subsequent Intellectual Development?" *Archives of Disease in Childhood* 38 (1963):546.

Templin, M. C. "Certain Language Skills in Children, Their Development and Interrelationships." *Institute of Child Welfare Monographs* Series 26. Minneapolis: University of Minnesota Press, 1957.

Thomas, A.; Chess, S.; Birch, H. G.; Hertzig, M. E.; and Korn, S. *Behavioral Individuality in Early Childhood.* New York: New York University Press, 1963.

Throne, J. M. "A Radical Behaviorist Approach to Diagnosis in Mental Retardation." *Mental Retardation* 8(1970):2.

———. "Genetic Structures in Mental Retardation: A Radical Behaviorist Point of View." *Mental Retardation* 10(1972):32.

———. "Learning Disabilities: A Radical Behaviorist Point of View." *Journal of Learning Disabilities* 6(1973):543.

Turk and Crowder. *Rural Development in Tropical Latin America.* Ithaca, N.Y.: New York State College of Agriculture, 1967.

Voronin, L. G., and Guselnikov, V. I. "On the Phylogenesis of Internal Mechanisms of the Analytic and Synthetic Activity of the Brain." *Pavlov Journal of Higher Nervous Activity* 13(1963):193.

Walzer, S., and Richmond, J. B. "The Epidemiology of Learning Disorders." *Pediatric Clinics of North America* 20(1973):549.

Waterlow, J. C.; Cravioto, J.; and Stephen, J. "Protein Malnutrition in Man." *Advances in Protein Chemistry* 15(1960):131.

Weir, M. W. "Developmental Changes in Problem-Solving Strategies." *Psychological Review* 71(1964):473.

Wilson, A. T. M. "Fostering Nutritional Change: Some Points from Social Research." *Proceedings of the Sixth International Congress of Nutrition,* edited by Mills and Passmore. Edinburgh: Livingstone, 1964.

Wilson, D.; Bressani, R.; and Scrimshaw, N. S. "Infection and Nutritional Status. 1. The Effect of Chicken Pox on Nitrogen Metabolism in Children." *American Journal of Clinical Nutrition* 9(1961):154.

Winick, M. "Malnutrition and Brain Development." *Journal of Pediatrics* 74(1969):667.

———, and Rosso, P. "The Effect of Severe Early Malnutrition on Cellular Growth of the Human Brain." *Pediatric Research* 3(1969):181.

Winitz, H. *Articulatory Acquisition and Behavior.* New York: Appleton-Century-Crofts, 1969.

Yatkin, U. S., and McLaren, D. S. "The Behavioral Development of Infants Recovering from Severe Malnutrition." *Journal of Mental Deficiency Research* 14(1970):25.

Zimmermann, R. R.; Geist, C. R.; Strobel, D. A.; and Cleveland, T. J. "Attention Deficiencies in Malnourished Monkeys." In *Early Malnutrition and Mental Development.* Twelfth Symposium of the Swedish Nutrition Foundation Stockholm, Sweden, August 20–23, 1973.

Editors' note: The specific focus of this chapter is on the neurological aspects of the psychological areas of perceptual and motor development in infancy through childhood and the critical need for the interchange of research information among scholars from different disciplines and different countries. Drs. Koupernik and Mac Keith, appropriate to their background, are primarily responsible for the section entitled "Neurological Correlates of Motor Development" while Lady Jessie Francis-Williams has contributed the final section on perceptual development. Issues germane to the diagnosis of neurological integrity are dealt with. Hard and soft signs of brain damage are discussed. A much-needed discussion of the concept of minimal brain dysfunction outlines the problems related to this issue as well as the controversy concerning the hyperactivity syndrome. With the information presented in this chapter and the one by Dr. Gaddes on "Neurological Implications for Learning" of Volume 1, the reader should become aware of the issues and research pertaining to the neurological aspects of learning problems.

Cyrille Koupernik, M.D., is Associate Member of the Medical College of Paris Hospitals and Consultant Psychiatrist, the American Hospital of Paris. He was formerly Visiting Ittleson Lecturer, Washington University, St. Louis, Missouri, and a Fellow at the Yale Child Study Center under Professor Arnold Gesell, Chef de Clinique Neuropsychiatrique Infantile à la Faculté de Médecine de Paris. He was Assistant Secretary General and then Vice President of the International Association of Child Psychiatry and Allied Professions and is presently Secretary of the International Study Group of this body.

Ronald Mac Keith, M.D., a British pediatrician, was formerly Director of Pediatric Teaching and Director of Newcomen Clinic at Guy's Hospital in London. He received his medical training at Oxford, St. Mary's Hospital, London, and at Bellevue Hospital in New York. Since 1958 Dr. Mac Keith has been the Editor of *Developmental Medicine and Child Neurology.* He has served as president to the Association for Child Psychology and Psychiatry, the Section of Pediatrics of the Royal Society of Medicine, and the Medical Association for Prevention of War. He is an honorary member of the American Academy of Cerebral Palsy, American Academy of Pediatrics, the Association of Child Psychology and Psychiatry, the British Pediatric Association, the Catalan Pediatric Society, and the Societé de Pédiatrie de la lague française. In 1972 Dr. Mac Keith received the British Pediatric Association's highest honor, the James Spence Medal, and in 1974 the Rosen von Rosenstein Medal of the Swedish Paediatric Society.

Lady Jessie Francis-Williams, M.A., is Research Psychologist, Newcomen Centre for Handicapped Children, Guy's Hospital, London, where lately she has also been Consultant Psychologist. She was formerly Senior Psychologist, Hospital for Sick Children, Great Ormond Street, London, and sometime Psychologist, University College Hospital, and Lecturer, University College, London. She is a member of the British Psychological Society and the author of books on psychology for student nurses, assessment of cerebral palsied children, children with specific learning difficulties, and a volume on the use of the Rorschach with children.

2

Neurological Correlates of Motor and Perceptual Development

Cyrille Koupernik, Ronald Mac Keith, and Jessie Francis-Williams

NEUROLOGICAL CORRELATES OF MOTOR DEVELOPMENT

An increasing capacity to move one's body and its several parts, whether for enjoyment, necessity, or some planned goal, is part of general development. The main characteristics of motor development are (1) It appears to be an inherent quality. This might seem to make motor development independent of environmental influences; but, while there is an element of truth in this, for realizing its full potential, motor skill requires a favorable milieu and adequate training. (2) Motor development seems to be independent of psychological and emotional factors, which is equally debatable. (3) Motor development can be studied by a purely medical approach, that of the classical clinical examination which today includes the qualitative procedures of the pediatric developmental assessment (Egan, Illingworth, and Mac Keith 1969). (4) Motor development includes the unicity of brain function and of its reactions toward external stimuli, including things such as aggression.

The study of motor development thus provides us with a privileged, largely objective insight into childhood psychopathology. This approach contrasts with psychoanalysis.

Although Freud wrote a classical and brilliant study of Little's disease (cerebral palsy) he was, later, not interested in brain impairment, and his followers were even less concerned. Freud was concerned neither with movement nor muscles; he was fascinated by the early developmental role of the two endodermic orifices—mouth and anus—and later with the role of the penis. He restricted personal psychology to where it belongs—to relationships, whether between mother and child or patient (whether child or adult) and therapist. Studying motor development brings the study of development back to its classical medical sources. By this approach each symptom (disability) is, as we shall see, correlated to others; the resultant syndromes imply the impairment (disorder) of a given neural activity; the cause of the impairment is then sought. Finally, the total diagnosis is reviewed and the appropriate treatment, including medication, among other therapies, is given. To be complete every diagnosis must include statements about the patient, the patient's disabilities, their underlying disorder, and their cause.

This approach antedated the great psychoanalytic invasion of child psychology and psychiatry. One result of this invasion has been a school of thought which sees motor impairments as due to neurotic conflicts. There is certainly a direct and even an etymological relationship between movement (motion) and emotion and between muscular tonus and emotion, as Wallon (1934, 1948) has shown, and has also been discussed for cerebral palsy (Mac Keith 1958). But it is difficult to see how to confine the origins of the variety of impaired motor performance and motor symptoms and signs to this one type of cause. Besides, philosophically, every symptom, as Abercrombie (1962) has shown, is necessarily multifactorial in origin in the sense that any symptom can be produced by a variety of causes. "One symptom therefore one cause" is an error of thinking. None of us being a psychoanalyst, we have no need to protest against abandonment of a one-psychoanalytic-track approach to the child. Equally, to equate all unusual movements or behavior with a lesion or damage in the brain is wrong. Our point is that any limited approach to understanding the child will have only limited usefulness. The bodily, organic, intellectual, emotional and social aspects—all of them—of each and every child need always be fitted together to make the picture of the child, also adding consideration of the child's current status and the relation of this to the pattern of optimum development.

THE CHILD DEVELOPS IN MOTOR CAPACITIES

The child differs from the adult because the child develops. This statement is clearly a truism, but at a time when much psychological writing is tenebrous and tenuous, platitudinous truth may be preferable to possibly faulty understanding.

A second truism: this development—derived from inherited tendencies—is programmed in the brain, whence the rule of the "normal sequence" of development, of the occurrence in every individual of a succession of states in the same order.

A third truism: this development is fully realized only if the environment plays its role of interacting physically and psychologically with the inherited tendencies.

Let us now apply these truisms to motor development by comparing the two extremes of childhood—the newborn infant and the adolescent.

The Newborn Infant

At birth the infant shows a number of responses to stimuli—the rooting and sucking responses, the Moro response, and primary walking. Responses which are stereotyped and inevitable are called *reflexes*. The word should not be applied to a response like the asymmetric tonic neck response, which is never an obligatory one. (This is the response in which, when the infant's head is turned to one side, the limbs on the side to which the face is turned extend while those on the "occipital" side flex.) The newborn infant is unable to perform voluntary movements or at any rate voluntary movements which serve a useful purpose that we adults can determine. To this there is one essential exception: he can suck.

Some predetermined archaic responses are present at birth and these are called the primary primitive responses. Others emerge later and are called the secondary primitive responses. These include the "propping" reaction, whereby an infant of six or eight months puts out his upper limb in the direction he is falling. This response is not learned; it appears without practice or teaching. Balancing is another inherent secondary primitive reaction which appears at about the same time.

The Moro response is elicited either by rapidly moving the head, thereby stimulating the labyrinth (Peiper 1960), or by suddenly changing the position of the head in relation to the trunk (André-Thomas, Chesni, and Saint-Anne-Dargassies 1960). The result of either stimulus is the same: first the infant abducts and extends his flexed limbs and trunk; the infant then returns to the posture of general flection. This response serves no useful purpose and will disappear at the age of two or three months. (This illustrates that in infancy normal development includes the losing of certain responses as well as the emergence of other new ones). When the Moro response disappears it is replaced by the startle response, which reveals the infant's state of vigilance which is subserved by the reticular formation in the upper brain stem. (The reticular formation influences general body tone and posture and is played upon by inhibitory and facilitory impulses from the sensory inflow and from the cerebral cortex. It is suggested that in the absence of facilitory impulses from the cerebral cortex, there is hypotonia and that such a condition of "cerebral zero" accounts for the hypotonia common in extreme mental deficiency.)

Another archaic response is the automatic walking which has been well studied by McGraw (1943), Peiper (1963), André-Thomas and Saint-Anne-Dargassies (1952). When the newborn infant is held under the arms in a vertical position and the soles of his feet touch the ground, he begins to walk and will walk upstairs and, held upside down, will walk across the ceiling. But this walking is not accompanied by any ability to balance and has no obvious usefulness. This response disappears at about two months. It has been shown that, in two-thirds of children, it can, up to the end of the first year, still be evoked if the infant's head is passively extended (Mac Keith 1964*a,b*). By twelve or fifteen months definitive walking has usually appeared.

Let us reflect for a moment. In this primary walking we have—inscribed in the central nervous system, probably in the brain stem, possibly in the cortex—a pattern of organization of movement which disappears and then reappears again, first as a conscious movement (one has only to see the efforts made by the toddler to achieve his first steps), and then becomes once again automatic in its mechanisms (for who spends time thinking about how to do walking). Though now automatized, this method of locomotion has a purpose and can be modified by the will (the adult steps, walks faster, runs, changes direction). The automatization of a laboriously learned motor skill is within the memory of everyone who has learned to ride a bicycle or to drive an automobile.

Using a wealth of evidence from studies of animals and birds, Peiper (1960) argued that the behavior of walking is an inherently determined skill which, once maturation has occurred, would appear spontaneously without teaching. It is true that parents "teach" their children to walk, but whether the child learns from this teaching is open to some doubt. It has also been argued that nocturnal bladder control, another motor skill, is similarly inherently determined and in the absence of adverse factors will appear spontaneously once maturation has occurred (Mac Keith 1973). We mention these possibilities to remind our readers that teaching and learning are not necessarily synonymous, and that if a change occurs in a child during treatment, the change may be the result of the passage of time and consequent maturation and not of the treatment.

A second topic for reflection which brings us back to our third truism: African Ugandan infants brought up in the traditional way, that is to say carried by the mother on her back, stand at six months of age, while European infants stand at ten to twelve months old, and the African infants walk at eight or nine months (Geber and Dean 1957*a,b*). This is not a racial characteristic: Ugandan infants brought up in the European manner follow the same pattern as little Europeans so far as motor development is concerned. What is inherited is a potential for response to environmental influences. What in fact happens is the result of the interaction of potentialities and life experiences. A concept of an either/or antithesis of heredity and environment is an outmoded idea. Both play their part in every biological event.

A third primary primitive response is the tonic finger flection reflex, as André-Thomas calls it, or the grasping reflex, as it is more commonly called. When one stimulates the palm of the hand or the palmar aspect of the four ulnar fingers, the hand of the neonate closes firmly. This primitive response also serves no useful purpose for the infant, unless one supposes, as does Peiper (1963), that it is an inheritance from some distant apelike ancestor who swung through the trees clinging to his mother's fur. This response also disappears at about two months to be replaced shortly afterwards by true prehension, which has been rigorously studied by Halverson (1943).

Looking forward to a later stage of development, we stress the special importance for human existence of standing and the use of the hands (Koupernik and Dailley 1972). It is the human hand, characterized from a functional point of view by the ability to oppose the thumb against the other fingers, which permits the full use of tools and which is, with language, at the basis of our civilization. The newborn infant has a very specific distribution of muscular tone. In the limbs, there is hypertonia of the flexor muscles. On the other hand, in the neck and trunk there is hypotonia. The head of the newborn dangles, and the infant cannot sit. We shall later have occasion to extend this discussion of tone.

At this point one should add that the brain of the newborn infant is small, his or her head circumference being about 36 cm. (though at one year it will reach 46 cm.) In a boy the brain weighs about 330 grams; in a girl 283 grams. In adult men it weighs about 1375 grams and in women 1245 grams. The difference is probably related to the greater maturity at all ages of the female, a consequence of which is that the female progresses more quickly through the period of most rapid brain growth (Ounsted and Taylor 1973). (Perhaps by energetic action members of the Women's Liberation Movement will somehow achieve the equality women deserve). The secondary sulci of the cerebral cortex are not yet developed in the newborn. Many of the nerve fibers which later will interconnect the various areas of the brain are still unformed.

The Adolescent

In contrast with the newborn, let us now look at the adolescent and his motor capacities. The adolescent is master of his own body. One has only to think of the extraordinary modern swimming champions, many only in mid-adolescence, or the virtuosity of the skiers who have barely left childhood, of the grace of juvenile dancers. Master also of his hands, he is skillful in drawing, writing, and in making and repairing things.

Man is bipedal and erect, that is to say, an animal in a posture of extension. For this, among other reasons, the adult differs from the newborn infant he once was. Each of his movements is a synergy between the agonist and the antagonist muscles. (During a flection movement of the hand, the finger extensor muscles curb and hence make smooth the flection movement and make it precise.) In the neonate the transition from flection to extension at the joints was made abruptly and was a total reaction, with the whole limb extending—or flexing—at every joint.

But not all adolescents are champions. Most of them are grouped around the average or ordinary level of motor competence. But some are clumsy, whether in the upper or lower limbs or in articulation. Most show an ordinary level of general motor activity, some show low motility and some a high level of motility which, if it is more than two standard deviations above the mean, will deserve the label hyperactivity.

MATURATION AND DEVELOPMENT

Arnold Gesell noted that children show development—a sequence of emergence of behaviors, for example, sitting, standing, walking, and running—and that the ages at which these skills were achieved varied in different children but the sequence was always the same. He postulated that for each behavior to emerge, links had to be formed in the central nervous system to provide the necessary pathways for the neural messages subserving the behavior. These anatomical changes he called maturation, which is a process of morphogenesis (Gesell and Ilg 1943). Maturation is inherently determined by inherited factors in the DNA of the genes. It is possible that maturation can be speeded; it certainly can be delayed by injury, e.g., perinatal anoxia of the brain.

The mechanisms which underlie maturation are not exactly known. The growth of nerve fibers to link with other nerve cells plays a part, as does the myelinization of the main pathways of conduction and association. But changes also take place within the nerve cells affecting intracellular structures such as the organelles, Nissl's bodies, and the neurofibrils. It is in this way and for this reason, that to take an example, the cerebellum, which plays an essential role in the coordination of movement, only reaches maturity toward the fourth year.

In recent years, more and more interest is being focused not only on anatomical but on physiological aspects of maturation and particularly on the cerebral bioamines—serotonin, noradrenaline, and dopamine—which, at the level of the synapses, play the role of mediators of nervous impulses and also on the enzyme systems which control the production and breakdown of these substances. Our knowledge is still far from exact, and while hypotheses are rightly being advanced about the parts played by such substances in thought and movement, such hypotheses are largely conjectural.

VARIATIONS IN MOTOR DEVELOPMENT

When the pediatrician makes a neurological assessment of a child's motor status, he does two things. He finds what the child can do and then evaluates this by comparing the child's capacities with those of his peer group and so obtains a developmental assessment. This may show the child as advanced, average, or delayed. The pediatrician also discovers whether there are any abnormalities in the child's motor functioning. From abnormal signs he can infer particular disorders of neurological function.

Among ordinary children there will be variation in motor abilities; there will be a normal range because some children are more and some less skilled in movement. Factors affecting motor capacity include inheritance, opportunity, encouragement, example, and the child's inherent drive. Motor delay arises not only from motor disorder; it can arise from disorder of other systems. The blind child stands but is late in walking "into the unknown"; the child with a mental handicap is often, but not always, late in motor development; emotional and social handicap can show themselves in motor delay.

When we consider the variation in capacity and skill of different persons, a major factor, and one which is of considerable importance for motor function, is training. The living conditions in the African savanna, the body science of Asiatics, produce better results than life in the big cities of the Western world. French school children, exhausted by superhuman educational programs, develop less harmoniously physically than do little Scandinavians or young East Germans, and ten years ago it was found that young Austrians have better motor capacity than the general run of young people in the USA.

When a child is late he may be a "late normal" child or he may have an unusual but nonetheless normal pattern of motor development. Robson (1970) has shown that 10 percent of children do not crawl, but between sitting and walking they move about on their bottoms. This trait is genetically transmitted in dominant fashion. While there is variation within the group of "shufflers," many of them have, in the second year, hypotonia of the lower limbs and walk late, but are perfectly normal once they do walk at the late age of twenty-one or twenty-four months. The presence of this trait may affect the evolution of motor conditions such as spastic cerebral palsy (Mac Keith and Robson 1971).

Motor delay is, of course, at times due to motor disorder, including the varieties of cerebral palsy and the muscle dystrophies. The earliest evidence of cerebral palsy is often motor delay which may be present before there are any abnormal signs such as alteration in tone.

THE DIAGNOSIS

Before going on to further description of motor development we shall make a rather lengthy digression to remind our readers of the need for clear thinking in the matter of diagnosis, for failure in this has produced much confusion, notably in relation to the term "minimal brain damage."

Although at times we all use abbreviations, we shall do well to remember that in order to be complete a diagnosis must have four parts. The patient comes to the doctor and presents a symptom or disability (the complaint). The doctor takes a full history and makes an examination (in which he finds the neurological and other signs). On the basis of these and, usually, some further tests, he decides by inferences the disorder, anatomical and pathophysiological, underlying the disability. He then tries to establish the cause of the disorder. He wants to know this because there may be a special treatment and also because disorders cannot be prevented unless we know their causes.

To be complete a diagnosis must include four statements:

1. about *the person involved,* for "there are no diseases, only sick people," as Trousseau said;
2. about *the disability* (the symptom or dysfunction);
3. about *the disorder* underlying the disability; and
4. about *the cause* of the disorder.

Let us give an example, that of a boy of four years who is brought because he is less able to run than he was formerly. His symptom or disorder of function can be stated as increasing motor disability. After taking a history and eliciting the signs (by a pediatric and a neurological examination) and conducting a test of the creatine-phospho-kinase level in the blood, and an electromyogram, we decide he has progressive weakness with muscular dystrophy of the Duchenne type. The cause of this is a recessively inherited genetic abnormality. What does the doctor do to help the child? He treats the dysfunction by ensuring the boy's activities are not pushed to fatigue, but he has as yet no treatment for the neuromuscular disorder; he treats the cause inasmuch as he gives the parents genetic counselling with the aim of preventing the birth of another patient. (This example is of special interest in that after we have assumed for a hundred years that this is a disorder of muscle, we find we may have to change to considering it to be neuronal in origin; medicine is a provisional, ever-changing subject.)

Let us take another example, that of a girl of nine months who is not yet sitting up, i.e., her symptom is delayed development. It could be immediately concluded that because she has motor disability, she has motor disorder. But every physician knows that the same motor disability could be due to other causes, notably mental handicap or social deprivation, and that there are children later perfectly normal who show early slow development. The inherited familial "shuffling" trait, a variant of normal development which can be observed in 10 percent of children, has been mentioned above.

Let us suppose the physician concludes the child has some degree of spastic cerebral palsy plus some degree of mental handicap. These are the disorders underlying the disability. The search for the cause of both cerebral palsy and of mental handicap is not always rewarding because in half of the cases, no cause is identified.

When we construct our fourfold diagnosis, the difference between observations and inferences must always be kept clear. Observation is subject to a variety of influences but agreement between observers should be possible. Inferences are far more uncertain. It may be better to stay on the certainty of observation. An inference of motor disorder from an observation of motor delay is risky. Other evidence is needed. An inference that a newborn baby with Down's Syndrome will later have an IQ below 50 has probability on its side but it will not necessarily be true about any individual child with Down's Syndrome. A baby born after a long and difficult labor will not necessarily be mentally or physically handicapped. The baby will be to some extent "at risk" but many infants "at risk" show no evidence of damage later.

This leads us to another point, that when the doctor is asked to help with a disability, he finds it intellectually satisfying to identify an underlying disorder and to identify the cause of this, but such inferred knowledge is in fact often unnecessary. The symptom or disability can be treated without knowledge of the disorder or its cause. Treatment of symptoms is often unwise in acute disorders, but where the disorder is nonprogressive, as so often is the case in cerebral palsy and learning difficulties, accurate analysis and treatment of the disabilities is often the best approach.

Considerations such as the above led the 1962 Oxford International Study Group on Child Neurology (Bax and Mac Keith 1963) to point out that the label "minimal brain damage" was frequently applied with no good evidence to support it and that it was wiser to consider only the observed disabilities and use the term "cerebral dysfunction." The study group also noted the variety of meanings given to "minimal brain damage" and suggested that the various disabilities should be listed as a basis for planning treatment.

THE CAUSES OF BRAIN DEFECTS

The study of etiopathogenesis includes ideas of cause and of mechanism. Trauma may be the cause of a brain defect, the mechanism being the bleeding caused by the trauma—a bleeding which destroys a particular part of the brain or interrupts its connections and hence produces interference with the function subserved by that part of the brain.

Defects may be caused by failure or distortion of development of the brain or by brain injury. The effects of injury of the brain in an adult and a child may differ because in the young child it is sometimes possible for other areas of the brain to take over the functions of an area destroyed.

Causes can be divided simply into prenatal, perinatal, and postnatal. Prenatal causes include causes in the genome, whether a dominant gene such as in Huntington's chorea which produces cerebral deterioration in middle life or a chromosomal anomaly such as occurs in Down's Syndrome. Other prenatal causes act in the first three months when organogenesis is most active. An example is rubella infection of the embryo or thalidomide taken by the mother. Later in pregnancy, toxoplasmosis, a benign disease in the woman, is a danger when it affects the fetus and its developing brain. Illnesses in the mother, such as poorly controlled diabetes, severe toxemia, and malnutrition, may lead to limitation of the growth of the brain, which grows fastest in the last few months of fetal life and the first six months after birth.

Perinatal causes include lack of oxygen from placental disorder, the hazards of delivery which may cause anoxia and brain injury, and the neonatal effects of iso-immunization disorder of which the commonest was Rhesus disorder. This last is, however, today largely prevented, and if it occurs is treated with good results. In a baby delivered too early, the liver may be immature and a similar hyperbilirubinemia result.

To be born early puts a baby's brain at risk, but today it seems that with good intensive care 80 percent of small preterm babies will be normal as compared with 50 percent some years ago.

The post-term infant is liable to intrauterine anoxia from placental insufficiency. Once again it must be noted that not all children who are postmature show evidence of damage.

During any delivery there will be some anoxia as the head of the baby is molded through the birth passages. On the other hand caesarean section does not evade all the risks of delivery.

Postnatal causes include trauma to the head whether in traffic collisions, by falling, or by the non-accidental injury of child abuse. Infections include meningitis, and meningitis occurring in the first year of life is more likely to be followed by lasting sequelae such as epilepsy, cerebral palsy, or mental handicap. Encephalitis is often blamed but is probably a rarity. The encephalitis lethargica which struck at the end of World War I still influences the thoughts of physicians who recall the behavioral and physical illness it left in its wake. We may remember that similar epidemics preceded the one of 1918 to 1920, that these came at intervals of fifty years, and that it is fifty years since the last major epidemic.

Head injury and meningitis may produce effects directly or by influencing the attitude of the parents to their child. However, after any birth episode or postnatal trauma, even when there was a clinical picture of a cerebral lesion, one can hope for complete recovery. The parents should be informed that this is so.

There are progressive cerebral disorders, degenerations, inflammations, and storage disorders which may affect motor development, but these are rare.

In conclusion we return to our earlier statement that where the brain lesion or disorder is a nonprogressive one, there is often no advantage in treatment to identifying the cause or the anatomical or physiological disorder. All the child's various abilities and disabilities must be evaluated and then treatment given for his visual, auditory, language, motor, learning, emotional, and social deficits; his pre-, peri-, or postnatal insult is in the past and is untreatable.

ABNORMAL MOTOR SYMPTOMS AND SIGNS

Symptoms

Symptoms are the disabilities related by the parents. They are commonly of a nature and severity that is far from minimal. (The 1962 Oxford meeting, unfortunately, in wisely moving from minimal brain damage to minimal cerebral dysfunction, did not make clear that the symptoms might well be major but that it is the signs that are commonly minimal.)

In assessing any child the doctor looks at many facets of the child—motor, visual, auditory, language, learning, drive, emotional, and social. The motor symptoms may be of poor movement, for example, the "palsy" of cerebral origin. This may be revealed by developmental motor delay and by slow stiff movements which later examination shows to be accompanied by spasticity. There may be abnormal movements. These may be slow—distal in the limbs and "majestic" when they are called athetosis—or quick, nonrepetitive, predominantly proximal in the limbs when they are called choreic. Because of a difference between European and North American terminology, the two are best grouped together as choreoathetosis. Between chorea and tics the nonmedical observer may find it difficult to differentiate, but not the neurologist. Choreoathetotic movements are often called "involuntary" movements. A full discussion of the will and of free will would be out of place here. The adjective, however, is unsuitable because these movements are absent when the child is asleep, relaxed, or at rest and appear only when the child wants and tries to do something. In fact they are a superfluous accompaniment of willed movements. The label "involuntary" is an inference and very likely erroneous. The purely descriptive label choreoathetoid or dyskinetic is much safer.

The parent may complain that the child is clumsy. By this he means the child is less adroit than the parent expects him to be for his age and his group. This is a symptom and like all symptoms it has a variety of possible underlying anomalies. The child may be at an extreme of ordinary variation. This may be familial. He may have a sensory or perceptual disorder. He may have delay in motor maturation, motor weakness (e.g., from muscle dystrophy), or minor motor disorder. This may be minor spastic, athetoid, or ataxic cerebral palsy. He may have delay in lateralization. He may have an intellectual handicap or emotional disturbance, inadequate training or social handicap. Those around him may have an infantilizing attitude toward the child. Clumsiness is rarely complained of by older children or by adults. Perhaps further motor maturation has occurred or perhaps they have learned to avoid situations in which their motor maladroitness produces problems.

There are children whose parents complain that they are hyperactive. At this stage we emphasize only that "hyperactivity" is a statement about the child's level of motor activity, and that we do not refer to any syndrome which may be inferred to exist in a child who shows a high level of motor activity. We shall discuss hyperactivity in greater detail later in this chapter.

Neurological Signs

The neurological examination assesses the *developmental capacities* of the child.

It then explores the *muscular strength* of the segments of each limb, paying particular attention to a comparison between one side and the other.

It explores the *tendon reflexes* on which the classical example is the patellar reflex or knee jerk. Here we emphasize that increase of tendon reflexes (hyperreflexia) is of no significance unless there is inequality between the two sides or other evidence of an upper motor neurone lesion.

The normal patellar reflex results in a single jerk (of extension of the leg); the reaction does not spread to other groups of muscles, and in particular not to the contralateral thigh adductors. Furthermore, the reflexogenic zone is confined to the anterior surface of the patellar tendon. Nevertheless, in people who do not have a cerebral lesion, one can see anomalies of the tendon reflexes. In particular, in patients who are described as "spasmophilic" and also in those who are emotionally tense or close to being hysterical, one can establish the presence of a wider reflexogenic zone and of a wider spread of the response, which in such cases does not indicate a permanent neurological lesion but an increased neuromuscular sensitivity, a low threshold of muscle excitability.

The third clinical aspect to be explored is *muscular tone.* We stress there is a difference in character and degree of severity between neurological dystonias (hypertonia and hypotonia) and maturative dystonias (paratonia) of Ernest Dupré and the hypotonia characterized by hyperextensibility described by André-Thomas, Chesni, and Saint-Anne-Dargassies (1960).

The *coordination* of movement is tested by watching the child at play building with wooden cubes, 2 or 2.5 cm along their edge, and by watching him moving his forefinger from the examiner's hand to his own nose. When there is tremor which is regular, transverse, and terminal (increasing as the hand or nose is reached), a poor ability to perform rapid alternating movements (dysdiadochokinesia)—e.g., tapping with the fingers or alternate supination and pronation of the forearm and hand—the incoordination is described as ataxic or cerebellar and ascribed to a disorder of the cerebellar–red nucleus system. Cerebellar function is only fully attained by the fourth year. Children with ataxic cerebral palsy are difficult to recognize in the first three years of life, although some, but not all, show hypotonia and late sitting and standing. Some children with ataxic cerebral palsy show symptoms and signs predominantly of tremor, others of disequilibrium. A child of ten who holds on to the stair rails in descending stairs is to be suspected of dysequilibric cerebral palsy.

Here we may suggest that the word *clumsiness* is used for the symptom, and the doctor will identify the disorder sometimes as weakness and sometimes as incoordination and that *ataxia* is usually applied only to the incoordination with terminal intention tremor and dysdiadochokinesia.

Synkinesias

Etymologically, synkinesias are associated movements, but the term is applied only to noncontributory associated movements. The tennis player when serving performs a complex association of movements—throwing the ball in the air, performing with the other hand a complex accelerating movement with the racket, so that the racket meets the ball at a given point in space and time and all the time moving to retain his balance—but these are not called synkinesias.

Fog and Fog (1963) described standardized tests of associated movements spreading from the acting to the other hand and also from the acting feet to the hands. In this ingenious observation they showed that the hand-to-hand and feet-to-hand associated or synkinetic movements are present in 80 percent of normal children at age six and a half years but in only 20 percent of normal children at age eight and a half years. In children with motor or mental handicap, the percentage showing associated movements is higher than in normal children. If on examination a child has such associated movements at, say, age ten, it can be said that he shows delay in motor maturation.

While doing the voluntary movement with one upper limb, the child may do similar (mirror) movement with the limb of the opposite side. If a right-handed child is asked to do an imitative movement with his left hand, the contralateral associated movements will be all the more evident. This can be useful in establishing which is the preferred hand for movement.

On the subject of synkinesia, Ajuriaguerra (1970) has made a valuable contribution deserving our attention. He describes two types: synkinesias of tonic diffusion and generalized stiffness, and synkinesias of tonico-kinetic diffusion, or imitative synkinesias.

Tonic synkinesia persists unchanged from six to ten years and can be found in varying intensity in a certain proportion after the age of ten. Tonico-kinetic synkinesis gradually becomes less evident between six and twelve years, when it disappears, and persistence after twelve years is one of the signs of motor immaturity.

A valuable but insufficiently employed test for exploring the child's motor abilities is the *Imitation of Gestures* test described by Bergès and Lézine (1965) which is available in an English translation. A series of standardized "gestures" or positions of the upper limb and hand are described. The examiner makes a gesture and the child is asked to imitate it, for example extending the upper limb forward with the forearm flexed into a vertical position. By observation of the child's success or failure, much information of which classical neurology is ignorant can be gleaned. The mechanisms involve the relatively unexplored territory of neuropsychology and are not always identifiable. But as the norms for children up to age ten have been established and as other normative tests of evolving motor function between age five and ten are scanty, the Imitation of Gestures test is of great value even if its mechanisms are not yet fully known.

In responding to the examiner's request the child may hesitate between using his right and his left upper limb. This could signify that when the examiner, facing him, uses his right upper limb to demonstrate the movement the child is to imitate, the child does not know whether or not to use the limb (his left one) immediately opposite the examiner's right upper limb. Younger children are happy to imitate with their left upper limb what the examiner facing them has done with his right upper limb. The child's hesitation between using his right or left upper limb may arise because he is partially or totally left-handed. (It may be noted that an unusually high proportion of children with cerebral palsy are, for some as yet poorly understood reasons, left handed. The child may have difficulty in analyzing the gesture he is asked to imitate or in the constructional (praxis) part of making his movement.

The Bergès-Lézine test of Imitation of Gestures is soon learned by the pediatric neurologist and a selection of the tests forms a useful addition to his routine examination.

An interesting attempt to devise a method of studying the child's motor function is the Oseretsky test and its modifications. This test describes the child's motor abilities under the following headings: (1) static coordination; (2) dynamic coordination of the hands; (3) general dynamic coordination; (4) speed of movements; (5) simultaneous movements; and (6) presence or absence of synkinesias.

The test is attractive, but we have doubts about the standardization of the test, and the way in which synkinesias are dealt with seems inadequate.

The Electroencephalogram

The electroencephalogram (EEG) is a widely used complementary method of investigating the electrical activity of the brain. It can sometimes tell us something about disorder of the brain; it cannot tell us about the person's abilities and disabilities (which are what are of interest to him). It cannot, except in rare instances, tell us whether a person has a brain lesion or epilepsy but it may tell us what sort of epilepsy he has. The patient's pediatrician or his psychologist or social worker would not be helped by being given the electroencephalographic tracing. What is needed is, as is usually the case, the *opinion* of an expert experienced in the particular field. The EEG is the recording, from electrodes attached to the scalp, of electrical potentials developed in the brain. There are several variables in the electroencephalogram.

The number of oscillations in the tracing observed per second is the rhythm. The various upward and downward deviations represent simultaneous discharges from large numbers of nerve cells. The rhythms vary with age, and a knowledge of development of the EEG is needed by the interpreting expert; otherwise rhythms of no significance in the infant EEG may be wrongly interpreted.

The "normal" alpha rhythm is that obtained from the brain with the person at rest with his eyes closed. It is occipital in origin with a frequency of 8 to 12 cycles per second. It disappears when the eyes are opened.

Certain stimuli produce changes in the EEG. Overbreathing, which removes too much carbon dioxide from the blood and produces an alkalosis, can produce disorganized EEGs which nevertheless do not signify any brain abnormality. But on occasion, overbreathing can lead to a typical "absence" (petit mal) attack or to a 3 cycles per second spike and wave curve indicative of petit mal. This still only shows that the child, under chemical stress, has petit mal; it does not prove, though it increases the possibility, that the child has petit mal, clinical or sub-clinical at other times.

In an analogous way, flickering light can evoke anomalous electrical discharges in the brain waves. It is known that some children sitting near a flickering television screen can have fits and the EEG response to photic (light) stimulation gives further information to be fitted into the EEG report.

There are other electrophysical tests used in the study of motor capacity; the speed of motor-nerve conduction and the electromyograph which gives information about the electrical discharges in stimulated muscles.

The EEG has been studied in children labeled as having minimal brain dysfunction. Satterfield (1973) found the EEG abnormal in eighteen of fifty-seven children. Twenty-nine of the fifty-seven had abnormal neurological signs. Seventy percent of the children showed 30 percent improvement on methyl phenidate treatment. The presence of both EEG and neurological impairment predicted what the author described as a "good" response to this drug treatment. These studies give probability indications, but no certainties can be drawn from the responses of individual patients as to their symptoms or (usually) about the treatment they need or indeed whether or not there were lasting effects on either the EEG or behavior from the chemotherapy.

"Debilité Motrice"

There are children whose histories, symptoms, and signs do not match those typical of specific cerebral lesions, although the children differ noticeably from their "ordinary" peers. It should be possible to describe such children by listing their symptoms, i.e., their disabilities, and then to try to help them. But the inclination of the medical mind has been to postulate underlying disorders, and this has periodically led to bold (but unbased) extrapolations which have often led to an impoverishment of our understanding and hence of our capacity to help the "difficult" child—who is often difficult for the doctor's diagnostic inclinations as well as difficult for parents and teachers to care for.

We propose to discuss a concept which has remained curiously unknown in Angolo-Saxon countries but which had a profound influence on psychiatric thought in France, and it is one of the forefathers of the North American concepts of minimal brain damage and minimal brain dysfunction.

In 1925, Ernest Dupré, Professor of Mental Disease at the Hospital of St. Anne in Paris, in a publication entitled *Pathologie de l'imagination et de l'emotivité,* contributed a chapter devoted to the concept of *debilité motrice.* (The translation into English presents some difficulties; "motor weakness" and "motor handicap" are clearly unsuitable; "motor debility" is a possibility, but it may be least misleading to use Dupré's own phrase, "*debilité motrice.*")

This adults' psychiatrist tended to try to take the whole field of psychiatry back to organic anatomical and physiological disorders. According to Dupré, the emotional constitution is explained by deep-seated vasomotor and visceral motor disorders. *Debilité motrice* is explained as a peripheral motor disorder. There is also a close relationship between this motor failure and mental failure. Finally, and it is in this respect that Dupré, with good reason, can be considered the creator of the minimal brain damage concept, everything is to be traced back to lesions of the central nervous system. The lesions he invokes are no more fanciful than those postulated much later by other authors under other skies, and include intrauterine encephalopathy and cerebral hypogenesis. It is doubtful, however, whether he used these terms in the sense that would be more acceptable to us today, i.e., of factors which lead to slow development of motor capacities.

Above all, Dupré asserts that, in many mental defectives, there is, alongside their psychic deficits, motor deficit which is equally attributable to cerebral malgenesis or agenesis. From this he extrapolates to the concept of *debilité motrice* and also to *debilité mentale,* thus classifying both into one category of motor plus mental inferiority.

Upon what criteria did Dupré identify *debilité motrice*? In particular he cited exaggeration of the tendon reflexes. This is a finding whose value we have been at some pains to deny. He also said that patients with *debilité motrice* show a disturbance of the plantar response, though he gave no specific details. He spoke of synkinesias, but this is not very helpful to us today as he provided no details of the ages of children showing this sign. He brought in one sign of considerable interest but of whose complexity he was manifestly unaware. This symptom is paratonia with involuntary movements and hypertonia which diminishes relaxation and hence interferes with the objective assessment of reflexes. But in fact, this is the sort of sign which results almost directly from emotional tension in the subject.

We spend sometime in discussion of Dupré's ideas because they have widely influenced the thought of psychiatrists on the continent of Europe toward assuming that behavioral disorders always have a basis in an anatomical lesion of the brain.

High Activity and Hyperactivity

In April 1970, "hyperactivity" as a diagnostic label carrying implications of learning difficulties and abnormality of temperament received the scientific accolade of an article in the *Scientific American.* Here we propose to consider in some detail the motor aspects only.

Many children are brought to notice because a parent or teacher considers them to be overly active. It is not a complaint made by the children concerned. It is the commonest reason for referral of children to child guidance clinics in the USA. The first step in diagnosis should be the decision or judgment whether this is high activity or hyperactivity. Many children are highly active and in theory the decision that hyperactivity exists involves measurement of the activity and establishing that the child's level of activity is more than two standard deviations above the mean for children of the patient's age and peer group. In practice, the judgment is made on the impression the child's activity makes on the observer. This judgment will be affected by the impression made on the observer by the parents' story and the child's activity as seen by the observer. This judgment will be affected by the examiner's personality, experience, and prejudices and his patience with children. For some parents, teachers, and doctors, a child's function is to minister to the adult's needs. Others see the child more as a person in his own right. The examiner's judgment will also be affected by the qualitative aspects he sees in the child's high activity. He may judge it as pointless, as failing to respond to training, reproof, and punishment. He may be influenced, though he should not be, by whether he also notices distractability, impulsivity, or learning difficulties or by whether he elicits a history of being "at risk" for brain damage.

Kenny, Clemmens, Hudson, Lentz, Cicci, and Mair (1971) reported on a multidisciplinary approach to one hundred children referred for hyperactivity. Three separate clinical examinations were made on each child. There was close agreement among examiners. Over half of the children were not considered hyperactive by any examiner; a third were by majority opinion deemed hyperactive. There was close agreement among examiners. It appears that two-thirds of these children judged by parents and teachers to be abnormally active were, judged by their behavior in the clinic, not excessively active.

As all symptoms have of necessity a variety of causes (Abercrombie 1961), high activity will also have a variety of possible origins. In medical terms, it will have a differential diagnosis. Certainly not all high activity is associated with distractibility, impulsivity, learning difficulties (Koupernik 1972). Some of the situations in which high activity is seen are:

1. most normal two- or three-year-old children;
2. other children with mental age of two or three years;
3. highly intelligent children with a strong exploratory drive;
4. children reacting to environmental influences such as nagging by a parent or teacher;
5. anxious children;
6. some depressed children;
7. many deprived children, especially those who are also mentally handicapped;
8. some children with infantile autism;
9. some children with epilepsy, especially if it is temporal lobe epilepsy; and
10. children with sub-clinical epilepsy, e.g., with sub-clinical petit mal.
11. There are also some children who have high activity as part of a syndrome which includes: high activity serving no useful purposes, distractibility, impulsivity, explosivity of mood, variability of mood from day to day, failure to respond to training or punishment, specific learning difficulties, and anxiety.

The Syndrome of Hyperactivity-Distractibility

Some of these children are of average intelligence; some have global mental handicap. Some have a major neurological disorder such as epilepsy or cerebral palsy; in some there are no abnormal neurological signs, and in some there are minor or minimal signs of neurological disorder. These have been listed by Millichap (1968) as motor impersistence, incoordination, dysdiadochokinesia, ataxia, inability to hop, extensor plantar responses, synkinetic movements, choreoathetosis, and speech impairment. This syndrome is sometimes called the "hyperactivity syndrome." Two points need to be made. One is that not all children with hyperactivity have the associated disabilities present in this syndrome. The other is that between the ages of six and sixteen, the subjects having the syndrome lose their excessive motor activity but the other disabilities persist. The syndrome is sometimes called the hyperkinetic syndrome, to which name the same objections apply.

It has been called the syndrome of minimal brain damage, but in half of the subjects there is no good evidence of any organic lesion of the brain. It has been called minimal cerebral dysfunction. This is more accurate in that it is based on manifest disabilities, but the label has disadvantages, because there are many minimal cerebral dysfunctions that are not associated with distractibility or learning disorders. The adjective *minimal* is open to more than one interpretation. The syndrome can be very disrupting to family and school life and the disability is certainly not minimal. It was used for children with this syndrome of major behavioral troubles to make the point that many of them have minimal abnormal neurological signs. But the same distractibility syndrome is seen in children with severe epilepsy, cerebral palsy, or mental deficiency. Their troubles are minimal neither as regards their behavior nor as regards their neurological signs. Probably the problem of giving the syndrome a name is best solved by eponymously labelling it the Strauss-Lehtinen syndrome.

The Strauss-Lehtinen Syndrome and the Concepts of Minimal Brain Damage and Minimal Brain Dysfunction

In 1947 Strauss and Lehtinen described children with this pattern of high activity, distractibility, explosivity, etc., and made the assumption that they all had lesions in the brain and called it "minimal brain damage." A further offensive in its favor was launched by Laufer and Denhoff in 1957. But a study of the literature shows that the clinical pictures described are so varied that a large variety of children are given this label and diagnosis by various authors and that agreement on the predominant components has been continuously lacking. For Bender (1949) and Eisenberg (1957) anxiety is never absent. In 1962, the Oxford meeting pointed out the great variety of interpretations given to the term "minimal brain damage" and the frequent absence of evidence of damage. They suggested the child's disabilities be listed and treated and that if the syndrome is given a name, it must refer to dysfunction and not to damage. In doing so much, the meeting failed to notice the need to get rid of the adjective *minimal.*

In the last ten years many articles have been published on the subject of minimal brain damage/dysfunction. There are two good reports, edited by Clements, which emphasized the need to avoid the assumptions commonly made when the label MBD is used, by identifying the areas in which each child needs help, i.e., his disabilities. In 1972 Wender selected three traits of the MBD syndrome as being particularly noteworthy—a poor capacity for experiencing pleasure, anxiety, and an insubordinate attitude to disciplinary measures. The names "minimal brain damage" and "minimal cerebral dysfunction" continue as in 1962, to imply different things to different authors.

The 1973 report of the conference on minimal brain dysfunction at the New York Academy of Sciences (de la Cruz *et al.* 1973) is found on reading the report to be a meeting on learning disorders.

We wish to make certain further comments on the current concept of minimal brain dysfunction.

1. *Its syndromatic obscurity.* This proposes a link between a variety of symptoms, their association being due not to chance but to having a cause in common. But there is only irregular agreement about the symptoms

comprising the syndrome, and in half the cases, etiological explanations are lacking. Hyperactivity is perhaps the most frequently described symptom, and indeed just as the Cheshire Cat sometimes disappeared except for his grin, so the syndrome seems to disappear except for hyperactivity. Conversely some older subjects lose their hyperactivity and have only "hyperactivity syndrome *sine* hyperactivity" (Weiss, Minde, Werry, Douglas, and Nemeth 1971).

2. *Its epidemiological obscurity.* Some have noted that hyperactivity was for years the most commonly made diagnosis in pediatrics. Wender (1971) quotes epidemiological studies on school populations in the USA as yielding figures from 4 to 20 percent of children, mostly between 5 and 10 percent. On the other hand, in the United Kingdom, Rutter, Graham, and Yule (1970) found that among children of nine to eleven years of age, if children with overt neurological disorders or epilepsy were excluded, only two of 2,189 children could justifiably be classified as hyperkinetic. (It could be argued that by this age hyperactivity would often have disappeared). Bax (1972, unpublished data), in a study of twelve hundred five-year-olds living in the Isle of Wight, did not find a single case of "hyperkinetic syndrome."

There are epidemiological differences among different countries when other behaviors are studied. For example, at age five, 8 percent of children in Sweden wet their beds while in the United States the figure is 25 percent. The differences are considerable, but those in relation to the frequency of "hyperactivity" are of totally different order. There is urgent need for resolving this epidemiological difference. Do North American authors include under MBD the other causes of hyperactivity? This would have important implications with regard to treatment.

3. *The pathogenic mechanism obscurity.* To recognize a syndrome, it is not necessary to understand the pathogenic mechanisms, but there is no agreement in the case of the syndrome we are considering.

On the one hand, based on learning theory, the children with minimal brain dysfunction are unable to respond to external rewards and have a deficient system of internal rewards.

On the other hand, the function of arousal subserved by the reticular formation is disordered. One author writes that "clinical inspection of minimal brain dysfunction children produces the clinical impression that they are over activated or hyperaroused" and on the next page concludes they are underaroused (Wender 1972).

A third idea suggests that there is a biochemical disorder in the brain. We are beginning to learn something about the chemical mediators of brain activity, but we are still very far from understanding them and further still from knowing the brain biochemistry of the Strauss-Lehtinen syndrome.

To argue that because two of the chemical mediators are catecholamines and chemically similar to amphetamine and because some cases improve with amphetamine treatment that the pathogenetic mechanism of the disorder is chemical, is not securely based. As Rutter (personal communication) has noted, the fact that electroshock is effective in combatting depression does not mean that depression is due to lack of electricity in the brain. We echo Gomez (1967) in his equating minimal cerebral dysfunction with maximal neurological confusion.

Drug Treatment of Hyperactivity

Amphetamine and methylphenidate which are brain stimulants are commonly used for treating hyperactivity. We do at times use these drugs, and for certain children we find them valuable. We have certain reservations, however, about drug treatment when it is so widely used as appears to be the case in some clinics and schools in the USA.

Consideration of the differential diagnosis of the disorders underlying the symptom of hyperactivity quickly reveals that for ten out of the eleven disorders listed, cerebral stimulants are contraindicated.

The phrase "one symptom, one cause, one treatment" embodies a not uncommon medical heresy. Despite its attractive simplicity, it needs to be guarded against. It reveals an attitude which would like to reduce all child psychiatry to structural or biochemical disorder, and does not even have the merit of being a sane reaction to the other extreme attitude which for decades confused child psychiatry to an exclusively psychoanalytic concept. It is a regression to the positions held by Bradley (1937) and Dupré (1925).

Another medical reservation is that amphetamines have certain side effects—anorexia, insomnia, growth retardation—even in the young child. They should never be prescribed as a strait-jacket intended to guarantee the peace of parents or teachers.

Amphetamines are in second position on the list of hard drugs. What guarantee do we have, with the current spread of drug dependence and lowering of the age at which it starts, that some individuals will not progress from therapeutic to addictive use? And would the benefits outweigh even the occasional production of that disastrous consequence?

There is a current tendency based on our use of antibiotics and headache tablets to believe that for every ill that flesh is heir to, a tablet is needed. The young are trained to think that stimulation comes from bottles, whether of tablets or alcohol. They, and too often doctors, forget the powerful effects of other approaches, personal and environmental.

The Future Approach to Hyperactivity and to MBD

The current publications on hyperactivity are a mixed bag. The enthusiastic recommendations of amphetamine by authors like Wender (1972) are depressing. But for us, as for the anonymous student of philosophy in Boswell's Johnson, we find that cheerfulness keeps breaking through. Fish (1971) criticizes the idea that hyperactivity should lead to a reflex prescription of cerebral stimulant drugs, arguing that differential diagnosis among the various possible underlying causes is needed if appropriate treatment is to be given. She notes that the term "hyperactivity" should not be used interchangeably with "minimal brain dysfunction" which implies multiple disorder or cerebral function. Kenny *et al.* (1971) also observed that decisions on treatment require identification of the underlying behavioral disorder. Wolff and Hurwitz (1973a) have made a careful study of the relationship of choreiform movements to behavior disorders in a population of thirteen hundred presumptively normal children and found that such choreiform movements can identify children whose classroom behavior is significantly different. This is an exemplary study of the functional significance of an individual abnormal neurological sign.

Finally, we support the statement of Wolff and Hurwitz (1973*b*) that "if experience can teach us anything, it is more than likely that a concept as vague and global as minimal brain dysfunction will sooner or later be hypostatized, just as similar diagnoses were in the past. The concept MBD will then begin to demand respect in its own right, without ever having been subjected to the tedious work of classification that is necessary to determine the concept's actual significance." Consulting the Oxford English Dictionary, in three sizes, including the seventeen-volume edition, was an enjoyable adventure from which we found that *hypostasis* derives from a deeply theological term implying the essence as opposed to what is attributed. Certainly in relation to MBD the appeal for separation between essence and attributes is welcome and so is this appeal for a reexamination of the label MBD (and maybe for discarding it). What is needed for each child is a list of disabilities so that suitable treatment for each can be planned and provided. We strongly support Wolff and Hurwitz's appeal for a reexamination of the term MBD. Increasingly it is more and more widely realized that MBD is an empty term, used to save us the trouble of thinking clearly about what we are talking about. The young of our era are right to decry thoughtless labeling; this is not to be dismissed as part of the anti-authority movement. Real danger lies in facile labeling; consider the effect of the label "*Juden*." We do not need or want labels which have no useful clinical relevance. No increasing of our understanding comes from the continued use of the MBD group of labels.

Meanwhile we look forward to fruitful cooperation in the study of motor development among parents, teachers, and doctors, with further studies of population such as have been provided by Rutter *et al.* (1970*a* and *b*), Robson (1970), and Wolff and Hurwitz (1973*a*). For we need to look at our "normal" children. There are more of them than of our clinic children, and if we look at them we may find many whom we can help and for whom we can improve the quality of their lives.

NEUROLOGICAL CORRELATES OF PERCEPTUAL DEVELOPMENT

It is helpful for those who are concerned with learning disabilities in children whose difficulties are possibly related to cerebral dysfunction to think of learning in terms of three stages. These are: (1) the reception of experience; (2) the central organization of received experience; and (3) its expression in terms of behavior and the capacity to build further learning on the experiences that have been integrated in this way.

In the education of normally developing, unhandicapped children, these three processes are generally taken for granted and, indeed, are interdependent in the course of a child's development, but in seeking to evaluate the ability and the special needs of damaged children, it is important to investigate separately these three developmental processes in order to see at what stage the child's learning capacity is being impaired.

If these three stages are considered separately, the extent to which the various disciplines are interdependent in making a proper evaluation of a child's educational needs becomes clearer.

The Reception of Experience—Input

In the beginnings of learning, experience comes to us all primarily through the channels of our senses. We learn about our world from what we see, from what we hear, from the experiences gained through touching and feeling and handling objects, and, later, through all the various experiences gained through movement. If any of these means of gaining experience are faulty, or if the opportunity for the child to gain experience in these ways is lacking, the possibility for development will be impaired to some extent.

In order to be able to make an adequate learning program for a child who is in difficulties, it is essential to know his physical condition, whether he suffers any sensory handicaps, particularly in vision or hearing, and also to what extent he suffers limitations in his capacity for movement or for learning through fine hand manipulation. The first phase of learning through experience is also affected by the limitations in life experience that can be caused through intermittent periods of hospitalization and limits on normal social learning in association and play with normal unhandicapped children. Children learn also through communication verbally and in other ways with other people. The development of communication beginning first of all between mother and baby makes a very important contribution to the experience through which a child learns. When we are considering learning disabilities thought to be related to cerebral dysfunction in the perceptual field, it is important to have as much information as possible about the availability of the normal channels for input of experience, knowing how greatly this affects a child's ability to learn.

Central Organization of Received Experience

Central organization is the process by which input gained through the sensory channels and experiences developed in ways described above is structured and organized to become meaningful and capable of providing understanding on which to build further experiences and extend learning. The capacity for central organization involves the formation of associations and the understanding of relationships, the ability to recall previous experiences, to form concepts, to integrate information gained through one sense modality with what has been gained through another, and to relate new experiences in a meaningful way with what the child has learned through previous experiences. This ability depends upon the integrity of the brain and its level of maturation.

The quality of the child's ability to use his capacity for the intellectual processes subsumed under the term "central organization" can only be judged through the third stage, described as output.

Output

Output is the expression by means of behavior and other channels of communication through which a child demonstrates his capacity to use his intellectual processes which lead to further learning.

Here we are concerned with the second stage—that is "the central organization of received experience"—which is what is understood by the term "perception." The correct and useful organization of received experience can become disorderly if the child suffers dysfunction in any of the following areas of stimulus—hearing, vision, fine and gross motor coordination, and language. These areas will be discussed separately and then the importance of the capacity to integrate these modalities will be assessed.

Auditory Perception

Hearing is measured clinically by free-field testing with voice and other sounds and by pure-tone threshold audiometry which determines the threshold of sensation for a number of frequencies. Deafness tends to be equated with hearing loss defined in terms of frequency and intensity. Results from this type of assessment can answer the question "How much sound is heard," but not "How are sounds being heard." From his wide experience of hearing, particularly in young children, Martin (1973) noticed that the investigation of hearing in young children produces a number of problems which cannot be explained by the results of pure-tone threshold audiometry. He gives as an example certain children who are slow in learning to talk. He says, "Their difficulty seems to consist not so much of an alteration of auditory threshold, but of an impaired ability to sort out or make sense of acoustical events."

Among the four main varieties of language codes—i.e., using words, pictures, mime or three-dimensional models—Sheridan (1972) placed the Recognition of Codemes as one of the important factors in understanding a child's process. Discussing this, she said, "The normal child is able to echo and understand words said to him several months before he can spontaneously speak them. . . . In young children with language disorders, the time-lag between ability to interpret the spoken word and ability to reply may be very prolonged." It is this delay in development of interpretation of the sensory stimulus—in this case the spoken word—in children who are not deaf that is understood as "auditory imperception."

Writing of this condition in children, Gordon (1964) describes it as "an abnormal response to auditory stimuli due to a disorder of function within the central nervous system, proximal to the auditory nuclei in the brain stem." Gordon stresses the practical importance of recognizing this condition of auditory imperception, since, particularly in young children, auditory imperception may easily be misdiagnosed as a condition caused by peripheral deafness. If this happens the child could then be mistakenly taught as if he were a peripherally deaf child. This would not serve his learning needs, since he should be taught by a quite different type of program which emphasizes the need for intensive training in the use of the tools of communication and the understanding and use of language.

Disorders of Visual Perception

Here we are concerned with the young child's understanding of and information about his world that comes through what he sees.

Perception has been described by Strauss (1947), a pioneer in finding methods of teaching brain injured children, as "the mental process which gives particular meaning and significance to a given sensation and therefore acts as a preliminary to thinking. It is the means by which the individual organizes and comes to understand the phenomena which constantly impinge upon him."

Writing in the days when psychology was still a branch of philosophy, William James described the infant as being conscious only of a "big, booming, buzzing confusion."

During the past fifteen years, however, this view has been modified by the tremendous advances in our knowledge of the development of visual perception in young children which have been made by experimental psychologists.

The conflict of opinion whether a person's ability to perceive the form of objects is inherent or whether must be learned from scratch, as it were, would seem to have been resolved by means of careful experimental observations of the visual interests of quite young babies.

Careful recordings of the extent to which an infant consistently turns its gaze toward some forms more than others demonstrate that young babies from birth show a differential response to pattern, and they suggest that some degree of form perception is inborn.

The Swiss pediatrician Stirnimann (1940, 1944) found that babies from one to fourteen days old fixated longer and showed preference for patterned cards rather than plain colors. Studies carried out by Fantz (1961) and his coworkers of human infants tested at weekly intervals from one to fifteen weeks show that at all ages they make a differential response to pattern. This was seen in the infant's "looking response," that is, his selective attention to patterned over plain surfaces and the increase in the length of time during which infants visually fixated on a patterned card.

While it is possible through careful experimental observations to learn much about the visual interests of quite young babies, the learning process in young babies is not so easy to study. Experiments with animals, however, have demonstrated that if animals are deprived of the visual stimuli of patterns for a period immediately after birth, their capacity for visual perception is impaired.

For example, it was found that monkeys reared in darkness after birth for varying lengths of time behaved, on being exposed to light, almost as if blind. They bumped into things, could not locate objects visually and had to be taught to see.

The shorter the period of deprivation of visual stimuli the more quickly they developed spatial orientation, but if the period of deprivation was too long, the monkeys remained permanently more interested in color, brightness, and size than in pattern and shape.

Similarly, adults who have been blind from birth and who have recovered sight after an operation have reported how difficult it was to distinguish visually one object from another or one shape from another without long and painstaking learning.

Vernon (1962) has described the young infant as being conscious only of a "random set of lights, noises, touches, taste and so on without any known cause." Because almost from birth the infant finds patterning interesting to him, however, pattern discrimination stimulates him to explore his environment and gradually increase his knowledge of his world.

By the time an infant is three months of age he is beginning to relate what he sees to past experience and gradually to select from his environment what is significant and has the beginnings of meaning for him.

It is not possible for a person to take notice equally of all the sights and sounds that impinge on his senses at a given moment. It is part of the action of our brain to select from all the varying sensations what is important and meaningful for us at that time and to relegate the less important to the background of our consciousness. It is only in that way that we can develop the power to concentrate on what is significant for us at the time.

Like all human skills, the ability to organize for ourselves a stable and understandable perceptual world is subject to maturation and developmental growth. The very young child more easily misjudges the distance of his head from the table and is more subject to bumps in consequence. He is less able to recognize and match differing forms and shapes. He cannot concentrate on any one task for long, but is easily distracted by all the noises and sights and movement around him. But the capacity to relate himself to his world and cope with the demands it makes on him develops as he grows in his understanding of it.

The teacher of young children knows that no child is ready to begin formal learning until he has had ample opportunity to learn about his world through his own exploration of it. It is through his sensory experience that a young child gains knowledge of size and shape, of degrees of temperature and intensities of sound, of the differences between things that feel rough or smooth, hard or soft.

He gradually learns about position and distance, that one object is nearer to him than another. He can reach out and pick up one, but in order to grasp another that is further away, he must himself move toward it. In the early learning stages, visual perception plays a very important part.

Over the past ten years, work with cerebral palsied children has brought to teachers and psychologists an awareness of the variety of visuo-perceptual disorders that handicap some of these children. This does not apply to all cerebral palsied children, and the severity and extent of the disorders among these children also varies greatly. It takes the form of such difficulties as the recognition of shapes and patterns, sorting or matching according to shape, copying forms or reproducing forms from memory.

Some damaged children who can copy printed shapes cannot reproduce the simplest structure built in bricks and cannot put together a jigsaw consisting of only three pieces, even when first shown the completed puzzle.

Visuo-perceptual disorders also give rise to difficulties in spatial orientation, in recognizing position and in distinguishing foreground from background in interpreting pictures and, indeed, among young children, in distinguishing nearness and distance of furniture and other objects as they move about the room.

Teachers working in schools for cerebral palsied children have found how greatly this "spatial inability" hinders normal educational progress. Particularly in the early stages of school learning, spatial ability plays an important part in the process of learning to read and write and in the ability to manipulate numbers.

These difficulties are fairly common in certain groups of cerebral palsied children. But similar disabilities have also been recognized in children without cerebral palsy and without any known history of illness in fetal life or other events which might have produced brain damage.

These children who show no severe disorder of movement and are not obviously spastic or athetoid have been described by Illingworth (1964) as having "minimal cerebral palsy" where the cerebral dysfunction is more crippling to the child than the palsy or paralysis.

Such children find their way into ordinary schools and often, because at home they have been awkward, clumsy, and uncoordinated, they have already developed disturbed patterns of behavior. Because their perceptual world is so confusing they are often restless and distractible and are mistakenly treated as naughty children, so that they start school life with the scales heavily weighted against them.

Whatever the cause, therefore, visuo-perceptual disorders not only interfere with and delay the learning of basic school subjects, but also impair the child's happiness and distort his behavior pattern.

Motor Dysfunction

Many children who are seen as having visuo-perceptual difficulties, such as an inability to recognize shapes and sizes, are also noticeably clumsy with a clumsiness that is out of context with their chronological age and overall level of intelligence. Clumsiness of movements out of context with other areas of development can be regarded as a specific developmental disorder, though it is more often found in conjunction with other aspects of perceptual dysfunction.

Writing of these children who show organic neurological factors related to learning disorders, Paine (1965) describes them as having "irregularly impaired cerebral function usually referred to as an 'organic' pattern which could conceivably exist as a uniform disability in different areas of function but which usually show striking discrepancies from one area to another." And he continues, "these are the difficulties which often constitute the principal barrier to academic performance in children with cerebral palsies or epilepsy and which can exist also by themselves in a borderline or (almost) 'sub-clinical' form."

Many children who would be included in Paine's definition have been noticed as being unusually clumsy. Illingworth (1963) defines this condition as one of "minimal cerebral palsy." Among a total of five hundred children with cerebral palsy seen by him in a children's hospital, he noticed twenty-seven of these children who fell into his descriptive category as "clumsy children." Signs of this clumsiness included (1) abnormal unsteadiness in standing on one leg; (2) slight hypertonia with minimal signs of involvement in the pyramidal tract; (3) very slight ataxia on building a tower of cubes; and (4) slowness and abnormal pattern of movement in standardized tests of repetitive movements involving the use of fingers.

These disabilities make life very hard for these children in school, in play, and in ordinary social relationships at home.

Good motor development and, particularly, fine motor coordination is necessary for normal achievement in many areas of school learning. Fine motor coordination appears to relate quite closely to perceptual disorders which create many special learning disabilities.

Sensory Integration

One of the striking characteristics of many cerebral palsied children is seen in the very real difficulty they have in integrating information derived from one sense modality with that gained from others. Denhoff and Robinault (1960) suggest that many of these children are damaged in their "central coordinating equipment." Failure in intersensory integration appears to be at the core also of the problem of many non-physically handicapped children who have special learning difficulties at school and show wide discrepancies in different areas of achievement in standardized intelligence tests such as the Wechsler Intelligence Scales.

In a recent follow-up study of children of very low birth weight (Davies and Francis-Williams 1974), a high percentage of these children, particularly those of eight or nine years of age who had failed to make any beginning in learning to read, strongly showed this characteristic of very discrepant levels of functioning.

Out of experience gained from many research studies, Birch and his co-workers have demonstrated how the central organization of received experience is dependent on the development of increasing liaison among separate sensory modalities. From a study of Visual-Auditory Integration (Birch and Belmont 1965) he suggests that many of the perceptual and visuo-motor disturbances found in children with neurodevelopmental disorders may be underlain by disturbed intersensory patterning. Many children with specific learning disabilities show themselves to be significantly defective in their ability to integrate information derived from the auditory, visual, tactile, and kinesthetic sense modalities with one another. The "clumsy" child, whose motor development is also delayed, lacks in his ability to learn, the essential contribution of sensorimotor integration.

The following case histories illustrate the learning problems of children with perceptual disorders.

1. Joanna—age nine years eleven months.

Joanna was referred to a hospital clinic by her doctor at the request of her "remedial" teacher, because of her complete inability to understand numbers.

Joanna was a friendly, happy little girl. Small for her age, she walked with a very awkward gait. Her balance and movements were poor and she presented as a typically "clumsy" child.

Tested on the Wechsler Intelligence Scale for Children, she did quite brilliantly on all the subtests in the Verbal Scale except for Arithmetic, in which she could only make a score of 4. When this was omitted and the score prorated, her Verbal IQ was 136. She found the Performance Scale tests impossibly difficult. She could only manage the designs A and B. Similarly her efforts in Object Assembly were hopelessly poor and her Performance Scale IQ was 78.

Joanna read extremely well. Her reading age for Accuracy was eleven years ten months and for Comprehension it was twelve years nine months. Her scores on the Frostig test were uniformly poor—she did not make any score above six and a half years, and her lowest score on Figure-Ground relationships was four years and nine months. She was completely defeated by Schonell's Mechanical Arithmetic Test, only managing success in three of the easiest sums. She knew all her tables by rote, but had no idea how to apply her knowledge. In the three sums—very simple additions—which she managed, she had to count up slowly using her fingers.

In the Bender Gestalt she made a high average score using the Koppitz developmental scoring method. She also did the Coloured Matrices test by Raven. This is a test of nonverbal reasoning, and on this test her score was low average (25th percentile).

This is a little girl with very severe visuo-spatial problems and with a very variable range of ability and disabilities. Her difficulty in developing any kind of number concept is related to her very real difficulty in patterning, and she gets no help in this from motor skills. In setting down a sum, she has no idea at all where to put the figures in relation to each other, despite the fact that she has had very specialized individual remedial teaching for over a year. She loves horse-riding, but has to be shown every time how to hold the reins. If she loses her hold, the reins have to be placed properly in her hand again.

2. Andrew—age eleven years.

Andrew was referred to the hospital clinic because he had made no beginning in reading. He was tested on the Wechsler Intelligence Scale for Children and was shown to be a boy of superior intelligence—Full Scale IQ 124. His achievement on the Verbal and Performance Scales was very even. The psychologist who tested this boy remarked on his delay in answering questions or responding in any way to her conversation with him. She thought that he had some hearing loss and referred him for audiometric testing. He was found to have no peripheral hearing loss, but was thought to have a very severe auditory imperception. When this was explained to the school and suggestions were made for giving him time to respond to what was said to him or asked of him, he made fairly rapid progress with the help of individual remedial teaching in reading.

3. Ian—age eight years.

This boy was referred to the hospital by his doctor, in response to his mother's anxiety. He was not doing well at school and his teachers complained that, although he seemed reasonably intelligent, he was "different" from other boys. His mother felt this also, though she found it hard to be more explicit.

His mother said she had had a bad pregnancy and very long labor at Ian's birth. She had very greatly looked forward to having her baby, but she said that he disappointed her because he seemed to make no response to all her nursing and talking to and loving him. Her description of him was very reminiscent of an autistic child. Ian was very late in speaking and did not really communicate in speech until he was four years old.

On tests (WISC) Ian was of average intelligence—Verbal Scale IQ 103, Performance Scale IQ 96, Full Scale IQ 99. His age for reading accuracy was high—nine years ten months, but his score on comprehension was much below his chronological age level. He read very quickly, never seeming to give himself time to comprehend what he was reading. He made a very high score on the Arithmetic subtest.

In his referral letter, his doctor wrote, "His speech is sometimes indistinct and he stammers under stress. His coordination is very poor and he has an awkward gait. He is slow to understand new concepts and his reasoning powers are poor."

This boy would seem to have an auditory imperception related to a severe language delay. He was held back also by perceptuo-motor disability.

These three children demonstrate differing perceptual disorders which in turn have created different learning problems, each of which demand a special and different approach to remedial teaching help for them.

References

Abercrombie, J. *Perceptual Visuo-Motor Disorders in Cerebral Palsy.* London: Heinemann, 1964.

Abercrombie, M. "Causes in Biology and Medicine." In *Psychosomatic Aspects of Paediatrics,* edited by R. C. Mac Keith and J. Sandler. London: Pergamon, 1961.

Ajuriaguerra, J. de *Manuel de Psychiatrie de l'Enfant.* Paris: Masson, 1970.

André-Thomas, and Saint-Anne-Dargassies, S. *Études neurologiques sur le nouveau-né et le jeune nourisson.* Paris: Masson and O. Perrin, 1951.

______; Chesni, Y.; and Saint-Anne-Dargassies, S. *The Neurological Examination of the Infant.* London: Heinemann, 1960.

Bax, M. "The Active and the Overactive School Child." *Developmental Medicine and Child Neurology* 14 (1972):83.

______, and Mac Keith, R., eds. *Minimal Cerebral Dysfunction.* London: Heinemann, 1963.

Bender, L. "Psychological Problems of Children with Organic Brain Disease." *American Journal of Orthopsychiatry* 94 (1949):494.

Bergès, J., and Lézine, I. *The Imitation of Gestures.* London: Heinemann, 1965.

Birch, H. G., and Belmont, L. "Auditory-Visual Integration in Brain-Damaged and Normal Children." *Developmental Medicine and Child Neurology* 7 (1965).

———, and Lefford, A. "Intersensory Development in Children." *Child Development Publications.* Lafayette, Indiana, 1963.

Bradley, C. "The Behavior of Children Receiving Benzedrine." *American Journal of Psychiatry* 94 (1937):494.

Clements, S. D., ed. *Minimal Brain Dysfunction in Children.* Washington, D.C.: NINDB Monographs, U.S. Department of HEW, Public Health Service, USGPO, 1966, 1968, 1970.

Davies, P., and Francis-Williams, J. M. In press, 1974.

De la Cruz, F. F.; Fox, B. H.; and Roberts, R. H., eds. "Minimal Brain Dysfunction." *Annals of New York Academy of Sciences* 205:1–396.

Denhoff, E., and Robinault, I. *Cerebral Palsy and Related Disorders.* New York: McGraw-Hill, 1960.

Dupré, E. *Pathologie de l'imagination et de l'emotivité.* Paris: Pavot, 1925.

Egan, D.; Illingworth, R. S.; and Mac Keith, R. C. *Developmental Screening 0–5 years.* London: Heinemann, 1969.

Fantz, R. L. "The Origin of Form Perception." *Scientific American* (May 1961).

Fish, B. "The One Child, One Drug Myth of Stimulants in Hyperkinesis." *Archives of General Psychiatry* 25 (1971):193.

Fog, E., and Fog, M. "Cerebral Inhibition Examined by Associated Movements." In *Minimal Cerebral Dysfunction,* edited by M. Bax and R. Mac Keith. London: Heinemann, 1963.

Geber, M., and Dean, R. F. A. "Gesell Tests on African Children." *Medicine* 20 (1957*a*):1055.

———, and Dean, R. F. A. "The State of Development of African Children." *Lancet* (1957*b*):1216.

Gesell, A., and Ilg, F. L. *Infant and Child in the Cultures of Today.* New York: Harper and Row, 1943.

Gomez, M. R. "Minimal Cerebral Dysfunction (Maximal Neurologic Confusion)." *Clinical Pediatrics* 6 (1967): 589.

Gordon, N. *The Concept of Central Deafness in the Child Who Does Not Talk.* London: Heinemann, 1964.

Graham, F. "Development Three Years After Perinatal Anoxia and Other Potentially Newborn Experiences." Psychological Monograph No. 522, American Psychology Association, 1962.

Halverson, H. M. "Development of Prehension in Infants." In *Child Behavior and Development,* edited by R. G. Barker *et al.* New York: McGraw-Hill, 1943.

Illingworth, R. S. "The Clumsy Child in Minimal Cerebral Dysfunction." In *Minimal Cerebral Dysfunction,* edited by M. Bax and R. Mac Keith. London: Heinemann, 1963.

———. *The Normal School Child.* London: Heinemann, 1964.

Kenny, T. J.; Clemmens, R. L.; Hudson, B. W.; Lentz, G. A.; Cicci, R.; and Mair, P. "Characteristics of Children Referred Because of Hyperactivity." *Journal of Pediatrics* 79 (1971):618.

Laufer, M. S., and Denhoff, E. "Hyperkinetic Behavior Syndrome in Children." *Journal of Pediatrics* 50 (1957):463.

Mac Keith, R. "The Characteristics of Spasticity in Children." *Cerebral Palsy Bulletin* 1 (1958): part 5, 5.

———. "Primary Walking Response and Its Facilitation by Passive Extension of the Head." *Acta Paediatrica Latina* (1964*a*): Supplementum 17, 710.

———. "Primary Walking Response of the Newborn." *Developmental Medicine and Child Neurology* (1964*b*):309.

______. "The Causes of Nocturnal Enuresis." In *Bladder Control and Enuresis*, edited by I. Kolvin, R. Mac Keith, and S. R. Meadow. London: Heinemann, 1973.

______, and Robson, P. "Shufflers with Spastic Diplegic Cerebral Palsy: A Confusing Clinical Picture." *Developmental Medicine and Child Neurology* 13 (1971):651.

Martin, J. A. M. "Auditory Perception." *British Medical Journal* (May 26, 1973).

McGraw, M. B. *The Neuromuscular Maturation of the Human Infant*. New York: Columbia University Press, 1943.

Millichap, J. G. "Drugs in the Management of Hyperkinetic and Perceptually Handicapped Children." *Journal of the American Medical Association* 206 (1968):1527.

Ounsted, C., and Taylor, D. C., eds. *Gender Differences: Their Ontogeny and Significance*. Edinburgh: Churchill-Livingstone, 1973.

Paine, R. S. *Organic Neurological Factors Related to Learning Disorders*. Vol. 1. Seattle: Special Child Publications, Seattle Sequin School, 1965.

Peiper, A. *Cerebral Function in Infancy and Childhood*. New York: Consultants Bureau, 1963.

Robson, P. "Shuffling, Hitching, Scooting and Sliding: Some Observations in 30 Otherwise Normal Children." *Developmental Medicine and Child Neurology* 12 (1970):608.

Rutter, M.; Graham, P. H.; and Yule, W. *A Neuropsychiatric Study in Childhood*. London: Heinemann, 1970.

______; Tizard, J.; and Whitmore, K. *Education, Health and Behaviour*. London: Longman, 1970.

Satterfield, J. H. "EEG Issues in Children with Minimal Brain Dysfunction." *Seminars in Psychiatry* 5 (1973):35.

Sheridan, M. *The Child's Acquisition of Codes for Personal and Interpersonal Communication in the Child with Delayed Speech*, edited by M. Rutter and J. A. M. Martin. London: Heinemann, 1972.

Stirnimann, F. *Psychologie des neugeborenen Kindes*. Zurich, 1940.

______. *Annals Paediatrica* (Basel) 163 (1944).

Strauss, A. A., and Lehtinen, L. E. *Psychopathology and Education of the Brain-Injured Child*. New York: Grune and Stratton, 1947.

Verson, M. D. *The Psychology of Perception*. New York: Penguin Books, 1962.

Wallon, H. *Les origines de charactere chez l'enfant*. Paris: Boivin, 1934.

Walzer, S., and Wolff, P. H., eds. *Minimal Cerebral Dysfunction in Children*. New York: Grune and Stratton, 1973.

Weiss, G.; Minde, K.; Werry, J. S.; Douglas, V.; and Nemeth, E. "Studies of the Hyperactive Child: Five-Year Follow-up." *Archives of General Psychiatry* 24 (1971):409.

Wender, P. H. *Minimal Brain Dysfunction in Children*. New York: Wiley Interscience, 1971.

______. "The Mininal Brain Dysfunction Syndrome in Children." *Journal of Nervous and Mental Diseases* 155 (1972):53.

Wolff, P. H., and Hurwitz, I. "Functional Implications of the Minimal Brain Damage Syndrome." *Seminars in Psychiatry* 5 (1973*a*):105.

______, and Hurwitz, I. In *Minimal Cerebral Dysfunction in Children*, edited by S. Walzer and P. H. Wolff. New York: Grune and Stratton, 1973*b*.

Editors' Notes: With advances occurring rapidly in the technology and measurement of early stages of learning, psychologists are beginning to unravel the complexities of development in infancy, and within the past few years, a great deal of research has accumulated on perceptual and attentional development. It is, of course, imperative that we have an understanding of the development and abnormal development of the infant.

Michael Lewis provides us with a review of the literature pertaining to perception in infancy, with particular focus on the variable of attention. Lewis places the study of infant development in historical perspective by outlining the major directions this field has taken. He builds a case for the developmental precedence of visual perception before motor development (this particular aspect of the chapter should be read in conjunction with Dr. Kephart's chapter in Volume 1 and Dr. Gyr's chapter in this volume). Dr. Lewis considers the various problems in the measurement of attention and argues that attention can be used to measure cognitive development. Data are presented on groups and individual subjects which indicate that the variable of attention may be a critical one in the early identification of learning problems.

Michael Lewis, Ph.D., is Director of the Infant Laboratory and a Senior Research Psychologist in the Educational Testing Service's Institute for Research in Human Development. He is also Professor of Developmental Psychology at the University of Pennsylvania's Graduate School of Education and the Graduate Center of the City University of New York and Clinical Professor of Pediatric Psychology at Columbia University Medical Center. He is a consulting editor for the monograph series of the Society for Research in Child Development and the journal *Sex Roles*, and he is on the board of consultants of the American Foundation for Maternal and Child Health. In addition, he is a consultant reviewer for many specialized journals and a consultant reader for the National Science Foundation. Dr. Lewis is a fellow of the American Psychological Association and a member of the Society for Research in Psychophysiology, the Society for Research in Child Development, and the New York Academy of Science. He has contributed chapters to at least eight volumes on such topics as psychophysiological responses, language development, affect, and mother-infant interaction, and has edited two books in the series The Origins of Behavior—*The Effect of the Infant on its Caregiver* and *The Origins of Fear*. He is also the author or co-author of more than a hundred journal articles.

3

The Development of Attention and Perception in the Infant and Young Child

MICHAEL LEWIS

The present discussion is divided into several fairly distinct sections. The first section of the chapter is concerned with some historical as well as empirical data related to the issue of infants' central nervous system functioning, and the theoretical approach growing out of these data. In the second section we will review the attentional literature with an emphasis on the problem of how to measure central nervous system function and dysfunction in the very young. The third section contains some of the data which have been gathered on the measurement of central nervous system functioning and several individual case histories highlighting the techniques and procedures used.

THE NATURE OF THE INFANT'S MIND

At the turn of the century, the psychologist William James (1895) characterized the mental life of the infant as a blooming, buzzing mass of confusion. Although Darwin (1897) at about the same time was making observations about the infant's ability to track and pay attention to interesting objects dangled before it, and Preyer in the 1880s had written about tests of the infant's sensory capacity, the primary view expressed by James's statement was the view which was to take hold and to prevail in terms of the subsequent interest and research in infant mental behavior. In prevailing, it prevented any systematic research from taking place for the next fifty years or so. Why James's view should have won out over that of Darwin or Preyer, for example, is somewhat of a mystery. Perhaps one reason was the fact that the sensory physiologists tended to support James's view. A more plausible explanation probably has to do with the *Zeitgeist*. Historically, the view of a *tabula rasa*—that the development of mind was due solely to experience—was a powerful position which allowed for no consideration of

Support for this study in attention comes from National Science Foundation Grant #GB28105. Appreciation for data collection and analysis is given to Eileen Scott.

innate structure. It was necessary to argue for either innate structure or blooming confusion. Confusion won out and the observation of Darwin went unnoticed. Although we now know better, it was a commonly held view that the infant's sensory systems were immature and could not lead to any accurate perception of the infant's world. Thus, for example, for all intents and purposes, the infant for the first six weeks of life was blind. It is interesting to note that it is possible to postulate a non-nativist position and still allow for very early function. If we propose only that many trials (much experience) may *not* be necessary for the formation of structure, it is then possible to argue for both an interactionist and early functioning position.

If we accept for the moment the premise that the infant's sensory systems are immature and essentially nonfunctioning, then, of course, we cannot help but accept James's view. One way of understanding the infant's cognitive structure is by discussing it in terms of an information system having an input and output function and some type of as yet undefined intermediate function which converts input to output. This model is useful in our analysis of the very young infant's cognitive structure. Figure 3.1 presents this model. The sensory systems can be considered input, and the responses of the infant can be considered output. If we believe that the sensory system is immature and that the infant has almost no voluntary motoric responses, then it is reasonable to assume that the intermediatory or processing function—we can call it higher cerebral function—is also nonexistent. Thus, James's blooming, buzzing mass of confusion would be a highly accurate description of the infant's mental life.

However, we know this analysis to be wrong. Interestingly, it fails because of what we initially have learned about the sensory systems. Preyer and Darwin were right in their observations of the newborn. Although the sensory apparatus of the newborn infant is immature, it is capable of functioning, and functioning at a high degree. Perhaps it was this discovery, chiefly in the work of Fantz in the later fifties and early sixties, which has led

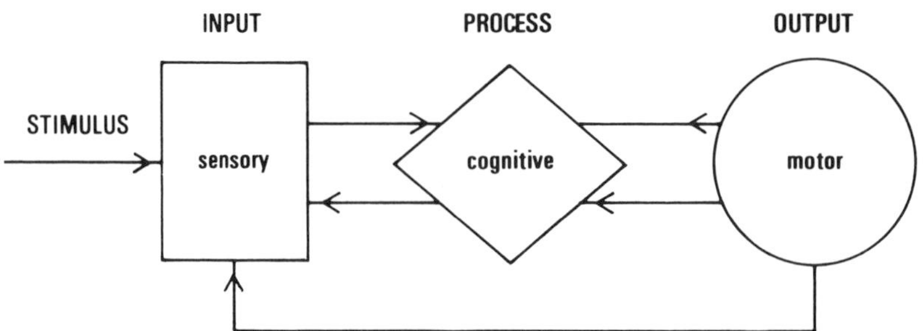

Figure 3.1. Schematic representation of an information model. Note the stimulus information enters the system through the input or sensory systems, is processed, and is expressed by the output or action systems. It is more than possible that this is not a linear model—that is, that output can move back to the sensory or cognitive systems for more information.

to the renaissance of interest in infancy research (Fantz 1961, 1963; Fantz *et al.* 1962). Fantz's experiments were simple and ingenious. Working in the visual modality, Fantz was able to demonstrate not only that the infant could see and discriminate between different kinds of stimuli, but in fact had preferences; for example, even newborns preferred the more complex over the simple. While it is true that the infant cannot accommodate well and that it does not have monocular vision, the infant is visually capable, and, given certain limitations, it can see its world.

One such limitation, for example, is the newborn's ability to track moving targets visually. It is clear that the infant is not capable of this sophisticated tracking procedure and it may be this incapacity which to this day leads many people to believe that initially the infant cannot see. Visual tracking of the face as it moves in conversation is one of the most salient clues used to determine whether we are being looked at. That newborn and young infants have trouble doing this may result in the conclusion of their blindness.

The demonstration of the newborn's ability to see was quickly followed by a demonstration that it could hear and respond differentially to sounds (Bartoshuk 1962*a,* 1962*b*), that its olfactory systems were operational, and that it could discriminate different olfactory experiences (Engen and Lipsitt 1965). Thus, by the early 1960s enough data had been gathered to demonstrate that the newborn and infant's sensory systems, although immature, were sufficiently capable of allowing the child to experience its world.

With this knowledge it becomes possible to review the input, output, and processing functions of the infant in order to explore the organism's cognitive process. From the data, it is possible to state that there is a sophisticated input system; that is, even the very young infant is capable of experiencing the world around him. Turn now to the output systems. Here one finds, as we had expected, that the output system—the motoric responses—of the infant are immature. It is in the lack of motoric response that one of the grossest differences exists between an adult and infant. The newborn infant can barely lift its head off the pillow when placed prone, let alone perform any sophisticated motoric acts—be they language or simple motor eye-hand coordination.

This information processing system is thus rather unique—an input function with little output function. We have a sophisticated sensory system capable of very complex sensory acts, yet a totally immature (even nonexistent) output system in terms of its motor or response behavior. What import do these facts have for the processing function, cerebral activity, and its development? A variety of theories about the growth of mental development have been put forth, most prominent of which has been Piaget's sensorimotor theory of intelligence (Piaget 1952). The construct of sensorimotor activity is one of interaction with the environment through which the cognitive structure of the infant is formed. Sensorimotor activity is intended to imply that perceptual as well as physical action is necessary in order for the infant to form structure. Moreover, assimilation and accommodation are possible only through this active interaction of the infant's present status with the demands of the environment.

Within this theoretical framework, then, motor activity plays a vital role in cognitive growth and cannot be considered incidental to the process of development. This view of a sensorimotor intelligence precludes the view that infants are capable of cognitive growth and the creation of structures solely through the use of sensory (not motor) activity. It is to be noted that sensory activity can be considered sensory as well as motor; that is, looking requires not only seeing but moving the eyes. If this is true, then we have reduced the notion of sensorimotor to a nonusable distinction, one which adds little to our discourse. No, sensorimotor behavior refers to the use at least of the hands and arms. In fact, most of the examples usually used in discussing sensorimotor activity refer to the limb and head movement.

This discussion is rather reminiscent of the S-R, S-S arguments of thirty years ago when S-R theorists would argue that in order for the formation of structure (in Hull's system, habit strength, H), a response was necessary (Hull 1943; Spence 1951). The S-S theorists argued that, to the contrary, no response was necessary for the formation of structure (Tolman 1949). As an explanation of their position, imitation learning was used wherein an organism *A* would first observe the behavior of *B* and *without* responding be able, at some future time, to carry out the task originally done by *B*. The S-R theorists responded that in fact there was a response, using eye movement as the criterion of that response. Thus S-R or S-S theory could not be refuted, and as others have pointed out, it is no longer a scientific discourse.

Likewise, we maintain that by sensorimotor activity we shall mean *motor* to refer more than just to the motor activity of the sensory activity. Anything else blurs the meaning and renders the discussion useless. If we are to refer to motor activity *per se* as important in the growth of structure, it is necessary that we consider part of the evolutionary history of our species, for it is here that we discover rather interesting and distinct motoric features which the anthropologists have claimed mark us from other organisms along the phylogenetic scale and which account for some of our cognitive activity. Here I am referring to the use of the arms and hands made possible by the upright position. It would appear that while we learn about our world through experience with all of our body, the arms and hands are those parts of the anatomy which give us the maximum information. Moreover, there is every reason to suggest that there is some relationship between this physical feature and our cognitive structure.

Given that Piaget's theory requires sensorimotor activity and given the infant's limited motoric capability, it is natural to conclude that most of the infant's cognitive structures (the more elaborate ones at least) must await the development of this motoric ability. Moreover, it would not seem unreasonable to conclude that given a failure of motoric development, the very young child's cognitive growth should be considerably restricted.

We shall now argue that neither of these assumptions are necessary or correct. Let us, for the sake of argument, suggest that it may be biologically advantageous for an organism at birth (or soon after) to be able to experience the world around it, form cognitive structures, and yet be unable to act in that world. Moreover, let us further suggest that the physical inability to act does not necessarily prevent the organism from forming structures. Thus, infants who are physically handicapped should not necessarily show the severe cognitive handicap suggested by a theory of sensorimotor intelligence.

In terms of the model presented in Figure 3.1, what we suggest is that the infant has both a sensory and cognitive function while at the same time little or no output or motoric capacity. Thus, unlike a theory requiring a motoric function in order to have a cognitive function, it is our belief that for some, if not all, cognitive structure—a sensory function—is all that is necessary.

How might one be able to test the hypothesis that motor activity is not necessary for the growth of cognitive structure? Fortunately for our discussion, Décarie (1969) was able to obtain data on a group of thalidomide infants and young children. Because thalidomide does not act on the central nervous system (CNS) but on the formation of the limbs, we have an unfortunate sample who, while having severe loss of the use of limbs, have little CNS impairment. This sample could be used to demonstrate the need of limbs in the formation of cognitive structure in very early childhood. We would expect that the loss of the proper use of arms and hands should result in some cognitive structure deficit. Decarie (1969) reports that while all the studies to date show no intellectual loss in thalidomide children, none report the actual testing of the children. In her report, Décarie discusses the children's performance on an object permanence task as well as on the Griffiths. The results clearly indicate no cognitive deficit. The point seems well made; there is no or little cognitive deficit when the most prominent and evolutionarily significant aspect of motoric exploration is absent or deformed. It would appear that if motoric activity is necessary for cognitive structures this severe loss would be reflected in performance. That no deficit is found would appear to be proof that the sensory system is sufficient for the formation and development of cognitive structures.

It is interesting to note that the data suggest that the absence of sensory capacity results in a more severe loss of cognitive function and structure (Fraiberg 1968; Furth 1966). Thus one might argue that in sensorimotor activity it is the sensory activity which is both vital and dominant.

Having argued that cognitive structure is possible without motoric capacity, it becomes necessary to demonstrate the infant's cognitive capacities. This presents some difficulty since in nonverbal organisms motoric behavior is usually required to demonstrate function. The failure of infant intelligence tests may reside precisely in their attempts to look at intellectual abilities by measuring sensorimotor activity, more specifically motor, rather than relying on sensory functions. It tells us little about intellectual ability to know when the infant sits up or to know whether or not it will reach for a red ring.

Our argument would be enhanced if in some way we could enable the young organism to act motorically. It should be able to show fairly complex cognitive function since it is in neither the input nor in the processing systems where the immaturity lies, but rather in the output or motoric systems (see Figure 3.1). Some sort of prosthesis is necessary. We might pause for a moment in our discussion and view a Buck Rogers world of the future where we attach all sorts of output systems to the organism and watch the infant act. But where to attach these prostheses; where is the phantom limb? What we have to do is find some response system that the newborn has and use that to attach the prosthesis. One such response system which is quite sophisticated at birth is the sucking response. As is well known, an infant can suck in one of two fashions, either by pressing the nipple against the roof of his mouth with his tongue or by creating a vacuum in the oral cavity and extracting the liquid in that fashion (Sameroff 1965). Both techniques are available to the newborn child and in a series of fairly ingenious experiments, it has been repeatedly demonstrated that if the environmental demand only allows the child to suck with vacuum, then the child's sucking behavior quickly switches to vacuum sucking. If, however, pressure sucking is called for, the newborn can quickly switch his behavior to pressure sucking (Bruner 1968; Sameroff 1965). Here then is the first example of the infant's ability to alter its behavior as a function of environmental demands. This would appear to involve some cognitive activity; however, it could also be considered simple reflexive behavior. Thus, in order to demonstrate more elaborate cognitive behavior, we need to use this sucking response. Siqueland (1968) and Bruner (1968) both report research where the sucking response was used to alter the visual field by increasing the illumination of a picture on a screen in one case and focusing a picture in the other. In these cases, planned, intentional, organized, sophisticated cognitive activity was demonstrated without the organism having the motoric capacity to carry out the action!

Many other examples less experimental come to mind where motoric action does not seem necessary or where its limitation did not result in cognitive deficit. Language is a good example of the former. While not completely settled as an issue, it does appear that language comprehension precedes language production by many months. Thus the infant has the semantic of words and phrases prior to being able to produce them. Swaddling is still another example of where the restriction of motoric behavior does not seem to result in the loss of cognitive structure and functioning.

It is important to consider one further aspect of cognitive activity as it relates to motor performance. If our analysis is correct, namely that motor activity may not be necessary for cognitive functioning, might it be that precocious motor activity may be detrimental to development? If one observes the ascending phylogenetic scale, one finds increasing periods of helplessness where the organism is unable to act motorically. If one requires an organism to act motorically at birth, then it is necessary to build into that organism those behavioral responses necessary for its action. That is to say, the organism which can act motorically at birth is an organism which did not need to learn how to act, but rather an organism in which action was predetermined. Thus, early motoric action in some sense is antithetical to elaborate and varied cognitive behavior and parsimonious with a prewired, predetermined system of behavior. It becomes clearer why it is inappropriate for the human infant to act, since, in fact, man above all species is most determined by what he learns rather than what is predetermined. What we have in the human infant is an organism unable to move its limbs, reach for, or ask for things—thus, an organism which is forced to "sit and think."

Using this approach one would expect to find not only a zero correlation between motoric capacity and cognitive function but a negative one. Unfortunately, there are few data on this subject, although Bayley (1970) presents some data—albeit weak—that show negative correlation between early motoric activity and later intellectual functioning.

A related issue is the training of precocious motor development and its negative relationship to cognitive functioning. While there is no evidence to support this view, it is clear that we must consider and investigate the relationship between the new infant toys (which enable the infant to show precocious activity) and the infant's subsequent cognitive development. If our view has any merit, cognitive harm may be the result of our toy technology.

In the preceding discussion we have stressed the lack of need for a motor activity component in the infant's acquisition of cognitive structure. Clearly such a statement is too strong. No one could argue that certain schema do not require motoric action. For example, it would seem that learning to ski would require more than just watching someone skiing. Likewise, any motor-action schema would require motor experience. In addition, the type of knowledge about objects and relationships would be incomplete without motor experience with them. I may know many things about a pencil by looking at it and watching others use it, but I can only know the feel of the pencil by touching it. Thus, a more moderate position is that the absence of action results in the limitation but not in the absence of knowledge. The function of our preceding comments is to suggest that motor activity, especially as used in the sensorimotor stage of genetic epistemology, has received too prominent a role.

This discussion serves as an introduction to the statement that we must guard against looking at motoric behavior when we try to assess the intellectual ability of the newborn and very young. In fact, in the next section we shall devote considerable time, given these facts, to talking about how one ought to go about studying individual differences in cognitive skills in the newborn and very young child.

ATTENTION AS A MEASURE OF COGNITIVE CAPACITY

In the previous section we tried to stress the point that it is necessary to look at the newborn and young child's sensory or input systems for cognitive functioning rather than somewhere else. Thus, it became our strategy to look at the attentional distribution of the infant and infer from that some of the infant's cognitive structures anp capacities as well as individual differences in these functions. For all the work that has been and continues to be generated, *attention* is not easily definable. In its general sense, it seems to be the process by which an organism directs its sensory and elaborating (cognitive) systems. This direction is in the service of all subsequent action, thought, or affect. Researchers have attempted to define *attention* more carefully through such physiological and behavioral observations as receptor orientation, decreases in ongoing activity such as moving, decreases in talking and vocalization and sucking. Several specific autonomic nervous system changes such as decrease in heart rate, galvanic skin response, vasodilation in the head and vasoconstriction in the extremities, breathing rate, and finally cortical changes (see Lewis 1971) usually indicate attention to external events and enable the organism subsequently to act, think, or feel. It seemed clear to us, therefore, that attending was a central process and as such vital in the study of cognitive and mental functioning.

Infants attend for many reasons. One kind of attention is what James has called "passive, immediate sensorial attention." In this type of attending the organism is forced to attend regardless of intent. A loud explosion, a loud tone, or a flash of light forces the organism to attend. Usually this type of attention is elicited by stimulus intensity and causes the organism, often without desire, to attend. In the second type of attending, which James called associational attending, the organism attends because of the relationship of the stimulation to his ongoing functions. A relationship between the event and the organism's cognitive structure is crucial. Thus, the infant attends to its mother's face because of certain knowledge, motives, and affects. The nature of the stimulus has relevance only as the organism chooses it. This type of attending is voluntary and under the control of the subject. Studies of passive attending usually are focused on the dimensions of intensity, number of variations, and complexity. Studies of associational or voluntary attending explore surprise, familiarity, novelty, and incongruity. The important issue for our consideration is this: how can one define familiarity or novelty along scaling dimensions which are independent of the organism. Unlike intensity or complexity, novelty and familiarity are completely dependent on the cognitive structures of the subject. Indeed, they are defined by the organism, by past experiences and cognitive structures.

An extremely important corollary to the investigation of this type of attending is that by observing what causes attending behavior one may determine the associational value of the event to the organism. It is by means of this corollary that the study of attending behavior, specifically associational attending behavior, becomes meaningful for our purposes. The researcher is provided with a channel through which he is able to observe the organism's internal processes. Moreover, by studying these attentional differences over age, he can come to understand the growth and development of cognitive structures themselves. Thus, this type of attending is ideally suited for our study of cognitive processes and individual differences in these processes in the newborn and young infant.

The research on attention can be divided into two categories. The first deals with the study of attention as a measure of the development of cognitive structures themselves—these have been called schemata. The second is a way of observing individual differences as they relate to or predict subsequent cognitive development. Before continuing, let me give examples of each and then present the kind of model which has been used extensively to study attention. Attention has been used to study cognitive development in infants by adopting a basic assumption: when the input from the environment matches a recently or nearly formed schema, that is, an internal representation of the external event, the infant will spend long periods of time looking or attending to this input. After the schema is well developed the infant will lose interest in stimuli which too well approximate it. Thus, if the stimulus array partially violates an existing schema, the violation will elicit attention. It is the distribution of the infant's attention that provides the clue to the nature of his cognitive structure. For example, before a child is familiar with a human face, it spends a great deal of time looking at faces. However, after it has become familiarized to human faces it spends relatively little time looking at faces. The amount of time the organism spends looking or attending informs us as to its cognitive structures.

It must be pointed out that there are several important issues in this discussion that have not been touched upon. For example, it is possible for the organism to spend more time attending to the familiar than to the novel. This is often a function of needs other than information; for example, security, as in the case where the child wants to hear the same (familiar) story over and over again at bedtime. Still another difficulty for the theory would be the case where the familiar serves to arouse, as in the case of hearing one's own baby cry in the middle of the night. Lewis (1971) has presented an alternative model for attending which rests on a two-phase process involving both alerting and cognitive aspects to an attending behavior.

Alternatively, the study of attention can be viewed as a measure of the capacity of the organism's central nervous system. For example, observe the infant who shows longer fixations or looks longer at a visual array than another infant—is this not indicative of the first infant's ability to sustain his attention and take in more of the environment? Stechler (1964) showed that in the newborn this difference in amount of attending was directly related to the amount and type of medication given to the infant's mother during labor. Infants whose mothers have less or no medication showed longer fixation times than did infants whose mothers received heavy medication. This attentional process was clearly influenced by medication affecting central nervous system functioning. Whether this type of individual difference reflects basic cognitive differences or whether these differences lead to cognitive differences via differential ability to process information—or both—remains to be explored.

These two kinds of models for studying the attentive behavior of newborn and young infants have been reported extensively in the literature. It is the former, that is, attention as a measure of the acquisition of cognitive structures, that we wish to consider. We shall do this by studying the attentional process, more specifically, by studying the infant's habituation to redundant information and its recovery to stimulus change.

RESPONSE DECREMENT AND RECOVERY MODEL

A simple experimental paradigm has been employed for investigating cognitive structures and processing in the newborn and very young infant. Figure 3.2 points out this experimental paradigm. An event, S_1, is repeatedly presented for *n* trials, following which some new event, an alteration of S_1—S_2—is presented on trial $n + 1$. Response decrement, having the form of a negative exponential function, should occur to the repeated event, S_1 (Lewis and Goldberg 1969; Thompson and Spencer 1966). The presentation of S_2 on trial $n + 1$ should result in response recovery. Both the response decrement and recovery data should reflect internal representation acquisition, with greater rate or amount of decrement and greater amount of recovery reflecting faster acquisition.

The explanation of response decrement is particularly germane to the question of whether or not the phenomenon under study is indeed a mental process. Response decrement can be attributed to receptor, effector, or general organism fatigue, and occurs because there is progressive physiological loss of the ability to respond. These phenomena are not related to what is considered cognitive processes. On the other hand, the Russian Sokolov (1963*b*), as well as American investigators such as Engen and Lipsitt (1965) and Thompson and Spencer (1966), would argue that response decrement is indicative of a cognitive process. Razran (1961), in his review of the Russian work on attending, states: "there is little doubt that if any [acquired] pattern is accorded cognitive status, the attending pattern is surely the most likely candidate" (p. 119).

Before going on to discuss the use of response decrement as a measure of individual differences in the acquisition of internal representations, let us first consider some alternative causes of response decrement. According to one fatigue model, response decrement reflects a general condition of the organism and is unrelated to the stimulus. Thus, a change in the stimulus after *n* repetitions would not alter the pattern of decreasing attention. The Sokolovian model assumes that response decrement is stimulus-specific and predicts response recovery to stimulus change. Indeed, an orienting reflex is defined as those responses which habituate (show response decre-

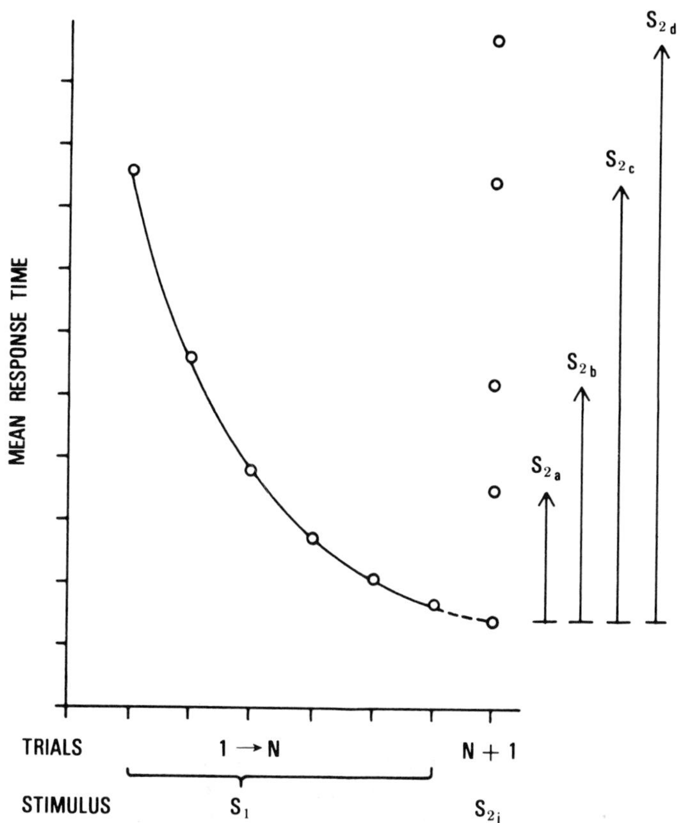

Figure 3.2. An experimental paradigm for investigating cognitive structures which involves the measurement of response recovery versus decrement.

ment) to repeated presentation of a stimulus (S_1) and which reappear when the stimulus is altered (S_2). The assumptions about S_2 in this model are limited to (1) S_2 is discriminable from S_1 and (2) S_2 is equal to or less intense than S_1. The intensity of S_2 must be less than S_1 in order to eliminate receptor fatigue (adaptation) and recovery as alternative hypotheses. Thus, both a fatigue and receptor adaptation hypothesis could be rejected by demonstrating response recovery to a stimulus change (S_2) after a period of response decrement produced by stimulus repetition. The recovery to S_2 has been demonstrated by many investigators using young children and infants as subjects (Bartoshuk 1962*a*, 1962*b*; Engen and Lipsitt 1965; Lewis 1969; Lewis *et al.* 1967; Lewis and Goldberg 1969; Pancratz and Cohen 1970).

A similar fatigue model suggests that response decrement is caused by the organism's becoming physically restless. This too has been rejected

(Cohen 1969*b*). In addition to the earlier extensive work (see Razran 1961; Sokolov 1963*a*, 1963*b*; and Thompson and Spencer 1966 for reviews), there is a growing body of neurophysiological data which strongly suggest that CNS changes such as negative slow potential change in the human cortex occur while the organism is acquiring expectations (that is, the memory, model, or internal representation of some event) through repetitive stimulus presentation (Rebert, McAdam, Knott, and Irwin 1967; Walter 1964; Walter, Cooper, Aldridge, McCallum, and Winter 1964). Thus, the composite of the research effort to date supports the theory that response decrement is a cognitive process related to the growth of internal representations against which external events are compared. *It then follows that if response decrement is a measure of the speed of model acquisition, then the amount or rate of this decrement should be associated with a more efficient system of forming representations, such that those infants who show more rapid response decrement are those who build internal representations faster.*

In this model we see an infant build up an internal representation of the external event, a memory if you like, and use that memory for making a decision on what it shall do on subsequent trials. The infant is capable of building up a representation, the utilization of representation in comparison with a new event, and volition—three clear elements to indicate sophisticated cognitive structures and processing.

In a series of experiments completed in our laboratory, as well as several others conducted elsewhere, the attentional model has been used to observe mental development and individual differences in this development. In the following discussion we will present this material, first describing those studies which observed variables characteristically associated with superior cognitive and CNS functioning and which related them to response decrement differences.

EMPIRICAL EVIDENCE FOR INDIVIDUAL DIFFERENCES IN RESPONSE DECREMENT AND RECOVERY

For the past ten years research has been conducted to demonstrate response decrement effects as a function of a wide variety of subject variables. The first of these—age differences in response decrement—can be demonstrated across at least two modalities. Figures 3.3 and 3.4 present response decrement by age for three-month to forty-four-month-old infants. Observation of the data indicates that response decrement increases with increasing age. Thus, three-month-old infants show relatively little response decrement, whereas older infants show increasingly greater amounts of response decrement.

Figure 3.5 presents data on response recovery when a change in the stimulus takes place. The data like response decrement clearly indicate an age-related function such that older infants show greater response recovery.

Figure 3.6 shows age differences in response decrement to auditory stimuli, this for another sample of subjects in the first two years of life. Again we see, this time for heart rate response, an age-related response

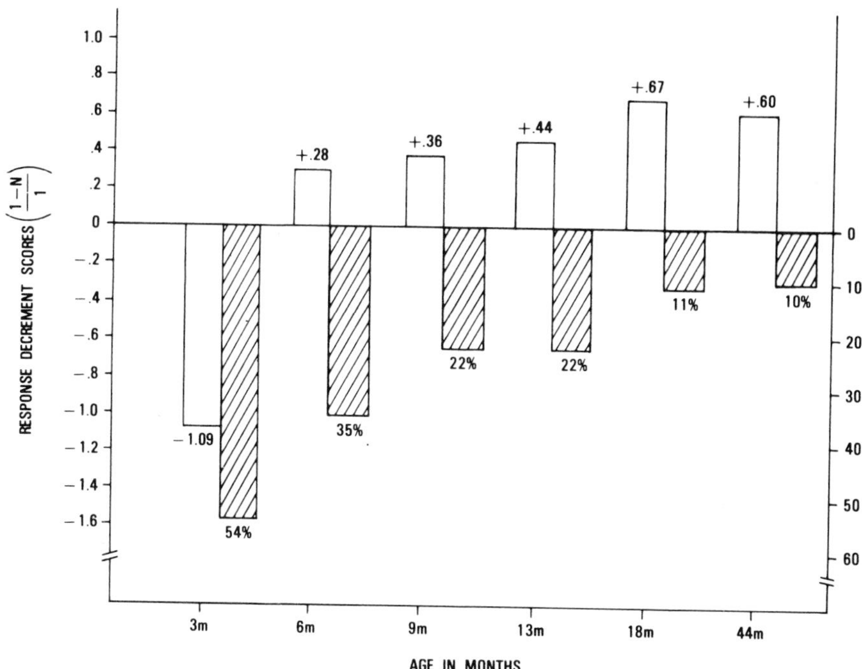

Figure 3.3. Response decrement as a function of age. The white bars represent the percentage of decrement over six trials of a repeated visual stimulus, while the striped bars represent the percentage of *S*s who failed to show decrement.

decrement function, especially for the auditory simple stimuli, where older infants show greater response decrement.

Response decrement has also been shown to be related to such mental operations as concept formation and discrimination learning in three to four-year-old children where a variety of standard psychological tests were given to a group of infants and response decrement scores to visual stimuli were obtained. In general, significant relationships were found such that infants who showed greater response decrement were the same infants who showed faster learning. Finally, response decrement in the first year of life was related to full-scale Stanford-Binet scores at age of four such that the greater the response decrement within the first year, the higher the Stanford-Binet scores at age four. The correlation was .46 for girls and .50 for boys, and as such higher than any correlations obtained by standard psychometric testing.

To summarize briefly some of the data, varying degrees of response decrement and recovery to repeated and varied signals, both visual and auditory, were found for infants within the first four years of life. Response decrement and recovery were directly related to the age of the infant, the younger infants showing less response decrement and recovery than the

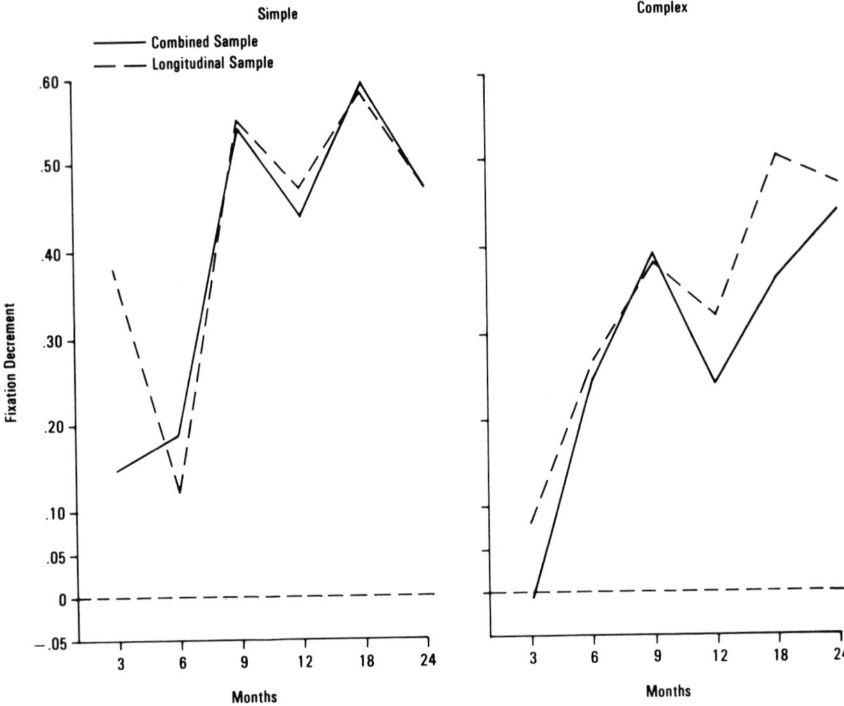

Figure 3.4. Response decrement as a function of age. Sample II. Percentages represent the amount of fixation decrement over six trials. Simple and complex refer to the nature of the visual stimulus.

older ones. Response decrement was also shown to be related to other individual difference variables, such as the state of the subject, the mother-infant interaction, measures of satiation such as play behavior, and the socioeconomic status of the father. Finally, response decrement was directly predictive of performance on cognitive tasks and predictive of IQ scores on a full-scale Stanford-Binet intelligence test (see Lewis *et al.* 1969).

CENTRAL NERVOUS SYSTEM DYSFUNCTION AND ATTENTION

We have been discussing CNS functioning and response decrement. Also of interest is the research relating CNS dysfunctioning to attentional processes. In 1966 Thompson and Spencer reviewed the literature on response decrement and cited numerous studies showing that decrement of attention differs markedly as a function of cortical involvement. There is reduced rate of response decrement after total decortication in dogs and chronic decerebration in cats. More specifically, in terms of local brain involvement, lesions in the auditory cortex in cats, frontal or temporal lesions

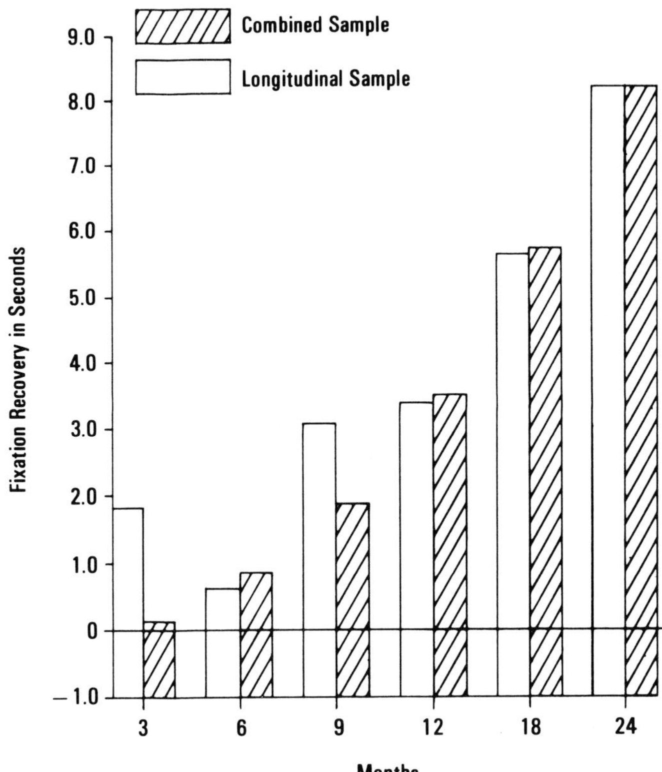

Figure 3.5. Response decrement of the heart rate responses as a function of age. The amount of heart rate is in beats per minute (BPM) and reflects the differences in deceleration. For the simple auditory signal—a pure tone—there is a lawful age function, with increased decrement directly related to age. For the complex signal there is little age relationship, though the groups 3 + 6, 9 + 12, and 18 + 24 months do show a significant age function (−2.17 BPM; −2.45 BPM; and −4.75 BPM).

in monkeys, cats, rats, and man, and bilateral amygdalectomy all reduce the rate of decrement. Thus, attending, and specifically response decrement, seems to be related to central nervous system dysfunction in animals.

Initially the research with humans was done mostly by the Russians. This is due to the formulations of Pavlov and Sokolov on the subject. Reviewing the Russian work on attending reveals that cortical function has been strongly implicated in the role of response decrement. From the very first work on the orienting response (OR), Pavlov (1949) demonstrated that response decrement was a cortical response and disruption of cortical function would affect the *rate* of decrement, as well as whether or not the organism showed response decrement at all.

Bronstein, Itina, Kamenetskaia and Sytova (1958) report on the attending response in the newborn child. Using both auditory and tactile

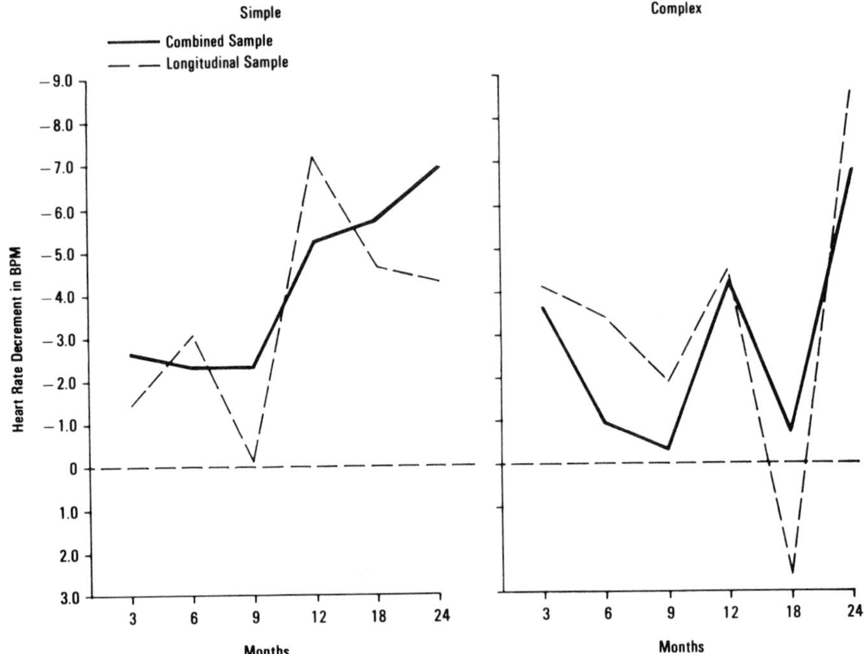

Figure 3.6. Response recovery as a function of age. Sample II. Fixation and response recovery were determined by subtracting the fixation scores from the seventh trial (a new event) from the sixth trial (the last redundant event).

stimulation and normal and traumatized children (children with birth injury), the investigators found large differences in rate of response decrement to repeated stimulation. For normal children, the response to sound disappeared after one trial in almost 12 percent of the healthy children but in only 4 percent of the injured ones. Moreover, 50 percent of the injured children showed no decrement at all over all the given trials. Bronstein *et al.* also refer to the work of Itina, who studied prematurely born babies. In these subjects, frequently it was not possible to produce response decrement, and for two children, both hydrocephalics, no decrement was shown after "a great number of test trials." Brackbill (1971) investigated the habituation pattern of an anencephalic infant and found no evidence of response decrement even after two hundred trials.

Polikania and Probatova (1958) also investigated the attending response in premature infants who were ten to thirty days old when the study was begun. Sound and light stimuli were used and approximately sixty infants were studied. Control *S*s, as old postnatally as the premature infants, were obtained, and the result indicated that for the premature *S*s there was no tendency toward response decrement of the autonomic components of the OR. This was true for the very premature children, and remained so even when the children were older. The experimenters also report cases of "pathological conditions of the cortex, or where the cortex was underdeveloped or destroyed." In these conditions, the data all reveal that response decrement was most difficult—at times impossible—to obtain. Adult subjects with more severe cortical involvement were studied by Briullova (1958) and Gamburg (1958*b*). Significant differences between normals and experimental subjects in response decrement again were obtained.

Thus, there is a large and impressive quantity of literature linking CNS dysfunction and response decrement in animals as well as infants and adult humans. While much careful mapping of the particular areas of the cortex responsible for response decrement need be conducted, it is clear that there are important relationships between CNS function or dysfunction and response decrement. Vedyayev and Karmanova (1958) conclude from their study of the phylogenesis of the OR that the "characteristics of the higher nervous activity of various animals that have been well studied at present are reflected by such indicators as the speed of extinction of the OR." In other words, rate of response decrement varied as a function of higher nervous system activity as seen in different animals along the phylogenetic scale. This idea was first expressed by Pavlov (1949) when he stated that the reflex arc of the OR is projected in the cortex as well as in the subcortical structures. For Pavlov, the speed of response decrement must be dependent "on the corticalization of the functions in the given animal on one hand, and on the relationship among the basic neural process on the other" (Vedyayev and Karmanova 1958).

These facts, together with the earlier data on individual differences in response decrement, supply clear evidence for CNS involvement in decrement, and, moreover, indicate that the degree of response decrement can be used as an important indicator of CNS dysfunction as well as of cognitive development and learning. It is evident, then, that individual differences in response decrement have important implications for predicting the growth of cognitive capacity.

Recently, American psychology has begun to explore attending differences as they relate to differences in CNS functioning/dysfunctioning and cognitive development. For example, Cohen, Offner, and Blatt (1965) have investigated the production and distribution of contingent negative variation (CNV) between normal and dyslexic children. Working under the assumption that the CNV is related to the buildup of a neuronal model, differences between these groups of children in terms of internal representation of external events, acquisition, and therefore CNV would be predicted. Differences were obtained such that the E-waves of the dyslexic children's response, in anticipation of the stimulus, were of a lesser magnitude than those the normal subjects showed. Fenelon (1968) also found differences in normal and dyslexic children in their CNV production.

More directly related to CNS dysfunction and response decrement is the study by Hutt (1968). Hutt was interested in individual differences in the exploration of novelty and used both normal and brain damaged (general cerebral lesions) children four to seven years of age. Her results agree with the earlier work indicating that an intact cortex is necessary for response decrement to occur. Hutt found that the proportion of time spent investigating a specific object, as opposed to other objects in the room, was longer for the brain lesioned subjects. After two weeks, the children were returned to the playroom, and while the brain damaged subjects maintained their level of interest as before, the normal children's interest had fallen off. These more molar behaviors involving children's play, rather than some molecular behavior such as an autonomic response, are totally consistent with earlier findings using those molecular responses. Moreover, the play data conform to the work of Lewis (1967*b*), who found that children from higher socioeconomic levels—children who probably are more intelligent as measured by our standard tests—spent more time in varied play than playing with a single toy.

Another area of inquiry into individual differences has been the effects of medication (given to the mother in labor) on the development of the infant. Stechler (1964) in an early study demonstrated that attentional differences (in terms of amount of looking time) in the newborn could be affected by the level of medication given the mother. However, because the infants were seen two to four days after birth, it is not possible to talk about attention differences as produced by structural changes caused by the medication. The medication itself might still be in effect so short a time after birth.

Bowes, Brackbill, Conway, and Steinschneider (1970), in a recent study of attention and medication, were able to show some very stable and long-lasting effects. These experimenters were interested in response decrement as an index of cortical integrity in the newborn. Sound stimuli were presented and response decrement observed two and five days and one month after birth. At two and five days, highly medicated infants required three to four times as many trials to habituate as did the lightly or nonmedicated infant. Moreover, since the drugs themselves were no longer potent by a month (Moya and Thorndike 1962), any differences observed would suggest that cortical structure and integrity might have been affected. Bowes *et al.* found that the significant difference between the medicated and nonmedicated groups still held one month after the medication, a strong indication of the potency of medication during labor and its long-term effects on cortical functioning and response decrement. Recently Brackbill, Kane, Manniello, and Abramson (1974) were again able to show the relationship between medication and infant habituation rates. Further, it was the habituation scores, not any of the standard infant tests, which showed the medication effect.

In all studies—Stechler (1964), Bowes *et al.* (1970), and Brackbill *et al.* (1974)—attentional responses were used to demonstrate individual differences in cortical function as it relates to certain experimental variables. These studies suggest that response decrement as a measure of individual differences may be a valuable diagnostic device for evaluating differences in a variety of areas of pathology. Moreover, since the medicated groups showed no visible clinical trauma, response decrement seems to be a more sensitive measure capable of detecting individual differences in groups with subclinical deficits. Two recent studies support this contention.

Rather than studying gross differences between children with severe cortical dysfunction and those with none, Lewis *et al.* (1967) chose to observe attention distribution of a sample in which all of the subjects were considered normal. Successful observation of differences in this sample would provide evidence that response decrement can be used as a measure in samples with little pathology. Subclinical problems may be thereby investigated. Given that a relationship does exist between subclinical problems and subsequent difficulties in development, the diagnosis of these differences may be anticipated: evidence exists relating such problems as behavioral disorders in school with difficult deliveries (Knobloch and Pasamanick 1959).

In the Lewis *et al.* study, the Apgar birth score was used as the measure of birth trauma continuum (Apgar, Holaday, James, Berrien, and Weisbrot 1958; Apgar and James 1962). The Apgar score, although deficient in certain respects, has been found to be related to subsequent mental and motor performance (Edwards 1968; Kangas and Butler 1966). Approximately forty infants were seen at three and at nine to thirteen months after birth. Apgar scores, all of them in the normal range (see Drage and Berendes 1966), were available as were measures of response decrement to a redundant visual stimulus. The children were divided on the basis of their Apgar scores into those with perfect scores and those with less than perfect scores but within the normal range. The results revealed that at three months response decrement was significantly different between the two groups and indicated greater decrement for the perfect-scoring group. Parenthetically, it is to be noted that the group differences also supported Stechler's results. Total looking time, as in Stechler's (1964) study, was also available and indicated more looking for the perfect-scoring group. In a replication of the Lewis *et al.* study, the results strongly support the earlier findings, the subjects with Apgar scores of 10 exhibiting greater response decrement than those with scores of 6 to 9.

The results of all the studies reviewed clearly indicate that rate of response decrement is affected by CNS dysfunction, medication, psychosis, and other variables affecting cortical functioning. That some of these variables are subclinical suggests that the theoretical and technological advances are ready to offer a highly reliable and sensitive measure of cortical involvement and pathology. The use of response decrement as a diagnostic measure clearly is called for. Moreover, since measures of response decrement reflect more efficient CNS functioning, any intervention program, such as drug therapy or learning enrichment, can be evaluated by increases in rate of response decrement (as measured by both prior and subsequent performance) as well as by comparison with a control or healthy group of subjects. The practical considerations only await the investigator. Thus, the use of attention promises to afford the investigator of early individual differences in cognitive processes an opportunity to explore individual differences and their etiology. In the following section I should like to present some individual subject data as an illustration of how these techniques might be applied.

Case history of R.B., nine months. We first saw R.B. when she was thirty-seven weeks old. Her mother responded to a news announcement asking for subjects by calling and asking if she could make an appointment to see us with her abnormal child. Upon examination, R.B. was discovered to be a healthy, alert nine-month-old female infant. However, her weight, physical stature and motor capabilities were those of a three-month-old infant. R.B.'s mother was a woman in her early fifties who informed us that R.B. was a menopause baby, the last of five children with a fifteen or sixteen-year spread between the last child and R.B. The mother reported, confirmed by the obstetrician, that the pregnancy and delivery were uneventful, and except for the curling of R.B.'s small fingers and the very small stature, R.B. seemed to be perfectly normal. R.B.'s mother reported that R.B. played with her older sibs and seemed to be a contented, happy child. However, as one might imagine, the mother was quite concerned since R.B. seemed developmentally far behind what her chronological age would indicate. Indeed, psychometric testing with a wide variety of standard infant intelligence tests (Bayley Scales of Infant Development), as well as some of the sensorimotor tests developed from Piagetian theory (Escalona and Corman's Scales of Sensorimotor Development) all revealed a severely retarded child. Motorically the child was six months behind her chronological age: she could not reach for a block or look under an object for another hidden object as required in the Bayley or in the Corman and Escalona tasks. The pediatrician could offer the mother no advice except that he could find nothing wrong with the child. Had we had no other procedure to utilize we too would not have been able to offer the mother anything but our sad counsel and our hope that the child would catch up with other infants. However, we have collected a large amount of normative attentional data on nine-month-old infants' responses to the kind of redundant visual situation that have been described previously. R.B.'s data on these standard perceptual tasks revealed that, although her motoric capabilities rendered her intellectual functioning scores severely retarded *vis-à-vis* other nine-month-olds, her visual perception data indicated habituation patterns much like that of other nine-month-old infants. On the basis of these it was predicted that R.B., although severely motorically retarded, should in fact have subsequent normal intellectual capabilities. Fortunately, R.B. was followed and at last visit she was thirty months old. By this time she has caught up considerably in terms of her body stature and motoric ability although, on the basis of these skills, one would still consider her behavior retarded *vis-à-vis* other thirty-month-olds. However, her performance on standard intelligence tests at this point, such as the Stanford-Binet, indicates a normal intellectual functioning. Thus, the utilization of attention in perceptual-cognitive tasks enabled us to predict normal intellectual functioning on the part of this child rather than the prediction which would have resulted had we only had her sensorimotor scores.

We are currently working with the problem of infant prematurity, anoxia and central nervous system dysfunction. This study has been conducted in collaboration with Suzanne Schimpeler and John Driscall of the Columbia University Medical Center. To study this problem we continue to use the attention paradigm of response decrement to redundant auditory signals and response recovery to stimulus change. Figure 3.7 presents the mean data on more than forty infants ranging in gestational age from thirty-four to forty-one weeks. Ten trials of a 65 decibel auditory signal (a human voice reciting a poem), each fifteen seconds long with a thirty-second intertrial interval, were presented. The eleventh trial consisted of a section of a musical piece also with an average of 65 decibels. The infant response observed was sucking rate. The number of sucks during stimulus presentation was subtracted from the number of sucks during the fifteen seconds immediately prior to stimulus onset. A positive score indicates sucking suppression; that is, during the auditory stimulus the infant sucked less than during the base period. Sucking suppression has been shown to be a correlate of attentive behavior (Siqueland 1969). The data indicate that

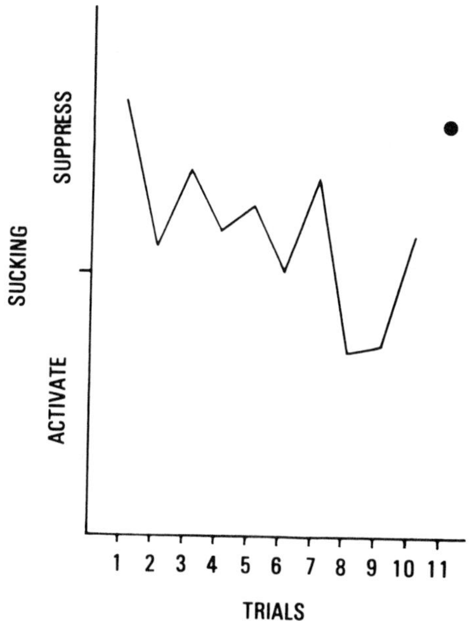

Figure 3.7. Change in number of sucks as a function of trials. Trials 1 through 10 were the same auditory event, while trial 2 was a new event. Sucking suppression indicates less sucking during stimulation than in the base period preceding it, while activation indicates an increase in sucking.

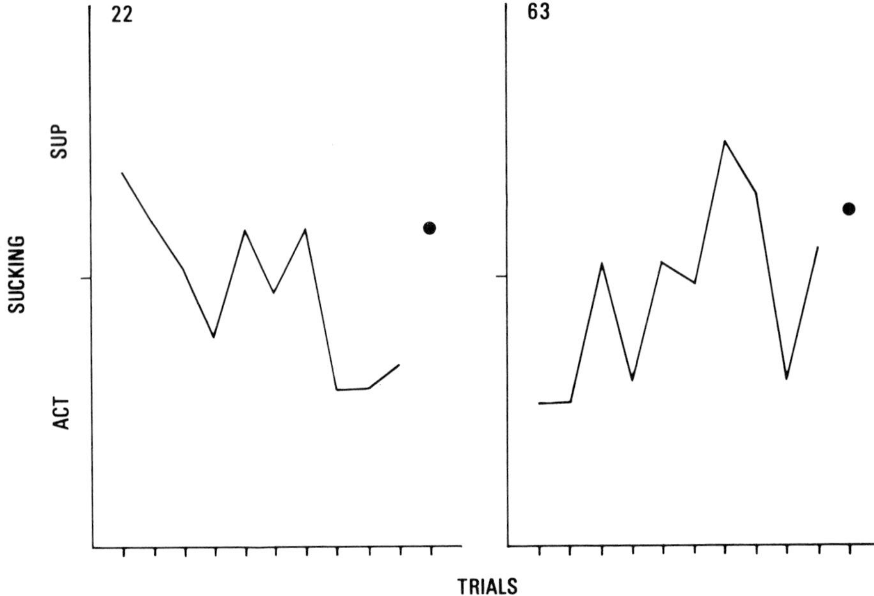

Figure 3.8. The sucking data of two subjects by trial.

with repeated exposure sucking suppression, attentive behavior, declines. However, there is attention recovery when the new stimulus is presented. Thus, as expected, the attentional paradigm appears to be appropriate for this type of clinical population.

Figure 3.8 presents the sucking data for two premature infants (thirty-nine–forty weeks gestation). Subject #22 is a healthy premature while subject #63 is not only premature but a methadone addicted infant. Observe the difference in response to this attentional situation when both infants were seen on the first day after birth. Subject #22 shows considerable sucking suppression over the first few trials, indicating attentive behavior. In addition, there is a gradual habituation of the sucking suppression over trials with a return of the sucking suppression when the stimulus was altered. Now consider the pattern of subject #63. There is little sucking suppression; indeed, amount of sucking seems to increase during stimulation, although the subject seems to become increasingly interested (rather than disinterested) in the stimulus. Stimulus change does not produce much response recovery. The pattern of #22 suggests a more appropriate CNS functioning than #63 and the data on these subjects support this pattern. Thus, it would appear that this technique can be used successfully with a wide variety of attentional measures (beside heart rate and fixation) and across a wide variety of settings. The use of this paradigm in a clinical setting should be most helpful in diagnosing possible CNS dysfunctioning within the minimal brain damage range.

Given that response decrement to redundant information and response recovery to change do measure central nervous system function and dysfunction, we now have a most valuable research tool for the investigator of individual differences in the opening months and even days of life. In addition, it is not an age specific test, at least in the opening two or three years of life. This enables us to explore developmentally many areas of inquiry and at the same time keep constant our experimental tests. Moreover and most importantly, we need not measure motoric function in our search for cognitive structure and process. This should prove a more accurate picture of the child's cognition, one which may be related to future behavior (see Lewis 1973; Lewis and McGurk 1972). Past work on attention and processes, especially response decrement and recovery, should excite us to continue investigating this most interesting topic, both for its clinical implications and its theoretical import.

References

Apgar, V.; Holaday, D. A.; James, L. S.; Berrien, C.; and Weisbrot, I. M. "Evaluation of the Newborn Infant: Second Report." *Journal of the American Medical Association* 168, (1958): 1985–88.

———, and James, L. S. "Further Observations on the Newborn Scoring System." *American Journal of Diseases of Children* 104 (1962): 419–28.

Bartoshuk, A. K. "Human Neonatal Cardiac Acceleration to Sound: Habituation and Dishabituation." *Perceptual and Motor Skills* 15 (1962*a*): 15–27.

———. "Response Decrement with Repeated Elicitation of Human Neonatal Cardiac Acceleration to Sound." *Journal of Comparative and Physiological Psychology* 55 (1962*b*): 9–13.

Bayley, N. "Development of Mental Abilities." In *Carmichael's Manual of Child Psychology*, edited by P. H. Mussen. Vol. 1. New York: Wiley, 1970.

Bowes, W. A.; Brackbill, Y.; Conway, E.; and Steinschneider, A. "The Effects of Obstetrical Medication on Fetus and Infant." *Monographs of the Society for Research in Child Development* 35 (4) (1970): Serial No. 137.

Brackbill, Y. "The Role of the Cortex in Orienting: Orienting Reflex in an Anencephalic Human Infant." *Developmental Psychology* 5 (1971): 195–201.

———; Kane, J.; Manniello, R. L.; and Abramson, D. "Obstetric Premedication and Infant Outcome." *American Journal of Obstetrics and Gynecology* 118(3) (1974): 377–84.

Briullova, S. V. "On Some Aspects of the Orienting Reflex in Persons Having Suffered a Covert Trauma of the Brain and in Neurotic Persons." In *Orienting Reflex and Exploratory Behavior*, edited by L. G. Voronin, A. N. Leontiev, A. R. Luria, E. N. Sokolov, and O. S. Vinogradova. Moscow: Academy of Pedagogical Sciences of RSFSR, 1958.

Bronstein, A. I.; Itina, N. A.; Kamenetskaia, A. G.; and Sytova, V. A. "The Orienting Reactions in Newborn Children." In *Orienting Reflex and Exploratory Behavior*, edited by L. G. Voronin, A. N. Leontiev, A. R. Luria, E. N. Sokolov, and O. S. Vinogradova. Moscow: Academy of Pedagogical Sciences of RSFSR, 1958.

Bruner, J. S. *Processes of Cognitive Growth: Infancy* (Volume III, Heinz Werner Lecture Series). Worcester, Mass.: Clark University Press with Barre Publishers, 1968.

Cohen, J.; Offner, F.; and Blatt, S. "Psychological Factors in the Production and Distribution of the Contingent Negative Variation (CNV)." Paper presented at the Sixth International Congress of Electroencephalography and Clinical Neurophysiology, Vienna, September 1965.

Cohen, L. B. "Observing Responses, Visual Preferences, and Habituation to Visual Stimuli in Infants." *Journal of Experimental Child Psychology* 7 (1969): 419–33.

Darwin, C. *The Descent of Man and Selection in Relation to Sex.* New ed. New York: Appleton, 1897.

Décarie, T. G. "A Study of the Mental and Emotional Development of the Thalidomide Child." In *Determinants of Infant Behavior IV,* edited by B. M. Foss. London, Methuen, 1969.

Drage, J. S., and Berendes, H. "Apgar Scores and Outcome of the Newborn." *Pediatric Clinics of North America* 13 (1966): 635–43.

Edwards, N. "The Relationship between Physical Condition Immediately after Birth and Mental and Motor Performance at Age Four." *Genetic Psychology Monographs* 78 (1968): 257–89.

Engen, T., and Lipsitt, L. P. "Decrement and Recovery of Responses to Olfactory Stimuli in the Human Neonate." *Journal of Comparative and Physiological Psychology* 59 (1965): 312–16.

Fantz, R. L. "The Origin of Form Perception." *Scientific American* (May 1961): 66–72.

———. "Pattern Vision in New Born Infants." *Science* 140 (1963): 296–97.

———; Ordy, J. M.; and Udelf, M. S. "Maturation of Pattern Vision in Infants During the First Six Months." *Journal of Comparative and Physiological Psychology* 55(6) (1962): 907–17.

Fenelon, B. "Expectancy Waves and Other Complex Cerebral Events in Dyslexic and Normal Subjects." *Psychonomic Science* 13 (1968): 253–54.

Fraiberg, S. "Parallel and Divergent Patterns in Blind and Sighted Infants." *Psychoanalytic Study of the Child, Volume XXIII.* New York: International Universities Press, 1968.

Furth, H. G. *Thinking without Language: Psychological Implications of Deafness.* New York: Free Press, 1966.

Gamburg, A. L. "Orienting and Defensive Reactions in Post-Traumatic Cerebroasthenia and Encephalopathy (second communication)." In *Orienting Reflex and Exploratory Behavior,* edited by L. G. Voronin, A. N. Leontiev, A. R. Luria, E. N. Sokolov, and O. S. Vinogradova. Moscow: Academy of Pedagogical Sciences of RSFSR, 1958.

Hull, C. L. *Principles of Behavior.* New York: Appleton-Century, 1943.

Hutt, C. "Exploration of Novelty in Children with and without Upper C.N.S. Lesions and Some Effects of Auditory and Visual Incentives." *Acta Psychologica* 28 (1968): 150–60.

James, W. *The Principles of Psychology.* New York: Henry Holt, 1890.

Kangas, J., and Butler, B. "Relationship Between an Index of Neonatal Delivery Room Conditions and Pre-school Intelligence." Paper presented at the American Psychological Association meeting, New York, 1966.

Knobloch, H., and Pasamanick, B. "Syndrome of Minimal Cerebral Damage in Infancy." *Journal of the American Medical Association* 170 (1959): 1384–87.

Lewis, M. "Infant Attention: Response Decrement as a Measure of Cognitive Processes, or What's New, Baby Jane?" Paper presented at the Society for Research in Child Development Symposium on the Roles of Attention in Cognitive Development, New York, 1967.

———. "Infants' Responses to Facial Stimuli During the First Year of Life." *Developmental Psychology* 1 (1969): 75–86.

———. "Individual Differences in the Measurement of Cognitive Development." In *Exceptional infant, 2,* edited by J. Hellmuth. New York: Brunner/Mazel, 1971.

———. "Infant Intelligence Tests: Their Use and Misuse." *Human Development* 16 (1973): 108–18.

———; Bartels, B.; Campbell, H.; and Goldberg, S. "Individual Differences in Attention: The

Relation Between Infants' Condition at Birth and Attention Distribution within the First Year." *American Journal of Diseases of Children* 113 (1967): 461–65.

———, and Baumel, M. H. "A Study in the Ordering of Attention." *Perceptual and Motor Skills* 10 (1970): 52–56.

———, and Goldberg, S. "The Acquisition and Violation of Expectancy: An Experimental Paradigm." *Journal of Experimental Child Psychology* 7 (1969): 70–80.

———, Goldberg, S.; and Campbell, H. "A Developmental Study of Learning within the First Three Years of Life: Response Decrement to a Redundant Signal." *Monographs of the Society for Research in Child Development* 34 (9) (1969): Serial No. 133.

———, and McGurk, H. "Evaluation of Infant Intelligence: Infant Intelligence Scores—True or False?" *Science* 178(4066) (1972): 1174–77.

———, and Scott, E. "A Developmental Study of Infant Attentional Distribution Within the First Two Years of Life." Paper presented at the XX International Congress of Psychology, Symposium on Learning in Early Infancy, Tokyo, Japan, August 1972.

Moya, F., and Thorndike, V. "Passage of Drugs across the Placenta." *American Journal of Obstetrics and Gynecology* 84 (1962): 1778–98.

Pancratz, C. N., and Cohen, L. B. "Recovery of Habituation in Infants." *Journal of Experimental Child Psychology* 9 (1970): 208–16.

Pavlov, I. P. *Complete Works* Moscow: USSR Academy of Sciences Press, 1947–49.

Piaget, J. *The Origins of Intelligence in Children.* New York: International Universities Press, 1952.

Polikania, R. I., and Probatova, L. E. "On the Problem of Formation of the Orienting Reflex in Prematurely Born Children." In *Orienting Reflex and Exploratory Behavior,* edited by L. G. Voronin, A. N. Leontiev, A. R. Luria, E. N. Sokolov, and O. S. Vinogradova. Moscow: Academy of Pedagogical Sciences of RSFSR, 1958.

Preyer, W. T. *The Mind of the Child, Volume I.* New York: Appleton, 1888; originally published 1882.

Razran, G. "The Observable Unconscious and the Inferable Conscious in Current Soviet Psychology: Interoceptive Conditioning, Semantic Conditioning, and the Orienting Reflex." *Psychological Review* 68 (1961): 81–147.

Rebert, C. S.; McAdam, D. W.; Knott, J. R.; and Irwin, D. A. "Slow Potential Change in Human Brain Related to Level of Motivation." *Journal of Comparative and Physiological Psychology* 63 (1967): 20–23.

Sameroff, A. J. "An Experimental Study of the Response Components of Sucking in the Human Newborn." Unpublished doctoral dissertation, Yale University, 1965.

Siqueland, E. R. "Conditioned Sucking and Visual Reinforcers with Human Infants." Paper presented at Eastern Regional meeting, Society for Research in Child Development, Worcester, Massachusetts, April 1968.

———. "The Development of Instrumental Exploratory Behavior During the First Year of Human Life." Paper presented at the Society for Research in Child Development meeting, Santa Monica, California, March 1969.

Sokolov, E. N. *Perception and the Conditioned Reflex,* translated by S. W. Waydenfeld. New York: Macmillan, 1963.

Spence, K. W. "Theoretical Interpretations of Learning." In *Handbook of Experimental Psychology,* edited by S. S. Stevens. New York: Wiley, 1951.

Stechler, G. "Newborn Attention as Affected by Medication During Labor." *Science* 144 (1964):315–17.

Thompson, R. F., and Spencer, W. A. "Habituation: A Model Phenomenon for the Study of Neuronal Substrates of Behavior." *Psychological Review* 173(1) (1966):16–43.

Tolman, E. C. *Purposive Behavior in Animals and Men.* New York: Appleton-Century-Crofts, 1932; 1949.

Vedyayev, F. P., and Karmanova, I. G. "On the Comparative Physiology of the Orienting Reflex." In *Orienting Reflex and Exploratory Behavior,* edited by L. G. Voronin, A. N. Leontiev, A. R. Luria, E. N. Sokolov, and O. S. Vinogradova. Moscow: Academy of Pedagogical Sciences of RSFSR, 1958.

Walter, W. G. "The Convergence and Interaction of Visual, Auditory, and Tactual Responses in Human Nonspecific Cortex." *Sensory Evoked Response in Man,* edited by H. E. Whipple. *Annals of the New York Academy of Sciences* 112 (1964): 320–61.

———; Cooper, R.; Aldridge, V. J.; McCallum, W. C.; and Winter, A. L. "Contingent Negative Variation: An Electric Sign of Sensorimotor Association and Expectancy in the Human Brain." *Nature* 203 (1964):380–84.

Editors' note: One of the most fruitful areas of research and theory which has burgeoned in child development over the past decade has been that related to the ability of children to attend selectively to stimuli in their environment. At one time dismissed as a construct too nebulous in definition, attention has once again become a viable area for study, assuming in fact, a critical role in the psychological development of children.

In this chapter, Dr. John Hagen and Mr. Robert Kail present the reader with an account of the research conducted on selective attention in children. Hagen's work, as well as that of others, is reviewed. An up-to-date account is given of the central role of attention in the psychological development of children. While the major focus of the chapter is upon the normal development of selective attention and its relationship to perception and cognition, the discussion also includes implications regarding abnormal development. Hagen and Kail present an excellent research and theoretical foundation on issues pertaining to the education and psychology of distractible children. Hagen and Kail have made progress toward what they have noted as a critical need in the area of attentional research—a bridging of the gap between basic and applied research.

John W. Hagen, Ph.D., is Professor of Psychology and Chairman, Developmental Program, at the University of Michigan. He has served as a consultant to numerous projects as well as on the Commission on the Age of Majority, State of Michigan. His research interests include the development of attention and the effects of verbal processes on memory. He has studied cognitive development in deviant and retarded as well as normal children.

Robert V. Kail, Jr., who received his B.A. from Ohio Wesleyan University and his M.A. from the University of Michigan, is a Ph.D. candidate in the program in developmental psychology at the University of Michigan. His current research interests focus on the development of memory and on the relationship between various cognitive processes and the ability to read. Mr. Kail is an associate member in the Society of Sigma Xi and maintains student memberships in the American Psychological Association and the Society for Research in Child Development.

4

The Role of Attention in Perceptual and Cognitive Development

JOHN W. HAGEN AND ROBERT V. KAIL, JR.

In recent years, attention has been rediscovered as a psychological concept. Much of the renewed interest can be traced to Broadbent's book, *Perception and Communication* (1958). Since its appearance, a multitude of articles, books, and symposia have been devoted to one aspect or another of attention. The vast array of definitions, operational or otherwise, and the variety of measures of attention that have been used attest to the lack of a concise meaning of the concept. It seems appropriate, then, to begin with a consideration of the historical and contemporary definitions of attention. Then, those which have been most useful to developmental psychology will be examined before we begin a review of the empirical developmental literature. This review will focus on development in normal children but will include studies of atypical or abnormal perceptual and cognitive development when they are available. Our own view of attentional processes includes the notion that the child becomes an increasingly active participant in the process with development, and that at least some cognitive difficulties are due to deficits in the development of "attentional strategies" (Hagen and Hale 1973). The case for this view will be made as we proceed.

According to E. G. Boring (1970), "attention is a *dynamic* concept, an *anticipatorily selective* principle." The major question concerns how the individual selects the important information and ignores the unimportant from the vast amount of input that is available to the individual at any given time. "Attention" was accused of being too mentalistic a construct by the Behaviorists and thus was excluded from their accounts, but the construct has been included by most of the major schools of experimental psychology since the time of Wundt (Boring 1950). The Gestalt psychologists viewed attention as an active, ongoing part of the perceptual process. It has been the rise to prominence of the cognitive theories—with their stress on cues, feedback loops, and information-processing "models of the mind"—that has fostered the reinstatement of attention as a viable, and even a key, construct. Because Broadbent's model has made the major impact, and has influenced our thinking on the concept of attention, it is described here. It should be kept in mind that other theories on attention have attained prominence—e.g., Moray (1970) and Mostofsky (1970)—but it would distract from the purpose of this chapter to attempt to provide a critique of them here.

Broadbent's information-processing model incorporates "filters" that operate on incoming information. Information comes into the system through the sense organs and is then subjected to filtering. Only that information passing through the filter (or successive filters) is processed further. Various cue properties of stimuli determine the aspects of information that are retained and eliminated. For example, if an individual is presented a message in a man's voice to the left ear and a message in a woman's voice to the right ear, and then told to learn the content of the message to the left ear, he will later be unable to recall any of the message spoken by the woman's voice. Quite obviously, the individual must perceive enough of this message to identify it as the unwanted message, but according to the model the single cue of voiceness is enough to exclude the message from further processing. Under conditions of information overload, selectivity becomes increasingly important to the individual because there is a finite amount of information that can be processed at any given time. This limitation is the channel capacity, and the efficiency of the channel is dependent upon the efficiency of the filters in selecting out the relevant from the irrelevant messages. While Broadbent has not attempted in his model to account for the development of the ability to process incoming information efficiently, other investigators have done so (Hagen 1967; Maccoby 1967; Maccoby and Hagen 1965). These studies are reviewed in the next section of this chapter.

A particularly rich aspect of Broadbent's model for those interested in cognitive processes is that attention is a multi-level process. Filtering does not occur only once in the processing of information; rather, information may be successively refined. At various stages filters act upon the incoming stimuli to eliminate the irrelevant information from relevant information. Accordingly, attentional processes play a role in information processing at several levels rather than at just a single level. Soviet psychologists have emphasized the role of the orientation of the receptors in attention, certainly one of the first levels of attention (Sokolov 1963). At a later point some of the information striking the receptors is not processed further. Finally, from the information that received further processing, critical components may be selected, while others are ignored. Obviously, the role of attention must be multifaceted. In this chapter, we propose to examine these different conceptions of attention by tracing their development in normal children.

THE DEVELOPMENT OF SELECTIVE ATTENTION

Do children improve with development in the ability to attend selectively to relevant information and to ignore irrelevant information? While one would quite confidently answer this question in the affirmative, it is more difficult to describe just how this improvement comes about. Jeffrey (1968) has proposed that the infant responds to only a limited number of stimuli that have innate salience, such as form or motion; with development, environmental factors provide for increased stimuli to which he may attend. Further, routine patterns of responding to cues emerge, and the child develops schema of his or her environment. These act as stable events that can be used in subsequent learning situations. A considerable amount of empirical evidence supports this general view of Jeffrey, and it is reviewed in Chapter 3 by Michael Lewis in this volume. We shall consider what is known about development in the ability to attend selectively from the preschool through the teenage years.

An obvious hypothesis is that the young child learns to orient the receptor organs, the eyes for example, in order to select certain information from the environment. An unpublished study by Mackworth and Bruner (1966, cited in Maccoby 1969) used eye photography to compare eye movements of six year olds and adults viewing visual stimuli. As compared to the children, the adults spent more time with their eyes focused on the most informative parts of the pictures. In another study, eye movements were compared in children at four age levels from three to nine years (Vurpillot 1968). The children were asked to look at pairs of pictures of houses, each having six windows with certain objects in them. For half the pairs, the windows in the two houses were identical and in half they were different. The task was to determine whether a given pair showed two identical or two different houses. The eye scans of children under six years of age were limited, and judgments were made before sufficient information had been obtained. Children over six years performed quite differently. They more often compared a set of windows of each house, and then proceeded to compare other sets. It is apparent, then, that with age children improve in their use of visual selection of information and attend to those aspects of stimuli that are most informative.

Studies of auditory attention (Maccoby 1969) suggest that selectivity improves with age even when sensory orientation cannot be employed. Auditory messages are presented to the subjects via headphones or stereophonic speakers. The message of simple words to one ear is in a man's voice and the message to the other ear is in a woman's voice, and both are presented simultaneously. The child is told to repeat either the words of the man or of the woman. Between the ages of five and fourteen years, the ability to report the correct message improves considerably (Maccoby 1967, 1969). In subsequent studies, it was found that the older child can attend to a greater range of stimulus cues than the younger child (Maccoby 1969). Linguistic properties of words, both semantic and syntactic, were found to increase the discriminability of the words. Thus, in audition, where it is generally agreed that the sense organs themselves cannot be focused on certain stimuli and "shut off" to others, selective attention has been found to improve with increasing age.

The Central-Incidental Paradigm

To study the development of the ability to select task-relevant (central) information, from task-irrelevant (incidental) information, a task was devised that became the basis of a major research program. In the first experiment (Maccoby and Hagen 1965), picture cards with distinctively colored backgrounds were shown to first, third, fifth, and seventh grade children in arrays that varied in length from four to seven. After a brief exposure, the cards were covered and a cue card of the same color as the background of one of the presentation cards was shown. The task was to identify the hidden card with the matching background color. The picture on the card was not in any way used in this part of the task. A series of such test trials was presented, and on each trial the picture cards were in a different order so there was no learning of position across trials. The number of correct card identifications constituted the *central* task measure. Then a set of pictures with the background color removed was shown along with a set of solid color cards, and the child's task was to match the colors with the pictures with which they had previously appeared. The score on this task constituted the *incidental* measure.

The predictions were derived from Broadbent's theory (1958) reviewed previously. First, central performance was expected to improve with increasing age because it had been found to do so in other studies using a similar task (Atkinson, Hanson, and Bernbach 1964). Second, under conditions in which the task demands are great, some information is excluded, and older subjects should be able to exclude incidental information better than younger subjects. A distractor task was administered to half the subjects at each age level to increase the informational demands of the task situation and thereby insure that both central and incidental information could not be learned. The distractor consisted of a taperecording of piano notes, mostly in the upper register of the keyboard. However, on the average of once every eleven seconds a very low note appeared, and the subject then was required to tap the desk with a small hammer.

As expected, performance on the central task improved with increasing age as did the proportion of central relative to total recall. Incidental performance remained constant until the seventh grade level, where it declined. Next, the effect of the distractor was considered. For the central scores, performance was significantly lower under distracting as compared to nondistracting conditions. However, all ages were affected equally on central recall, so the second prediction was only partially confirmed by the findings. Incidental performance was affected only at the seventh grade level, where it declined.

In a subsequent study, new stimuli were used (Hagen 1967). For the original cards, if the pictures were used as the central objects and the colors as the incidental, there was little or no incidental learning. There may have been some peculiar properties of the figure-background relation that was responsible for the central-incidental task interaction. The new stimuli consisted of pairs of animals and household objects on each card, so the figure-background problem was avoided. Half of the children at each age level were instructed to recall the locations of the animals and half were to recall the household objects. For the incidental measure, separated animals and household objects were given to the subject for pairing. The grade levels tested were the same as the previous study. The major findings of the initial study were replicated. Central recall improved as a function of age level, while incidental performance did not. The auditory distractor lowered central recall about equally at all age levels but decreased incidental recall at the oldest level only. Further, the new stimuli proved to be an improvement over the old: It did not matter whether the subjects were "set" for animals or household objects; incidental performance was the same in either condition.

An interesting pattern emerged when the central and incidental scores were correlated. At the younger age levels those children who did well on the central task tended also to do well on the incidental, while at the oldest age level, high central performance was associated with low incidental performance. It appears, then, that with increasing age the ability to maintain central task performance by excluding certain incidental information improves. The major evidence of this change did not occur until the twelve to thirteen year age range, however. During the grade-school years, improvement in central task recall is not a result of increasing selectivity of task-relevant information.

Perhaps selectivity was not found at earlier ages because the stimuli used were difficult for the younger children to separate perceptually. Hence, in subsequent studies a number of modifications were made in the stimulus configurations. In one study (Hagen and Frisch 1968) the presentation of the incidental stimuli was varied in three ways. In one condition, the earlier method of presentation was replicated, i.e., the incidental picture always appeared with the same central picture. In the other two, pairings were not constant. In the second condition, pairing was random and in the third, the *same* incidental picture was paired with each central picture for a given trial. Recognition rather than recall was tested because the latter could not be used in the two new conditions. It was expected that when the incidental pictures were not always paired with the same central pictures that central recall would improve, especially for the younger subjects. The major results of the earlier studies were replicated, but no differences in central task performance occurred as a result of the pairing conditions. Apparently, younger children are distracted by the mere presence of the incidental pictures; simply being paired with the central pictures is sufficient to cause attention to be directed toward the incidental pictures.

In another attempt to alter performance by changing the configurations of the stimuli, Druker and Hagen (1969) made two changes. In one condition the two pictures on a card were separated spatially from each other, rather than touching each other as in the standard condition. In the second condition, alternating versus nonalternating spatial arrangements were used. In the standard condition it was randomly determined whether the central or the incidental picture appeared in the upper position on the card. A nonalternating arrangement was used here to determine if the incidental stimuli could be more easily differentiated from the central when the central could be scanned visually across the top (or bottom) of the cards. The spacing condition did result in a decrease in incidental recall, but the decline was equal across age levels, from third through ninth grade. Central recall was not affected. The stimuli in the nonalternating arrangement did not affect performance on either task.

Two interesting findings occurred in a post-test questionnaire. Both specific verbal labeling and focused visual scanning of the central pictures were reported more often at the older age levels. It seems that there is a developmental change in the tendency to employ actively certain encoding strategies to facilitate selection of the to-be-learned stimuli, but the changes introduced experimentally in the stimuli have little effect on the employment of these strategies.

In a recent study, Sabo and Hagen (1973) introduced two variations—one aimed at improving perceptual discriminability and one aimed at facilitating the use of encoding strategies. For the first, the central pictures were all of one color and the incidental pictures were all of another color. Color did improve children's simple recognition of the pictures but the effect was the same across age levels which were at the third, fifth, and seventh grades. In the other condition, a ten-second delay was imposed between the presentation of the stimuli and viewing of the cue card. For half the subjects the delay was unfilled, but for the other half the subjects were required to count out loud. The younger subjects were not affected in their performance by this manipulation, but the older subjects were: Recall was considerably better when the delay was unfilled than when the distracting task had to be performed. This finding is consistent with our above suggestion that, with development, children begin to employ task-relevant strategies. Another recent study (Hagen and Kail 1973) confirms that if these strategies are interfered with by the imposition of a distraction task central performance of older children is reduced to a level of performance similar to that of children several years younger. Because young children (at six to eight years) do not use these strategies anyway, their performance is not affected. Hence, in tasks requiring selective attention for effective performance, there is evidence that the requisite skills do not simply emerge passively but rather they come to be used actively as the child develops. Whether younger children cannot, or simply do not, use these encoding strategies remains to be demonstrated.

Related Evidence

At this point, one may wonder if the findings cited concerning the central-incidental paradigm have any generality beyond the tasks used. There have been a number of studies by other investigators that add substantial support to our findings. In one study, second and sixth graders were compared in the ability to attend to cues of relevant as compared to irrelevant dimensions in a visual discrimination task (Crane and Ross 1967). After initial learning, additional practice was given in which both relevant and previously irrelevant dimensions could be used. Then a new learning problem was introduced using the same stimuli from both dimensions. The younger children were found to be using cues from both dimensions in this task, but the older children used cues primarily from the original relevant dimension. A discrimination task that had both central and incidental cues was also used by Siegel and Stevenson (1966). An increase in incidental learning was found between the ages of seven and twelve years, and a decline occurred between ages twelve and fourteen years.

Baker (1970) used Hagen's central-incidental stimuli and varied the number of trials presented at age levels eight, ten, and twelve years. She found that incidental scores were higher at the two younger levels with increased exposure to the stimuli, but there was no increase in incidental performance at the oldest age level. Thus younger children continued to attend to these stimuli through the task, but the twelve year olds increased their selectivity as the task progressed.

A naturalistic presentation of a stimulus situation was employed by Hale, Miller, and Stevenson (1968). A film that had an interesting plot was shown to grade-school children. After viewing the film, the subjects answered a series of questions, some pertaining to issues central to the main plot and others referring to incidental features. Recall of incidental details increased somewhat with increasing grade level until the seventh grade, where a drop occurred. Thus, once again, a decline of incidental learning, reflecting less processing of task-irrelevant information, occurred at just about the same age level where it has been found to occur in the great majority of the previously cited studies.

To conclude this section, the recent work of Gordon Hale and his colleagues at the Educational Testing Service is described. Hale also has been interested in the effects of varying systematically certain aspects of the stimuli. Hale and Piper (1973) used pictures of animals and objects similar to those used by Hagen, but they were paired in varying degrees of action relationships. For example, in the standard condition, a bear and a broom appeared on the card. In one variant, the bear was holding the broom; in the next, the bear was sweeping with it. The latter arrangement should form a unitary scene that should be more salient or meaningful for all subjects, but in particular it was expected to increase incidental learning in the older subjects. It was found that increasing the action relationship did increase incidental learning, but not more so at the older ages.

In one study, however, incidental learning was increased, especially at the oldest age level (Hale and Piper 1974). Geometric shapes were used as the central stimuli and colors were used as the incidental. The colors were varied in their relation to the shapes. In one condition, for example, a yellow card contained a black outline drawing of a triangle, but in another the triangle itself was yellow, the incidental color. In the former condition incidental learning showed the relation to age found previously, but in the latter condition, both central and incidental scores increased markedly between ages eight and twelve years. It is apparent here that the key difference in the conditions must be in the relation between the central and incidental features. In both instances it is not possible to focus the eyes only on the central features at the expense of the incidental. However, upon viewing these stimuli it is obvious that the incidental component is "integrally contained within the central stimulus elements, while for the shapes on colored backgrounds, the incidental information was independent of the central feature" (Hagen and Hale 1973, p. 126).

This seemingly anomalous finding provides for a refined interpretation of the situation. If the central and incidental components can readily be recognized as elements independent of each other, there is an increasing tendency to do so with development. However, when the components cannot easily be regarded as separate entities, to attempt such separation is no longer a task-appropriate strategy. The more efficient approach here may well be to attend to all aspects of the stimuli rather than to try to separate the relevant from the irrelevant features. This interpretation, then, still views the older child as a more efficient processor of information. Further, selectivity in attention of children in the age range under investigation here clearly comes about through the employment of task-appropriate encoding strategies rather than through the use of increasingly finer perceptual discriminations of the stimuli themselves.

Deficits in Attention

Do children with deficits in perceptual and cognitive task performance show deficits when tested on these tasks designed to measure the ability to selectively attend to task-relevant information? In his chapter on distractibility in the learning disabled child (Chapter 5 of this volume) Hallahan reviews many studies that bear on the issues, and we shall not attempt to review these again here. Rather, only those studies are considered that provide direct evidence on the major points emphasized in this chapter.

The central-incidental task has been administered to retarded children (Hagen and Huntsman 1971). The retardates attended special education classes, and the normal control children were in nursery school or regular public school classrooms. The normal children had average IQ scores of approximately 100, while there were two levels of IQ in the retarded group, mean scores of approximately 50 and 75. In terms of CA, the normal children ranged from four to eight years, while the retardates ranged from eight to twelve years. Four MA levels were used with approximate means of four, six, seven, and nine years, and there were equal numbers of retardates and normal children at each level. The results showed that selective attention improved as MA level increased for both the normal and retarded groups. In fact, retardates performed as well as normal subjects at the same MA level, though their performance was significantly lower when compared to normal subjects of equivalent CA level.

The findings are consistent with results reported by Zeaman and House (1963) who assessed the role of attention in discrimination learning. In their studies, even when retardates' performance is compared to younger, normal children of equivalent MA levels, their attention deficit appears. However, it should be pointed out that Zeaman and House's retardates have been institutionalized, while ours lived at home. A sample of institutionalized retardates was tested next. It was found that when MA comparisons were made, the performance of these children was lower than that of either the normal or the noninstitutionalized retardates. It appears that institutionalization is the factor more strongly related to poor selective attention in the central-incidental task. Zigler (1966) has argued that motivational and emotional factors attributable to institutionalization rather than retardation *per se* contribute to deficits in performance. We also believe that institutional environments are not conducive to good cognitive growth and that retardation *per se* is not the only explanation for lower performance in the central-incidental task.

A subsequent study provides evidence on the trainability of mildly retarded children in the selective attention task (Hagen and West 1970). A modification in the procedure provided for a primary and a secondary dimension rather than the central and incidental components. The subjects were instructed to remember pictures of both dimensions, and pennies were earned for correct recall, but the payoff was five times as great for the primary pictures as compared to the secondary. A much greater proportion of primary than of secondary pictures were recalled. For those subjects with a mean MA level of eight years, the differential payoff proved to be very successful: Their recall of primary pictures improved steadily as a function of the number of trials given. An older group, with a mean MA of 10.6 years, did not show this improvement in selectivity of attention to the primary dimension over trials, but their initial performance was considerably better in the initial trials, so perhaps the training was not needed for them. The findings of this study do provide evidence that retardates can profit from differential reward and improve their performance in a task requiring attention to cues of different reinforcement values.

A cross-cultural study of selective attention by Daniel Wagner (1974) of our laboratory provides some further evidence on sources of differences in task performance. The central-incidental task was administered to children and adults in Yucatan, Mexico, in a version using pictures from a game well known to the people there. Developmental comparisons were made among both urban and rural residents. The interaction between age and central-incidental performance was replicated for the urban sample, although the decline in incidental performance did not occur until just after sixteen years. The findings for the rural sample were very different. There was no increase in central recall, although an age span of over twenty years was tested! Incidental performance showed some increase, and declined only at the oldest age level, twenty-seven years. For both measures, performance was considerably lower in the rural than in the urban groups.

It is provocative to note here that two types of environmental variation have been found to have strong effects on performance in the selective attention task: urban versus rural cultural settings, and institutional versus noninstitutional living among retarded children. There are so many differences among these settings that it is not possible to offer any sound explanations for the crucial differences. However, the implication that environmental or ecological factors play critical roles in determining how attention is deployed is indeed clear.

Hallahan (Chapter 5) has concluded, although very tentatively, that children with learning disabilities perform less well in tasks measuring selective attention than do mentally retarded children of the same MA level. If this conclusion is borne out in subsequent research, there are some very important implications. First, it suggests that the search for specific deficits in the performance of the learning disabled child may well prove to be fruitful and may help to provide an organizing theme in this search. Second, we believe the evidence supports the view that the ability being measured by the central-incidental and similar tasks is more cognitive than perceptual. Third, the employment of encoding strategies is essential in the development of selective attention. If at least a part of the problem of the learning disabled child is cognitively based, then training programs must be designed to deal specifically with techniques that will foster the use of encoding strategies. The research on retarded subjects has helped to pave the way for studies on learning disabilities, and Hallahan's research has provided the initial link that should lead to a better rapprochement among the various studies of populations with cognitive deficits.

ATTENTION AND DISCRIMINATION LEARNING

In the discussion of selective attention, we concluded that with development children become more adept at attending to task-relevant stimuli at the expense of incidental or task-irrelevant stimuli. In this section we will examine the role of attention in a similar situation, that of discrimination learning. In this case, a particular attribute of a stimulus is relevant to the solution of a problem, and the child must attend to that characteristic, instead of another, irrelevant feature of the stimuli. For example, if the child is learning to discriminate between the letters *b* and *h,* the child cannot differentiate the central from the incidental stimuli. Both the *b* and *h* are central stimuli, and the child must attend to each. But to learn this discrimination requires the child to attend to the critical attribute that differentiates these stimuli, in this case, the shape of the bottom of the letter.

A discrimination learning task typically involves the simultaneous presentation of two stimuli. The child is shown these stimuli and is asked to choose the correct one. The child receives a marble, token, or similar reward for each correct response. The stimuli used may vary along a single dimension. For example, they may differ only in their shape, or they may

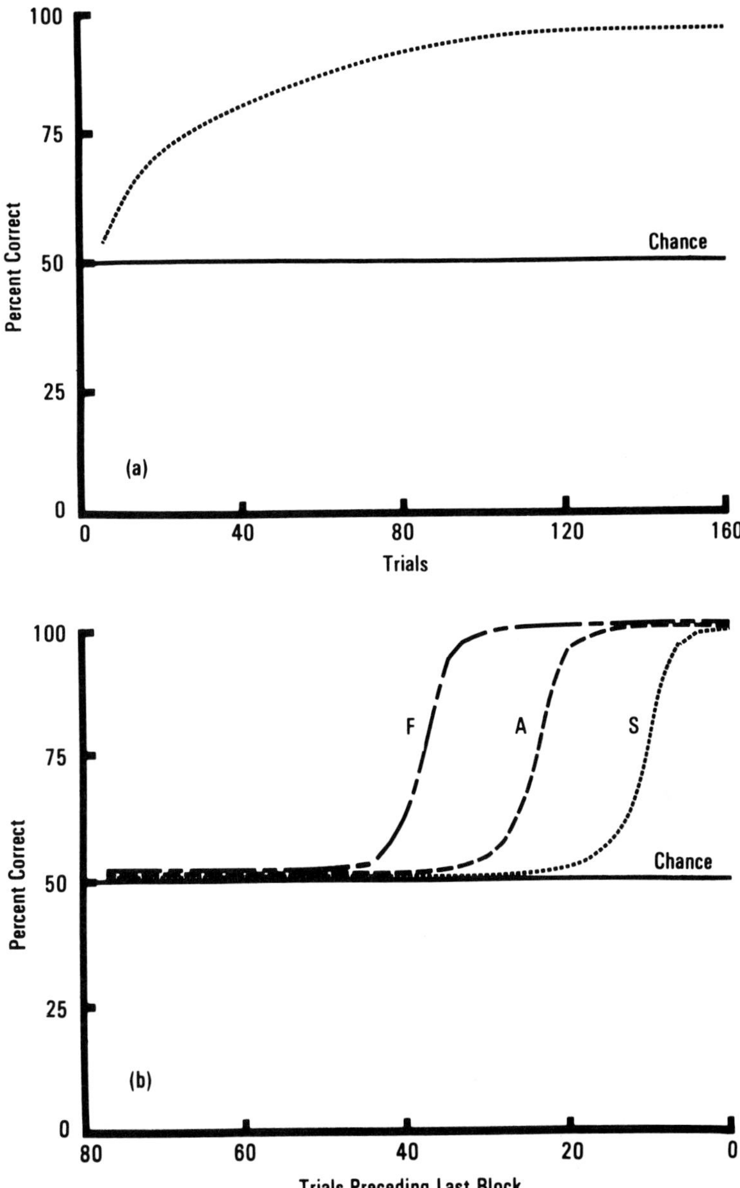

Figure 4.1. Theoretical learning curves for simple discrimination tasks: (*a*) a forward learning curve based on grouped data; (*b*) a backwards learning curve for a fast, average, and slow learner.

differ along several additional dimensions (e.g., color, size) as well. Of course, initially the child can only guess because the experimenter has arbitrarily determined the correct stimulus. After several trials the child ceases making errors as he or she starts responding on the basis of the proper cue of the stimulus, rather than guessing on the basis of some irrelevant cue. It is assumed that the child has learned the discrimination when the child makes a series of consecutive correct responses.

According to a stimulus-response, associationist explanation (Spence 1956), discrimination learning occurs gradually as a hierarchy of habit strengths develops (see Figure 4.1*a*). On each presentation of the stimuli, certain stimuli are reinforced and others are not, resulting in a gradation of habit strength based upon the number of reinforcements received. The discrimination will be learned when the habit strength for the correct stimulus is reliably greater than the strength for all other stimuli.

However, these analyses of performance were typically based on the data from groups of subjects rather than individuals. Zeaman and House (1963) examined the performance of individuals in this task using a technique known as a "backwards learning curve." In this procedure, a single subject's data is analyzed backwards from the point at which the subject learned the discrimination. In this manner, the performance of subjects who learned the discrimination at different rates is more readily compared. Using this form of analysis, it is evident that the group data do not reflect individual performance (see Figure 4.1*b*). Instead of a gradual rise in performance over trials, correct responding remains at chance level for several trials, then rapidly increases to nearly perfect for the duration of the experiment.

An Attentional Theory of Discrimination Learning

An associationistic model cannot easily account for this abrupt improvement in performance, and Zeaman and House (1963) proposed an alternative explanation.* They suggested that discrimination learning actually involves two successive processes: an attentional response and an instrumental response. In the first stage, the child attends to a stimulus dimension; in the second, the child makes an instrumental response to a stimulus cue. If the stimuli vary on more than a single dimension, it is assumed that the child attends to only one dimension on a particular trial.

*A third theory that proposes to explain learning in a discrimination task is the verbal mediation theory proposed by Kendler and Kendler (1962). Like the Zeaman and House (1963) model, it is a two-stage theory that postulates a mediating link in the learning of discriminations. Unlike the attentional model, Kendler and Kendler propose that the mediating link is verbal. On an empirical level it is difficult to differentiate between the two approaches; in many situations they make identical predictions. At a theoretical level, they are also difficult to separate. Stevenson has suggested that for older children, "verbalization may have a directing influence on attention, and conversely, the appearance of salient cues may be conducive to verbalization about these cues" (1972, p. 253). Nevertheless, the results of various studies with younger, presumably preverbal children suggest the utility of the attentional rather than the mediational model (Wolff 1967).

In terms of the data depicted in Figure 4.1*b*, it is assumed that the child is not yet attending to the correct stimulus dimension while his or her performance remains at chance level. The rapid improvement in the number of correct responses reflects the child's attention to the relevant dimension and subsequent learning of the appropriate instrumental response to the positive cue.

The relative importance of the attentional versus the instrumental responses in learning has been examined in a large body of research using various "shift" procedures. In these experiments, subjects first learn a discrimination to criterion. When the child has reached this advanced level of learning, the experimenter changes the rules of reinforcement *without* telling the child that such a change has occurred. By changing these rules in specific ways it is possible to test the influence of the different responses on the rate of learning the discrimination.

In an *intradimensional shift* the relevant dimension during original learning remains relevant following the shift. However, two totally novel stimuli are introduced on this relevant dimension. For example, green may have provided the positive and red the negative cue during original learning. Following an intradimensional shift, two new colors are arbitrarily associated with positive and negative outcomes. In this type of shift, the probability of attending to the relevant dimension is quite high because it has not changed from original learning. The probability of making a correct instrumental response is at chance level, because neither has been presented or reinforced previously.

In an *extradimensional shift,* the relevant dimension from original learning now becomes irrelevant to the solution as a new, previously irrelevant dimension becomes the key to learning the discrimination. Thus, color may be replaced by form as the relevant dimension, and two stimuli differing in form are assigned to the positive and negative outcomes. In this case, the likelihood of the child's attending to the new relevant dimension is initially very low, while the probability of making a correct instrumental response is at chance level, as in the intradimensional shift.

A comparison of the learning curves following these shifts would indicate the importance of each type of response in discrimination learning. If attention to the relevant dimension is the critical component, then the intradimensional shift should result in a much higher rate of learning than the extradimensional shift. In general, intradimensional shifts are easier to learn than extradimensional shifts, for retardates (Campione, Hyman, and Zeaman 1965), preschool children (Trabasso, Deutsch, and Gelman 1966), and older children (Furth and Youniss 1964). Changes in the positive and negative cues associated with reward result in only a minor decrement in the child's correct responding. However, a change in the dimension that is relevant to the solution leads to a marked decline in performance that is eliminated only after an extended series of post-shift trials.

While the associationistic and attentional theories clearly differ in their explanation of discrimination learning, they are similar in their conceptualization of the subject's activity during the task. In both cases, the subject's role consists of passively attending to stimuli and subsequently making a response. An alternative model suggests that the subject is actively testing and rejecting hypotheses throughout the experiment, in order to find a solution that will lead to consistent reinforcement.

This model was tested by Eimas (1969*a*) in a way that differed from the typical discrimination learning experiment in that the subject was not told on every trial if he or she had made a correct choice. Rather, on four of every sixteen trials the subject was told of the correctness of the response; on the remaining twelve trials (called "blank" trials) this information was not provided. By analyzing the child's pattern of responding during the blank trials, it was possible to determine if the child was using hypotheses. For example, if the large stimulus appeared on the left side of the display on trials 5, 7, 9, 11, 13, and 15 and on the right side on trials 6, 8, 10, 12, 14, and 16, we would assume that the child is testing the hypothesis that the large stimulus is correct if he alternated his choices between left and right. Similarly, if the triangle was on the left for trials 5–10 but on the right for trials 11–16, the child apparently had hypothesized that the triangle was the positive cue if he made six left followed by six right responses. Eimas found that second, fourth, sixth, and eighth grade children all demonstrated hypothesis testing on the blank trials. Thus, the conception of attention in discrimination learning may also involve the deployment of strategies similar to those found to be used in selective attention.

It is apparent that the associationistic model cannot readily explain these abrupt changes that occur in the course of discrimination learning. On the other hand, the attention theory of Zeaman and House (1963) predicts the obtained results quite well. The critical factor determining the ease with which discriminations are learned is the likelihood that the child will attend to the relevant dimension.

Variables Influencing the Attentional Response

To a certain extent the probability that the child will sample the relevant dimension is determined by chance. But it is also true that experimentally it is possible to create situations that are likely to facilitate the child's attending to the relevant dimension and, consequently, can facilitate the child's learning of discriminations. Similarly, we can make it highly unlikely that the child will select the appropriate dimension and can make the discrimination very difficult as a result. We shall now examine some of the means of facilitating or distracting the child's attention.

Stimulus variables. One straightforward implication of the attentional parameter of the Zeaman and House (1963) model is that the difficulty of the discrimination should increase as the number of irrelevant dimensions increases. (An irrelevant dimension is defined as being not correlated with reward.) This difficulty would be predicted because the probability that the child will correctly sample the relevant dimension by chance is inversely related to the number of irrelevant dimensions. These predictions were tested in an experiment by Lubker (1969). In her experiment, there were three dimensions—color, size, and form—with the latter always the relevant dimension. The stimuli presented to the seven- and eleven-year-old children differed according to the number of irrelevant dimensions present in the stimuli. For one group, there were no irrelevant dimensions, and stimuli differed only along the relevant dimension. A second group of subjects was presented stimuli that differed with respect to an irrelevant dimension—brightness—as well as the relevant dimension—form. For a third group of children, the stimuli varied on all three dimensions, thus yielding two irrelevant dimensions—(brightness and size)—in addition to the relevant form dimension. The results were in accord with the predictions made by the attentional model. Learning was facilitated by the *absence* of irrelevant dimensions. In fact, after all fifty-six training trials were completed, the performance of those children who were tested with either one or two irrelevant dimensions present did not differ strikingly from chance levels.

Because added irrelevant dimensions interfere with learning, an obvious question we might ask is whether added relevant cues can facilitate learning. That is, if we provide cues that are redundant (e.g., the correct stimulus is always large *and* white), will this help the child learn more rapidly? Several experiments (Crane and Ross 1967; Eimas 1969*b*) have demonstrated that such redundancy in the stimulus display does facilitate discrimination learning.

In terms of the Zeaman and House model, this facilitation occurs because the probability that the child will attend to a correct dimension by chance is increased as redundant relevant dimensions are added. An alternative explanation suggests that the child can attend to more than a single dimension at a time, and that such compound dimensions provide more effective cues than single dimensions. This "multiple-look" model (House and Zeaman 1963) is merely an elaboration of the original Zeaman and House (1963) "single-look" model and shares the other assumptions of the attentional theory. Eimas (1969*b*) trained kindergarten, second and fourth grade children on a two-choice simultaneous discrimination with either two, three, or four redundant relevant cues. After successfully mastering the initial discrimination, the child was given test trials that measured performance on the discrimination using each relevant cue separately. Children at all ages demonstrated learning of at least two separate dimensions, and the fourth graders were able to use three of the four individual dimensions in the test sequence.

However, the results also demonstrated that the relationship between the number of redundant relevant cues and the learning of individual cues is not linear. When trained with two or three relevant cues, kindergarten children responded correctly to two of these cues in the test trials, but could discriminate only along a single dimension on the test trials when initially trained with four redundant relevant cues. Furthermore, although the initial discrimination was learned more rapidly when there were three or four redundant cues, these differences were not significant. Thus, it appears that while the child may benefit from the presence of multiple cues, too much redundancy adds little to improve learning and actually interferes with the learning of individual dimensions.

Because it is critical for the child to attend to the relevant dimension, one way that we could facilitate learning would be to highlight the relevant cue for the child. Thus, if we can induce the child to attend to the relevant cue immediately, then the child need only learn the instrumental response to the positive cue. One way that near errorless learning has been achieved is through the use of a "fading-in" technique. In this procedure the critical components of the stimuli are first presented in isolation. Then, as the experiment progresses, other irrelevant aspects of the stimuli are also presented. With these procedures even animals can achieve errorless discrimination learning (Terrace 1966).

Using this technique Caron (1968) taught three-year-olds to discriminate between figures on the basis of their angularity or curvature. Initially the critical angles and curves of the stimuli were marked with black ink and the irrelevant aspects of the stimuli were barely perceptible. In a series of five graded steps the outlines of the stimuli became darker and the ink used for highlighting purposes was eliminated. Children trained with this fading technique made fewer errors in learning the discrimination and did so in fewer trials than did a control group.

Subject variables. To this point we have followed the assumptions made by Zeaman and House (1963) that on each trial the child randomly samples from the pool of available dimensions. However, this assumption was made to clarify the quantitative aspects of the model and need not typify the performance of an individual child as he or she tries to learn the discrimination. On the contrary, we would expect that individual children certainly have various idiosyncratic preferences for different stimuli that initially affect their rate of learning.

Everyday observation would seem to suggest that children like novelty, and these observations have been supported experimentally (Cantor 1969). For example, when given the opportunity to choose between playing with a novel or familiar toy, children will generally select the novel toy (Endsley 1967). Would the presence of novel stimuli affect children's attention in a discrimination task? White (1966) compared the discrimination learning of children of four different ages in three conditions. In the two experimental groups, one stimulus was the same on all trials, while the second stimulus was always a completely novel stimulus on each trial. For one experimental group the varying stimulus was the positive cue; for the second experimental group, it served as the negative cue. With the nursery school children, both experimental conditions were more difficult than the control condition in which neither stimulus varied. The varying negative experimental condition was more difficult than the varying positive and control conditions for the kindergarten, first, and second grade children. At the fourth grade level, all differences were eliminated between the three conditions. The presentation of a novel stimulus can result in a decrement in performance, but this result is not stable across all ages. Stevenson (1972) has suggested that repeated presentation of the positive cue may induce habituation and, consequently, a decline in the effectiveness of this cue to elicit attentional and instrumental responses in comparison to a completely novel stimulus. Thus we have the paradoxical situation that once having achieved a level of perfect or near-perfect performance, the child's rate of correct responding may decline due to the very effectiveness of the positive cue!

Another way that children could conceivably differ might be in their preference for the various attributes or dimensions of the stimuli used in these experiments. If children prefer a particular characteristic of stimuli, such as color, they may be more likely to attend to that dimension than to a less preferred dimension. Preferences for different dimensions of stimuli were tested by Suchman and Trabasso (1966). Nursery school and kindergarten children were allowed to choose stimuli that varied according to form, color, and size. More than 90 percent of the children tested were consistent in choosing stimuli according to a particular dimension, and there were developmental differences in the typically preferred dimension. The younger children generally preferred color and the older children preferred form, with the transition occuring at approximately age four years. To determine if these preferences could influence the rate of discrimination learning, Trabasso, Stave, and Eichburg (1969) first determined preschoolers' preferences for form or color, then tested them on a two-choice color-form discrimination. In two experiments, children whose preferred dimension was relevant solved the discrimination more rapidly than did the children for whom the unpreferred dimension was relevant. Preference for the relevant dimension evidently facilitated attention to the relevant dimension, resulting in a higher rate of discrimination learning for these children.

These results were replicated in a study by Seitz and Weir (1971). The primary difference between this experiment and the Trabasso *et al.* (1969) study is that a more elaborate procedure was used to assess the dimension preferences of the four-and-one-half-year-old subjects. There were two important results from the use of the more refined procedure. First, though some children preferred either form or color, there was a large number of children with equal dimensional preference. This suggests that many of the children classified as preferring either form or color probably had equal dimensional preference. More important, only one-third of those children for whom the preferred dimension was irrelevant solved the discrimination within 100 trials. Clearly dimensional preferences not only influence the rate at which children begin to attend regularly to the relevant dimension, but also strongly determine whether the problem will be solved at all.

Thus we conclude that there are many ways to facilitate or disrupt the child's learning in these tasks. As stimuli in the task become more complicated with the addition of irrelevant dimensions the discrimination becomes increasingly difficult. Whether this is a consequence *only* of the low probability of the child's sampling the relevant dimension or of the distracting presence of the irrelevant dimensions is unclear. We can facilitate the child's attention to the relevant stimulus characteristics by adding redundant relevant dimensions, but only to a limited extent. Two or three redundant dimensions seem to yield a maximal facilitation of learning, and there are diminishing returns as additional dimensions are added. These added dimensions, though relevant, may possibly distract some children in certain situations. To eliminate the distracting cues provided by irrelevant stimulus dimensions, errorless learning can be induced using a fading-in technique. Finally, an examination of the child's preferences showed that presentation of novel stimuli could have detrimental effects on the rate of learning, and that congruence between the subject's preferred dimension and the task-relevant dimension may be essential for discrimination learning.

Discrimination Learning in the Mentally Retarded

A fortunate circumstance for researchers working with exceptional children is that the Zeaman and House (1963) attentional model was originally developed as a theory of retardate discrimination learning. As a consequence, a systematic and thorough research program has been devoted to the investigation of the role of attention in retardate learning. In this concluding section on discrimination learning the variables that were found to influence the rate of learning of the normal child are examined to see if they have similar effects on the learning of retarded children.

Before catáloging these effects, however, it is important to determine if the basic processes postulated in the attentional model operate in the discrimination learning of the retardate as they do with the normal child. Zeaman and House (1963, pp. 162–64) tested eleven- and twelve-year-old retardates of two different mental ages (two, four years) on a simple color-form discrimination. Several conclusions are readily apparent from their data. First, the children at the higher MA did learn the discrimination more rapidly, but the shapes of the learning curves are almost identical. Both groups show the abrupt, rapid learning followed by near-perfect performance, and differed only in the number of trials during which performance remained at chance levels. Second, the performance of those children who failed to learn the task was consistently at a steady chance level of responding. There was no indication that these nonlearning children were merely slower in forming approach and avoidance responses than the learners, as the associationistic position might suggest. Rather the performance of the nonlearners was marked by an apparent inability to attend continuously to the relevant dimension.

Thus, as with normal children, the rate of learning a discrimination is primarily a function of the rate that the child learns to attend to the relevant dimension. Furthermore, a retardate attention deficit seems to be a principal factor in the difference between children of varying degrees of MA and one of the differences between normal and retarded children. Learning rates, once the subject is attending to the relevant dimension, do not differ between retardates with IQs as low as 25 and normal children. However, even when the performance of retardates is compared to younger, normal children of equal mental age, the attention deficit appears (House and Zeaman 1963). Clearly, the attending response is a problem area for the retarded child.

Given this degree of attentional deficit in the retardate, how well does the child respond to the manipulations described in the previous section that were so effective in facilitating or distracting the normal child's learning? Ullman and Routh (1972) compared the ability of retarded and nonretarded subjects matched on mental age (MA = six years) to utilize relevant redundant cues in discrimination learning. While the retarded subjects made more errors overall than did the normal children, both groups benefited equally from the presence of the redundant cues. Most of the improvement in learning for both groups occurred with the addition of the first redundant relevant dimension, replicating separate findings with normal children (Eimas 1969*b*). Further, House and Zeaman (1963) found that retarded children with higher mental ages use compound cues formed by redundant relevant dimensions more than do children of lower mental age.

Bricker, Heal, Bricker, Hayes, and Larsen (1969) have demonstrated the effectiveness of the fading-in technique (Caron 1968) to induce very high levels of performance in retardates (MA = 1.4–4.6 years). In this experiment the stimuli were presented in illuminated windows. At the start of the experiment, the window containing the positive cue was at maximum illumination, while the negative cue was illuminated at the minimum intensity. Following each correct response the illumination of the positive window was decreased and increased in the negative window in a sequence of nine steps. The group trained with the fading technique had significantly fewer errors during learning than did the control group.

A preference for novel over familiar stimuli has also been demonstrated in the discrimination learning of retardates. House and Zeaman (1958) presented a single stimulus on the first trial that was reinforced exactly 50 percent of the time. On the second trial this stimulus and a second, novel, stimulus were presented. When the single stimulus on the first trial had not been reinforced, subjects selected the novel stimulus more frequently on trial 2. However, these results also were obtained when the stimulus on trial 1 *was reinforced;* again subjects preferred the novel stimulus on the second trial. Thus, with retardates, novelty is an attribute of stimuli that can exert strong control over the attentional component of discrimination learning.

Similar effects have been obtained from investigations of the role of subject preferences in retardate discrimination learning. Heal, Bransky, and Mankinen (1966) first assessed retardates' dimensional preferences, then tested their discrimination learning. Their results replicated findings by Trabasso *et al.* (1969) with normal children in that the rate of learning was much higher when the subject's preferred dimension was the relevant dimension. In fact, the magnitude of the difference is probably even larger than these results indicate, because Heal *et al.* employed a very general index of dimensional preference, rather than the more sensitive procedures employed by Seitz and Weir (1971). Consequently, these data most likely present a conservative estimate of the detrimental effect of subject preference–task relevance incongruity.

Discrimination learning has been the subject of considerable investigation by psychologists, and from the material reviewed here it is apparent that attention to relevant cues is an essential component in this type of learning situation. The fact that much learning occurs abruptly, or in an all-or-none fashion, is at first surprising, but when one considers that the typical task consists of various dimensions that may be considered, accepted, or rejected individually in attempting to find the "correct" cue, then all-or-none learning makes intuitive sense. An incorrect dimension cannot provide relevant information about the correct response, so the individual must start over in the quest for problem solution. The two components identified in discrimination learning emphasize the importance of careful diagnosis of the specific aspects of deficit found in the child with learning disability. The developmental changes found to occur in children's discrimination learning are consistent with our model that the ability to pay attention improves as active, deliberate strategies to cue selection emerge and become refined with increasing age.

ATTENTION AND COGNITIVE STYLES

Any observer of children is aware that great individual differences can be readily observed in the way children go about solving problems that confront them. Some seem more concerned with getting through the task as quickly as possible, while others take a deliberate, organized approach to the situation. Apparently children differ in their general strategies for processing information, and in many tasks the child's success depends to a large degree on how the child proceeds with the task at hand. We have already examined a considerable amount of literature on the development of selective attention, and we shall now consider cognitive styles as relevant to attention, an area in which the focus has been on individual differences as well as on developmental differences.

One theorist has offered a developmental framework within which the various cognitive styles may be organized. Santostephano (1969, 1971) proposed that four dimensions, each typified by a certain information-processing style, can be ordered in terms of their emergence. As the child matures, he moves through each of these control dimensions and on to the next. The dimensions are called: focal attention, field articulation, leveling-sharpening, and equivalence range. It is the second that is closely related to attentional processes as considered here. At the second control level, field articulation, attention can be directed to relevant information and at the same time withheld from irrelevant. While it is obvious that even at a young age the child can employ this control to a degree, from the research using the central-incidental task it is evident that improvement in this ability continues at least into the adolescent period.

More than two dozen different cognitive styles have been identified and studied, and the interested reader is referred to Kagan and Kogan (1970) and to Santostephano (1969, 1971) for thorough reviews of this literature. Two of the best known and most thoroughly studied of these are considered here, each of which has a clear link to attentional abilities. It should be emphasized before we begin that while individuals differ in the way they employ these dimensions, there is no necessary "right" or "wrong" end to the dimensions, and under some conditions an individual may respond in a style that occurred developmentally earlier in his or her history. The important point is that there is a consistency in the use of the style that can be identified as characteristic of a particular phase in development or of a particular individual.

The dimension of reflection-impulsivity was identified by Kagan (Kagan and Kogan 1970) as basic to the way children approach many of the everyday tasks they encounter. The test used to assess the child's position on this dimension is called the Matching Familiar Figures Test (MFF). A standard picture, such as a teddy bear sitting on a chair, is shown. Another set of pictures is then shown that includes an exact replica of the standard and others containing slight variations. On one, an ear may be positioned differently than in the standard. On another, the chair may have only three legs. The child must identify the picture that is identical to the original. Both the child's speed of responding and the child's accuracy are recorded. Within the age range of five to twelve years, errors decrease and response time increases. At each age level, the children who take longer to make their responses also make the fewest errors. Individual children are remarkably stable in their tendency to be either reflective (low error rate and longer response times) or impulsive (high error rate and shorter response times). Attempts to train children to be more reflective have been successful at increasing response latency but not in reducing errors (Kagan and Kogan 1970).

Performance on this task is also predictive of performance in other situations. Children found to be reflective performed better in an inductive reasoning task in which information was presented aurally than did impulsive children (Kagan, Pearson, and Welch 1966). Recently preschool reflective and impulsive children were tested on recognition memory (Siegel, Kirasic, and Kilburg 1973). For easy items, the two groups did not differ in their recognition scores, but for difficult items, which according to the authors required more detailed analysis of differentiating features, the reflective children performed better than the impulsive children.

To determine why some children respond impulsively while others take a more reflective approach, strategies used in visual scanning of the stimuli have been studied. Drake (1970) recorded eye movements and found that the number of fixations made by the eyes and the time spent looking at the standard and its variants were greater among reflective as compared to impulsive children. This finding is not surprising since these children spend more time at the task than do impulsive children. When proportion of time spent looking at the standard as compared to the variants was considered,

Drake found that third grade reflective children had higher standard/variant proportions than did impulsive children, but Siegelman (1969) found the opposite result for fourth grade boys. The apparent contradiction here is clarified somewhat in a more recent study of third grade children (Zelnicker, Jeffrey, Ault, and Parsons 1972). Both groups of children made visual comparisons between the standard and its variants, but the reflective children spent a greater proportion of their time making paired comparisons between the standard and its variants than did the impulsive children. It is apparent that these children approached the problem with a systematic strategy. The particular aspects of the stimuli focused upon apparently are not as important as the systematic comparisons made among these aspects.

Perhaps the best-known of the cognitive styles is field differentiation. Witkin and his associates (Witkin, Lewis, Hertzman, Machover, Meissner, and Wapner 1954) have described this dimension on which individuals differ in their approach to perceptual tasks. The two ends of the dimension are identified as field dependence and field independence. At the field dependence end, limited differentiation of perceptual fields occurs; discriminations are made globally. At the field-independence end, differentiation is much more precise and small differences are noticed.

Three different measures have been used to assess the individual's position on this dimension. In the first, an individual is seated on a chair in a chamber. Both the chair and the chamber can be tilted. The chamber is placed in a tilted position considerably off from the vertical, as is the chair. The subject can change the position of the chair, and he is instructed to orient himself so that he is sitting at the "true vertical." This task is not easy because the chamber completely occupies his visual world. The second measure uses a portable apparatus to accomplish the same purpose as the first. A frame, like a picture frame, contains a vertical rod that can be adjusted to various angles within the frame. The frame is placed at various angles in relation to the true vertical by the experimenter, and the subject's task is to adjust the angle of the rod to the vertical in spite of the tilted appearance of the frame that surrounds it. The testing room is darkened to eliminate visual cues and the subject's accuracy in orienting the rod is measured. The third measure is somewhat different, and has become the most-often used measure. A simple geometric figure is shown, followed by a complex figure in which the simple figure is embedded. Hence, the test is known as the embedded figures test (EFT). Twenty-four different sets of figures are presented and the average time taken to locate each figure is recorded. The scores on these three measures correlate very highly among themselves, and of the three the EFT has proved to be the most useful single measure.

An individual's performance on these tests is remarkably stable from one testing to another, even over a number of years (Witkin, Goodenough, and Karp 1967). With increasing age, there is a progression from the global, relatively undifferentiated mode of perceptual-cognitive responding to the articulated, more differentiated mode. An individual's relative position on this dimension remains relatively stable, but his absolute performance moves toward increasing differentiation with development. Hence, on this dimension we see once again a developmental progression toward increased ability to separate relevant cues from irrelevant, in tasks that involve kinesthetic and vestibular as well as visual information.

Scores have been found to correlate with a number of different abilities and characteristics. The field-independent person scores high on certain subtests of intelligence, especially those involving perceptual performance. Also, the field-independent person makes a more sophisticated drawing of the human body than does the field-dependent person.

Witkin's studies have also provided some valuable clues regarding the etiology of the child's performance on the tasks of field differentiation. Grade school boys and their mothers were tested (Witkin, Dyk, Faterson, and Karp 1962). The mothers were also evaluated on certain personality characteristics as well as their interactions with their sons. Ratings of the mother's tendencies to either foster or inhibit differentiation in their sons were made, based on the amount of protectiveness, independence training, and attempts at facilitating impulse control displayed by the mothers. While the mothers' and sons' differentiation scores were not strongly correlated, the maternal ratings were related to the son's performance on the field differentiation tasks in the expected direction. That is, maternal behaviors that increased independence and ability to control impulses in the sons were positively associated with field independence.

These findings were essentially replicated with mothers and fathers and daughters and sons (Corah 1965). However, it is interesting that the results held only for cross-sex comparisons. That is, mothers and sons scored in a similar manner as in the first study as did fathers and daughters. Positive relations were not found either for mothers and daughters or for fathers and sons.

In both of these studies the data are correlational, so no firm conclusions can be made concerning the direction of causality implied by the findings. While it is tempting to conclude that parents play an important role in shaping their children's use of a particular cognitive style, it is premature to do so. The child's habitual use of a particular style may well influence the parents' interactions with him or her. The cross-sex findings indicate that the relationship is not a simple one.

Recently children with learning disabilities have been evaluated on some measures of cognitive style. Keogh and Donlon (1973) employed the Rod and Frame Test (Witkin *et al.* 1954) to compare normal and learning disabled grade school boys on their ability to adjust the rod to the true vertical, i.e., to exhibit field-independence. The learning disabled subjects were found to show considerably less field-independence than normal subjects of equivalent age levels.

A task designed to measure Santostephano's dimension of field articulation (1971) was used in two studies of children who had behavior problems in school and were diagnosed hyperactive (Campbell, Douglas, and Morgenstern 1971; Cohen, Weiss, and Minde 1972). The Fruit Distraction test contains series of pictures of fruit. In the standard condition, each is pictured in its appropriate color. In one distracting condition, several achromatic distracting pictures appear with each fruit. In the second distracting condition, the fruit appear in inappropriate colors. The child's task in each condition is to say the colors of the fruits as quickly as possible. Both the amount of time taken to identify the colors and the number of errors are recorded. The hyperactive subjects of both studies were found to be deficient in performance under the two distracting conditions. Because the distractors in this task require one to ignore certain information competing with the task at hand and in the same sense modality, it is reasonable to speculate that performance here should be related to the embedded figures test and the central-incidental task. However, these comparisons have not yet been made. If hyperactive children were found to be deficient on all three measures, it would provide a clue to at least a part of their difficulty.

CONCLUDING REMARKS

The development of attention is certainly better understood today than it was a decade ago. Tasks to measure attention have been defined, and numerous research programs have identified consistencies and emerging patterns in the way children approach and differentially process information. We have found repeatedly that there is developmental improvement in the ability to attend selectively. Incidental learning was found to change little from the early grade school years to adolescence, while at the same time central performance increased considerably during this time. There appears to be an emerging tendency to employ task-appropriate strategies during this period that certainly involve perceptual processing but also involve a central, cognitive component. Children's discrimination learning improves with development and seems to be less dependent on situational or extra-task considerations at older age levels. Strategies also seem to be used by children in at least some of the learning tasks used containing multiple cues. Among the numerous cognitive styles that have been identified, a developmental hierarchy has been proposed that orders the various styles into a set of dimensions, beginning at the level of simple stimulus selection exhibited by young children and progressing to the complex, organized styles revealed by adolescents and adults (Santostephano 1971).

It is clear that significant changes occur with development in the efficiency with which attention is deployed, and the implications of these changes for both the researcher and the practitioner are enormous. At the same time, though, we must admit that the phenomena are better described than they are understood. Little evidence can be offered concerning the role played by specific environmental factors in the development of attention. While direct training has been found to be of some benefit in certain task situations, there is not much that can be said concerning the longevity or generality of the effects due to training. It should not be surprising, then, that very little research has focused on the development and training of attention in the child with learning disabilities. Children with problems in perceptual and cognitive development have been found to be deficient in many of the measures of attention reviewed here, but the emerging picture is by no means clear.

Three recommendations are offered as challenges to the researcher interested in these problems. First, much more information is needed concerning the interrelations among the various tasks of selective attention, and longitudinal data to show the degree of stability in these measures is also needed. The difficulties inherent in this type of research are recognized, but the outcomes would justify the effort. Secondly, studies employing very clearly specified and defined populations of learning disabled children and carefully matched control children would facilitate greatly the generalities that could be drawn across studies. Finally, the need for greater cooperation and collaboration between the applied and the basic researchers has become even more clear to us in reviewing the literature for this chapter. Each has important contributions to make, and the efficiency as well as the quality of the research could be improved if more knowledge of each other's work, appreciation for each other's problems, and interest in each other's ideas and theories could be fostered.

In summarizing her observations of the hyperactive child, Virginia Douglas comments: "These youngsters are apparently unable to keep their own impulses under control in order to cope with situations in which care, concentrated attention, or organized planning are required" (1972, p. 275). Further, they seem to react to the first feature of a situation that compels their attention, instead of taking a planful approach. The young child and the child with cognitive deficiencies fit her description rather well. There is no doubt that only through the study of both normal as well as atypical development will a final accord be reached in the quest to understand the complex phenomenon we have chosen to call attention.

References

Atkinson, R. C.; Hansen, D. N.; and Bernbach, H. A. "Short-Term Memory with Young Children." *Psychonomic Science* 1 (1964): 255–56.

Baker, S. J. "A Developmental Study of Variables Affecting the Processing of Task-Relevant and Task-Irrelevant Information." Unpublished doctoral dissertation, University of Michigan, 1970.

Boring, E. G. *A History of Experimental Psychology.* New York: Appleton-Century-Crofts, 1950.

———. "Attention: Research and Beliefs Concerning the Conception in Scientific Psychology Before 1930." In *Attention: Contemporary Theory and Analysis,* edited by D. Mostofsky. New York: Appleton-Century-Crofts, 1970.

Bricker, A.; Heal, L. W.; Bricker, D. D.; Hayes, W.; and Larsen, L. A. "Discrimination Learning and Learning Set with Institutionalized Retarded Children." *American Journal of Mental Deficiency* 74 (1969): 242–48.

Broadbent, D. E. *Perception and Communication.* New York: Pergamon Press, 1958.

Campbell, S. B.; Douglas, V. I.; and Morgenstern, G. "Cognitive Styles in Hyperactive

Children and the Effect of Methylphenidate." *Journal of Child Psychology and Psychiatry* 12 (1971): 55–67.

Campione, J.; Hyman, L.; and Zeaman, D. "Dimensional Shifts and Reversals in Retardate Discrimination Learning." *Journal of Experimental Child Psychology* 2 (1965): 255–63.

Cantor, G. N. "Effects of Stimulus Familiarization on Child Behavior." In *Minnesota Symposia on Child Psychology*, edited by J. P. Hill. Vol. 3. Minneapolis: University of Minnesota Press, 1969.

Caron, A. "Conceptual Transfer in Preverbal Children as a Consequence of Dimensional Training." *Journal of Experimental Child Psychology* 6 (1968): 522–42.

Cohen, N. J.; Weiss, G.; and Minde, K. "Cognitive Styles in Adolescents Previously Diagnosed as Hyperactive." *Journal of Child Psychology and Psychiatry* 13 (1972): 203–209.

Corah, N. L. "Differentiation in Children and Their Parents." *Journal of Personality* 33 (1965): 300–308.

Crane, N. L., and Ross, L. E. "A Developmental Study of Attention to Cue Redundancy Introduced Following Discrimination Learning." *Journal of Experimental Child Psychology* 5 (1967): 1–15.

Douglas, V. "Stop, Look, and Listen: The Problem of Sustained Attention and Impulse Control in Hyperactive and Normal Children." *Canadian Journal of Behavioral Science* 4 (1972): 259–82.

Drake, D. M. "Perceptual Correlates of Impulsive and Reflective Behavior." *Developmental Psychology* 2 (1970): 202–14.

Druker, J. F., and Hagen, J. W. "Developmental Trends in the Processing of Task-Relevant and Task-Irrelevant Information." *Child Development* 40 (1969): 371–82.

Eimas, P. D. "A Developmental Study of Hypothesis Behavior and Focusing." *Journal of Experimental Child Psychology* 8 (1969*a*): 160–72.

______. "Multiple-Cue Discrimination Learning in Children." *Psychological Record* 19 (1969*b*): 417–24.

Endsley, R. C. "Effects of Differential Prior Exposure on Preschool Children's Subsequent Choice of Novel Stimuli." *Psychonomic Science* 7 (1967): 411–12.

Furth, H. G., and Youniss, J. "Effect of Overtraining on Three Discrimination Shifts in Children." *Journal of Comparative and Physiological Psychology* 57 (1964): 290–93.

Hagen, J. W. "The Effect of Distraction on Selective Attention." *Child Development* 38 (1967): 685–94.

______, and Frisch, S. R. "The Effect of Incidental Cues on Selective Attention." Report No. 57, USPHS Grant HD 01368, Center for Human Growth and Development, University of Michigan, 1968.

______, and Hale, G. A. "The Development of Attention in Children." In *Minnesota Symposia on Child Psychology*, edited by A. Pick. Vol. 7. Minneapolis: University of Minnesota Press, 1973.

______, and Huntsman, N. "Selective Attention in Mental Retardates." *Developmental Psychology* 5 (1971): 151–60.

______, and Kail, R. V., Jr. "Facilitation and Distraction in Short-Term Memory." *Child Development* 44 (1973): 831–36.

______, and West, R. F. "The Effects of a Pay-Off Matrix on Selective Attention." *Human Development* 13 (1970): 43–52.

Hale, G. A., and Piper, R. A. "Developmental Trends in Children's Incidental Learning: Some Critical Stimulus Differences." *Developmental Psychology* 8 (1973): 327–35.

______, and Piper, R. A. "The Effect of Pictorial Integration on Children's Incidental Learning." *Developmental Psychology* 10 (1974): 847–51.

______; Miller, L. K.; and Stevenson, H. W. "Incidental Learning of Film Content: A Developmental Study." *Child Development* 39 (1968): 69–77.

Heal, L. W.; Bransky, M. L.; and Mankinen, R. L. "The Role of Dimension Preference in Reversal and Nonreversal Shifts in Retardates." *Psychonomic Science* 6 (1966): 509–10.

House, B. J., and Zeaman, D. "Reward and Nonreward in the Discrimination Learning of Imbeciles." *Journal of Comparative and Physiological Psychology* 51 (1958): 614–18.

———, and Zeaman, D. "Miniature Experiments in the Discrimination Learning of Retardates." In *Advances in Child Development and Behavior*, edited by L. P. Lipsitt and C. C. Spiker. Vol. 1. New York: Academic Press, 1963.

Jeffrey, W. E. "The Orienting Reflex and Attention in Cognitive Development." *Psychological Review* 75 (1968): 323–34.

Kagan, J., and Kogan, N. "Individual Variation in Cognitive Processes." In *Carmichael's Manual of Child Psychology*, edited by P. Mussen. 3rd ed. New York: Wiley, 1970.

———; Pearson, L.; and Welch, L. "Conceptual Impulsivity and Inductive Reasoning." *Child Development* 37 (1966): 583–94.

Kendler, H. H., and Kendler, T. S. "Vertical and Horizontal Processes in Problem Solving." *Psychological Review* 69 (1962): 1–16.

Keogh, B. K., and Donlon, G. "Field Independence, Impulsivity, and Learning Disabilities." *Journal of Learning Disabilities* 5 (1972): 331–36.

Lubker, B. J. "The Role of Between- and Within-Setting Irrelevant Dimensions in Children's Simultaneous Discrimination Learning." *Child Development* 40 (1969): 957–64.

Maccoby, E. E. "Selective Auditory Attention in Children." In *Advances in Child Development and Behavior*, edited by L. P. Lippsitt and C. C. Spiker. Vol. 3. New York: Academic Press, 1967.

———. "The Development of Stimulus Selection." In *Minnesota Symposia on Child Psychology*, edited by J. P. Hill. Vol. 3. Minneapolis: University of Minnesota Press, 1969.

———, and Hagen, J. W. "Effects of Distraction Upon Central Versus Incidental Recall: Developmental Trends." *Journal of Experimental Child Psychology* 2 (1965): 280–89.

Mackworth, N. H., and Bruner, J. S. "Selecting Visual Information During Recognition by Adults and Children." Unpublished manuscript, Center for Cognitive Studies, Harvard University, 1966.

Moray, N. *Attention: Selective Processes in Vision and Hearing*. New York: Academic Press, 1970.

Mostofsky, D. *Attention: Contemporary Theory and Analysis*. New York: Appleton-Century-Crofts, 1970.

Sabo, R. A., and Hagen, J. W. "Color Cues and Rehearsal in Short-Term Memory." *Child Development* 44 (1973): 77–82.

Santostephano, S. "Cognitive Controls and Cognitive Styles: An Approach to Diagnosing and Treating Cognitive Disabilities in Children." *Seminars in Psychiatry* 1, 3 (1969): 291–317.

———. "Beyond Nosology." In *Perspectives in Child Psychopathology*, edited by H. E. Rie. Chicago: Aldine, 1971.

Seitz, V., and Weir, M. W. "Strength of Dimensional Preferences as a Predictor of Nursery-School Children's Performance on Concept-Shift Task." *Journal of Experimental Child Psychology* 12 (1971): 370–86.

Siegel, A. W., and Stevenson, H. W. "Incidental Learning: A Developmental Study." *Child Development* 37 (1966): 811–17.

———; Kirasic, K. C.; and Kilburg, R. R. "Recognition Memory in Reflective and Impulsive Preschool Children." *Child Development* 44 (1973): 651–56.

Siegelman, E. "Reflective and Impulsive Observing Behavior." *Child Development* 40 (1969): 1213–22.

Sokolov, Y. N. *Perception and the Conditional Reflex*, S. W. Waydenfeld, trans. New York: Pergamon, 1963.

Spence, K. W. *Behavior Theory and Conditioning*. New Haven: Yale University Press, 1956.

Stevenson, H. W. *Children's Learning*. New York: Appleton-Century-Crofts, 1972.

Suchman, R. G., and Trabasso, T. "Color and Form Preference in Young Children." *Journal of Experimental Child Psychology* 3 (1966): 177–87.

Terrace, H. S. "Stimulus Control." In *Operant Behavior: Areas of Research and Application*, edited by W. K. Honig. New York: Appleton-Century-Crofts, 1966.

Trabasso, T.; Deutsch, J. A.; and Gelman, R. "Attention and Discrimination Learning of Young Children." *Journal of Experimental Child Psychology* 4 (1966): 9–19.

______; Stave, M.; and Eichburg, R. "Attribute Preference and Discrimination Shifts in Young Children." *Journal of Experimental Child Psychology* 8 (1969): 195–209.

Ullman, D. G., and Routh, D. K. "Discrimination Learning in Mentally Retarded and Nonretarded Children as a Function of the Number of Relevant Dimensions." *American Journal of Mental Deficiency* 76 (1971): 176–80.

Vurpillot, E. "The Development of Scanning Strategies and Their Relation to Visual Differentiation." *Journal of Experimental Child Psychology* 6 (1968): 632–50.

Wagner, D. A. "The Development of Short-Term and Incidental Memory: A Cross-Cultural Study." *Child Development* 45 (1974): 389–96.

White, S. H. "Age Differences in Reaction to Stimulus Variation." In *Experience, Structure, and Adaptability*, edited by O. J. Harvey. New York: Springer, 1966.

Witkin, H. A.; Goodenough, D. R.; and Karp, S. A. "Stability of Cognitive Style from Childhood to Young Adulthood." *Journal of Personality and Social Psychology* 7 (1967): 291–300.

______; Dyk, R. B.; Faterson, H. F.; Goodenough, D. R.; and Karp, S. A. *Psychological Differentiation*. New York: Wiley, 1962.

______; Lewis, H. B.; Hertzman, M.; Machover, K.; Meissner, P. B.; and Wapner, S. *Personality Through Perception*. New York: Harper, 1954.

Wolff, J. L. "Concept Shift and Discrimination-Reversal Learning in Humans." *Psychological Bulletin* 68 (1967): 369–408.

Zeaman, D., and House, B. J. "An Attentional Theory of Retardate Discrimination Learning." In *Handbook of Mental Deficiency*, edited by N. R. Ellis. New York: McGraw-Hill, 1963.

Zelnicker, T.; Jeffrey, W. E.; Ault, R.; and Parsons, J. "A Comparison of Search Strategies of Impulsive and Reflective Children on the Matching Familiar Figures Test." *Child Development* 43 (1972): 321–35.

Zigler, E. "Mental Retardation: Current Issues and Approaches." In *Review of Child Development Research*, edited by L. Hoffman and M. Hoffman. Vol. 2. New York: Russell Sage Foundation, 1966.

Editors' note: While the last chapter focused upon the normal development of attentional mechanisms, the present chapter deals specifically with faulty attention in children. Research on and practical interest in such variables as attention span, hyperactivity and impulsivity have evolved. One of the most frequently cited psychological characteristics of children who have learning problems, whatever their particular diagnostic category, is that of distractibility.

In this chapter, Dr. Daniel P. Hallahan extends the research of the previous chapter to include consideration of deviant populations. Stimulus variables—auditory and visual distractors, proximal and distal distractors—are dealt with. The research on cognitive tempo, modeling, and locus of control is discussed with regard to the variable of distractibility. Hallahan also presents some data from a study of distractibility and hyperactivity in children with learning problems. The data suggest, among other things, a need to look more closely at laboratory and naturalistic measures of attention. This echoes one of the conclusions of the previous chapter concerning a need for more interchange between basic and applied research.

Daniel P. Hallahan, Ph.D., is Assistant Professor of Special Education at the University of Virginia. Dr. Hallahan completed his doctorate in the Combined Program in Education and Psychology at the University of Michigan, where he served as a Research Associate at the Institute for the Study of Mental Retardation and Related Disabilities. He is the author of numerous books and articles in the field of learning disabilities and mental retardation.

5

Distractibility in the Learning Disabled Child

DANIEL P. HALLAHAN

SELECTIVE ATTENTION

Teachers of children identified as having various kinds of learning problems frequently comment upon the inability of some of these children to attend to the academic tasks assigned them. It is the purpose of the present chapter to review research relevant to the issue of distractibility in children who are nonlearners. The research emanating from our research group as well as from others' will be reported.

Over the past few years we have been involved in the investigation of selective attention in normal and deviant populations. Primarily, we have focused on the ability of intellectually and behaviorally deviant children to process relevant information in the face of irrelevant stimuli. The primary stimuli for our own research has been the research and writings of two individuals—John W. Hagen and William M. Cruickshank. The latter, in a now classic study (Cruickshank, Bice, Wallen, and Lynch 1965), was the first to document the existence of attention deficits in deviant subjects of normal intelligence; the former, focusing on selective attention, has charted the development of attending abilities in both normal and retarded children.

For our own studies we have often used the experimental task first devised by Maccoby and Hagen (1965) and later modified by Hagen (1967). Originally based upon the stimulus filter theory of Broadbent (1958), this task has two components—central recall and incidental recall. In the particular paradigm we have used, the subject first has twelve trials in which he or she is required to remember the serial position of a particular card from an array of from three to six cards, each of which contains line drawings of an animal and a familiar household object. On these trials the subject is told

A number of individuals from the Special Education Department at the University of Virginia have participated with me in an informal research team. Chief among these individuals have been Drs. James Kauffman and Donald Ball, as well as Bette Heins, Dr. Cecil Mercer, and Sara Tarver. Each of these individuals has contributed time and thought to some of the conduction of the studies reviewed in this section.

to pay attention to the animals only. The total number of correct trials constitutes central recall performance.

After these initial trials, the subject must match the animals to the household objects with which each had always appeared. The total number of correct pairings is termed incidental recall—incidental in the sense that the child had not been instructed to pay attention to the incidental information, i.e., household objects. (For a fuller description of the task and the rationale behind it, the reader is referred to Hagan and Kail's chapter in this volume.)

In a variety of experimental situations, Hagen and his colleagues have found a developmental increase in the ability of normal children to attend to central information and to ignore incidental material (Drucker and Hagen 1969; Hagen 1967; Hagen and Huntsman 1971; Hagen and Sabo 1967; Maccoby and Hagen 1965). Using the central and incidental tasks as repeated measures, Hagen repeatedly has found an interaction between type of recall (central versus incidental) and age. Interestingly, the major change usually has occurred rather dramatically at about twelve to thirteen years of age, when, although the recall of central information continues to increase uniformly, incidental recall generally drops markedly. Furthermore, positive correlations between central and incidental recall are found at the younger ages, whereas negative correlations between the two are obtained by about twelve years. The direction of these correlations strengthens the assumption that older children have developed a strategy whereby they give up incidental information in order to recall central material.

In our studies with normal children and our studies using control groups of normal children, we have found essentially the same developmental change (Hallahan, Kauffman, and Ball 1974; Hallahan, Stainback, Ball, and Kauffman 1973). In addition to the repeated measures design, we have calculated what can be considered an index of selective attention efficiency—the proportion of central correct minus the proportion of incidental correct (%C – %I). This %C – %I has led to essentially the same results as those obtained using Hagen's repeated measures analysis and has been used primarily because of its conceptual simplicity and clarity.

Studies With the Mentally Retarded

The first study using Hagen's central-incidental task with the retarded was conducted by Hagen and Huntsman (1971). In this investigation, it was found that institutionalized, educable mentally retarded children were inferior to normals of the same mental age in their ability to attend selectively to central information over incidental information. Educable retardates who were not institutionalized, however, were found to perform similarly to normals. Hagen and Huntsman proposed two possible explanations for these results. The first hypothesis, and the more appealing one in terms of previous research, was that institutionalization may result in inferior selective attention performance. This argument was consistent with Zigler's (1966) findings that institutionalization results in motivational problems in children. The other alternative mentioned by Hagen and Huntsman was that social class variables may be responsible for the findings—the institutionalized retardates were predominantly from the inner city of Detroit prior to their institutionalization.

Parenthetically, it ought to be added that many of the children in this particular institution are there because of frequent behavior problems commonly associated with juvenile delinquency. In other words, the retarded children of Hagen and Huntsman's experiment were more typical of socially deprived delinquents than they were of the usual institutionalized retardate. The fact that they were institutionalized but scored as high as the educable range in intelligence suggests that they were not typical institutionalized retardates.

Another plausible explanation for the institutionalized group's poorer selective attention performance also arises. Since none of the retarded children was diagnosed differentially, the institutionalized group could have contained proportionately more subjects from one diagnostic group—e.g., brain damaged—than from any other. Our research group noted that organic factors were also uncontrolled in other studies wherein institutionalized retardates exhibited an attention deficit—e.g., Zeaman and House (1963)—and that the methodologically questionable but suggestive evidence of Werner and Strauss (1940, 1941) posited that brain damaged retardates were characterized by attentional problems. Thus, in order to determine if brain damage is indeed a depressor of selective attention performance, we decided to explore the central-incidental performance of cerebral palsied retardates.

With previously mentioned considerations in mind, Hallahan, Stainback, Ball, and Kauffman (1973) administered the central-incidental task to younger and older non-institutionalized, educable retarded, spastic, cerebral palsied children and to two groups of younger and older normal children equated on mental age with the two groups of cerebral palsied. Results indicated that both normal and cerebral palsied children develop the ability to attend selectively. However, the brain damaged group did not differ from the normals when the two were equated on mental age. These results suggest that brain damage was not a factor which, even if present in Hagen and Huntsman's institutionalized group, would have led to poorer performance. Hagen and Huntsman's speculations regarding the factor of insitutionalization or social class still remained the most viable hypotheses.

An unpublished study (Hagen and Hallahan 1972) has provided data which lead to some questioning of the explanation that institutionalization accounts for poor selective attention. In this study, a group of institutionalized retarded children with a mean IQ of 53.82 was compared with a normal group equated on mental age and a group of normal controls equated on chronological age. Although the CA control group was superior to the retarded group, the MA controls were not different from the retardates. Furthermore, length of institutionalization and the proportion of his life that each retardate had been institutionalized both correlated *positively* with the selective attention index—proportion of central correct minus proportion of incidental correct (.39 and .42 respectively). The latter was significant at the .05 level; the former approached significance at this level. A possible explanation for this unexpected finding involves the effect of institutionalization on the retardate's motivation to follow instructions. It could be that the institutional regime is quite effective in training retardates to do as they are told. In other words, when instructed to pay attention only to the animals, they tend to do just that because of past reinforcement associated with doing what they are told to do.

While the above *post hoc* explanation can be used to explain the Hagen and Hallahan data, the contradiction between these results and those of Hagen and Huntsman still remains to be explained. As noted above, the retardates of Hagen and Huntsman were primarily from lower social class backgrounds, while the retardates of Hagen and Hallahan were from a wider range of social class backgrounds. Social class, therefore may be the factor which influenced poor selective attention by Hagen and Huntsman's subjects.

Another variable also differentiated the retardates of Hagen and Huntsman and Hagen and Hallahan. The retardates of the latter study were of a lower IQ (M = 53.82) than those of the former (M = 76.3). Consequently, it may be that selective attention performance is poorer in retardates of higher IQs than in those of lower IQs when both groups are compared to MA controls.

Studies with the Learning Disabled

Additional evidence suggests that at even higher levels of IQ than the retarded range, selective attention performance suffers in children who are deviant with regard to learning. When Hallahan, Kauffman, and Ball (1973) compared low-achieving and high-achieving sixth grade boys on the central-incidental task, results indicated that the low achievers were poorer in their ability to recall relevant information. This finding supports the frequent observation of teachers of the learning disabled that these children are often distractible and exhibit an inability to focus their attention.

The fact that the mean IQ of the low achievers was 100 also lends additional support to the previously discussed notion that children deviant in learning ability are more likely to be deficient on the central-incidental task if their IQs are high than if they are low. Data collected on learning disabled children in a study by Mercer, Cullinan, Hallahan, and LaFleur (in press) also indicates that learning disabled children perform poorly on the selective attention task. Also, we have recently collected data on learning disabled subjects which indicate that their selective attention performance is extremely deficient.

The summary in Table 5.1 presents a closer look at the selective attention performance of learning disabled children versus mentally retarded versus normal children equated on mental age. All groups selected for inclusion in this table were equated for MA because numerous investigations

Table 5.1
Performance of Learning Disabled, Mentally Retarded, and Normals Equated on MA on Hagen's Central-Incidental Task

Population	IQ	MA	%C	%I	%C – %I
Learning Disabled*	88	10.71 yrs.	.58	.59	–.01
Mentally Retarded,†					
Cerebral Palsied	74	10.68 yrs.	.51	.31	.20
Normals†	98	10.46 yrs.	.82	.43	.39

*This group was formed by combining the data of Mercer *et al.* and data recently collected by colleagues and myself.

†These groups were from the Hallahan, Stainback, Ball, and Kauffman (1973) study.

have indicated that MA is a more crucial variable than CA for selective attention performance (Hagen and Huntsman 1971; Hagen and Hallahan 1972; Hallahan, Stainback, Ball, and Kauffman, 1973). While interpretation of the table *must remain guarded* due to the fact that the groups were from different studies with different experimenters and different settings, the results are provocative. Also, institutionalization is a possible confounding variable since the LD *S*s were all in residential settings. The data presented in this crude table, however, lend additional support to the general notion that deviant (in terms of learning) children who are of higher IQ (i.e., learning disabled) perform more poorly than those of lower IQ on Hagen's selective attention task.

Further replications, however, are needed to substantiate the *post hoc* tentative conclusion that learning disabled children are more deficient in selective attention performance than are mentally retarded children. (The evidence suggests, in fact, that community-reared, mentally retarded children of middle class status are *not* deficient in selective attention performance when equated on MA with normals.) This relatively cautious statement regarding the comparison between learning disabled and mentally retarded children should not be confused with the relatively strong evidence indicating that learning disabled do not perform as well as normals on Hagen's task.

If further replications support the position that learning disabled are more deficient than mentally retarded children in selective attention, at least two explanations may be advocated. As noted previously, a high score on the central relative to the incidental task may be highly dependent on the subject's ability and motivation to follow instructions. Higher intelligence children who are having problems in school may be inclined to be less motivated to follow the instructions of the experimenter. The task itself may be of little interest to them and the simple instructions to pay attention to the animals may not hold enough incentive for them to follow directions. Studies using various incentives would be appropriate to attack this problem of motivational factors. Another explanation would be that the ability to attend to relevant information, while ignoring irrelevant stimuli, is simply more deficient in learning disabled than in mentally retarded children.

Selective Attention and Other Cognitive Variables

Our studies have also provided information regarding selective attention performance in relation to other areas of psychological functioning. In the Hallahan, Kauffman, and Ball (1973) study, for example, in addition to Hagen's task, Kagan's Matching Familiar Figures Task (MFF) was also administered to the low-achieving and high-achieving groups. Briefly, this task requires the subject to choose, from among a number of variants, the one stimulus figure which is exactly like the standard. "Impulsive" children respond quickly and make many errors, while "reflective" children respond slowly and make fewer errors. Past research had revealed more reading problems among the impulsives than among the reflectives (Kagan 1965), and Hallahan *et al.* additionally found more impulsives than reflectives among the low achievers and more reflectives than impulsives among the high achievers. Also, evidence was found for a relationship between the reflectivity-impulsivity dimension and Hagen's selective attention task. Good performance on Hagen's selective attention task corresponded with reflective performance on Kagan's task. Likewise, impulsive subjects did the most poorly on Hagen's task. There thus appears to be a link between selective attention and cognitive tempo.

Administering the selective attention task along with a modeling task to twenty learning disabled boys, Mercer, Cullinan, Hallahan, and LaFleur (in press) found that performance on the modeling task was significantly correlated with central recall. Thus, imitative learning, thought to be of great importance in children's development (Bandura 1969), appeared to be related to selective attention skills. A logical deduction here is that a child must be able to attend to the relevant features of a model's performance before the child can imitate it.

Proximal versus Distal Distractors and the Learning Disabled

The central-incidental task of Hagen, discussed above, is constructed in such a way that the potential distractors are a part of the stimulus materials. The incidental information is on the same card with the central information, so that irrelevant, distracting stimuli are in close proximity to the central material to which the subject must attend. Other experiments also have presented learning disabled subjects with tasks which have the potentially distracting stimuli in close proximity with the material to be focused upon. Another series of investigations has used distractors which are at some distance from the subject. These studies using distal distractors typically have employed bright flashing lights, colored objects, and/or loud noises.

Tarver and Hallahan (1974) have reviewed a number of studies requiring the subject to perform in the presence of proximal and distal distractors. The deviant subjects used in these studies were classified in a variety of ways by the different investigators—e.g., learning disabled, underachieving, reading disabled, or minimally brain-injured. All of the groups, however, used subjects which would fall under the general rubric of "learning disabled" in that the children were of normal or near-normal intelligence and were experiencing academic problems.

The results of the studies investigating proximal distractors are in general agreement with the data presented above on Hagen's central-incidental task: learning disabled children attend less well in the face of distracting information near the material to be focused upon. Mondani and Tutko (1969), for example, gave junior high school subjects a test of social responsibility. On the test forms, the experimenters wrote in pencil various irrelevant doodle-like stimuli—e.g., question marks or flowers. After the test was administered, the subjects were asked to recall the irrelevant stimuli. Mondani and Tutko found that low achievers recalled more of this incidental information than did high achievers.

Silverman, Davids, and Andrews (1963) compared underachievers and achievers on the Stroop Color-Word test (Stroop 1935). The Stroop test requires the subject to name as quickly as possible the colors in which color names are printed. For example, the word *red* printed in green ink would call for the response *green*. A subject who would be distracted by the color name would thus make more errors and be slower. Silverman *et al.* found that the achievers were more accurate and completed the task faster than the low achievers. Unfortunately, because the achievers were older and because there were no IQ data available on them (they may have been of higher intelligence than the under-achievers), there are weaknesses in the conclusion that under-achievers are more distractible on this task.

Elkind, Larson, and Van Doorninck (1965), studying the performance of retarded readers and normals on a task involving the differentiation of figures embedded in extraneous backgrounds, found that retarded readers from the third through sixth grade were less able than average readers to differentiate the figures. In addition, in a training phase of the study, the reading disabled group needed more cues for solution and benefitted less from the training.

Keogh and Donlon (1972), in their study, were interested in Witkin's (Witkin, Dyk, Faterson, Goodenough, and Karp 1962) construct of field-independence, dependence. Using a variety of perceptual tasks, Witkin and his associates identified individuals as those who are not influenced by the perceptual field around them (field independents) versus those who are affected by the context of the stimulus field (field dependents). Keogh and Donlon used a portable rod and frame test which assessed the child's ability to position a movable rod at the true vertical even when it was placed in a context which provided misleading cues. The learning disabled boys of this study, when compared to the norms for their age group, were found to be highly field dependent. Thus, the evidence from this study also corroborates the findings of the above studies. The learning disabled subjects were more influenced by irrelevant, extraneous cues and were unable to focus on the relevant cues in isolation.

Another study supporting the hypothesis that some learning disabled children are more prone to distraction by the cues of an embedded context is that of Sabatino and Ysseldyke (1972). After dividing learning disabled children into those who were normal readers and those who were retarded in reading, the authors gave the Bender-Gestalt under standard administration and again with the Bender designs embedded in extraneous backgrounds. The two groups did not differ under the standard administration, but the non-readers were inferior to the readers when the designs were presented within an extraneous background.

Atkinson and Seunath (1973) have also noted the proximal versus distal distinction and conducted a study wherein the irrelevant stimuli were contained within the stimulus array. In their task, subjects were presented with slides containing squares of different colors. The subjects were required to identify those slides (about 20 percent of them) which contained a red square with a black dot within it. Two stimulus conditions were used: (1) a constant condition in which the squares stayed in the same position from one slide to the next and (2) a stimulus change condition in which the squares varied in position from slide to slide. Atkinson and Seunath found the learning disabled children to commit more errors of omission than normals under the stimulus change but not the constant condition. The low number of errors for both normals and learning disabled children in the constant condition suggest that ceiling effects may have been operating to produce the non-significant results for this condition. As Atkinson and Seunath note, the fact that errors of omission and not errors of comission separated the learning disabled from normals indicates that the learning disabled children were attending to the irrelevant stimuli: Attending to irrelevant stimulation would decrease the probability of responding to the discriminative stimulus and result in more errors of omission. However, attending to either relevant or irrelevant stimulation should not increase the probability of falsely detecting a discriminative stimulus (an error of commission). It was noted that the frequency of errors of comission was essentially inconsequential for both groups of children" (p. 573).

The results of the above studies (Atkinson and Seunath 1973; Elkind *et al.* 1965; Keogh and Donlon 1972; Mondani and Tutko 1969; Sabatino and Ysseldyke 1972; Silverman *et al.* 1963) are consistent with the notion that, as a group, learning disabled children are distracted by proximal irrelevant cues. These findings also corroborate data collected by our research group using Hagen's central-incidental task. Tarver and Hallahan (1974), however, have noted that those studies on learning disabled children which have used distal distractions (Browning 1967*a*; Douglas 1972) have not found the same negative effect.

While further replications are in order to substantiate the negative findings under the distal distraction conditions, the fact that results thus far are in opposition to those obtained under proximal conditions leads to some interesting, and perhaps theoretically profitable, hypothesis building. At least two explanations can be advanced. Browning (1967*b*) himself has posited why he found multi-colored flashing lights to be ineffective as distractors for minimally brain injured children. He has hypothesized that some of the subjects exhibit hyporesponsiveness—a reduced propensity to respond. In other words, some children who fall under the classification of learning disabled may be harder to arouse than are normal children. Thus, bright flashing lights surrounding hyporesponsive subjects may arouse them to respond. These hyporesponsive subjects therefore would react in a manner opposite to that of hyperresponsive children; and under conditions of intensive, extraneous stimulation, the effects of the distractors would be washed out. Some limited physiological evidence supports the notion that the orienting response of some learning disabled children may be deficient (Cohen, in Douglas 1972; Dykman, Ackerman, Clements, and Peters 1971).

Two other investigations on normal (Turnure 1970) and mentally retarded children (Stainback, Stainback, and Hallahan 1973) have obtained results which are consistent with Browning's notion of the arousing nature of extraneous distractors. Turnure found visual distractors to depress performance in children at 5.5 years of age but to influence performance positively by the age of 7.5 years. He hypothesized that the potential distractor acted as a mobilizer of attention in the older children. Stainback *et al.* found that mentally retarded children performed the best on Hagen's central-incidental task under the condition of music with distractors (tape-recording of typical school hall noises) in comparison with music alone, distractor alone, and a control condition. These results can be interpreted to suggest that the two variables, music and distractors, may reach a point of such salience that they arouse the subjects to respond.

Another plausible interpretation of the failure of intensive, extraneous distractors to affect negatively the performance of learning disabled children involves the ability to recognize which aspects of a stimulus situation are relevant. When placed within a laboratory situation wherein irrelevant information may stand out for the subject when it is placed in the proximal-distraction studies), learning disabled subjects are distracted by the interferring stimuli. In this kind of situation, there is little aid (in terms of stimulus parameters) given to the subject with regard to what is relevant and what is not. When bright flashing lights are presented as distractors, however, the learning disabled subject may be helped by these *obvious* distractors to determine what is relevant and what is not. The most bland relevant information may stand out for the subject when it is placed in the context of bright distractors. It may thus be that studies using distractors high in saliency are serving to aid some subjects to discriminate between relevant and irrelevant stimuli.

Auditory Distractors and the Learning Disabled

The studies considered so far have used tasks requiring the subject to attend to visual stimuli. The distractors, too, have been primarily of a visual nature. There have been fewer developmental studies concerned with auditory than visual selective attention in normals (c.f. Hallahan, Kauffman, and Ball 1974; Maccoby 1967; Maccoby and Konrad 1966) and even fewer auditory than visual studies in the learning disabled. Lasky and Tobin (1973) conducted an experiment in which subjects were required to listen to auditory messages while auditory distractors were provided. In three separate tasks, the child was required to respond verbally to questions about his worksheet, to make a written response to auditory questions, and to make a written response to written material. For each of the three kinds of tasks, there were three distinct auditory distraction conditions: no distraction, linguistic messages (children reading prose and number facts), and nonlinguistic messages (white noise). The auditory distraction conditions were presented on tape over three loudspeakers behind the subjects. On all three tasks, Lasky and Tobin found that learning disabled first graders did not differ from their normal peers in the quiet or white noise conditions. Performance by the learning disabled subjects was adversely affected, however, in the linguistic distractor condition, whereas that of the normals was not. This study indicates, then, that auditory stimuli similar to those encountered in the classroom are most likely to affect the performance of learning disabled children. Before any definite conclusions can be made regarding the meaningfulness or linguistic component of distractors, however, there must be further studies using various kinds of non-linguistic distractors—e.g., car horns, traffic sounds, slamming doors. Because white noise, which was used by Lasky and Tobin, has been found in previous studies to act as a buffer in blocking out extraneous auditory stimuli, it probably is not a very good choice as an auditory "distractor."

Using an auditory-visual analog of Maccoby's dichotic listening tasks (Senf 1969; Senf and Feshbach 1970; Senf and Freundl 1971), Senf and his colleagues have reported a number of studies with learning disabled children. Senf's task typically involves the simultaneous presentation of an auditory and visual stimulus. After each auditory-visual presentation comes a pause—an interpair interval—followed by another auditory-visual pair, and after three or four such pairs, the subject is asked to recall the stimuli. The subject can be directed to recall the stimuli in pairs (pair recall), in one modality then the other (modality recall), or in free recall. Senf has found an interaction among age, type of directed recall, and learning disabled versus normal children. At older age levels (CA about 14.5 years) the learning disabled perform equally to normals in modality recall but are deficient in pair recall. At the early elementary grades, however, learning disabled children recall pairs just as well as normals but do more poorly than normals in modality recall.

With regard to the poorer modality recall of the learning disabled at early elementary school ages, Senf offers a number of explanations, one of which is germane to the present discussion of auditory distractors. In his studies, he has found that learning disabled children show a marked preference for the auditory modality. This preference may explain why the younger children do more poorly on modality recall. "Assessing the modality of the bisensory stimulus first to be reported in free recall, we found that both learning disabled and culturally deprived children are heavily auditorially preferant. It is possible that this preference indicates that the retarded readers are stimulus bound, that their attention is captured by auditory stimulation. As a result, they may be unable to deploy sufficient attention to visual material when auditory stimulation is present. Whether the retarded reader is less able to exclude irrelevant stimuli (auditory distraction) or is stimulus bound by aural input (auditory dominance) requires further experimentation" (Senf and Freundl 1971, p. 105).

Although further studies will be needed in order to determine the extent of auditory distraction, Senf's experiments do suggest that auditory stimuli may prove to be more distracting than visual stimuli. Future research efforts should explore the learning disabled child's ability to process auditory information and to focus attention in the presence of auditory distractors. The visual-motor emphasis seen in the field of learning disabilities as a whole (Hallahan and Cruickshank 1973) no doubt has influenced interest in aspects of visual attention to the relative exclusion of auditory attention. Investigations of auditory selective attention and auditory distractors hold promise for an understanding of language disabilities in children.

In summary, studies to date generally support the notion that proximal visual distractors are more influential than distal visual distractors in depressing the performance of learning disabled children. In addition, there is some evidence to indicate that auditory stimuli are more distracting than visual ones. This latter possibility suggests the need for more research in conjunction with the variables of proximity and meaningfulness.

Internal-External Locus of Control and Distraction in the Learning Disabled

As yet, there are no definitive statements regarding causative factors of distractibility in learning disabled children. The possible causes run the gamut from condiseration of neurological factors to strictly motivational ones. Except for studies investigating the influence of brain damage on attention, very few studies have addressed themselves to the question of why a child is distractible. The studies concerning brain damage are not only inconclusive but likely to remain so for some time because of the relatively crude nature of the instruments available to detect brain damage (Hallahan and Cruickshank 1973).

One line of research, however—that concerned with internal versus external locus of control—is gaining momentum as an explanatory construct for a number of deviant behaviors. This research deals with the manner in which an individual views his own ability to control what happens to himself. The person high in external control believes that he has very little to do with what happens to himself. He believes, too, that others in his environment are in control over his rewards and punishments. The person high in internal control, on the other hand, asserting that he is responsible for his own success and failures, relies relatively little on others for an explanation of his behavior. Closely aligned with these studies of internal versus external locus of control are studies dealing with the motivational variables of inner-directedness and outer-directedness. The inner-directed individual is said to rely upon his own performance, while the outer-directed person is dependent upon cues from others.

Evidence accumulated thus far supports the position that children who have had a history of failure in learning are characterized by personalities high in external locus of control and outer-directedness. For example, Turnure and Zigler (1964) have found mentally retarded children to be more outer-directed than normal controls. A number of studies also have found evidence that children who might fall under the label of "learning disabilities" are more apt to have a high external and low internal locus of control orientation. Shaw and Uhl (1971) found that in white, upper middle-class children there was a relationship between low reading ability and external locus of control. Also, McGhee and Crandall (1968) have cited a number of studies (Cellura 1963; Chance 1965; Crandall, Katkovsky, and Preston 1962) which found internal locus of control to correlate with high achievement. McGhee and Crandall themselves found that an internal locus of control was asociated with achievement.

Also relevant to the discussion here is the discovery of a relationship between distractibility and outer-directedness. Turnure and Zigler (1964), for example, found that retarded subjects, in addition to being high in outer-directedness, also glanced away from problem-solving tasks toward the experimenter more often than normals. Ruble and Nakamura (1973), in fact, have used glancing away behavior as their only measure of outer-directedness. The hypothesis is that glancing behavior correlates with outer-directedness because the child who is not sure that he can rely upon his own problem-solving skills is apt to look around for external cues from adults. Turnure (1973) has found, in fact, that retarded children glance away more in the presence of an experimenter than when the experimenter is not present.

While the studies relating academic achievement to internal and external control have not used glancing behavior as a dependent measure, it is reasonable to consider that the distractibility noted in learning disabled children may be connected to their looking about for external cues. It could be that some of the distractible behavior of learning disabled children results from their outer-directedness. Of course, there is still no definite answer to the question of whether outer-directedness causes poor academic performance or vice versa. There is logic in the adoption of either position with regard to the direction of causation; further research is in order to determine which causes which.

This discussion of internal and external locus of control raises the question of motivational variables in general. In studying the distractibility of learning disabled children, it is well to keep in mind the possibility that motivation may be playing some part in distractibility. Poor motivation to succeed, a high expectancy of failure, and previous failure experiences on problem-solving tasks may all combine to influence the child to become more interested in attending to stimuli other than the ones designated by the experimenter as important.

RELATIONSHIP BETWEEN DISTRACTIBILITY AND HYPERACTIVITY IN LEARNING DISABLED CHILDREN

Besides the characteristic of distractibility, learning disabled children are frequently said to exhibit hyperactivity. The position advanced by clinical judgment is that distractibility and hyperactivity are correlates of each other. However, empirical evidence for the association between the two, especially in learning disabled children, has been mostly indirect. Kagan and his colleagues, working with normal populations, have found some evidence for an association between the two. Kagan (1966) observed that those boys who displayed an analytic response style were not as likely to exhibit hyperactive behaviors in the laboratory and on the playground. If one can assume a relationship between an analytic response style and freedom from distractibility, then Kagan's observation is evidence for the relationship between distractibility and hyperactivity. Indirect evidence for a relationship between hyperactivity and distractibility in the learning disabled also comes from a study by Sroufe, Sonies, West, and Wright (1973). Sroufe *et al.* found that when activity levels were reduced in learning disabled subjects there was an increase in anticipatory heart rate deceleration (an indicator of attention).

> More objective evidence for the association between hyperactivity and lack of attention comes from the Fels longitudinal study's finding that hyperactive behavior in children from 3 to 6 years of age was inversely correlated with involvement in intellectual activity during adolescence and adulthood (Kagan and Moss, 1962). Kagan et al. (1964) also found that a boy rated as hyperactive between ages 4 and 8 is unlikely to use analytic concepts at age 10. Kagan noted, too, that Schaefer and Bayley's (1963) classic longitudinal study determined that hyperactive infants tested later at ages 5 and 6 were inattentive to intellectual problems. (Hallahan and Cruickshank 1973, p. 233)

Sykes and his colleagues have also found evidence for a negative relationship between attention skills and hyperactivity (Sykes, Douglas, and Morgenstern 1973); Sykes, Douglas, Weiss, and Minde 1971). They have found that subjects labeled as hyperactive perform more poorly on the continuous performance test—a test of sustained attention. One limitation of their studies, however, is that the subjects were determined to be hyperactive by clinical reports and not by any objective criteria.

Our research group has collected some data, the preliminary analyses of which have some bearing upon the question of the relationship between distractibility and hyperactivity. Besides studying this relationship, the investigation had at least three other purposes. Since there exists a paucity of data on learning disabled children collected through observational recording techniques, we wanted to collect data on motor and attending behaviors within a classroom setting. We also wanted to obtain an indication of the frequency of these behaviors over time, since no longitudinal data exist on hyperactivity and attending behaviors. Furthermore, we were interested in the relationship between a laboratory measure of selective attention (Hagen's central-incidental task) and behavioral observation measures of attention and hyperactivity.

The twenty-nine children in this study were all diagnosed as having learning disabilities and were residing in an institution for learning disabled children.* At the beginning of the study, the children ranged in age from 9.08 to 14.83 years of age (M = 11.92 years), and the mean IQ was 82.41.† All of the children were deficient in academic achievement. In order to quantify the extent of the learning disabilities for these children, "learning: potential for learning" ratios were computed for each child for reading and arithmetic. This was done by converting the grade level obtained on a standardized achievement test to a chronological age equivalent. This figure was then divided by mental age. The resulting ratio was an index of the degree to which the child was achieving below his or her hypothesized potential. As a group the children had a "learning: potential for learning" ratio of 81.92 in reading and 87.60 in arithmetic. The children were selected for inclusion in the study on the basis of their likelihood of staying in the institution for more than the academic year in which the first data were taken. The first data on the behavioral measures were collected from February through May of 1973, and the same behavioral measures were obtained from October through November of 1973. The Hagen task was administered once, in November. It was not administered twice because the incidental task requires the subject to do something he was not expecting to do.

For each child seven behaviors were recorded. Two of these were considered to be within the realm of attention, and five were indicative of amount of motoric activity. The seven behaviors were:

1. Percent of Time Attending—This was defined as the proportion of the time spent attending to the task at hand.
2. Attention Shifts—This referred to the number of times the subject switched his attention from one activity to another.
3. Out of Seat—This was recorded every time the child's buttocks left the chair.
4. Foot off Floor—This was counted whenever a child lifted a foot off the floor without getting out of his seat.

*Thanks are extended to Dr. Martin Mayfield, Headmaster Robert Stieg, and the teachers of Grafton School, Berryville, Virginia. This research was partially supported by funds awarded the author through the University Research Policy Council of the University of Virginia.

†The low mean IQ of these children should caution the reader from concluding that these children were all learning disabled in the strictest sense of the term. While for ease of communication these children will be referred to as "learning disabled," it should be kept in mind that some of them scored very close to or in the educable retarded range of intelligence.

5. Change of Position—This was defined by any change in posture which did not accompany getting out of seat.
6. Inappropriate Manipulation of Objects—This referred to a child's fidgeting or handling an object inappropriately. For example, a child might rub a pencil continuously between his hands.
7. Touching Others—This category was marked whenever a subject touched another child or an adult.

All the above measures were obtained while the children were supposed to be engaged in seatwork activity related to arithmetic or language arts skills. If at any time a teacher directed a child to engage in a response which required him to act in such a way that his behavior would be counted in one of the above categories, the response was not recorded by the experimenter. Each child was observed individually for a thirty-minute session, half of which was devoted to the collection of data on the first two attending measures and the other half of which was used to record the frequency of the five motor behaviors. Each child was observed for two thirty-minute sessions occurring approximately one month apart in the spring of 1973. Two more data collection sessions, again about one month apart, were run in the fall. One observer collected both the spring and the fall data. An estimate of reliability was obtained in the spring by having a second observer record the same behaviors on the same child. Percentage of agreement ranged from 75 to 100 percent. In the fall, data for reliability estimates were collected twice. The percentage of agreement for these children again ranged from 75 to 100 percent.

Table 5.2 presents the means obtained on the two attention measures and four of the motor measures (Touching Others was eliminated from analysis because it occurred so infrequently) obtained over thirty minutes in the spring and the thirty minutes in the fall. For example, for Percent of Time Attending, the mean for all twenty-nine of the subjects was 71 percent in the spring and 72 percent in the fall. For attention shifts, there were on the average 23.72 shifts of attention in thirty minutes for each subject in the spring and 21.69 shifts in the fall. Table 5.2 also contains correlations of the observations obtained in the spring with the same observations taken again in the fall.

Table 5.2
Spring and Fall Means and Pearsonian Correlations
Between Spring and Fall Measures of Attention and Hyperactivity

Behavior Observed	Spring	Fall	*r*	Sig. Level of *r*
Percent of Time Attending	71%	72%	.25	(ns)
Attention Shifts	23.72	21.69	.44	(.05)
Out of Seat	3.96	2.41	.63	(.01)
Foot off Floor	41.96	49.41	.72	(.01)
Change of Position	18.10	16.58	.50	(.01)
Inapprop. Manip. of Objects	8.62	11.75	.19	(ns)

With regard to the latter correlations, four were quite high, while those of Percent Attending ($r = .25$) and Inappropriate Manipulation of Objects ($r = .19$) were low. There are two ways of interpreting these low correlations: either the measures taken were not reliable, or these behaviors were not stable in these individuals. For several reasons, the latter interpretation seems the more plausible. First of all, the reliability estimates based upon percentage of agreements between independent observers were of sufficient magnitude in both the spring and fall. Also, as is discussed later, both measures, especially that of Percent of Time Attending, intercorrelate highly with the other measures in a consistent and interpretable manner. In connection with the intercorrelation of the measures there was no evidence of a depression of the correlations between these measures and others which would occur if the two measures were unreliable. Considered within the context of stability, then, results suggest that the percentage of time which learning disabled children spend on task and the frequency with which they manipulate objects inappropriately may not remain stable over time. An interesting observation here is that although not remaining stable for individual children the means in Table 5.2 show that both behaviors, especially Percent of Time Attending, remain at about the same levels in terms of the group. In other words, the group as a whole spent an equal amount of time in attending in both sessions, but individual children in general did not. Another factor which should not be ignored with regard to the low stability coefficients for the Percent of Time Attending and Inappropriate Manipulation of Objects is the relatively short time period covered by the behavioral observations. Each behavior was only observed within two thirty-minute sessions. Observations over an extended duration might provide more evidence of stability.

Although the lack of a normal control group precludes any definitive statements regarding the extent of attention problems and hyperactivity in learning disabled children, a few tentative comments can be made about the means presented in Table 5.2. It would appear that, as a group, these learning disabled children did not evidence *great* difficulty in control of motor behaviors or attentional responses. The means of 71 and 72 for Percent of Time Attending does not seem to be excessively low. Patterson, Cobb, and Ray (1972) have reviewed some literature which substantiates the position that our group was not unduly inattentive:

> Data presented by Werry and Quay (1968) indicated that the deviant child was out of his seat over twice as much as the normal child; he made noise 25 times as often; he vocalized inappropriately twice as often. While the normal child attended to his task about 77% of the time, the deviant child was on task only 54% of the time. These data are in essential agreement with the figure of 39% provided by Walker, Mattson, and Buckley (1969) for a class of disturbed boys. Similarly, Hammerlynck, Martin, and Rolland (1968) showed that a special class of retarded children spent an average of only 45% of their classroom time "on task." (p. 153)

Thus, the children in this chapter were attending about as much as the normal children of Werry and Quay. Also, Bryan and Wheeler (1972) found a group of normal children from kindergarten, first, second, fourth, and sixth grades to engage in task-oriented behavior 70 percent of the time. While this is quite comparable to our learning disabled subjects, Bryan and Wheeler did find their learning disabled group to attend only 57 percent of the time and to be significantly less task oriented than normals. To complicate matters further, Bryan (1974) has found a group of third grade learning disabled children to be task oriented 68 percent of the time, but to be significantly less task oriented than normals who were attentive 87.7 percent of the time. These conflicting results regarding the percentage of on-task behavior for both normals and learning disabled children point to a need for further research in this area. While a number of variables should be investigated in future studies in order to untangle the contradictory results obtained so far, a few come immediately to mind. As has been pointed out, the learning disabled subjects of this chapter had fairly low IQs; since the studies by Bryan and Bryan and Wheeler did not report IQs, this could be a distinguishing variable. Also the normal subjects in Bryan's study were selected by teachers, and the teachers could have chosen their best students instead of their average pupils which would account for their being on-task 87.7 percent of the time. Studies which consider the variables of IQ, age, and subject selection are warranted.

The rate of shifting of attention (about once every 1.3 minutes) appears not to be extraordinary either. The only motor activity mean which seems to border on being excessive is that of leaving the seat almost seven times (when not called upon to do so by the teacher) in the course of an hour. The means certainly are not low, but the picture one obtains of this group is that they are not excessively hyperactive or nonattentive in class. Examination of the data indicates that there may be subgroups of hyperactive and hypoactive children which would coincide with Browning's notions based upon laboratory experimentation.

Table 5.3 shows the intercorrelations of the six behavioral measures and the scores from the central-incidental task of Hagen. The behavioral scores used for this matrix were obtained by taking a combination of the spring and fall data. For the Percent of Time Attending, an average was taken for spring and fall. For the rest of the measures, the spring and fall sessions were simply combined.

The first noticeable aspect of the matrix is that the two behavioral measures of attention are not correlated. While at first glance it would seem that these two categories—Percent of Time Attending and frequency of Attention Shifts—should be negatively correlated, further reflection upon the relationship between the two produces an explanation. An individual may shift his attention frequently yet keep his attention off task only for short periods of time. This response would be characterized by the child who makes quick but momentary glances away from the task. Likewise, a child

Table 5.3
Intercorrelations Among the Two Behavioral Measures of Attention, the Four Behavioral Measures of Motor Activity, and the Laboratory Measure of Selective Attention

	AS	OS	FF	CP	IMO	C	I	%C – %I
Percent Attending (%A)	–.06	–.29	–.44*	–.60†	–.51†	–.01	–.14	.11
Attention Shifts (AS)		.00	.22	.04	.08	–.20	.09	–.21
Out of Seat (OS)			.71†	.60†	.19	.00	.15	–.13
Foot off Floor (FF)				.63†	.29	.00	.01	–.01
Change of Position (CP)					.39*	–.02	.16	–.15
Inapprop. Manip. of Objects (IMO)						.17	.24	–.15
Central Recall (C)							.05	.46*
Incidental Recall (I)								–.84†

*$p < .05$
†$p < .01$

who looks away from the assigned task may also keep his attention focused away from the task for a lengthy duration. Apparently, both of these distraction "styles" were operating in the present sample.

The correlations of Table 5.3, however, do reflect a strong relationship among the four categories of motoric behavior. The Pearsonian *r*s not to reach significance among the hyperactivity categories were that between Out of Seat and Inappropriate Manipulation of Objects and between Foot off Floor and Inappropriate Manipulation of Objects. The non-relationship between Out of Seat and Inappropriate Manipulation of Objects suggests that leaving one's seat prohibits sitting at one's desk and playing with objects. It is our observation that most of the inappropriate manipulation of objects occurred while the child was seated. Thus, even this non-relationship may have been to some degree a result of some incompatibility between the two classes of behaviors. If a child gets out of his seat, he may not be in as advantageous a position as is the seated child to engage in such activities as tapping a pencil, rolling marbles, or bending the binding of a book. However, in general, the intercorrelations show that behaviors indicative of hyperactivity (if exhibited to a marked degree) possess a strong tendency to appear simultaneously.

With regard to the relationship between ability to focus attention and motor activity, the matrix shows a clear and consistent negative relationship between the hyperactivity measures and Percent of Time Attending. However, the frequency of Attention Shifts did not correlate with any of the hyperactivity categories. Evidently, the learning disabled child who glances away frequently is not any more apt to display hyperactivity than the child who is seldom distracted. Nevertheless, the percentage of time during which the learning disabled child attends is very negatively correlated with hyperactivity.

The finding of the independence of Attention Shifts and Percent of Time Attending and the opposing findings with regard to hyperactivity and these two measures of attention merit further study. An interesting line of research, for example, would be to explore the relative importance of frequency of shifts to the duration of the glancing away behavior. It may be that the learning disabled child is unable to tolerate (in terms of their effect on learning) frequent interruptions of attention, brief though they may be. On the other hand, it is possible that the total proportion of time the learning disabled child attends, regardless of the number of off-task glances, is crucial.

Finally, the data here underscore the need for more research using naturalistic observation techniques. None of the behavioral measures correlated with any of the three scores obtained from the laboratory measure of selective attention. While laboratory measures are useful in their own right, the lack of correlation especially between the field-based measures of attention and the laboratory measure of attention points to a need for more behavioral observation measures of attention. Perhaps the laboratory and classroom definitions of attention are different. This statement does not imply that either setting has the "correct" definition. While intuitively one may wish to lean toward data collected in a classroom setting because they are obtained from the "real world," the precision which can be gained from laboratory studies should not be discounted. In the study presented here, for example, the behavioral measures of attention relied upon observable responses of the subject's head and eyes. That a child has his eyes pointed in the direction of the assigned task is no guarantee of his "attention" to the information in the sense of *processing* the relevant stimuli.

SUMMARY AND CONCLUSIONS

While the characteristic of distractibility has occupied much space in clinically oriented literature, it has just begun to be investigated systematically. Conclusions drawn in this chapter are therefore tentative. Results of the various studies on distractibility in learning disabled children are far from reaching the state of consensus necessary for the development of a theory of distractibility in learning disabilities. Any inferences drawn from the studies can at this point contribute only to hypotheses regarding distractibility in learning disabilities.

One relatively consistent line of evidence apparent in reviewing the studies of this chapter concerns the differential effects of proximal and distal distractors on the performance of learning disabled children. When relevant and irrelevant stimuli are presented in close proximity, learning disabled children are more distracted than normals to attend to the irrelevant distractors. Those experiments employing extraneous distractors (e.g., bright flashing lights, mirrors, toys) on the periphery of the child's intended line of sight have not found these distractors to decrease learning disabled children's performances. Some evidence, in fact, suggests that these distal distractors improve the performance of learning disabled children, educable mentally retarded children, and young normal subjects. With regard to the learning disabled children, Browning has formulated a hypothesis that for one subgroup of hyporesponsive learning disabled children excess stimulation helps to arouse a response. Another explanation states that extraneous distal distractors may be used by some learning disabled children as a crutch to help them discriminate the relevant from irrelevant aspects of the task.

There is also some evidence to indicate that learning disabled children are more distractible in the presence of proximal distractors than are other groups of children deviant in learning—e.g., mentally retarded or brain damaged. This provocative evidence can be used as indirect, tentative support for the notion that the learning problems of learning disabled children may in some cases be primarily due to distractibility, whereas learning problems of the mentally retarded may be due more to lowered intelligence.

Although not much data have been collected thus far, it also appears that there is a tendency for auditory distractors to be more distracting than visual ones for learning disabled children. Studies are needed to investigate the interaction of sensory mode of the distractor, sensory mode of input required for correct completion of the experimental task, intensity of the distracting stimuli, and proximity of the distracting stimuli.

Studies on distractibility also underline the need for consideration of motivational variables in the performance of learning disabled children. Some data show that children who are not confident in their own ability to control their behavior are more apt to look around for helpful cues from adults. Evidence indicating that learning disabled children are likely to exhibit an external locus of control suggests that they may be glancing away from the task (whether it be toward the experimenter or toward incidental, irrelevant stimuli) in an attempt to pick up additional cues for solution.

The variable of motivation to perform (in the sense of desire to do well) must also be considered within the context of distractibility studies. A subject's disinterest in learning tasks may precipitate inattentiveness to what the experimenter has defined as important. The ever-elusive construct of motivation thus remains a possible causal factor in the distractibility of learning disabled children.

Clinical evidence suggests a correlation between hyperactivity and distractibility. Indirect empirical support for this relationship also has materialized. In this chapter we reported the results of a study which investigated in learning disabled subjects two behavioral-observation measures of attention, five behavioral-observation measures of motor activity, and a laboratory test of attention. The data showed a negative association between the percentage of time the learning disabled child attended and the amount of irrelevant, motoric activity in which he engaged. No relationship was found, however, between motoric activity and number of times the learning disabled child glanced away from his assigned task. This differential relationship between the two attentional behaviors and hyperactivity measures, coupled with the finding that the two attention measures were not correlated, indicates that future studies should treat the two measures of attention—percentage of time attending and attention shifts—separately. Significant correlations were found among the behavioral measures of motoric behavior. There was no relationship between the laboratory measure of selective attention—Hagen's C-I task—and the behavioral measures of attention and hyperactivity. Although at first glance it perhaps seems appropriate to question the utility of Hagen's task in predicting or explaining relevant behaviors of learning disabled children, the task has differentiated learning disabled from normal children and has correlated with such important behaviors as modeling and cognitive tempo. One must recognize, however, that the results suggest that a learning disabled subject may be assessed on a different dimension of attention in Hagen's task than he is in behavioral observations of attending behavior.

The review here points out the need for further naturalistic studies focusing on the antecedent and consequent events of distractibility and hyperactivity. At least two questions worth pursuing arise: (1) What situations evoke distractible and hyperactive behavior? (2) What role does the behavior of other children and the teacher play in influencing when and how a child will not attend or will exhibit hyperactivity?

More research is needed also to assess the interrelationships of laboratory measures of distractibility. The majority of investigations considered in this chapter have used Hagen's selective attention task. Studies are needed to determine the interrelationship of a variety of laboratory tasks designed to measure distractibility as well as tasks purporting to measure in some way various features of the global construct of attention, e.g., Zeaman and House's discrimination task (1963), Cruickshank's Syracuse Visual Figure-Background Test (Cruickshank, Bice, Wallen, and Lynch 1965), Rosvold's Continuous Performance Test (Rosvold, Mirksy, Sarason, Bransome, and Beck 1956), and the digit-span subtest from IQ tests (Huelsman 1970).

References

Atkinson, B. R., and Seunath, O. H. M. "The Effect of Stimulus Change on Attending Behavior in Normal Children and Children with Learning Disorders." *Journal of Learning Disabilities* 6 (1973): 569–73.

Bandura, A. *Principles of Behavior Modification.* New York: Holt, Rinehart & Winston, 1969.

Broadbent, D. E. *Perception and Communication.* New York: Pergamon Press, 1958.

Browning, R. M. "Effect of Irrelevant Peripheral Visual Stimuli on Discrimination Learning in Minimally Brain-Damaged Children." *Journal of Consulting Psychology* 31 (1967*a*): 371–76.

______. "Hypo-Responsiveness as a Behavioral Correlate of Brain Damage in Children." *Psychological Reports* 20 (1967*b*): 251–59.

Bryan, T. S. "An Observational Analysis of Classroom Behaviors of Children with Learning Disabilities." *Journal of Learning Disabilities* 7 (1974): 26–34.

______, and Wheeler, R. "Perception of Learning Disabled Children: The Eye of the Observer." *Journal of Learning Disabilities* 5 (1972): 484–88.

Cellura, A. R. "Internality as a Determinant of Academic Achievement in Low SES Adolescents." Unpublished manuscript, University of Rochester, 1963.

Chance, J. E. "Internal Control of Reinforcements and the School Learning Process." Paper given at Society for Research in Child Development, Minneapolis, Minn., 1965.

Crandall, V. J.; Katkovsky, W.; and Preston, A. "Motivational and Ability Determinants of Young Children's Intellectual Achievement Behaviors." *Child Development* 33 (1962): 643–61.

Cruickshank, W. M.; Bice, H. V.; Wallen, N. E.; and Lynch, K. S. *Perception and Cerebral Palsy.* 2nd ed. Syracuse: Syracuse University Press, 1965.

Douglas, V. I. "Stop, Look and Listen: The Problem of Sustained Attention and Impulse Control in Hyperactive and Normal Children." *Canadian Journal of Behavioural Science* 4 (1972): 259–82.

Druker, J. F., and Hagen, J. W. "Developmental Trends in the Processing of Task Relevant and Task Irrelevant Information." *Child Development* 40 (1969): 371–82.

Dykman, R. A.; Ackerman, P. T.; Clements, S. D.; and Peters, J. E. "Specific Learning Disabilities: An Attentional Deficit Syndrome." In *Progress in Learning Disabilities,* edited by H. R. Myklebust. Vol. II. New York: Grune & Stratton, 1971.

Elkind, D.; Larson, M.; and Van Doorninck, W. "Perceptual Decentration Learning and Performance in Slow and Average Readers." *Journal of Educational Psychology* 56 (1965): 50–56.

Hagen, J. W. "The Effect of Distraction on Selective Attention." *Child Development* 38 (1967): 685–94.

———, and Hallahan, D. P. "Selective Attention in Retardates: A Validation Study." Report No. 17, Developmental Program, Department of Psychology, University of Michigan, 1972.

———, and Huntsman, N. J. "Selective Attention in Mental Retardates." *Developmental Psychology* 5 (1971): 151–60.

———, and Sabo, R. "A Developmental Study of Selective Attention." *Merrill-Palmer Quarterly* 13 (1967): 159–72.

Hallahan, D. P., and Cruickshank, W. M. *Psychoeducational Foundations of Learning Disabilities.* Englewood Cliffs, N.J.: Prentice-Hall, 1973.

———; Kauffman, J. M.; and Ball, D. W. "Developmental Trends in Recall of Central and Incidental Auditory Material." *Journal of Experimental Child Psychology,* 17 (1974): 409–421.

———; Kauffman, J. M.; and Ball, D. W. "Effects of Stimulus Attenuation on Selective Attention Performance of Children." *Journal of Genetic Psychology* 125 (1974): 71–77.

———; Stainback, S.; Ball, D. W.; and Kauffman, J. M. "Selective Attention in Cerebral Palsied and Normal Children." *Journal of Abnormal Child Psychology* 1 (1973): 280–91.

Hammerlynck, L. A.; Martin, J.; and Rolland, J. "Systematic Observation of Behavior: A Primary Teacher Skill." *Education and Training of the Mentally Retarded* 3 (1968): 39–42.

Huelsman, C. B. "The WISC Subtest Syndrome for Disabled Readers." *Perceptual and Motor Skills* 30 (1970): 535–50.

Kagan, J. "Reflection-Impulsivity and Reading Ability in Primary Grade Children." *Child Development* 36 (1965): 609–28.

———. "Developmental Studies in Reflection and Analysis." In *Perceptual Development in Children,* edited by A. H. Kidd and J. H. Rivoire. New York: International Universities Press, 1966.

———, and Moss, H. A. *Birth to Maturity: A Study in Psychological Development.* New York: Wiley, 1962.

———; Rosman, B.; Day, D.; Albert, J.; and Phillips, W. "Information Processing in the Child: Significance of Analytic and Reflective Attitudes." *Psychological Monographs* 78 (1964) (Whole No. 578).

Keogh, B. K., and Donlon, G. "Field Independence, Impulsivity, and Learning Disabilities." *Journal of Learning Disabilities* 5 (1972): 331–36.

Lasky, E. Z., and Tobin, H. "Linguistic and Nonlinguistic Competing Message Effects." *Journal of Learning Disabilities* 6 (1973): 243–50.

Maccoby, E. E. "Selective Auditory Attention in Children." In *Advances in Child Development and Behavior*, edited by L. P. Lippsitt & C. C. Spiker. Vol. III. New York: Academic Press, 1967.

———, and Hagen, J. W. "Effects of Distraction upon Central versus Incidental Recall: Developmental Trends." *Journal of Experimental Child Psychology* 2 (1965): 280–89.

———, and Konrad, K. W. "Age Trends in Selective Listening." *Journal of Experimental Child Psychology* 3 (1966): 113–22.

McGhee, P. E., and Crandall, V. C. "Beliefs in Internal-External Control of Reinforcements and Academic Performance." *Child Development* 39 (1968): 91–102.

Mercer, C. D.; Cullinan, D.; Hallahan, D. P.; and LaFleur, N. K. "Modeling and Attention in Learning Disabled Children." *Journal of Learning Disabilities*, in press.

Mondani, M. S., and Tutko, T. A. "Relationship of Academic Underachievement to Incidental Learning." *Journal of Consulting and Clinical Psychology* 33 (1969): 558–60.

Patterson, G. R.; Cobb, J. A.; and Ray, R. S. "Direct Intervention in the Classroom: A Set of Procedures for the Aggressive Child." In *Implementing Behavioral Programs for Schools and Clinics*, edited by F. W. Clark, D. R. Evans, and L. A. Hammerlynck. Champaign, Ill.: Research Press, 1972.

Rosvold, H. E.; Mirksy, A. F.; Sarason, I.; Bransome, E. D.; and Beck, L. H. "A Continuous Performance Test of Brain Damage." *Journal of Consulting Psychology* 20 (1956): 343–52.

Ruble, D. N., and Nakamura, C. Y. "Outerdirectedness as a Problem-Solving Approach in Relation to Developmental Level and Selected Task Variables." *Child Development* 44 (1973): 519–20.

Sabatino, D. A., and Ysseldyke, J. E. "Effect of Extraneous 'Background' on Visual-Perceptual Performance of Readers and Non-Readers." *Perceptual and Motor Skills* 35 (1971): 323–28.

Senf, G. M. "Development of Immediate Memory for Bisensory Stimuli in Normal Children and Children with Learning Disorders." *Developmental Psychology Monographs* 1(6) (1969): 1–27.

———, and Feshbach, S. "Development of Bisensory Memory in Culturally Deprived, Dyslexic, and Normal Readers," *Journal of Educational Psychology* 61 (1970): 461–70.

———, and Freundl, P. C. "Memory and Attention Factors in Specific Learning Disabilities." *Journal of Learning Disabilities* 4 (1971): 94–106.

Shaw, R. L., and Uhl, N. P. "Control of Reinforcement and Academic Achievement." *Journal of Educational Research* 64 (1971): 226–28.

Silverman, M.; Davids, A.; and Andrews, J. M. "Powers of Attention and Academic Achievement." *Perceptual and Motor Skills* 17 (1963): 243–49.

Sroufe, L. A.; Sonies, B. C.; West, W. D.; and Wright, F. S. "Anticipatory Heart Rate Deceleration and Reaction Time in Children with and without Referral for Learning Disability." *Child Development* 44 (1973): 267–73.

Stainback, S. B.; Stainback, W. C.; and Hallahan, D. P. "Effect of Background Music on Learning." *Exceptional Children* 40 (1973): 109–10.

Stroop, J. R. "Studies in Interference in Serial Verbal Reactions." *Journal of Experimental Psychology* 18 (1935): 643–61.

Sykes, D. H.; Douglas, V. I.; and Morgenstern, G. "Sustained Attention in Hyperactive Children." *Journal of Child Psychology and Psychiatry* 14 (1973): 213–20.

______; Douglas, V. I.; Weiss, G.; and Minde, K. K. "Attention in Hyperactive Children and the Effect of Methylphenidate (Ritalin)." *Journal of Child Psychology and Psychiatry* 12 (1971): 129–39.

Tarver, S. G., and Hallahan, D. P. "Attention Deficits in Children with Learning Disabilities: A Review." *Journal of Learning Disabilities* 7 (1974): 560–69.

Turnure, J. E. "Children's Reactions to Distractors in a Learning Situation." *Developmental Psychology* 2 (1970): 115–22.

______. "Outerdirectedness in EMR Boys and Girls." *American Journal of Mental Deficiency* 78 (1973): 163–70.

______, and Zigler, E. "Outer-directedness in the Problem Solving of Normal and Retarded Children." *Journal of Abnormal and Social Psychology* 69 (1964): 427–36.

Walker, H. M.; Mattson, R. H.; and Buckley, N. K. "Special Class Placement as a Treatment Alternative for Deviant Behavior in Children." In *Modifying Deviant Social Behaviors in Various Classroom Settings*, edited by F. A. M. Benson. Eugene, Ore.: University of Oregon, 1969.

Werner, H., and Strauss, A. A. "Causal Factors in Low Performance." *American Journal of Mental Deficiency* 45 (1940): 213–18.

______, and Strauss, A. A. "Pathology of Figure-Background Relation in the Child." *Journal of Abnormal and Social Psychology* 36 (1941): 236–48.

Werry, J. S., and Quay, H. "Observing the Classroom Behavior of Elementary School Children." Paper presented at the meeting of the Council for Exceptional Children, New York, April 1968.

Witkin, A. A.; Dyk, R. E.; Faterson, H. F.; Goodenough, D. R.; and Karp, S. A. *Psychological Differentiation*. New York: Wiley, 1962.

Zeaman, D., and House, B. J. "The Role of Attention in Retardate Discrimination Learning." In *Handbook of Mental Deficiency*, edited by N. R. Ellis. New York: McGraw-Hill, 1963.

Zigler, E. "Mental Retardation: Current Issues and Approaches." In *Review of Child Development Research*, edited by L. Hoffman and M. Hoffman. Vol. 2. New York: Russell Sage Foundation, 1966.

Editors' note: The last chapter was concerned primarily with research on the psychological aspect of distractibility; the present chapter deals specifically with research into the education of distractible and hyperactive children.

Drs. Daniel P. Hallahan and James M. Kauffman have systematically reviewed this bulk of literature. They have drawn from applied research studies directly related to teaching methods for distractible children and have also reviewed basic research pertinent to the problem. The classroom parameters of environmental stimuli and teaching materials are discussed. The literature pertaining to each indicates that the teacher can have a great deal of impact on children's attention skills by careful consideration of the kinds of materials and environment provided the pupils. The powerful influence of *language* is also noted and reviewed, as is modeling as a possible teaching strategy. The crucial role of behavior modification techniques as they relate to the education of attention and motor control skills are discussed. The use of reward and punishment in the teaching situation is considered.

After reading this chapter, as well as Dr. William Cruickshank's chapter, "The Learning Environment" and Ms. Evelyn Marshall's chapter "Teaching Materials for Children with Learning Disabilities" of Volume 1, the teacher should have a sound research base as well as practical suggestions for teaching the distractible and hyperactive child.

Daniel P. Hallahan, Ph.D., is Assistant Professor of Special Education at the University of Virginia. Dr. Hallahan completed his doctorate in the Combined Program in Education and Psychology at the University of Michigan, where he served as a Research Associate at the Institute for the Study of Mental Retardation and Related Disabilities. He is the author of numerous books and articles in the field of learning disabilities and mental retardation.

James M. Kauffman, Ed.D., is Associate Professor of Education, Department of Special Education, at the University of Virginia. He is a member of the Council for Exceptional Children, the Association for the Advancement of Behavior Therapy, and the Society for Research in Child Development. Dr. Kauffman's experience with children includes teaching emotionally disturbed children at the Menninger Clinic, Topeka, Kansas, and instructing disturbed and normal children in public schools. He is the co-author of many books and journal articles in special education.

6

Research on the Education of Distractible and Hyperactive Children

DANIEL P. HALLAHAN AND JAMES M. KAUFFMAN

One of the most disconcerting things that can happen to a teacher is to have a child (or a group of children) in the class who is disruptive. While a child can be disruptive in any number of ways for any number of reasons, the disturbing behaviors we are concerned with in this chapter are those that are frequently subsumed under the labels of "distractibility" and "hyperactivity." In this chapter, we will present a review of research that focuses on using various educational techniques for distractible and hyperactive behavior. In addition, we will formulate educational strategies based upon research from the literature of experimental child psychology.

The most notable educational program to be developed specifically for the purpose of training the attentional skills of children evolved from the work of Werner and Strauss (1940, 1941) with distractible, hyperactive, mentally retarded children. The skeletal structure of this educational approach was later published in the now classic works—Strauss and Lehtinen's *Psychopathology and Education of the Brain-Injured Child* (1947), and Strauss and Kephart's *Psychopathology and Education of the Brain-Injured Child. Vol. II. Progress in Theory and Clinic* (1955).

Cruickshank, a former colleague of Werner and Strauss, refined Strauss and Lehtinen's techniques and extended these procedures for use with distractible, hyperactive children of normal intelligence. Cruickshank's project (Cruickshank, Bentzen, Ratzeburg, and Tannhauser 1961) modified Strauss and Lehtinen's institutional program to make it applicable for a public school setting. Cruickshank based his program on what he considered to be four essential educational components for the unique psychological characteristics of the distractible child: (1) reduced environmental stimuli, (2) reduced space, (3) a structured school program, and (4) an increase in the saliency of teaching materials.

No one of the above four elements was considered to be more crucial than any of the others; however, the concept of reduced environmental stimuli was certainly the most radical departure from the traditional educational routine. Among other things, the following alterations were made: windows were opaque; ceilings and walls were sound-treated; the color of walls, ceiling, and floor were the same; the floor was carpeted; bulletin boards were used only for specific learning experiences; the amount of furniture was decreased; the number of children in the class was kept small; teaching materials, when not in use, were placed in closed cupboards; the teacher wore plain clothes with a minimum of flashy jewelry. In short, every possible effort was made to reduce extraneous stimulation.

Considering space to correlate positively with opportunity for stimulation, Cruickshank placed the children in as small a physical space as possible. The size of the room was reduced and cubicles were constructed in which the children did their seat-work. At first, the child did all of his work within the environment of his cubicle, or "office space." Gradually, he was given more and more opportunity to do his work at an unenclosed desk or table with other children.

With regard to structure, Cruickshank believed that these distractible children, so much at the mercy of their own impulses, were in need of a tightly structured life style. A highly teacher-directed program was the result. The program was set up to reduce the number of decisions required of the child. Thus, it was thought, the number of failure experiences would be minimized for the child. Only after a period of some time was the child gradually given more and more responsibility for deciding what he wanted to do with his time.

While the physical environment was generally devised to be non-stimulating, the teaching materials definitely were not. Whenever possible the stimulus value of the materials was enhanced. By creating a sharp contrast between the bland surroundings and the striking materials it was hypothesized that the child would be better able to focus on the relevant stimuli to the exclusion of the extraneous.

Cruickshank's program has not gone without controversy. No aspect of the Strauss-Lehtinen and Cruickshank educational approaches has caused more debate than their firm beliefs in the beneficial results of reducing the amount and intensity of environmental stimuli in the classroom. Indeed, back in the late 1950s and early 1960s, when Cruickshank and others began to popularize this kind of educational environment, there was probably no more intense a debate about the education of exceptional children than the one surrounding the benefits of stimulus reduction. Unfortunately, advocates and critics alike reacted on raw emotions rather than on the basis of objective evidence. Advocates were quick to climb aboard the bandwagon and critics were all too eager to throw roadblocks in its way.

Like other innovative educational ideas before and after it (e.g., open classrooms, perceptual-motor training), Cruickshank's program fell prey to overzealous supporters who overextended its application. While Cruickshank championed a reduced-stimuli environment only for those children exhibiting distractibility and hyperactivity, the educational consumers in the field frequently used it with children with a variety of learning and behavioral problems. Also, educators often make the critical mistake of relying upon etiological classifications in deciding whether to include a child in a Strauss-Lehtinen-Cruickshank classroom. Because the original program of Strauss and Lehtinen was recommended for use with brain injured children and because some of the children in the Cruickshank *et al.* (1961) project displayed evidence of brain injury, reduced environmental-stimuli programs were employed with children simply because they were diagnosed as brain injured.

As has been pointed out, however, some of the children included in Strauss and Lehtinen's program were quite possibly not brain injured (Sarason 1949). This possible misdiagnosis, coupled with the fact that brain injury is still extremely difficult to diagnose reliably and validly, points to the gross error committed by those who have assumed that any child labeled as brain injured should be shielded from normal environmental stimuli in the classroom.

The misuse of the Strauss-Lehtinen-Cruickshank procedures has no doubt contributed to the vociferous criticisms which they have received. Opponents of the program also were prone to equate the reduced-stimuli approach with barbaric treatment of the child. Such illogical, emotional reactions, while surprising at first glance, are perhaps more understandable when one considers that the Cruickshank project was the first structured approach to gain widespread use. Also, Cruickshank's suggestion of a structured, directive program came at a time when the prevailing attitude was to provide these children with an unstructured, open approach. Predating the application of behavior modification programs of today, it is not surprising that a program suggesting the reduction of irrelevant environmental stimulation was seen as cruelly depriving children of sensory excitation.

Critics have, in addition, pointed to the inconclusive results of the Cruickshank project. The success was less than what was hoped for. After one year in the program the experimental children had made significant gains on six of ten scoring categories of the Bender-Gestalt and on the amount of distractibility shown on the Syracuse Visual Figure-Background Test. However, no gains were found on measures of intelligence and academic achievement. After the year-long project was completed, the children returned to traditional classroom designs and the few gains noted above were eliminated.

This latter finding, as has been noted elsewhere (Hallahan and Cruickshank 1973), is not unlike the findings regarding preschool compensatory programs—any advances made are generally reversed when the child begins regular public schooling. The generally disappointing findings after one year on the experimental project, however, are more difficult to explain. It should be remembered that the project was initiated as a demonstration-pilot study. While this does not completely justify the inconclusive results, it is a fact of life that field-based research is extremely difficult to conduct and seldom yields unambiguous evidence. When the complexity of the undertaking reaches the proportions of the Cruickshank project, the difficulties multiply. This is attested by the fact that there have been no replications of the *total* program reported in the literature. The researcher is thus confronted with a most vexing dilemma. Because of the looseness of control over crucial variables—e.g., teacher competency and motivation, administrative cooperation, parental cooperation—field studies must rely on a greater number of replications than laboratory research before any definitive conclusions can be reached. However, the difficulty of developing an exact educational program strongly mitigates against conducting field-based replications.

There have been studies since the Cruickshank project which have focused on two matters germane to the program—manipulation of the environmental surroundings and manipulation of stimulus materials. For the most part the former studies have been undertaken for the purpose of assessing the efficacy of the Strauss-Lehtinen-Cruickshank procedures, while studies relevant to the importance of the teaching materials have come from the domain of experimental child psychology. We will now explore each of these areas.

MANIPULATION OF ENVIRONMENTAL SURROUNDINGS

In terms of studies pertaining to the exploration of the effectiveness of reduced stimulation, only seven studies were located for this review—one in a laboratory and six in naturalistic settings. As noted above, none of the field-based investigations was even a close approximation of Strauss and Lehtinen or Cruickshank's *total* program. Reduction of environmental stimulation was the variable under scrutiny. This point is often overlooked by the authors of these studies themselves.

The first study pertaining to the efficacy of Cruickshank's educational techniques happened by chance (Frey 1961). In a study for his dissertation, Frey began to compare the reading abilities of brain injured and non-brain injured children of near normal and normal intelligence. Finding the brain injured children to have superior reading skills compared to the controls, even though the two groups were matched in IQ and age, Frey looked into the situational variables of both groups in order to account for this curious finding. He conjectured that the particular program that the brain injured children were enrolled in—a non-stimulating environment based upon Strauss-Lehtinen-Cruickshank concepts—was superior to the traditional programs of the control group children in promoting reading skills. This evidence, however, must be kept within the confines of speculation since the interpretation of the findings is purely *post hoc*.

Unfortunately, the other studies of the effects of stimulus reduction (Gorton 1972; Jenkins, Gorrafa, and Griffiths 1972; Rost and Charles 1967; Shores and Haubrich 1969; Slater 1968; Somervill, Warnberg, and Bost 1973) are contradictory and inconclusive. Three of the six studies indicated success on such various dependent variables as attending behavior (Shores and Haubrich 1969), computation of arithmetic problems (Gorton 1972), and completion of unspecified worksheets (Jenkins *et al.* 1972). On the negative side, however, investigators have also found no significant changes in academic achievement (Rost and Charles 1967; Shores and Haubrich 1969; Slater 1968) and time to complete perceptual-motor tasks (Somervill *et al.* 1973).

Table 6.1 summarizes information regarding the dependent variables of the five studies as well as other pertinent data. From this summary of information an explanation for the generally inconsistent results can be posited. The children under investigation have ranged from normals to brain injured, mentally retarded. Only three of the studies (Rost and Charles 1967; Shores and Haubrich 1969; Somervill *et al.* 1973) attempted to study children displaying behavioral characteristics of distractibility and/or hyperactivity. Two of these studies (Rost and Charles 1967; Shores and Haubrich 1969) were vague in their specification of how it was determined that the children were hyperactive and distractible. The other study by Somervill *et al.* relied upon teacher ratings, and an astounding 35 percent of the population was found to be distractible. This high percentage causes one to question how severe the distractibility was in many of the "distractible" subjects. The contradictory findings might thus be the result of this wide heterogeneity of subjects studied by the different investigators. In addition, the amount and kind of stimulus reduction has ranged from the separation of the total classroom but not individuals within it to the total seclusion of individual subjects within an enclosed cubicle. Duration of the experimental procedures, too, has varied and has been for relatively short periods of time.

Although the results have been generally conflicting, when one examines the dependent measures under scrutiny, some tentative conclusions can be advanced. For the most part, whenever attention was measured or tasks appeared to rely upon attentional skills (simple arithmetic problems of Gorton, completion of work sheets of Jenkins *et al.*, attending behavior of Shores and Haubrich), there has been a favorable effect of stimulus reduction. On higher level measures, however, stimulus reduction has not faired as well. One possible exception to this trend was the study of Somervill *et al.* which found no differences on the time required to complete a number of perceptual-motor tasks—tasks that undoubtedly required a great deal of attention. Aside from the question raised above regarding subject selection for this study, other methodological concerns can be raised. Although the subjects were instructed, "We'll try to keep everything quiet so you can do your best and finish as fast as possible" (p. 177), the authors did not indicate that the subjects were encouraged in any other way to perform quickly. Since time to complete the task was the dependent variable, this is crucial. In addition, the child was given a reward after the allotted period of time on each task whether the child completed it or not. Thus, after the first task or two, the child could very easily have recognized that completing the task as soon as possible was not necessary for reward.

Table 6.1
Summary of Pertinent Information Regarding Six Field-Based Studies of the Effectiveness of Reduced Environmental Stimuli

Study	Population	N	Type of Stimulus Reduction	Length of Program	Approx. Total No. of Hrs. in Experimental Setting(s)	Dependent Variables	Results
Gorton 1972	EMR, brain injured; EMR, non-brain injured; Normals	14 14 14	Total seclusion in enclosed cubicle; Visual seclusion; Auditory seclusion	6 weeks	12 hours	Simple arithmetic problems	Non-brain injured, EMRs did best under visual seclusion; brain injured were best under total seculsion; normals did best under total and visual seclusion
Jenkins et al. 1972	Undifferentiated EMRs	8	Isolation in small rooms	1 week	25 hours	Completion of unspecified work sheets	Positive
Rost and Charles 1967	EMR, about half diagnosed brain injured, the other half displayed hyperactivity and distractibility	10	Three-sided cubicles	4 months	140 hours	Wide-Range Achievement Test	No significant differences

Shores and Haubrich 1969	Emotionally disturbed, hyperactive children with academic retardation	3	Three-sided cubicles	16 days	32 hours	Attending behavior; arithmetic rate; reading rate	Attending behavior increased; arithmetic and reading rate did not
Slater 1968	Normal 7th graders	101	Classroom isolated from other classrooms and children in the building	2 days	6 hours	Reading test	No significant difference
Somervill, Warnberg, and Bost 1973	Distractible children from regular classrooms and nondistractible children from regular classrooms	8 8	Three-sided cubicles	10 days	2½ hours	Time to complete perceptual-motor tasks	No significant differences for either group

At first glance this trend of no effects on cognitive tasks but effects on attending skills would seem particularly damaging to the utility of the reduction of extraneous stimuli in the environment. For higher cognitive abilities to be affected, however, it would seem logical that the length of the programs would have to be longer than most of the studies. In some studies the cubicles were introduced for very short periods of time. In these situations, in particular, it is conceivable that the introduction of cubicles, itself, would prove distracting for some children. Placing a child in any new situation, even though it might be designed to aid the child, will require a period of adaptation. In addition, it must be repeated that these studies manipulated only one aspect—stimulus reduction—of the Strauss-Lehtinen-Cruickshank approach. This technique of stimulus reduction is devised to help the distractible child in attending behaviors. Once attending is under control, the teacher must then teach the child the higher cognitive skills involved in academic achievement. Thus, if stimulus reduction is shown to increase children's abilities to attend to the task at hand, then it has served its major purpose. The teacher must then do the job of teaching. While the evidence is *far* from conclusive, the results of the field studies generally suggest that attending skills are enhanced by stimulus-reduction procedures.

In a laboratory study of stimulus reduction using normal and cerebral palsied subjects, Fassler (1970) compared the effects of normal auditory input (placebo "ear protectors") and reduced auditory input (ear protectors). It was found that the cerebral palsied gained significantly from the reduced auditory input on measures of memory and attention whereas the normal children showed no gains. The improved performance for cerebral palsied, but not for normals, is not surprising since there is strong evidence to indicate that cerebral palsied individuals, especially spastics as were mainly used in this experiment, are likely to be more distractible than normals (Cruickshank, Bice, Wallen, and Lynch 1965). Thus, the importance of matching educational procedure with the particular psychological needs of the child is once again underlined.

Because the use of cubicles has become a widely recommended and widely employed means of controlling the environmental surround in special classes, caution should be taken in their use. It is our observation that whether or not the use of cubicles is successful in increasing children's learning seems to depend on precisely *how* they are constructed and used. Cubicles that are flimsy, poorly constructed, or easily moved about by children are of little value, for they themselves become a source of additional distracting stimuli. Furthermore, if children are allowed to write graffiti or post pictures, their work, etc., on the cubicles, distractions are multiplied, not attenuated. Only when cubicles are a fixed, stable, uncluttered part of the classroom environment can they serve their intended purpose. Cubicles should become a special part of the environment that is associated with study and work behaviors, i.e., they should become discriminative stimuli for productive academic behavior. In order for them to function as such, the teacher must make certain that children use the cubicles *only* when they are engaged in academic tasks. Cubicles should never, therefore, be used as "time out" or isolation areas, and any child observed to engage in nonstudy behaviors while in a cubicle should be immediately removed. The teacher must make it clear that the cubicles are places in which to work—they are not for playing, sleeping, daydreaming, or other nonstudy behaviors.

MANIPULATION OF TEACHING MATERIALS

Besides advocating certain changes in the more global aspects of the distractible child's environmental surround, Strauss and Lehtinen and Cruickshank also recommended numerous modifications of the teaching materials themselves. These changes were made with the major psychological characteristics of the hyperactive-distractible child in mind. Extraneous information was eliminated and aspects of the task which required the child's attention were emphasized. Observing that such children, when presented with a page filled with math problems, were unable to concentrate on these tasks, Cruickshank suggested that the teachers give the child one problem per page. Also, reading books displaying colorful pictures on the same page as the text was assumed to be distracting. Such potential distractors as colors, however, were used to capture the child's attention. For example, in a math problem deviced to teach the child numbers, the numeral *3* and three dots might be red in color and the numeral *8* and eight dots might appear in blue. By adding the additional cue of color, the discrimination would be made easier for the child. Also the mathematical signs—+, −, ÷, ×—would be printed in different colors to highlight the mathematical operation required for solution. On word-recognition tasks, the letters of words were printed in colors in order to draw the child's attention to them.

Whereas the reduction of environmental stimuli has received a modest amount of research, the procedures outlined above for constructing teaching materials for distractible children have received none. This is indeed unfortunate since it would actually be easier to conduct research which assessed teaching materials rather than cubicles. The latter are certainly more expensive to make and more difficult to implement appropriately within the confines of a public school setting. The concreteness and specificity of teaching materials would also be easier to manipulate as an independent variable in comparison to the global variable of "reduction of environmental stimuli."

Even though special educators have not addressed themselves in a research effort to the efficacy of the above teaching materials, researchers within experimental child psychology have been involved in extensive research on the effects of different kinds of stimulus cues on a variety of laboratory tasks. The literature involves normal children, but the implications for deviant populations are apparent.

Dimensional Preferences

First of all, it has been demonstrated that children have definite preferences for either form or color. When asked to sort or match objects or pictures differing in form and color, children will choose one or the other dimension on which to base their judgments. Developmental studies have consistently found preferences to vary with age—children from preschool through six years of age prefer or attend to the dimension of color while form has more stimulus value for older children (see Pick and Pick [1970] for a review of these studies). That preferences are important for the performance of children has been demonstrated. Odom and Corbin (1973), for example, found that children were better able to perform on memory tasks when the dimensions critical for solution matched the preferences of the children.

It is important to note, also, that the early stages of learning to read, a process requiring the discrimination of stimuli based on form, occurs during a developmental period when color still has greater saliency than form. If it were found that distractible children were developmentally retarded in their perceptual preferences (as they are in other ways), the color preference would be even more dramatic.

There is some evidence that preferences can be changed. Gaines (1970) first determined subjects' preferences for color or form and then trained the children with oddity problems (i.e., "Pick the one of three that is different from the other two") to make choices based on the non-preferred dimension. With a readministration of the preference test, she found that preferences could be changed.

The literature on dimensional preferences has obvious educational implications which coincide with those previously recommended by Strauss, Lehtinen, and Cruickshank. Teachers should be ready to take advantage of the preferences of children. For example, children who are color-dominant could be given characters in different colors in order to help in the discrimination of letters, words, and numbers. The results of Gaines also indicate that teachers could teach preference for form which must ultimately be accomplished. In other words, those children who did not originally attend to form could be taught gradually to discriminate on the basis of form alone. It is important that teachers first determine the particular dimensional preference for *each individual child.* While developmental studies have found age-related shifts in preferences, these are *group differences.* Individual children may exhibit preferences the opposite of other children of the same age. Without research regarding attention to dimensions on distractible children it is all the more imperative that teachers explore the particular attentional responses of these children. Besides form and color mentioned above, the dimension of texture might also be investigated. The sandpaper letters employed in the VAKT (visual, auditory, kinesthetic, tactual) method of Fernald have received clinical support as appropriate teaching materials; and, thus the tactual sense warrants consideration (cf. Massad and Etzel 1972).

Cue Saliency and Discrimination Learning

Stevenson (1972) has reviewed a number of studies in which various dimensions have been presented as either relevant or irrelevant to the visual discrimination to be learned (Lubker 1967; 1969; Osler and Kofsky 1965).

Using the three dimensions of brightness (black versus white), size (big versus small), and form (square versus circle), Lubker (1967, 1969) presented a number of discrimination trials to children in which form was the relevant dimension (i.e., attention to form resulted in reward). Stevenson concluded:

> The conclusions from these studies are straightforward. We can make learning easier for children, especially for young children, by eliminating irrelevant information, for they have a hard time doing this for themselves. We also can be helpful if we heighten the differences among stimuli by having them differ consistently in more than one aspect. The beginning reader, for example, might be confused less often by letters such as "b" and "d" if, in his first encounters with the letters, they differed in color or size as well as in direction. When irrelevant information is redundant it may be helpful; otherwise it is a hindrance. (p. 230)

The example chosen by Stevenson is an excellent one. Reversals of letters and words such as *b* and *d* and *was* and *saw* are frequently reported by teachers of learning disabled children. By presenting those letters or words which the child often confuses in different bright colors, discrimination should be made easier.

Research also suggests that, if, for example, color is used, the color should be a part of the letter itself rather than merely associated with it (e.g., a colored dot on the flashcard containing the letter). House (1970), using educable and trainable retarded children, found that additional relevant cues are more helpful "if they are attributes of a single stimulus but retard learning if they are spatially separated cues from the same relevant dimension" (p. 403).

Using as a theoretical base the work of Gibson (1969), another procedure can be suggested to the teacher. Gibson has put forth a theory of perceptual development which states that a child learns to make discriminations based upon the distinctive features of stimuli. In the example of *b* and *d* the particular side of the *o* on which the *l* falls is the distinctive feature with regard to the particular name of the letter. Since attention to such distinctive features are so important to learning, it can be suggested that rather than printing the whole letter in color the teacher might highlight the *l* of *b* and *d* by presenting it in a bright color. The hypothesized result would be that such a technique would draw the child's attention to the crucial portion of the two letters which differentiates them.

Fading Techniques

Once the teacher has presented the child with stimuli which have been made (through the use of color or size) to capture the child's attention, the teacher is faced with the task of re-deploying the child's attention to the form of the object. This must be accomplished since the child is not going to be presented for the rest of his life with materials to read which are color or size-cued. The study by Gaines discussed above suggested that the teacher could directly train the child to attend to form by presenting oddity problems requiring attention to form for solution. Another method has also been used quite successfully in the experimental discrimination literature—fading procedures. A body of literature has accumulated which suggests that a gradual fading out of the additional salient cue is a useful procedure (Moore and Goldiamond 1964; Terrace 1968; Trabasso and Bower 1968).

These experiments have, with a wide variety of subject populations, presented subjects with objects varying on two dimensions such as brightness and form, e.g., a white square and a black rectangle. Once the subject has learned, for instance, to choose the black rectangle, the blackness is gradually faded out over trials so that eventually the two objects vary only in form. The subject has thus been trained to make the discrimination based on form alone in that he is able to choose a white rectangle over a white square.

The application to the educational forum suggests that the teacher could first have the child learn the difference between a red *b* and black *d* and a large *was* and a small *saw*. By gradually fading the redness of the *b* and reducing the size of the *was*, the discriminations would be made easier. There is also evidence to indicate that fading out of critical cues, e.g., *l* of *b* and *d*, would be of more value than fading out color cues contained in the whole letter (Schwartz, Firestone, and Terry 1971).

Besides the fading out procedures discussed above, "fading in" techniques have also been used. In this procedure the child is first presented the correct stimulus alone. Gradually, the incorrect stimulus is faded in. Stevenson (1972), in his review of the "fading in" technique, presents a variety of studies which have demonstrated that fading in the incorrect stimulus has a beneficial influence of helping children to make discriminations (Bijou and Baer 1963; Caron 1968; Cole, Dent, Eguchi, Fujii, and Johnson 1964; Spiker 1959). As noted by Stevenson, Caron's experiment demonstrated that fading in procedures have also been successful when emphasizing the criterial features of the stimuli. This procedure focuses the child's attention on the distinctive features of the task.

The use of fading in procedures should prove useful to the classroom teacher of the distractible child. For example, the teacher might give the child a *b* by itself. Then *d* would be given in conjunction with *b* but *d* would be printed in very light ink so it would be difficult to see. The ink of the *d* would be darkened gradually over many presentations.

The particular advantage of both fading out and fading in procedures is that they make it difficult for the child to make inappropriate responses. These procedures can be used to result in what has been called "errorless" learning. Especially with the fading in procedure, there is little opportunity for error. The child from the very beginning is responding to the correct stimulus. Such a technique gives the child little chance to choose the incorrect stimulus. Future research is needed to compare the relative effectiveness of fading in and fading out procedures and the use of both procedures focusing on distinctive features. The results already obtained hold relevance for the educational setting.

Studies of Central-Incidental Learning

Hagen, using a short-term memory format devised by Maccoby and Hagen (1965), has investigated the development of selective attention in children. The task materials typically consist of cards upon which are a line drawing of an animal and a household object. The same animal always appears with the same household object. The child is first given a number of trials in which a series of cards is presented to him, and the child is then asked to recall the serial position of the animals. The number correct constitutes a central recall score. After these trials, the child is asked to pair the animals with the household objects with which they had always appeared. The number of correct matchings comprises an incidental learning score. It has consistently been found that central recall increases with age, whereas incidental performance remains the same or declines (Druker and Hagen 1969; Hagen 1967; Maccoby and Hagen 1965; Hallahan, Kauffman, and Ball 1974*b*). Furthermore, with age children attend more to the central or relevant stimuli, relative to the incidental or irrelevant stimuli. The same general findings have been replicated in an auditory analog of the task (Hallahan, Kauffman, and Ball 1974*a*). In addition, it has been found that institutionalized mentally retarded (Hagen and Huntsman 1971) and underachieving children are deficient in selective attention to the central materials. Non-institutionalized, cerebral palsied children have been found to be inferior to CA controls but not MA matched controls (Hallahan, Stainback, Ball, and Kauffman 1973).

Relevant to the discussion here, experiments have been conducted which have attempted to affect selective attention by manipulating the task materials. In the first place, Hagen (1967), after administering a condition in which only the animals were present, found children to perform better than when the incidental household objects were included. This finding that a child's performance is impaired when irrelevant stimuli are included is consistent with the studies of House (1970) and Lubker (1967, 1969) discussed previously. The addition of stimulus elements which are not relevant to the task at hand are detrimental to central task performance. For the child who is already distractible and thus likely to attend to inessential stimuli, one can only guess at the effects of extraneous information.

Druker and Hagen (1969) modified the usual task materials by varying the spatial separation of the relevant and irrelevant stimuli. They found that there was a significant effect upon incidental recall only, with fewer incidental stimuli being recalled when the central and incidental materials were separated spatially. Since the central scores were not affected, the selective attention performance of the children was not really improved by spatial separation. However, it can be hypothesized that, if the central task were to be increased in complexity and/or distractible subjects were used, the greater attention to incidental stimuli in the contiguous condition might impair central task performance.

The use of brightness and color cues has also not resulted in much change in selective attention performance. Hallahan, Kauffman, and Ball

(1974*b*) found that reducing the saliency of the incidental stimuli had no affect on central or incidental performance. Sabo and Hagen (1973) found that using black line drawings of both the central and incidental stimuli increased recognition of the central stimuli but had no influence on serial position recall. A possible explanation for the disappointing results of the above two studies is that altering the color or brightness of the stimuli may, for some children, arouse them to attend to both central and incidental stimuli. In the Hallahan *et al.* experiment, for example, even though the incidental stimuli were decreased in saliency, they were still visible to the subjects. The very fact that the irrelevant stimuli were reduced in discriminability may have resulted in some children responding more intensely to them in order to perceive what they were. Since there was no tangible reinforcement given the subject for attending to the relevant stimuli, it is possible that the low discriminability and novelty of the incidental stimuli could have actually made the incidental stimuli more salient for some of the poorly motivated and/or highly distractible children.

The results of the above studies of the manipulation of the task materials in central-incidental learning are not as clear cut as those which have used fading and the use of cues and cue preferences in discrimination learning.

CHANGING THE CHILD'S ATTENTIONAL STRATEGY

The two general approaches to training attentional skills discussed thus far—manipulation of the environmental surroundings and manipulation of teaching materials—have focused primarily on objects or materials external to the child. These techniques can be considered to be centered on changing environmental stimuli rather than on the child himself. In contrast to this focus on the stimuli rather than on the child, there have also been explorations of ways to encourage the child to reorient the way in which he deploys his attention. This latter approach, emphasizing the importance of changing the child's attentional strategies, views the individual as a potentially active participant in the attending process rather than as a passive organism completely under the influence of environmental stimuli.

Instructions Regarding Relevant Aspects of the Task

One seemingly obvious method of helping a child to pay attention is to instruct him with regard to what he should pay attention to. Pick, Christy, and Frankel (1972), for example, found that informing normal sixth graders beforehand of what relevant conceptual category to attend to was of great benefit in lowering reaction times on a task requiring subjects to make a "same-different" judgment. On her dichotic listening tasks, Maccoby (1967) has found that preparing subjects beforehand to pay attention to a particular voice (male or female) greatly increases the child's auditory selective attention. In addition, Lovitt and Smith (1972) found that instructions had a significant influence on the linguistic responses of a learning disabled child to certain aspects of visual stimuli.

Instructions given to the child can exert a powerful influence on the child. It is important to note that all the above studies employed specific instructions. The teacher who claims "But I'm always telling Johnny to pay attention" may not be doing enough. For the distractible child, especially, it would seem imperative that he specifically know what is expected of him and what aspects of the array of stimuli in his environment he should focus his attention on.

Verbal Labelling and Rehearsal

Verbal instructions, of course, have their limitations. Most importantly, the teacher is not able to be aware of when a child is in need of specific attentional instructions. The child must eventually work independently. One approach which has proven successful in encouraging independent attentional skills has been that of instructing the child in the use of verbal labels (Balling and Myers 1971; Furth and Milgram 1973; Hagen, Hargrave, and Ross 1973; Hagen and Kingsley 1968; Hagen, Meacham, and Mesibov 1970; Kingsley and Hagen 1969; Yussen 1972).

A generally consistent finding of these studies is that inducing the child to label and rehearse relevant aspects of the task improves the child's performance on a variety of tasks. There is also some limited data to suggest that verbal highlighting (requiring the child to label) is more effective than visual highlighting on discrimination tasks (Yussen 1972). In addition, in terms of memory abilities, there is evidence pointing toward verbal rehearsal as being more effective than mere labeling (Kingsley and Hagen 1969).

There is also evidence, however, that at certain ages induced labeling is deleterious. As Hagen, Meacham, and Mesibov stated after consideration of results of a number of studies by Hagen and his colleagues:

> Irrelevant stimuli have a detrimental effect at younger CA levels but no effect at older; imposed labeling facilitates at younger but inhibits performance at older CA levels. It seems that at younger ages the child is more dependent upon immediate stimuli in his environment, and has not developed strategies for coping with specific task demands. The older child becomes more dependent upon his own information processing strategies; he can ignore stimuli that are irrelevant unless they conflict with his strategies. Verbal labels which are imposed externally are irrelevant, and even distracting, for the individual who does not utilize them in task performance. (p. 57)

In terms of implications for the education of the distractible child, it would appear that training in verbal labeling and rehearsal would be of benefit. Conclusions must be tentative, however, since no experiments have been done with the inattentive child. From the literature on distractible children it can be inferred that they are frequently deficient in verbal coding strategies. Thus, training in the use of verbal strategies should be profitable. The results of Hagen, Hargrave, and Ross (1973), however, showing that prompting subjects rather than merely inducing them to label was of benefit, should serve as a cautionary note. The teacher should not be satisfied with simply telling the child to label relevant aspects of stimuli. In the early stages of learning at least, the teacher may have to monitor the child's use of labels to insure that the child is using them appropriately.

Modifying Impulsive Behavior

Numerous studies have investigated the effects of various procedures on changing the impulsive behavior of some children. Most of these studies have been conducted using the Matching Familiar Figures test (MFF) of Kagan (Kagan, Rosman, Day, Albert, and Phillips 1964) to identify impulsive and reflective children. Impulsive children are those who score below the median on response time but above the median in errors; the reflectives, on the other hand, are above the median in response time but below it in number of errors. The task itself requires the child to match a standard familiar figure with one correct choice from among a number of alternatives, all but one of which differ from the standard in some way. Thus, the impulsive child matches quickly and has a greater likelihood of selecting the wrong figure.

The simplest method of changing an impulsive cognitive tempo which comes to mind is to require the child to delay his response. This has been done, but what happens is that the impulsive child slows his response but he still maintains a high rate of errors (Kagan, Pearson, and Welch, 1966). In other words, merely slowing down the impulsive child's response time does not guarantee that he will use this extra time efficiently in the solution process. Merely saying to Johnny, "Slow down, take your time," is evidently not sufficient.

Those studies which have been successful in improving the accuracy of impulsive children have manipulated the particular attentional strategy the child uses. Noting the studies of Siegelman (1969) and Drake (1970), which have shown that impulsives' scanning strategies of the various alternatives are deficient in comparison to those of reflectives, Zelniker and colleagues (Zelniker, Jeffrey, Ault, and Parsons 1972; Zelniker and Oppenheimer 1973) have focused on modifying the information-seeking behavior of impulsive children. They have trained impulsive subjects to attend to the ways in which the alternatives differ from one another. This differentiation training has generalized to improved performance on a discrimination task (Zelniker and Oppenheimer 1973) as well as greater accuracy on the MFF (Zelniker *et al.* 1972). In the latter case, fewer errors were made with no change in response time.

Modeling has also been used to change the performance of impulsives (Debus 1970; Denney 1972; Ridberg, Parke, and Hetherington 1971). Impulsives who have viewed a reflective model have been influenced to perform like the model. As with the studies on forced latency, however, response times have proven easier to change than has accuracy. Having the model use scanning (the model points to where his eyes focus) and/or verbal cues (the model tells the subject what he is doing) has been the most effective way of increasing accuracy as well as increasing his decision time (Ridberg *et al.*

1971). Particularly pertinent to teachers of impulsive children in special classes, Ridberg et al. found that for their lower IQ children (those below 118) the combined use of both scanning and verbal cues was the most effective. Apparently, children of lower intellectual ability need many direct aids to successful performance. In other words, the more the performance of the child with lower intelligence is structured for him the better he is likely to do.

The above laboratory studies have clear implications for the classroom setting. Instructing children to slow down or to think before they respond may be a necessary but not sufficient teaching technique. The teacher must also be equipped to instruct specific ways in which the child should use his attention. Merely delaying a response still gives the distractible, impulsive child an opportunity to be distracted to irrelevant stimuli. In teaching letters of the alphabet to the impulsive child, for example, the teacher can encourage the child to slow down but also should be prepared to use visual and verbal cues as to what the child should look for (i.e., distinctive features) in discriminating one letter from another.

The teacher should also be aware of the powerful influence the teacher can be in terms of a model. Yando and Kagan (1968), for instance, in a field-based study found that impulsive children decreased their response times after a year of exposure to an experienced, reflective teacher. That accuracy of responses of the MFF was not influenced in this study is not of critical importance here since the teachers were not instructed in any way to encourage their children to use more appropriate attentional strategies. The implication of the laboratory studies and the naturalistic study of Yando and Kagan (1968) is that teachers who can act as reflective models and also provide children with instruction on what to attend to can improve the performance of impulsive children. It is also important that teachers be careful to engage in appropriate behaviors which help the child to attend to relevant aspects of tasks. Stevenson (1972), in his review of incidental learning studies, has concluded that children are more likely to model the incidental behaviors of adults who are perceived by the child to be nurturant and to have control over the reinforcers for the child. It is, thus, paradoxical that those teachers with personalities which would be assumed to be conducive to good teaching (i.e., warm and nurturant) are perhaps the ones who must be most careful in their teaching behaviors around children. If these teachers are disorganized and perform irrelevant behaviors (i.e., are not task-oriented) when showing children how to solve a problem, they may influence their students to imitate behaviors which are irrelevant.

BEHAVIOR MODIFICATION OF ATTENTION

The pioneering studies of Cruickshank *et al.* (1961) and Haring and Phillips (1962) with hyperactive, brain injured, and emotionally disturbed children set the stage for the development of behavior modification techniques with children who exhibit inattentive or disruptive behavior. Among other features, some of which have already been discussed, these early studies emphasized the necessity for clear directions regarding academic tasks and classroom behavior, firm expectations of task completion and appropriate behavior, and consistent consequences for the child's performance and deportment. The elaboration and refinement of these basic ideas, particularly the notion of consistent consequences, in part provided the basis for present-day behavior modification procedures (cf., Haring 1974; Kauffman 1970; Whelan 1974).

The use of consistent consequences to modify academic and behavioral deficits in the early 1960s is typified by the report of Zimmerman and Zimmerman (1962). They described the use of consequences to change the classroom behavior of two emotionally disturbed boys in a residential treatment center. In the case of the first child, an eleven-year-old of normal intelligence, whenever he was asked to spell a word which he had previously studied "he would pause for several seconds, screw up his face, and mutter letters unrelated to the word" (p. 59). Subsequently, the teacher would ask him to sound out the word or provide other cues and give him encouragement. This procedure consumed an inordinate amount of the teacher's time and apparently maintained the child's incorrect responses. When the teacher changed her procedure by directing the child to spell the word correctly and then withholding all attention until the child complied, after which she responded with smiles and praise, the child's behavior changed: "As a result of a month of this treatment, the frequency of bizarre spelling responses . . . declined to a level close to zero per class session" (p. 59). The second boy, also an eleven-year-old of normal intelligence, frequently exhibited tantrums, irrelevant verbalizations, and baby talk. Again, the teacher ignored such inappropriate responses and attended positively to the child only when his behavior was acceptable. "After several weeks, class tantrums disappeared entirely. . . . Furthermore the frequency of irrelevant verbal behavior and of baby-talk declined almost to the point of elimination following the procedure of withholding attention after the emission of such behavior" (p. 60).

Since the early 1960s there has been an increase in the explicitness with which the learning environment and behavioral consequences are arranged to modify inadequate educational performance and maladaptive behavior (Haring and Whelan 1966). More important, however, has been the increase in precision with which behavioral change and academic progress are measured and evaluated (Haring 1974). No longer are anecdotal reports, behavior rating scales, and standardized achievement tests considered adequate tools for the assessment of psychoeducational interventions. Current behavior modification procedures include frequent (usually daily) direct measurement of the child's academic performance or other behavior. (See Kauffman's chapter in this volume and Haring's chapter in Volume I for further discussion of behavior modification methodology.) The behavior modification technology now available to teachers of children with special learning difficulties (cf. Bushell and Brigham 1971; Haring and Lovitt 1967; Lovitt 1968; Wallace and Kauffman 1973) does not invalidate the simpler applications of learning principles practiced more than a decade ago, but it does offer a more precise set of tools for dealing with difficult educational situations.

The behavior modification approach to problems of attention assumes that attending is comprised, at least in part, of behaviors that can be measured directly. Behaviors such as looking at the teacher, following directions, engaging in a single activity, writing answers, or in some other manner giving correct responses or exhibiting task-oriented activity have been recorded as measures of attention in the classroom. A behavior modification analysis of attention implies that such attending responses are a function of specific consequences which can be varied systematically to increase or decrease attending behavior (Martin and Powers 1967). A number of studies have shown that task attention, study behavior, or orientation to teacher can be increased by reinforcing those behaviors with teacher attention or other social or material consequences. These studies have demonstrated the effectiveness of a variety of reinforcement procedures in different settings and with children varying in age, behavioral description, and diagnostic label.

In several early experiments, the consequences of attention were manipulated for children described as hyperactive. Patterson (1965) increased task attention (and reduced hyperactive behaviors) in a nine-year-old boy in a second grade classroom by using a "magic teaching machine," a small box with a light and counter which could be controlled remotely by the experimenter. The box, which was placed on the child's desk, was used to signal the child that he had exhibited appropriate attending behavior. Contingent on the child's attending for a brief interval, the experimenter would cause the light to flash and the counter to turn (and click) and would also place one M&M candy or penny on the child's desk. At the end of each experimental session, the child shared the candies or pennies he had earned with his classmates. Quay, Sprague, Werry, and McQueen (1967) used somewhat the same procedure with a group of five six-to-nine-year-old hyperactive, aggressive boys in a special public school class for conduct problem children. Each child was provided with a box containing a light. The box was placed on the child's desk, and the light was flashed by the experimenter contingent on a brief interval of attention (visual orientation) to the teacher during story time. At first, both social reinforcers (praise) and M&M candies were given for the number of light flashes. After visual orientation was conditioned, however, social reinforcers alone (praise and pats on the head for the number of light flashes) were used to maintain attention. In another study Allen, Henke, Harris, Baer, and Reynolds (1967) controlled the attending behavior of a four-year-old boy who, although apparently well adjusted in other respects, tended to "flit from activity to activity" in his preschool classroom. He typically spent less than one minute engaged in any one activity in the preschool, and his "flightiness" also caused his parents concern at home. By ignoring quick shifts in activity and making adult social reinforcement (i.e., teacher attention—looking, smiling, touching, praising) contingent on first one and later two unbroken minutes of attention to an activity, the child was taught to change activities at a markedly lower rate.

Several investigators have modified attending behavior by using points or tokens. Walker and Buckley (1968) used a clicking sound, which represented points that could be exchanged for a model, to increase attending behavior in a bright nine-year-old boy who exhibited a high rate of inappropriate and inattentive behaviors. Training sessions were held in a controlled setting. Subsequent to the training sessions in which the child's task attention was increased, the regular classroom teacher was taught to administer points contingent on relatively long (average thirty minutes) periods of attending. This generalization program maintained the child's attention in the regular class. Similarly, Novy, Burnett, Powers, and Sulzer-Azaroff (1973) modified attending-to-work behavior in a nine-year-old boy in a special class for learning disabled children by presenting light flashes and token reinforcers contingent on study behavior. Ten students in a special class for children with learning disabilities were the subjects of a study by McKenzie, Clark, Wolf, Kothera, and Benson (1968). These ten-to-thirteen-year-old students had histories of distractible, disruptive behavior. The teacher used grades, which were based on specific academic performance criteria, as tokens which the children could exchange for money (allowances) at home. Attention to reading and arithmetic tasks increased with the use of this procedure. Bushell, Wrobel, and Michaelis (1968) applied "group" contingencies involving tokens to the modification of the study behavior of preschoolers. Plastic washers were distributed to children for study behaviors, and these tokens were later exchangeable for a "special-event ticket" and snack foods. When the tickets and foods were contingent on having earned enough tokens to purchase them, study behaviors occurred at a higher rate than when the special events and snacks were provided noncontingently. Hewett (1968) developed a highly structured "engineered classroom" in which attending behaviors were the first in a hierarchy of educational tasks to be acquired by emotionally disturbed children. Based on his experiences teaching inattentive and disruptive students at the Fernald School and the Neuropsychiatric Institute School at UCLA, he devised a checkmark or point system for reinforcing attentive behavior as well as progress in academic and social areas (cf. Hewett 1974). The evaluation of his Santa Monica Project showed that attention to task increased significantly in the classes where task attention was systematically reinforced.

The use of lights, timers, and tokens contingent on attending and study behavior has been elaborated and extended in other investigations. Surratt, Ulrich, and Hawkins (1969) trained a fifth grade student to control a timer and lights mounted on boxes on the desks of four first grade children. The fifth grader successfully modified the younger children's study behavior by turning on and off the lights contingent on the younger children's behavior. Accumulated "study time" was exchangeable for special privileges.

Coleman (1970) used a portable radio control apparatus to present a counter click contingent on the study behavior of four elementary students who exhibited low rates of study and high rates of disruptive behavior. Each click represented an earned M&M candy which the subject shared with his classmates. This procedure increased study behavior and decreased inappropriate behavior. When the counter click was withdrawn, the behavioral gains of all four pupils were maintained by candy reinforcement alone. Willis and Crowder (1972) employed a portable wireless switch controlling a clock to increase the attention of an entire class of first graders. Attending behavior resulted in the accumulation of time on the clock, and a movie was made contingent on accumulating a specific number of minutes. In Packard's (1970) study, four elementary teachers controlled a light, which signaled their observations that all the children were "paying attention," and a timer, on which time attending accumulated. Packard found that teachers' instructions to attend had little effect on children's attention. However, token reinforcement for attention, contingent on a gradually increasing criterion, increased attending behavior to 70 to 85 percent for the entire group and 90 to 100 percent for individuals. Finally, Glynn, Thomas, and Shee (1973) showed that elementary pupils could be taught to maintain their own on-task or study behavior by evaluating their own attention at auditorially signaled intervals. The children began the self-control procedure after their on-task behavior had first been reinforced by the teacher with contingent free time and activities. As part of the self-control procedure, the children engaged in self-assessment, self-recording, self-determination of reinforcement, and self-administration of reinforcement.

Another group of investigations has shown that attention and study behavior can be modified merely by providing teacher attention for the desired pupil response. Hall, Lund, and Jackson (1968) and Cossairt, Hall, and Hopkins (1973) showed that the study behavior of elementary pupils could be increased by having the teacher ignore nonstudy and attend to study behaviors. Schutte and Hopkins (1970) found that kindergarten children attended to (followed) the teacher's instructions more often if the teacher ignored children who did not follow the teacher's instructions and attended positively to those who did. The effects of teacher attention on children in proximity to the "target" child, whose attending behavior was to be modified, was investigated by Broden, Bruce, Mitchel, Carter, and Hall (1970). Differential teacher attention was given to a child for attending behavior, and the attending behavior of another child at an adjacent desk was simultaneously recorded. Broden *et al.* concluded that "as teachers have long surmised, increasing the appropriate behavior of one pupil tends to be associated with increased appropriate behavior of a pupil seated at an adjacent desk" (p. 203). Kazdin (1973) replicated the finding of Broden *et al.* but found in addition that reinforcement of *inattention* in the target child also increased attentive behaviors in the child's adjacent peers.

The foregoing studies show rather conclusively that the classroom teacher can arrange consequences to shape and maintain attending, on-task, or study behaviors when these behaviors are defined as visual orientation to the teacher or task. It is quite possible, however, that such apparent attending behaviors do not serve to improve children's educational performance. Haring (1968) suggested that the only way to *know* a child has attended is to observe the child's responses. A child may be looking at a stimulus (e.g., a book) but not be attending to it; therefore, one can verify that the child is attending only by noting his observable responses (e.g., calling the title or color of the book). Although anecdotal or suggestive evidence of an accelerating effect on achievement has been offered in some studies of the modification of attending behavior (e.g., Cossairt *et al.* 1973; Hall *et al.* 1968; O'Leary, Becker, Evans, and Saudargas 1969), these investigations did not examine experimentally the effects of increased levels of attending behavior on academic responses.

The results of a study by Ferritor, Buckholdt, Hamblin, and Smith (1972) suggest that increasing attention (i.e., task orientation) *per se* does not necessarily produce an increase in academic work. When third graders were reinforced with tokens for "attending behaviors, which included a child looking at or writing on his test paper or on a scrap of paper, asking a question, looking toward the teacher when she was talking, counting on his fingers or softly counting aloud, sharpening his pencil, or passing out papers" (p. 9), attending behaviors increased, but the quantity and accuracy of academic responses (arithmetic problems) did not increase. When tokens were given for correct responses, however, correct responses increased and attending behaviors dropped. Only when both attending behaviors and correct responses were required to obtain token reinforcers were both attending and accuracy maintained at high levels.

There are at least two reasons to question the results of Ferritor *et al.* (1972), at least as they apply to children with attention deficits. First, the pupils in that study were attending, on the average, approximately 75 to 80 percent of the time during baseline sessions. Studies of attention have shown that normal children attend to task approximately 75 percent of the time (Patterson, Cobb, and Ray 1972). Furthermore, the experimenters never succeeded in increasing significantly the number of academic responses given, although percentage completed correctly was greatly increased. Thus, the subjects apparently did not exhibit marked attention deficits, and they appeared to be working at a rate near their capacity. If one were to reinforce the attending behaviors of children whose usual level of attention and performance were much lower (e.g., children who usually attend only 40 percent of the time and who work at a very slow pace), the results might be quite different. Increasing attending behavior may have no significant effect on the performance of children whose attention is already high, but it may have a profound influence on the performance of children who seldom attend to tasks. Second, in another study (Kirby and Shields 1972) it was found that praise and immediate accuracy feedback for arithmetic responses increased collaterally the attending behavior of a seventh grade pupil. (It is notable that this pupil attended to task only about

50 percent of the time during baseline sessions.) This finding, that modification of academic responses resulted in a concomitant increase in attending behavior, is in direct contradiction to the results of Ferritor *et al.*

The finding of Kirby and Shields that reinforcement of correct responses results in an increase in attending behaviors is consonant with Skinner's (1968) observations on the nature of attention: "To attend to something as a form of self-management is to respond to it in such a way that subsequent behavior is more likely to be reinforced. . . . There are two stages: (1) attending to a given state of affairs and (2) responding to it in some other way. In the normal course of events the reinforcement of the second stage strengthens the first" (p. 122). Thus, it would be expected that reinforcement of correct academic responses would strengthen attention to the academic tasks or materials involved.

At this point it may seem reasonable to conclude that: (a) there is no convincing evidence that reinforcement of attending behaviors will result in improved academic performance and (b) in order to increase attending behaviors one need only reinforce academic performance. The first conclusion appears to receive further support from the findings of several studies (e.g., Debus 1970; Denney 1972; Kagan, Pearson, and Welch 1966; Yando and Kagan 1968) in which teaching children to increase their attention (i.e., increase response latency) to a task did not increase their accuracy. The second conclusion seems clearly to obtain additional support from informal observation of the relation between attending behavior and appropriate responses (i.e., it is impossible to learn a discrimination or perform correctly without attending to the relevant stimuli) and from Skinner's (1968) description of how reinforcement of performance ordinarily strengthens attention. Nevertheless, neither conclusion is justified.

It is important to recognize that there are situations in which direct reinforcement of attending behaviors is desirable or necessary. As Skinner (1968) has commented further:

> some techniques of attending to a stimulus are learned only slowly, if at all, when reinforcement is confined to the second stage. . . . Simply reinforcing a child when he reads a text correctly may be much less effective than special contingencies which induce him to read from left to right or to read a block of words at a glance. Another way to attend to stimuli so that one may respond to them more effectively is to construct supplemental stimuli. We do this when we point to words we are reading or follow a voice in a recorded fugue by singing or beating time with it or by moving our eyes along a score. Techniques of this sort are not likely to be learned simply because behavior which presupposes them is reinforced.
>
> In short, much of the elaborate art of looking and listening cannot be taught simply by reinforcing the student when he responds in ways which show that he has previously looked and listened carefully. Direct instruction is needed. (p. 123)

Several investigations have shown that when children are trained explicitly and directly *how* to attend, not merely to look at the task materials, they do improve their performance (Heider 1971; Ridberg, Parke, and Hetherington 1972; Zelniker and Oppenheimer 1973). Such training provides the child with an attention *strategy* and modifies the function of his attending behavior, not merely its topography. One can safely conclude, then, that there are both circumstances under which it would be most efficient to reinforce the desired academic response and conditions under which one should reinforce a specific attending strategy.

In summary, the teacher can use behavior modification techniques, such as contingent teacher attention or token reinforcement, to improve children's attentional skills. If the child does not have marked, specific attentional deficits, it may be sufficient to reinforce only correct or appropriate responses in order to increase attending behaviors. On the other hand, if the child lacks the ability to respond adequately because the child has not learned a successful attention strategy, the specific attentional skill must be taught directly in order to improve the child's performance.

HYPERACTIVITY

The discussion thus far has focused on methods of increasing the distractible child's attention. Implicit in many of the studies reviewed has been the view that distractibility and excessive amounts of motor activity go hand in hand. Many of the techniques and methods presented for increasing attentional skills have also been advocated for decreasing hyperactivity. The Strauss-Lehtinen-Cruickshank orientation, for example, has been recommended as an aid to controlling inappropriate motoric behavior. The studies relating to the effectiveness of different training techniques which we have reviewed above have not provided any data bearing directly on the control of hyperactivity. Indirect evidence only can be inferred from some of the above studies. For instance, it can be speculated that in order for a child to be attending to the task at hand the child must also be able to control excessive amounts of irrelevant motor activity. Alabiso (1972), for example, in a literature review has suggested that attention has an inhibitory function in reducing hyperactive behaviors. This line of reasoning would lead one to the conclusion that any method that increases task attention would also be effective in decreasing hyperactivity. Such a conclusion must remain within the realm of speculation, however, since the studies in question did not include any direct measures of behaviors specifically detailed as hyperactive in nature.

Investigations that relate directly to the control of motor activity generally fall into two categories—verbal control of motor activity and behavior modification.

Verbal Control of Motor Activity

Most of the work investigating the effects of language on motor behavior has sprung from the theoretical formulations of Luria (1961). Luria has posited that as the child develops he acquires the ability to use internalized speech to regulate his own actions. Initially, the child is considered to be at the mercy of his own motoric impulses. The verbal commands of others can at times influence the child's behavior, but not until about five years of age is the child capable of using internalized language appropriately in directing his own motor activities. Wolff and Wolff (1972), using teacher-rating data, obtained evidence to substantiate Luria's theory. They found a correlation between quantity of verbal output and gross motor activity in four and five-year-olds. In addition, there was a correlation between the quality of language expressed by the children and the amount of fine motor activity engaged in. Hallahan, Kauffman, and Mueller (in press), in a group of younger (M = 3 years, 8 months) children than those studied by Wolff and Wolff, found, using naturalistic observation data, that the amount of verbalization correlated with physical contact with peers but not with gross or fine motor activity. At this younger age, it appears that language is elicited by social interaction (i.e., contact with peers). The evidence suggests that verbal behavior is not yet used to regulate motor behavior.

Numerous studies have shown that training children to use verbal cues can help them to exert control over their motor movements (Bem 1967; Birch 1966; Lovaas 1964; Meichenbaum and Goodman 1969; Palkes, Stewart, and Freedman 1971; Palkes, Stewart, and Kahana 1968). Typically, these studies have trained the child to verbalize aloud what he is to do motorically (e.g., "do" or "do not push" a lever, depending upon the color of the light presented).

Only three of the studies have been concerned with children who would be considered overactive. Meichenbaum and Goodman (1969) found that impulsives (as determined by the MFF task of Kagan) were less able than reflectives to perform well on a task requiring the child to depress a foot pedal for a blue light but not for a yellow light. Training in saying aloud *push* and *don't push* eliminated differences between impulsives and reflectives. Palkes and associates have taught boys identified as hyperactive to perform more accurately on the Porteus Maze (Palkes, Stewart, and Freedman 1971; Palkes, Stewart, and Kahana 1968). Requiring them to verbalize the self-directed commands of stopping and thinking before responding was found to be effective. Merely reading the instructions without overtly verbalizing them was not effective.

In general, the above evidence indicates that training hyperactive children to verbalize may be one method of reducing inappropriate motoric behavior. In the early stages, it may be necessary to require the severely hyperactive child to verbalize each of the steps in a sequence of behaviors before attempting each step. It may be that only after much training in this overt verbalization can the child gradually come to use these language cues covertly. The use of overt and covert verbalization also has the added advantage, as was reviewed above, of helping the child to attend to the relevant aspects of the task.

Behavior Modification of Hyperactivity

Because of the apparent relationship between deficits in attending behavior and hyperactivity, many of the studies which have dealt with modification of attending behavior have also provided evidence of concomitant changes in hyperactive or disruptive behaviors. Other behavior modification studies have investigated ways to reduce or eliminate directly behaviors associated with hyperactivity: out-of-seat behavior, unnecessary movement, inappropriate noise-making, talking-out, excessive talking, arguing, holding tantrums, fighting, or other aggressive or disruptive behaviors. Indeed, studies of such behaviors have become so numerous that some writers have suggested behavior modifiers may be preoccupied with stillness, quietness, and docility (Winett and Winkler 1972). It is undeniable, however, that the teacher of learning disabled children will be confronted with the need to manage disruptive, disturbing behavior. Consequently, we will outline briefly the behavior modification techniques which have been found to be most effective in controlling hyperactivity and behaviors inimical to classroom control or learning.

Making Rules, Praising, Ignoring, and Reprimanding

It has been found that elementary classroom control can be increased by the use of four basic elements: (a) making clear rules for behavior, (b) praising frequently the children who follow the rules, (c) ignoring all but dangerous or intolerable infractions of the rules, and (d) softly disapproving or reprimanding children for specific infractions (Madsen, Becker, and Thomas 1968; Madsen, Madsen, Saudargas, Hammond, Smith, and Edgar 1970). Classroom rules should be made, if possible, with the participation of the children. The rules should be simple, direct, positively stated, and frequently reviewed, particularly when children are not misbehaving. In short, pupils must be told frequently, explicitly, and in positive terms how the teacher expects them to behave. It is essential also for the teacher to give frequent praise, positive attention, or approval to children who are following the rules. Teacher praise must be given very frequently and be made contingent on appropriate, rule-following behavior in order to be effective. On the other hand, misbehavior should be ignored unless it simply cannot be tolerated. As Kauffman, Vicente, Benton, McKnight, and Mende (1972) have noted, "most misbehavior which irritates the teacher and other students does not demand intervention for the sake of safety. After such misbehavior, the bodies of the persons involved and the property of the school are left undamaged. Any suffering caused by the misbehavior is psychological and transitory" (p. 194). If the teacher attends to misbehavior of this kind (e.g., if the teacher responds to inappropriate standing or out-of-seat behavior with "sit-down" commands) an increase in undesirable behavior may result (Madsen, Becker, Thomas, Koser, and Plager 1972). When behavior is dangerous or intolerable and must be stopped, soft, private reprimands are likely to be more effective than loud, public disapproval (O'Leary and Becker 1968; O'Leary, Kaufman, Kass, and Drabman 1970).

Numerous other studies (e.g., Brown and Elliot 1965; Hall and Broden 1967; Hall, Fox, Willard, Goldsmith, Emerson, Owen, Davis, and Porcia 1971; Hall, Panyan, Rabon, and Broden 1968; Pinkston, Reese, LeBlanc, and Baer 1973; Thomas, Becker, and Armstrong 1968) have shown that contingent teacher attention (i.e., approval or other social reinforcement) to appropriate behavior is a powerful means of increasing desirable behavior and reducing disruptive behavior for most children. In essence, during the past ten years research has supported the assertion of Haring and Phillips (1962) and others that hyperactive, disruptive behavior in the classroom is best managed, in most cases, by several relatively simple techniques: clear direction, firm expectations, and consistent follow-through in applying consequences. However, there are behavior management situations which require the use of more powerful procedures than rules, contingent teacher attention, and soft reprimands.

Tokens, Contracts, Games, and Novelties

A number of procedures or behavior management systems which make reinforcement of appropriate behavior stronger (i.e., more extrinsic or more explicit) have been applied in classrooms. Extensive reviews of the use of token reinforcement systems (Axelrod 1971; Kazdin and Bootzin 1972; O'Leary and Drabman 1971) show rather conclusively that a properly operated token economy can contribute much to the management of disruptive and disturbing behavior (see Stainback, Payne, Stainback, and Payne 1973, and Walker and Buckley 1974, for step-by-step methods for establishment of a classroom token economy). Contingency contracting, a method of making an explicit, formal agreement with a child regarding the consequences of the child's behavior, has also been used to reduce behavior problems (Cantrell, Cantrell, Huddleston, and Woolridge 1969; Homme 1969; Patterson, Cobb, and Ray 1972). A number of researchers have devised games involving reinforcement for appropriate behavior (Barrish, Saunders, and Wolf 1969; Harris and Sherman 1973; Medland and Stachnik 1972; Wolf, Hanley, King, Lachowicz, and Giles 1970). Others have found that time to play with toys, to obtain novel reinforcers, or to experience novel contingencies are effective in controlling disruptions and increasing the desirable behavior of children (e.g., Kauffman and Hallahan 1973; Kubany, Weiss, and Sloggett 1971; Wasik 1970). Thus, there is ample evidence that reinforcement techniques stronger than contingent social attention and praise may be employed in the classroom with salutary effects on children's behavior.

Punishment and Time Out

Occasionally, a child's undesirable behavior persists in the face of powerful reinforcement for appropriate behavior. Under such circumstances, other techniques designed specifically to reduce the problem behavior may be indicated. Punishment may involve one of two techniques for reducing the frequency of a behavior: (a) presenting an aversive stimulus contingent on the behavior or (b) removing a positive reinforcer contingent on the behavior. Both types of punishment may be used in the classroom, and both have been shown to be effective when properly used. For example, Hall, Axelrod, Foundopoulos, Shellman, Campbell, and Cranston (1971) found that the teacher pointing at a child and shouting "*No!*" contingent on the child's biting or pinching someone effectively reduced the frequency of the child's biting and pinching. They also found that taking away a slip of paper with the child's name written on it and keeping the children after school for specific behavioral offenses were effective in reducing specific problem behaviors. Time out involves the use of both types of punishment simultaneously. The child is removed for a specified period of time from a situation in which the child can obtain reinforcement (hence, "time out" from positive reinforcement) and placed in an unstimulating (and, hence, aversive) environment. Ordinarily, this means that the child is removed from the classroom or activity and placed in an isolation area or room. Although time out and other forms of punishment can be used effectively in the classroom, it is necessary to take care to avoid using punishment as the primary means of control and to avoid procedures which might have undesirable side effects. O'Leary and O'Leary (1972) have suggested the following guidelines: "In order to avoid negative side-effects, one should (1) use punishment sparingly, (2) make clear to a child why he is being punished, (3) provide the child with an alternative means of obtaining some positive reinforcement, (4) reinforce the child for behaviors incompatible with those you wish to weaken, (5) avoid physical punishment if at all possible, (6) avoid punishing while you are in a very angry or emotional state, and (7) punish at the initiation of a behavior rather than at its completion" (p. 152).

Parent-, Peer-, and Self-Control

The enlistment and training of a disruptive child's parents or peers to manage his behavior are now methods of proven value. Manuals for parents and parent training, based on a considerable volume of research, are now available (e.g., Becker 1971; Madsen and Madsen 1972; Patterson 1971). Additionally, it has been clearly shown that with adequate training the peers of disruptive children can become effective contingency managers (e.g., Nelson, Worell, and Polsgrove 1973; Solomon and Wahler 1973; Suratt, Ulrich, and Hawkins 1969) and that disruptive children can manage their own behavior (e.g., Bolstod and Johnson 1972; Glynn, Thomas, and Shee 1973). The evidence that parents, peers, and children themselves can be taught to change disruptive behavior suggests that: (a) classroom behavior management can be made more efficient by using individuals other than the teacher, (b) one can deal with disruptive behavior by intervening in the psychological ecology of the child, and (c) it is possible to humanize behavior management techniques by extending knowledge and use of behavior modification technology to students themselves. Two recently published volumes contain papers in which each of these suggestions is pursued (Ramp and Hopkins 1971; Semb 1972).

Observational Learning

Learning by observing a behavioral example or model has received relatively little attention in the management of disruptive classroom behavior. In a review of research on the use of observational learning in special education Cullinan, Kauffman, and LaFleur (in press) noted:

> In contrast to the many applications of operant learning principles . . . the potentially useful findings on imitative learning have not been widely employed in special education settings. Further, they receive unduly small emphasis in many expositions of behavior change techniques. It is often pointed out that reinforcement principles function in the classroom whether they are systematically utilized or not. Similarly, modeling influences are ubiquitously operative within social situations; the teacher or other alterative agent who fails to apply them in an orderly fashion risks foregoing a powerful force for change.

Although a few recent reports have investigated peer models (Csapo 1972) or vicarious reinforcement (Broden, Bruce, Mitchell, Carter, and Hall 1970; Kazdin 1973) or disruptive or inattentive classroom behavior, observational learning clearly is an area in which more experimentation is needed.

There are thus a number of methods which the teacher can employ to decrease hyperactive behavior in children. Providing the child with strategies of verbalization has received support as a method of controlling motor behavior. The research literature also points out that a teacher well versed in behavior modification techniques will be more likely to have success in dealing with hyperactive children. There is also logical justification for the notion that there is an interaction between training attention and motor control.

References

Alabiso, F. "Inhibitory Functions of Attention in Reducing Hyperactive Behavior." *American Journal of Mental Deficiency* 77 (1972):259–82.

Allen, K. E.; Henke, L. B.; Harris, F. R.; Baer, D. M.; and Reynolds, N. J. "Control of Hyperactivity by Social Reinforcement of Attending Behavior." *Journal of Educational Psychology* 58 (1967):231–37.

Axelrod, S. "Token Reinforcement Programs in Special Class." *Exceptional Children* 37 (1971):371–79.

Balling, J. D., and Myers, N. A. "Memory and Attention in Children's Double-Alternation Learning." *Journal of Experimental Child Psychology* 11 (1971):448–60.

Barrish, H. H.; Sauders, M.; and Wolf, M. M. "Good Behavior Game: Effects of Individual Contingencies for Group Consequences on Disruptive Behavior in a Classroom." *Journal of Applied Behavior Analysis* 2 (1969):119–24.

Becker, W. C. *Parents Are Teachers.* Champaign, Ill.: Research Press, 1971.

Bem, S. L. "Verbal Self-Control: The Establishment of Effective Self-Instruction." *Journal of Experimental Psychology* 74 (1967):485–91.

Bijou, S. W., and Baer, D. M. "Some Methodological Contributions from a Functional Analysis of Child Development." In *Advances in Child Development and Behavior,* edited by L. P. Lippsitt and C. C. Spiker. Vol. 1. New York: Academic Press, 1963.

Birch, D. "Verbal Control of Nonverbal Behavior." *Journal of Experimental Child Psychology* 4 (1966):266–75.

Bolstod, O. D., and Johnson, S. M. "Self-Regulation in the Modification of Disruptive Behavior." *Journal of Applied Behavior Analysis* 5 (1972):443–54.

Broden, M.; Bruce, C.; Mitchell, M. A.; Carter, V.; and Hall, R. V. "Effects of Teacher Attention on Attending Behavior of Two Boys at Adjacent Desks." *Journal of Applied Behavior Analysis* 3 (1970):205–11.

Brown, P., and Elliott, R. "Control of Aggression in a Nursery School Class." *Journal of Experimental Child Psychology* 2 (1965):103–107.

Bushell, D., and Brigham, T. A. "Classroom Token Systems as Technology." *Educational Technology* 11 (4) (1971):14–17.

______; Wrobel, P. A.; and Michaelis, M. L. "Applying 'Group' Contingencies to the Classroom Study Behavior of Preschool Children." *Journal of Applied Behavior Analysis* 1 (1968):55–61.

Cantrell, R. P.; Cantrell, M. L.; Huddleston, C.; and Woolridge, R. "Contingency Contracting with School Problems." *Journal of Applied Behavior Analysis* 2 (1969):215–20.

Caron, A. J. "Conceptual Transfer in Preverbal Children as a Consequence of Dimensional Training." *Journal of Experimental Child Psychology* 6 (1968):522–42.

Cole, R. E.; Dent, H. E.; Eguchi, P. E.; Fujii, K. K.; and Johnson, A. C. "Transposition with Minimal Errors during Training Trials." *Journal of Experimental Child Psychology* 1 (1964):355–59.

Coleman, R. "A Conditioning Technique Applicable to Elementary School Classrooms." *Journal of Applied Behavior Analysis* 3 (1970):293–97.

Cossairt, A.; Hall, R. V.; and Hopkins, B. L. "The Effects of Experimenter's Instructions, Feedback, and Praise on Teacher Praise and Student Attending Behavior." *Journal of Applied Behavior Analysis* 6 (1973):89–100.

Cruickshank, W. M.; Bentzen, F. A.; Ratzeburg, F. H.; and Tannhauser, M. T. *A Teaching Method for Brain-injured and Hyperactive Children.* Syracuse: Syracuse University Press, 1961.

______; Bice, H. V.; Wallen, N. E.; and Lynch, K. S. *Perception and Cerebral Palsy.* 2nd ed. Syracuse: Syracuse University Press, 1965.

Csapo, M. "Peer Models Reverse the 'One Bad Apple Spoils the Barrel' Theory." *Teaching Exceptional Children* 5 (1) (1972):20–24.

Cullinan, D.; Kauffman, J. M.; and LaFleur, N. K. "Observational Learning: Research with Implications for Special Education." *Journal of Special Education*, in press.

Debus, R. L. "Effects of Brief Observation of Model Behavior on Conceptual Tempo in Impulsive Children. *Developmental Psychology* 2 (1970):22–32.

Denney, D. R. "Modeling Effects upon Conceptual Styles and Cognitive Tempo." *Child Development* 43 (1972):105–19.

Drake, D. M. "Perceptual Correlates of Impulsive and Reflective Behavior." *Developmental Psychology* 2 (1970):202–14.

Druker, J. F., and Hagen, J. W. "Developmental Trends in the Processing of Task-Relevant and Task-Irrelevant Information." *Child Development* 40 (1969):371–82.

Fassler, J. "Performance of Cerebral Palsied Children under Conditions of Reduced Auditory Input." *Exceptional Children* 37 (1970):201–209.

Ferritor, D. E.; Buckholdt, D.; Hamblin, R. L.; and Smith, L. "The Noneffects of Contingent Reinforcement for Attending Behavior on Work Accomplished." *Journal of Applied Behavior Analysis* 5 (1972):7–17.

Frey, R. "Reading Behavior of Public School Brain Injured and Non-Brain Injured Children of Average and Retarded Mental Development." Doctoral dissertation, University of Illinois, 1961.

Furth, H. G., and Milgram, N. A. "Labeling and Grouping Effects in the Recall of Pictures by Children." *Child Development* 44 (1973):511–18.

Gaines, R. "Children's Selective Attention: Stage or Set?" *Child Development* 41 (1970): 979–91.

Gibson, E. J. *Principles of Perceptual Learning and Development.* New York: Appleton-Century-Crofts, 1969.

Gorton, C. E. "The Effects of Various Classroom Environments on Performance of a Mental Task by Mentally Retarded and Normal Children." *Education and Training of the Mentally Retarded* 7 (1972):32–38.

Glynn, E. L.; Thomas, J. D.; and Shee, S. M. "Behavioral Self-Control of On-Task Behavior in an Elementary Classroom." *Journal of Applied Behavior Analysis* 6 (1973):105–13.

Hagen, J. W. "The Effect of Distraction on Selective Attention." *Child Development* 38 (1967):685–94.

———; Hargrave, S.; and Ross, W. "Prompting and Rehearsal in Short-Term Memory." *Child Development* 44 (1973):201–204.

———; and Huntsman, N. J. "Selective Attention in Mental Retardation." *Developmental Psychology* 5 (1971):151–60.

———; and Kingsley, P. R. "Labeling Effects in Short-Term Memory." *Child Development* 39 (1968):113–21.

———; Meacham, J. A.; and Mesibov, G. "Verbal Labeling, Rehearsal, and Short-Term Memory." *Cognitive Psychology* 1 (1970): 47–58.

Hall, R. V.; Axelrod, S.; Foundopoulos, M.; Shellman, J.; Campbell, R. A.; and Cranston, S. S. "The Effective Use of Punishment to Modify Behavior in the Classroom." *Educational Technology* 11(4) (1971): 24–26.

———, and Broden, M. "Behavior Changes in Brain-Injured Children through Social Reinforcement." *Journal of Experimental Child Psychology* 5 (1967): 463–79.

———; Fox, R.; Willard, D.; Goldsmith, L.; Emerson, M.; Owen, M.; Davis, F.; and Porcia, E. "The Teacher as Observer and Experimenter in the Modification of Disputing and Talking-Out Behaviors." *Journal of Applied Behavior Analysis* 4 (1971): 141–49.

———; Lund, D.; and Jackson, D. "Effects of Teacher Attention on Study Behavior." *Journal of Applied Behavior Analysis* 1 (1968): 1–12.

———; Panyan, M.; Rabon, D.; and Broden, M. "Instructing Beginning Teachers in Reinforcement Procedures Which Improve Classroom Control." *Journal of Applied Behavior Analysis* 1 (1968): 315–22.

Hallahan, D. P., and Cruickshank, W. M. *Psychoeducational Foundations of Learning Disabilities.* Englewood Cliffs, N.J.: Prentice-Hall, 1973.

———; Kauffman, J. M.; and Ball, D. W. "Developmental Trends in Recall of Central and Incidental Auditory Material." *Journal of Experimental Child Psychology* 17 (1974*a*):409–21.

———; Kauffman, J. M.; and Ball, D. W. "Effects of Stimulus Attenuation on Selective Attention Performance of Children." *Journal of Genetic Psychology* 125 (1974*b*):71–77.

———; Kauffman, J. M.; and Mueller, C. S. "Behavioral Observation and Teacher Rating Correlates of Motor and Vocal Behavior in Preschoolers." *Journal of Genetic Psychology,* in press.

———; Stainback, S.; Ball, D. W.; and Kauffman, J. M. "Selective Attention in Cerebral Palsied and Normal Children." *Journal of Abnormal Child Psychology* 1 (1973): 280–91.

Haring, N. G. *Attending and Responding.* San Rafael, Calif.: Dimensions, 1968.

———. "Norris G. Haring." In *Teaching Children with Behavior Disorders: Personal Perspectives,* edited by J. M. Kauffman and C. D. Lewis. Columbus, Ohio: Merrill, 1974.

———, and Lovitt, T. C. "Operant Methodology and Educational Technology in Special

Education." In *Methods in Special Education,* edited by N. G. Haring, and R. L. Schiefelbusch. New York: McGraw-Hill, 1967.

———, and Phillips, E. L. *Educating Emotionally Disturbed Children.* New York: McGraw-Hill, 1962.

———, and Whelan, R. J. "The Learning Environment: Relationship to Behavior Modification and Implications for Special Education." *Kansas Studies in Education* 16 (1966) (Whole No. 2).

Harris, V. W., and Sherman, J. A. "Use and Analysis of the 'Good Behavior Game' to Reduce Disruptive Classroom Behavior." *Journal of Applied Behavior Analysis* 6 (1973): 405–17.

Heider, E. R. "Information Processing and the Modification of an 'Impulsive Conceptual Tempo.'" *Child Development* 42 (1971): 1276–81.

Hewett, F. M. *The Emotionally Disturbed Child in the Classroom.* Boston: Allyn & Bacon, 1968.

———. "Frank M. Hewett." In *Teaching Children with Behavior Disorders: Personal Perspectives,* edited by J. M. Kauffman and C. D. Lewis. Columbus, Ohio: Merrill, 1974.

Homme, L. *How to Use Contingency Contracting in the Classroom.* Champaign, Ill.: Research Press, 1969.

House, B. J. "A Decremental Effect of Redundancy in Discrimination Learning." *Journal of Experimental Child Psychology* 10 (1970): 403–12.

Jenkins, J. R.; Gorrafa, S.; and Griffiths, S. "Another Look at Isolation Effects." *American Journal of Mental Deficiency* 76 (1972): 591–93.

Kagan, J.; Pearson, L.; and Welch, L. "The Modifiability of An Impulsive Tempo." *Journal of Educational Psychology* 57 (1966): 359–65.

———; Rosman, B.; Day, D.; Albert, J.; and Phillips, W. "Information Processing in the Child: Significance of Analytic and Reflective Attitudes." *Psychological Monographs* 78 (1964) (Whole No. 578).

Kauffman, J. M. "Recent Trends in the Behavioral Approach to Educating Disturbed Children." *Journal of School Health* 40 (1970): 271–72.

———, and Hallahan, D. P. "Control of Rough Physical Behavior Using Novel Contingencies and Directive Teaching." *Perceptual and Motor Skills* 36 (1973): 1225–26.

———; Vicente, A. R.; Benton, J. F.; McKnight, M. W.; and Mende, R. H. "A Resource Program for Teachers and Their Problem Students." *Academic Therapy* 8 (1972): 191–98.

Kazdin, A. E. "The Effect of Vicarious Reinforcement on Attentive Behavior in the Classroom." *Journal of Applied Behavior Analysis* 6 (1973): 71–78.

———, and Bootzin, R. R. "The Token Economy: An Evaluative Review." *Journal of Applied Behavior Analysis* 5 (1972): 343–72.

Kingsley, P. R., and Hagen, J. W. "Induced versus Spontaneous Rehearsal in Short-Term Memory in Nursery School Children." *Developmental Psychology* 1 (1969): 40–46.

Kirby, F. D., and Shields, F. "Modification of Arithmetic Response Rate and Attending Behavior in a Seventh-Grade Student." *Journal of Applied Behavior Analysis* 5 (1972): 79–84.

Kubany, E. S.; Weiss, L. E.; and Slogett, B. B. "The Good Behavior Clock: A Reinforcement/Time Out Procedure for Reducing Disruptive Classroom Behavior." *Journal of Behavior Therapy and Experimental Psychiatry* 2 (1971): 173–79.

Lovaas, O. I. "Cue Properties of Words: The Control of Operant Responding by Rate and Content of Verbal Operants." *Child Development* 35 (1964): 245–56.

Lovitt, T. C. "Operant Conditioning Techniques for Children with Learning Disabilities." *Journal of Special Education* 2 (1968): 283–89.

———, and Smith, J. O. "Effects of Instructions on An Individual's Verbal Behavior." *Exceptional Children* 38 (1972): 685–93.

Lubker, B. J. "Irrelevant Stimulus Dimensions and Children's Performance on Simultaneous Discrimination Problems." *Child Development* 38 (1967): 119–25.

———. "The Role of Between- and Within-Setting Irrelevant Dimensions in Children's Simultaneous Discrimination Learning." *Child Development* 40 (1969): 957–64.

Luria, A. R. *The Role of Speech in the Regulation of Normal and Abnormal Behavior.* New York: Liveright, 1961.

Maccoby, E. E. "Selective Auditory Attention in Children." In *Advances in Child Development and Behavior,* edited by L. P. Lippsitt and C. C. Spiker. Vol. III. New York: Academic Press, 1967.

———, and Hagen, J. W. "Effects of Distraction upon Central versus Incidental Recall: Developmental Trends." *Journal of Experimental Child Psychology* 2 (1965): 280–89.

Martin, G. L., and Powers, R. B. "Attention Span: An Operant Conditioning Analysis." *Exceptional Children* 33 (1967): 565–70.

McKenzie, H. S.; Clark, M.; Wolf, M. M.; Kothera, R.; and Benson, C. "Behavior Modification of Children with Learning Disabilities Using Grades as Tokens and Allowances as Back Up Reinforcers." *Exceptional Children* 34 (1968): 745–52.

Madsen, C. H.; Becker, W. C.; and Thomas, D. R. "Rules, Praise, and Ignoring: Elements of Elementary Classroom Control." *Journal of Applied Behavior Analysis* 1 (1968): 139–50.

———; Becker, W. C.; Thomas, D. R.; Koser, L.; and Plager, E. "An Analysis of the Reinforcing Function of 'Sit-Down' Commands." In *Classroom Uses of Behavior Modification,* edited by M. B. Harris. Columbus, Ohio: Merrill, 1972.

———; Madsen, C. K.; Saudargas, R. A.; Hammond, W. R.; Smith, J. B.; and Edgar, D. E. "Classroom RAID (Rules, Approval, Ignore, Disapproval): A Cooperative Approach for Professionals and Volunteers." *Journal of School Psychology* 8 (1970): 180–85.

Madsen, C. K., and Madsen, C. H. *Parents/Children/Discipline.* Boston: Allyn & Bacon, 1972.

Massad, V. I., and Etzel, B. C. "Acquisition of Phonetic Sounds by Preschool Children." In *Behavior Analysis and Education—1972,* edited by G. Semb. Lawrence, Kan.: Kansas University Department of Human Development, 1972.

Medland, M. B., and Stachnik, T. J. "Good-Behavior Game: A Replication and Systematic Analysis." *Journal of Applied Behavior Analysis* 5 (1972): 45–51.

Meichenbaum, D., and Goodman, J. "Reflection-Impulsivity and Verbal Control of Motor Behavior." *Child Development* 40 (1969): 785–97.

Moore, R., and Goldiamond, I. "Errorless Establishment of Visual Discrimination Using Fading Procedures." *Journal of the Experimental Analysis of Behavior* 7 (1964): 269–72.

Nelson, C. M.; Worell, J.; and Polsgrove, L. "Behaviorally Disordered Peers as Contingency Managers." *Behavior Therapy* 4 (1973): 270–76.

Novy, P.; Burnett, J.; Powers, M.; and Sulzer-Azaroff, B. "Modifying Attending-to-Work Behavior of a Learning Disabled Child." *Journal of Learning Disabilities* 6 (1973): 20–24.

Odom, R. D., and Corbin, D. W. "Perceptual Salience and Children's Multidimensional Problem Solving." *Child Development* 44 (1973): 425–32.

O'Leary, K. D., and Becker, W. C. "The Effects of the Intensity of a Teacher's Reprimands on Children's Behavior." *Journal of School Psychology* 7 (1968): 8–11.

———; Becker, W. C.; Evans, M. B.; and Saudargas, R. A. "A Token Reinforcement Program in a Public School: A Replication and Systematic Analysis." *Journal of Applied Behavior Analysis* 2 (1969): 3–13.

———, and Drabman, R. S. "Token Reinforcement Programs in the Classroom: A Review." *Psychological Bulletin* 75 (1971): 379–98.

———; Kaufman, K. F.; Kass, R. E.; and Drabman, R. S. "The Effects of Loud and Soft Reprimands on the Behavior of Disruptive Students." *Exceptional Children* 37 (1970): 145–55.

_____, and O'Leary, S. G., eds. *Classroom Management: The Successful Use of Behavior Modification.* New York: Pergamon Press, 1972.

Osler, S. F., and Kofsky, E. "Structure and Strategy in Concept Learning." *Journal of Experimental Child Psychology* 4 (1966): 198–209.

Packard, R. G. "The control of 'Classroom Attention': A Group Contingency for Complex Behavior." *Journal of Applied Behavior Analysis* 3 (1970): 13–28.

Palkes, H.; Stewart, M.; and Freedman, J. "Improvement in Maze Performance of Hyperactive Boys as a Function of Verbal-Training Procedures." *The Journal of Special Education* 5 (1971): 337–42.

_____; Stewart, M.; and Kahana, B. "Porteus Maze Performance of Hyperactive Boys after Training in Self-Directed Verbal Commands." *Child Development* 39 (1968): 817–26.

Patterson, G. R. "An Application of Conditioning Techniques to the Control of a Hyperactive Child." In *Case Studies in Behavior Modification,* edited by L. P. Ullmann and L. Krasner. New York: Holt, Rinehart & Winston, 1965.

_____. *Families.* Champaign, Ill.: Research Press, 1971.

_____; Cobb, J. A.; and Ray, R. S. "Direct Intervention in the Classroom: A Set of Procedures for the Aggressive Child." In *Implementing Behavioral Programs for Schools and Clinics,* edited by F. W. Clark, D. R. Evans, and L. A. Hamerlynck. Champaign, Ill.: Research Press, 1972.

Pick, A. D.; Christy, M. D.; and Frankel, G. W. "A Developmental Study of Visual Selective Attention." *Journal of Experimental Child Psychology* 14 (1972):165–75.

Pick, H. L., and Pick, A. D. "Sensory and Perceptual Development." In *Carmichael's Manual of Child Psychology,* edited by P. H. Mussen. 3rd ed. New York: Wiley, 1970.

Pinkston, E. M.; Reese, N. M.; LeBlanc, J. M.; and Baer, D. M. "Independent Control of a Preschool Child's Aggression and Peer Interaction by Contingent Teacher Attention." *Journal of Applied Behavior Analysis* 6 (1973): 115–24.

Quay, H. C.; Sprague, R. L.; Werry, J. S.; and McQueen, M. M. "Conditioning Visual Orientation of Conduct Problem Children in the Classroom." *Journal of Experimental Child Psychology* 5 (1967): 512–17.

Ramp, E. A., and Hopkins, B. L., eds. *A New Direction for Education: Behavior Analysis 1971.* Lawrence, Kan.: Kansas University Department of Human Development, 1971.

Ridberg, E. H.; Parke, R. D.; and Hetherington, E. M. "Modification of Impulsive and Reflective Cognitive Styles through Observation of Film-Mediated Models." *Developmental Psychology* 5 (1971): 369–77.

Rost, K. J., and Charles, D. C. "Academic Achievement of Brain Injured and Hyperactive Children in Isolation." *Exceptional Children* 34 (1967): 125–26.

Sabo, R. A., and Hagen, J. W. "Color Cues and Rehearsal in Short-Term Memory." *Child Development* 44 (1973):77–82.

Sarason, S. B. *Psychological Problems in Mental Deficiency.* New York: Harper, 1949.

Schutte, R. C., and Hopkins, B. L. "The Effects of Teacher Attention on Following Instructions in a Kindergarten Class." *Journal of Applied Behavior Analysis* 3 (1970): 117–22.

Schwartz, S. H.; Firestone, I. J.; and Terry, S. "Fading Techniques and Concept Learning in Children." *Psychonomic Science* 25 (1971): 83–84.

Semb, G., ed. *Behavior Analysis and Education—1972.* Lawrence, Kan.: Kansas University Department of Human Development, 1972.

Shores, R. E., and Haubrich, P. A. "Effect of Cubicles in Educating Emotionally Disturbed Children." *Exceptional Children* 36 (1969): 21–26.

Siegelman, E. "Reflective and Impulsive Observing Behavior." *Child Development* 40 (1969): 1213–22.

Skinner, B. F. *The Technology of Teaching.* New York: Appleton-Century-Crofts, 1968.

Slater, B. R. "Effects of Noise on Pupil Performance." *Journal of Educational Psychology* 59 (1968): 239–43.

Solomon, R. W., and Wahler, R. G. "Peer Reinforcement Control of Classroom Problem Behavior." *Journal of Applied Behavior Analysis* 6 (1973): 49–56.

Somervill, J. W.; Warnberg, L. S.; and Bost, D. E. "Effects of Cubicles versus Increased Stimulation on Task Performance by First-Grade Males Perceived as Distractible and Nondistractible." *Journal of Special Education* 7 (1973): 169–85.

Spiker, C. C. "Performance on a Difficult Discrimination Following Pretraining with Distinctive Stimuli." *Child Development* 30 (1959): 513–22.

Stainback, W. C.; Payne, J. S.; Stainback, S. B.; and Payne, R. A. *Establishing a Token Economy in the Classroom.* Columbus, Ohio: Merrill, 1973.

Stevenson, H. W. *Children's Learning.* New York: Appleton-Century-Crofts, 1972.

Strauss, A. A., and Kephart, N. C. *Psychopathology and Education of the Brain-Injured Child.* Vol. II. *Progress in Theory and Clinic.* New York: Grune & Stratton, 1955.

———, and Lehtinen, L. E. *Psychopathology and Education of the Brain-Injured Child.* New York: Grune & Stratton, 1947.

Surratt, P. R.; Ulrich, R. E.; and Hawkins, R. P. "An Elementary Student as a Behavioral Engineer." *Journal of Applied Behavior Analysis* 2 (1969): 85–92.

Terrace, H. S. "Discrimination Learning with and without 'Errors.'" *Journal of the Experimental Analysis of Behavior* 6 (1963): 1–27.

Thomas, D. R.; Becker, W. C.; and Armstrong, M. "Production and Elimination of Disruptive Classroom Behavior by Systematically Varying Teacher's Behavior." *Journal of Applied Behavior Analysis* 1 (1968): 35–45.

Trabasso, T., and Bower, G. H. *Attention in Learning: Theory and Research.* New York: Wiley, 1968.

Walker, H. M., and Buckley, N. K. "The Use of Positive Reinforcement in Conditioning Attending Behavior." *Journal of Applied Behavior Analysis* 1 (1968): 245–50.

———, and Buckley, N. K. *Token Reinforcement Techniques.* Eugene, Ore.: E-B Press, 1974.

Wallace, G., and Kauffman, J. M. *Teaching Children with Learning Problems.* Columbus, Ohio: Merrill, 1973.

Wasik, B. H. "The Application of Premack's Generalization on Reinforcement to the Management of Classroom Behavior." *Journal of Experimental Child Psychology* 10 (1970): 33–43.

Werner, H., and Strauss, A. A. "Causal Factors in Low Performance." *American Journal of Mental Deficiency* 45 (1940): 213–18.

———, and Strauss, A. A. "Pathology of Figure-Background Relation in the Child." *Journal of Abnormal and Social Psychology* 36 (1941): 236–48.

Whelan, R. J. "Richard J. Whelan." In *Teaching Children with Behavior Disorders: Personal Perspectives,* edited by J. M. Kauffman and C. D. Lewis. Columbus, Ohio: Merrill, 1974.

Willis, J., and Crowder, J. "A Portable Device for Group Modification of Classroom Attending Behavior." *Journal of Applied Behavior Analysis* 5 (1972): 199–202.

Winett, R. A., and Winkler, R. C. "Current Behavior Modification in the Classroom: Be Still, Be Quiet, Be Docile." *Journal of Applied Behavior Analysis* 5 (1972): 499–504.

Wolf, M. M.; Hanley, E. L.; King, L.; Lachowicz, J.; and Giles, D. K. "The Timer-Game: A Variable Interval Contingency for the Management of Out-of-Seat Behavior." *Exceptional Children* 37 (1970): 113–17.

Wolff, P., and Wolff, E. A. "Correlational Analysis of Motor and Verbal Activity in Young Children." *Child Development* (1972): 1407–11.

Yando, R. M., and Kagan, J. "The Effect of Teacher Tempo on the Child." *Child Development* 39 (1968): 27–34.

Yussen, S. R. "The Effects of Verbal and Visual Highlighting of Dimensions on Discrimination Learning by Preschoolers and Second Graders." *Child Development* 43 (1972): 921–29.

Zelniker, T.; Jeffrey, W. E.; Ault, R.; and Parsons, J. "Analysis and Modification of Search Strategies of Impulsive and Reflective Children on the Matching Familiar Figures Test." *Child Development* 43 (1972): 321–35.

———, and Oppenheimer, L. "Modification of Information Processing of Impulsive Children." *Child Development* 44 (1973): 445–50.

Zimmerman, E. H., and Zimmerman, J. "The Alteration of Behavior in a Special Classroom Situation." *Journal of the Experimental Analysis of Behavior* 5 (1962): 59–60.

Editors' note: Beginning in 1941, with an early study reported by Heinz Werner and Mable Bowers which dealt with auditory perception in exogenous mentally retarded children, there have been but a few investigators who have turned their attention to the auditory aspect of human perception. Helmer Myklebust has been one of these significant persons, and Joseph M. Wepman has been another. Dr. Wepman has spent the major portion of his professional life exploring the parameters of auditory perception and attempting to understand the relationship between perceptual distortions and oral communication. The study of auditory perception is costly and more elusive than the study of visual perception. A child's learning involves so much auditory-motor activity that the dynamics of these perceptual deficits must become more thoroughly understood, and ameliorative procedures must be perfected.

There are varieties of viewpoint regarding the interpretations of perceptual disorders. The chapter by A. Jean Ayres is concerned with visual perception, that of Joseph M. Wepman, with auditory perception. The fact that these chapters are juxtaposed in this volume does not imply that the authors employ the same orientation in writing about the two sensory systems. The discerning reader will observe differences of opinion between the two authors which involve both differences in theoretical orientation and philosophical approach to the problem. These differences, while making interesting reading, emphasize the point that research in both modalities needs to be undertaken which will ultimately minimize differences and isolate commonalities between these two sensory systems and as well among all sensory systems in the human organism.

Joseph M. Wepman Ph.D., holds numerous appointments at the University of Chicago, among them: Professor of Psychology and Surgery, Director of the Speech and Language Clinic and Research Laboratory, and, since 1969, Professor of Education. He is also Chairman of the Department of Psychology at the University of Chicago. Dr. Wepman has been active nationally and has held appointments on numerous study sections and councils in the U.S. Office of Vocational Rehabilitation, the National Institutes of Health, and the National Advisory Council of Veterans Administration. He is a Diplomate in Clinical Psychology, American Board of Professional Examiners in Psychology, American Psychological Association, and a member of numerous professional organizations. Dr. Wepman has written widely in various areas of audiology, particularly in those pertaining to auditory perception.

7

Auditory Perception and Imperception

JOSEPH M. WEPMAN

"The intellectual life of man consists almost wholly in his substitution of a conceptual order for the perceptual order in which his experience originally comes." William James, *Essays in Radical Empiricism*

INTRODUCTION—THEORY

In order to portray the role of auditory perception in the overall process of learning to comprehend and use verbal symbols in communication, it is necessary to consider a number of concurrently developing physiological and psychological characteristics of the individual child. Learning is an individualized process differing in many ways from child to child in the rate and manner of acquisition of the ability. While every child develops the same perceptual processes, some of the aptitudes essential for learning to use the language code of the community develop rapidly and early in some children, while in others the onset and progression is delayed.

Perhaps the most important thing to say about children is that they must all learn to use (decode, recode, and encode) language. Each child does so in his or her own way, at his or her own rate by natural adaptation of innate characteristics and environmental conditions. The individual differences to be discussed are unrelated to class, ethnicity, opportunity, or intelligence. While these factors and others play an important role and must be given due recognition, this chapter confines itself largely to the major readiness factors—to those processes which must reach a stage of adequacy of function before the child can be said to be ready to adapt to the task of learning to comprehend and use verbal symbols.

In the viewpoint expressed here perception itself is divisible into at least two levels or stages in a developmental hierarchy. As the schematic model of Figure 7.1 indicates, perception functions at both a *perceptual* or subliminal, imitative, or echoic level and at a *conceptual* meaningful, comprehension level where the output is consciously expressive of the individual's thought processes.

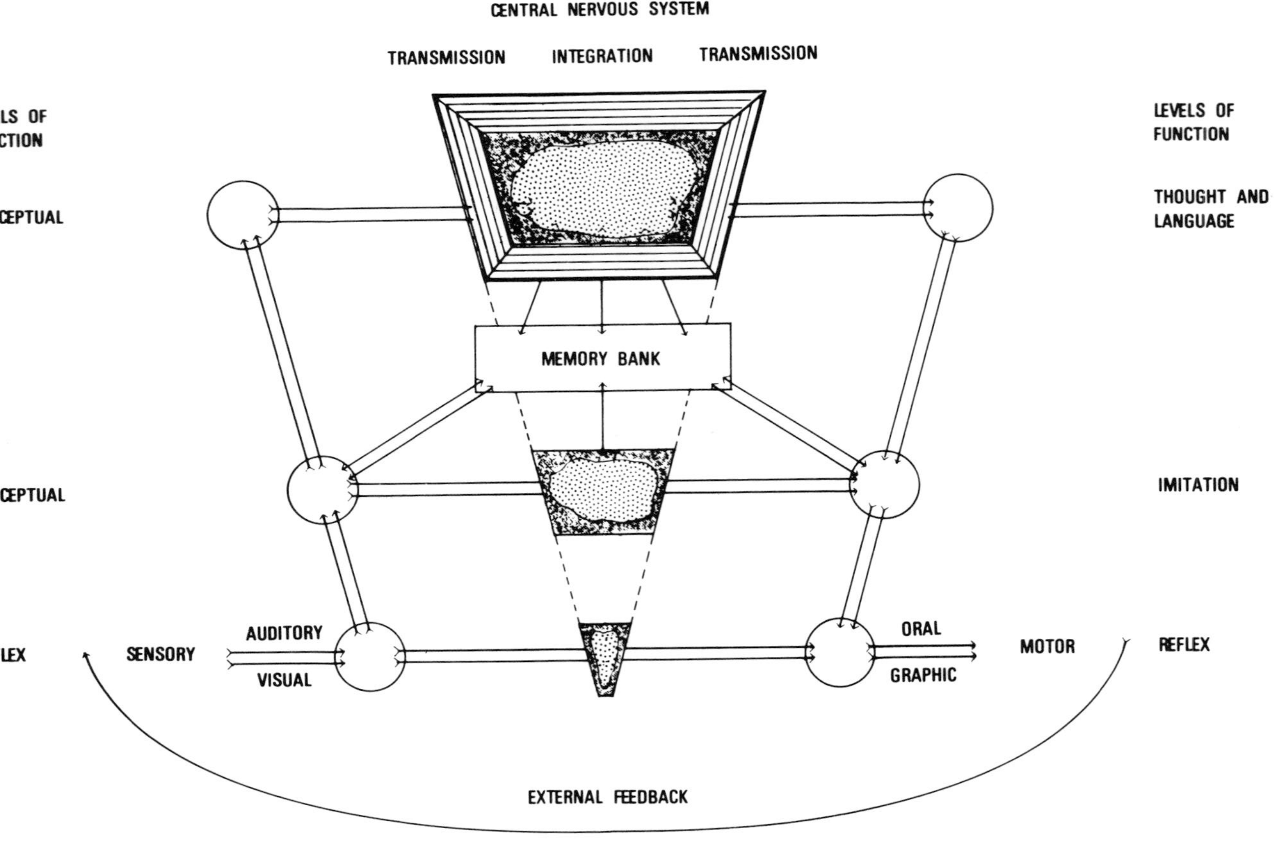

Figure 7.1. An operational diagram of the levels of function of the CNS.

Auditory perception has a vital role in both perceptual and conceptual language learning—and as will be seen, its maldevelopment plays a vital role in determining a learning disability.

This model of language development stresses the separation of the modalities by and through which children learn. While schematically each stage or level is portrayed as separable from each stage above it, in actuality the stages blend into one another. This is especially true of the perceptual and conceptual levels related to language acquisition and use.

The model indicates the separate pathways of audition and vision which become integrated in the central processing of stimuli through a cross-modality interaction or a unimodal effect. Outputs, the motor acts, depend upon a progressive maturation of motor controls. In simpler terms, auditory input functions as a singular pathway via the external receptor, the ear, and its connection to the eighth cranial nerve which transmits auditory stimuli to the central auditory process. Similarly, the visual modality transmits visual stimuli via the end organ, the eye, and its varied connections to the central nervous system (CNS).

While the model is restricted to auditory and visual pathways, a concurrent development of tactile/kinesthetic reception develops, and its end product is added to the central matrix. Furthermore, on the output side, coordination of the musculature of expression, as in speech (Liberman *et al.* 1967) or writing (Myklebust 1965), has its own developmental rate.

This difference in developmental rates between and within the modalities of both reception and expression is the cornerstone of individual differences in learning. While reception and comprehension of verbal symbols always precedes expression, the auditory pathway becomes partially functional before the visual sensory process begins its development. Muscular coordination—the control over fine muscle systems as in speech—begins and continues its development independent of the other modalities. Thus, speech which may begin as an unintelligible phonetic output (jargon) becomes intelligible as the sixty-seven muscles necessary for accurate articulation become a coordinated set of sequentially ordered movements. Developmentally, this occurs at different times and at different rates in children and in consequence adds to individual differences in maturation of communication skill.

Each of these modality-bound input and output pathways are unique in the rate of their development. Research evidence indicates that the processes involved with the perceptual level develop according to an innate, genetically determined pattern. Once the processes begin their development, the progression appears to be inviolate—only differing in rate between children.

Thought processing, the ability to comprehend and formulate a response, is a sensory central integration synthesis at the conceptual level. Until the child has acquired a sufficient perceptual mastery of the phonemic/phonetic alphabet to permit expression in form of the language code of his or her community, however, the product may not be intelligible.

The child learns this code and is able to decode messages long before he or she is able to encode responses. This is evident in the abortive attempts children make to communicate orally with the melody or stress of spoken attempts at language usage, producing unintelligible jargon. Until a sufficient perceptual discrimination provides the child with an alphabet of sounds through imitation, as this alphabet is discriminated—vowels separated from consonants, vowels separated from other vowels, and consonants from other consonants—language can be decoded for meaning but not encoded for meaningful expression.

When it is said that a given word is not in the vocabulary of a child, it is meant that by the child's behavior the thought process which generates the expected word has insufficient power to organize that word for expression or that the stimulus word or action perceived has insufficient power to stimulate the desired thought processes. Yet, the child may indicate by imitative or echoic action that the word in question can be received, integrated, recalled, and produced perceptually.

A parrot, for example, can produce a word meaningful to its auditor but be only imitative or echoic to its producer. The parrot speaks perceptually—the parrot hears and integrates by transforming the input signal into an intelligible motor pattern without an intervening thought process—without meaning. Children, like parrots, learn this perceptual decoding and encoding process before they learn to synthesize the signal into a meaningful state prior to a purposeful output. The child parrots the environment, and the parroted word, while not meaningful, indicates the intactness of the perceptual process. As the word parroted becomes reinforced, secures need satisfaction, and makes it worthwhile that it be repeated, the perceptual echoed word becomes conceptualized and expressive of a meaningful state. The word is repeated by the child to satisfy a behavioral environmental need-reducing result. The word then becomes part of the child's vocabulary. Note: the learning that has occurred—the structure and the form it takes. An auditory stimulus is discriminated and imprinted as a unit; after stimulation, it is transformed (probably through trial and error initially) into a specific motor act of speech without meaning. This output is then reacted to and brings a need-reducing result. This behavior is noted, stored, and available for recall and use when the same or a similar situation occurs.

Symbolic verbal behavior—a substitute for action or a command for attention—is produced as the need arises. This order of events is largely unrelated to intelligence *per se* but rather is related to survival in the sense of need reduction regardless of the intellectual process involved. The part intelligence plays in these first steps of acquisition of semantic and syntactic substitution relates only to the degree of self-recognition that the production creates the desired or needed result. Nonverbal behavior—a smile, a frown, crying, gurgling with apparent satisfaction, grasping at an observed object—occurs prior to the verbalized use of words.

The developmental rate seems unquestionably related to a similar growth and maturation of the CNS. As that system differentiates vertically from spinal to brain stem to subcortex and cortex, it becomes capable of controlling more and more complex behavior. At the reflex level, for example, the CNS with a minimum of integration between input and output transmits a specific sensory signal into a preordained specific motor act. In audition, the auropalpebral reflex is an important example. Here a sound signal is transmitted from the external end organ—the ear—via the eighth nerve, to the spinal nervous system, which transmutes it into a motor signal causing the eyes to blink. No learning occurs at this level; as the model indicates there is no connection between reflex behavior and memory. No matter then how many times a particular reflex is activated, it performs no better due to the repetition.

The reflex level is important to a full understanding of the model. The reflex behavior indicates the intactness of the CNS as well as its receptor and effector mechanisms. Any failure to produce the expected motor output after the stimulus points to an impairment. Thus, if a loud noise is introduced into a subject's ear and the subject fails to blink his or her eyes, (the auropalpebral reflex) the examiner knows that either (1) the ear may not be functioning, (2) the sensory reception and transmission of sound in the nervous system may be faulty, (3) the central integrative process translating sensory to motor function may be at fault, (4) the transmission of nervous impulses to the muscles may be impaired, or (5) the musculature of the eyelids producing the blink may be at fault. By further examination these alternative factors can be studied and the specific cause of the reflex failure isolated.

It is at this level of reflex behavior that a determination of an organic physiological impairment can most simply be demonstrated. The brain injured child with problems in learning will most often show an impairment at the reflex level. Learning problems of demonstrable organic etiology are relatively uncommon. The noted behavior, however, of the brain injured child, his apparent lack of attention to certain stimuli, is commonly seen. Because of this commonality of behavior the so-called minimal brain impairment syndrome is identified—the children are treated as though they were indeed organically impaired. (As an aside, it should be noted that this classification—minimal brain impairment—is an over-used and a most often inaccurately used category. By using it there is a tendency to exploit the organic nature of a learning problem, tending to stigmatize the child and to identify his exceptionality as an organic fault when no organic deficiency exists. Minimal brain impairment is a pejorative term that this writer believes should be eliminated from any categorization of learning disabilities.)

The interrelationship between physiologic and psychological factors in development are recognizable at this juncture. Learning in one sense is a neuropsychological manifestation where the mechanism of learning is accomplished through CNS action. If the neuroanatomy is faulty, the product—language usage—will be faulty; it takes an adequate machine to produce an adequate ability to process thought and produce language as an end product.

Eisenson (1966), discussing perceptual disturbances in children with

CNS dysfunctions, itemizes four perceptual processes, any one of which may be instrumental in producing aphasia in children if they are physiologically impaired: "(1) The capacity to receive stimuli that are produced in sequential order; (2) The capacity to hold the stimuli in mind, to hold the sequential impression so that its components may be integrated into some pattern; (3) The capacity to scan the pattern from within so that it may be compared with other impressions or other remembered patterns; and (4) The capacity to respond differentially, meaningfully to the perceptual impression" (p. 25).

Learning or learning to learn is a psychoeducational task—an educational not a medical process—yet, the adequacy of the physiological mechanism is essential to language development. When the fault is organic in the sense used here, resolution of the problem should be with the cooperation of a medical consultant.

At this point it may be most important to recognize that a very small percentage of learning disabled children show underachievement due to organic pathology. However, when CNS impairment does exist, the likelihood of a language learning problem is materially enhanced. This is especially true when the physiologic impairment involves the left cerebral hemisphere. In such instances aphasia—the language deficit caused by cortical damage—is common. If the impairment is located elsewhere, other forms of language deficiency such as the agnosias (receptive defects) or the apraxias (expressive defects) are more common. Eisenson (1966) lists deficits in auditory discrimination, sequencing difficulty, auditory span, and localization of sound as specific and common deficiencies in aphasic children.

In our consideration of the role of auditory perception and imperception in learning, the intactness of the basic reflexes using auditory stimuli may be most important; for perception to occur the auditory mechanism must be functional as must the sensory transmission of sound waves. The input or sensory system of audition uses the same common pathway for all levels of behavior—reflex, perceptual, and conceptual. A breakdown of an auditory reflex might negate further analysis of the auditory perception since one can only perceive centrally what is received and transmitted peripherally. Perception is a CNS function; sound signals must be received to be perceived. The auditory system in all its aspects, whether at the most simplified reflex level or at the higher levels, is dependent on the stimulus being received and transmitted.

Auditory imperception, then, may be the product of inadequate development or malfunction of the receptive mechanism either at the peripheral end organ or in the nervous system responsible for transmitting the sound patterns. Learning, of course, can only occur when and if and to what degree the stimulus is received.

A particular case in point are the children who are profoundly deaf from birth—the auditory pathway is nonfunctional for them. All learning must be achieved through other sensory pathways. Hearing loss that takes place after speech has developed or partial hearing loss in children that blocks the full use of sensory pathway should not exclude further study of the perceptual or conceptual abilities. It may be most important to know the extent of development along the other modalities since it is through their media that compensatory education must occur.

A behavioral myth about people with hearing loss sufficient to create a learning problem is that when the auditory modality is blocked the other modalities become more expert—a deaf child sees better, a blind child hears better. No evidence exists for this compensatory modality. The deaf see better only because they attend better with less distraction to visual and tactile stimuli. In the early stages of learning, this adaptation to a handicap is often the best indication of a good or superior intelligence. Most often if a child has one modality blocked and the child is unable to adapt without considerable directed intervention, the indication of an average or below average intellectual ability exists. Unfortunately, there is no physiological compensation or restitution for the loss or impairment of any of the specific modalities.

This point of lack of compensatory physiological processing ability can be noted in observing the learning attempts of profoundly deaf preschool children. Some such children learn to lip-read and even develop some useful deaf-oral speech while others of essentially the same adequate native intelligence fail to do so. It is here postulated that the early lip-readers, those that appear to learn to lip-read almost automatically, are children with an innate preference for learning visually. They are "visile" children in Charcot's (1953) terms. While those who fail to learn to lip-read without marked and lengthy instruction do poorly because they are innate auditory learners or "audile" children, with their major learning pathway nonfunctional. Such children are often erroneously classified as "mentally retarded" or "emotionally disturbed."

Intervention here needs to take the compensatory form early in their learning. Whatever strengths they possess—whether they be "tactile"/kinesthetic alone or visual-tactile-kinesthetic—too often it has been observed that schoolrooms for preschool deaf children limit their training to an imaginary, impractical program and fail to explore the value of sign language. It should be axiomatic that when a pathway is not available for whatever reason all of the possible compensatory pathways should be used, not limiting the child to a particular modality because of some theory that deaf-oral speech is the only means of expression worth working toward.

The schematic model of the developmental hierarchy of learning is perhaps more readily understood if one pictures a series of independently developing but constantly converging lines. As these lines converge they interact more and more—each line's maturation effecting each other line through the matrix of immediate memory and thereby enhancing the maturational pattern.

The hierarchy of interlocking processes from the genetic endowment at birth through the critical formative years exemplifies ontogenetic likenesses between people but also indicates the potential for individual differences. During a child's very early years, innate capacity and structure is most evident. With time, opportunity, experience, and stimulation the effect of environmental conditioning becomes more apparent.

It is at the preschool and early school level that intervention becomes a salient factor.

Implied but not apparent perhaps in Figure 7.2 is the increasing degree of interaction as the child approaches the stage of formal operations—of abstract thought and language. Figure 7.2 presents schematically five major lines of development during the vital critical periods of maturation. It shows the independence of each as the child matures and the interrelation between the different characteristics through the process of memory. While each of the lines are capable of wholly independent and individually unique rates of development, their interdependence for full utilization is apparent.

The origin of each line is seen to be in the genetic endowment with the environment playing an increasing role as time ensues. Each line begins as a gross, roughly undifferentiated characteristic and progresses both through an extension of innate capacity and environmental opportunity and conditioning.

No exact chronological timetable mirrors the development; wide variations occur both because of differential endowment and the variable forces of the environment.

Of the five concurrently developing processes, the neurological (which also includes the neuroanatomical) is probably the most absolute in its development. The increasing capacity of the neural structure from spinal reflex through brain stem function to the highest level of subcortex and cortex indicates clearly the potential limitations placed on the development of other pathways when impairment occurs. Any interruption due to pathological or developmental factors will create a reduction in the adequacy of development of all of the other lines. A birth defect, for example, affecting neurological maturation will not only show as a reduction in the complexity of neural activity, but will also have a negative effect upon the development of cognition, perceptual processing, and motor coordination. This is less true of the other lines of development. Perceptual processing—subliminal learning via the different modalities—may show lags in developmental rate, yet cognition—the conceptual pathway related to thought process development and meaningful reception and reaction—may be affected only in the sense of adequacy of verbal expression.

Most importantly in studying the child it is vital to recognize the interaction of the various vectors through the process of retention and recall.

Each of the developmental lines may and most often are studied separately, yet no true picture of a child's capacity at any time in his or her maturation can be obtained if the particular line of development is not considered in the light of the stage of development of the other vectors. Cognition, for example, depends upon perceptual processing development

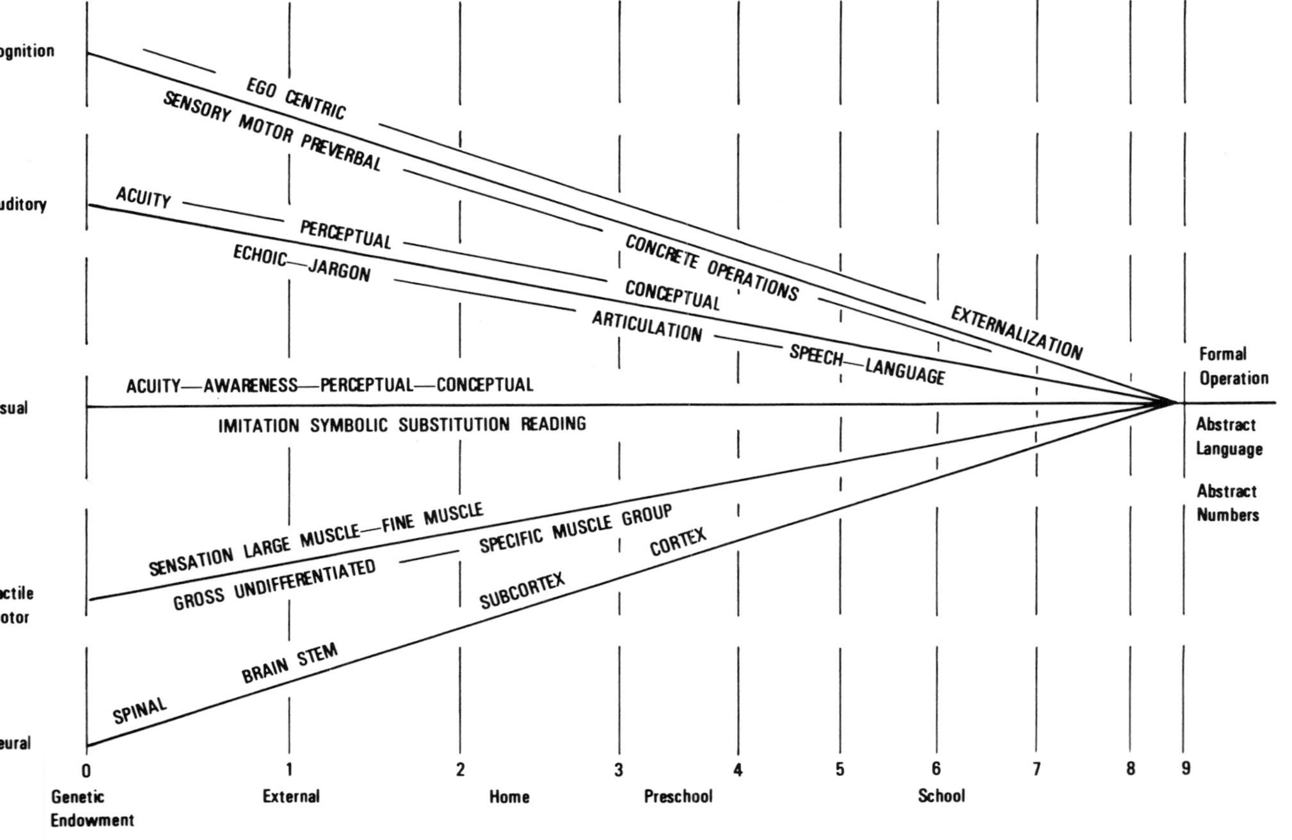

Figure 7.2. Independent converging pathways: interaction through memory; short-term memory, long-term memory, increased interaction.

for efficiency in language formulation and use. Language usage, which is often equated with intelligence, is wholly dependent on the child learning the phonemic/phonetic patterns making up the code of communication of the society in which the child is reared. Equally as the child reaches the stage of orthographic substitution for previously learned phonemic/phonetic patterns—as the child learns to read and write using the linguistic code that has made the child's speech intelligible—the degree of perceptual visual and auditory processing is the basis of the child's formulation of graphic verbal symbols. It provides the child with the alphabets needed to formulate intelligible language.

The perceptual processes include the ability to discriminate, to retain, and to recall the alphabets of phonemes and graphemes. The ability to imitate and to echo the stimuli of visual and auditory signals are not totally or irrevocably essential to cognitive development, since the deaf child develops a thought-processing ability without a phonemic/phonetic alphabet. Yet for the most part, the unimpaired child utilizes these lower-level functions in bringing his or her cognitive capacities to their highest level of development.

Independence of development and maturational capacities is a key to individual differences, yet interdependence is the keystone of maximal development. Each child reaches the stage of concrete operations, but not all go beyond that stage. In the early forties Goldstein (1941) recognized insightfully the effect of brain impairment on the cognitive process. He pointed out that the mode of thought after brain injury was not only a focal disturbance of a specific capacity impaired by cortical trauma but a total regression to a state of concretistic thought from whatever level of abstract thought the individual had achieved.

The model presented in Figure 7.2 shows no separate line of language development. Language, the comprehension and use of verbal symbols for communication, is without question a higher mental process. Through language use the individual child or adult displays his or her intellectual capacity in a sense; yet it is at best a poor indicator of thought. It is this writer's observation and belief that language development is the product of all the separate converging lines. It serves man as a means toward an end—societal interaction—yet by its own constraints, the rigidity of its syntactic structure and the automaticity of its production, it serves the individual intellect but is not coequal with it. Language in this sense is the servant of thought, not its mirror. Man can and does survive without language—but verbal language cannot and does not exist without man (Furth 1966).

Learning disabilities are easily depicted in the model. Any interruption in the progression to the state of formal operations will produce a learning problem, not only because each of the separable lines of development are necessary to reach the culminating level of symbolic behavior but also because society expects that each line must be achieved equally in a temporal, chronological sense. This environmental expectancy—on the part of both parents and educators—sets the goals of each stage of development, most often without consideration of the individual differences involved. It is commonly held that the child must speak by one or at least by one and a half years. He must add vocabulary and word groupings by two or two and a half years. He must be intelligible, speak in sentences by three, and so on, yet by the nature of the progression of neurological, perceptual, and conceptual processes of development, by the very fact of differential growth and maturation, these specific goals are often ephemeral. Actually they more closely approximate the mean of development, not the accomplishment of every child. If this viewpoint were true, every child whose development is below the statistical mean would be considered a failure, would need special attention, would have emotional or intellectual or physical problems. In a world where the lowest acceptable achievement is at the mean, one half of the population becomes, by definition, problem children.

The perceptual level of function which as we have seen is modality bound in both input and output is thought to be innate—or at least the preference for one modality over another appears to be so. This follows Charcot's (1953) principle of inborn learning types—"audile," "visile," and "tactile." Development of each modality, however, appears to relate closely to the concurrent development of the necessary neural structures. At the same time, the environment plays a considerable role at both the imitative/echoic level and at the higher level of conceptualization.

From the environmental sound patterns the child acquires the aurally stimulated stress or intonation patterns sometimes called the melody of speech. In some children seen clinically this first auditory sensory step in learning what is later to become intelligible speech occurs during the first year of life. No research is available on this point, yet many observations indicate its occurrence at this early age. It is to be noted that as children babble—that is, seem to use sound for the pleasure of it—no intonation pattern is observed, but as the babble turns to jargon, children attempt to speak by using the stress and melody of the auditory models, of the speech they hear. Dialects and accents are formed at this time by imitating sound patterns. They may and most often do become so overlearned that they remain the melody of speech throughout life.

Some dialectically speaking children and adults are capable of changing their speech patterns as they learn a second language or as they move into a different geographical community where the melody of speech is quite different. These latter are thought to be "audile" learners—or at least they have a highly developed auditory learning capacity even though their modality preference may be visual.

The retention of a dialect or foreign accent, then, relates to the innate subconsciously acquired perceptual auditory ability—it does not indicate a handicap or a learning disability but is the natural developmental process in action. The failure to change should not be held as a negative consideration of the child's ability (nor should it be so considered in the adult). Whether or not a change can be instituted through intervention must today be considered as moot. No research on the subject has been reported.

At the perceptual level the child acquires an alphabet of sounds and accurate articulation. These depend in large part upon the degree of development of the child's auditory discrimination and auditory memory for the sounds the child hears and makes. "Audile" children develop good articulation early in life; as each phoneme becomes functional (i.e., discriminated), "audile" children are able to compare the sounds they hear and to differentiate them from other sounds. If at the same time the child's motoric coordination is adequate to the task, the child's articulation of speech as oral language is acquired will be accurate in production. A self-monitoring system develops internally and permits the child to self-correct errors in articulation through both internal and external feedback. This perceptual function, the accurate production of sounds, occurs at different rates in different children; however, as Templin (1957) has shown, by eight years of age most children have acquired adequate intelligible speech.

While learning in general is subsumed here as an entity, specific acts or processes of learning to communicate using verbal symbolic forms (oral language as in speech, graphic language as in writing, comprehensive reading and spelling of orthographic forms) constitute the framework used in the present discussion of the auditory contribution to the total act.

Audition as a major sensory pathway must be viewed at two levels: the first is the function of the external mechanism of hearing (acuity), and the second is the neural level of perception of what is heard.

From clinical experience with the aftereffects of brain injury in adults, auditory perception is known to operate on two levels in the processing of neurally received auditory signals. Subjects were seen who were capable only of imitating or echoing auditory stimuli and unable from their behavior to comprehend the same stimuli. Other subjects were able to comprehend what they heard and to act appropriately but were incapable of imitating or echoing the stimuli. To accommodate these two levels of perception, the modality-developmental theory postulates a lower-level function of perception (the *perceptual level*) and a higher level of perception (the *conceptual level*).

The perceptual level of perception is a rough approximation of Piaget's (1959) stimulus-response and preoperational levels. It functions naturally in a subliminal fashion, the subject being unaware of the learning taking place. The subject can be made aware of the type of behavior, however, through a testing procedure which calls for an imitative or echoic response—neither stimulus or response requiring the attachment of meaning for adequate performance. It is then within this multi-modal framework of independent yet interacting pathways that the auditory role in learning is depicted in the acuity of hearing and the perceptual and conceptual levels. The interrelation of these three characteristics of audition are discussed separately.

Auditory imperception as a cause for learning disabilities will be seen as any impairment or limitation—pathological, developmental, or psychological—of the capacity to react to an auditory signal appropriately either at the perceptual (imitative) level or at the conceptual (meaningful) level. The central focus of the present chapter is on the first of these—the perceptual level—which, because of the likelihood that it most closely reflects a child's innate characteristics, is felt to represent the true nature of a child's manner or type of learning rather than does the conceptual level, which is seen as being more closely related to environmental conditioning. (For a more complete discussion of the theoretical model see Wepman 1963; Osgood 1963; Wepman 1968; Piaget 1959.)

ACUITY

While not itself a direct part of auditory perception, auditory acuity bears upon it in a most important sense. Since people can perceive only those auditory signals they receive, any limitation of the stimulus will constrain, reduce, or distort their perception.

A series of important and unresolved questions are brought to mind by this relationship between the loss of auditory acuity and its effect on auditory perception. There is little definitive research in the area, but audiological as well as perceptual researchers might address themselves to such questions as the following:

1. Does partial hearing loss (of what degree) affect the time and rate of acquisition of accurate speech articulation?

2. Templin (1957) and others have amply demonstrated that accuracy of articulation is acquired progressively through the first eight years of life. Could a partial congenital hearing loss account in part for a delay in speech accuracy? How much of a role might it play? Could a temporary, intermittent hearing loss due to infection or other pathological factors at or during the time a child is learning to speak affect the manner and rate of such learning?

3. Morency *et al.* (1970) have shown a typical pattern of the acquisition of articulatory accuracy related to the adequate development of the child's auditory perception. In that pattern, the sounds acquired last by children with unimpaired hearing are by and large sounds produced at the upper end of the hearing range, thus *th* (voiceless), *b*, *v*, *s*, *sh*, and *th* (voiced) are developmentally the last sounds produced accurately in unimpaired children.

In children with hearing loss at the upper end of the frequency scale, which either limits or distorts the auditory signal and therefore the perception of sounds involved, it is commonly assumed that a relationship exists between the two—the poor hearing and poor speech. However, no research has been reported verifying this assumption. Again, how much of a loss of acuity is necessary to account for inaccurate speech?

Poor auditory discrimination or delayed discrimination is held to be accountable for delays in accuracy of speech production. The role of permanent or transient hearing loss or the amount or degree of that loss on the development of the perceptual processes is not presently known. This area of research is a most challenging one facing both the audiologist and the child development specialist. Equally searching questions need to be studied in the area of the onset and acquisition of spoken language. Acuity loss affects perception by reducing perceptual adequacy, yet little rigorous research has been reported bearing on this admixture of peripheral and central audition.

Gaines (1969) makes a very valid distinction between those children she defines as "perceptually deprived" and children who are "perceptually handicapped." She notes that "*the term 'perceptually deprived' children refers to children who have a sensory limitation and cannot receive perceptual information in a normal way either because of blindness, deafness, a neurological disorder or mental retardation.*"

From this viewpoint, it would appear that the perceptually deprived child represents an exclusively different problem in learning from the "perceptually handicapped," where the difficulty lies solely in the CNS. Yet it should be noted that a "perceptually deprived" child may also be "perceptually handicapped." A partially deaf child may also have a poorly developed visual learning capacity, in which case learning to lip-read or learning to sign- or finger-spell might be equally difficult for the child to master.

Another case in point are the children whose perceptual deprivation was seen as being due to mental retardation. A mentally retarded child (especially if exogenously retarded) may have very good auditory sensory perceptual abilities and indicate so by his or her ability to imitate or echo auditory stimuli. If this strength is recognized, an auditory emphasis to learning may stimulate the child while a visual approach or a traditional smorgasbord approach, where the child selects from a multi-modal stimulus, might fail. In point of fact, many children identified as mentally defective may indeed be suffering from a perceptual handicap and have been misdiagnosed as retarded. This raises so many problems related to labeling and mislabeling children that it is urgently suggested that the state of the child's perceptual development be studied before the label is used. A child with very slow developing auditory perception, for example, might well be diagnosed as mentally retarded simply because the child could not at the time examined follow oral instructions; the same might well be true of the child with a partial hearing loss and consequent imperception. It seems to this writer that any categorical labeling of children as deficient should be avoided until all of the factors which might lead to the child's deficiency are definitively explored. Cruickshank (1972) has held for many years that "mental retardation" is too general a term, that adequate description of a child's strengths and weaknesses in learning is more important than the stigmatizing label of "mental deficiency."

Until the past decade the great majority of studies of audition have emphasized the acuity factor. Two excellent reviews of the literature in this area bear testimony to the fact that this still remains true in the field of study called audiology. Katz's excellent *Handbook of Clinical Audiology,* published in 1972, and Jergers' *Modern Developments in Audiology* (second revised edition 1973) are mainly concerned with new approaches to the study of hearing acuity. In the former, however, attention should be called to an excellent chapter by Berlin and Lowe on "Central Auditory Disorders" which deals with perceptual and conceptual auditory processing problems.

In their chapter in Jergers' (1973) book, O'Neill and Oyer (p. 211) discuss aural rehabilitation for the deaf or deafened child in terms of lipreading, auditory training, and conservation of speech. They point out the paucity of research studies in auditory communication with those whose hearing is impaired. They illustrate, moreover, what can be done with the "verbatonal method" where "the basic approach is an auditory one with band-passed speech sounds being used to determine auditory threshold of detection and identification with relatively good results."

O'Neill and Oyer also comment on "frequency transposition" research which studies communication in the hearing impaired using amplified sound. "Much of the recent interest," they say, "is the result of developments in instrumentation that allow for certain manipulation of the auditory signal" (p. 232). Time-compressed speech has also been experimentally used, with some success, to modify the auditory signal (Zemlin 1966).

While the immediate interest of the present chapter lies in the central processing of auditory signals, new studies, largely medically oriented, have attracted audiological researchers in improving the assessment of hearing ability which has the effect of increasing our knowledge of the perceptual problems of the hearing impaired. Studies utilizing computer analyses of the auditory signal called the "evoked auditory potential" (Tepas 1974), the use of dichotic listening techniques (Jerger 1970), of "sound localization" (Butler 1973), and lateralization of auditory dominance (Kimura 1961) should not be overlooked in considering the auditory role in learning. Audiology as a science is active in many ways that help to clarify and extend our knowledge in this regard.

Tepas (1974) reviews the work on computer analysis of the electroencephalogram which he subtitles "evoking, promoting, and provoking." Studies using this method of signal detection have become numerous in recent years. Since the evoked potential is an assessment of the signal strength within the nervous system, it represents a stage between acuity and perception and may provide us with some of the information presently lacking in the complex interrelationship between acuity and perception.

A challenge for researchers in this area is to explore the relationship between such "evoked auditory potentials" and the auditory perceptual processes. Do specific patterns of evoked potentials relate to specific patterns of auditory perception? or to particular patterns of auditory imperception? These might be the most revealing questions to study and yield presently unknown data.

Audiometry, the study of hearing thresholds, is further extending the accuracy and objectivity of the assessment of hearing loss through studies using electrocochleography (Hooper 1973) to replace the older classical but subjective threshold measurements. Researchers using this device point to the accuracy of their assessments which are beyond the control of the individual being tested. Such studies, since they are at the very borderline between acuity and perception, should be followed with increasing interest by the students of child development.

These are but a few of the recent areas of acoustic research bearing essentially on the critical aspect of acuity or hearing loss.

Publications in the *Journal of Hearing and Speech Research* indicate the growing amount of research reported in the area of audition. While most emphasize the acuity factor, there is a growing tendency to explore some of the relationships between acuity and perception. In one issue of the *Journal,* for example (September 1974), appear articles dealing with "Comprehension of Relativized Sentences by Deaf Students (Quigley *et al.*, pp. 325–41); "Performance of Young Hearing Impaired Children on a Test of Basic Concepts" (Davis, pp. 342–51); "Durational Aspects of Vowel Production in the Speech of Deaf Children" (Monsen, pp. 386–98); "Categorical Encoding in Short-Term Memory by Deaf and Hearing Children" (Hoeman *et al.*, pp. 426–31); and "Performance of Severely Hearing Impaired Children on a Closed Response, Auditory Discrimination Test" (Jones and Studebaker, pp. 531–48). Thus, a broad range of acuity/perceptual/conceptual studies are beginning to surface to fill the previously noted gap in our fund of information. The future should bring considerable clarification of what has until very recently been a relatively unresearched area.

Finally, in the study of the hearing impaired is the monumental book by Furth, *Thinking Without Language* (1966). This keen student of language and hearing explored in detail the relationships between cognitive development and hearing loss. While primarily concerned with the profoundly deaf, Furth's studies also include the partially deafened. The author is a student of the Piagetian viewpoint of development, and he points out that "logical thinking develops gradually from its first manifestations in object formation around age one to the first evidence of logical operations at age six. In this period of transition pre-logical thinking is tied to perceptual presentation." "The deaf," Furth concludes, "illustrate some of the effects of linguistic deficiency, however, the basic development and structure of intelligence of the deaf in comparison with the hearing is remarkably unaffected by the absence of verbal language."

Furth's conclusion that the deaf reach the level of formal operations of abstraction in thought despite their impairment in language is in contradistinction to the generally held view that the thought processes of the profoundly deaf are concretistic and rarely reach the abstractive level of their hearing peers. If Furth's view is supported, a greater emphasis on the level of expectation one can hold for the deaf and their capacity to think without hearing and think without language should be forthcoming.

The next decade might well show further replication of Furth's view, confirming or denying his conclusions. From the viewpoint of the student of auditory perceptual problems it should be noted that where the pathway is totally blocked compensatory sensory pathways (other modalities) will be found useful in education and remediation with aims as high as for the hearing—the capacity for formal operations and abstract language.

AUDITORY PERCEPTION AND LANGUAGE

Communication through the use of verbal symbols takes different forms. Speech or oral language is followed chronologically by reading, writing, and spelling. The role of auditory perception in each of these acquired functions is somewhat different. Speech is a more or less natural acquisition in the hearing child. Sociologically, man developed oral forms of communication as the need for inter-species relations became necessary. As a species seeking survival in a predatory world where all or many of the other species were individually and collectively more powerful, man needed a method for collective defensive action. Speech as the outward signal of language performed this function. It served to bind together for fight or flight the constituent members into a society. Within limits it could perform its function beyond the limits of visual signals. Man could produce sound, and it was natural for him to turn this sound-producing facility into a linguistic system—a language where words had concrete as well as symbolic meaning.

Reading and its correlated writing and spelling, however, are artificial acquisitions. No survival needs justify their existence other than the convenience in communication. As communication skills they serve to extend the species' capacity to learn from the past and plan for the future. Phylogenetically, writing probably developed with reading almost simultaneously, with pictographic communication in ancient caves thought to be graphic messages which carried meaning and served as the basis for formal language (Ardrey 1966).

Reading in an alphabetic rather than pictorial form followed the pattern established by spoken language. Oral language has a flexibility, however, not present in reading. Children will learn to talk without instruction following the development of their auditory perceptual abilities, but reading always (or nearly always) requires instruction. Put more simply, children talk at an early age because their needs are great to interrelate with society.

Learning the orthographic elements—the alphabet—of verbal symbols is an indication of what has become a cultural sophistication. Society has become more complex, and complex technology increases the need for literacy. Social status as well as culture demands it. Yet the act is artificial, not natural, and certainly not as essential to survival as it may be to social mobility.

Having at hand a method for communication using verbal-symbol substitution for action through spoken language, man adapts this already formulated system to written language. Speech precedes reading and writing in the normal progression of communication skill; phonemic/phonetic alphabets always precede orthographic alphabets in acquisition. That aspect of audition which provides the basis for speech is originally imitative but becomes conceptual at the higher level of spoken language with meaning.

Learning to read, write, and spell, since these activities have their base in spoken language, is closely related to auditory perception. Failure to perceive adequately provides a faulty structure on which to establish the phonics of the printed form. While reading is initially a visual skill, it soon requires an auditory counterpart—especially for those children who are strongly "audile" in learning type. There are many who hold that all children learn to read phonically whether that is the method of formal instruction or not. If this is true, then the importance of auditory perception to reading is magnified. Naturally, a corollary to this would be that auditory imperception would be equally important as a cause for reading disability.

The role of auditory perception, then, in all aspects of communication using verbal symbols—whether the act be speech, reading, or writing—is of central importance. Since learning disabilities are usually thought of as the source of underachievements by the school-age child as the child learns to read and write, auditory imperception may well be at the very root of the problem. Certainly, where oral language is the matter of concern, auditory imperception can be shown to be most clearly related as Eisenson (1966) indicates.

FUNCTIONAL STRUCTURE OF AUDITORY PERCEPTION

The sound wave collected at the external ear is transformed into neural energy through the medium of the organ of corti. It is then transmitted to a reception area in the temporal lobe.

Many researchers have postulated theoretical schema for the internal analysis of signals within the cortex after the signal is received. Konorski (1967) postulated a functional structural mechanism, such as shown in Figure 7.3, which appears to account for the major functional components of a central modality-bound auditory mechanism performing its role. While this is only one of many such hypothetical models of brain function, it does account for the steps that must occur between sensory-receptive input and transmission of the signal, its analysis at the perceptual and conceptual levels, and the eventual motor response.

As an example of the interaction between two independently developing perceptual modalities, consider the acquisition of accuracy in speech production. For many of the sounds of English in the phonemic/phonetic alphabet the continuation of phoneme substitution may be purely a reflection of inadequate auditory processing. An example of this might be the common substitution of the sound /t/ for /k/. These two phonemes are voiceless plosive stops differing only in tongue placement—a single discriminating feature. The poor or inadequate discriminator may substitute one for the other, the word /k-a-t/ pronounced as /t-a-t/. Auditory imperception may then be held accountable for many single discriminating

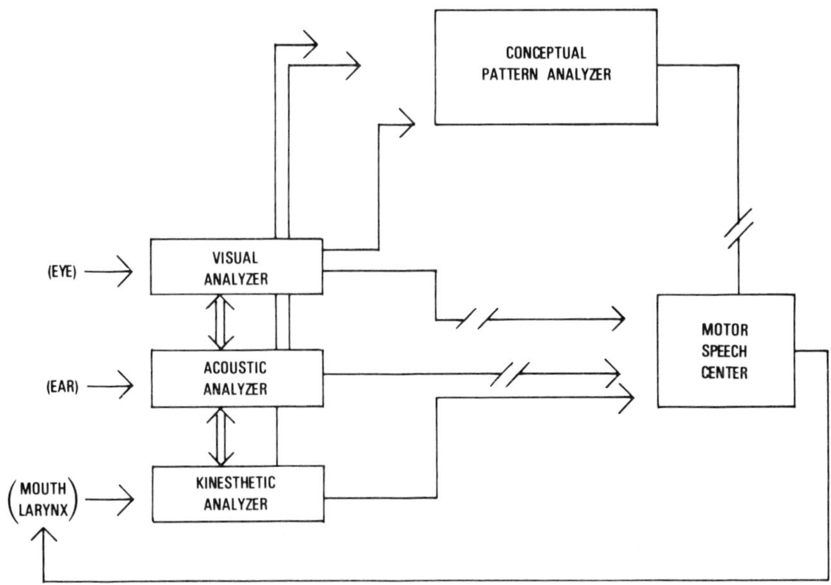

Figure 7.3. Functional-structural model of brain function. From (Konorski 1967)

feature substitutions. (/th/ for /s/; /f/ for /th/; /m/ for /n/, etc.). However, certain sound pairs are substituted not because of auditory imperception but rather because of a lag in the development of motor coordination or the ability to make rapid repetitive muscular movements in the flow of speech. The substitution of /w/ for /r/ as /wed/ for /red/ or /y/ for /l/ as in /yet/ for /l-e-t/ are good examples. Here the auditory imperception plays at most a minimal role, while the major source of the inaccuracy is in the poor or inadequately developed motoric capacity. The lag in motor movement maturation interacting with the auditory perception lies at fault.

The ability to discriminate sounds progresses from gross widely differentiated phonemes (such as vowels from consonants or stops from continuants) to sounds which are differentiated by a single discriminating feature. This area of auditory processing is presently receiving considerable attention in the speech and psycholinguistic literature.

Parnell and Korzeniowski (1972) report that auditory disturbances are to be found in 40 to 70 percent of children with learning disabilities. They recommend "structural experiences in listening, attention increasing activities, fine sound difference activities, sequential order exposure and specific training for memory."

Morency (1968) showed a continuing significant relationship between auditory discrimination and auditory memory as measured at the first grade level and school achievement at the third grade level.

Flower (1968), studying the evaluation of auditory abilities in children with reading problems, concluded that "auditory processing plays a major role in the mastery of this activity. The reconstruction of a spoken message from a printed page involves the transformation of visual stimuli into auditory stimuli. Graphemes are transformed into phonemes; printed words into spoken words. If a child is unable to receive phonemes clearly, respond to them discretely, retain them in accurate sequences and organize them into linguistic signs, he is likely to encounter formidable difficulties in learning to read."

Van Atta (1973), in a study comparing auditory skills of dyslalic and normal-speaking children in grades one through three, found auditory discrimination and auditory memory difficulties in combination more prevalent in the poorer speaking children.

Distinctive feature differences have come under scrutiny in a variety of studies since the classical paper of Jacobson, Font, and Halle (1952). They held that such features may well tap noncognitive (nonlinguistic) aspects of speech stimuli. Chananie and Tikovsky (1969) studied choice response time and distinctive features in speech discrimination.

Murch (1973) differentiated speech perception from pitch perception, intensity duration, and complex tone through spectographic research. He pointed out that these auditory processes were functions of the peripheral auditory mechanism where speech perception was a CNS function.

These are but a few of the many contributions to the literature in the area of auditory perception and learning, indicating that it is of growing interest.

Readiness to read—or readiness to develop one's own attack on reading—can now be safely assumed from the evidence to be as closely related to auditory perceptual factors as to visual. The remedial teacher as well as the psychoeducational specialist responsible for individual programming of intervention for the learning disabled child can and should benefit from a more complete understanding of the role of auditory perceptual development. Speech and hearing specialists have understood reading with regard to speech accuracy development for some time. Yet, these specialists in specific therapy or intervention have tended to overlook the developmental nature of the relationship. Too often children who are still developing adequate perceptual skills and in consequence demonstrate certain speech inaccuracies are advised to undergo corrective therapies. A study of children in one public school system where children below the age of nine with articulatory inaccuracies were split into two matched groups, in which Group A received speech therapy while Group B did not for the three first grades of school, revealed that no difference existed in articulation at the end of the three-year trial period. Interestingly enough, in this same study no significant relationship was found between speech inaccuracy, its recovery with or without therapy, and school achievement. The study provided additional interesting data—certain children showed auditory-processing difficulty and related speech deficiency as would be predicted;

however, not predicted was the fact that certain other children showed auditory imperception and reading achievement difficulty in significant numbers (Wepman 1960).

Returning now to the Konorski (1967) model, the potential is presented for (1) limited sensation analysis with its imitative or echoic response at the primary stage, and (2) the more extensive analysis and integration at the secondary stage. While Konorski was interested mainly in describing the processes necessary to explain the behavior of the brain injured aphasic subjects with their consequent language problems, the model seems equally appropriate to suggest the functional mechanism necessary for modality-bound learning in the unimpaired. Its divisions also serve as well for an understanding of the focal points which must be considered in understanding the mechanism underlying specific learning disabilities.

At stage one of the model the signals transmitted through each of the modality receptors (eye, ear, kinesthetic) are processes. In terms of our immediate interest such processing would include (1) discriminating the signal into its phonemic elements, (2) storing each element discriminated in memory (short and long term), and (3) the sequential order in which each element is received. These processed sound elements then could immediately or in a delayed fashion be transmitted directly to the motor speech center where a corresponding phonetic response would ensue directly related to the sensory stimulus—an imitation or echoing of the stimulus.

Auditory imperception at this level would be the result of the individual not yet having developed a mature and accurate auditory processing ability in either discrimination or memory. The sound signal would then be perceived or recalled inaccurately, i.e., not discriminated from other sounds similar to it or not recalled accurately when recall was required. The imitation or echo of the input signal would then be heard as inaccurate production. For example, if the signal was the phonemic array /k-a-t/ and discriminated inaccurately as /t-a-t/ the product in speech would reflect the misperception. The word phoneme cluster /tat/ would be produced rather than /kat/—the stop /t/ would be substituted for the stop /k/. If the /k/ were properly discriminated from /t/ but the auditory memory or recall were insufficient or inadequate, the phoneme /t/ might also be produced because the /k/ and /t/ have so many discriminating features in common.

Auditory discrimination and auditory memory are known to be developmental in nature (Turaids, Wepman, and Morency 1972). As the child's vocabulary increases, the need for more and more phonemic constitutent elements increase in number and type—the child needs more and more of the phonemic alphabet to be able to imitate the sensory input. Templin (1957), Morency, Wepman, and Hass (1967), and others have shown the progressive acquisition of the phonemic alphabet as expressed in speech through the first eight years of life. The acquisition order is not inviolate; that is, certain sounds may appear in the production pattern prior to others for a number of reasons, but the general order seems to be the same for most children. Lags in the development of auditory discrimination ability or pathologies affecting the clear perception of sounds produce different patterns of acquisition as demonstrated by the typical articulatory inaccuracies of children with differing etiologies (Morency, Wepman, and Weiner 1967).

In the widely used Auditory Discrimination Test devised by the present writer (Wepman 1958, 1973) thirty word-pairs, each differing in a single discriminating feature, are read to children who are asked to indicate whether the word pairs are the same word repeated or two different words. Each of the possible phonemically balanced sounds of English, including initial and final consonants and medial vowels, are presented. By comparing the scores obtained (the number of word-pairs correctly identified as same or different) with age-related norms, a relatively reliable estimate can be made of the child's auditory discriminatory ability. The developmental nature of this ability is seen by the increasing number of correct judgments or discriminations with each age from five through eight years. Further, from the standardized data collected on unselected population of unimpaired children the ability to discriminate becomes asymptotic after eight years of age. Older children make approximately the same number of errors as do the eight-year-olds (Wepman 1973).

Auditory memory span at the perceptual level shows a similar developmental progression through the five- to eight-year span. A test exploring the ability to recall discrete word units of increasing length shows the expected increase with age in the unimpaired child (Wepman and Morency 1973).

Auditory memory span inadequacy is described by a child's inability to match his age peers in span of recall. When memory span inadequacy is coupled with poor auditory discrimination, the likelihood of a handicapping condition affecting learning is accentuated.

The third auditory factor found to relate statistically to verbal symbolic learning—especially to learning to spell—is the specialized recall of sequential ordering of sounds. Again, research has demonstrated the increasing capacity for recall of sequential order at the perceptual level with age (Wepman and Morency 1973).

These three perceptual processes—discrimination, memory span, and sequential recall—have been found to have a positive correlation to reading, writing, and spelling achievement (Morency 1968). Inadequate development of any one of the three at the time that formal education is undertaken may be at the root of the problem. When inadequate development includes more than a single feature—such as poor discrimination and short memory span or poor discrimination and inadequate sequential recall—the likelihood is increased. Naturally, if all three factors are inadequate, the potential for a learning disability is very high. Experience in one extensive study (Dubuque not yet completed in its longitudinal design) indicates very strongly that children who are consistently poor auditorizers—who learn poorly by ear regardless of age—are most likely to have difficulty in learning to use verbal symbols as needed in most school subjects requiring reading. Especially to be noted in this regard is the effect such delay or pathology in auditory perception has on learning to read through phonics.

Many studies in the literature of the last decade point to the importance of the auditory factor in reading readiness. A reference list of many such studies is attached at the end of the chapter. The number of children involved who show auditory imperception has been found to be varied in different studies. Williams (1972) reported that of forty-eight children studied at the first grade level eighteen showed inadequate discrimination. She further found that in those same populations specific errors of discrimination related from .40 to .70 to specific errors in articulation. Morency (1968), in a longitudinal six-year study of 179 children, demonstrated that "significant relationships exist between first grade auditory perception and school achievement" at each of the six succeeding grades. While the relationship decreased after the third year (about the age of nine), it remained statistically significant throughout the study.

THE CONCEPTUAL LEVEL

The role of auditory perception at the conceptual or meaningful level of communication is as important as its role at the perceptual or imitative level. The comprehension of verbal symbols, while ultimately an integration of sensory-motor learned and imprinted individual phonemic-phonetic patterns following the linguistic code of the speaking environment, has its origins in the use of language forms within the totality of behavior of the speaker—most often of the mother. As she performs the necessary and constant tasks of being motherly, she speaks to the child. Words and sentences accompany need-reducing behavior. As she feeds the infant, satisfying his "hunger" needs, changes him from a state of discomfort, plays with him, coddles him, and rocks him to sleep, she speaks to the child. From this continuous verbal behavior the infant obtains a melody, an intonation pattern which as has been seen becomes his melody and pattern. While this is perceptual learning, it becomes a part of meaningful learning. Speech intonation patterns come to the child in the form of words, at least most of the time, or sufficiently often at least that the two—the verbal structure and the melodic pattern—form a unit. As the child begins to imitate the words in an attempt to imitate the mother—or to respond in kind to the mother—the child's first attempts fail to meet the criteria of intelligibility. The child's attempts are a jargon of unintelligible speech but almost from the outset are produced in a reasonable imitation of the intonation pattern used by the mother. Comprehension of the mother's spoken language begins with the totality of the stimulus: words accompany every act therefore words become a part of every act.

Without dwelling on the concept of "how" language is acquired, about which many theories have been developed (Flavell 1963; McNeill 1974), it is easy to recognize the importance of audition in the act. In company with the variety of nonverbal activities and the need-reducing satisfaction of the total situation, the child hears the words being spoken.

Soon in the developmental sequence, perhaps the most telling juncture between infancy and childhood, is the individual's recognition that words not only accompany the reception of rewards but can by their use bring on the rewards in some magical way (to the child) he begins to experiment with their use. As the phoneme structure of words becomes available the potential for verbal symbolic output becomes possible. The hearing child with normal acuity and normal central auditory processing has the where withal to begin his own spoken language efforts.

Impairment of auditory acuity or any reduction in auditory perception which limits the auditory process also reduces the capacity to gain comprehension. If the impairment is developmental—if it has not yet obtained the level of adequacy in discrimination or memory—it may limit comprehension and delay the process of language formulation. Severe lags in auditory-processing development or pathologies affecting its development produce two major effects on learning. First, the child's attempted speech will reflect the auditory imperception by the inaccuracy of the child's articulation. Second, because the articulation is inaccurate and the child's early speech attempts are unrewarded, language development is likely to be delayed since unreinforced behavior tends to become extinct.

The non-"audile" child—one who learns best by other than auditory means, in part because of the slower development of the child's auditory perception—is most often reported by concerned parents as either being slower or older when speech is attempted. Or, if the child does attempt to speak, the results are unintelligible.

It is perhaps unfortunate that so much attention has been given to so-called authoritative observations and statistics in this regard. Blind wish-fulfilling acceptance of speech and language acquisition by or near the first birthday as stated by Gesell and his associates (1940) has been interpreted to mean that every child should, if normal, begin to speak at that time in his life. This allows for no individual differences in the adequacy of development of the preverbal perceptual factors which have clinically been noted as becoming adequate as late as the third year of life. Nor does it permit the wide variations in onset of speech because of differential verbal environments—children whose mothers for any of a number of reasons have not used speech as an active part of mothering. Reports are multiplying, for example, on the lack of verbal stimulation in the inner cities of our large urban communities (Hess and Shipman 1965).

From years of clinical experience with the onset of speech and language in children, it seems safe to estimate that adequate development of speech and language can come as late as three or even three and a half years without affecting the child's later use of oral communication.

The development of auditory perception is dependent on auditory stimulation. Auditory imperception or lack of auditory stimulation may each, then, play an important role in the onset and development of speech and language. The lack of comprehension of spoken language will almost certainly delay the development of cognition as well. The non- or partial-hearing child, whether the impairment is in acuity or in perceptual imitation, will lack the values accruing from auditory feedback and be solely dependent on direct auditory stimulation or the capacity of the individual child to obtain meaning from the nonverbal clues of a message.

Cognitive development at this early age is at least in part encouraged by the child's self-monitoring of his own speech and language efforts.

McNeill (1974), whose work in the development of language is noteworthy for its clarity of exposition, compares the onset and use of speech to that of a camera. At given moments the child's shutter is open, and the child is amenable to reception. Upon being stimulated aurally, the shutter in effect closes while the child rehearses internally the spoken stimulus. When the internal rehearsal produces what the child believes to be a meaningful situation, he formulates a response. Stimulation-rehearsal-production is the sequence of acquisition according to McNeill. The production may be imitation at the perceptual level without meaning or it may be understanding followed by an appropriate imitative response indicating that the behavior is on the conceptual level. Imitation as the response, if not accompanied by appropriate nonverbal behavior, would indicate that the verbal stimulus had not evoked a conceptual state but had simply resulted in a repetition.

This concept of language development is almost wholly auditory in nature. Meaningless imitation after rehearsal indicates that the child was not yet ready for higher-level conceptualization. Language usage is a form of intellection, a form of cognitive portrayal by the use of verbal symbols in the code of communication. Imitation often repeated may lead to that end result, but only after external reward.

In a later exposition on language development McNeill (1974) makes this telling observation about articulation: "The speech production mechanisms of adults are relatively narrow in their conceptual adaptation and are not fundamentally different from the mechanisms available to young children whose mental functioning is at the sensory-motor and early representational levels." This view stresses the interrelationship between perceptual and conceptual functioning in speech production. Regardless of the abstract nature of adult language, its oral expression is limited to the articulation mechanism of the child. No additional phonemes are added after the child acquires his perceptually based discriminated and memorized basic alphabet. In order to express the more abstract, higher-level thought, the adult can do so only by more complex grammatical forms.

Research reports on the conceptual level of speech and language usage are becoming more and more evident in the literature but do not all support the conceptualization of sound difference. La Reviere, Winitz, Reed, and Herriman (1974), seeking to explore the conceptual reality of selective distinctive features, concluded that "features may tap noncognitive (nonlinguistic) aspects of speech stimuli since no conceptual aspects were statistically relatable to the results achieved."

In the area of memory for sounds in short- and long-term sensory storage, Miller's (1956) magical number of seven units maintained simultaneously in short-term memory remains a subject of interest to researchers. Murch (1973) comments, after reviewing a number of research reports, that "probably the actual amount depends more on the presentation rate and the type of material" than on the total number of units presented. "Miller," Murch notes, "pointed out that the magical number refers to chunks of information rather than number of items."

Auditory sequencing recall using digit order repeated has also been reported in the literature as a conceptual factor. Our routine use of numbers for the telephone, street addresses, social security numbers, and so on makes sequencing recall a daily event. Sequencing of this nature is becoming so automatized by constant use, in fact, that in short-term memory it takes on the nature of perceptual processing, even though meaning is attached to each sequence.

In a series of very excellent studies of sequential auditory recall, Aaronson (1968) found the expected influence of presentation rate in the recall task in which errors increased as did speed of presentation. Monitoring the recall effort, however, she found unaffected by presentation rate.

Much of the work with the ITPA (Kirk, McCarthy, and Kirk 1968) indicates the conceptual level of achievement, both auditory and visual.

Before leaving the area of speech and language development—the first of the verbal symbol acquisitions, both receptive and expressive in nature, that the unimpaired child learns to use—a word must be said about the effect on the total learning process when the auditory conceptual process is impaired. So important is auditory reception in stimulating the development of the cognitive process at this early age in the child's life that a lasting effect on later apparently unrelated communication skills must be noted.

Learning disabilities at any age may well result from a failure to develop adequate auditory conceptualization at the expected time in a child's life. Delays in language development may directly upset the timetable of acquisition of reading skill and fluency. The auditory role in oral reading is, of course, evident. The same articulatory accuracy is demanded in this form of expression as it is in speech, where the approach to reading, for example, is through phonics. The demands for adequate understanding of the auditory stimulus is used as the comparative base for the orthographic, visually presented material. Mispronounciations, syllable inversions, and sound substitutions, to name only three paraphasic type of errors, have their direct roots in auditory perception.

Eisenson (1966), in discussing the aphasic child, not only explored the auditory perceptual processing abilities, as previously noted, but extended his examination into the auditory conceptual level, noting such factors as "what kind and how much material presented auditorially can the child process?" and "how well can the child reproduce a sequence of auditory events to which he has been exposed?" He noted further that "those of our patients who, however impaired, had some expressive language, nevertheless, found great difficulty in managing the reproduction of a digit series."

"Sequencing," Eisenson concluded, "is below what we expect on the assumptions we make about their intellectual potential." He relates this to a belief that it may not be the mechanical seriation of repeated digits in order but, that it is "probably related to impairment of categorical ability . . . they may well be related to the lack of inner language to permit self-talking or thinking as an approach to *arrive at and maintain* a mode of behavior required to deal with a meaningful sequential situation."

Luria (1961), in his consideration of mental deficiency, commented: "The effect produced by an early disturbance of a certain function depends primarily on the role played by this function in the general mental development of the child, as well as on the period of development during which the given disturbance occurred."

Auditory perception in both its perceptual and conceptual aspects during the early stages of development is so vital to the normal maturation of cognitive function that impairment or even serious delay may establish in the minds of concerned adults the likelihood of permanent deficiency. Such children may become categorized as deficient and forever after be treated as though the retardation were irreversible.

It should be noted, however, that, as Luria points out, if the auditory misperception occurs during the years when cognitive processing is changing to more complex activities, the error or fault in learning may create lasting inadequacies extending into the later learning of the comprehension and use of language through its effect on reading and other school-age achievement. A wide range of intervention to offset this type of deficiency in learning has been suggested. Lloyd and Fulton (1972) comment, in their work on audiology's contribution to communications programming with the retarded, that "logic and data clearly indicate that the ability to hear is a basic prerequisite for normal speech and language development; and perhaps as suggested by Luria (ibid.) a prerequisite to intellectual development." With reference to language, Luria states that "disturbances of the auditory system deter the assimilation of the system of language, and that the deranged formation of a strictly differentiated phonemic system causes retardation in the development of active articulated speech. . . . The consequence most evident . . . is the inadequate development of a communication system."

The reported work on the mentally retarded is subject to the same criticism that Furth (1966) has made relative to abstract learning in the profoundly deaf. Reinterpretation of the meaning of mental retardation from the viewpoint of perceptual inadequacies at the critical time when cognition is also at its critical early stage of development, establishing not only the weaknesses but the strengths of the child, might well reduce the number of children misclassified as retarded and place them in the more hopeful category of having a specific learning disability. Certainly many so-called mentally retarded children show modality strengths that provide a basis for directed intervention which has the chance of maximizing their performance sufficiently to warrant their reclassification.

An illustrative case in point is that of a previously diagnosed severely mentally retarded child of twelve seen clinically who demonstrated an almost total lack of auditory perception. He could neither imitate an auditory stimulus nor recall it, nor could he gain meaning from it. He was recognized on our examination as possessing, however, adequate visual perception both in discrimination and in memory. He could also respond appropriately to visual cues requiring problem-solving solutions if the target and the expected response were clearly delineated. His level of behavior was reinterpreted following our examination as one of severe unimodal deficiency—a specific learning disability in auditory perception processing affecting discrimination, memory, and sequencing recall. Training was advised building on the adequate visual skills, coupled with visuomotor training. Reevaluated one year later his measurable IQ had been raised thirty points. He was no longer considered mentally retarded.

It should be pointed out, however, that so much frustration reaction behavior had been built up within him through his previous years of failure that in addition to directive educational intervention he was in need of and received psychological counseling. At the same time the counselor needed to work through with both his parents and his teachers the relationships they had unfortunately permitted to develop. In many ways this was the more difficult part of the total treatment program. The parents had become accustomed to treating the child as deficient. They found it difficult to accept his problem in learning as being due to a severe auditory imperception. His teachers had similar difficulties in acceptance and understanding but did after many consultations understand the problem and change their attitude toward the child, providing him with a more rewarding climate for learning in which he could succeed.

Perhaps the most difficult change to encompass, however, was at the administrative level. His school record carried the label "severely mentally retarded" and removing that stigma from the record proved almost impossible.

For reasons such as the above the task force whose mission it was to define specific learning disabilities included in their guidelines protection of the rights of parents and child alike by being made aware of (1) the classification made and the evidence for it; (2) the right to appeal the classification made and to seek if necessary additional professional opinion to verify the finding; (3) the right of review at periodic intervals to be certain that a child not be kept in a special class or school beyond the time of his or her need; (4) the right to seek professional guidance beyond directive education if it was indicated but not provided by the school (Wepman *et al.* 1974).

AUDITION AND COGNITION

Recalling Figure 7.2, the concept of converging lines of development indicates how impairment of auditory comprehension through providing an inadequate experiential base for language development will play an important role in delaying cognitive maturation. Cognition progressing from sensorimotor and preverbal intellection to the stage of concrete operations needs the input from auditory comprehension to foster its rate and degree of growth. Without the auditory input the cognitive progression is retarded because of the lack of oral language usage and the consequent feedback and monitoring of the effects of language usage. Cognitive development becomes mixed at the preverbal, preoperational level. Nonverbal symbols at this early stage of development are too concrete to provide the necessary stimulation for intellectual comprehensive thought.

At the later stage where learning to read is the task requirement, this retardation in cognition becomes instantly recognizeable. Children having demonstrable cognitive delays will be found to be unequal to the task, because intellectually they are capable of function only at the preverbal level and not beyond it. Auditory inadequacy then directly effects cognitive development by denying to the child the advantages that accrue through verbal symbolization. The necessary interaction between the two lines of independent development, the dependence of cognitive development on auditory comprehension, and its consequent effect on language usage may well lie at the root of what is later interpreted as a learning disability.

READING AND AUDITION

The "why" of auditory perception preceding visual perception in language learning or why speech and oral spoken language precedes reading may be most easily understood by the work of Sinsheimer (1971). While listening and comprehension (conceptualization) or listening without comprehension (perception) requires the analysis and integration of complex acoustic features, it is accomplished, this author points out, by some 100 million cells in the CNS devoted exclusively to the hearing act. Vision, on the other hand, Sinsheimer notes, has over 540 million cells devoted to the registration and interpretation of visual signals. Reading, then, which originates as a visual signal, may require the combined cellular activity of some 540 million visual cells and 200 million auditory cells or a ratio of close to 5:1 in favor of visualization over auditorization to achieve meaning.

The auditory role in reading is like that in speech—one of discrimination isolation and storage of the phonemic/phonetic alphabet with its forty-odd parts against which the newly learned arbitrary twenty-six letters of the alphabet can be compared (not accounting here for all of the allophonic sound differences, the intonation pattern, the blends, and the regional variations which make up some of the units of spoken language). This phonic reconstruction of visual-to-auditory-to-visual process is accomplished only when the two modalities have some degrees of equality of discrimination and recall in perceptual development.

Reading disability becomes apparent when the complexity of the task is beyond the capacity of the child. If either auditory or visual discrimination or memory factors are immature or undeveloped, the task is further complicated and the learning-to-read task more difficult. If the imbalance remains or the task is pressured, the expectation is too high and simple difficulty or delay in learning to read becomes a real disability.

This account of acquiring the skill or aptitude of reading with increasing comprehension becomes even more complex if the phonemic discrimination and memory is related, as it must be, to phonetic development in the act of oral reading.

Some research and some researchers (Edfeldt 1960) insist that even in silent reading a covert articulatory muscular activity occurs which would add the complexity of phonetic development whenever the task is attempted. All reading, Edfelt insists, whether oral or silent, has this articulatory undertone, at least at the initial stage and probably throughout life, though with time and facility it becomes less evident—more covert than overt.

From a modality-oriented viewpoint, it would be expected that the child with strong and well-developed auditory perception would be inclined to "overtly or covertly" subarticulate whenever he or she reads. This pattern for verbal structure is so strongly fixed—so much a part of any attempt to use the phonemic/phonetic combination in production—that it may be deleterious in the child's instruction or in any special educational intervention to attempt to suppress it. Yet, it is one of the best-held myths of teaching reading to all children that it should be repressed. No research is available to verify this assertion, but clinical experience with some very "audile" children who were poor readers indicates that not only should the muscular movements of speech not be suppressed for these children, but, rather, they should be encouraged. At least it can be said that when these children were taught to articulate and were freed of suppression, their reading difficulty was reduced.

The combined phonemic/phonetic alphabet of speech is a good example of the interaction hypothesis proposed here. The congruent but independent motor and auditory perceptual processes that interact to provide a system capable of being stored and recalled as a unit serve as a base for speech and later as a base for the comparisons necessary between graphemes and phonemes in reading.

Reading with comprehension is an instance where the close relationship between the perceptual and conceptual is apparent. Reading with comprehension is part of the cognitive developmental structure. Until the child begins to read with meaning, the child's cognitive development remains at best at the level of concrete operations. Reading is in one sense the ultimate abstractive use of verbal symbols. Reading disabilities or failure to progress in reading skill and facility are often seen in the child with good general intellection when perceptual development is retarded. That appears to be the case where children in the age range of nine to fifteen continue to show reading achievement at the first, second, or third grade level, as though the attack on learning to read was insufficient or misdirected.

A case in point which can be multiplied by similar cases seen by learning disabilities specialists or remedial reading specialists is the child referred for examination because of a marked underachievement only in reading. Most often such children will show aggravated secondary psychological problems. Depending on their personality types they may either act out and be difficult to handle in the regular classroom or they may passively withdraw from the reading task because of continued failure. The child in question showed average intellectual ability, excellent motivation for physical activities such as sports, but a marked reduction in auditory perceptual processing. In all of the individual subtests we employed to explore perceptual development (discrimination, memory span, and sequential memory) his scores indicated that these capacities had not developed beyond the average of a seven year old. (Parenthetically, his visual perceptual abilities were markedly improved over the auditory processes; in visual discrimination, memory and orientation, he showed adequate development.) Studying his educational background, it was discovered that the approach to reading that he had been exposed to was through phonics—an auditory approach.

Attempted remediation had further extended the phonic approach without apparent recognition that this pathway to reading was, if not totally blocked, so deficient that failure was to be expected. At our suggestion a tutorial exposure to visual sight training was established with the following result—he enjoyed reading for the first time. He advanced in reading achievement in one year to within a year of his grade and age expectation. His acting out behavior almost disappeared. As a result no need was seen for special psychotherapy or counseling. He was able to resume his education in a normal classroom.

For such children reading is a visual to visual process—not, as previously noted, a visual-auditory-visual sequence.

Not all children who have specific reading disabilities respond so well. Not all show the almost total auditory imperception or the compensatory visual perceptual skill. But when they do, the answer is not in their attempting to overcome the auditory deficiency—at this child's age, fifteen, this could not be expected—but by concentrating on the child's strengths his maximal potential could be accomplished.

It is not the opinion of this writer or of anyone studying the underachieving school-age child that perceptual inadequacies are the only reason for failure. It does seem, however, that in a sizeable number of instances the perceptual approach has merit and should be explored.

Vernon (1971), discussing this factor in his book *Reading and Its Difficulties*, devotes the first half of his book to the role of impairment of perceptual processing development and reading. While he stresses visual perceptual processing at greatest length, he recognizes the individual differences that may be involved and the deleterious effect of auditory imperception at both the perceptual and conceptual level of reading.

LEARNING DISABILITIES AND AUDITION

The evidence of the past decade is relatively clear. The term "learning disability" describes any or all conditions which impair the capacity to learn. Auditory imperception, both at the perceptual (imitative) and conceptual (meaningful) level, plays an important role in the total development of the child, especially in the child's capacity to comprehend and use verbal symbols. Through auditory perception speech and language become available to the child and through the interaction of spoken language and cognitive development add materially to the normal maturation of cognition. Impairment of auditory perception by lags in the developmental process or by pathology at either level reduces the child's capacity to learn in a natural way. Auditory imperception has been found to play an important role in the acquired act of reading and writing since it is the basis for phonic instruction felt by many to be the essential method for all reading instruction.

The student of the cause (and resolution) of learning disabilities has a series of alternatives available in conceptualizing the problem. For some, the maldevelopment of sensorimotor integration is the source of much of the deficiency (Frostig 1968); for others, the incapacity is best seen as an interruption of the development of coordination (Kephart 1964). Others have argued for neurophysiological inadequacies which affect the basic progression of the necessary qualities for learning (Wepman 1968). Still others insist that reading and its cognate writing and spelling difficulties are attributable to emotional or family rearing practices. While still others believe that learning requires the development of adequacy in certain prereading, preverbal skills (Wepman 1968; Morency 1968). There is probably no single cause or single view which solely explains either the cause or the cure.

Following the dictates discussed at length in previous pages devoted to theory and to the findings of the task force on learning disabilities, the present writer believes that an arbitrary definition must be established to rid us of the chaotic condition in which the field of learning disabilities finds itself at the present. In consequence, the following definition of a specific learning disability is suggested. A learning act is inadequately developed or the processes essential to the learning act is inadequately developed or pathologically impaired to the degree that it interferes with the normal acquisition and development of the comprehension and use of verbal symbols.

Auditory perception has been shown to be developmentally acquired. Its roots lie in auditory perceptual process development, i.e., in the subliminal acquisition of the inherent skill of the phonemic discrimination and recall. Impairment of this skill by either developmental lags or by pathology can be determined, and in many instances, if a prescribed training program is followed reflecting a child's strengths, it will have a material effect on the act of learning.

It is a corollary of this concept that while intelligence (cognitive development) may play a role it is more likely the case that auditory imperception deleteriously affects cognitive development than vice versa. It is a further corollary that the development of discrimination of fine differences in the phonemic/phonetic alphabet is directly related to neurophysiological development. As the central nervous system matures the individual is capable of making the necessary auditory discriminations and is capable of imprinting these in memory available for recall as needed. The consequences of inadequate neurophysiological development affects all of the other developmental processes.

The literature is replete with research reports bearing on this perceptual-conceptual modality concept both directly and indirectly. Relative to auditory processing space permits direct reference to only a few. Thompson (1963) found, for example, that auditory discrimination was often inadequate in children of six to seven years of age. About a quarter of the children tested at eight years still showed poor discrimination, and half of these children were poor readers. On the other hand Thompson found that the majority of those who became good readers had adequate auditory discrimination. This is in keeping with our own findings as reported by Morency (1968) and Wepman and Morency (1973).

Sequential memory has been reported as being closely related to spelling. Peters (1967) cites the work of Ahlstrom, who demonstrated that children's ability to predict the pronunciation of written nonsense words and the spelling of spoken nonsense words was closely associated with sequential recall ability.

Gibson (1969) concluded from the study of infants that the initial stage in the understanding of speech is the discrimination of contrasting phonemes from the total phonemic pattern. Vowel consonsant contrast is discriminated first, then labial versus dental contrasts and breaks in the continuous sound pattern are apprehended at an early age. Consonants within words and consonant clusters are learned later. "Discrimination," Gibson wrote, "improves with increase in age; and those phonemes which possess the most distinctive features are most accurately discriminated."

Tekafsky and McInish (1968) showed that even at seven years of age, "pairs of words are most often confused in auditory discrimination when there was a difference of only one phoneme feature between them." This is in keeping with Wepman's (1966) demonstration of the relation between perceptual auditory discrimination and articulation in children up to eight years of age.

Lory (1966) pointed out that any weakness in auditory discrimination tends to impede not only speech but reading-spelling skills.

The list of research articles bearing on the perceptual skills including the auditory is too long to include here. A selected group of references on the subject is included at the end of this chapter. Klasen's (1972) comment in her book, *The Syndrome of Specific Dyslexia,* is most appropriate. After a review of many research studies she said, "In short, much more research on learning processes is needed for more factual understanding and more effective treatment of learning disabilities" (p. 38).

SUMMARY—CONCLUSIONS AND IMPLICATIONS

A theory of learning related to a modality-oriented hierarchy of perceptual and conceptual processing of environmental signals explanatory of normal growth and maturation has been presented. Against the backdrop of converging independent vectors of physiological and behavioral contributors to the culminating achievement of abstract reasoning at the critical age of nine, the interaction between the various developing lines through integrative memory stresses the importance of subliminal-perceptual learning to the eventual end of maximal cognitive functioning. Each of the lines of development are seen as making its own contribution in a unimodal sense, but also extending its influence depending on the learning task itself by its interaction with other lines of development.

Auditory perception is seen as one of the important developmental vectors. At the conceptual level it adds materially to language and speech acquisition and, with their growth, to cognitive maturation. At the perceptual level it provides the alphabet of sounds which are essential to conceptual verbal symbol formulation. Three empirical sub-processes at the perceptual level were identified as being essential to learning whenever the task is one of a verbal symbolic nature; the processes identified are auditory discrimination, memory, and sequential recall.

Auditory imperception at both the perceptual and conceptual level was seen to be implicated in learning disabilities whether in the sense of spoken language impoverishment or delay or in the acquisition of the skills of reading, spelling, or writing.

Specific learning disabilities were attributed to perceptual auditory processing deficiencies. The literature of the past decade indicates the importance of the auditory perceptual processing abilities to the total development of the abstract use of verbal symbols as a major contributor to abstract thought.

The implications of these findings for the future are manifest. Research identifying as early as possible the modality preference of children and applying the knowledge of such identification to the early educational process seems essential. Homogeneous grouping for educational purposes in kindergarten through third grade, both by modality preference of the children and by the modality orientation of the instructional method—auditory versus visual—seems an imperative area to study.

By an understanding of modality differences—and differential rates of modality-bound development—a reconsideration of current classification of exceptional children is suggested. Are the so-called mentally retarded actually perceptually handicapped children who might benefit from a modality-oriented educational opportunity? How often does failure to match a child's early learning abilities with the child's modality propensity produce the behavior which labels the child as "emotionally disturbed"?

How often does the educational effort which undertakes to guide a child during the learning-to-learn stage begin before the child's perceptual processes have developed to a state of adequacy? What are the relationships between perceptual development and achievement?

If learning to read, to write, or to spell is based on a pre-knowledge of phonemic discrimination, memory span, and sequential recall, at what point in the educational process should phonics be introduced?

These and other research questions need to be answered before the term "specific learning disability" can become meaningful. In each of the answers to be sought the part that auditory perception plays is seen as essential—as one of the common pathways to learning.

With an acceptance of the definition of a specific learning disability as indicative of a perceptual handicap because of developmental or pathological reasons it is hoped that the present state of disarray in the field from the multiplicity of overlapping and often nonuseful labels will find psychologists, educators, parents, and physicians able to discuss the problems of learning on a higher level of understanding.

References

Aaronson, D. "Temporal Course of Perception in an Immediate Recall Task." *Journal of Experimental Psychology* 76 (1968): 129–40.

Ardrey, R. *The Territorial Imperative.* New York: Dell, 1966.

Butler, R. A. "The Relative Influence of Pitch and Timbre on the Apparent Location of Sound in the Median Sagittal Plane." *Perception and Psychophysics* 14 (1973): 255.

Chananie, J. P., and Tikovsky, R. S. "Choice Response Time and Distinctive Features in Speech Discrimination." *Journal of Experimental Psychology* 81 (1969): 161–63.

Charcot, J. M. "New Lectures, 1886." In *On Aphasia,* edited by S. Freud. New York: International Universities Press, 1953.

Cruickshank, W. "Some Issues Facing the Field of Learning Disability." *Journal of Learning Disabilities* 5 (Aug./Sept. 1972): No. 7.

Davis, Julia. "Performance of Young Hearing Impaired Children on a Test of Basic Concepts." *Journal of Speech and Hearing Research* (September 1974): 342–51.

Edfeldt, A. W. *Silent Speech and Silent Reading.* Chicago: University of Chicago Press, 1960.

Eisenson, J. "Perceptual Disturbances in Children with Central Nervous System Disfunctions and Implications for Language-Development." *British Journal of Disorders of Communication* 23 (1966).

Flavell, J. H. *The Developmental Psychology of Jean Piaget.* New York: Van Nostrand, 1963.

Flower, R. M. "The Evaluation of Auditory Abilities in the Appraisal of Children with Reading Problems." In *Perception and Reading,* edited by H. K. Smith. Proceedings of the 12th Annual Convention, International Reading Association. Newark, Del. (1968): 21–24.

Frostig, Marianne. "Visual Modality Research and Practice." In *Perception and Reading,* edited by H. K. Smith. Proceedings of the 12th Annual Convention, International Reading Association, Newark, Del. (1968): 25–33.

Furth, H. G. *Thinking without Language: Psychological implications of Deafness.* New York: The Free Press, 1966.

Gaines, Rosslyn. "Experiencing the Perceptually-Deprived Child." *Journal of Learning Disabilities* (1969): No. 11.

Gesell, A. *The First Five Years of Life.* New York: Harper & Row, 1940.

Gibson, E. J. "Perceptual Learning." *Annual Review of Psychology* 14 (1963): 29–56.

Goldstein, K., and Scheerer, M. "Abstract and Concrete Behavior: An Experimental Study with Special Tests. In *Psychological Monographs*, edited by J. Dashiell, Evanston, Ill.: American Psychological Assn.

Hess, R. D., and Shipman, V. "Early Blocks to Children's Learning." *Children* 12 (September/October 1965): 189–94.

Hoemann, H. W.; Andrews, C. E.; and DeRosa, D. V. "Categorical Encoding in Short-Term Memory by Deaf and Hearing Children." *Journal of Speech and Hearing Research* 17 (September 1974): 426–31.

Hooper, R. "Electrocochleagraphy." *Journal of Laryngology Otolaryngology* 87(10) (1973): 919–27.

Jakobson, R.; Font, G. M.; and Halle, M. "Preliminaries to Speech Analysis." MIT Tech. Report 13 (1952).

Jerger, J., ed. *Modern Developments in Audiology*. 2nd ed. New York: Academic Press, 1973.

Jones, K., and Studebaker, G. "Performance of Severely Hearing Impaired Children on a Closed Response, Auditory Discrimination Test." *Journal of Speech and Hearing Research* (September 1974): 531–41.

Katz, J., ed. *Handbook of Clinical Audiology*. Baltimore: Williams & Wilkins, 1972.

Kephart, N. C. "Perceptual-Motor Aspects of Learning Disabilities." *Exceptional Child* 31 (1964): 201–206.

Kimura, D. "Cerebral Dominance and the Perception of Verbal Stimuli." *Canadian Journal of Psychology* 15 (1961*b*): 166–71.

Kirk, S.; McCarthy, J.; and Kirk, W. *Illinois Test of Psycholinguistic Abilities*. Urbana, Ill.: University of Illinois Press, 1968.

Klasen, E. *The Syndrome of Specific Dyslexia*. Baltimore: University Park Press, 1972.

Konorski, J. *Integrative Activity of the Brain*. Chicago: University of Chicago Press, 1967.

LaReviere, C.; Vinitz, H.; Reeds, J.; and Herriman, E. "The Conceptual Reality of Selected Distinctive Features." *Journal of Speech and Hearing Research* 17 (1974): 122–33.

Liberman, A. M.; Cooper, F. S.; Schankweiler, D. P.; and Studdert-Kennedy, M. "Perception of the Speech Code." *Psychology Review* 74 (1967): 431.

Lloyd, L. L., and Fulton, R. T. "Audiology's Contribution to Communications Programming with the Retarded." In *Language Intervention with the Retarded*, edited by J. McLean, D. Yoder, and R. Schiefelbush. Baltimore: University Park Press, 1972.

Lory, P. *Die Leseschwach. Entstehung und Formen, ursachliche Zusammenhange, Behandlung*. Munchen/Basel: Reinhardt Verlag, 1966. (Band 44, Erziehung und Psychologie, Beihefte der Zeitschrift Schule und Psychologie, Luckert, H. R., Hrsg.)

Luria, A. R. *The Role of Speech in the Regulation of Normal and Abnormal Behavior*, edited by J. Tizard. New York: Liveright, 1961.

McNeill, D. "Semiotic Extension." Speech presented at Loyola Symposium on Cognition, April 30, 1974, Chicago, Ill.

______. Personal communication, 1974.

Miller, G. A. "The Magical Number Seven, Plus or Minus Two: Some Limits on Our Capacity for Processing Information. *Psychology Review* 63:81–97; Bobbs-Merrill Reprint P-241, 1956.

Monsen, R. B. "Durational Aspects of Vowel Production in the Speech of Deaf Children." *Journal of Speech & Hearing Research* (September 1974): 386–98.

Morency, A. "Auditory Modality: Research and Practice." In *Perception and Reading*, edited by H. K. Smith. Proceedings of the 12th Annual Convention, International Reading Association, Newark, Del. (1968): 17–21.

______, and Wepman, J. M. "Early Perceptual Ability and Later School Achievement." *Elementary School Journal* 73 (March 1973): 323–27.

______; Wepman, J. M.; and Hass, S. "Developmental Speech Inaccuracy and Speech Therapy in the Early School Years." *Elementary School Journal* 73 (January 1970): 219–24.

______; Wepman, J. M.; and Weiner, P. S. "Studies in Speech: Developmental Articulation Inaccuracy." *Elementary School Journal* 67 (March 1967): 329–37.

Murch, G. M. *Visual and Auditory Perception.* New York: Bobbs-Merrill, 1973.

Myklebust, H. R. *Development and Disorders of Written Language.* Vol. 1 New York: Grune & Stratton, 1965.

O'Neill, J. J., and Oyer, H. J. "Aural Rehabilitation." In *Modern Developments in Audiology,* edited by J. Jerger. New York: Academic Press, 1973.

Osgood, C. E., and Miron, M. S. *Approaches to the Study of Aphasia.* Urbana, Ill.: University of Illinois Press, 1963.

Parnell, P., and Korzeniowski, R. "Auditory Perception and Learning, Part II." *Remedial Education* 4(4) (1972): 20–22.

Peters, M. L. *Spelling: Caught or Taught?* London: Routledge & Kegan Paul, 1967.

Piaget, J. *The Language and Thought of the Child.* New York: Meridian, 1959.

Quigley, S. P.; Smith, N. L.; and Wilbur, R. B. "Comprehension of Relativized Sentences by Deaf Students." *Journal of Speech & Hearing Research* (September 1974): 325–41.

Sinsheimer, R. L. "The Brain of Pooh: An Essay on the Limits of Mind." *American Scientist* 59 (1971): 21–28.

Templin, M. C. *Certain Language Skills in Children.* Minneapolis, Minn.: University of Minnesota Press, 1957.

Tepas, D. I. "Computer Analysis of the Electroencephalogram: Evoking, Promoting and Provoking." *Behavioral Research Methods & Instrumentation* 6(2) (1974): 95–110.

Thompson, B. B. "A Longitudinal Study of Auditory Discrimination." *Journal of Educational Research* 56 (1963): 376.

Tikofsky, R. S., and McInish, J. R. "Consonant Discrimination by Seven-Year Olds." *Psychonometric Science* 10 (1968): 61.

Turaids, D.; Wepman, J. M.; and Morency, A. "A Perceptual Test Battery: Development and Standardization." *Elementary School Journal* 72 (April 1972): No. 7.

Van Atta, B. "A Comparative Study of Auditory Skills (Sensitivity, Discrimination and Memory Span) of Dyslalic and Normal Speaking Children in Grades 1–3. *Aviso* 4(1) (1973): 1–7.

Vernon, M. D. *Reading and Its Difficulties.* New York: Cambridge University Press, 1971.

Wepman, J. M. *The Auditory Discrimination Test—Manual.* Chicago: Language Research Associates, 1958.

______. "Auditory Discrimination, Speech and Reading." *Elementary School Journal* (March 1960): 325–33.

______. "The Modality Concept: Including a Statement of the Perceptual and Conceptual Levels of Learning." In *Perception and Reading,* edited by H. K. Smith. Proceedings of the 12th Annual Convention, International Reading Association, Newark, Del. (1968): 1–6.

______. *The Auditory Discrimination Test—Revised Edition. Manual.* Chicago: Language Research Associates, 1973.

______; Cruickshank, W.; Deutsch, Cynthia; Morency, A; and Strothers, C. "Learning Disabilities." In *Issues in the Classification of Children,* edited by N. Hobbs. San Francisco: Jossey-Bass, 1974.

______, and Morency, A. *Auditory Memory Span Test—Manual.* Chicago: Language Research Associates, 1973.

______, and Morency, A. *Auditory Sequential Memory Test—Manual.* Chicago: Language Research Associates, 1973.

Williams, P. E. "An Investigation of the Relationship between Auditory Discrimination and Speech Patterns." Unpublished doctoral dissertation, University of Chicago, 1972.

Zemlin, W. R. "The Use of Bandwidth and Time Compression for the Hearing Handicapped." Proceedings of Louisville Conference on Time Compressed Speech, Center for Rate Controlled Recordings, University of Louisville, 1966.

References For Perceptual Modality Studies, 1960–72

Ables, B. S.; Aug, R. G.; and Loof, D. H. "Problems in the Diagnosis of Dyslexia: A Case Study." *Journal of Learning Disabilities* 4 (1971): 409–17.

Arnold, R. D., and Wist, A. H. "Auditory Discrimination Abilities of Disadvantaged Anglo- and Mexican-American Children." *Elementary School Journal* 70 (1970): 295–99.

Bateman, B. "The Efficacy of an Auditory with a Visual Method of First Grade Reading Instruction with Auditory and Visual Learners." *Perception and Reading* 12 (1968): 105–12.

Berlin, C., and Dill, A. C. "The Effects of Feedback and Positive Reinforcement on the Wepman Auditory Discrimination Test Scores of Lower-Class Negro and White Children." *Journal of Speech and Hearing Research* 10 (1967): 384–89.

Birch, H. G. "Auditory-Visual Integration, Intelligence and Reading Ability in School Children." *Perceptual and Motor Skills* 20 (1965): 295–305.

Blank, M. "Cognitive Processes in Auditory Discrimination in Normal and Retarded Readers." *Child Development* 39 (1968): 1091–101.

Bruininks, R. H. "Teaching Word Recognition to Disadvantaged Boys." *Journal of Learning Disabilities* 3 (1970): 28–37.

Christine, D., and Christine, C. "The Relationship of Auditory Discrimination to Articulatory Defects and Reading Retardation." *Elementary School Journal* 65 (1964): 97–100.

Clark, A. D., and Richards, C. J. "Auditory Discrimination Among Economically Disadvantaged and Non-Disadvantaged Preschool Children." *Exceptional Children* 33 (1966): 259–62.

Dellirsch, K.; Jansky, J.; and Langford, W. S. "The Oral Language Performance of Premature Children and Controls." *Journal of Speech and Hearing Disabilities* 29 (1964): 60–69.

Deutsch, C. "Auditory Discrimination and Learning." *Merrill-Palmer Quarterly of Behavior and Development* 10 (1964): 277–96.

Doehring, D. G., and Rabinovitch, M. S. "Auditory Abilities of Children with Learning Problems." *Journal of Learning Disabilities* 2 (1969): 467–75.

Dykstra, R. "Auditory Discrimination Abilities and Beginning Reading Achievement." *Reading Research Quarterly* 1 (3) (1966): 2–34.

Flynn, P., and Byrne, M. "Relationship Between Reading and Selected Auditory Abilities of Third Grade Children." *Journal of Speech and Hearing Research* 13 (1970): 731–40.

Frank, L. "A Survey Comparison Between Auditory Development, Severity of Articulation and Reading Level." *Illinois Journal of Education* (December 1967): 18–21.

Frostig, M.; Lefever, D. W.; and Whittlesey, J. R. B. "A Developmental Test of Visual Perception for Evaluating Normal and Neurologically Handicapped Children." *Perceptual and Motor Skills* 12 (1961): 383–94.

———, and Horne, D. *The Frostig Program of Visual Perception.* Chicago: Follet, 1964.

Goetzinger, C. P.; Dirks, D. D.; and Baer, C. J. "Auditory Discrimination and Visual Perception in Good and Poor Readers." *American Otolaryngology, Rhinology, and Laryngology* 69 (1960): 121–37.

Goldman, R.; Fristoe, M.; and Woodcock, R. W. "A New Dimension in the Assessment of Speech Sound Discrimination." *Journal of Learning Disabilities* 4 (1971): 364–68.

Gottesman, R. L. "Auditory Discrimination Ability in Negro Dialect-Speaking Children." *Journal of Learning Disabilities* 5 (1972): 94–101.

Hunter, E. J., and Johnson, L. C. "Developmental and Psychological Differences Between Readers and Non-Readers." *Journal of Learning Disabilities* 4 (1971): 572–77.

Irwin, R. B. "The Effects of Speech Therapy Upon Certain Linguistic Skills of First Grade Children." *Journal of Speech and Hearing Disabilities* 28 (1963): 375–82.

Irwin, R. B.; West, J. F.; and Trombetta, A. "Effectiveness of Speech Therapy for Second Grade Children with Misarticulations—Predictive Factors." *Exceptional Children* 32 (1966): 471–78.

Katz, J., and Burge, C. "Auditory Perception Training for Children with Learning Disabilities." *Menorah Medical Journal* 2 (1971).

Lingren, R. "Performance of Disabled and Normal Readers on the Bender-Gestalt, Auditory Discrimination Test and Visual-Motor Matching." *Perceptual and Motor Skills* 29 (1969): 152–54.

Lowell, R. E. "Reading Readiness Factors as Predictors of Success in First Grade Reading." *Journal of Learning Disabilities* 4 (1971): 563–67.

Lowry, L. M. "Differences in Visual Perception and Auditory Discrimination Between American Indian and White Kindergarten Children." *Journal of Learning Disabilities* 3 (1970): 360–63.

Millman, H. L. "Minimal Brain Dysfunction in Children: Evaluation and Treatment." *Journal of Learning Disabilities* 3 (1968): 91–98.

Morency, A. "Auditory Modality and Reading: Research and Practice." In *Perception and Reading,* edited by H. K. Smith. Newark, Del.: International Reading Association, 1968.

———. "School Achievement as Related to Developmental Speech and Perceptual Handicaps: A Review of a Longitudinal Study." *Journal of Northern Illinois Association of Educational Research* 4 (1969).

———, and Wepman, J. M. "The Relationship of Early Perceptual Ability and Later Elementary School Achievement." *Elementary School Journal* (in Press).

———; Wepman, J. M.; and Hass, K. "Developmental Speech Inaccuracy and Speech Therapy in Early School Years." *Elementary School Journal* 70 (1970): 219–24.

———; Wepman, J. M.; and Weiner, P. S. "Studies in Speech: Developmental Articulation Inaccuracy." *Elementary School Journal* 67 (1967): 329–37.

Oakland, T. D. "Auditory Discrimination and Socio-Economic Status as Correlates of Reading Ability." *Journal of Learning Disabilities* 2 (1969): 33–37.

Payne, J. S.; Cegelka, W. J.; Cooper, J. O. "Headstart: Yesterday, Today and Tomorrow." *Training School Bulletin* 68 (1971): 23–48.

Perozzi, J., and Kunze, L. M. "Relationship Between Speech Sound Discrimination Skills and Language Abilities of Kindergarten Children." *Journal of Speech and Hearing Research* 14 (1971): 382–90.

Prins, T. D. "Relations Among Specific Articulatory Deviations and Responses to a Clinical Measure of Sound Discrimination Ability." *Journal of Speech and Hearing Disabilities* 28 (1963): 382–87.

Rechner, J. K., and Wilson, B. A. "Relation of Speech Sound Discrimination and Selected Language Skills." *Journal of Communication Disabilities* (1967): 26–30.

Rice, D. "Learning Disabilities: An Investigation in Two Parts." *Journal of Learning Disabilities* 3 (1970).

Richards, H., and Fowler, R. "Helping the Learning Disabled Through Existing Community Services." *Journal of Learning Disabilities* 3 (1970): 563–70.

Rosner, J., and Simon, D. "The Auditory Analysis Test: An Initial Report." *Journal of Learning Disabilities* 4 (1971): 384–92.

Sabatino, D. A. "The Information Processing Behaviors Associated with Learning Disabilities." *Journal of Learning Disabilities* 1 (1968): 440–50.

______. "Identification of Neurologically Impaired Children Through a Test of Auditory Perception." *Journal of Consulting Clinical Psychology* 33 (1969): 184–88.

______. "An Evaluation of Resource Rooms for Children with Learning Disabilities." *Journal of Learning Disabilities* 4 (1971): 84–93.

______, and Hayden, D. L. "Prescriptive Teaching in a summer Learning Disabilities Program." *Journal of Learning Disabilities* 3 (1970): 220–27.

______, and Hayden, D. L. "Variation in Information Processing Behavior." *Journal of Learning Disabilities* 3 (1970): 404–12.

Schiller, J.; Schiller, J.; and Deignam, M. "An Approach to Diagnosis and Remediation of Learning Disabilities." *Journal of Learning Disabilities* 2 (1969): 509–19.

Schlanger, B. B., and Galanowsky, G. "Auditory Discrimination Tasks Performed by Mentally Retarded and Normal Children." *Journal of Speech and Hearing Research* 9 (1966).

Schwalb, E., and Blau, H. "Child with Brain Dysfunction." *Journal of Learning Disabilities* 2 (1969): 182–88.

Sherman, D., and Geith, A. "Speech Sound Discrimination and Articulation Skill." *Journal of Speech and Hearing Research* (1967): 277–81.

Shipe, D., and Solveiga, M. "A Pilot Study in the Diagnosis and Remediation of Special Learning Disabilities in Preschool Children." *Journal of Learning Disabilities* 2 (1969): 579–92.

Sommers, R. K.; Meyer, W. J.; and Furlong, A. K. "Pitch Discrimination and Speech Sound Discrimination in Articulation Defective and Normal Speaking Children." *Journal of Audiology Research* 9 (1969): 45–50.

Thompson, B. B. "A Longitudinal Study of Auditory Discrimination." *Journal of Educational Research* 56 (1963): 376–78.

Turaids, D.; Wepman, J. M.; and Morency, A. "A Perceptual Test Battery: Development and Standardization." *Elementary School Journal* (1972): 351–61.

Weiner, P. S.; Wepman, J. M.; and Morency, A. "A Test of Visual Discrimination. *Elementary School Journal* 65 (1965): 330–37.

Wepman, J. M. "Auditory Discrimination, Speech and Reading." *Elementary School Journal* 60 (1960): 325–33.

______. "The Interrelationship of Hearing, Speech and Reading." *The Reading Teacher* 14 (1961): 245–47.

______. "The Perceptual Basis for Learning." In *Meeting Individual Differences,* edited by H. Robinson. *Supplementary Educational Monograph* (1964):25–33.

______. "Auditory Discrimination: Its Role in Language Comprehension, Formulation and Use." *Pediatric Clinics of North America* 15 (August 1968).

______. "The Modality Concept: Including a Statement of the Perceptual and Conceptual Levels of Learning." In *Perception and Reading,* edited by H. K. Smith. Newark, Del.: International Reading Association, 1968.

______, and Morency, A. "School Achievement as Related to Developmental Speech Inaccuracy: Final Report." *ERIC Catalog* #ED 024-694 (1967).

______, and Morency, A. "School Achievement as Related to Speech and Perceptual Handicaps: Final Report." *ERIC Document Reproduction Service* (1971).

Wyatt, G. *Language Learning and Communication Disorders in Children.* New York: Free Press, 1969.

Editors' note: In volume 1, Drs. Newell Kephart and Marianne Frostig presented chapters dealing with the broad issue of perceptual-motor development in children, with particular concern for research relevant to the classroom setting. In this chapter, Dr. A. Jean Ayres, writing from a slightly different perspective, provides an extensive review of the research dealing with the sensorimotor foundations of childhood development and maldevelopment.

Dr. Ayres focuses especially on the motor development of infants and young children. Her own pioneering work, as well as that of others, is extensively reviewed, especially the area of tactual perception and the construct of tactile defensiveness. She has also related the motor integrity of the child to neurological constructs. This chapter, along with that of Koupernik, Mac Keith, and Francis-Williams of this volume, provides the reader with a thorough discussion of the complexity of the neurological aspects of learning disabilities. It is also interesting to compare this chapter with that of Lewis in this volume. They differ considerably with regard to the role of sensorimotor development. Treatment approaches are also considered within a research framework. Dr. Ayres gives an up-to-date account of applied research pertaining to the training of sensorimotor development.

A. Jean Ayres, Ph.D., is Adjunct Associate Professor of Education, Department of Special Education, University of Southern California. She is also associated with the Center for the Study of Sensory Integrative Dysfunction. Formerly, she was with the Department of Occupational Therapy of the University of Southern California. Dr. Ayres has received the two highest awards of the American Occupational Therapy Association and was named to the 1971 edition of *Outstanding Educators of America*. Her research and publications are in the field of sensory integrative dysfunction in learning disabled children. Dr. Ayres is a member of the Society for Research in Child Development, the American Psychological Association, the American Educational Research Association, and the American Occupational Therapy Association.

8

Sensorimotor Foundations of Academic Ability

A. JEAN AYRES

The most elementary human behavior and the ontogenetically earliest learning are primarily sensorimotor in nature. Sensation and movement are so intimately related that they are expressed in the single word *sensorimotor* and cannot be considered separately in analyzing the problems of the learning disabled child.

Early sensorimotor learning is sometimes claimed to provide a basis for later learning in the early school years. Deficits in academic learning may be associated with faulty processes in sensory development and resultant motor growth. These deficits have given rise to theory, discussion, and action in seeking the solution to this complex and obscure relationship. "The ways of life are made possible by abilities, and each ability is made possible by inputs, internal coordination, and skilled performance" (Washburn and Harding 1971, p. 45). Early academic ability is no exception, but the ways in which sensorimotor functions fit into this schema are not easily determined.

The large amount of data on human sensory and motor growth and development does not, in itself, lead to an answer about how that development contributed to the abilities needed to master early academic learning. Rather, a more fruitful approach to the question appears to be in noting the sensorimotor deficits of learning disabled children as well as the sensorimotor procedures which have been found most effective in enhancing academic success. Information from neurobiological research is added to these observations to enable the elaboration of hypotheses about the relationship with the objective of providing more precise and effective remediation.

The sensorimotor problems of learning disabled children do not lie in input but in internal coordination or processing of that input. The output or

The author thanks Anna M. Doudlah, Ph.D., for reading and making suggestions regarding the manuscript.

motor aspect is a problem only because it is dependent upon the processing of input.

Some of the current ideas concerning sensorimotor function and learning disorders will be reviewed, with emphasis on what appear to be fundamental problems in conceptualizing, especially as shown in the educational research. Some attempts will be made to present a more accurate conceptualization by suggesting a theory which may move the field of education closer to its objective of ameliorating learning disabilities.

REVIEW AND CRITIQUE OF THE LITERATURE

The challenge of determining the relation of sensory and cognitive processes to motor functions extends to all disciplines concerned with the dilemmas encountered in attempting to influence human behavior. In an attempt to cope with learning disabilities, man has tended to separate sensory, motor, and cognitive functions. Sperry (1952) has commented that current thinking suffers from a one-sided preoccupation with sensory channels and from a failure to view mental activities in relation to motor behavior. He recommends that study of mental processes be supplemented by attention to what can be inferred from motor patterns regarding the nature of associative and sensory functions.

General Relationships

Influence of Motor Activity on the Developing Brain

Research on the effects of an enriched sensorimotor program on the anatomy and chemistry of rat brains has import not only for the learning disabled child but for all aspects of child development. Experiments (Rosenzweig, Krech, Bennett, and Diamond 1962; Rosenzweig 1966; Bennett, Diamond, Krech, and Rozenweig 1964; Rosenweig, Bennett, and Diamond 1972; Rosenweig and Bennett 1972; Riege 1971; Rosenzweig, Bennett, and Diamond 1973) have compared the weight and thickness of the cerebral cortex of laboratory rats and their biochemical activity when provided with toys and equipment which encouraged sensorimotor exploration with litter mate control rats in a nonenriched environment. Rats exposed to climbing, running mazes, and crawling over brushes and other objects demonstrated increased weight and thickness of the cerebral cortex (especially in the visual cortex) and increased chemical activity which the research workers believed was due to synaptic transmission, gains in problem-solving ability, and an increased quantity of spines on dendrites of the neurons of the rats. Comparable changes were found in the hippocampus, a limbic system structure involved in long-term memory and higher order discriminative abilities (Walsh, Budtz-Olsen, Penny, and Cummins 1969).

The findings may be compared to the pressure on a child resulting from a natural drive to explore or encountered during perceptual-motor training of the learning disabled child. Pressure is either self-imposed or externally imposed when a child is expected to perform in a situation making greater demands on the child than those the child has previously met and mastered. The average child supplies that pressure by eagerness to respond to a natural challenge. Left to his own devices, the child with a neurological problem is not usually able to self-impose and to respond to normal pressure. The therapeutic situation provides the appropriate amount of pressure for the learning disabled child.

It is not only the quantity but the variety of stimuli that produce changes. Brown and King (1971) found that increments of variety of visual stimuli had a greater effect on enzyme activity and learning performance than did an increase in amount of stimuli.

Insofar as the results of rats can be extrapolated to human beings, sensorimotor activity resulting in purposeful interaction with the environment would appear to have considerable influence on the development of that part of the brain which is intimately concerned with learning. Children with certain types of irregular brain development need therapeutic intervention in order to enable them to react appropriately to the environment, a condition which differentiates their behavior from that of the rats involved in the research. Kalverboer (1971) determined that boys with minor neurological signs played less constructively with toys that were not motivating than did control children. The neurologically involved children needed more variation in stimuli than did those with better neurological integrity. An enriched environment will not necessarily lead to a more effective learning capacity unless the child can be enabled to interact appropriately with it.

Piaget (1952) has described how the sensorimotor phase of infancy provides a general basis for later developing perception and cognition. The most obvious and easily understandable relationship between motor activity and perceptual-cognitive development is the opportunity mobility affords in exploring and learning about the environment. For example, in comparing cerebral palsied children with a control group Wedell, Newman, Reid, and Bradbury (1972) found an association between length of experience, independent mobility, and perception of size constancy at a distance. While such experiences no doubt are important aspects of development of perception, the sensorimotor foundation of academic ability is considerably more complex.

Analysis of the effect of motor activity on the electrical activity of the brain leads to a humbling recognition of the discrepancy between the sensorimotor activity which takes place and the information which is utilized for educational purposes. Paxinos and Bindra (1970) found that gross motor activity involving postural adjustment as opposed to fine motor activity such as licking and grooming elicited theta rhythm in the hippocampus area of the brain of rats. The hippocampus is an important mediator of learning. Motor activity also influences alpha activity. Using simple movements such as turning a handle or swinging a leg, Scheich and Simonova (1971) altered alpha activity in college students. It is reasonable to hypothesize that, under certain conditions, sensorimotor activity may help normalize electrical activity in a dysfunctioning brain, but specific conditions remain to be determined.

Motor Activity as a Reflection of More Extensive Neural Function

Motor phenomena are more than just an indication of motor ability. The clinician employs motor expressions as accurate and easily observable expressions of the state of neurological growth and integrity, including that necessary to academic learning. (See, for example, Saint-Anne Dargassies 1972; Egan, Illingworth, and MacKeith 1969; Casaer and Akiyama 1971; Touwen & Prechtl 1970; Rutter, Graham, and Yule 1970; Reitan 1971; and Drillien 1972). As Prechtl (1971) points out, it is the motor system that reflects the systematic developmental changes that are a function of the maturational process of the nervous system.

As the child grows to school age, more behavioral parameters become available for checking the status of brain function, but motor processes continue to be observable and measurable expressions of the status of neural activity, especially that concerned with integration of sensory information. Birch and Lefford (1967) and Lefford (1970) have demonstrated that skilled motor development is a reflection of sensory, perceptual, and intersensory processing and patterning of sensory inputs. Motor, especially visuomotor, tests continue to be among the best predictors of the type of dysfunction which influences academic success. (See, for example, Denhoff, Hainsworth, and Siqueland 1968; de Hirsch and Jansky 1968; Hertzig 1969; Eaves, Kendall, and Crichton 1972; L. S. Brown 1971; and Norfleet, 1973.) The status of postural reflexes is also becoming a helpful diagnostic tool (Ayres 1969, 1971, 1972*c*; Pyfer 1972; and Rider 1972, 1973). Of the tests measuring postural reflex maturation, standing balance is the most common, though there are other manifestations of reflex maturation which may be used in differential diagnosis and which will be discussed later.

Significant relationships have been found between motor performance involving gross motor coordination, perceptual-motor ability, balance, and academic aptitude and achievement (Chissom 1971; Sommers, Joiner, Holt, and Gross 1970; Skubic and Anderson 1970; Aichele 1972; Ismail and Gruber 1967; Charlton 1971; Kalakian 1971; K. L. Fisher 1970; Lauten 1970; Upchurch 1972; and Kaufman and Kaufman 1972). However, other studies have failed to support a relationship between motor competency and academic or intellectual achievement (Budde 1971), perceptual-motor scores, or reading achievement when vocabulary skill was controlled (DuBois 1972). Evidence indicates that sensory integrative factors common to both motor and cognitive functions account for part of this relationship. The same common factors appear to underlie associations between motor processes and learning disorders. Levine and Fuller (1972) discuss that association.

There are, of course, other important associations. The appropriate question to raise is not whether sensorimotor functions are related to early academic skill but: *What* sensorimotor functions are related to early academic learning and in *what* way? Sensory integrative processes subserve some aspects of cognition; for this reason sensorimotor activity has meaning for the field of learning disabilities.

The study of motor development alone will not clarify the relationship of motor development to academic learning. Rather, the study of the motor performance of the child with learning disorders, when judged against the developmental sequence, indicates that motor functions are observable manifestations of neural processes to which academic learning is closely related. The relationship is evident where sensory integrative dysfunction is present. Once a given level of sensory integration is reached, other factors—for example, the ability to conceptualize and abstract—appear more important in shaping cognitive development and academic achievement. Furthermore, sensorimotor deviations are not always linked to learning disorders. Other factors are involved, especially in certain types of dyslexia (for example, Critchley 1964).

Some Emerging Theories in the Literature

The association between motor function and the development of the capacity of learning readiness has given rise to a number of theories and resultant programs aimed at improving academic achievement through sensorimotor activity. A brief look at some of the major tenets, their evolution, differences, likenesses, and effectiveness, can clarify the proposed nature of the perceptual-cognitive-motor interaction and promote development of procedures more effective than those now employed.

As one of the early explorers of the motor basis of academic achievement, Kephart (1960) recognized the importance of learning laterality (the internal awareness of the two sides of the body and their difference) by actually experimenting through movement. He considered readiness for learning to involve not a "loosely-organized bunch of skills," but "a hierarchical build-up of generalizations which allows the child to deal increasingly effectively with his environment" (Dunsing and Kephart 1965, p. 81). Learning disabilities were viewed as difficulties in the developmental sequence which limited or distorted future learning. Activities designed to remediate the problems reflected the sequential development of motor generalization and fostered internal awareness through tasks such as standing balance and chalkboard activities using both hands in symmetrical and asymmetrical acts. Kephart's concepts and remedial procedures have found support in a number of correlational and experimental studies (Lewis, Bell, and Anderson 1970; Plack 1971; Sullivan 1972; M. D. Fisher and Turner 1972). These studies identified the following problem areas in poor readers: locomotion, bilateral movement, synchrony, sequencing, and many items on the Purdue Perceptual Motor Survey.

Applying Kephart's sensorimotor training to hospitalized retardates, Maloney (1969) found that training did promote body-image development but did not demonstrate the principle of generalizability to higher level abilities such as intelligence. Similar results were obtained in a group of educable mentally retarded by K. L. Fisher (1970). Meckler (1972) found training in fine motor activities using the Kephart principles generalized to other fine motor tasks in adolescent retardates. Kephart, of course, did not base his theoretical formulations on mentally retarded children, but on learning disabled children who had more potential for demonstrating higher cognitive skills than do most retarded children, although they exhibited specific developmental gaps relating to balance, bilaterality, and generalization of motor function.

Building largely on the previously developed neural constructs of Temple Fay, three clinicians—Doman, Doman, and Delacato (Delacato 1963; Delacato 1959; and LeWinn 1969)—employed concepts of the hierarchical organization of the brain and emphasized evaluation and recognition of each level of ontogeny. The most critical to reading was considered to be the establishment of dominance of the eye, hand, foot, and speech in one cerebral hemisphere. Remedial methods for establishing cerebral dominance included creeping and emphasis on the use of one hand and homolateral eye as dominant. Delacato, to whom most of the treatment procedures are attributed, placed special emphasis on "cross-patterned" creeping or advancing the contralateral arm and leg simultaneously. Doman, Spitz, Zucman, Delacato, and Doman (1960) reported positively on the treatment of seventy-six severely brain damaged children whose treatment stressed "patterning," which is essentially the passive manipulation of the child in a motor pattern similar to crawling and the establishment of dominance. In addition to locomotor processes, the theory considered many aspects of sensory processes and automatic functions. The concept of "patterning" may be related to recent neurobiological views (DeLong 1972; Bizzi and Evarts 1972) that many motor patterns are programmed or stored in the central nervous system and may be triggered by sensory input.

The Doman-Delacato theory of neurological organization is best viewed as an approach to solving learning problems rather than as an assortment of procedures to be used in isolation. Their concept that nervous system organization can be modified to assist cognitive functions followed by about a decade the work of Kabat and Knott (1948), and later that of Bobath and Bobath (1955) and Rood (Stockmeyer 1967), all of whom have utilized central nervous system mechanisms to modify neuromuscular dysfunction. The concept of neural organization, while popularized among educators by Delacato, is common in neurobiology and was first stressed by Sherrington (1906). The concept might be advanced by noting that both the neuromuscular and the learning theorists are concerned with the child with neurodevelopmental disorders.

While positive effects on visual perception and language development from procedures given according to the rationale of Delacato were reported by Lavin (1972), a number of other experiments (Robbins 1966; O'Donnell and Eisenson 1969; McLees 1970) failed to show that the Delacato procedures increased reading scores. Cornish (1970) also reported negative results from a program consisting of three minutes per day of cross-patterning exercises using a mechanical device with intact kindergarten classes with perceptual-motor deficits. On the basis of his results, Cornish suggested "that a neurological training program does not significantly improve the psychomotor functioning of kindergarten children" (p. 15).

The contrast of the tremendous complexity of the nervous system with Cornish's simplistic approach, though comprehensive conclusions, reflects the difficulties and confusions rampant in the thought and practice of enhancing learning through sensorimotor processes.

Frostig (Frostig and Horne 1964; Frostig 1970) developed a program of sensorimotor skill development, emphasizing both gross and fine motor activity as well as direct visual perception development. Several studies (Gamsky and Lloyd 1971; Bishop, Gayton, and Bassett 1972; Walsh and D'Angelo 1971; Beck and Talkington 1970; Talkington 1968; Jessen 1970) have supported hypotheses that the Frostig program enhanced performance on perceptual tests, but the training appeared to be closely related to the test tasks. Malehorn (1971) found the program increased reading readiness and education ability, but J. L. Brown (1970) failed to demonstrate significant gains in reading accuracy or comprehension.

Dividing poor readers into groups receiving either the Frostig visual perception training or an auditory program resulted in no significant differences in scores on a word recognition test (Buckland and Balow 1973). There was no attempt to differentiate the children with auditory-language problems from those with visual perception problems. Chance factors alone would tend to relegate an equal number of children with different difficulties to each group, thus canceling out the influence of what may have been two equally effective means of ameliorating learning problems.

Barsch's (1967) theory of Movegenics stressed development through movement in space, proposing that it optimizes learning. He shares with others a view of movement as a survival function as well as the importance of transforming sensory input into information on which the organism can act, the significance of the developmental sequence, and the need for adequacy of the sensory feedback system.

The physical education program of Cratty (1970, 1971) approaches academic-motor liaison by actually involving academic material in motor games. Movement is considered to enhance perceptual and intellectual processes if it encourages the child to think. Although the program does not profess to improve reading through use of large skeletal muscles, it has been reported to improve some aspects of visual perception in children with moderate motor problems. Activities involve balance, ball skills, and use of the trampoline (Cratty, Ikeda, Martin, Jennett, and Morris 1970).

Rather than stressing the role of physical movement in relation to learning, Ayres (1972*b*) focuses on the sensory integrative aspect of sensorimotor functions. Physical activity is viewed primarily as the source of and a means for organizing sensation. She proposes that the aspect of early academic learning that is dependent upon sensory integration relates it to certain aspects of motor development in children. There is limited evidence that if the theory is carefully applied to learning disabilities it can bring demonstrable results (Ayres 1972*a*). However, when utilized with kindergarten children, results were reported as encouraging but not reaching statistical significance (Wilbarger 1971). Portions of the theory are presented later.

Other studies of the effect of sensorimotor approaches not identified with any of the previously discussed theoretical systems have generally demonstrated improvement in fine motor coordination, visual perception, and perceptual-motor performance (Haring and Stables 1966; Kannegieter 1970; Rice 1972; McCormick and Schnobrich 1971; August 1970); in reading readiness skills (Pryzwansky, 1972; Lipton, 1970); and in cognitive functions or academic achievement (Feriden, Van Handel, & Kovalinsky 1971; Patrinakou 1970; Leithwood and Fowler 1971; Deutsch 1971; Halliwell and Solan 1972).

Other studies of children with or without identified perceptual deficiencies reported lack of statistically significant results in improving intelligence, perceptual-motor development, or reading readiness (Hedges and Hardin 1972; Keim 1970; McRaney 1971). Belmont, Flegenheimer, and Birch (1973) found neither perceptual training nor remedial instruction superior in advancing the reading level in children at risk for reading failure. No attempt was made to match training to the child's underlying problem in any of these studies.

Several studies (Chasey and Wyrick 1970; Alley and Carr 1968; Hawarth 1971; Harkins 1971; Richardson 1970) employing physical education-like activity with mentally retarded children failed to demonstrate significant change in perceptual-motor skill or cognitive function, although Beter (1970) found improvement in the areas of reading comprehension and arithmetic in a comparable sample following a combined program of concentrated physical education and an auditory and visual perceptual reading program. On the whole these studies make little attempt to relate the nature of the program theoretically to the neural condition expected to change.

Analysis of Theories Reported in the Literature

Analysis of the methods employed by the various studies and of the results helps clarify the relationship of sensorimotor functions to learning disability. Hammill's (1972) review of related research led him to conclude that current programs were not effective in improving reading and possibly not visual perception. Hammill gave little attention to critique of design or the theoretical formulations. That negative results may be a function of inadequacy of research methodology or implementation of the remedial program seems seldom to occur to the researchers or their reviewers. Assuming that a relationship does not exist because a hypothesis was not supported at the customary level of significance may interfere with progress toward determining a possible relationship.

From a review of studies emphasizing perceptual (as opposed to gross motor) training, Halliwell and Solan (1972) found that perceptual training when added to the reading program occasionally brought results. These authors commented on the frequent failure of schools to select students with measurable perceptual deficits and the inadequacy of training of personnel for program implementation.

Footlik's (1970) summary of the experimental evidence of effects of perceptual-motor training and cognitive achievement focuses on studies associated with the Reading Research Foundation. Consistently significant improvement in reading by slow learners was demonstrated. The symptoms for which the program was designed were hyper- or hypoactivity, distractibility, auditory and visual memory, discrimination, motor coordination, body image, and laterality. The theoretical rationale stressed the developmental hierarchical organization of behavior relative to the different senses. The sequence utilized was: proprioceptive, tactile, auditory, visual, and language. This program not only acknowledges the developmental sequence but employs the concept of central nervous system patterns of sensory and motor activity and their interaction. The orienting reflex and exercises involving crossing the midline of the body received emphasis.

The most common limitations of the studies failing to demonstrate effectiveness of perceptual-motor programs were: (a) a tendency to test a few isolated procedures derived from a larger theoretical framework dependent upon a more comprehensive approach which, at best, overlooks most of the neurobiological research on sensorimotor function, (b) insufficient understanding of the original theory by the individuals who implemented the program, and (c) perhaps because of limited understanding of the theoretical rationale, a failure to match the remedial program to the child's specific type of sensorimotor dysfunction, if, indeed, the child has a difficulty. When an attempt was made to match treatment to dysfunction, it was done without regard to the neurological processes involved in either treatment or the dysfunction. Too often all learning disorders are considered to be alike, so all children are given essentially the same intervention program, a practice which may be compared to administering the same medicine to all "sick" patients. It is unrealistic to expect to learn much about the sensorimotor foundations of academic ability from such work.

A source of confusion in thinking which relates sensorimotor activity to academic learning is the seldom recognized difference in two educational approaches. The conventional educational approach teaches the specific skill which the child is expected to learn. On the other hand, approaches based on understanding how the brain develops and learns maintain the objective of changing the brain function so that the learning capacity increases. Auxter (1972) confused the latter approach with the former approach when he proposed that laterality is appropriately taught through motor activities in which one side of the body must balance with the other side, and that balancing in an anterior-posterior manner is irrelevant to development of laterality. Each of the two approaches has a place, but when procedures developed upon constructs of enhancing neural integration are employed by researchers who adhere to the philosophy of teach-to-the-specific-skill, studies yield (at best) confusing and unconvincing evidence.

Intervention programs yielding positive results vary in approach but hold some characteristics in common, due, apparently, to the fact that most of them have been derivations of the major theories described above. Rationales form a continuum, at one end of which is direct or cognitive training to a specific skill, such as a visuomotor task, and at the other end is an approach that employs neural constructs in an effort to enhance the functioning of the neural substrate of early academic learning. The majority of the studies propose a program employing constructs that are related to hypothesized function but are expressed in terms that can be directly related to tasks seen as relevant to the reading process without recourse to understanding neurobiological processes.

There is some common rationale in the concepts and remedial procedures employed in the studies that apparently succeeded in meeting the objective of remediating some of the underlying neurobiological conditions which interfere with academic learning. It is from the common focus of these studies that hypotheses are deduced relative to just which aspects of sensorimotor development are critical in learning to read and calculate. Most commonly employed concepts among the successful studies are directionality of movement, gross motor learning, motor planning, balancing and other postural reflexes, the developmental sequence, proprioception, touch, spatial awareness, bilaterality of function (including crossing the midline of the body), the orienting reflex, and training in all of the senses, including intersensory training. Most of the investigators recognize that lateralization of function in the brain is in some way related to learning.

Synthesizing these ideas results in the postulation that the capacity to read and calculate is in part dependent upon prior development involving the processing of input from many sensory sources and the intersensory association of that input.

The sensory processing appears to enable maturation of postural responses, the ability to motor plan, awareness of space, and the relationship of the two sides of the body to each other. Lateralization of cerebral functions is fostered by these sensorimotor processes. It is possible that each of these aspects of development is linked in a developmental sequence in which the optimum development of each step is dependent upon a certain amount of maturation of previous steps. Some of the skills required for academic success in the first school years may be part of this developmental sequence.

The studies yielding positive results were usually implemented by those who either developed the theoretical rationale or were thoroughly familiar with it. Studies which were less successful frequently utilized isolated procedures as a "recipe" rather than applying professional judgment based on knowledge of sensorimotor development and on the nature of the problem and response of each individual child. Such studies were usually designed by a person not involved in the construction of the underlying theoretical rationale. Kephart (1971) rightly questioned whether the nature of most of the hypotheses regarding the effect of sensorimotor activity on learning disorders accurately reflected the nature of the problem which many researchers believed they were studying.

When the characteristics of the studies which obtained statistically significant results, but did not train specifically to the test, are compared with those which failed to obtain demonstrable results, the former are found to have far more complex, comprehensive, and logical rationales. The characteristics of the statistically significant studies relate a number of interrelated behavioral parameters in a logical fashion to the task of reading.

The studies cited reflect not only the inevitable problems of the youth of a growing body of theoretical knowledge, but also a great discrepancy between the sophisticated mathematical model of the design and the theoretical model under test. Emphasis on the experimental method as the most sophisticated research tool has led to an uncritical reverence for the results regardless of the amount of thought undergirding the theory from which hypotheses are derived. Kass (1969) reviewed the research on learning disabilities and concluded that the traditional experimental designs do not always provide the most successful approach to bridging the gap between diagnosis and remediation of learning disorders. In many cases, the emphasis on experimental design has forced premature judgment of the relationship between sensorimotor functions and learning disabilities.

After reviewing the research on the neurophysiology of learning, Thompson, Patterson, and Teyler (1972) succinctly concluded that understanding of the neurobiology of learning has only just begun. Considering how little is known, researchers who have brought about apparent neural changes resulting in enhanced capacity in disabled learners have done remarkably well. In view of the complexity of the brain, it is almost presumptuous that they would even try, but apparently the need to do so remains. The American Association of Health, Physical Education and Recreation (1971) stated the situation plainly: a stronger scientific base for operations is needed.

The Developmental Sequence

The proposition that certain perceptual or sensory integrative development associated with motor concomitants must occur before a child is optimally prepared to read is central to most of the theories that relate sensorimotor function to academic learning. The basic assumption holds that incorporating some aspects of the developmental sequence in the remedial situation may assist the child in more adequate realization of potential rather than focusing only on the end product or capacity. The rationale is implied in Prechtl's (1969) definition of ontogenetic development as *"sequential changes which continuously transform any biological system of relatively simple organization into one of increasing complexity and differentiation until a final stable stage is reached"* (p. 4). By carrying this thought a step further, the concept is developed that each sequence in development, beginning with conception, not only increases the adaptive capacity of the child but places the child in a better position for taking the next sequential step, with each step more complex than the previous step.

The 1940s produced some of the most classical, detailed, and accurate descriptions of motor development (for example, Gesell *et al.* 1940; McGraw 1945). Since that time, as Mussen (1970) has commented, developmental psychology has focused on explanations or mechanisms accounting for psychological changes and has emphasized cognitive development. The field of medicine, on the other hand, has increased its production of publications describing methods of examining the young child's neurological integrity. Since sensorimotor function and its sequential development are an accurate reflection of many aspects of neurological integrity, these examinations provide an account of motor development in the early and most important years (Beintema 1968; Grant, Boelsche, and Zin 1973; Andre-Thomas and Autgaerden 1966; Paine and Oppé 1966; Prechtl & Beintema 1964; Illingworth 1962; Andre-Thomas, Chesni, and Saint-Anne Dargassies 1960; Touwen 1971). The work of Milani-Comparetti and Gidoni (1967) provides an especially thorough account of the development of postural responses, that is, the ontogeny of anti-gravity control of the body axis. Some detailed comments on discrete aspects of motor development by various researchers and clinicians may be found in a publication edited by Connolly (1970).

Comprehensive reviews of motor development from the psychoeducational standpoint tend to present the more obvious relationship of motor development to cognitive development, that is, the ability to move about within the environment in order to learn about it (for example, Hurlock 1972; Lisina and Neverovich 1964). According to Fowler and Leithwood (1971), the diminished amount of recent psychological research in gross motor development of the young child may be partly attributed "to lack of conceptual constructs and accompanying analytic-evaluative instruments" (p. 523). Conceptual constructs are imperative to link sensorimotor development to cognitive learning.

Piaget (1952) proposed a link between perception and conceptualization when he suggested a certain amount of dependence of the ability to conceptualize upon a prior perceptual-motor stage. This stage, in turn, was dependent upon the early sensorimotor stage of development.

Some of the sources of research that are most helpful in determining the critical aspects of the sequence of sensorimotor development are those concerned with fetal and infant development. Carmichael (1970) thoroughly reviews the literature on fetal sensorimotor development and Kessen, Haith, and Salapatek (1970) cover the research on infant motor activity. As the latter authors point out, the literature offers little on the nature of the continuity between early reflexive behavior and later cognitive functions. If these data are to be used for understanding learning disorders, the clinician must make the leap from fact to remediation via hypotheses.

The complexity and intricacy of the developmental process makes it both difficult to test and to follow in remedial work. Bibace and Hancock (1969) questioned the assumption that perceptual-motor readiness was an essential precursor to certain aspects of school learning. They tested the assumption using a design involving a few eight-year-old subjects and a narrow range of complex perceptual-motor tasks. They found support for their assumption as well as instances contrary to the assumption. Until more is known of the specific developmental steps critical to optimum development of perception and other sensory processing underlying reading and calculating, any hypotheses regarding perceptual or sensorimotor precursors to academic learning cannot be tested with finality.

The concept of the developmental sequence is easily distorted into a lock-step, rigid hierarchy in which a later step cannot develop before complete mastery over an earlier step is achieved. Such an interpretation overlooks the constant reciprocal interweaving of the developing behavioral domains. Developmental steps overlap. They are not discontinuous; rather they tend to be spiral. Most importantly, probably some of the sequences of neural development which are especially important in preparing a child for early academic learning are not yet recognized, as suggested by the demands of the activities commonly employed in the studies reporting enhancement of reading ability through sensorimotor means. Furthermore, the plasticity of the young brain may enable some (but not necessarily all) children to use compensatory abilities to assist in academic learning. While each developmental step provides a basis for the next developmental step, the dependence is relative rather than absolute, and certain neural systems may show a stronger dependence upon a hierarchical sequence than do other neural systems. There may be a minimal level of certain types of sensory integration essential to some of the basic demands of early academic learning, but beyond that basic level, further development in those parameters is not as important as other factors, such as the capacity for abstract thinking. These basic demands are normally met in the average child through the usual experiences of childhood. In the learning disabled child, the usual experiences have been insufficient.

Fetal Sensorimotor Development

Any consideration of sensorimotor development must consider that which occurs in fetal and neonatal life. In these instances the sequences of development, especially in response to sensory input, are often more clear cut, and may be considered guides to sequences occurring later in life. T. Humphrey (1969) found that the first year of normal, postnatal motor development followed sequences which first made their appearance in fetal development. The sequence also may be repeated perinatally. The tendency toward repetition of motor sequences is, in part, due to neuroanatomical arrangements. Humphrey comments that the anatomical arrangements make it inevitable that the earlier stages of development are used as "building blocks" for later stages. It is assumed that the general anatomical arrangements remain constant and that circuitry establishing a developmental sequence early in life will be more easily activated later in life than alternate circuitry. Stated otherwise, the basic assumption underlying recapitulation of some aspects of sensorimotor development in a remedial situation is that the building block that served earlier will be likely to serve again for more mature development.

From an unpublished experiment with fetal development by L. Bergström, cited by R. M. Bergström (1969), some inference can be made with regard to factors other than maturation which can enter into increasing the probability of appearance of an ontogenetically later response. When electrical stimulation was given to the fetal brain slightly earlier in the developmental sequence than the time at which a given motor performance should appear spontaneously, the electrical stimulus appeared to elicit the later developmental stage. It was implied that the application of the stimuli to the brain reduced randomness of neural function and increased the amount of information in the brain. This process is essentially what is attempted therapeutically; that is, the sensory input is intended to enhance the adaptiveness, orderliness, and specificity of motor response and to increase the information that enables the brain to emit a response of greater adaptiveness or maturity.

While human postnatal motor development has been observed and recorded in detail, the sequence of development of the sensory systems is less well known, but it is critical to any theory that attempts to incorporate the developmental sequence into a therapeutic program of sensory integration. Much of the research on fetal or neonatal development is based on subhuman species although the human fetus is also studied. The status of sensory development is determined by response of the organism to the mode of sensory stimulation.

Research quite consistently reports the tactile system as among the first, if not the first, sensory system to mature (T. Humphrey 1969; Carmichael 1970; Volokhov 1970; Fox 1970). The response to tactile input was reflex motor activity, the earliest centering around the neck and mouth, followed by arms, legs, and trunk (Bergström 1969; Carmichael 1970).

From his review of related research, Carmichael (1970) found that responses that can be attributed to stimulation of the vestibular system are also seen early in fetal development. Vestibular control of eye movement develops before visual control, and interpretation of vestibular input is necessary for the development of postural reaction. Postural reactions are quite mature at birth in many subhuman species; the survival of the animal is dependent upon postural reactions. Similarly, muscle receptors respond to percussion in early prenatal life. By the time of birth, proprioceptors in muscles, tendons, and joints are "among the best-organized receptor fields so far as the initiation and control of behavior are concerned" (p. 523).

At least in lower animals, olfaction is fairly mature just after birth (Volokhov 1970; Carmichael 1970). There is quite general agreement that the phyletically older systems (tactile, olfactory, gustatory, vestibular, and proprioceptive) mature before the younger auditory and visual systems (Volokhov 1970; Fox 1970; Carmichael 1970).

Motor responses begin at the neck and mouth followed by head and body righting reflexes and eye movements (Bergström 1969). Carmichael (1970) states that there is reason to believe that the first eye movements are a response to bodily position. Flexor tone is present before extensor (Fox 1970) and phasic motor activity is present first proximally, then distally in the limbs (Bergström 1969). Another order of appearance of motor function observed by Bergström (1969) is related to quickness of response and cessation of response to a stimulus. The first fetal motor behavior is slow in both respects, and this sustained response is in contrast to later fetal motor responses which are more phasic.

Carmichael (1970) found that most students of fetal development agree that locomotion, sucking, and breathing are three of the earliest essential behavior systems of the animal at birth. Carmichael notes that, in its developed form, each of these responses may involve proprioceptive stimulation. He considers postural responses, including those of eye muscle, to be among the more significant prenatal activities. These actions may be considered preparation for postnatal walking and movement of arms, trunk, and legs. Several of the procedures commonly found in studies reporting success in remediating learning disorders are consistent with sensory development in the fetus, namely: (a) consideration of all of the sensory systems, especially those receiving input from the body as opposed to only the visual or auditory channels, (b) emphasis on postural reflexes, and (c) gross motor learning.

The first fetal motor output is random (Bergström 1969), with action preceding reaction (Hamburger 1970). What brings orderliness to this random action? Bergström (1969) suggests attributing the advent of orderliness to the appearance of central inhibitory mechanisms, while Hamburger (1968) found that in the young chick embryo movement became organized when it became responsive to sensation. The control of sensory input and activation of inhibitory mechanisms in the remedial situation is consistent with both schools of thought.

Many questions about the embryonic development of motion remain unanswered. Hamburger (1970) notes two schools of thought, neither of which he considers completely satisfactory. One school holds that actions of a segment of the body individuate out of actions involving a larger portion of the body; the second school, based largely on the mammalian fetus, holds that local motor responses are combined into an integrated whole. Both schools of thought are reflected in procedures for remediation of sensory integrative dysfunction. Although individual reflexes or nervous system networks containing a programmed motor pattern that does not require sensory input for elicitation are activated, they are activated in order to obtain a more normal volitional pattern involving the entire body. More discrete volitional movements are individuated out of the more gross motion. This principle is also consistent with phylogeny. Evolution proceeded from the diffuse to local forms or neural activity (for example, see Karamyan 1968). Hamburger (1970) comments on the interesting theoretical implications of the precedence of action over reaction in embryonic development of behavior, but he admits that he cannot finalize the idea at this point.

The complexity of sensorimotor development which underlies the foundation of academic ability obviously exceeds the current knowledge of it. The recognition that some aspects of sensorimotor development provided important building blocks to cognitive learning has led to a tendency to oversimplify the relationship and to hypothesize a simple, single cause for any given effect rather than a complex interaction process.

A THEORY OF SENSORY INTEGRATIVE DYSFUNCTION: ITS RELATIONSHIP TO LEARNING DISABILITIES AND THEIR AMELIORATION

The balance of this chapter presents a theory of the sensorimotor foundations of learning and a review of related research. The theory has been tested and found effective with some learning disabled children when appropriately applied (Ayres 1972*a*). The theory is not considered final; rather, it is seen as a continually evolving formulation of ideas to incorporate information from neurobiological research.

The Sensory Integrative Process

Perception and purposeful movement are largely dependent upon sensation, especially sensation from several different modalities integrated into a meaningful whole that informs the human organism about the status of its body and the environment in which the body is interacting. Equally important is the *production* of sensation and *integration* through movement. In fact, sensation and movement are so intimately related they are expressed together in the single word *sensorimotor* and cannot be considered separately when involved with remediation for the learning disabled child.

That higher integrative functions evolved from and operate through mediation of sensorimotor experience is not a new idea in the field of neurobiology (see, for example, Sherrington 1955; Herrick 1956). This viewpoint is basic to current theories purporting to influence certain kinds of learning disabilities through sensorimotor activity. It is also basic to the theory presented in this chapter.

Perception and learning are not dependent upon a simple cortical interpretation of auditory or visual stimuli at the moment. The final encoding process is dependent upon many previous processes, most of which are involved with intersensory integration, or the association of sensations from several different sensory sources. That many learning disabled children have disorders in cross-modality association has been shown repeatedly (Birch and L. Belmont 1964, 1965*a*, 1965*b*; Birch and I. Belmont 1964; Belmont, Birch, and Karp 1965; Beery 1967; Bryden 1972). Vande Voort, Senf, and Benton (1972), however, found in their sample of children with deficient reading skills that the cross-modal task was not reliably different from the within-modal task, i.e., visual to visual and auditory to auditory. The investigators interpreted their findings to mean that attentional and encoding processes were more critical factors than sequencing, memory, or simultaneous matching of stimuli through different channels. This interpretation requires investigation of the encoding procedure, especially initial processing.

There is a great deal more interaction among the senses than is commonly recognized from simple observation of a child beginning academic work, yet this interaction may well be one of the more critical processes eventually resulting in the perceptual capacity necessary for academic learning.

The capacity for intersensory integration increases as one ascends the phylogenetic scale, and may account for man's superior capacity over lower animals in adaptive responses. A great deal of intermodality association occurs through the convergence of sensory input from several different sources on polysensory or convergent neurons, or on nuclei or other structures which are designed to associate input from several different modalities (Fessard 1961; Jung, Kornhuber, and DaFonseca 1963; Eccles 1966; Buser and Imbert 1961; Albe-Fessard and Fessard 1963; Bental, Dafny, and Feldman 1968; Spinelli, Starr, and Barrett 1968).

The fact that a single neuron can and does respond to more than one sensory modality, and sometimes requires input from more than one sensory source in order to discharge, points up the fact that the brain is designed to organize and utilize input from several simultaneous sources. Convergence of sensory input can also, under certain conditions, prevent neural discharge. Intermodality convergence occurs at all levels of the brain, including the brain stem, cortex, and intermediate sources.

The most commonly reported sensory modalities showing convergence are visual, auditory, tactile, vestibular, and other proprioception. That most tactile, vestibular, and other proprioceptive input is largely elicited through movement of the body gives motor activity much of its importance to sensory integrative development. One of the major reasons that movement is employed in remediation of sensory integrative dysfunction is for its sensory-producing effect.

Sensation from the skin, muscles, joints, gravity, and movement receptors of the body have a widespread distribution to academically relevant areas, including the auditory, visual, and motor areas of the cortex. Melzack, Konrad, and Dubrovsky (1969), for example, demonstrated that rubbing the paw of a cat that was lightly anesthetized influenced electrical discharge in the visual, somatic, and auditory systems and the pyramidal tract under certain conditions.

Neurobiologists in general hold that multisensory stimuli are more effective than messages from only one modality. Albe-Fessard (1967) hypothesizes that the widespread dispersion of sensory input from the body, especially that traveling up the spinal column from the body, is employed for unconscious control of sensory as well as motor activities. This relatively recent view emphasizing input from the skin, muscles, and related structures is similar to Schilder's (1933) earlier conception of the vestibular system as having a coordinating or uniting function on the other senses.

The implication for the academic world is that auditory and visual perception necessary to school learning does not develop in isolation from the other senses but is dependent upon integrative functions of the tactile, vestibular, and other proprioceptive systems. This dependency, then, indicates a need for normalizing integrative processes in the sensory systems in order that other sensory systems more directly related to academic work may function optimally.

The potential influence of input from one sensory channel on the brain as a whole is illustrated in an experiment in which Wenzel and Salzman (1968) permanently prevented olfactory stimuli from reaching the brains of pigeons. Following the deprivation, the birds were significantly slower in learning visual-motor tasks. The authors suggested that the olfactory system participated in limbic system functions in some general way. In the pigeon the limbic system mediates some of the highest forms of their adaptive behavior. It is not necessarily implied that the human brain is similarly influenced by olfactory stimuli, but that it might be stimulated by other sensory modalities.

Brain Stem Contributions to Sensory Integration

One of the most fundamental principles of neural development is that the lower parts of the brain develop before the higher structures. Accordingly, brain stem functions mature before cortical functions, as was true in the phyletic sequence. When higher structures evolved, they did not lose their dependence upon the lower structures. Cortical functions, then, are in some respects still dependent upon brain stem functions.

The brain stem is one of the major structures in which sensory integration occurs. Wherever there is considerable convergence of input. there is also the possibility of pervasive influence over the rest of the brain. Both the tactile and vestibular systems send large quantities of input to the brain stem and through it can exert influence over cortical function.

In addition to this generalized influence on sensory integration, there are specific motor and visual processes mediated through brain stem structures that are particularly important in the development of visual perception. While educators are understandably concerned with the visual perceptual demands of reading, it is necessary to recognize that the type of visual perception in reading is dependent upon some mastery of visual perception of the environmental scheme.

As information from the vestibular and other proprioceptors arising from moving about within the environment becomes associated with visual input, a model or map develops of the environment to which the body relates. This environmental scheme, which initially is proprioceptive, eventually becomes essentially visual. The environmental scheme is analogous to the body scheme, i.e., the brain's model or plan of how the body is designed and functions as a mechanical structure. The nature of each scheme is dependent in part upon the nature of the other. The body is the center of the environmental scheme and the environmental plan exists only in relation to the body relating to the environment. The organism is located within the environmental scheme and it acts within it according to that scheme.

The environmental scheme changes each time the head or body

changes position, for it is a spatial relationship between the body and the earth and objects in the environment. Lord Brain (1963) expressed the relationship thus: "All action in the external world requires and implies information as to the existing orientation of the body in relation to it, and of the parts of the body to one another" (p. 398).

Learning to perceive the environmental scheme visually evolved over millions of years through association with the vestibular, locomotor, and oculomotor processes. These three functions and visual perception of the environmental scheme have come to perform essentially as one united system, each aspect of the system giving meaning to all other aspects. Thus, the evolution of visual perception began with perceiving gravity and the sense of movement, and using that information to make postural and locomotor responses relating self to environment, with the eye muscles providing an essential aspect of the musculo-skeletal-postural system.

It is proposed that this combination of sensorimotor processes still functions essentially as a unit in the midbrain of man, although it does so in connection with the neocortex. The newly evolved structures never quite lose their dependence upon older structures.

The importance of the contribution of the midbrain to visual functions was first and most forcefully put forth by Trevarthen (1968), with some additional support at the time from Held (1968). At that time the proposition of dual modes of vision was proposed, one being "ambient." The ambient mode is the perception of space to which the body is relating and is largely a function of the midbrain. The second mode proposed was "focal." The focal mode perceives a small area in great detail and is largely a function of the neocortex (Trevarthen 1968).

Later, Held (1970), in a theoretical paper strongly supported with data from lower animals and human beings, further clarified the duality of the visual system, attributing interpretation of contour or making figural judgments to the neocortex and assigning the locus of a visual stimulus to the brain stem. Locating a visual stimulus is related to visual-motor control, that is, reaching for an object or directing one's hand or foot in space.

A number of other studies support the contention of extensive visual processing in the midbrain, especially at the superior colliculus of the midbrain. In the lower animal, the midbrain receives significant projection from the optic tract, and that projection has a definite organization in the superior colliculi (Trevarthen 1968; Masland, Chow, and Stewart 1971; McIlwain 1972).

The visual processes that have been associated with the midbrain, especially in lower animals, include eye fixation (Brown and Berkson 1970); visually guided behavior and pattern discrimination (Sprague, Berlucchi, and DiBernardino 1970); direction selectivity (McIlwain 1972); movement or motion detection (Schaefer 1970; Gordon 1972; Richards 1971); visuospatial function, visual, tactile, and pattern discrimination (Voneida 1970); oculomotor and orienting movements (Schaefer 1970; Sterling and Wickelgren 1970); guidance of the direction of movement (Riss 1968).

N. K. Humphrey (1970) demonstrated that monkeys without a visual cortex had accurate visually guided reaching for objects, suggesting acute subcortical vision insofar as sensitivity to spatial location was concerned, although the monkeys could not attribute abstract meaning to what they saw. Gordon (1972) made the observation, the full significance of which may not yet be recognized, that retinal input to the colliculus is primarily from the contralateral eye, with relatively little input from the ipsilateral eye. She also found that the superior colliculus, while primarily an organ of visual processing, also processes auditory and somatosensory input. Of particular relevance is the fact that the topographical maps of the three sensory channels were superimposed, contributing to the integration of these three types of sensation, especially in locating, orienting, searching, and tracking related to any of the sensory inputs.

Richards (1971) submits that the midbrain visual function is similar in process from fish to man. Most researchers hold the opinion that brain stem visual processing in man is probably similar to that observed in lower animals. In studying split-brain human beings, Trevarthen (1970) obtained responses which led him to conclude that in the absence of the cerebral commissures, the midbrain served to unify some general aspects of form and motion of the two visual half-fields.

Of current concern among basic scientists is whether the brain stem and neocortical systems function with relative independence or interdependence. While Held (1970) and Trevarthen (1968) tend to favor relative independence of the two systems, McIlwain (1972) and Sterling and Wickelgren (1970) take an interdependence point of view. A position somewhat between these two extremes—and more helpful to the professional concerned with the child with a visual perception problem—is expressed by Berlucchi, Sprague, Levy, and DiBernardino (1972). They maintain that what might appear to be two visual systems identified by the two major neuroanatomical levels at which the major processing occurs is really one system with crucial interaction between cortex and midbrain, even during complex visual functions. They have demonstrated that lesions in the midbrain of the cat result in perceptual problems—not sensory or motor—and that the difficulties are similar to those following visual cortical ablations provided testing is of original learning and not of retention.

The ontogenetic sequence of these two aspects of the visual system holds significance for the therapeutic process. In the human infant, the brain stem processing develops earlier than the neocortical process (Bronson 1969; Gibson 1970). Bower (1969) found young human infants especially capable of perceiving motion, space, and size constancy before they could discriminate patterns.

It seems reasonably safe to assume that visual perception in man is in one way or another dependent upon brain stem functions and that in providing visual perception training, brain stem visual processing must be considered.

To what extent are brain stem processes involved in crossing the street, in locating and following material on a chalkboard, in eye-hand activity, in following a line of words, or in returning one's eyes to the next line of reading material? Such a question accurately focuses on the problem.

The Developmental Sequence as Therapeutically Applied

While the literature supplies adequate information on the sequence of development, especially motor development, it does not, in itself, indicate which of these steps is most critical to the development of cognitive processes upon which early academic learning is dependent. It is nearly impossible to replicate every developmental step. The following sequence is proposed as one which serves theoretical formulation, but it is not comprehensive. Emphasis on the various steps is varied in accordance with the type of dysfunction of the child.

The gross steps are: improve sensory integration in general, especially of the tactile and vestibular systems; enhance maturation of postural responses and related proprioceptive mechanisms; develop praxis or the capacity to motor plan; encourage interaction of the two sides of the body and space; develop form and space perception.

Improving Sensory Integration in General

A procedure employed with children who show signs that the vestibular and tactile systems are not entering into the total sensory integrative process to an adequate degree involves providing general stimulation through those sensory channels. The practice is consistent with the early maturation of the tactile and vestibular systems and the possibility that their development will provide a foundation for the development of the other senses. The child who shows reduced nystagmus or dizziness on rotation around his longitudinal axis when sitting, head slightly flexed, is assumed to have a disorder in the vestibular system that results in inadequate involvement of input from that system. Brain stem sensory integrative processing suffers at least as much as cortically mediated integrative processes, and the brain stem is one of the more important locales for sensory integration.

If there is evidence that a child's vestibular system may not be providing adequate input and if the child's emotional response to the procedure is positive, he is spun or spins himself by sitting or lying in a net hammock, both ends of which are suspended from a common point, or by lying on a scooter board—a short board on freely moving casters—and spinning. Some of the value in trampoline activities may lie in their strong activation of the vestibular system. It is the clinical impression that, when used appropriately, general vestibular stimulation can be profoundly effective. The child's subsequent response to treatment suggests that dormant or insufficiently active neuronal connections may have been activated by the right combination of events. The observation of influence on the child is consistent with current concepts of the developmental sequence and intersensory integration.

There are definite hazards to vestibular stimulation resulting from rapid rotation. It has an immediate and direct depressing effect on the respiratory system and quickly influences the vasomotor neurons (Yemel'yahov and Razumeyev 1972). The vasomotor reaction results in blanching or flushing of the skin. Vestibular stimulation can also decrease heart rate (Pomerleau-Malcuit, and Clifton 1973), which may or may not be desirable, depending upon the status of the child. Korner and Thoman (1972) found vestibular stimulation had a highly soothing effect on infants. The effect of vestibular input on other aspects of the autonomic nervous system causing nausea are better known. Any child receiving vestibular stimulation, especially passively, should be watched closely for flushing or blanching of the face, sweating, nausea, a lowered level of consciousness, or any indication of reduced respiration. If any of these signs appear, the vestibular stimulation should be stopped and its duration shortened in future therapeutic sessions. Another potential negative side effect is hyperexcitability to the point of disorganization. On the other hand, slow rhythmical motion such as swinging back and forth, or in an orbit of about twenty-five revolutions per minute, can be inhibitory and organizing to a hyperactive child.

Stimulation of the vestibular receptors also may precipitate seizures in seizure-prone children. Costin, Hafeman, Elazar, and Adey (1970) cite research to the effect that certain types of vestibular stimulation in lower animals resulted in an electroencephalogram indicating epileptic seizure activity in the temporal lobe. There are a few unpublished clinical reports of seizure-prone children having a seizure at a time when vestibular stimulation could have contributed to the situation. The seizure may even occur several days after the stimulation.

Learning disabled children show a wide variety and range of responses to vestibular stimulation; each child's response should guide the director of activity in selecting the appropriate use of this powerful tool. Some children cannot organize an adaptive response to any unaccustomed pattern of vestibular input, especially from the motion receptors. Their inability to respond in a manner that leads to postural security results in an understandable feeling of threat and fear of changes in posture or movement. Only as much vestibular input as the posturally insecure child can organize, and to which the child can respond, should be provided. Emphasis should be placed on developing all of the basic and reflex-based motor patterns that enable a child to control the dynamic relationship among gravity, movement, and the child's body. It is essential that the posturally insecure child not be threatened by an overzealous therapist who has little concept of how it feels to be the victim of a tyrannical gravitational force or an unmodulated "blast" of vestibular input.

As the child gains control, he will explore within his own capacity to master the situation. Sitting in the net hammock and slowly pushing himself back and forth with his feet may be as much input as the child can organize. Most children are accustomed to the pattern of sensory input entering the brain when in the seated position. The child's control over the additional amount of sensation resulting from pushing himself with his feet against the floor assists him in being able to organize the resultant input. Maintaining contact with the stable floor helps give him the orientation to space that a normally functioning vestibular system ordinarily provides a child. Rolling on the floor is another beginning activity more acceptable to the posturally insecure and fearful child, provided he activates the rolling himself as opposed to being rolled. When the child has developed the capacity to organize vestibular input reasonably well, he can proceed with the therapy suggested for some of the major syndromes. That proposed for apraxia is usually most appropriate.

Tactile stimuli are generated by rubbing the skin with a terry cloth or with a brush in the manner developed by Rood (see Stockmeyer 1967). In addition to contributing to the sensory integrative processes in general, tactile stimulation may have a regulatory effect on the total central nervous system excitatory state, either energizing the child or reducing his arousal level. The effect of tactile stimuli is best judged by the immediate emotional response of the child to the procedure and his behavior for a twenty-minute period following. Treatment through the tactile system should be modified according to his response.

Both tactile and vestibular stimuli strongly affect the reticular system which has a prolonged influence on the rest of the brain and on muscle tone. This influence must be taken into consideration when using tactile stimuli. When some muscles are hypertonic, increasing tone may be contraindicated, but when muscles are hypotonic, increasing tone results in increased afferent discharge from the muscles which can contribute to the more comprehensive sensory integrative process.

Worldwide professional opinion and research (for example, Zaporozhets 1965; Papoušěk 1965; Riesen 1961; Fair 1965) supports the idea that sensory integrative mechanisms do not mature in isolation but in association with adaptive motor interaction with the environment. Adaptive motor responses impose organization upon sensory input, and this may be one of the major ways in which motion contributes to the foundations of learning. Adaptiveness implies "successful" or appropriate response to the situation; response implies a reaction to a situation—in this case a pattern of sensory input—from which meaning must be gleaned. The adaptive response is the action or reaction of the organism to the environment. A reflex, such as an equilibrium or balancing response, is a simple adaptive response. Wandering aimlessly about the classroom is less adaptive and usually is the result of inability to make adaptive responses to classroom demands. A procedure is therapeutic if it enables a child to make a response to his environmental input that is more adaptive (or mature) than previous responses. Otherwise, activity is simply exercise.

Effectiveness of response is partly dependent upon accuracy or precision of the sensory input and feedback from the response. The child with disordered perception is not receiving precise information about his environment and, therefore, has greater difficulty in organizing and emitting an adaptive response. The therapeutic situation simplifies the environment at the same time it enhances the brain's capacity to organize sensory input so as to increase the probability of adaptiveness of response to sensory input. By following the ontogenetic sensorimotor sequence, more mature or complex adaptive responses are enabled to develop.

Enhancing Maturation of Postural Responses

Postural responses involve the body's dynamic relationship with the earth's gravitational force. Posture is seldom static. Movement is the rule rather than the exception. These responses involve automatic or reflex-based reactions which are programmed into the nervous system, or patterns of motion which are basic to the developmental sequence. One of the ontogenetically earliest responses is flexion of the arms, legs, and head so that the child is essentially "curled up" while lying in the supine position. The next step is lifting the head up when lying prone, an antigravity response called the labyrinthine head-righting reflex. This step is followed developmentally by lifting up both ends of the body into an extended position when lying prone. The supine flexion and prone extension postures were once noted as significant steps in motor development by Rood (Ayres 1963), who referred to them as the withdrawal and pivot prone positions. Gesell and associates (1940) and K. Bobath (1966) have also noted the signal role of the prone extensor posture.

Both the prone extensor and the supine flexor positions are generally thought to be the reverse of the position facilitated by the tonic labyrinthine reflex (TLR), one of the many postural responses mediated by the labyrinth. Commonly the effect of the TLR is facilitation of flexor tone in all four extremities when the head is prone and facilitation of extensor tone when the head is supine (see Fiorentino 1972). This pattern or reflex response has been observed in infants up to six months of age (O'Neill 1946), after which it becomes integrated into the sensorimotor system and is not easily demonstrable, though it continues to contribute to sensorimotor integration. Its presence early in life, followed by its assimilation, defines it as a primitive reflex. Tokizane, Murao, Ogata, and Kondo (1951) found that in healthy adults the maximal extensor tone elicited from the TLR occurred when the head was upside down and that minimal extensor tone occurred when the head was upright.

If the TLR does facilitate flexion when the head is prone and extension when the head is supine, and if the reflex is poorly integrated in the learning disabled child, the difficulty in mastering the supine flexion and prone extensor postures, both basic to more mature postural reactions, is increased.

The degree to which a child can assume and hold the basic motor patterns of flexion when supine and prone extension is one of the indices of his sensorimotor development. The prone extensor posture requires contraction of tonic muscles designed to hold a position for a considerable period of time. A school-age child past six years of age usually can hold it for twenty seconds. The flexor pattern involves contraction of muscles designed for phasic contraction or a contraction followed almost immediately by relaxation. Young children should not be expected to hold the supine flexor position for more than a few seconds.

Another primitive postural reflex, the tonic neck reflex (TNR), may also interfere with development of postural responses unless it is sufficiently integrated into the sensorimotor system. The asymmetrical TNR is manifested by increased tone in the extensor muscles in the arm on the side toward which the head is turned and a corresponding reduction in extensor tone in the other arm. The change in tone is most easily detected when the child is in the quadruped position with elbows slightly flexed. Opinions vary regarding the effect of the symmetrical TNR. The most common opinion, based largely on animal research, is that when the neck is flexed so that the head is bent down, the arms tend to flex and the legs extend; when the neck is extended or the head is tilted backward in relation to the trunk, the arms tend to extend and the legs flex. Simons (1953), however, observed that in many human subjects bending the head backward increased flexor tone in the upper extremities while bending the head forward increased extensor tone. Brain (1927) perceived that when a human subject with neurological dysfunction was in the quadruped position the extension of the neck led to increased extensor tone in the arms and flexion of the neck diminished it. When the patient was erect, the effect of extension and flexion of the neck was reversed. In studying healthy adult human beings, Tokizane and associates (1951) found that head flexion resulted in flexion of all four extremities. Reports of wide variations of responses to the symmetrical TNR necessitates careful evaluation of the response of each child if therapeutic procedures are to be related to the symmetrical TNR. Further description of other postural reflexes are given by Fiorentino (1972). Evidence of too much residual or poorly integrated reflexes suggests a poorly integrated motor system. When this is the case, integrating those reflexes through activating more mature responses is an initial step in sensory integrative therapy.

Fostering integration of the postural responses begins with activation of two basic total body responses to gravity—the supine flexor and prone extension patterns. These positions are the reverse of positions commonly assumed to be elicited by the TLR. They represent a more mature level of response, a condition that encourages integration of the primitive reflex.

The course of events in the life of the learning disabled child with disorder in the postural system has been insufficient to develop normal postural patterns. To be therapeutic, then, activity must provide something other than that which the child has encountered previously. Providing an activity which elicits a postural response is the most obvious and essential component of an intervention program. Several procedures based on basic brain research involve the use of sensory input and should be used to modify the central nervous system to increase the probability of the optimum postural reaction. Rood (Stockmeyer 1967) developed the therapeutic procedure of providing tactile stimulation by brushing over the muscle in which a response is desired. She also pointed out that quick stretch to a muscle activates the stretch reflex and encourages response to subsequent resistance. According to Granit (1970), postural reflexes are mediated through polysynaptic neural circuits. Part of this circuit is the small fusimotor (gamma) system and alpha-gamma co-innervation loop which includes the muscle spindles. The small fusimotor neurons that innervate the fibers of the muscle spindle cause the spindle muscle fibers to contract, eliciting discharge of the muscle spindle receptors. The afferent discharge flows back to the central nervous system where it influences the motor discharge to the skeletal muscles. Both sensory input, such as tactile, proprioceptive, and vestibular, as well as central conditions act upon the fusimotor neurons.

Granit (1970) has summarized the research on the influence of vibration over the muscle tendon or belly on the fusimotor system and through it to the polysynaptic neural circuits. He concluded that the vibratory reflex acts on one of the muscle spindle receptors in such a way that its afferent flow mobilizes the polysynaptic organization that is specific to postural reflexes. In order for vibration to affect this polysynaptic circuit, previous activation of it over the fusimotor loop is required. Clinical experience suggests that vestibular or tactile stimulation can provide this activation. Simply contracting or trying to contract the muscle during the application of vibration is sufficient to optimize the effect of vibration in preparing the nervous system to emit a postural response. Pal'tsev and El'ner (1972) scientifically demonstrated that neuromuscular reflexes are more easily excitable after vestibular stimulation. Vibration also has a tendency to enhance muscle tone, resulting in the activation of primitive postural reflexes, as well as the more mature reflex response. Care must be taken to avoid activating the primitive postural responses and to facilitate specifically the desired postural response by means of an activity which naturally demands it. Vibration provides an effective means of facilitating the prone extensor posture. Vibration is applied in the correct frequency over the belly of a muscle in which a contraction is desired.

The most effective activity for reflex activation of the prone extension posture is to ride a scooter board prone down an inclined ramp. The acceleration provided by rolling down the ramp, for example, appears to be a source of stimuli able to activate the prone extensor posture by reflex. Use of the various types of sensory input described above prepares the nervous system to emit a response which the nervous system has previously found difficult to emit. Lack of nervous system response interferes with the natural course of development of postural responses and those functions related to them. A prevailing professional opinion holds that the primitive postural responses must be integrated into the sensorimotor system before the ontogenetically more mature and normal postural reactions can develop. Stressing equilibrium reactions in the standing position prior to integration of the primitive reflexes may not be as effective in bringing about change in academic learning capacity as introduction of equilibrium reactions after the ontogenetically earlier postural responses are normalized.

Current principles involved in bringing about assimilation of the TNR are similar to those used to assimilate the TLR and to develop the basic normal postural responses. When the TNR is predominant it represents a tendency of the central nervous system toward a prevailing response to a given stimulus. To alter this tendency so that more mature postural responses are possible, the child is placed in the quadruped position, with the head rotated to the side and the arm toward which the jaw is facing flexed. The weight of the body is borne on the opposite hand, thus activating the positive supporting reaction in that hand. When one leg is lifted, equilibrium reactions are required to maintain balance. Both the positive supporting reaction and the equilibrium reactions in the quadruped position are more mature postural reactions which, by nature of their greater maturity, help integrate the primitive reaction. The reversed position of head and forearms tends to reduce the tendency of the muscle spindle to mediate the TNR. Thus, if this posture, which may be facilitated through vibration (and other proprioceptive means) is followed by an activity such as rolling, the turning of the head is less apt to activate the TNR and more apt to activate the neck-righting reflex or the body-righting reflex acting on the body. The neck-righting reflex consists of an automatic turning of the body from the supine to the prone position when the head is turned. Its emergence within the early months of life helps the child learn to roll over. When rolling over has been fairly well mastered on a mature level, the neck-righting reflex and body-righting reflex acting on the body become integrated so that rolling over is not triggered by the sensory input that activates these reflexes. In the therapeutic process, these reflexes are appropriately activated through rolling that replicates these early motor patterns. It is possible that the tendency for children with minimal brain dysfunction who have difficulty rotating on the longitudinal axis of the body may be related to a deficiency in the maturational stage during which the righting reflexes are predominant.

Continuing to follow the developmental sequence, the intervention program then involves the child in activities eliciting equilibrium reaction in the prone, quadruped, and seated positions. Protective extension of the arms is another important developmental milestone. While kneeling and squatting are not discrete phases in postural development, they are motor patterns which receive some emphasis in the therapeutic recapitulation of the developmental sequence of postural responses. Of less importance, equilibrium reactions in the standing position are elicited. It is essential that they not be emphasized before the earliest steps are mastered.

All of the procedures for developing more mature postural reactions have been described in greater detail elsewhere (Ayres 1972*b*).

The extraocular muscles are skeletal muscles and operate as part of the postural responses. It was noted earlier that during ontogeny, vestibular control of eye movement developed before visual control. The vestibular system, of course, is critical to the postural response system. All of the therapeutic endeavors directed toward normalization of the vestibular system and postural mechanisms also have a positive influence on the extraocular muscles at the same time. The cranial nerve nuclei that serve the extraocular muscles make direct connections with the vestibular and neck receptors. In turn, these connections enable eye muscles to enter into postural adjustment, simultaneously being normalized through the more normal postural responses. The capacity to direct the eyes accurately contributes to the effectiveness of visually directed responses, such as required in reading or crossing a street. For example, Zangwill and Blakemore (1972) recorded the eye movements of a twenty-three-year-old dyslexic subject as he tried to read. He made frequent fixational pauses with many regressive movements and had a strong tendency to scan from right to left. The investigators suggested that the eye movements might explain errors in the order of words and syllables when reading.

The neck muscles are key targets for remediation. In fetal development they are among the first muscles to respond. Neck muscles are especially involved in scooter board activity, in eliciting the neck-righting reflex, and in demanding equilibrium reaction in the prone, supine, and quadruped positions. These muscles are influenced by vestibular input (Brodal 1964), and, in turn, proprioception from the neck muscles has been found to be important in helping the brain to interpret vestibular functions. Cohen (1961) found that lower primates did not show equilibrium problems following detachment of extraocular muscles, but when the neck proprioceptors were anesthetized, they had severe problems in balance, orientation, and motor coordination. There is constant interaction among the extraocular muscles, vestibular system, and the neck muscles. The vestibular system is the mediator of the TLR and many of the righting and equilibrium reactions. These comments have special meaning in view of the fact that many learning disabled children show poor ability to stabilize their neck musculature.

The muscle spindle, which is intimately involved in all postural reactions, sends a great deal of information to the cerebellum where it is used to regulate, guide, and coordinate movement. The cerebellum also is concerned with the regulation of saccadic eye movement.

Developing Capacity to Motor Plan

Motor planning or praxis is dependent upon sensory integration. Developing praxis, then, is approached through attempts to normalize sensory processes and improve the capacity for skilled sensorimotor responses. Several principles discussed earlier guide therapy. The sensory systems that mature earliest receive emphasis. These systems provide input from the body for unconscious neural control of sensorimotor activity and to convergent neurons for intersensory association. Gross postural responses are elicited before more individuated skilled movements are required. Variety of activity is provided to promote growth of sensory integration in general and to develop a generalized ability to motor plan.

Enhancing neural integration through the tactile system is encouraged by rubbing the skin with cloth or a soft brush or involving the child in activities in which the skin comes in contact with a tactually stimulating surface. The procedure is recommended for some, but not all, children. Responses to tactile input varies widely among learning disabled children, and their responses should be respected and used as a guide for the appropriateness of the procedure.

Occasionally certain types of tactile stimuli or certain methods of stimulation are contraindicated. The apraxic child often has a low threshold to tactile stimuli and responds with irritation. The manner in which the receptors are activated helps determine how the brain interprets the stimulation. Lying on a rough carpet or wearing a wool sweater elicits an occasional light stimulus as the child moves. The child's brain may interpret the light stimulus as arousing and uncomfortable, but the same wool cloth rubbed against the skin with pressure provides the kind of tactile input that will tend to normalize the tactile system and reduce the discomfort of the tactile input. Some apraxic children are so tactually defensive that almost any rough texture leads to discomfort and a negative behavioral reaction. For those children a smooth-surfaced fabric is more appropriate than a coarse fabric.

Several concerns enter into the rationale for use of tactile stimuli to promote praxis. The skin is closely associated with muscle action from early in life. The first motor response in the human fetus is elicited by tactile stimulation. In fact, most of the fetal reflexes reported are elicited by exteroceptive stimuli of which touch is the main source (T. Humphrey 1969). Reflexes contribute to the basis for later skilled, differentiated tasks.

Tactile stimuli acting on the nervous system at levels below the cortex normally act upon the neural tracts in a manner which strengthens the ability to recognize form and contour (Jabbur and Banna 1970) and encourages exploratory movements that lead to further tactile input and information (Wall 1970; Wall and Dubner 1972).

The tactile system makes extensive connections with many associative zones in the cortex, cerebellum, thalamus, basal ganglia, and reticular formation. In these structures stimuli from different parts of the body converge to provide a basis for motor planning (see Albe-Fessard 1967). The motor cortex is one of these areas and is critical to mediation of the motor plan. Auditory and visual stimuli also project to the motor cortex (see Blakemore, Iverson, and Zangwill 1972).

Because of their pervasive and unifying effect, vestibular stimuli elicited through both gravity and movement are purposely included early in the development of motor planning ability. The proprioceptive input is usually the result of the activities in which the child engages, but it may be appropriate to provide vestibular input directly through the methods described earlier. Again, the child's response must be the guide. The young and disordered nervous system may be sensitive and unable to organize the input.

Enhancement of kinesthesia through joint receptor activation is approached through activities which involve joint compression and traction as well as cocontraction of antagonistic muscles. Ability to cocontract muscles is essential to the tonic response in muscles; the tonic response is an important aspect of postural reactions. Cocontraction also gives the stability proximally that enables skill in distal segments of the body. Since muscle spindles contribute to the sense of kinesthesis (Goodwin, McClosky, and Matthews 1972*a*, 1972*b*), those procedures described as effective in increasing spindle afferent discharge, such as tactile, vestibular, and vibratory stimulation, may enhance conscious perception of movement and position of the various anatomical segments.

With strengthened sensory integrative processes, the child is better able to master the basic gross motor patterns from which the finely individuated motor skills may be differentiated. The most basic motor patterns are, first, total flexion when in the supine position and second, extension when in the prone position. These positions are the same as those utilized to promote interhemispheral integration and may be activated the same way, but, in addition, portions of the basic flexion and extension synergies need to be repeated many times in a large variety of circumstances. *Synergy* refers to a group of muscles that work together to perform a given motion.

Portions of the flexor synergy or pattern are elicited in rocking back and forth while seated on a piece of equipment that rocks. The child should assist the rocking by holding on to some part of the equipment and pulling with his arms at the same time he flexes his neck and trunk. The flexor synergy is involved at a more advanced level when the child swings from a trapeze and with both feet knocks the top box off a tower of cartons. Variations of the extensor synergy are most easily elicited when the child rides a scooter board prone. In that position, he can be asked to ride down a ramp and reach up and touch an overhanging object as he goes under it. The protective extension of the arms is elicited when the child rolls crosswise over a barrel and catches himself by placing both hands on the floor.

Gross motor patterns that involve rotation of the trunk and diagonal motions of the extremities from one side of the body to the other were utilized by Kabat and Knott (1948) because the contraction of the muscles results in proprioceptive facilitation of the rest of the muscles in the synergy, particularly if resistance was given to the muscle contraction. Such facilitation will optimize the response and provide the brain with increased proprioceptive input from the musculature. Many learning disabled children are quite deficient in planning movement which involves rotation of the trunk; they tend to cross the midline of the body with difficulty.

Eliciting the gross diagonal patterns is recommended as part of the basic motor repertoire to be developed in the apraxic child. A simple method of eliciting gross diagonal patterns of motion in the upper extremities involves use of a small piece of wood with two handles on top and three ball-bearing casters on the bottom which allow the equipment to be moved freely across the floor. The child kneels, grasps the device with both hands, and moves it in a large figure eight that wraps around his body, requiring rotation of the trunk of the child. Rotation of the trunk activates the tonic lumbar reflex in such a way that when the right arm is in a position over the left leg, both of those extremities receive increased extensor tone. Rotation in the other direction facilitates extensor tone in the other extremities.

Activation of the tonic lumbar reflex (described in detail by Tokizane *et al.* 1951) may contribute to the reflex substrate of praxis. Easton (1972), a theoretical biologist, has suggested and supported with sound logic the concept that the postural reflexes, including such reactions as the placing and supporting reaction, "form the basic language of the motor program" (p. 598). Easton means that the central nervous system may use reflexes as the raw material to build the more complex volitional movements necessary for highly adaptive responses. Sensorimotor organization may even be based on reflexes—an economical and efficient use of these prearranged, stereotyped responses. Easton's observations and conclusions are consistent with observations of apraxic children. While there is undoubtedly a reflex substrate to most volitional acts, many automatic motor patterns are less accurately termed reflexes than centrally controlled motor patterns (see Schmitt, Adleman, Melnechuk, and Worden 1972). Not all motions have a reflex basis. Bruner (1970), for example, states that early hand skills do not come from earlier hand-arm reflexes.

As the basic flexor, extensor, and rotatory synergies become automatic, gross but more individuated partial movements of the body which require more motor planning are elicited through purposeful activity. An example of an activity which elicits considerable sensory input at the same time it requires a planned individuated motion superimposed on a more basic motor pattern is riding a scooter board down a ramp, coasting under a strip of inner tube (both ends of which are attached to stable points), and catching that inner tube strip with one leg flexed at the knee. A variety of similar scooter board activities are described elsewhere (Ayres 1972*b*), and variety is necessary to avoid training in "splinter skills" only. Variety also keeps the child interested and motivated; involvement is necessary for optimal brain development.

Only after the child has shown some mastery of the basic motor synergies is emphasis placed on planning simple actions that are not strongly supported on a sensory, automatic, or reflex basis. These activities should be simple at first and expect a non-habitual but natural motion. For example, standing with one's back to a hanging ball and kicking it poses a motor planning problem which may not be encountered when standing in front of it and kicking it. The latter position usually has been learned and no longer requires planning.

Activation of the postural reflexes and contraction of the neck muscles against resistance helps develop the extraocular muscle eye control frequently deficient in the apraxic child. Studies with split-brain humans (Gazzaniga 1970) show that eye position contributes a great deal to the overall accuracy of eye-hand tasks. The eye-hand task begins with a general orientation toward a stimulus involving eye, head, and neck position, and the feedback from these sources sets and resets the motor apparatus.

If these procedures for the development of praxis are successful, the child is then ready to be involved in manipulatory tasks and, finally, in drawing and writing.

Encouraging Interaction of the Two Sides of the Body and Space

If the postural reactions are normalized and the capacity to motor plan developed in a gross manner, the nervous system will automatically begin to integrate the function of the two sides of the body and body-centered space. (There are exceptions to this generalization, especially when unilateral disregard is part of the symptomatology.) As better bilateral coordination is made possible by maturation of prior developmental steps, especially maturation of the postural responses, the child often demonstrates an interest in simple bilateral activity. This increased ability and interest may be maximized by providing the child with activities which enable him to express this sensorimotor skill. The activity described as developing the ability to motor plan gross diagonal motor patterns is especially appropriate for this stage because of the proprioceptive facilitation achieved through activating the motor pattern which automatically involves one side of the body interacting with contralateral space.

Simple gross bilateral activities which require both hands to work together, either symmetrically or reciprocally, in similar motions are also appropriate. Many of the chalkboard exercises recommended by Kephart (1960) encourage bilateral sensorimotor integration. Waving flags bilaterally and across the midline is another example of the level of bilaterality of function that may need to be fostered.

Development of Form and Space Perception

Consistent with the concept of the developmental sequence, form and space perception are seen largely as an end product of sensorimotor integration. The neural processes concerned with this end product are rather closely related to the developmental steps concerned with postural responses and praxis. There are, however, some cases of poorly developed form and space perception that do not seem to fit into this conceptualization. Although the treatment of visual perception disorders entails attention to the previously described developmental steps, some recapitulation and elaboration of procedures and theoretical formulations underlying both procedures and research are in order.

Space perception is fundamental to all phyletic levels. Before an organism can relate itself to the environment, it must have some concept of space. In man, the concept of space begins with the vestibular system, activated by gravity and motion, conveying information to the brain. Information of vestibular derivation is soon followed by additional spatial information from the other proprioceptive and tactile receptors, all of which become associated with and contribute to meaningful visual reception. Vision, then, ultimately becomes one of the major ways by which the human organism relates himself to space. It is recognized, however, that many skilled movements attempted later in life are first directed visually and later kinesthetically.

Form and space perception are dependent upon both cortical and brain stem processes. The fact that many learning disabled children show symptoms of inadequate brain stem functions leads to placing emphasis on brain stem mechanisms in the therapeutic situation.

Cats with somatosensory tracts cut at the midbrain were found to have visual deficits (Sprague, Chambers, and Stellar 1961). The investigators concluded that visual functions may depend upon midbrain mechanisms receiving input over the somatosensory tracts. Schaefer (1970) noted that the brain stem visual areas are modified more by motor activity than the visual cortex. There is considerable evidence that active movement is important in the development of certain visual processes (Held 1968; Held and Hein 1963; Gleitman 1963; Eccles 1966). Furthermore, both Held (1968) and Trevarthen (1968) are convinced that visual feedback from actions is essential to integration of visual and motor processes attributed to the brain stem. In a study with kittens, Hein and Diamond (1972) found that visual direction of a paw was not learned until after visually directed locomotion in space was learned. The authors concluded that the visual feedback information was not meaningful until after the kittens had learned to direct themselves in body-centered space. They saw this succession of events as a normal developmental sequence. If the same sequence holds true in man, brain stem processes, including the motor component, should be utilized in therapy to promote the development of perception at the neocortex. The effect of enriched sensorimotor activity on the development of the rat visual cortex in the studies initiated by Rosenzweig and associates was cited earlier.

In view of the functional unity of locomotor, oculomotor, visual, vestibular, and other proprioceptive brain stem processes, the remedial procedures utilized for normalization of the vestibular mechanisms and of disordered postural and ocular mechanisms are the appropriate initial procedure for enhancing visual perception. This approach is particularly appropriate where there are other signs of poorly integrated brain stem function. It is also consistent with the principles of recapitulating the developmental process and enhancing organization of lower brain functions before higher brain functions.

In addition to the specific brain stem and neocortical visual processing structures, there are nonspecific brain stem influences on visual perception through the reticular formation. Buser's (1970) study of the research has led him to hypothesize that the nonspecific brain stem system has an essential role in visual processes such as pattern recognition, memorization, and association. Some of this influence is mediated through the lateral geniculate nucleus (Doty 1970), a subcortical visual structure which modifies the ongoing processing of visual stimuli. The excitability of the lateral geniculate nucleus is also modified by the superior colliculi of the midbrain and by activity in the vestibular nuclei (Doty 1970). Vestibular nuclei are, of course, activated by gravity and motion which, in turn, are determined by the position of the head in space and by movement.

It then follows that sensory input which influences the reticular nonspecific system can and will affect visual processing, probably at all levels. This fact necessitates production of optimal conditions in the reticular system through other sensory channels when directing therapy toward visual form and space perception. Movement is one of the means through which sensory input can help to normalize the nonspecific reticular system and, through it, visual processing at the lateral geniculate nucleus.

The role of the visual cortex is central to higher perceptual processes. In addition to the previously cited research which indicates some of the factors acting on the cortex, there are other influences to be considered. Most important is the recognition of the many different types of stimuli that act upon visual areas of the neocortex. Research in the laboratory of Jung (1961) and Jung, Kornhuber, and DaFonseca (1963) demonstrated that neurons in the visual cortex of cats show integration of information from the eye, the vestibular system, and the nonspecific reticulo-thalamic system. Vestibular stimulation activated 90 percent of the neurons in the cat's visual cortex. The investigators suggested that cortical neurons convergent for visual and vestibular stimuli were precoordinated in the brain stem.

The visual cortex also receives somatosensory input (Horn 1965). This association is not to be interpreted that all stimuli facilitate visual perception, for sometimes the experimental effect is not in that direction. That it can be facilitating is supported by an experiment by Sperry (1958) in which he found that the visual discrimination of cats was seriously impaired when somatosensory input to the cortex was prevented. The important point is that sensorimotor activity which gives rise to somatosensory and vestibular input has a varied and profound influence on cortical processing of visual stimuli.

Just as brain stem visual processes are closely associated with brain stem mediated motor activity, so also is cortical visual processing associated with cortically mediated motor activity, such as manipulatory motions. Trevarthen (1968) is among those who hold to this assumption. The fact that some of the neurons in the motor cortex respond to visual stimuli (Buser and Imbert 1961) suggests that motion is an integrator of visual stimuli. Another association of somatosensory input and cortical visual processing is suggested by Luria (1966). From a review of the literature and his own observations, he concluded that frontal lobe lesions which interfere with the function of the systems regulating the head, neck, and eyes will inevitably lead to disturbance of visual perception.

Additional aspects of visual perception and sensorimotor interrelationships are emerging as the role of the inferotemporal cortex in monkeys comes under exploration (for example, Kover and Stamm 1972; Wilson,

Kaufman, Zieler, and Lieb 1972). Attentional mechanisms appear to be involved. Wilson and colleagues (1972) cite Gross as suggesting that the inferotemporal cortex serves to integrate the two visual systems as described by Trevarthen. It seems likely that future research will reveal greater precision in the extension and manner in which sensorimotor integration in general influences the development of ongoing visual perception.

Types of Sensorimotor Dysfunction and their Specific Treatment

The effectiveness of intervention programs may be directly related to the degree to which they are specific to the type of dysfunction interfering with learning, yet these types are not clearly or consistently identified. In fact, clarifying the varying constellations of symptoms of sensory integrative problems appears to be the current stage of development of knowledge of sensorimotor dysfunction in learning disabled children.

Although the brain tends to function as a whole, there is sufficient differentiation among neural processes to result in different symptom complexes among children with learning disorders. It is difficult to associate any one type of dysfunction with low academic performance (see Walker 1965), suggesting that learning is dependent upon many different brain functions.

There is growing evidence that children with minimal brain dysfunction or learning disorders show different patterns of sensory integrative disorder (Clements 1966; Birch and Walker 1966; Ball and Wilsoncroft 1967; Satz, Rardin, and Ross 1971; Kalverboer 1971; Crinella and Dreger 1972; Crinella 1973; Silberzahn, unpublished study 1972; Bortner, Hertzig, and Birch 1972; Newcomer and Hammill 1973; and Ayres 1965, 1966, 1971, 1972*c*).

Categorizing, at this stage, varies largely with the orientation of the researcher, types of observations made, and the age and nature of the sample. Critchley (1968) differentiated only between "specific developmental dyslexia" as a "genetically determined constitutional disorder" and "developmental dyslexia" where there are other problems such as perceptual or postural problems.

Bannatyne and Wichiarajote (1969) identified three types of brains among fifty "normal" third-grade children: an efficient one; a less efficient one characterized by mirror imaging, verbal incompetence and left-handedness; and one that was visuospatially inept, but not necessarily given to mirror imaging. These authors thought the second type of brain may be caused by a maturation lag while the third type may result from minimal brain dysfunction. A similar suggestion of etiology was found by Silver and Hagin (1964), who identified a developmental group characterized by visual, tactile, and auditory perceptual deficits, right-left discrimination defect, and lack of clearly established cerebral dominance. A second "organic" group with similar deficits had additional evidence of organic defects. The Silver and Hagin grouping was similar to that of Ingram, Mason, and Blackburn (1970). A group with less evidence of brain damage or dysfunction had more trouble with reading and auditory phonic synthesis than in other academic areas, while the group with more positive neurological findings had more general learning problems.

Three types of syndromes have been proposed by Denckla (1972) from observations of learning disabled children: specific language disabilities; specific visuospatial problems including poor tactile perception and sometimes "strange" behavior; and dyscontrol syndrome. All three syndromes were considered to reflect neurological impairment. Crinella and Dreger (1972) identified syndromes of brain dysfunction as: high visuomotor integrity and fast manual reaction with relatively less skill in the serial synthetic and tactile-motor abilities; deficiencies "across the board" but especially in tactile-motor and visual-motor areas; and predominantly left-handed children with greatest deficiencies in general cognitive maturation with poor tactile-kinesthetic ability but good rhythmic skills. Most of the children with symptoms described by the second factor had confirmed neurological lesions. While categorization through factor analysis has been accomplished with young school-age children, it is reasonable to hypothesize that similar syndromes exist in younger children but the means to their identification are not known at this time.

It is clear that not only do learning disabled children vary in their symptomatology but also that attempts to differentiate the types of symptom constellations do not result in clear-cut types, easily identified from another professional orientation. Some common associations, however, are found by a number of investigators.

Repeated statistical analyses (Ayres 1965, 1966, 1969, 1971, 1972*c*; M. Silberzahn, unpublished study 1972) designed to identify the symptom complexes in learning disabled children have resulted in identification of reasonably consistent, but not mutually exclusive, syndromes found among learning disabled children. Interpreting these syndromes as neural systems provides a means of planning an intervention program to help normalize disorder in the system, thereby providing more effective sensory integrative foundations for learning. These neural systems, while sufficiently independent to show differential vulnerability, are nevertheless not completely discrete. A child with a disorder in one neural system is apt to have some disorder in another system, particularly if he is moderately or severely involved. Some neural systems seem to be more closely associated than others. The identification and differentiation of these syndromes is most easily accomplished in the child five through eight years of age, for this is an age when sensory integrative processes are in ascendancy in development and differentiation, and are easily evaluated objectively. The more subtle symptoms have not yet become obscured.

The neural system disorder most frequently observed in children with reading—and sometimes in other academic—disorders is concerned with the lack of integration of function of the two sides of the body, which is presumed to reflect inadequate communication between the two cerebral hemispheres. Related symptomatology includes disorder in postural and ocular mechanisms, and usually, but not invariably, auditory-language problems, poor right-left discrimination, and deficits in visual form and space perception. Deficits in visual form and space occur especially, but not only, in differentiating mirrored or rotated figures. This symptom complex shows similarities to the type of brain identified by Bannatyne and Wichiarajote (1969) as having a tendency to mirror imaging. There are also similarities between the syndrome characterized by lack of integration of function of the two sides of the body and the Ingram *et al.* (1970) group that showed less evidence of brain damage or dysfunction but trouble with reading and auditory phonic synthesis, to Silver and Hagin's "developmental" group, and Crinella's group with high visuomotor integrity but less skill in serial synthetic and tactile-motor abilities. Many of the procedures developed by Kephart (1960) and by Kaluger and Heil (1970) appear directed to remediation of disorder in this neural system.

Dysfunction in the neural subsystem subserving praxis results in similar symptoms, but the major problems lie in motor planning and disorder in tactile and less frequently kinesthetic perception. Integration of function of the two sides of the body and space are not a particular problem except insofar as apraxia interferes. Postural reactions are usually poorly developed and many visuospatial tasks are difficult, but differentiating mirror images is no more troublesome than other visual perception tasks. Auditory-language deficits may be present in the more severe cases but are not considered a symptom of this syndrome except as it affects articulation. Academic problems are of a general nature, as a rule. Clinical impression suggests that this syndrome is related to the third type of brain (visuospatially inept but not especially with mirror images) identified by Bannatyne and Wichiarajote (1969). The "organic" type recognized by Silver and Hagin (1964), Denckla's group (1972) with visuospatial and tactile disorders, and Ingram's (1970) group with more positive neurological findings are also related to the third type of brain.

While statistical analyses consistently link visual form and space perception as a factor identifiable from the other factors interpreted as neural syndromes, the special educational situation sees few children with isolated visual perception problems. This observation is consistent with attempts to differentiate types as reported by other investigators.

Disorder in these three neural subsystems—namely, those concerned with interhemispheral integration, praxis, and form and space perception—will be discussed in detail. Other syndromes, identified but not under discussion in this chapter, are: auditory-language problems not associated with lack of adequate communication between the two cerebral hemispheres; tactile defensiveness, which is associated with hyperactivity and distractibility; and unilateral disregard associated with other symptoms suggesting right hemisphere involvement. Discussion of tactile defensiveness and unilateral disregard may be found elsewhere (Ayres 1972*b*).

Deficit in Interhemispheral Integration

Bilateral symmetry of the body characterizes the simplest vertebrates as well as all of the higher animals. In man, the highest level of the vertebrate scale, the bilateral symmetry at the neocortical level gives way to asymmetry in order to localize function for greater specialization and adaptiveness. It appears that a disorder in this developmental step—among the highest and the latest in sensorimotor ontogeny—is involved in some learning problems. The more recently acquired evolutionary developments are more vulnerable to dysfunction.

That which has been gained in evolution supposedly represents a functional gain. The capacity to specialize function in the cerebral hemispheres, especially language and language-related auditory functions in the left cerebral hemisphere and visuospatial tasks in the right cerebral hemisphere, is generally considered an optimum neural basis for learning. Failure to establish "dominance" of one hemisphere for language and skilled hand usage has long been a controversial issue relative to learning disorders. The consequences of failure to specialize functions of the right hemisphere are possibly just as important but they are largely unrecognized at this time.

If it is assumed that specialization of function is important, then a corollary assumption holds that optimizing cerebral function is enabled only when the two cerebral hemispheres are free to differentiate and specialize because information from one hemisphere is available to the other. The simplest illustration of the need for interhemisphere communication is the tendency for visual functions to localize in the right hemisphere and language in the left hemisphere. Without communication between the two processes reading would be virtually impossible. Furthermore, each half of the visual field of each eye goes to a different hemisphere. Coordination of the two halves of the visual field from any one eye is dependent upon interhemispheral integration, most commonly attributed to the corpus callosum.

When the corpus callosum, a major means of communication between the two hemispheres, is congenitally absent, the performance of the individual suggests that both hemispheres tend to develop similar functions and that this method of neural organization is not as effective as having interhemispheral communication (Ettlinger, Blakemore, Milner, and Wilson 1972; Sperry 1970). Sperry (1970), who has specialized in the study of differences in function of the two cerebral hemispheres and their interaction, has pointed out that without the kind of cross-integrational functions enabled by the corpus callosum, the faculties that suffer are those associated with cerebral dominance, such as the lateral differentiation of higher mental processes, especially spatial orientation and abstract thinking.

Supporting evidence that children with reading problems have diminished localization of language and linguistic auditory functions in the left hemisphere comes from studies of dichotic listening (Zurif and Carson 1970; Bryden 1970) and tachistoscopic presentation of words to one visual field (Olson 1973). Dichotic listening studies also help confirm the localization of language in the left hemisphere and nonlanguage auditory perception in the right hemisphere in individuals who are right-handed (Knox and

Kimura 1970; Spreen, Spellacy, and Reid 1970; Netley 1972). Bryden (1970) found that the familial left-handers were somewhat less likely to be right ear (left hemisphere) dominant than non-familial left-handers in dichotic listening. Studies of individuals with total agenesis of the corpus callosum indicate a tendency toward left ear (right hemisphere) superiority. Partial agenesis has been found to lead to tendency toward right ear (left hemisphere) superiority, but in these cases handedness was mixed (Ettlinger, Blakemore, Milner, and Wilson 1972). Annett's finding (1970) that children with mixed handedness had lower vocabulary scores than those of consistent handedness also supports the need for lateralization of cerebral function for optimum language development.

The findings by Levine and Fuller (1972) that children with reading deficits had more trouble perceiving bilateral auditory, visual, and tactual stimuli than unilaterally presented stimuli could be related to poor interhemispheral integration. If the two hemispheres cannot work together, they are apt to interfere with each other (Kinsbourne 1972; Sperry 1970). If hemispheres cannot specialize in their functions, they are apt to develop similar functions.

Levy, Trevarthen, and Sperry (1972) reviewed a number of studies and interpreted the results to partially confirm the hypothesis that the tendency to develop language function in both hemispheres is done so at the expense of developing visual space perception, a frequent concomitant of learning disorder. It is advisable to consider the hypothesis that other higher functions attributed to the right hemisphere might also fail to develop optimally. These right hemisphere functions center around synthesizing visual and tactile stimuli from part to whole relationships and memory for tasks involving stimuli over those sensory channels (Blakemore, Iverson, and Zangwill 1972; Levy, Trevarthen, and Sperry 1972; Nebes 1972, 1973; De Renzi, Scotti, and Spinnler 1969; Corkin 1965; Gazzaniga 1970; Milner and Taylor 1972; Dee and Fontenot 1973). Furthermore, appositional thinking, or the ability to check or cross-check propositions, as well as creativity have been attributed to the right hemisphere (Bogen 1969*a*, 1969*b*; Bogen and Bogen 1969; Gazzaniga 1970). There may well be additional complex functions mediated through the right hemisphere which would have a better opportunity to mature if adequate opportunity for lateralization of function in the hemispheres were present.

Evidence from basic brain research suggests that inadequate interhemispheral communication resulting in each hemisphere's working independently slows the process of certain types of learning. Sechzer (1970) found that cats required at least twice as long to learn a visual or somatosensory task when only one hemisphere was learning the task as opposed to the normal intercommunication of both hemispheres through the unsectioned corpus callosum and the optic chiasma. The investigator suggested the results might be explained on the basis of the amount of brain tissue available for learning. Similarly, Dimond and Beaumont (1971) reported that when the perceptual load was distributed between the two cerebral hemispheres of college students, the total output was increased. The use of two information channels was superior to the use of one.

Interaction between the two hemispheres through the corpus callosum allows the two hemispheres to assist each other in somatosensory learning and resultant bilateral motor coordination (Deuel, Mishkin, and Semmes 1971; Preilowski 1972), but at higher levels of ideation and complex processes, each hemisphere may work independently (Lishman 1971). Clearly, interhemispheral integration is essential to lower functions as well as to higher functions.

In addition to the inferences made from the dichotic listening studies, there are other symptoms of lack of adequate integration of function of the two cerebral hemispheres of children with this syndrome. Using the two hands together in a coordinate manner is usually difficult (Ayres 1965). Such actions, of course, require interhemispheral communication. There is a tendency to avoid crossing the midline of the body with the hands and to use one hand on one side of the body and the other hand on the other. This tendency may contribute to the reduced inclination to establish strong hand dominance.

In one study (Ayres 1971) more left-handedness was found among children with disorder in this neural system than among children with apraxia. This difference is not so great, however, that it appears consistently or to a significant degree. If there is poor interhemispheral communication, it may be easier for the young child to draw and do other visuospatial tasks with his left hand than his right hand. When he is then presented with the necessity of learning to write, he may continue to use the hand that previously served him best for drawing. The idea is presented as highly conjectural but worthy of consideration when the question of hand dominance arises.

Chapman and Wedell (1972) reported that children who write with many reversals scored poorly on tests of crossing the midline of the body and on the Position in Space subtest of the Frostig Test. They scored relatively better on other types of perceptual-motor tests. Reversals in writing and difficulty with mirror image perception are considered likely symptoms of disorder in the neural system concerned with brain stem interhemispheral integration.

Kephart (1960) was one of the first clinicians to suggest that right-left discrimination or a sense of directionality developed only after the body was able to function as two integrated halves. One of the most consistently occurring non-motor indices of disorder in this neural system is difficulty in right-left discrimination (Ayres 1965, 1971). Silver and Hagin (1960), Belmont and Birch (1965), and Croxen and Lytton (1971) have found an association between right-left discrimination and reading disability, although Coleman and Deutsch (1964) failed to find such a relationship in children about ten years of age. Wechsler and Hagin (1964) found rotational errors were associated with reading achievement but that left-right rotation was not the most frequent type. Rosenblith's study (1965) suggests that perception of mirror image likenesses or differences is more difficult than perceiving up-down differences in general. In a profile analysis of symptoms associated with brain dysfunction, Crinella and Dreger (1972) found right-left discrimination, rail walking, rhythm tapping of both hands, and auditory-vocal functions shared variance. Problems in all of these parameters are typical of the child with poor interhemispheral integration.

These symptoms, which are interpreted as reflecting inadequate interhemispheral integration, lead to a search for the means by which interhemispheral communication occurs. There are two major means known by which the two cerebral hemispheres communicate with each other. The corpus callosum is essential for communication between the two cerebral cortices. That the two cerebral hemispheres also communicate through mechanisms in the brain stem has been recognized in recent years, especially in research with lower animals (Black and Myers 1965; Ebner and Myers 1962; Nelson and Lende 1965; Glickstein and Sperry 1960; Hamilton 1967; McCleary 1960; Trevarthen 1965; Rutledge 1965; and Mosidge, Rizhinashvili, Totibadze, Kevanishvili, and Akbardia 1971).

More specifically, at the midbrain level there are interneurons between the nuclei of cranial nerves III, IV, and VI that assist in eye movements. Observations of individuals with congenital absence of the corpus callosum show that the two hemispheres probably cross-communicate through other pathways which are most likely in the brain stem (Sperry 1970; Akelaitis 1943; and Ettlinger *et al.* 1972). Although the brain stem integrating mechanism is usually thought to be more limited in its capacity for complex functions than is the corpus callosum, others (Ettlinger *et al.* 1972; Doty 1966) hypothesize that bilateral interhemispheral integration of complex phenomena occurs in the midbrain reticular formation.

While the superior and inferior colliculi of the midbrain reach maturity a few months after birth (Prechtl 1971) and the postural mechanisms of the brain stem mature within the early years of life, the corpus callosum does not reach full myelinization before the seventh to tenth year of life (Prechtl 1971). The degree to which the maturation and function of the corpus callosum is dependent upon, or interdependent with, the brain stem interhemispheral integrating mechanism is not known, but one of the more consistent principles of neural processing is the functional dependence of higher neural structures upon lower neural structures.

It is proposed that the brain stem interhemispheral mechanism serves a critical role in this neural system and that it is frequently malfunctioning in the learning disabled child. This hypothesis derives not only from the data presented above but also from some of the symptoms that are almost invariably associated with this syndrome (Ayres 1965, 1969, 1971, 1972*c*; Rider 1972, 1973; and Silberzahn, unpublished study 1972). These symptoms include poorly integrated postural and oculomotor mechanisms which are mediated largely through the midbrain (see Denny-Brown 1962). The so-called primitive reflexes, especially the tonic neck and tonic labyrinthine reflexes, tend to be poorly assimilated into the sensorimotor system.

General professional opinion assumes that when these reflexes fail to become well integrated, their presence interferes with the maturation of more advanced and normal postural and equilibrium reactions (for example, see Bobath and Bobath 1955, 1964). These reflexes continue to be active in normal adulthood, but they contribute to, rather than interfere with, sensorimotor function.

Central to the theory and treatment of this syndrome is the postulate that the brain stem interhemispheral integrating mechanism is functionally associated with the brain stem postural reflexes and reactions and, furthermore, that inadequate maturation of the brain stem mediated postural reactions interferes with maturation of the interhemispheral integrative mechanism at that level. The resultant dysfunction interferes with the development of specialization of function in the cerebral cortex.

Since the major gap in the early developmental sequence in this syndrome lies in the maturation of the postural mechanisms, focus is placed at this point. The first step in obtaining a generalized sensory integration is emphasized according to the symptoms of the child. The second step, integrating function of the two sides of the body, is particularly pertinent to this syndrome. While the therapeutic emphasis may be on gross sensorimotor development, the objective is promoting higher cognitive functions.

The fact that learning disabled children receiving a remedial program based on this theoretical formulation improved in reading performance (Ayres 1972*a*) lends some support to the procedures. Kawar (1973) also found that a comparable therapeutic program increased the tendency for right ear (left hemishere) superiority in dichotic listening in learning disabled children, a result consistent with these formulations.

Developmental Apraxia

Apraxia is a disorder of encoding a new, as opposed to a habitual, motor response strategy. The difficulty in formulating the motor plan is considered primarily a reflection of inadequate sensory integration, especially of tactile and kinesthetic input. The motor centers of the brain may also be involved. Planning an unfamiliar task or one that never becomes automatic—such as writing—requires a sensorimotor awareness of the different anatomical elements of the body and their potential movements, especially in relation to each other. This internal postural model or body scheme is gradually built during the early years of life by associating the sensations from the body with motions and the results of those motions. The innate neural connections serving the postural reflexes and centrally patterned responses provide a foundation for the more cortically planned motions.

The body scheme is the neurophysiological substrate of which a person is generally only semiconscious and from which plans are formulated. It is an end-product of intersensory integration, a pool of experiences enabling an intact although constantly changing model from which any plan can be implemented. The body scheme is more than the sum of somatosensory input. It is an integration of that input. Schilder (1950) explored the concept in a comprehensive manner. "When the knowledge of our own body is incomplete and faulty, all actions for which this particular knowledge is necessary will be faulty too. We need the body image to start movements. We need it especially, when actions are directed towards our own body" (p. 45).

Of the sensory systems involved in the apraxic child, the discriminative tactile system is the most consistently deficient, but kinesthesis or the perception of joint position and movement is not infrequently poor (Ayres 1965, 1969, 1971, 1972*c*). Postural responses are usually poorly developed, suggesting involvement of the vestibular and possibly other proprioceptive systems.

Lacking adequate neural processing of tactile and kinesthetic input, the child has only a hazy idea as to the physical design and operation of his body. He has difficulty knowing where he is touched and the exact nature of the object he holds in his hand. He often cannot tell which finger is being touched without looking. The child with poor finger identification cannot be expected to use those fingers very dexterously.

The problem is not one of reduced awareness of sensation. In fact, many apraxic children have a lowered threshold to sensation. A similar association was found by Bell, Weller, and Waldrop (1971). In their study infants with low tactile threshold later showed clumsiness and incoordination. The apraxic child's difficulty is one of recognizing the spatial and temporal aspects of sensation. The hazy body scheme results in imprecise motor plans and a clumsiness in motor activity, such as that required in drawing, cutting, pasting, assembling, and in utilizing playground equipment. Yet the apraxic child can and does learn to perform specific tasks and in performing them tends to confuse the educator as to his capacity to undertake an unfamiliar motor task or the degree of effort required to accomplish it.

Even though lacking an adequately developed body scheme, the bright apraxic child can figure out how to peform a task using cognitive instead of perceptual-motor processes. Again the educator can mistake the child's ability and fail to recognize the large amount of effort necessitated in cognitive function. "He can do it if he tries!" may be correct, but trying is not the answer to the situation. Neither is destruction of the materials of the situation the answer, but it is an approach which an apraxic child commonly uses when his desire to play or work constructively does not result in the accomplishment he has in mind.

While the motor problem resulting from the sensory integrative dysfunction is fairly evident, of equal concern but less well understood is the association between the disordered sensory function and the behavior of the child. The neurological condition in itself results in the child's being especially vulnerable to the vicissitudes of life; the frustration encountered in attempting to deal with perceptual-motor tasks places further stress on a brain poorly prepared to cope in the first place.

As a sensory integrative problem, the first step in treating apraxia is obtaining better integration in the tactile and vestibular systems, followed by emphasis on improving proprioception. Since most apraxic children have poorly developed postural mechanisms, the next emphasis is on that area followed by helping the child engage in a considerable number of activities requiring motor planning.

Visual Form and Space Perception.

Identification of a visual perception problem is the easiest of sensory integrative problems to detect and hardly needs elaboration in this chapter. Although factor analyses show form and space perception as a separate functional unity, seldom is a child seen whose sensory integrative dysfunction is restricted to visual perception. These observations are consistent with the proposal that visual perception is one of the later developmental steps. As such, remediation of many (but not all) visual perception problems is largely attempted by treating the two syndromes with which it is most commonly found, namely, poor interhemispheral integration and apraxia. When found with unilateral disregard to the left, the situation is far more complex.

The earlier discussions on visual functions, both at the brain stem and neocortical levels, make it clear that any approach to enhancing visual perception must take into consideration the neurophysiological foundations that lie in motion and sensations associated with it. The appropriate sequence of steps in developing visual perception are: (a) normalization, insofar as is possible, of the reticular mechanisms through such stimuli as tactile, vestibular, and other proprioceptive input; (b) activating and bringing to appropriate maturity for the age of the child postural and ocular mechanisms mediated by the brain stem; (c) involving the neck musculature in contraction against resistance; (d) engaging in activities which relate the body to objects in space and provide extra sensory input from the body related to that activity; (e) eye-hand manipulatory activities involving form and space and space visualization; and (f) requiring differentiation of visual stimuli on the basis of a configuration or perception of a small focal area.

We are at the beginning, not at the end, of understanding sensorimotor processes and learning disorders. Ideas are new, highly theoretical, and individualistic. Few well-considered and comprehensive studies are available for checks and guides. The blossoming field of neurobiology offers data for use in understanding, but few professionals are prepared to utilize it, and those that are prepared find it difficult. But within the field of neurobiology may lie the best hope for increased knowledge of the means for remediation of the underlying conditions interfering with academic learning. It is a time to look forward to what may be accomplished, not backward to what has not been done.

REFERENCES

Aichele, R. L. "A Longitudinal Study of Predictive Validity of the Aichele Perceptual Motor Forms Copying Test." *Dissertation Abstracts* 32 (1972):3817-A–3818-A.

Akelaitis, A. J. "Studies on the Corpus Callosum: VII. Study of Language Functions (Tactile and Visual Lexia and Graphia) Unilaterally Following Section of the Corpus Callosum." *Journal of Neuropathology and Experimental Neurology* 2 (1943):226-62.

Albe-Fessard, D. "Organization of Somatic Central Projections." In *Contributions to Sensory Physiology,* edited by W. D. Neff. Vol. 2. New York: Academic Press, 1967.

———, and Fessard, A. "Thalamic Integrations and Their Consequences at the Telencephalic Level." In *Progress in Brain Research,* edited by G. Moruzzi, A. Fessard, and H. Jasper. Vol. 1. *Brain Mechanisms.* New York: Elsevier, 1963.

Alley, G. R., and Carr, D. "Effects of Systematic Sensory-Motor Training on Sensory-Motor, Visual Perception and Concept Formation Performance of Mentally Retarded Children." *Perceptual and Motor Skills* 27 (1968):451–56.

American Association of Health, Physical Education and Recreation. "Perceptual-Motor Development: Action with Interaction; Report of an AAHPER Conference." *Journal of Health, Physical Education and Recreation* 42 (1) (1971):36–39.

Andre-Thomas, and Autgaerden, S. *Locomotion from Pre- to Post-Natal Life.* Clinics in Developmental Medicine, No. 24. London: Heinemann, 1966.

———; Chesni, Y.; and Saint-Anne Dargassies, S. *The Neurological Examination of the Infant.* Little Club Clinics in Developmental Medicine, No. 1. London: National Spastics Society, 1960.

Annett, M. "The Growth of Manual Preference and Speed." *British Journal of Psychology* 61 (1970): 545–58.

August, I. "A Study of the Effect of a Physical Education Program on Reading Readiness, Visual Perception and Perceptual-Motor Development in Kindergarten Children." *Dissertation Abstracts International* 31 (1970):2212-A.

Auxter, D. "Evaluation of Perceptual Motor Training Programs." *Teaching Exceptional Children* 4 (1972):89–97.

Ayres, A. J. "Occupational Therapy Directed toward Neuromuscular Integration." In *Occupational Therapy,* edited by H. S. Willard and C. S. Spackman. 2nd ed. Philadelphia: Lippincott, 1963.

———. "Patterns of Perceptual-Motor Dysfunction in Children: a Factor Analytic Study." *Perceptual and Motor Skills* 20 (1965):335–68.

———. "Interrelationships among Perceptual-Motor Functions in Children." *American Journal of Occupational Therapy* 20 (1966):68–71.

———. "Deficits in Sensory Integration in Educationally Handicapped Children." *Journal of Learning Disabilities* 2 (3) (1969):160–68.

———. "Characteristics of Types of Sensory Integrative Dysfunction." *American Journal of Occupational Therapy* 25 (1971):329–34.

———. "Improving Academic Scores through Sensory Integration." *Journal of Learning Disabilities* (1972*a*):338–43.

———. *Sensory Integration and Learning Disorders.* Los Angeles: Western Psychological Services, 1972*b*.

———. "Types of Sensory Integrative Dysfunction among Disabled Learners." *American Journal of Occupational Therapy* 26 (1972*c*):13–18.

Ball, T. S., and Wilsoncroft, W. E. "Perceptual-Motor Deficits and the Phi Phenomenon." *American Journal of Mental Deficiency* 71 (1967):797–800.

Bannatyne, A. D., and Wichiarajote, P. "Hemispheric Dominance, Handedness, Mirror Imaging, and Auditory Sequencing." *Exceptional Children* 36 (1969):27–36.

Barsch, R. H. *Perceptual-Motor Curriculum.* Vol. 1. *Achieving Perceptual-Motor Efficiency.* Seattle: Special Child Publications, 1967.

Beck, R., and Talkington, L. W. "Frostig Training with Headstart Children." *Perceptual and Motor Skills* 30 (1970):521–22.

Beery, J. W. "Matching of Auditory and Visual Stimuli by Average and Retarded Readers." *Child Development* 38 (1967):827–33.

Beintema, D. J. *A Neurological Study of Newborn Infants.* Clinics in Developmental Medicine, No. 28. London: Heinemann, 1968.

Bell, R. Q.; Weller, G. M.; and Waldrop, M. F. "Newborn and Preschooler: Organization of Behavior and Relations between Periods." *Monographs of the Society for Research in Child Development* 36 (1–2, Whole No. 142) (1971).

Belmont, I.; Birch, H. G.; and Karp, E. "The Disordering of Intersensory and Intrasensory Integration by Brain Damage." *Journal of Nervous and Mental Disease* 141 (4) (1965):410–18.

———; Flegenheimer, H.; and Birch, H. G. "Comparison of Perceptual Training and Remedial Instruction for Poor Beginning Readers." *Journal of Learning Disabilities* 6 (1973):230–35.

Bennett, E. L.; Diamond, M. C.; Krech, D.; and Rosenzweig, M. R. "Chemical and Anatomical Plasticity of Brain." *Science* 146 (1964):610–19.

Bental, E.; Dafny, N.; and Feldman, S. "Convergence of Auditory and Visual Stimuli on Single Cells in the Primary Visual Cortex of Unanesthetized Unrestrained Cats." *Experimental Neurology* 20 (1968):341–51.

Bergström, R. M. "Electrical Parameters of the Brain during Ontogeny." In *Brain and Early Development,* edited by R. J. Robinson. New York: Academic Press, 1969.

Berlucchi, G.; Sprague, J. M.; Levy, J.; and DiBerardino, A. C. "Pretectum and Superior Colliculus in Visually Guided Behavior and in Flux and Form Discrimination in the Cat." *Journal of Comparative and Physiological Psychology Monograph* 78 (1) (1972):123–72.

Beter, T. R. "The Effects of a Concentrated Physical Education Program and an Auditory and Visual Perceptual Reading Program upon Academic Achievement, Intelligence, and Motor Fitness of Educable Mentally Retarded Children." *Dissertation Abstracts International* 30 (11-A) (1970):4706–707.

Bibace, R., and Hancock, K. "Relationships between Perceptual and Conceptual Cognitive Processes." *Journal of Learning Disabilities* 2 (1969):17–29.

Birch, H. G., and Belmont, I. "Perceptual Analysis and Sensory Integration in Brain-Damaged Persons." *Journal of Genetic Psychology* 105 (1964):173–79.

———, and Belmont, L. "Auditory-Visual Integration in Normal and Retarded Readers." *American Journal of Orthopsychiatry* 34 (1964):852–61.

———, and Belmont, L. "Auditory-Visual Integration in Brain-Damaged and Normal Children." *Developmental Medicine and Child Neurology* 7 (1965*a*):135–44.

———, and Belmont, L. "Auditory-Visual Integration, Intelligence and Reading Ability in School Children." *Perceptual and Motor Skills* 20 (1965*b*):295–305.

———, and Lefford, A. "Visual Differentiation, Intersensory Integration, and Voluntary Motor Control." *Monographs of the Society for Research in Child Development* 32 (2, Whole No. 110) (1967).

———, and Walker, H. A. "Perceptual and Perceptual-Motor Dissociation." *Archives of General Psychiatry* 14 (1966):113–18.

Bishop, J. S.; Gayton, W. F.; and Bassett, J. E. "An Investigation of the Efficacy of the Frostig Program for the Development of Visual Perception." *Pediatrics* 50 (1972):154–57.

Bizzi, E., and Evarts, E. V. "Translational Mechanisms between Input and Output." In *Neurosciences Research Symposium Summaries*, edited by F. O. Schmitt, G. Adelman, T. Melnechuk, and F. G. Worden. Vol. 6. Cambridge, Mass.: MIT Press, 1972.

Black, P., and Myers, R. E. "A Neurological Investigation of Eye-Hand Control in the Chimpanzee. Ciba Foundation Study Group No. 20." In *Functions of the Corpus Callosum*, edited by E. G. Ettlinger. London: Churchill, 1965.

Blakemore, C.; Iverson, S. D.; and Zangwill, O. L. "Brain Functions." *Annual Review of Psychology* 23 (1972):413–58.

Bobath, K. *The Motor Deficit in Patients with Cerebral Palsy*. Clinics in Developmental Medicine, No. 23. London: Heinemann, 1966.

———, and Bobath, B. "Tonic Reflexes and Righting Reflexes in Diagnosis and Assessment of Cerebral Palsy." *Cerebral Palsy Review* 16 (5) (1955):3–10, 26.

———, and Bobath, B. "The Facilitation of Normal Postural Reactions and Movements in the Treatment of Cerebral Palsy." *Physiotherapy* (England) 50 (8) (1964):246–62.

Bogen, J. E. "The Other Side of the Brain I: Dysgraphia and Dyscopia Following Cerebral Commissurotomy." *Bulletin of the Los Angeles Neurological Societies* 34 (1969*a*):73–105.

———. "The Other Side of the Brain II: An Appositional Mind." *Bulletin of the Los Angeles Neurological Societies* 34 (1969*b*):135–62.

———, and Bogen, G. M. "The Other Side of the Brain III: The Corpus Callosum and Creativity." *Bulletin of the Los Angeles Neurological Societies* 34 (1969):191–220.

Bortner, M.; Hertzig, M. E.; and Birch, H. G. "Neurological Signs and Intelligence in Brain-Damaged Children." *Journal of Special Education* 6 (1972):325–32.

Bower, T. G. R. "Perceptual Functioning in Early Infancy." In *Brain and Early Behavior*, edited by R. J. Robinson. New York: Academic Press, 1969.

Brain, W. R. "On the Significance of the Flexor Posture of the Upper Limb in the Hemiplegic, with an Account of the Quadrupedal Extensor Reflex." *Brain* 50 (1927):113–37.

———. "Some Reflections on Brain and Mind." *Brain* 86 (1963):381–402.

Brodal, A. "Anatomical Organization and Fiber Connections of the Vestibular Nuclei." In *Neurological Aspects of Auditory and Vestibular Disorders*, edited by W. S. Fields and B. R. Alford. Springfield, Ill.: Thomas, 1964.

Bronson, G. "Vision in Infancy: Structure-Function Relationships." In *Brain and Early Behavior*, edited by R. J. Robinson. New York: Academic Press, 1969.

Brown, C. P., and King, M. G. "Developmental Environment: Variables Important for Later Learning and Changes in Cholinergic Activity." *Developmental Psychobiology* 4 (1971):275–86;

Brown, J. L. "The Frostig Program for the Development of Visual Perception in Relation to Visual Perception Ability and Reading Ability." *Dissertation Abstracts International* 30 (11-A) (1970):4872.

Brown, L. S. "Good and Retarded Readers Compared According to Performance on Visual-Motor, Simulated Language Learning and Memory Tasks." *Dissertation Abstracts International* 31 (1971):7566-B–67-B.

Brown, T. S., and Berkson, G. "Orienting Response of Kittens with Lesions of the Superior Colliculus." *Psychonomic Science* 18 (1970):153–54.

Bruner, J. S. "The Growth and Structure of Skill." In *Mechanisms of Motor Skill Development*, edited by K. Connolly. New York: Academic Press, 1970.

Bryden, M. P. "Laterality Effects in Dichotic Listening: Relations with Handedness and Reading Ability in Children." *Neuropsychologia* 8 (1970):443–50.

———. "Auditory-Visual and Sequential-Spatial Matching in Relation to Reading Ability." *Child Development* 43 (1972):824–32.

Buckland, P., and Balow, B. "Effect of Visual Perceptual Training on Reading Achievement." *Exceptional Children* 39 (1973):299–304.

Budde, E. H. "The Relationship between Performance of Kindergarten Children on Selected Motor Tests and the Metropolitan Readiness Tests—Otis-Lennon Mental Ability Test." *Dissertation Abstracts International* 31 (1971): 5820A–21A.

Buser, P. "Nonspecific Visual Projections." In *Early Experience and Visual Information Processing in Perceptual and Reading Disorders,* edited by F. A. Young and D. B. Lindsley. Washington, D. C.: National Academy of Sciences, 1970.

______, and Imbert, M. "Sensory Projections to the Motor Cortex in Cats: A Microelectrode Study." In *Sensory Communication,* edited by W. A. Rosenblith. New York: Wiley, 1961.

Carmichael, L. "The Onset and Early Development of Behavior." In *Carmichael's Manual of Child Psychology,* edited by P. H. Mussen. Vol. 1. New York: Wiley, 1970.

Casaer, P., and Akiyama, Y. "Neurological Criteria for the Estimation of the Post-Menstrual Age of Newborn Infants." In *Normal and Abnormal Development of Brain and Behavior,* edited by G. B. A. Stoelinga and J. J. Van der Werff ten Bosch. Baltimore: Williams and Wilkins, 1971.

Chapman, L. J., and Wedell, K. "Perceptual-Motor Abilities and Reversal Errors in Children's Handwriting." *Journal of Learning Disabilities* 5 (1972):321–25.

Charlton, N. W., II. "An Investigation of Selected Visual-Perceptual and Motor Parameters of Young Trainable Mentally Retarded Children." *Dissertation Abstracts International* 32 (1971):271A.

Chasey, W. C., and Wyrick, W. "Effect of a Gross Motor Developmental Program on Form Perception Skills of Educable Mentally Retarded Children." *Research Quarterly: American Association of Health, Physical Education and Recreation* 41 (1970):345–52.

Chissom, B. S. "A Factor-Analytic Study of the Relationship of Motor Factors to Academic Criteria for First- and Third-Grade Boys." *Child Development* 42 (1971):1133–43.

Clements, S. "Syndromes of Minimal Brain Dysfunction in Children: A Multidisciplinary Concern." In *Perceptual-Motor Dysfunction, Evaluation and Training. Proceedings of Occupational Therapy Seminar.* Madison, Wisc., June 1966.

Cohen, L. "Role of Eye and Neck Proprioceptive Mechanisms in Body Orientation and Motor Coordination." *Journal of Neurophysiology* 24 (1961):2–11.

Coleman, R. I., and Deutsch, C. P. "Lateral Dominance and Right-Left Discrimination: A Comparison of Normal and Retarded Readers." *Perceptual and Motor Skills* 19 (1964):43–50.

Connolly, K., ed. *Mechanisms of Motor Skill Development.* New York: Academic Press, 1970.

Corkin, S. "Tactually Guided Maze Learning in Man: Effects of Unilateral Cortical Excisions and Bilateral Hippocampal Lesions." *Neuropsychologia* 3 (1965):339–51.

Cornish, R. D. "Effects of Neurological Training on Psychomotor Abilities of Kindergarten Children." *Journal of Experimental Education* 39 (1970):15–19.

Costin, A.; Hafeman, D.; Elazar, Z.; and Adey, W. R. "Posture and the Role of Vestibular and Proprioceptive Influences on Neocortical, Limbic, Subcortical and Cerebeller EEG Activity." *Brain Research* 17 (1970):259–75.

Cratty, B. J. *Some Educational Implications of Movement.* Seattle: Special Child Publications, 1970.

______. *Active Learning: Games to Enhance Academic Abilities.* Englewood Cliffs, N.J.: Prentice-Hall, 1971.

______; Ikeda, N.; Martin, Sister M. M.; Jennett, C.; and Morris, M. *Movement Activities, Motor Ability and the Education of Children.* Springfield, Ill.: Thomas, 1970.

Crinella, F. M. "Identification of Brain Dysfunction Syndromes in Children through Profile Analysis: Patterns Associated with So-called 'Minimal Brain Dysfunction.' " *Journal of Abnormal Psychology* 82 (1973):33–45.

Crinella, F. M., and Dreger, R. M. "Tentative Identification of Brain Dysfunction Syndromes in Children through Profile Analysis." *Journal of Consulting and Clinical Psychology* 38 (2) (1972):251–60.

Critchley, M. *Developmental Dyslexia.* London: Heinemann, 1964.

Croxen, M. E., and Lytton, H. "Reading Disability and Difficulties in Finger Localization and Right-Left Discrimination." *Developmental Psychology* 5 (1971):256–62.

Dee, H. L., and Fontenot, D. J. "Cerebral Dominance and Lateral Differences in Perception and Memory." *Neuropsychologia* 11 (1973):167–73.

deHirsch, K., and Janksy, J. J. "Early Prediction of Reading Disability." In *Dyslexia: Diagnosis and Treatment of Reading Disorders,* edited by A. H. Keeney and V. T. Keeney. St. Louis: Mosby, 1968.

Delacato, C. H. *The Treatment and Prevention of Reading Problems.* Springfield, Ill.: Thomas, 1959.

———. *The Diagnosis and Treatment of Speech and Reading Problems.* Springfield, Ill.: Thomas, 1963.

DeLong, M. "Central Patterning of Movement." In *Neurosciences Research Symposium Summaries,* edited by F. O. Schmitt, G. Adelman, T. Melnechuk, and F. G. Worden. Vol. 6. Cambridge, Mass.: MIT Press, 1972.

Denckla, M. B. "Clinical Syndromes in Learning Disabilities." *Journal of Learning Disabilities* 5 (1972):401–406.

Denhoff, E.; Hainsworth, P. K.; and Siqueland, M. L. "The Measurement of Psychoneurological Factors Contributing to Learning Efficiency." *Journal of Learning Disorders* 1 (1968):636–44.

Denny-Brown, D. "The Midbrain and Motor Integration." *Proceedings of the Royal Society of Medicine* 55 (1962): 527–38.

DeRenzi, E.; Scotti, G.; and Spinnler, H. "Perceptual and Associative Disorders of Visual Recognition." *Neurology* 19 (1969): 634–42.

Deuel, R. K.; Mishkin, M.; and Semmes, J. "Interaction betweer the Hemispheres in Unimanual Somesthetic Learning." *Experimental Neurology* 30 (1971): 123–38.

Deutsch, C. "Patterns of Perceptual, Language, and Intellective Performance in Children with Cognitive Deficits." Final Report of Project No. 32-42-0920-1009, U.S. Office of Education, Bureau of Research, 1971. Mimeographed.

Dimond, S., and Beaumont, G. "Use of Two Cerebral Hemispheres to Increase Brain Capacity." *Nature* 232 (5308) (1971): 270–71.

Doman, R. J.; Spitz, E. B.; Zucman, E.; Delacato, C. H.; and Doman, G. "Children with Severe Brain Injuries." *Journal of the American Medical Association* 174 (1960): 257–62.

Doty, R. W. "On Butterflies in the Brain." *Abstract for Symposium on Higher Nervous Activity.* IVth World Congress of Psychiatry. Madrid, 1966.

———. "Modulation of Visual Input by Brain-Stem Systems." In *Early Experience and Visual Information Processing in Perceptual and Reading Disorders,* edited by F. A. Young and D. B. Lindsley. Washington, D.C.: National Academy of Sciences, 1970.

Drillien, C. M. "Abnormal Neurologic Signs in the First Year of Life in Low-Birthweight Infants: Possible Prognostic Significance." *Developmental Medicine and Child Neurology* 14 (1972): 575–84.

DuBois, N. F. "Selected Relationships between Reading Achievement and Visual Perceptual, Visual Motor and Intersensory Integration Abilities in a 2nd and 4th Grade Population." *Dissertation Abstracts International* 32 (1972): 3858A.

Dunsing, J., and Kephart, N. C. "Motor Generalizations in Space and Time." In *Learning Disorders,* edited by J. Hellmuth. Vol. 1. Seattle: Special Child Publications, 1965.

Easton, T. A. "On the Normal Use of Reflexes." *American Scientist* 60 (1972): 591–99.

Eaves, L. C.; Kendall, D. C.; and Crichton, J. U. "The Early Detection of Minimal Brain Dysfunction." *Journal of Learning Disabilities* 5 (1972): 454–62.

Ebner, F. F., and Myers, R. E. "Direct and Transcallosal Induction of Touch Memories in the Monkey." *Science* 138 (1962): 51–52.

Eccles, J. C. "Conscious Experience and Memory." In *Brain and Conscious Experience,* edited by J. C. Eccles. New York: Springer-Verlag, 1966.

Egan, D. F.; Illingworth, R. S.; and MacKeith, R. C. *Developmental Screening 0–5 Years.* Clinics in Developmental Medicine, No. 30. London: Heinemann, 1969.

Ettlinger, G.; Blakemore, C. B.; Milner, A. D.; and Wilson, J. "Agenesis of the Corpus Callosum: A Behavioural Investigation." *Brain* 95 (1972): 327–46.

Fair, C. M. "The Organization of Memory Functions in the Vertebrate Nervous System." *Neuroscience Research Program Bulletin* 3 (1) (1965): 27–62.

Ferinden, W. E., Jr.; Van Handel, D.; and Kovalinsky, T. "A Supplemental Instructional Program for Children with Learning Disabilities." *Journal of Learning Disorders* 4 (1971): 193–203.

Fessard, A. "The Role of Neuronal Networks in Sensory Communications within the Brain." In *Sensory Communication* edited by W. A. Rosenblith. New York: Wiley, 1961.

Fiorentino, M. R. *Normal and Abnormal Development.* Springfield, Ill.: Thomas, 1972.

Fisher, K. L. "Effects of a Structured Program of Perceptual-Motor Training on the Development and School Achievement of Educable Mentally Retarded Children." *Dissertation Abstracts International* 31 (1970): 1618A.

Fisher, M. D., and Turner, R. V. "Effects of a Perceptual-Motor Training Program upon the Academic Readiness of Culturally Disadvantaged Kindergarten Children." *Journal of Negro Education* 41 (1972): 142–50.

Footlik, S. W., for Reading Research Foundation, Inc. "Perceptual-Motor Training and Cognitive Achievement: A Survey of the Literature." *Journal of Learning Disabilities* 3 (1) (1970): 40–49.

Fowler, W., and Leithwood, K. A. "Cognition and Movement: Theoretical, Pedagogical and Measurement Considerations." *Perceptual and Motor Skills* 32 (1971): 523–32.

Fox, M. W. "Reflex Development and Behavioral Organization." In *Developmental Neurobiology,* edited by W. Himwich. Springfield, Ill.: Thomas, 1970.

Frostig, M., in association with Maslow, P. *Movement Education: Theory and Practice.* Chicago: Follett, 1970.

———, and Horne, D. *The Frostig Program for the Development of Visual Perception.* Chicago: Follett, 1964.

Gamsky, N. R., and Lloyd, F. W. "A Longitudinal Study of Visual Perceptual Training and Reading Achievement." *Journal of Educational Research* 64 (1971): 451–54.

Gazzaniga, M. S. *The Bisected Brain.* New York: Appleton-Century-Crofts, 1970.

Gesell, A.; Halverson, H. M.; Thompson, H.; Ilg, F. L.; Castner, B. M.; Ames, L. B.; and Amatruda, C. S. *The First Five Years of Life.* New York: Harper, 1940.

Gibson, E. J. "The Development of Perception as an Adaptive Process." *American Scientist* 58 (1970): 98–107.

Gleitman, H. "Place-Learning." *Scientific American* 209 (1963): 116–22.

Glickstein, M., and Sperry, R. W. "Intermanual Somesthetic Transfer in Split-Brain Rhesus Monkeys." *Journal of Comparative and Physiological Psychology* 53 (1960): 322–27.

Goodwin, G. M.; McCloskey, D. I.; and Matthews, P. B. C. "The Persistence of Appreciable Kinesthesia after Paralysing Joint Afferents but Preserving Muscle Afferents." *Brain Research* 37 (1972*a*): 326–29.

———; McCloskey, D. I.; and Matthews, P. B. C. "Proprioceptive Illusions Induced by Muscle Vibration: Contributions by Muscle Spindles to Perception?" *Science* 175 (1972*b*): 1382–84.

Gordon, B. "The Superior Colliculus of the Brain." *Scientific American* 227 (1972): 72–82.

Granit, R. *The Basis of Motor Control.* New York: Academic Press, 1970.

Grant, W. W.; Boelsche, A.; and Zin, D. "Developmental Patterns of Two Motor Functions." *Developmental Medicine and Child Neurology* 15 (1973): 171–77.

Halliwell, J. W., and Solan, H. A. "The Effects of a Supplemental Training Program on Reading Achievement." *Exceptional Children* 38 (1972): 613–20.

Hamburger, V. "The Beginnings of Co-ordinated Movements in the Chick Embryo." In *Growth of the Nervous System,* edited by G. E. W. Wolstenholme and M. O'Connor. Ciba Foundation Symposium. Boston: Little, Brown, 1968.

———. "Embryonic Motility in Vertebrates." In *The Neurosciences: Second Study Program,* edited by F. O. Schmitt. New York: Rockefeller University Press, 1970.

Hamilton, C. R. "Effects of Brain Bisection on Eye-Hand Coordination in Monkeys Wearing Prisms." *Journal of Comparative and Physiological Psychology* 64 (1967): 434–43.

Hammill, D. "Training Visual Perceptual Processes." *Journal of Learning Disabilities* 5 (1972): 552–59.

Haring, N. G., and Stables, J. M. "The Effect of Gross Motor Development on Visual Perception and Eye-Hand Coordination." *Journal of the American Physical Therapy Association* 46 (1966): 129–35.

Harkins, D. W. "The Effect of a Motor Development Program on Motor and Intellectual Abilities of Trainable Mentally Retarded Children." *Dissertation Abstracts International* 31 (1971): 3991A.

Haworth, M. A. P. "The Effect of Rhythmic-Motor Training and Gross-Motor Training on the Reading and Handwriting Abilities of Educable Mentally Retarded Children." *Dissertation Abstracts International* 31 (1971): 3991A–92A.

Hedges, W. D., and Hardin, V. B. "Effects of a Perceptual-Motor Program on Achievement of First Graders." *Educational Leadership* 30 (1972): 249–53.

Hein, A., and Diamond, R. M. "Locomotory Space as a Prerequisite for Acquiring Visually Guided Reaching in Kittens." *Journal of Comparative and Physiological Psychology* 81 (1972): 394–98.

Held, R. "Dissociation of Visual Functions by Deprivation and Rearrangement." *Psychologische Forschung* 31 (1968): 338–48.

———. "Two Modes of Processing Spatially Distributed Visual Stimulation." In *The Neurosciences: Second Study Program,* edited by F. O. Schmitt. New York: Rockefeller University Press, 1970.

Held, R., and Hein, A. "Movement-Produced Stimulation in the Development of Visually Guided Behavior." *Journal of Comparative and Physiological Psychology* 56 (1963): 872–76.

Herrick, C. J. *The Evolution of Human Nature.* Austin: University of Texas Press, 1956.

Hertzig, M. E.; Bortner, M.; and Birch, H. G. "Neurologic Findings in Children Educationally Designated as 'brain-damaged'." *American Journal of Orthopsychiatry* 39 (3) (1969): 437–46.

Horn, G. "The Effect of Somaesthetic and Photic Stimuli on the Activity of Units in the Striate Cortex of Unanaesthetized, Unrestrained Cats." *Journal of Physiology* 179 (1965): 263–77.

Humphrey, N. K. "What the Frog's Eye Tells the Monkey's Brain." *Brain, Behavior and Evolution* 3 (1970): 324–37.

Humphrey, T. "Postnatal Repetition of Human Prenatal Activity Sequences with Some Suggestions of Their Neuroanatomical Basis." In *Brain and Early Behavior,* edited by R. J. Robinson. New York: Academic Press, 1969.

Hurlock, E. B. *Child Development.* 5th ed. New York: McGraw-Hill, 1972.

Illingworth, R. S. *An Introduction to Developmental Assessment in the First Year of Life.* Little Club Clinics in Developmental Medicine, No. 3. London: National Spastics Society, 1962.

Ingram, T. T. S.; Mason, A. W.; and Blackburn, I. "A Retrospective Study of 82 Children with Reading Disability." *Developmental Medicine and Child Neurology* 12 (1970): 271–81.

Ismail, A. H., and Gruber, J. J. *Integrated Development, Motor Aptitude and Intellectual Performance.* Columbus, Ohio: Merrill, 1967.

Jabbur, S. J., and Banna, N. R. "Widespread Cutaneous Inhibition in Dorsal Column Nuclei." *Journal of Neurophysiology* 32 (1970): 616–24.

Jessen, M. S. "Reflections on Research Related to Reading Readiness." *Journal of the California State Federation, Council for Exceptional Children* 19 (2) (1970): 19–21.

Jung, R. "Neuronal Integration in the Visual Cortex and Its Significance for Visual Information." In *Sensory Communication,* edited by W. A. Rosenblith. New York: Wiley, 1961.

———; Kornhuber, H. H.; and Da Fonseca, J. S. "Multisensory Convergence on Cortical Neurons." In *Progress in Brain Research,* edited by G. Moruzzi, A. Fessard, and H. H. Jasper. Vol. 1. *Brain Mechanisms.* New York: Elsevier, 1963.

Kabat, H., and Knott, M. "Principles of Neuromuscular Re-education." *Physical Therapy Review* 28 (1948): 107–11.

Kalakian, L. H. "Predicting Academic Achievement from Perceptual-Motor Efficiency in Educable Mentally Retarded Children." *Dissertation Abstracts International* 32 (1971): 3122A.

Kaluger, G., and Heil, C. L. "Basic Symmetry and Balance—Their Relationship to Perceptual-Motor Development." *Progress in Physical Therapy* 1 (1970): 132–37.

Kalverboer, A. F. "Observations of Free-Field Behaviour in Preschool Boys and Girls in Relation to Neurological Findings." In *Normal and Abnormal Development of Brain and Behavior,* edited by G. B. A. Stoelinga and J. J. Van der Werff ten Bosch. Baltimore: Williams & Wilkins, 1971.

Kannegieter, R. B. "The Results of a Perceptual-Motor-Cognitive Learning Program Designed for Normal Preschool Children." *American Journal of Occupational Therapy* 24 (1970): 208–14.

Karamyan, A. I. "On the Evolution of the Integrative Activity of the Central Nervous System in the Phylogeny of Vertebrates." In *Progress in Brain Research,* edited by E. A. Asratyan. Vol. 22. *Brain Reflexes.* New York: Elsevier, 1968.

Kass, E. "Learning Disabilities." *Review of Educational Research* 39 (1) (1969): 71–82.

Kaufman, A. S., and Kaufman, N. L. "Tests Built from Piaget's and Gesell's Tasks as Predictors of First-Grade Achievement." *Child Development* 43 (1972): 521–35.

Kawar, M. "The Effects of Sensorimotor Therapy on Dichotic Listening in Children with Learning Disabilities." *American Journal of Occupational Therapy* 27 (1973): 226–31.

Keim, R. P. "Visual-Motor Training, Readiness, and Intelligence of Kindergarten Children." *Journal of Learning Disabilities* 5 (3) (1970): 256–59.

Kephart, N. C. *The Slow Learner in the Classroom.* Columbus, Ohio: Merrill, 1960.

———. "On the Value of Empirical Data in Learning Disability." *Journal of Learning Disabilities* 4 (7) (1971): 393–95.

Kessen, W.; Haith, M.; and Salapatek, P. H. "Human Infancy: A Bibliography and Guide." In *Carmichael's Manual of Child Psychology,* edited by P. H. Mussen. Vol. 1. New York: Wiley, 1970.

Kinsbourne, M. "Eye and Head Turning Indicates Cerebral Lateralization." *Science* 176 (1972): 539–41.

Knox, C., and Kimura, D. "Cerebral Processing of Nonverbal Sounds in Boys and Girls. *Neuropsychologia* 8 (1970): 227–37.

Korner, A. F., and Thoman, E. B. "The Relative Efficacy of Contact and Vestibular-Proprioceptive Stimulation in Soothing Neonates." *Child Development* 43 (1972): 443–53.

Kover, R., and Stamm, J. S. "Description of Short-Term Visual Memory by Electrical Stimulation of Inferotemporal Cortex in the Monkey." *Journal of Comparative and Physiological Psychology* 81 (1972): 163–72.

Lauten, D. A. H. "The Relationship between Intelligence and Motor Proficiency in the Intellectually Gifted Child." *Dissertation Abstracts International* 31 (1970): 1521B.

Lavin, C. M. "The Effect of a Structured Sensory-Motor Training Program on Selected Cognitive and Psycholinguistic Abilities of Preschool Disadvantaged Children." *Dissertation Abstracts International* 32 (1972): 1984A–85A.

Lefford, A. "Sensory, Perceptual and Cognitive Factors in the Development of Voluntary Actions." In *Mechanisms of Motor Skill Development*, edited by K. Connolly. New York: Academic Press, 1970.

Leithwood, K. A., and Fowler, W. "Complex Motor Learning in Four-Year-Olds." *Child Development* 42 (1971): 781–92.

Levine, M., and Fuller, G. "Psychological, Neuropsychological, and Educational Correlates of Reading Deficit." *Journal of Learning Disabilities* 5 (1972): 563–71.

Levy, J.; Trevarthen, C.; and Sperry, R. W. "Perception of Bilateral Chimeric Figures Following Hemispheric Deconnexion." *Brain* 95 (1972): 61–78.

Le Winn, E. B. *Human Neurological Organization.* Springfield, Ill.: Thomas, 1969.

Lewis, F. D.; Bell, D. B.; and Anderson, R. P. "Relationship of Motor Proficiency and Reading Retardation." *Perceptual and Motor Skills* 31 (1970): 395–401.

Lipton, E. D. "Perceptual-Motor Development Program's Effect on Visual Perception and Reading Readiness of First-Grade Children." *Research Quarterly, American Association of Health, Physical Education and Recreation* 41 (1970): 402–405.

Lishman, W. A. "Emotion, Consciousness and Will after Brain Bisection in Man." *Cortex* 7 (1971): 181–92.

Lisina, M. I., and Neverovich, Ya. Z. "Development of Movements and Formation of Motor Habits." In *The Psychology of the Preschool Child*, edited by A. V. Zaporozhets and D. B. Elkonin. Cambridge, Mass.: MIT Press, 1971; Moscow, 1964.

Luria, A. R. *Human Brain and Psychological Processes.* New York: Harper & Row, 1966.

Malehorn, H. A. "Some Effects of Specific Visual-Motor Training on the Perceptual Development of Kindergarten Children." *Dissertation Abstracts International* 31 (1971): 3173A–74A.

Maloney, M. P. "An Analysis of the Generalizability of Sensory-Motor Training." *Dissertation Abstracts International* 30 (3-B) (1969): 1362–63.

Masland, R. H.; Chow, K. L.; and Stewart, D. L. "Receptive-Field Characteristics of Superior Colliculus Neurons in the Rabbit." *Journal of Neurophysiology* 34 (1971): 148–56.

McCleary, R. A. "Type of Response as a Factor in Interocular Transfer in the Fish." *Journal of Comparative and Physiological Psychology* 53 (1960): 311–21.

McCormick, C. C., and Schnobrich, J. N. "Perceptual-Motor Training and Improvement in Concentration in a Montessori Preschool." *Perceptual and Motor Skills* 32 (1971): 71–77.

———; Schnobrich, J. N.; Footlik, S. W.; and Poetker, B. "Improvement in Reading Achievement through Perceptual-Motor Training." *Research Quarterly: American Association for Health, Physical Education and Recreation* 39 (1968): 627–33.

McGraw, M. *The Neuromuscular Maturation of the Human Infant.* New York: Columbia University Press, 1945.

McIlwain, J. T. "Central Vision: Visual Cortex and Superior Colliculus." In *Annual Review of Physiology*, edited by J. H. Comroe, A. C. Giese, and R. R. Sonnenschein. Vol. 34. Palo Alto, Calif.: Annual Reviews, 1972.

McLees, M. P. "The Effectiveness of Activities Designed to Improve Basic Perceptual-Motor Patterns for Increasing Achievement among Seventh Grade Remedial Reading Pupils." *Dissertation Abstracts International* 31 (1970): 2190A.

McRaney, K. A. "A Study of Perceptual Motor Exercises Utilized as an Early Grade Enrichment Program for the Improvement of Learning Activity and Motor Development." *Dissertation Abstracts International* 31 (1971): 3935A–36A.

Meckler, R. S. "The Effects of Perceptual-Motor Training on the Development of Fine Motor Proficiency of Trainable Mentally Retarded Adolescents." *Dissertation Abstracts International* 32 (1972): 1946A–47A.

Melzack, R.; Konrad, K. W.; and Dubrovsky, B. "Prolonged Changes in Central Nervous System Activity Produced by Somatic and Reticular Stimulation." *Experimental Neurology* 25 (1969): 416–28.

Milani-Comparetti, A., and Gidoni, E. A. "Routine Developmental Examination in Normal and Retarded Children." *Developmental Medicine and Child Neurology* 9 (5) (1967): 631–38.

Milner, B., and Taylor, L. "Right-hemisphere Superiority in Tactile Pattern-Recognition after Cerebral Commissurotomy: Evidence for Nonverbal Memory." *Neuropsychologia* 10 (1972): 1–15.

Mosidze, V. M.; Rizhinashvili, R. S.; Totibadze, N. K.; Kevanishvili, Z. Sh.; and Akbardia, K. K. "Some Results of Studies on Split Brain." *Physiology and Behavior* 7 (1971): 763–72.

Mussen, P. H., *Carmichael's Manual of Child Psychology*. 3rd ed. New York: Wiley, 1970.

Nebes, R. D. "Dominance of the Minor Hemisphere on Commissurotomized Man in a Test of Figural Unification." *Brain* 95 (1972): 633–38.

———. "Perception of Spatial Relationships by the Right and Left Hemispheres in Commissurotomized Man." *Neuropsychologia* 11 (1973): 285–89.

Nelson, L. R., and Lende, R. A. "Interhemispheric Responses in the Opossum." *Journal of Neurophysiology* 28 (1965): 189–99.

Netley, C. "Dichotic Listening Performance of Hemispherectomized Patients." *Neuropsychologia* 10 (1972): 233–40.

Newcomer, P., and Hammill, D. "Visual Perception of Motor Impaired Children: Implications for Assessment." *Exceptional Children* 39 (1973): 335–37.

Norfleet, M. A. "The Bender-Gestalt as a Group Screening Instrument for First Grade Reading Potential." *Journal of Learning Disabilities* 6 (1973): 383–88.

O'Donnell, P. A., and Eisenson, J. "Delacato Training for Reading Achievement and Visual-Motor Integration." *Journal of Learning Disabilities* 2 (9) (1969): 441–47.

Olson, M. "Laterality Differences in Tachistoscopic Word Recognition in Normal and Delayed Readers in Elementary School." *Neuropsychologia* 11 (1973): 343–50.

O'Neill, H. "A Study of the Attitudinal Reflexes of Magnus and de Kleijn in Thalamic Man." *Archives of Otolaryngology* 43 (1946): 243–82.

Paine, R. J., and Oppé, T. E. *Neurological Examination of Children.* Clinics in Developmental Medicine, No. 20/21. London: Heinemann, 1966.

Pal'tsev, Ye. I., and El'ner, A. M. "Change in Reflex Reaction of Human Muscles during Adequate Vestibular Stimulation." *Kosmicheskaya Biologiya i Meditsina* (USSR) 6 (2) (1972): 61–66.

Papoušek, H. "The Development of Higher Nervous Activity in Children in the First Half-Year of Life." In *Monographs of the Society for Research in Child Development*, edited by P. Mussen. 30 (2, Serial No. 100) (1965): 102–11.

Patrinakou, E. D. "A Study of the Effect of Motor Perceptual Training on Cognitive Abilities in Slow Learning Children with Implications for Educational Planning." *Dissertation Abstracts International* 31 (1970): 2220A.

Paxinos, G., and Bindra, D. "Rewarding Intracranial Stimulation, Movement and the Hippocampal Theta Rhythm." *Physiology and Behavior* 5 (1970): 227–31.

Piaget, J. *The Origins of Intelligence in Children.* New York: International Universities Press, 1952.

Plack, J. J. "An Evaluation of the Purdue Perceptual Motor Survey as a Predictor of Academic and Motor Skills." *Dissertation Abstracts International* 31 (1971): 5184A.

Pomerleau-Malcuit, A., and Clifton, R. K. "Neonatal Heart-Rate Response to Tactile, Auditory, and Vestibular Stimulation in Different States." *Child Development* 44 (1973): 485–96.

Prechtl, H. F. R. "The Problems for Study." In *Brain and Early Behavior,* edited by R. J. Robinson. New York: Academic Press, 1969.

———. "Motor Behaviour in Relation to Brain Structure." In *Normal and Abnormal Development of Brain and Behavior,* edited by G. B. A. Stoelinga and J. J. Van der Werff ten Bosch. Baltimore: Williams & Wilkins, 1971.

———, and Beintema, D. *The Neurological Examination of the Full Term Newborn Infant.* Little Club Clinics in Developmental Medicine, No. 12. London: Heinemann, 1964.

Preilowski, B. F. B. "Possible Contribution of the Anterior Forebrain Commissures to Bilateral Motor Coordination." *Neuropsychologia* 10 (1972): 267–77.

Pryzwansky, W. B. "Effects of Perceptual-Motor Training and Manuscript Writing on Reading Readiness Skills in Kindergarten." *Journal of Educational Psychology* 68 (1972): 110–15.

Pyfer, J. F., and Carlson, R. "Characteristic Motor Development of Children with Learning Disabilities." *Perceptual and Motor Skills* 35 (1972): 291–96.

Reitan, R. M. "Sensorimotor Functions in Brain-Damaged and Normal Children of Early School Age." *Perceptual and Motor Skills* 33 (1971): 655–64.

Rice, J. A. "Feasibility of Perceptual-Motor Training for Headstart Children: An Empirical Test." *Perceptual and Motor Skills* 34 (1972): 909–10.

Richards, W. "Motion Detection in Man and Other Animals." *Brain, Behavior and Evolution* 4 (1971): 162–81.

Richardson, R. E. "Effects of Motor Training on Intellectual Function, Social Competency, Body Image, and Motor Proficiency of Trainable Mentally Retarded Children." *Dissertation Abstracts International* 31 (1970): 2764A.

Rider, B. A. "Relationship of Postural Reflexes to Learning Disabilities." *American Journal of Occupational Therapy* 26 (1972): 239–43.

———. "Perceptual-Motor Dysfunction in Emotionally Disturbed Children." *American Journal of Occupational Therapy* 27 (1973): 316–20.

Riege, W. H. "Environmental Influences on Brain and Behavior of Year-Old Rats." *Developmental Psychobiology* 4 (1971): 157–67.

Riesen, A. H. "Studying Perceptual Development Using the Technique of Sensory Deprivation." *Journal of Nervous and Mental Disease* 132 (1961): 21–25.

Riss, W. "Overview of the Design of the Central Nervous System and the Problem of the Natural Units of Behavior." *Brain, Behavior and Evolution* 1 (1968): 124–31.

Robbins, M. P. "A Study of the Validity of Delacato's Theory of Neurological Organization." *Exceptional Children* 32 (1966): 517–23.

Rosenblith, J. F. "Judgments of Simple Geometric Figures by Children." *Perceptual and Motor Skills* 21 (1965): 947–90.

Rosenzweig, M. R. "Environmental Complexity, Cerebral Change, and Behavior." *American Psychologist* 21 (1966): 321–32.

———, and Bennett, E. L. "Cerebral Changes in Rats Exposed Individually to an Enriched Environment." *Journal of Comparative and Physiological Psychology* 80 (2) (1972): 304–13.

———; Bennett, E. L.; and Diamond, M. C. "Brain Changes in Response to Experience." *Scientific American* 226 (2) (1972): 22–29.

———; Bennett, E. L.; and Diamond, M. C. "Effects of Differential Experience on Dendritic Spine Counts in Rat Cerebral Cortex." *Journal of Comparative and Physiological Psychology* 82 (1973): 175–81.

———; Krech, D.; Bennett, E. L.; and Diamond, M. C. "Effects of Environmental Complexity and Training on Brain Chemistry and Anatomy: A Replication and Extension." *Journal of Comparative Physiology and Psychology* 55 (1962): 429–37.

Rutledge, L. J. "Facilitation: Electrical Response Enhanced by Conditional Excitation of Cerebral Cortex." *Science* 148 (1965): 1246–48.

Rutter, M.; Graham, P.; and Yule, W. *A Neuropsychiatric Study in Childhood.* Clinics in Developmental Medicine, Nos. 35/36. London: Heinemann, 1970.

Saint-Anne Dargassies, S. "Neurodevelopmental Symptoms during the First Year of Life." *Developmental Medicine and Child Neurology* 14 (1972): 235–64.

Satz, P.; Rardin, D.; and Ross, J. "An Evaluation of a Theory of Specific Developmental Dyslexia." *Child Development* 42 (1971): 2009–21.

Schaefer, K. P. "Unit Analysis and Electrical Stimulation in the Optic Tectum of Rabbits and Cats." *Brain, Behavior and Evolution* 3 (1970): 222–40.

Scheich, H., and Simonova, O. "Parameters of Alpha Activity during the Performance of Motor Tasks." *Electroencephalography and Clinical Neurophysiology* 31 (1971): 357–63.

Schilder, P. "The Vestibular Apparatus in Neurosis and Psychosis." *Journal of Nervous and Mental Disease* 78 (1933): 1–23, 137–64.

———. *The Image and Appearance of the Human Body.* New York: International Universities Press, 1950.

Schmitt, F. O.; Adelman, G.; Melnechuk, T.; and Worden, F. G., eds. *Neurosciences Research Symposium Summaries.* Vol. 6. Cambridge, Mass.: MIT Press, 1972.

Sechzer, J. A. "Prolonged Learning and Split-Brain Cats." *Science* 169 (1970): 889–92.

Sherrington, C. S. *The Integrative Action of the Nervous System.* New Haven, Conn.: Yale University Press, 1906.

———. *Man on His Nature.* Garden City, N.Y.: Doubleday, 1955; first published 1940.

Silver, A. A., and Hagin, R. "Specific Reading Disability: Delineation of the Syndrome and Relationship to Cerebral Dominance." *Comprehensive Psychiatry* 1 (1960): 126–34.

———, and Hagin, R. A. "Specific Reading Disability: Follow-up Studies." *American Journal of Orthopsychiatry* 34 (1) (1964): 95–102.

Simons, A. "Head Posture and Muscle Tone: Clinical Observations." Abstracted by Signe Brunnstrom. *Physical Therapy Review* 28 (1953): 102–106.

Skubic, V., and Anderson, M. "The Interrelationship of Perceptual-Motor Achievement and Intelligence in Fourth Grade Children." *Journal of Learning Disabilities* 3 (8) (1970): 413–20.

Sommers, P. A.; Joiner, L. M.; Holt, L.; and Gross, J. C. "Reaction Time, Agility, Equilibrium, and Kinesio-perceptual Matching as Predictors of Intelligence." *Perceptual and Motor Skills* 31 (1970): 460–62.

Sperry, R. W. "Neurology and the Mind-Brain Problem." *American Scientist* 40 (1952): 291–312.

———. "Physiological Spasticity and Brain Circuit Theory." In *Biological and Biochemical Bases of Behavior,* edited by H. F. Harlow and C. N. Woolsey. Madison: University of Wisconsin Press, 1958.

———. "Cerebral Dominance in Perception." In *Early Experience and Visual Information Processing in Perceptual and Reading Disorders,* edited by F. A. Young and D. B. Lindsley. Washington, D.C.: National Academy of Sciences, 1970.

Spinelli, D. N.; Starr, A.; and Barrett, T. "Auditory Specificity in Unit Recordings from Cat's Visual Cortex." *Experimental Neurology* 22 (1968): 75–84.

Sprague, J. M.; Berlucchi, G.; and Di Bernardino, A. "The Superior Colliculus and Pretectum in Visually Guided Behavior and Visual Discrimination in the Cat." *Brain, Behavior and Evolution* 3 (1970): 285–94.

———; Chambers, W. W.; and Stellar, E. "Attentive, Affective, and Adaptive Behavior in the Cat." *Science* 133 (1961): 165–73.

Spreen, O.; Spellacy, F. J.; and Reid, J. R. "The Effect of Interstimulus Interval and Intensity on Ear Asymmetry for Nonverbal Stimuli in Dichotic Listening." *Neuropsychologia* 8 (1970): 245–50.

Sterling, P., and Wickelgren, B. G. "Function of the Projection from the Visual Cortex to the Superior Colliculus." *Brain, Behavior and Evolution* 3 (1970): 210–18.

Stockmeyer, S. A. "An Interpretation of the Approach of Rood to the Treatment of Neuromuscular Dysfunction." *American Journal of Physical Medicine* 46 (1) (1967): 900–56.

Sullivan, J. "The Effects of Kephart's Perceptual-Motor Training on a Reading Clinic Sample." *Journal of Learning Disabilities* 5 (1972): 545–51.

Talkington, L. W. "Frostig Visual Perceptual Training with Low-Ability-Level Retarded." *Perceptual and Motor Skills* 27 (1968): 505–506.

Thompson, R. F.; Patterson, M. M.; and Teyler, T. J. "The Neurophysiology of Learning." *Annual Review of Psychology.* Vol. 23. Palo Alto, Calif.: Annual Reviews, 1972.

Tokizane, T.; Murao, N.; Ogata, T.; and Kondo, T. "Electromyographic Studies on Tonic Neck, Lumbar and Labyrinthine Reflexes in Normal Persons." *Japanese Journal of Physiology* 2 (1951): 130–46.

Touwen, B. C. L. "A Study in the Development of Some Motor Phenomena in Infancy." *Developmental Medicine and Child Neurology* 13 (1971): 435–46.

———, and Prechtl, H. F. R. *The Neurological Examination of the Child with Minor Nervous Dysfunction.* Clinics in Developmental Medicine, No. 38. London: Heinemann, 1970.

Trevarthen, C. "Functional Interactions between the Cerebral Hemispheres of the Split-Brain Monkey." Ciba Foundation Study Group No. 20. In *Functions of the Corpus Callosum,* edited by E. G. Ettlinger. London: Churchill, 1965.

———. "Two Mechanisms of Vision in Primates." *Psychologische Forschung* 31 (1968): 299–337.

———. "Experimental Evidence for a Brain Stem Contribution to Visual Perception in Man." *Brain, Behavior and Evolution* 3 (1970): 338–52.

Upchurch, W. B. "The Relationship between Perceptual-Motor Skills, and Word Recognition Achievement at the Kindergarten Level." *Dissertation Abstracts International* 32 (1972): 4497A.

Vande Voort, L.; Senf, G. M.; and Benton, A. L. "Development of Audiovisual Integration in Normal and Retarded Readers." *Child Development* 43 (1972): 1260–72.

Volokhov, A. A. "The Ontogenetic Development of Higher Nervous Activity in Animals." In *Developmental Neurobiology,* edited by W. Himwich. Springfield, Ill.: Thomas, 1970.

Voneida, T. J. "Behavioral Changes Following Midline Section of the Mesencephalic Tegmentum in the Cat and Monkey." *Brain, Behavior and Evolution* 3 (1970): 241–60.

Walker, M. "Perceptual, Coding, Visuomotor and Spatial Difficulties and Their Neurological Correlates: A Progress Note." *Developmental Medicine and Child Neurology* 7 (1965): 543–48.

Wall, P. "The Sensory and Motor Role of Impulses Travelling in the Dorsal Columns towards Cerebral Cortex." *Brain* 93 (1970): 505–24.

———, and Dubner, R. "Somatosensory Pathways." In *Annual Review of Physiology,* edited by J. H. Comroe, A. C. Giese, and R. R. Sonnenschein. Vol. 34. Palto Alto, Calif.: Annual Reviews, 1972.

Walsh, J. F., and D'Angelo, R. "Effectiveness of the Frostig Program for Visual Perception Training with Headstart Children." *Perceptual and Motor Skills* 32 (1971): 944–46.

Walsh, R. N.; Budtz-Olsen, O. E.; Penny, J. E., and Cummins, R. A. "The Effects of Environmental Complexity on the Histology of the Rat Hippocampus." *Journal of Comparative Neurology* 137 (1969): 361–66.

Washburn, S. L., and Harding, R. S. "Evolution of Primate Behavior." In *The Neurosciences: Second Study Program,* edited by F. O. Schmitt. New York: Rockefeller University Press, 1971.

Wechsler, D., and Hagin, R. A. "The Problem of Axial Rotation in Reading Disability." *Perceptual and Motor Skills* 19 (1964): 319–26.

Wedell, K.; Newman, C. V., Reid, P., and Bradbury, I. R. "An Exploratory Study of the Relationship between Size Constancy and Experience of Mobility in Cerebral Palsied Children." *Developmental Medicine and Child Neurology* 14 (1972): 615–20.

Wenzel, B. M., and Salzman, A. "Olfactory Bulb Ablation or Nerve Section and Behavior of Pigeons in Nonolfactory Learning." *Experimental Neurology* 22 (1968): 472–79.

Wilbarger, P., ed., for the Goleta Union School District. *The Identification, Diagnosis and Remediation of Sensorimotor Dysfunction in Primary School Children.* Final report of Project 5127, ESEA, Title III, P.L. 89–10, 1971.

Wilson, M.; Kaufman, H. M.; Zieler, R. E.; and Lieb, J. P. "Visual Identification and Memory in Monkeys with Circumscribed Inferotemporal Lesions." *Journal of Comparative and Physiological Phychology* 78 (1972): 173–83.

Yemel'yahov, M. D., and Razumeyev, A. N. "Role of Higher Autonomic Centers in the Mechanisms of Vestibular-Autonomic Reflexes." *Kosmicheskaya Biologiya i Meditsina* (USSR) 6 (1972): 55–61.

Zangwill, O. L., and Blakemore, C. "Dyslexia: Reversal of Eye Movements during Reading." *Neuropsychologia* 10 (1972): 371–73.

Zaporozhets, A. V. "The Development of Perception in the Preschool Child." In *European Research in Cognitive Development,* edited by P. H. Mussen. *Monographs of the Society for Research in Child Development* 30 (2, Serial No. 100) (1965): 82–101.

Zurif, E. B., and Carson, G. "Dyslexia in Relation to Cerebral Dominance and Temporal Analysis." *Neuropsychologia* 8 (1970): 351–61.

Editors' note: In the writings of some of the major theorists in the field of learning disabilities there is an intimate association noted between the areas of visual perception and motor development. Dr. Newell Kephart, most notably, based his treatment approach for children with perceptual-motor problems on the construct of the "Perceptual-Motor Match."

Dr. John W. Gyr presents a unique perspective on the interrelationship between visual and motor processes. While much of the research literature reviewed is based on adult studies, the implications for perceptual and motor development are important. Animal studies are also reviewed as they pertain to the issue of visual perception's relation to motor development.

Because of the technical nature of this chapter, footnotes have been provided to define terms.

John W. Gyr, Ph.D., is a Research Psychologist at the Mental Health Research Institute, Department of Psychiatry, at the University of Michigan, where he received his doctorate. In 1968, Dr. Gyr received a Killiam Fellowship at the Center for Advanced Study in Theoretical Psychology, University of Alberta. He is an Editorial Consultant for *Behavioral Science, Journal of Experimental Child Psychology, Journal of Personality and Social Psychology,* and *Psychological Review.* His research interests include computer simulation and cognitive development.

9

The Relationship Between Motor and Visual-Sensory Processes in Perception

JOHN W. GYR

This chapter discusses research aiming to show that motor and visual-sensory processes interact to produce percepts. Related issues, like developmental stages in perception or the dynamics of perceptual development, are not discussed, though these problems are not skirted entirely.

In addition to an introduction, the material in the chapter is divided into three main sections. The first section is designed to show that theories of visual perception which exclude the role played in perception by nonoptic events having to do with the organism's motor activity are limited theories of perception. That is, the former theories cannot account for a significant set of known perceptual effects.

Attempting to show that perception can be accounted for by purely optic parameters has, of course, always been very seductive to a large proportion of the fraternity of psychologists. The variables one has to deal with from the point of reference of such a more limited theory are relatively easy to observe and to control experimentally, and the internal psychobiological models one must assume are also simpler and more in accord with conventional S-R thinking (Teuber 1964). Alternatively, postulating an interaction between motor and sensory processes in perception leads to the need to consider additional experimental variables and requires the assumption of more complex psychobiological models. Whereas the former theories at best assume a retina-to-visual cortex pathway in the brain with certain by now fairly well-known properties, the latter theories are required to talk, in addition, about motor areas of the cortex and about motor-sensory connections and feedback. These latter processes and connections have, until recently, been relatively unexplored and are ill understood. The second section of the chapter presents some of the results of research which demonstrate that the assumptions about internal brain systems made by theorists who look on perception as a sensorimotor process appear not to be unreasonable even though they may be wrong in some of their details.

(The first and second sections of the chapter represent updated and modified versions of an earlier published paper of Gyr in 1972.)

In addition to showing how well a given theory of perception predicts specific perceptual events, or to indicating the extent to which it makes reasonable assumptions, a theory can also be evaluated by other criteria. These additional criteria are concerned with how well a given theory fits what might be called the epistemological *Zeitgeist*. Questions that can be raised in this regard are whether a theory perpetuates supposedly outmoded Mechanistic, Empiricistic, Vitalistic, or Positivistic models, or whether it falls in line with supposedly more current approaches to knowledge, such as, for example, structuralism[1] (for a definition of the latter see, for example, Piaget 1970). The third section of the chapter attempts to show that, not only are sensorimotor theories of perception in accord with a large amount of psychological data, they also appear to fit the criteria of wholeness, transformation, and self-regulation invoked by modern structuralism. Invoking the criterion of structuralism makes explicit two assumptions advanced here. One is that the introduction of epistemological issues is germane to the evaluation of a specific psychological theory. The other assumption is that modern theories of psychology should be structural. Bringing epistemology into the evaluation of a theory is to argue that a theory must not only fit the facts in its own special domain, but that it must be in harmony with some meta theory, which in this case is a meta theory of natural phenomena.

INTRODUCTION

The sensorimotor approach to perception is an approach which may be contrasted with theories which have been concerned mostly with the detailed analysis of the optic array for predicting specific perceptual events and which generally have not been interested in studying whether, with the optic array constant, other nonoptic events produce specifiably different perceptual effects—or, further, whether varying either optic or nonoptic parameters, singly or in combination, results in different perceptual effects in each case. More generally, the approach in this chapter is in contrast with what might be called purely visual-sensory theories of perception, that is, theories which restrict their attention to properties of the optic array or of the retina and/or the pathway from retina to visual cortex.

The beginnings of a broader approach to perception, which recognizes a role for motor movements in perception, can be seen in Gibson's (1966) theory—a theory of perception in which motor mechanisms figure in the procurement of stimuli. Gibson discusses the idea that ambient optic array[2] information is not available to a motorically passive organism but that it

[1]Structuralism is concerned with principles which will unify science. Structuralism suggests that, speaking very abstractly, the principles of *wholeness, transformation,* and *self-regulation* will accomplish these ends. For definitions of the latter terms see footnote 20, p. 386.

[2]Ambient optic array is Gibson's (1966) term for the dense interlocking network of light rays that are generated by reflecting surfaces in a visual environment.

must be obtained by active movements of the eyes, head, limbs, or body. For example, he argues that motion parallax cues can induce the perception of depth and that these cues obtain when the head moves, thereby causing near objects to move across the retina at a faster rate than far objects. Likewise, a cue for movement of the observer is a transformation with occlusion effects[3] of the total optic array. More generally, in all of perception, the visual information needs to be obtained by an actively moving eye or head. Gibson argues against the conception of a one-way visual system and stresses the circular character of the perceptual process in which retinal inputs lead to ocular adjustments and, in turn, to altered retinal inputs. Gibson even explores—to an extent—the properties of such a circular system. Thus, for example, he states that successive inputs under successive scans comprise a mathematical group, that is, that among other things, the same structure persists throughout the series. At this point, Gibson seems to say that the outer environment as such does not have properties of a mathematical group, but that such group properties become available as the ambient optic array is being transformed by the perceiver's own movements. That is, the organism's own actions help to construct, and thereby they help to define the stimulus. However, at this point Gibson seems to shy away from assigning a truly fundamental role to motor processes in the formation of percepts and confines his attention essentially to the structure of the optic array in explaining perception. Gibson states: "The available stimulus surrounding the individual has structure and this structure depends on sources *in the outer environment*" (emphasis added, p. 267). That is, despite the inclusion of motor movements as an essential part of the process of obtaining visual input, Gibson puts the whole burden of explaining perception on the optic array.

Because Gibson's theory is a good illustration of an attempt to formulate a limited, optic array, theory of perception, the theory will be discussed in some further detail. According to Gibson, there is permanent stimulus information in the ambient optic array. Gibson (in press) says: "The meanings of the edge, of a falling-off place, . . . are given in the optic array." More specifically (Gibson 1959), the effective stimulus for perception must be sought in a textured optic array, supplemented by the transformations relating a simultaneous pair of them and by transformations relating sequences of momentary arrays. According to Gibson (1966) it is this structure inherent in the optic array that organizes visual perception in conjunction with a brain that resonates to this ready-made structure. There is no further need for perception to be mediated by an internal model, let alone constructed by the organism. Nor are there internal processes correcting or interpreting this information. This is Gibson's conception of *direct* visual perception.

[3]Occlusion effects occur, for example, when the spatial relations between edges of surfaces in the visual environment change because of shifts in the station points of the eyes during movements of the observer.

To be sure, theories like the theory of direct visual perception recognize that optic array information does not exhaust the information received by the organism. It also receives input about its own movements, for example. Here again, however, it is generally argued that the relevant input, whether proprioceptive or exteroceptive,[4] is already structured. In addition to being structured, exteroceptive and proprioceptive information can in important ways be interchangeable. For example, movement on the part of the individual can be detected not only directly via proprioceptors, but also through motions of the ambient optic array. Notice that the point which is made here is not restricted to the notion of visual proprioception, which is that one's movements are usually seen as well as felt. In general, it seems fair to conclude that the theory of direct visual perception assumes that ambient optic array information will be *sufficient* for the perception not only of events happening in the outside environment but for the perception of the organism's movements as well.

On the matter of whether information from the ambient optic array has to be interpreted by the brain, consider what the theory says about the perception of motion in the environment and of movement by the observer (Gibson 1968). The stimulus for the motion of an object is a lawful set of optic relations at the eye having to do with a figure in an array transforming itself with occlusion effects. It is implied that this is *the* optic stimulus information for motion of an object in the environment. On the other hand, *the* optic stimulus for movement of the observer is a transformation with occulusion effect of a total optic array. This information need not be interpreted by the brain. Gibson (1966) was very explicit on this point when he discussed the difference between his theory of motion and movement and that by von Holst (1954) and von Holst and Mittelstaedt (1950). Because of the crucial importance of this issue, Gibson's statement is quoted in full:

> One theory suggests that whenever the brain sends out a command for a certain movement it stores a copy. When the input of any receptor reaches the brain, it is automatically compared with the current stored copy. If it matches, the input is taken to be a case of proprioception—a feed-in. *In this theory, the input does not itself specify its cause; the cause must be deduced* (von Holst and Mittelstaedt 1950).
>
> An alternative theory assumes that the neural input caused by self-produced action is simply different from the neural input caused by an intruding stimulus. The two kinds of input are different in their sequential properties; they are different kinds of transformation or change, and the simultaneous pattern of nerve fibers might be widely dispersed. In the long run, this second hypothesis may prove to be the simpler of the two, *for it does not presuppose a brain that copies, stores, compares, matches, and decides.* (emphasis added, Gibson 1966, p. 39)

This second hypothesis, of course, represents Gibson's own theory of the perception of motion and movement.

[4]As used here, *proprioception* refers to sensations in the end organs of muscles during movement; *exteroception* refers to sensations of external origin introduced via the eyes.

The overall impression left by the theory of direct visual perception is that despite the seemingly important statements about motor mechanisms in perception, the theory is essentially concerned with the ambient optic array. How the structure of the optic array is produced and by whom is, in the final analysis, not considered to be germane to this theory of perception. But what if in some way the organism were to have information about its own activity, that is, about its own contribution to the construction of the stimulus, quite independently from action-produced peripheral feedbacks? As will be shown, the organism may in fact have information about its actions or about its own plans for action at a central level of the nervous system, in addition to the information it receives about action-produced peripheral feedback. If such a central process were to operate, the organism's information about its own activity could be considerably more independent of peripheral inflow and notably of exteroception than Gibson assumed. Since, as was mentioned, the organism's actions help to construct and define the stimulus, not to include information which the organism might have about such actions into one's theory of perception may amount to constructing a theory that is unduly restrictive. Feedback from the central nervous system itself about the organism's own activity could have a direct effect *on perception,* possibly in the manner implied by von Holst (1954)—that is, this kind of information could be used by a brain that "copies, stores, compares, matches and decides," to use Gibson's (1966) phrase quoted earlier.

In order to explore whether, as the theory of direct visual perception claims, optic array information is sufficient for predicting a given perceptual process or whether nonoptic variables having to do with the organism's motor activity *interact* with optic information to produce a percept, a type of research is needed that has not been considered within this theoretical framework. As stated in the beginning of this chapter, it is necessary to study whether, with the ambient optic array constant, other nonoptic events produce specifiably different perceptual effects. More generally, it must be explored whether varying either optic or nonoptic parameters, singly or in combination, results in a different perceptual effect in each case. Several studies that have done this are mentioned in the following section. The argument is made that certain of the findings produced by this research would seem to require a modification of the theory of direct visual perception such that it becomes in effect a sensorimotor theory of perception.

EXPERIMENTAL FINDINGS ON THE INTERRELATION IN PERCEPTION BETWEEN OPTIC EVENTS AND THOSE NONOPTIC EVENTS HAVING TO DO WITH THE ORGANISM'S OWN MOTOR ACTIONS

The work of von Holst (1954) and von Holst and Mittelstaedt (1950) on the perception of motion and movement may first be mentioned as an example of an approach to the study of perception that explores the relation between optic and nonoptic variables in perception and thereby investigates the role played by these variables in the perceptual process. It should be recalled, first, that for the theory of direct visual perception (Gibson 1966) the information for the perception of the motion of an object is a lawful set of optic relations at the eye having to do with a figure in an array being transformed with occlusion effects. It is implied that this is the optic information for motion on the part of an object in the environment. On the other hand, the information for movement of the observer is a transformation with occlusion effects of a total optic array. At first glance, none of this seems debatable, given the normal everyday environment of the mature perceiver. However, the study by von Holst and Mittelstaedt (1950) with a fly is instructive because it shows that the same optic input can connote at one time movement of the observer and at another time motion by the environment. Of concern are a series of three experiments in which, under conditions where afferent[5] input from the optic array remains the same, entirely different perceptual interpretations of the afferent signals were made by the fly.

If a fly is put in the center of a black and white striated cylinder which is rotating to the right, the fly follows the movement of the cylinder by also rotating to the right. (If the cylinder is rotated to the left, tracking takes place to the left). Von Holst and Mittelstaedt proposed that the fly's eye contains specific neurons that control the observed optomotor reflex. This conclusion was derived from the additional finding that if the head of the fly is surgically rotated 180 degrees in relation to the body, so that left and right sides of the eyes are reversed and hence the visual signals are also reversed, the fly turns opposite to the direction of the rotation of the cylinder. In a second experiment, involving a normal fly, a stimulus such as smell was placed to the left of the fly. The fly then moved to the left in the direction of the new stimulus while the cylinder remained stationary and thus produced very nearly the same visual afferent inputs into its eye as in the first experiment when the cylinder moved to the right and the fly remained stationary—the only difference being that these inputs are now motion produced. Under this condition, the fly does not show the oculomotor reflex that it showed in Experiment I. That is, the same afferent input evidently no longer signifies a motion to the right by the environment and does not elicit a tracking motion in the appropriate direction. The fly merely initiates left movement and stops when it reaches the source of the smell. Von Holst and Mittelstaedt (1950) interpreted this result to mean that in this second experiment efferent information is somehow processed by the system and that

[5]Throughout this chapter a series of terms like *afferent, efferent, reafference, efference,* and *afference* will occur. *Afferent* input and *afference* refer to peripheral inflow information, say of proprioceptive or exteroceptive origin. *Efferent* and *efference,* on the other hand, refer to centrally available outflow information from the outgoing motor nerve impulses in the motor pathways to the periphery. *Reafference* refers to afferent information which is produced by, and is therefore correlated with, the efference accompanying motor movement.

it contributes to the *interpretation* which is placed on afferent input. In line with reflex theory, it could be claimed of course that, by locomoting, the optomotor reflex observed in the first experiment is simply blocked. To refute this possibility, a third experiment was performed that was identical to the second, except that the head was surgically rotated 180 degrees. In this case, if motion to the right on the part of the animal is started by a smell to the right of the fly, the fly—experiencing the same afferent input as in Experiment I and clearly the same as in Experiment 2—will continue to move to the right in small circles until exhausted. This, however, happens only if the environment is textured. In an optically homogeneous environment, the animal moves normally and stops at the location of the smell. These findings suggest that the optomotor reflex is not blocked during motion by the animal but, rather, that the behavior observed in both Experiments 2 and 3, and presumably in Experiment I, is a function of reafference and its relation to the motor activity or nonactivity of the organism.

Von Holst (1954) explained the results of the above experiments by postulating a built-in summation or comparison between monitored efferent and afferent signals. According to von Holst, if the normal animal moves to the left in a stationary environment, an efferent copy of left movement as well as the reafferent signals associated with such movement (i.e., a movement of the visual field from left to right across the retina) are compared in the central nervous system. In this case, these two types of signals, according to a convention assumed by von Holst, are of opposite sign and can cancel each other. This means that this particular reafferent input will not signify to the animal changes taking place in the environment itself, and it will not lead to optomotor action of tracking by the animal (Experiment 2). If the same afferent optic input is not accompanied by an efferent copy—as when the environment moves and the fly is stationary—the meaning to the animal of the afferent input is changed, and this case leads to tracking behavior to the right to follow the motion of the environment (Experiment I). If there is efference as well as reafference, but if the latter is reversed, these two types of signals have the same sign, summate, and produce the continued circling motion of the animal (Experiment 3). *What von Holst is thus saying is that the organism records relations between itself and the environment.*

McKay (1973) has since criticized the von Holst summation model on the grounds that it requires an unreasonable amount of accuracy in the efferent-copy signal. McKay believes a less quantitatively refined system, based on expectancy, might be all that is required. There is evidence supplied by Matin and Matin (1973) that an extraocular signal is involved in the role of a cancelling signal in the perception of visual direction, but that this copy signal is too sloppy to carry out by itself the functions required by von Holst's theory in exactly the way stated in the theory. These authors feel that what might work is a combination of the extraocular signal and a process called saccadic suppression (which "prevents perception at a time when there is a large and rapidly changing discrepancy between the extraretinal signal and eye position"). The source of the extraocular signal, whether peripheral or central (the latter was claimed by von Holst), was not determined by the study.

A set of findings similar to those of von Holst was reported by Sperry (1950). Working with fish, Sperry found strong circling tendencies to result from surgically rotating an eye 180 degrees. In connection with these findings, Sperry (1950) did a series of studies of brain ablation and extirpation of the vestibular system. On the basis of these studies alone, Sperry could not conclude in favor of a theory which asserts that the *relation* between optic and extraoptic factors is crucial. In fact, the findings that ablation of the optic tectum does interfere and that bilateral labyrinthectomy does not interfere with the optokinetic response decidedly ruled in the possibility of a purely optic explanation of the data. A labyrinthectomy—on the hypothesis of extraretinal kinetic factors—should have led to an interference with a circling response. However, the additional finding—as in the von Holst and Mittelstaedt (1950) study—that exactly the same pattern of excitations from the retina may, in one instance, arouse a circling movement and not in another, *depending entirely upon the direction of the animal's movement accompanying the retinal input*—made a purely optic hypothesis unlikely to Sperry. The movement itself had to be brought in as a necessary determiner of the perceptual process. This argument, coupled with the findings in regard to the negative effect of extirpation of the vestibular system on circling motion, led Sperry to formulate the idea that the kinetic component arises not peripherally but centrally, as part of the organism's efferent commands which elicit overt movement. He thus proposed what may be considered to be the equivalent of von Holst's "efferent copy" theory—namely, "any excitation pattern that normally results in a movement that will cause a displacement of the visual image of the retina may have a corollary discharge into the visual centers to compensate for the retinal displacement" (p. 488).

That the notions of corollary discharge and efferent copy are generally interpreted to be the same becomes evident from an examination of the literature (e.g., Paillard and Brouchon 1968; Rock 1966; and Teuber 1960).

As has already been mentioned the exact theory proposed by von Holst and by Sperry to explain their data may need to be modified. What needs to be pointed out here is that the results of their experiments contradict any hypothesis that categorically claims that ambient optic array information is sufficient to produce the perception of motion and movement and need never be interpreted by being related to other events arising in the organism itself. By showing that percepts can vary while the information in the ambient optic array remains constant, important parts of the theory of direct visual perception would seem to have been refuted. An argument which might still salvage the theory—namely, that differences in attentional processes might account for the differences in perception—would not seem valid in view of the fact that the animal's behavior in all experimental conditions shows that they were clearly attending to the stimulus. A final argument that Gibson has used is that von Holst and Sperry were concerned with retinal *sensations* which must be corrected by the brain. Gibson has always made it clear that sensations are irrelevant to his theory. Thus, it might be claimed that von Holst and Sperry used data that might be considered irrelevant to perception. Clearly, however, the "sensations" with which these authors are concerned are the result of the same families of transformations in the optic array upon which Gibson based his own theory.

The studies cited thus far have dealt with situations in which reafference is associated with head movement or with locomotion. There are some suggestive studies in the area of eye movement as well, reported by von Graefe (1878), von Helmholtz (1925), and von Holst (1954). Von Helmholtz' observation deals with the situation in which the external rectus muscle of the eye is paralyzed such that the eye cannot move in a given direction. It is found that in a situation in which the right eye cannot move to the right, a command to the subject to move his right eye to the right will produce a perception on his part of seeing the environment moving to the right. Again, then, here is a case in which there is perceptual change without any actual change in the input from the optic array.

The von Helmholtz data, while they were taken to support a position which said that an extraoptic event—namely, the feeling of innervation—enters into perception, have historically become subject to two interpretations. One is the interpretation by von Helmholtz, which said that there is central information that affects the perceptual process. The other interpretation, reviewed by Festinger and Canon (1965), was proposed by James (1950). James asserted that since it is well known that both eyes act in concert motorically, and since only one eye was immobilized in the case of the von Helmholtz experiment, the perceptual information for motion could have come not from a central source to the immobilized eye, but from the proprioceptive information due to the normal eye which *was* in motion during the perceptual act. At the time James made his point, it was generally assumed that, indeed, peripheral stimulation could therefore account for the results obtained by von Helmholtz. However, later developments have at least cast a certain amount of uncertainty on James's arguments. These will now be reviewed.

Whitteridge (1962) raised the question "whether the position of the eyes enters into judgments of position and movement, and if it does, how far proprioceptors are responsible" (p. 511). A direct test of the question whether there is useful proprioceptive information resulting from eye movement was made by Brindley and Merton (1960). These authors anesthetized the surface of the eyes as well as the inner surface of the eyelids. Moreover, they covered the corneas of the eyes with opaque caps so that no visual information was available to the subjects. They then mechanically moved the eyes singly as well as in concert and found the subjects were unaware that any such movement had taken place. They concluded that no information about the position of the eye is derivable from the sense endings of eye muscles. However, using somewhat different techniques and measures,

Skavenski (1972) showed that information about eye position was available to the organism from stretch receptors in the extraocular muscles of the eye. That the latter source of information is not completely free from error, however, is attested by an error rate of 20 and 32 percent in *S*s' judgments of right and left eye movements, respectively. It should be noted that these are errors in direction, of knowing whether the eye had turned left or right. Nothing is said about the usefulness of preprioceptive feedback in telling the eye which exact point in space it is looking at.

A study by Festinger and Canon (1965) was designed explicitly to ascertain whether information obtained from a record of certain *outgoing* motor nerve impulses is available and can be used by the organism to know where the eye is pointing. The hypothesis was tested that the organism knows the direction of the eye from knowing where it has been directed to go. Experimentally, this means that conditions had to be created in which, in one condition, the eye became directed at a certain point in space because of a specific efferent command and, in another condition, without such a command. To accomplish this, Festinger and Canon availed themselves of findings by Rashbass (1961) on the differences between saccadic and smooth tracking eye movements. The former's function, according to Rashbass, seems to be to move the eye to a specific location; the function of the latter is to match velocities of a moving target regardless of the target's position. The experiment thus involved having subjects fixate on a suddenly appearing target versus having them track a slowly moving target to a fixed position in space. In both experimental conditions, *S*s had to point out the location in space of the target by using a pointer operated by their index finger. The efferent outflow is different in these two conditions, while the proprioceptive information from extraocular muscles, if any, is the same. The major findings are that the accuracy of pointing at the location of the target is very significantly better in the condition in which the target suddenly appears than in the condition where the target slowly moves toward its ultimate destination. This finding supports Festinger and Canon's theory that efferent—that is, outflow—information is both available and useful for the subject in making perceptual judgments about radial direction. An alternative hypothesis, that *S*s in the "saccadic condition" were attending to position cues—and thereby obtained exteroceptive information—whereas the subjects in the smooth tracking eye-movement condition did not attend to these cues, is eliminated by the fact that there were no such cues, since the experiments were performed in the dark.

While the Skavenski (1972) findings indicate there is information about eye position from proprioceptors of the extraocular muscles, Festinger and Cannon's results would seem to show that information from efference is more useful in this regard.

However, regardless of the merits of central outflow theories (Brindley and Merton 1960; Festinger and Canon 1965; and Helmholtz 1925) or peripheral inflow theories (Skavenski 1972), the study by von Helmholtz suggests that the perception of movement takes place even though the ambient optic array remains constant. Since, in this case, there is no information due to changes occurring in the optic array, this perceptual event must be explained by assuming the intervention of certain efferent and/or proprioceptive events related to the motor activity of the organism which provide it with perceptual information about movement.

The conclusion to be drawn from all of this is that the data reported by von Helmholtz do not seem explainable in terms of purely peripheral visual excitation and that other mechanisms such as those proposed by von Helmholtz or by von Holst should at least be considered. A von Holst type explanation would be as follows: In a stationary environment, efference to the eye to move to the right is normally accompanied by a movement of the retinal image from right to left. Since, in fact, no such movement occurred in Helmholtz' experiment, the organism perceives a compensatory movement by the environment from left to right.

The study by Helmholtz has been elaborated further by von Holst (1954). In addition to performing the experiment reported by Helmholtz, von Holst carried out two additional and related studies to further test his theory. In one experiment, instead of commanding the subject to move his eye, he turned the subject's paralayzed eye mechanically to the right. He argued that in this case there is no efference nor is there an efference copy. There is, however, afference which now, unmatched by an efferent copy, is transmitted to a central integrating mechanism, according to the theory. The theory would predict that a perception of movement of the environment to the left will ensue, and it does. In a final study, the paralyzed eye is commanded to move and is also moved mechanically—thereby in effect simulating the voluntary movement of a normal eye, in which case there is both efference and reafference. In this case, the von Helmholtz effect and the effect of von Holst's second study cancel each other, and the environment is perceived as stationary. By means of this triplet of studies, one of which is a replication of the experiment by von Helmholtz, von Holst has thus demonstrated nicely the function of the *relation* between optic and extraoptic variables in perception. He has shown that the perception of no motion by the environment is based on an organism-environment relation, and his theory also explains the illusion of motion and, more precisely, the specific form that illusion takes.

Still further studies by von Holst (1954) are also relevant. These deal with the system of visual accommodation[6] rather than exploratory movements. If the circular muscle which allows the lens to round up is narcotized, vision will be accommodated for distant objects. Any intention for near accommodation will start a motor impulse which cannot be nullified by any change in reafference, and, hence, as in the previous cases with the von Helmholtz effect, certain predictable perceptions should ensue. That is,

[6]*Accommodation* refers to the process whereby the rounding of the lens of the eye is altered when the distance changes between the eye and an external object upon which the eye is focused. The purpose of the process is to keep the object in sharp focus.

projections will remain the same size on the retina despite accommodation commands, and it has long been known that under these conditions all objects in the visual field come to be seen as small. Von Holst argued that a similar set of phenomena can be produced in the case of a normal eye via the process of afterimages. If an afterimage is produced of a distant object which is then projected on a near surface, accommodation is again accompanied by a retinal projection which remains constant in size. Under these conditions, the object appears very small on the near surface. Von Holst argued that these false perceptions appear although the peripheral stimulus situation is unaltered. If, now, the peripheral stimulus situation does become altered and the accommodation remains unaltered—as when the subject looks first at a small and then at a large cross at the same distance—then the large cross looks larger. If, again, the situations of these two experiments are combined, and the eye looks at a given object being moved nearer to it, the object is perceived as being constant in size.

Von Graefe (1878) reported cases of paralysis of the rectus muscle of the eye in which the subject can move his eye only over an angle of, say, 20 degrees to the right. If such a subject is asked to look at an object which is at this given angle of 20 degrees to his straight ahead, the effort to do so is much greater than it would be normally. The prediction made by a Sperry or von Holst type of theory would be that this circumstance should affect the subject's perception of radial direction. Such is indeed the case. Under these conditions, subjects will judge an object at 20 degrees to the right of straight ahead to be located at an angle much greater than that. In fact, the angle indicated by subjects is approximately that which a normal eye would have traversed had it been moved to its extreme right position.

Further studies showing that information about the voluntary motion of the eye and its relation to reafferent input is important in perception have been concerned with the problem of the stabilized retinal image.[7] For example, Festinger, Burnham, Ono, and Bamber (1967) discussed a novel way of looking at the situation produced by the stopped or stabilized retinal image (Ditchburn and Ginsborg 1952). The effect of this treatment, which is temporary fading of the retinal picture, has traditionally been interpreted as neural "fatigue" or adaptation. The assumption that perception involves centrally available information about the organism's voluntary activity, however, allows consideration of a competing hypothesis. This hypothesis says that fading results, at least in part, because the ordinary relationship between efference and the response-produced stimulation or reafference, which in this case is the relationship between motion of the eye and resultant change of position of retinal input, is destroyed when the retinal image is stabilized. Festinger proposed that if the stabilized image could be moved in

[7] A retinal image is stabilized when—as a result of a variety of optic or nonoptic interventions—each movement of the eye effects a parallel movement of the visual array. The result is that saccades made during maintained fixation of a visual target no longer produce changes in projections of the target on the retina. Under these conditions the target has been found to fade rapidly.

a manner which is unrelated to any movement by the eye—perhaps by having an experimenter do the moving—the competing hypotheses should be testable. If fading effects continued under the latter treatment, the reafferent hypothesis would be strengthened since the neural adaptation effect should be minimal under these conditions. Observations reported by Campbell and Robson (1961), using the shadows of retinal capillaries[8] which are moved across the retina at certain amplitudes and frequencies, seem to support this new hypothesis. That is, the persistent fading of the capillary shadows reported by Campbell & Robson cannot be explained entirely in terms of fatigue or satiation of neural mechanisms. Festinger *et al.* also mentioned a study by Tepas (1962) in which complete "blank out"—that is, a complete disappearance of the sense of vision on the *ganzfeld,*[9] —was reported by subjects at the same time as they also manifested an absence of saccadic eye movements.

Up to this point it has been shown that information other than that stemming from the optic array enters into various types of perception. The next set of studies to be reported have tried to show that the extra-visual information must be due to information about *voluntary* activity, or the plans for activity, available in the CNS. This hypothesis takes off directly, of course, from the work of von Helmholtz and the later studies by Merton (1964) and Festinger and Canon (1965) which showed there was usable information about the efferent impulses issued from the CNS through the motor pathways. These studies explicitly have tried to rule out proprioception as a source of extraoptic information in perception.

The notion that centrally available information about voluntary activity is necessary in perception was already hinted at by the results in the Sperry (1950) study which has been reported. It receives additional support from a series of studies on perceptual learning. For example, studies by Festinger *et al.* (1967) are a direct test of the hypothesis that centrally available information about its own activity, about efference, is essential to the organism's visual adaptation to distortions produced by prisms. The major idea here is that if perception involves the building up of efferent-reafferent correlations and if distorting prisms require a systematic shift in such a correlation, adaptation to prism-induced distortions in contour should be facilitated by the presence of central efferent participation by the central nervous system in the adaptation process. In the experiment, prisms were used to induce curvature to objectively straight contours and straightness to objectively curved contours. The contours in most cases were parallel metal bars. In some experiments, during adaptation training a stylus had to be moved between the bars. In another study, the eye, now itself fitted with a contact lens on which a prism was mounted, had to focus along the length of the contours. In an additional experiment, a different experimental task (a "shooting gallery") was used, and arm movement had to

[8] Retinal capillaries are minute blood vessels connecting the arteries and veins.
[9] In a *ganzfeld* a completely uniform, structureless, visual field is produced.

be used to aim a light gun. In all experiments, the two major variations for comparison were (*a*) to move a stylus, shoot the "gun," or move an eye as a result of contour-specific efferent commands to move along specific paths in the field (e.g., to learn a smooth, fast, sweeping motion of the stylus between the apparently curved parallel rods); (*b*) to move without making contour-specific efferent commands regarding direction (e.g., to have the eye *follow* a target moving between apparently curved parallel rods, to learn a smooth stroking motion which must at all times maintain contact with one rod, etc.). The first variation, according to the authors, constituted an efferent or "learning" condition, while the second was designed as a nonefferent or "accuracy" condition.

The major findings are that the "efferent" conditions do lead to significantly greater adaptation (*adaptation* being defined as the extent to which an "apparently curved" but objectively straight contour is judged as less curved after the experiment and, similarly, the extent to which "apparently straight" but objectively curved is judged as less straight). This is measured by ascertaining changes in the setting of the metal rods to straight by the subjects wearing both prisms and plain glasses in pre- and post-tests. In several of the experiments, the efferent processes induced (i.e., moving a stylus with the arm and hand) are not as directly relevant to the final measure of *visual* adaptation to distorted contours as is an efferent process in which eye movement itself is involved. It is interesting to find, therefore, that Festinger *et al.* (1967) showed that one experiment which involved moving the eye along the contours, rather than the stylus, produced the highest (approximately 40 percent) adaptation. This work has since been replicated and extended by Burnham (1968), Gyr and Willey (1970), Gyr, Willey, and Gordon (1972), and Slotnick (1969). Gyr *et al.* ran a study similar to the Festinger *et al.* arm movement and parallel bar study but—because of a methodology which made use of a computer, cathode ray tube, and light pen—they were able to obtain complete records of arm movements and motor learning during the entire experiment. Gyr *et al.* established not only that voluntary activity played a role in adaptation, but—by showing the existence of a positive correlation between amount of motor learning during training and amount of visual adaptation—they verified more directly the hypothesis that in order to produce perception efferent-reafferent correlations have to be built up.

A suggestive set of evidence in regard to the hypothesis that central processes having to do with the organism's voluntary activity are necessary to perception has also been supplied by the studies on the relation between perception and voluntary motion contributed by Held (1964), Held and Bossom (1961), Held and Freedman (1963), Held and Gottlieb (1958), Held and Hein (1958, 1963), Held and Schlank (1959), and Hein and Held (1962). Held argued strongly against the assumption that "the neurological processing of sensory input is independent of the organization of motor action, that is, against the assumption that the analysis of sensory input preparatory to motor acts occurs solely in the course of a chain of neural events traversing the sensory projections but completed prior to impingement upon motor centers in the brain" (1964, p. 141).

In studies of perceptual displacement, Held and Bossom (1961) have shown that voluntary motion (as opposed to passively being moved about but ostensibly receiving the same visual inputs), with its concurrent train of sensory and motor feedback, provides the essential order required for compensation in such an environment. That is to say, spatial orientation in such an environment was only made if voluntary motion was allowed. Further evidence quoted from Held (1964) stated: "Hein & Held have reared kittens with one eye open during locomotion in an illuminated surrounding; the other eye was open during passive transport over an equivalent path. After several months of such exposure, stimulation of the eye that had been open during active movement produced normal visually-guided behavior but the other was functionally blind. These experiments clearly implicate the motor system in processes traditionally regarded as sensory" (pp. 308–309). Held and Hein (1963) found that self-produced movement is necessary for the development of visually guided behavior such as on the "visual cliff"[10] (Walk and Gibson 1961). Only those cats which had been allowed voluntary motion while given controlled inputs of patterned vision during training showed any behavioral evidence of depth discrimination when put on the visual-cliff, or evidence of visually guided paw placement. In the test involving visually guided paw placement, the subject's body was held in the experimenter's hands so that its head and forelegs were free. It was then slowly carried forward and downward toward the edge of a table. A normally reared animal shows visually mediated anticipation of contact by extending its paws as it approaches the edge. Held and Hein stated that peripheral astrophy resulting from lack of use of various organs is contraindicated by the presence of pupillary and pursuit reflexes and the rapid recovery of function of the passive subjects once given their freedom. Debility specific to the motor system can be ruled out, according to the authors, because the passive subjects showed the same tactual placing responses and other motor activities as the normals.

A somewhat more detailed inquiry into the mechanisms of adaptive change, and their central or peripheral origin, is manifest in two further studies (Hardt, Held, and Steinbach 1971; and Templeton, Howard, and Wilkinson, in press).

In the study by Hardt *et al.* predictions derived from a total of four alternative theories were tested. The data obtained were consistent only with a sensorimotor theory of adaptation. The four theories were: (1) a purely visual theory, (2) a response theory, (3) a proprioceptive theory, and (4) a sensorimotor theory.

[10]The *visual cliff* is a laboratory apparatus designed to study depth perception. It is composed of a board raised above the center line of a sheet of glass which extends beyond it. On the shallow side of the centerboard a textured material is attached to the underside of the glass. On the deep side the same textured material is attached to a platform with variable distance to the glass. The animal's preference to descend to one or the other side of the centerboard is studied.

The study was like many other studies on visual rearrangement of direction but differed from these in that it had a more elaborate repertoire of pre- and post-tests. The pre- and post-tests, given to different groups of *S*s, were of three kinds. In one kind of test *S*s had to point at visually available targets. All of the four theories proposed predict adaptation effects on this test. A second test required blindfolded *S*s to direct their head toward the tip of their arm which in turn was extended toward given environmental targets. A purely visual theory does not predict adaptation on this measure, since vision was excluded from the test. A response theory also does not predict adaptation, inasmuch as the response required in the test (directing the head) had not been made during the exposure phase of the experiment. On the other hand, both proprioceptive and sensorimotor theories predict measurable adaptation on this test. Finally, a third test required blindfolded *S*s to reposition their arm in several different postures defined in terms of the proprioceptively sensed position of the responding limb but independent of any spatially directed behavior. A proprioceptive theory predicts adaptation on this measure. On the other hand, a sensorimotor theory does not, inasmuch as such a theory argues that there can be changes in the internal spatial mapping of one element into another (of, perhaps, arm position in relation to eye position) at a central level without there being any change on tasks (such as the test) involving each element (e.g., the arm) taken separately.

The only predictions which were consistent with the findings in four different experiments were the predictions derived from sensorimotor theory. In general, adaptation was found to be specific to responses involving the exposed arm in spatially directed behavior. No adaptation was shown by *S*s on the measure in which the arm moved by proprioceptive cues alone. Furthermore, the changed response generalized to another response modality (i.e., directed eye movements). Moreover, change was evident when the exposed arm was used either as a target or target indicator. Hardt *et al.* (1971) concluded that the findings could be consistent only with a sensorimotor mechanism which recalibrates a *central* control system.

The research by Templeton *et al.* (in press) explored the same general question but via a different approach. It follows from the sensorimotor interpretation of the data by Hardt *et al.* (1971) that there can be situations in which the total adaptation in all the joints involved in an adaptation study (arm position, head position, etc.) do not add up to the total observed adaptation, as measured by the adaptive shift in pointing with unseen hand at a visual target. This is so because, as has already been stated in reviewing Hardt *et al.*, sensorimotor theory argues that there can be changes in the central internal spatial mapping of elements which are not reflected in the responses of the elements taken separately. Templeton *et al.* argued that, should all subadaptations add to the total observed adaptation in a given experiment, such a result would support a proprioceptive theory of adaptation. Since Hardt *et al.* had not in fact measured all elements involved in their adaptation task and hence had failed to exclude a purely proprioceptive interpretation of their data, Templeton *et al.* set out to correct this omission. In particular, Hardt *et al.* had omitted to study adaptation in the felt position of the neck. (Of course, it may be argued that the approach taken by Hardt *et al.*, which consisted of separating various theories by testing certain of their predictions, only required them to find a single instance in which a proprioceptive prediction was disconfirmed, thus making it unnecessary to study every single response system involved during exposure.)

Be this as it may, Templeton *et al.* found that *S*s who showed a gaze shift, in addition to at least an arm shift, manifested total additivity. *S*s which did not show a gaze shift had no additivity. The latter data thus implicated a central sensorimotor process in the adaptation process. Templeton *et al.* argued that the obvious function of sensorimotor processes in adaptation are to process current error feedback. It should be noted, however, that even in the case of *S*s which showed additivity it is not clear that a sensorimotor theory could not also account for the results. It would appear that in order to preclude sensorimotor mechanisms, it is necessary to study responses which are not specific to spatially directed behavior but which have only a proprioceptive base. This was done in the third pre- and post-test condition of the study by Hardt *et al.* (1971). Such a condition was not part of the study by Templeton *et al.* since *S*s' task in directing their gaze was to direct it to one of their visible toes, rather than to direct the eye in terms of whether it *felt* to be up, down, or whatever.

The position taken by the authors who have attempted to show that efference is *necessary* to visual adaptation has very important implications. If the organism has at its disposal information about the activities of the CNS, prior to the occurrence of the motor act itself and *prior* to the occurrence of motor-produced reafferent feedback, then there is a role for the motor system in perception. Teuber (1964) has suggested that, if the organism has information about its own motor contribution to the construction of the stimulus which is independent of action-produced peripheral feedbacks, one function of the response may be to "prepare the sensory structure for an anticipated change." In line with von Holst's theory, this anticipated change may then be compared with the obtained change.

As has just been shown, much research appears to support this general position of efferent involvement in perception. However, attacks against it are also present in the literature. One attack, specifically aimed at the work of Held and his associates, was made by Singer and Day (1966*a*, 1966*b*) in a series of four experiments. They attempted to show that adaptation to prism-produced distortion of localization occurs under both passive and active conditions and that it is not efference but other factors that play a role in adaptation. Of these other factors, two were selected for experimentation. They were a factor of judgment (the subject being required to make continuous judgments about the location of his seen arm during training), and a factor which dealt with the likeness of the task confronting the subject during training to the tasks he faced during the pre- and posttests. These factors were studied by superimposing them on Held's dimensions of active versus passive motor movement.

Singer and Day's findings may be summarized as follows: (*a*) The results reported by Singer and Day show that there are no statistically significant differences in adaptation between active and passive training conditions, while there are generally significant amounts of adaptation in each. The following comments, however, are in order in relation to these findings. One comment is that, while there were no significant differences between active and passive groups, the active groups had higher means both in Experiment I of the 1966*a* study as well as in Experiment I of the 1966*b* study. This fact would seem to point to the possibility that the reported divergence of their data from data reported elsewhere in the literature—which support the idea of an efferent contribution to perception—may be quantitative rather than qualitative. Moreover, in showing the lack of difference between active and passive groups in Experiment I of the 1966*a* study, the authors merely demonstrate the absence of a significant difference between active and passive conditions and a significant effect if both conditions are combined. They do not show whether either the active or passive condition alone manifested adaptation that were significantly different from zero. They did do this for Experiment I of the 1966*b* study and found that both active and passive conditions produced adaptation means significantly different from zero, though, again, the active condition mean was higher. That a passive condition can produce adaptation goes against the theory these experiments were designed to attack, namely Held's. It might of course always be argued that any passive condition in which the conventional technique is used, whereby the experimenter moves the subject's arm, may not be totally devoid of some efferent outflow. Even the authors themselves suggested this possibility and then conducted a second experiment (Singer and Day 1966*b*, Experiment 2) in which in one condition the subject merely judged the position of his passive arm during training. In this condition in fact no significant adaptation occurred. Thus, the evidence reported by Singer and Day on the issue of active versus passive dimensions in adaptation is, to say the least, less than conclusive. (*b*) Singer and Day (1966*b*, Experiment I) found that a judgment condition led to greater adaptation, regardless of whether it occurred under active or passive conditions. However, in the second 1966*b* study adaptation under conditions that were still more passive and involved a different visual task there was no significant difference in adaptation under judgment than under no-judgment conditions. Thus, the role of judgment in adaptation is still left unclear by these experiments. (*c*) Singer and Day (1966*b*) conclude that adaptation, regardless of activity or passivity, is heightened if the task (in spatial terms) which the subject confronts during training is like the tasks which he performs during testing. The generality of this finding, however, is weakened by a study performed by Pick and Hay (1965), who concluded that their data, at least indirectly, supported Held's hypothesis that active groups adapt more, regardless of whether the pre- and post-tests are active or passive. That kind of similarity between pretest and training at least appears to be irrelevant.

It should be pointed out, of course, that in any case neither items (*b*) or (*c*) above are directly related to efference theory and its verification or refutation.

Another study explicitly critical of Held's efferent position is by Weinstein, Sersen, Fisher, and Weisinger (1964). These authors argued that Held's research does not allow one to decide between the contributions made by adaptation by, on the one hand, *movement*, and, on the other, by *decisions* to move in one direction or another. The experiment by Weinstein *et al.* studied adaptation to displacement of the straight-ahead under decision-with-movement, decision only, movement only, and passive-movement only conditions, thus attempting to tease apart the role of movement versus decision. It is clear, however, that if movement is to be an active movement in Held's sense it should be that movement which ensues when a given command from the CNS occurs. If that command contains directional instructions, as it does in this particular study, the active movement condition should include directional features. This it does not do in the Weinstein *et al.* study. Rather, under the active condition the subject is told to turn the wheels of a wheelchair, but where the subject goes is decided by an attendant. The subject is not allowed to turn one wheel more than another and in so doing to control direction of the wheelchair. This illustrates the point that the content of an active movement cannot be divorced from the content of an active decision. If this precept is violated, as it is in the Weinstein *et al.* study, then the experimenter has in effect transformed an active-movement condition into a passive-movement condition. As to the decision-only condition, it is clear that neither Held nor several other investigators of extra optic dimensions in perception would insist that a decision must be accompanied by a motor movement. In fact, Festinger *et al.* (1967) and Taylor (1962) have noted explicitly that perception need not involve so much actual motor activity as a readiness to act. In short, it appears that from the point of view of efference theory the decision and the decision-with-movement conditions should show the most adaptation and that the active-movement condition and passive-movement group should show the least. Weinstein *et al.* reported significant adaptation in all groups and no significant differences between groups. However, when ordered by extent of adaptation, the decision group and active-movement-with-decision group fall in the order one and two, with the active-movement and passive groups being in third and fourth place. It could well be that, had the first two groups and the last two groups been combined, as they ought to have been, significant differences might have been obtained. As in the case of the Singer and Day studies, the results, as reported, are by no means conclusive refutations of efference theory.

Another approach presumably critical of efference theory is illustrated in studies by Howard, Craske, and Templeton (1965) as well as by

Weinstein *et al.* (1964). These studies are designed to show that adaptation to displacement can occur in the absence of any activity merely by providing clues to the subject about conflict within purely environmental inputs themselves, as when a perceiver collides with a moving object which, because it was visually displaced, he had judged to be out of range of his own body. As Taub (1968) had pointed out, however, these adaptations (in a pointing response) presume a prior well-established sensorimotor relation. Because they presume, rather than rule out, this relation, such studies cannot contribute to the decision as to whether the efferent motor signal is or is not necessary to adaptation.

In summary, it is judged that the weight of the experimental evidence listed in the chapter up to this point favors the idea that perception is a process which includes efference in the making of percepts.

If, then, motor and sensory processes are thought to interact prior to the formation of the percept itself, is there any psychobiological evidence which would make such a process feasible and therefore at least plausible? This is the question to which the next section of the chapter addresses itself.

EVIDENCE THAT ORGANISMS ARE ABLE TO MONITOR THEIR OWN MOTOR BEHAVIOR AT A CENTRAL LEVEL

The theories proposed by von Holst, Sperry, Held, Festinger, and others maintain that in addition to receiving optic input, the organism in some way also monitors its own behavior emitted to produce such input. One version of these theories is that information from monitored behavior prepares sensory structures for anticipated changes and compares anticipated with actual changes. This is done via the "efferent copy" or an equivalent mechanism. All of this suggests that the organism uses information from its own motor mechanism for interpreting visual input. The question may be raised whether there is any direct evidence from neuropsychology that can be marshaled in support of these kinds of theories. It appears that there are such data.

Research that is relevant has explored whether self-produced voluntary movement or instrumental activity can be learned without the benefit of peripheral proprioceptive or exteroceptive feedback. The kind of movement or activity under consideration here is that which is involved when the organism provides itself with new stimulation and consequently new perceptions by the performance of motor acts. It is what Konorski (1967) called Type II conditioning involving response-contingent stimulation. If an organism can, at a central level, be aware of and regulate its own behavior, the organization of action would not have to presuppose an already independently established peripheral perceptual process. Under these conditions there would be no reason to favor the assumption that motor activity is controlled by, organized by, or in the service of perception. The latter, nonetheless, has been the conventional assumption (see Sperry 1952, for a review). The mutual dependence between these two would be an equally good hypothesis. Perception thus might be a process from the outside in as well as from the inside out. Voluntary action and perception could be mutually affecting and possibly organizing each other. This would suggest that the theory proposed by von Holst and others could be tenable.

Evidence that voluntary activity can be organized relatively independently from peripheral input has been accumulating over a number of years. The evidence in question comes from the research on deafferented[11] animals. This work has been performed by numerous researchers producing largely similar results on two continents, and it has been summarized nicely by Konorski (1967) and Taub and Berman (1968). To anticipate the results, it may be stated that this work shows that voluntary motion is possible without essentially any peripheral feedback from movement taking place.

The deafferentiation work takes off from early findings reported by Mott and Sherrington (1895) and Sherrington (1931) that deafferentiation of a single limb leads to total incapacitation of that limb for any purposeful activity. These findings seemed to support Sherrington's theory of the reflex arc[12] based on the findings of the afferent and efferent spinal neuron. This research has since been superseded by very interesting further studies exploring conditions under which deafferented systems do manifest purposeful activity. The newer findings have forced a revision of the Mott and Sherrington interpretation.

The research that is reported was initially designed to insure, by deafferentiation of relevant parts of the spinal cord, that the animal does not get any direct proprioceptive feedback from its own voluntary movements. Subsequent research has also become concerned with eliminating all indirect peripheral feedback. Examples of such indirect feedbacks are the sound of a buzzer which terminates as the movement which is designed to avoid shock is initiated, the distension of the skin which occurs as the deafferented limb moves, and stimulation of the middle ear during voluntary activity. The concern with the elimination of indirect peripheral feedback from the animal's own activity has led later experimenters to expand the deafferentiation so as to wipe out most of the somatic and interoceptive feedbacks.[13] Moreover, there has been an interest not only in gross but in fine-grained movements. Finally, trace conditioning[14] has been used in an attempt to eliminate associations between voluntary movement and the conditioned stimulus.

[11]The term *deafferented* refers to an experimental procedure whereby all manner of peripheral (inflow) sensations (e.g., exteroceptive, proprioceptive) to the animal are eliminated.

[12]The *reflex arc* is a concept central to psychobiological theories which argue that innate reflexes (and higher forms of behavior) depend on the conduction of excitation from the periphery, through a set of receptors, to a set of effectors (motor neurons) through an intervening chain of neurons.

[13]In the context of the research reported, somatic and interoceptive feedbacks refer to those feedbacks derived from a functioning spinal chord which produce a large variety of body sensations.

[14]In trace conditioning the usual situation, in which a signal (CS) is produced upon the completion of a response (thereby providing a signal that the response has been made), does not obtain. Instead, a CS is used whose duration is too short for even the appearance of response termination.

It may be pointed out that findings contrary to those reported by Mott and Sherrington (1895) and Sherrington (1931) first appeared when experimenters began to use both fore or both hind limbs in producing voluntary instrumental activity or, if they used one limb only, the other limb was restrained. Earlier studies by Sherrington had used one limb only, while leaving the other limb free. Typically, in these newer studies animals like monkeys, cats, dogs, or rats are trained to produce instrumental responses involving one or two limbs or, alternatively, a fine grasping movement. Instrumental responses are used both to produce positive or to ward off negative effects. This training may either precede or follow the process of eliminating surgically, and otherwise, all of the relevant peripheral feedback. Normally, in addition to studying the animal under conditioning, it is also studied in a "free" situation to observe if normal functioning of the limb, singly and in concert with other body parts, will return following deafferentiation. The studies whose results are summarized below are by Berman, Teodoru, and Taub (1964); Bossom and Omaya (1968); Gorska and Jankowska (1959, 1961); Gorska, Jankowska, and Kozak (1961); Jankowska (1959); Knapp, Taub, and Berman (1958, 1963; Taub, Bacon, and Berman (1965); Taub and Berman (1963); Taub, Ellman, and Berman (1966); Vaughan, Gross and Bossom (1970); and Wynne and Solomon (1955).

The number of studies involved precludes a detailed review here. Instead, only a summary of the major findings is attempted. These are as follows: (*a*) Under conditions either of partial deafferentiation to prevent feedback from a given instrumental limb or pair of limbs, total deafferentiation plus blindfolding, or under conditions of the combined surgical and pharmacological interruption of the autonomic nervous system, the animals in question can be trained to produce the instrumental response, or, if trained previously, the animal retains the instrumental response or it can be retrained. (*b*) Both gross instrumental responses such as forelimb flexion and fine instrumental behavior such as finger movement are preserved or can be trained under the above conditions. (*c*) In the "free" situation and for both the partially deafferented and totally deafferented animals there is total restoration of function for the monkeys. Partially deafferented animals, for example, become successful at climbing the wire mesh fence within two to six months. Totally deafferented animals showed restoration of functioning of the forelimb. Because of the lack of sufficiently long-term survival of the totally deafferented animals, hind leg functioning was not restored, and it is therefore unknown if such restoration can be affected. (*d*) The only restriction to be placed on the findings under item (*c*) above is that if only one limb is deafferented, the animal's unaffected limb must be restrained during training. If it is not, the findings reported for the "free" situation under item (*c*) do not occur. The explanation for this, which is given by Taub and Berman (1968), is that the movements of the unaffected limb have an inhibitory effect on the other limb which, due to the operation, is no longer held in check by the ipsilateral segmental afferent inflow.[15] This problem does not arise, however, when both limbs are deafferented. (*e*) If a totally deafferented animal, which is deprived of all somatic feedback as well as all feedback from sympathetic and sacral parasympathetic pathways,[16] is now also deprived of feedback from most of the cranial parasympathetic system,[17] avoidance responses are still given. Elimination of all feedback, however, tends to put the animal to sleep.

The above studies show that response-produced feedback is not necessary for instrumental conditioning (Konorski 1967; Taub and Berman 1968). Konorski (1967) has shown elsewhere that such feedback is not sufficient—that is, he reported research on the general conditionability of passive movements and movements obtained by brain stimulation and predicted that these should not be conditionable on the assumption that peripheral feedback is neither necessary nor sufficient. As to the former, Konorski concluded that passive movements cannot be used in instrumental conditioning (Woodbury 1942). Konorski agreed that there seem to be exceptions to this rule, as in some experiments on larger animals like goats and big dogs. Exceptions also seem to occur in experiments in which animals are passively transported between a starting point and a goal but nevertheless are able to use this experience to proceed thereafter on their own to a goal box (Beritoff 1965). Finally, exceptions seem to arise in certain "insight" experiments (Konorski 1950). In each of these cases, however, Konorski suggested that more than purely peripheral information is available to the animals involved. Either the active intervention of reflexes such as myotatic reflexes[18] are involved in the work with large animals, or responses are made by the animal which go unnoticed by the observer, or, in the case of "insight" experiments, well-known responses tend to be involved which already have extensive internal representations that may be triggered off by, say, visual input and do not require feedback from actual locomotion.

In the case of movement obtained by brain stimulation, Konorski (1967) concluded that all movements produced by stimulation of the motor cortex which are produced by the efferent part of a reflex arc only cannot be instrumentally conditioned. Konorski argued: "only those movements can become instrumentalized which are accomplished by the intermediary of the central nervous system—in other words, which have a reflex character

[15]Ipsilateral segmental afferent inflow refers to interlimb inhibition which can cause a plastic rigidity in the animal. It is eliminated as a result of bilateral forelimb deafferentation.

[16]Sympathetic and sacral parasympathetic pathways are pathways in the autonomic nervous system with special reference to those in the sacrum.

[17]The cranial parasympathetic system is comprised of parts of the autonomic nervous system with pathways to the head. Deafferentation of this system, in its most extreme form, can lead to a shutting down of all background excitation in the brain.

[18]Myotatic reflexes are the sharp reflexes which contract a muscle after it has been stretched. An example of such a reflex is the kneejerk.

in the broad sense of the word" (p. 485). In short, only those movements can be instrumentalized which are mediated by the central behavioral system—that is, *which are performed by the organism itself and are not forced upon it.*

The cumulative impact of these studies is to suggest that voluntary activity can take place with little or no peripheral feedback and that such feedback by itself is not sufficient or necessary, except in a very marginal way. Thus, there must exist a system at a central level whereby the organism can be aware of its own activity, and this information must play a role in voluntary activity. This is the kind of system which von Holst (1954) perhaps alluded to and which is a candidate for an explanation of the data reported in the first part of this chapter.

Konorski (1967) referred to this central system which registers activity of the central nervous system under the rubric of kinesthesis. He distinguished kinesthesis from proprioception and exteroception on the basis that the latter can be controlled externally, whereas the former cannot. Kinesthesis, to Konorski, is concerned with the afferent system which inputs information, not about externally controllable events but about events produced by the central nervous system itself; it informs the central nervous system about its own activity. The kinesthetic analyzer which records muscular contractions is placed by Konorski at the level of the cerebellum. According to Konorski, the cerebellum provides the basic input to the motor (kinesthetic) cortex which thus obtains information about complex movements from such input. In turn, the cerebellum receives inputs from that motor cortex, as well as information from tendon and stretch receptors.

Taub and Berman (1968) also reported research (Chang 1955; Kuypers 1960; Levitt, Carreras, Liu, and Chambers 1964; and Li 1958) that has bearing on a mechanism with a purely central feedback mechanism which returns information concerning future movements to the central nervous system before the impulses which will produce these movements have reached the periphery, thereby allowing the animal to know the position of its limb even when there are no peripheral sensations. Taub and Berman stated that the mechanism "would seem to involve afferent collaterals from the medullary pyramidal tracts to the nuclei gracilis and cuneatus, thence back to the cerebral cortex through ventralis lateralis." Teuber (1964) reports research which implicates the frontal granular cortex as a center for the corollary discharge—that is, as a discharge from motor to sensory structures. On the basis of research with many frontal lobe and other patients, he concludes that patients with frontal lobe pathology tend to have trouble distinguishing those changes in sensory input resulting from their own movements from actual movements in the environment.

It appears that organisms do possess systems at the level of the central nervous system which tell them about their own activity. Moreover, this central information seems to be essential for the conduct of response-contingent voluntary activity. These findings, coupled with the findings reported in the first part of this chapter, would seem to make an explanation of perception that involves both information from the optic array and, centrally, from the organism's own activity at least potentially fruitful for perception theory. The modification of perception theory involved would be accomplished by adding the notion that perception requires the intermediary of an organism which decides and does not merely resonate.

It would appear from the combined findings of the first and second sections of this chapter that the separation between perception and voluntary activity as two functionally distinct processes can be brought into question. Perception is not imposed on a passive organism. Peripheral input and central inputs due to the organism's voluntary activity are both involved and may, to an extent, even be shaping or organizing each other, thus lending a feature of self-organization to the perceptual process. The hypothesis that behavior and peripheral visual inputs might be organizing each other has been a feature of computer simulation work in perception by Gyr, Brown, Willey, and Zivian (1966), and the hypothesis was proposed earlier by Platt (1962). Concrete evidence of possibilities for "functional" self-organizing activity of the brain (also proposed by Hebb 1948) has not been readily available until recently. The empirical fact of processes of functional organization in the tectum[19] and visual cortex has recently been reported, however, by Gaze, Keating, Szekely, and Beazley (1970); Hirsch and Spinelli, (1970); Hubel and Wiesel (1965); Pettigrew, Olson, and Berlow (1973); Schlaer (1971); and Wiesel and Hubel (1965).

Conceived as an interaction between central and peripheral inputs and feedback, whether preformed or functional, perception may be said to possess an "internal semantic" by which the organism can bridge the gap between the "inner" and "outer" since these two realms are, or can become, organized together. By conceiving of an organism that does more than resonate but also, rather, compares and decides, the model lends itself better to explaining attention and selection than does a model that discusses the "outer" in terms that are not organically related to the "inner."

PERCEPTION IN THE LIGHT OF EPISTEMOLOGICAL CONSIDERATIONS

The empirical grounds for the theory that visual-sensory as well as motor processes are interrelated in perception have been reviewed, and it has been concluded that the theory is generally supported by empirical fact. In addition, however, there is something else that can be said in favor of the sensorimotor theory of perception which goes beyond the issue of how well it is supported by psychological or psychobiological experimental results. That is, the theory appears to conform rather well to certain epistemological criteria which theories should possess—at least according to modern structuralists. Since these criteria are ones that characterize the thinking of

[19]The tectum is roof of the brain or the dorsal part of the midbrain.

a number of researchers in mathematics, physics, biology, psychology, language, and sociology and have been advanced as the great intellectual tools for penetrating to the heart of the phenomena covered by these disciplines, it is felt that this affinity between a theory of perception—conceived as a sensorimotor, active, and possibly self-organizing process—and structuralism should at least be mentioned. (For a review of structure and structuralism, see Piaget 1970).

As has already been stressed in previous sections of this chapter, the model of perception outlined here excludes the idea of an organism passively "reasonating" to peripheral input. Rather, in an active organism, peripheral input or, more specifically, peripheral input which is relevant to the organism, is that input which is related to the organism's voluntary activity. The theory states that input from the environment is normally obtained by a motorically active organism or, in the language of operant conditioning, that it is contingent with behavior. Stimuli thus are parts of transformations which actions put on the environment. In fact, the characteristic of transformation typifies this theory of perception, and it is this feature which structuralists consider to be truly interesting.

Structuralism suggests that what needs explaining, what is important to achieve in all areas of knowledge, is the discovery of the principles of how various elements and processes discovered fit together. Once this has been done, the feeling that a core truth has been discovered is realized. Structuralism suggests that, speaking very abstractly, the principles of wholeness, transformation, and self-regulation[20] are the core concepts to accomplish these ends. It is argued that every discipline must find, and that many have found, a place in their theoretical structures for such concepts. Especially important as a conceptual tool, according to structuralists, is the mathematical notion of the group of transformations, one of whose properties is that the transformations inherent in a structure never lead beyond the system but always engender elements that belong to it and preserve its laws. Because of this feature, the capacity to express laws of a

[20] *Wholeness* or *structure* is contrasted to the word *aggregate*, the latter being a composite formed of elements that are independent of the complexes into which they enter.

Transformation refers to the dynamic element in the concept of structure. Were it not for the idea of transformation, *structure* would lose all explanatory import, since it would collapse into static form.

Self-regulation conveys the idea that the transformations inherent in a structure never lead beyond the system but always engender elements that belong to it and preserve its laws.

The notion of self-regulation is represented rigorously by the notion of the group. A *group* is any system consisting of a set of elements together with a rule of combination, e.g., a rule of transformation. One of the properties of a group is that the transformations applied to elements of the system never lead beyond the system but preserve its laws. This is the property of *closure*. Other properties of groups are (1) that there is an *identity* transformation such that, when combined with any other transformation, it leaves the results of the latter unaffected; (2) that for every transformation there is an *inverse* transformation which, conjoined, have the same effect as the application of the identity transformation; and (3) that any three transformations t_1, t_2, t_3 are *associative*, i.e., $t_1 (t_2 t_3) = (t_1 t_2) t_3$.

discipline in the language of transformation groups amounts to the capacity to unify it—obviously the dream of every scientist.

For example, in mathematics, the notion of the group of transformations allowed Felix Klein (1939) to join into one vast structure previously isolated and purely descriptive geometries. This was accomplished by showing that geometries could be conceived as types of transformations, each of which formed a group and was characterized by a set of geometric properties which remained invariant under the given transformation. The geometries generated were motion, similarity, and affine, projective, and topological transformations. These were linked by their invariants. Topological transformations are the most general because they preserve only closure. Projective transformations, preserving both closure and rectilinearity, are next in line. Affine transformations preserve the above two invariances plus parallelness. A hierarchy of transformations can thus be built up with motion transformations being the most specialized.

The above is an example of a dramatic revolution in mathematics caused by the introduction of the concepts surrounding the notion of the group of transformations. It is believed that such concepts can also be fruitful to psychology. It was already stated that the sensorimotor theory of perception proposed here can be framed in structuralist terms. The application of the notion of the group of transformations to perception was in a sense natural once it was recognized that the active perceiver does not passively absorb input but obtains it through motor transformations put on the environment. As pointed out earlier, perception, conceived as a sensorimotor process, even in Gibson's restricted sense, was felt already to be compatible with mathematical notions of the group of transformations (Gibson 1966). More detailed elaborations of the group properties possessed by perceptual sensorimotor processes had been made earlier by the mathematician Poincaré (1952, 1958). As far as the motor transformations preceding visual reafference are concerned, Poincaré suggested that the movements in space which enter into the perceptual acts of obtaining stimuli—such as eye and head motions and locomotion—form a mathematical group—that is to say, these movements satisfy several conditions, including that a return to the starting point is always possible (the condition of reversibility), and that the same goal is attainable by alternate routes (the condition of associativity).

Further suggestions and findings are that inputs produced by an active perceiver in some ways resemble a group (Beth and Piaget 1966; Piaget 1969), and that in the course of perceptual information processing the mathematical structure of the input in terms of the group of transformation to which it belongs may be what is salient to the organism (Gyr, Willey, Gordon, Bram, and Davis, 1973; Gyr, Willey, and Kubo 1974; Hoffman 1966, 1970). In the case of studies by Gyr *et al.* (1974) it has been shown that the visual system in children responds to the group structure in a stimulus, at least in part, in the way a mathematical group theorist would.

Hoffman (1966, 1970) has applied group theory to hypothesized perceptual structures in the brain and has speculated that Lie pseudo-groups[21] of transformations are capable of representing the invariances associated with the familiar constancies. Thus, the possible usefulness of the idea of the group of transformation, which is suggested by the conception of perception as a sensorimotor and transformational process, appears to hold up when the responses of the visual-sensory system *per se* are studied.

Another principle of structuralism which is also characteristic of the sensorimotor theory of perception considered here is that no given structure stands by itself. In mathematics this principle is illustrated by another revolutionary theory produced this time by Kurt Gödel (1931). Gödel showed, among other things, that no mathematical system, such as elementary arithmetic, can by its own principles of reasoning demonstrate its own consistency: it has to appeal to principles of reasoning which are "stronger." This finding led to the idea of a hierarchy of structures and to the notion of construction. In biology, a perhaps similar notion is that of evolution. According to Piaget (1970) the idea of structure as a system of transformation becomes continuous with that of construction as continual formation. The process of construction can, in principle, go on indefinitely. Piaget states: "the number of operations open to human thought is not fixed and may, for all we know, grow" (p. 35). Change in a structure or evolution of structures can come about because of either combination or differentiation.

As has been evident throughout this paper, the concepts of wholeness (that no given structure stands by itself) and of construction are needed to describe the sensorimotor process of perception as well. This is as much true in the case of perceptual adaptation (the various experiments by Held *et al.* and by Festinger *et al.*) as in the experiments which concern themselves with "functional" changes in the makeup of the visual cortex or tectum when unusual visual environments are presented to the animal or when visual inputs are rechanneled by surgical procedures (Gaze *et al.* 1970; Hirsch and Spinelli 1970; Hubel and Wiesel 1965; Pettigrew, Olson, and Barlow 1973; Schlaer 1971; Wiesel and Hubel 1965). For it is clear from these studies that neither the organism's own biological structure nor the structure of its environment can be described or understood separately. Rather, only by the interaction of the two (i.e., of the whole) can the units (organism and environment) be understood. The interaction is the construction. Finally—and this is an application of Gödel's theorem to psychobiology—the system can neither be fully detailed in advance nor exhaustively described at any one moment.

In terms of combinations and differentiations of the broader class of sensorimotor process considered by Piaget and his collaborators (Piaget

[21]Lie groups are a special variety of groups. As contrasted to other groups, they are of a "continuous" or "infinitesimal" kind. In mathematical terms, a Lie group is not only a group but also a differentiable manifold. Because of such properties calculus is used extensively in Lie group theory.

1952*a*, 1952*b*, 1954, 1965, 1970; Piaget and Inhelder 1956), they too form structures that combine and differentiate. These authors suggest, for example, that the operations of later-developing stages of cognitive thought are derived from combinations of such sensorimotor structures. The elements of sensorimotor behavior they have in mind are acts or operations of "uniting," "ordering," "placing in one-to-one correspondence." Formal thinking, according to Piaget, combines both group and lattice structures. In the case of children's representation of space, Piaget and Inhelder show that topological structures ultimately become differentiated into the more restrictive projective, affine similarity, and motion structures, while at the same time preserving a topological "mother-structure." It should be pointed out that in each of the operations of combination and differentiation entirely new properties, not invariant before, emerge (Apostel, Grize, Papert, and Piaget 1963; Piaget 1970).

It may be concluded that not only are sensorimotor theories of perception generally supported by much empirical research, but these theories and their extensions also are compatible with conceptualization in terms of the potentially very rich constructs of wholeness, transformation, and self-regulation which form the foundations of at least one branch of modern epistemology. The implications of this are that thinking of these processes in sensorimotor terms may amount to not just a nice new idea or clever twist, but a conception with perhaps immense possibilities for integrating previously disparate phenomena. For example, it may make possible the integration of visual-sensory and visual-motor processes involved in perception, as well as the integration of lower-order sensorimotor phenomena such as perception and higher-order sensorimotor phenomena such as cognition. For once, work in psychology might thus lead not to more and more specialization of area of interest, but to integration.

References

Apostel, L.; Grize, J. B.; Papert, S.; and Piaget, J. *La filiation des structures.* Paris: Presses Universitaires de France, 1963.

Beritoff, I. S. *Neural Mechanisms of Higher Vertebrate Behavior,* edited and translated by W. T. Liberson. Boston: Little, Brown, 1965.

Berman, A. J.; Teodoru, D.; and Taub, E. "Conditioned Behavior Following Sensory Isolation in Primates." *Transactions of the American Neurological Association* 89 (1964):185–86.

Beth, E. W., and Piaget, J. *Mathematical Epistemology and Psychology.* Dordrecht-Holland: Reidel, 1966.

Brindley, G. S., and Merton, P. A. "The Absence of Position Sense in the Human Eye." *Journal of Physiology* 153 (1960):127–30.

Burnham, C. A. "Adaptation to Prismatically Induced Curvature with Nonvisible Arm Movements." *Psychonomic Science* 10 (1968):273–74.

Campbell, F. S., and Robson, J. G. "A Fresh Approach to Stabilized Retinal Images." In *Proceedings of the Physiological Society* (1961): 11P–12P.

Chang, H. T. "Activation of Internuncial Neurons through Collaterals of Pyramidal Fibers at Cortical Level." *Journal of Neurophysiology* 18 (1955):452–71.

Ditchburn, R. W., and Ginsborg, E. L. "Vision with Stabilized Retinal Image." *Nature* 170 (1952):36–37.

Festinger, L.; Burnham, C. A.; Ono, H.; and Bamber, D. "Efference and the Conscious Experience of Perception." *Journal of Experimental Psychology Monograph* 74 (4, Whole No. 637) (1967).

———, and Canon, L. K. "Information about Spatial Location Based on Knowledge about Efference." *Psychological Review* 72 (1965):373–84.

Gaze, R. M.; Keating, M. J.; Szekely, G.; and Beazley, L. "Binocular Interaction in the Formation of Specific Intertectal Neural Connexions." *Proceedings of the Royal Society* 175(B) (1970):107–47.

Gibson, J. J. "Perception as a Function of Stimulation." In *Psychology: A Study of a Science,* edited by S. Koch. Vol. I. New York: McGraw-Hill, 1959.

———. *The Senses Considered as Perceptual Systems.* Boston: Houghton Mifflin, 1966.

———. "What Gives Rise to the Perception of Motion?" *Psychological Review* 75 (1968):335–46.

———. "Outline of a Theory of Direct Visual Perception." In *The Psychology of Knowing,* edited by J. R. Royce and W. W. Rozeboom. New York: Gordon & Breach, in press.

Gorska, T., and Jankowska, E. "Instrumental Conditioned Reflexes of the Deafferented Limb in Cats and Rats." *Bulletin of the Academy of Polish Science* 7 (1959):161–64.

———, and Jankowska, E. "The Effects of Deafferentation on Instrumental (Type II) Conditioned Reflexes in Dogs." *Acta Biologiae Experimentalis* 21 (1961):219–34.

———; Jankowska, E.; and Kozak, W. "The Effects of Deafferentation on Instrumental (Type II) Cleaning Reflex in Cats." *Acta Biologiae Experimentalis* 21 (1961): 207–17.

Graefe, A. von. *Handbuch der gesammten Augenheilkunde* 6 (1878): 18–21.

Gyr, J. W. "Is a Theory of Direct Visual Perception Adequate?" *Psychological Bulletin* 77 (1972):246–61.

———; Brown, J. S.; Willey, R.; and Zivian, A. "Computer Simulation and Psychological Theories of Perception." *Psychological Bulletin* 65 (1966):174–92.

———, and Willey, R. "The Effects of Efference to the Arm on Visual Adaptation to Curvature: A Replication." *Psychonomic Science* 21 (1970):89–91.

———; Willey, R.; Gordon, D.; Bram, S.; and Davis, S. "Children's Attention to Mathematically Ordered Transforming Stimuli." *Perceptual and Motor Skills* 36 (1973):463–75.

———; Willey, R.; Gordon, D.; and Kubo, R. "Do Parameters of Group Structure Characterize the Perceptual Schema of Younger and Older Children?" *Human Development* 17 (1974): 176–86.

Hardt, M. E.; Held, R.; and Steinbach, M. J. "Adaptation to Displaced Vision: A Change in the Central Control of Sensorimotor Coordination." *Journal of Experimental Psychology* 89 (1971):9–39.

Hay, J. C., and Pick, H. L., Jr. "Visual and Proprioceptive Adaptation to Optical Displacement of the Visual Stimulus." *Journal of Experimental Psychology* 71 (1966): 150–58.

Hebb, D. O. *The Organization of Behavior.* New York: Wiley, 1948.

Hein, A., and Held, R. "A Neural Model for Labile Sensori-Motor Coordinations." In *Biological Prototypes and Synthetic Systems,* edited by E. E. Bernard and M. R. Kare. Vol. 1. New York: Plenum Press, 1962.

Held, R. "The Role of Movement in the Origin and Maintenance of Visual Perception." In *Proceedings XVII International Congress of Psychology* Amsterdam: North Holland, 1964.

———, and Bossom, J. "Neonatal Privation and Adult Rearrangement: Complementary

Techniques for Analyzing Plastic Sensory-Motor Coordinations." *Journal of Comparative and Physiological Psychology* 54 (1961): 33–37.

———, and Freedman, S. J. "Plasticity in Human Sensori-Motor Control." *Science* 142 (1963): 455–61.

———, and Gottlieb, N. "Technique for Studying Adaptation to Disarranged Hand-Eye Coordination." *Perceptual and Motor Skills* 8 (1958): 83–86.

———, and Hein, A. V. "Adaptation of Disarranged Hand-Eye Coordination Contingent upon Reafferent Stimulation." *Perceptual and Motor Skills* 8 (1958): 87–90.

———, and Hein, A. V. "Movement-Produced Stimulation in the Development of Visually Guided Behavior." *Journal of Comparative and Physiological Psychology* 56 (1963): 872–76.

———, and Schlank, M. "Adaptation to Disarranged Eye-Hand Coordination in the Distance-Dimension." *American Journal of Psychology* 72 (1959): 603–605.

Helmholtz, H. von. *Treatise on Physiological Optics,* edited and translated by P. C. Southall. Vol. 3, 3rd ed. Menasha, Wisc.: Optical Society of America, 1925.

Hirsch, H. V. B., and Spinelli, D. N. "Visual Experience Modifies Distribution of Horizontally and Vertically Oriented Receptive Fields in Cats." *Science* 168 (1970): 869–71.

Hoffman, W. C. "Higher Visual Perception and Prolongation of the Basic Lie-Transformation Group." *Mathematical Biosciences* 6 (1970): 437–71.

———. "The Lie-Algebra of Visual Perceptiom." *Journal of Mathematical Psychology* 3 (1966): 65–98.

Holst, E. von. "Relations between the Central Nervous System and the Peripheral Organs." *British Journal of Animal Behavior* 2 (1954): 89–94.

———, and Mittelstaedt, H. "Das Reafferenz-Prinzip." *Die Naturwissenshaften* 20 (1950): 464–76.

Howard, I. P.; Craske, B.; and Templeton, W. B. "Visuo-Motor Adaptation to Discordant Exafferent Stimulation." *Journal of Experimental Psychology* 70 (1965): 189–91.

Hubel, D. H., and Wiesel, T. N. "Binocular Interaction in Striate Cortex of Kittens Reared with Artificial Squint." *Journal of Neurophysiology* 28 (1965): 1041–59.

James. W. *Principles of Psychology.* Vol. 2. New York: Dover, 1950.

Jankowska, E. "Instrumental Scratch Reflex of the Deafferented Limb in Cats and Rats." *Acta Biologiae Experimentalis* 19 (1959): 233–42.

Klein, F. *Elementary Mathematics from an Advanced Standpoint: Geometry.* New York: Dover, 1939.

Knapp, H. D.; Taub, E.; and Berman, A. J. "Effect of Deafferentation on a Conditioned Avoidance Response." *Science* 128 (1958): 842–43.

———; Taub, E.; and Berman, A. J. "Movements in Monkeys with Deafferented Forelimbs." *Experimental Neurology* 7 (1963): 305–15.

Konorski, J. "Mechanisms of Learning." In *Phsyiological Mechanisms in Animal Behavior. Symposium of the Society for Experimental Biology* 4 (1950): 409–31.

Konorski, J. *Integrative Activity of the Brain.* Chicago: University of Chicago Press, 1967.

Kuypers, H. G. J. M. "Central Cortical Projections to Motor and Somatosensory Cell Groups." *Brain* 83 (1960): 161–84.

Levitt, M.; Carreras, M.; Liu, C. N.; and Chambers, W. W. "Pyramidal and Extra-Pyramidal Modulation of Somatosensory Activity in Gracile and Cuneate Nuclei." *Archives of Italian Biology* 102 (1964): 197–229.

Li, Ch-L. "Activity of Interneurons in the Motor Cortex." In *Reticular Formation of the Brain,* edited by H. H. Jasper, L. D. Proctor, R. S. Knighton, W. C. Norsbay, and R. T. Costello. Boston: Little, Brown, 1958.

Matin, L., and Matin, E. "Visual Perception of Direction and Voluntary Saccadic Eye Movements." In *Cerebral Control of Eye Movements and Motion Perception,* edited by I. Dichgans and E. Bizzi. New York: Karger, 1972.

Merton, P. A. "Absence of Conscious Position Sense in the Human Eyes." In *The Oculomotor System,* edited by M. B. Bender. New York: Harper & Row, 1964.

Mott, F. W., and Sherrington, C. S. "Experiments upon the Influence of Sensory Nerves upon Movement and Nutrition of the Limbs." *Proceedings of the Royal Society* 57 (1895): 481–88.

Paillard, J., and Brouchon, M. "Active and Passive Movements in the Calibration of Position Sense." In *The Neuropsychology of Spatially Oriented Behavior,* edited by S. J. Freedman. Homewood, Ill.: Dorsey, 1968.

Pettigrew, J.; Olson, C.; and Barlow, H. B. "Kitten Visual Cortex: Short-Term, Stimulus Induced Changes in Connectivity." *Science* 180 (1973): 1202–203.

Piaget, J. *The Psychology of Intelligence.* New York: Harcourt, Brace, 1950.

———. *The Child's Conception of Number.* New York: Humanities Press, 1952.

———. *The Construction of Reality in the Child.* New York: Basic Books, 1954.

———. *The Mechanisms of Perception.* New York: Basic Books, 1969.

———. *Structuralism.* New York: Basic Books, 1970.

Pick, H. L., and Hay, J. C. "A Passive Test of the Held Reafference Hypothesis." *Perceptual and Motor Skills* 20 (1965): 1070–72.

Platt, J. R. "Functional Geometry and the Determination of Pattern in Mosaic Receptors." *General Systems* 7 (1962): 103–19.

Rashbass, C. "The Relationship between Saccadic and Smooth Tracking Eye Movements." *Journal of Physiology* 159 (1961): 326–38.

Rock, I. *The Nature of Perceptual Adaptation.* New York: Wiley, 1966.

Sherrington, C. S. "Quantitative Management of Contraction in Lowest Level Coordination." *Brain* 54 (1931): 1–28.

Singer, G., and Day, R. H. "Spatial Adaptation and Aftereffect with Optically Transformed Vision: Effects of Active and Passive Responding and the Relation between Test and Exposure Responses." *Journal of Experimental Psychology* 71 (1966*a*): 725–31.

———, and Day, R. H. "The Effects of Spatial Judgments on the Perceptual Aftereffects Resulting from Prismatically Transformed Vision." *Australian Journal of Psychology* 18 (1966*b*): 63–70.

Skavenski, A. A. "Inflow as a Source of Extraretinal Eye Position Information." *Vision Research* 12 (1972): 221–29.

Slotnick, R. S. "Adaptation to Curvature Distortion." *Journal of Experimental Psychology* 81 (1969): 441–48.

Sperry, R. W. "Neural Basis of the Spontaneous Optokinetic Response Produced by Visual Inversion." *Journal of Comparative and Physiological Psychology* 43 (1950): 482–89.

———. "Neurology and the Mind-Brain Problem." *American Scientist* 40 (1952): 291–312.

Taub, E.; Bacon, R.; and Berman, A. J. "The Acquisition of a Trace-Conditioned Avoidance Response after Deafferentation of the Responding Limb." *Journal of Comparative and Physiological Psychology* 58 (1965): 275–79.

———, and Berman, A. J. "Avoidance Conditioning in the Absence of Relevant Proprioceptive and Exteroceptive Feedback." *Journal of Comparative Physiological Psychology* 56 (1963): 1012–16.

———, and Berman, A. J. "Movement and Learning in the Absence of Sensory Feedback." In *The Neuropsychology of Spatially Oriented Behavior,* edited by S. J. Freedman. Homewood, Ill.: Dorsey, 1968.

———, Ellman, S. J.; and Berman, A. J. "Deafferentiation in Monkeys: Effect on Contitioned Grasp Response." *Science* 151 (1966): 593–94.

Taylor, J. G. *The Behavioral Basis of Perception.* New Haven: Yale University Press, 1962.

Templeton, W. B.; Howard, I. P.; and Wilkinson, D. A. "Additivity of Components of Prismatic Adaptation." *Perception and Psychophysics,* in press.

Tepas, D. I. "The Electrophysiological Correlates of Vision in a Uniform Field." In *Visual Problems of the Armed Forces,* edited by M. A. Whitcomb. Washington, D.C.: National Academy of Science, National Research Council, 1962.

Teuber, H. L. "Perception." In *Handbook of Physiology,* edited by J. Field, H. W. Magoun, and V. E. Hall. Section 1. *Neurophysiology.* Vol. 3. Washington D.C.: American Physiological Society, 1960.

———. "The Riddle of Frontal Lobe Function in Man." In *The Frontal Granular Cortex and Behavior,* edited by J. M. Warren and K. Akert. New York: McGraw-Hill, 1964.

Walk, R. D., and Gibson, E. "A Comparative and Analytical Study of Visual Depth Perception." *Psychological Monographs* 75 (15, Whole No. 519) (1961).

Weinstein, S.; Sersen, A.; Fisher, L.; and Weisinger, M. "Is Reafference Necessary for Visual Adaptation?" *Perceptual & Motor Skills* 18 (1964): 641–48.

Whitteridge, D. "Afferent Mechanisms in the Initiation and Control of Eye Movements." In *Proceedings of the International Union of Physiological Science: XXII International Congress.* Amsterdam: Excerpta Medica Foundation, 1962.

Wiesel, T. N., and Hubel, D. H. "Comparison of the Effects of Unilateral and Bilateral Eye Closure on Cortical Unit Responses in Kittens." *Journal of Neurophysiology* 28 (1965): 1029–40.

Woodbury, C. B. "A Note on 'Passive' Conditioning." *Journal of Genetic Psychology* 27 (1942): 359–61.

Wynne, L. C., and Solomon, R. L. "Traumatic Avoidance Learning: Acquisition and Extinction in Dogs Deprived of Normal Peripheral Autonomic Function." *Genetic Psychology Monographs* 52 (1955): 243–84.

Editors' note: In Volume 1, Dr. Norris Haring presented an overview of the application of behavior modification to children with learning disabilities. In this chapter, Dr. James M. Kauffman deals more specifically with the research aspects of behavior modification.

Dr. Kauffman provides us with a general orientation to theory and methodology in behavior modification as an introduction to the use of this powerful approach. The various kinds of measurement techniques and devices are discussed, with special reference to the numerous problems encountered in measuring behavior and its change. Dr. Kauffman deals extensively with the various modes of research design employed in behavioral research. The use of behavior modification in various academic areas—reading, arithmetic, written language, and oral language—are covered thoroughly.

As has been pointed out in the chapters, "The Psychoeducational Match" and "The Learning Environment," by Dr. William Cruickshank in Volume 1, the need for structure in the teaching environment of many learning disabled children is apparent. Dr. Kauffman's chapter provides support for the notion that behavior modification as a technique of "structuring" is an extremely valuable technique.

James M. Kauffman, Ed. D., is Associate Professor of Education, Department of Special Education, at the University of Virginia. He is a member of the Council for Exceptional Children, the Association for the Advancement of Behavior Therapy, and the Society for Research in Child Development. Dr. Kauffman's experience with children includes teaching emotionally disturbed children at the Menninger Clinic, Topeka, Kansas, and instructing disturbed and normal children in public schools. He is the coauthor of many books and journal articles in special education.

10

Behavior Modification

James M. Kauffman

Behavior modification is the systematic control of environmental events to produce specific changes in observable behaviors. It is not restricted to the use of consequences or to the removal of maladaptive behaviors. Environmental events preceding the behavior in question (such as instructions, cues, models, and prompts) as well as events following the behavior (such as positive reinforcers or aversive stimuli) may be arranged to modify an individual's performance. Furthermore, procedures which strengthen appropriate behavior are equally as important as techniques designed to eliminate undesirable behavior. While traditional psychological methods of modifying children's behavior have sought rather global changes in personality, including alteration of internal psychic processes or other variables measurable only by inferential techniques, behavior modification seeks more limited and specific changes in behaviors which can be observed and measured directly. The studies reviewed in this chapter will be concerned with: (*a*) specific behaviors that are open to direct measurement, (*b*) manipulation of environmental events that are functionally related to those behaviors, and (*c*) evaluation of behavioral change that is open to empirical verification.

A number of basic principles of behavior management have been known and practiced for centuries—cf. Benjamin Franklin [B. F. Skinner] 1970; Ullmann and Krasner 1965; Wolpe and Theriault 1971—but the *systematic* application of those principles to problems of human behavior was not common until the late 1950s. Early studies in which basic principles of learning were systematically applied to the management and education of hyperactive, brain damaged, or emotionally disturbed children (e.g., Cruickshank, Bentzen, Ratzeburg, and Tannhauser 1961; Haring and Phillips 1962; Zimmerman and Zimmerman 1962) were remarkable for the clarity and simplicity with which behavioral and academic problems were approached. The method consisted of carefully controlling the educational environment and academic tasks, taking special care to make the teacher's directions clear, to make the teacher's expectations firm, and to keep the consequences of the child's behavior consistent. Such highly structured educational methodology was a significant precursor of current behavior modification procedures, but by current standards it lacked precision and an adequate evaluation component; behaviors were not measured continuously and directly, nor was any attempt made to analyze functionally the various techniques used to change behavior.

In the decade since Ullmann and Krasner published their now classic volumes (Krasner and Ullmann 1965; Ullmann and Krasner 1965), the behavior modification literature has grown enormously. A voluminous part of the literature deals with severely handicapped or deviant individuals. As Estes (1970) has observed, some of the most convincing evidence of the efficacy of behavior modification is to be found in cases where other methods have conspicuously failed, and conspicuous failure of other methods is common with the severely handicapped. Furthermore, because behavior modification evolved from laboratory research with infrahuman subjects, behaviorists have found many of their research methods particularly well suited to the study of simple instrumental responses of severely limited humans. However, there is no evidence of an essential discontinuity between the principles governing manipulation of animal behavior and those governing control of the behavior of mildly handicapped or normal humans (Ferster and Perrott 1968; Skinner 1953; Whaley and Malott 1971). Consequently, behavior modification research with mildly handicapped and normal individuals is increasing. This chapter will focus primarily on behavior modification studies with normal children and children who are mildly or moderately handicapped.

Because behavior modification principles have been found to apply in essentially the same fashion to all organisms, behavior modifiers have been little concerned about the categories, labels, or classification of their subjects. Techniques which successfully eliminate tantrums or increase task attention often appear to apply equally as well to children labeled emotionally disturbed or mentally retarded as they do to children considered learning disabled. The essential consideration in selecting a behavior modification procedure is not etiology or psychiatric nosology but the child's behavior and its responsiveness to specific environmental modulations. Nevertheless, this chapter will be primarily concerned with studies of children who are described as having learning disabilities. Both the sheer quantity of recent behavior modification research and the purpose of this volume suggest such restriction of the topic. Additionally, a recent survey by Hallahan and Cruickshank (1973) of the learning disabilities literature has found behavior modification with learning disabled children to be a relatively neglected area of research.

The behavior modification literature is replete with studies of the control of disruptive, hyperactive, aggressive, inappropriate, and inattentive behaviors (see chapters by Hallahan and Kauffman in Volume 2 and Haring in Volume 1 for a partial review of this literature). In fact, studies of this sort have been published in such quantity that the usefulness of additional similar research has been questioned (Winett and Winkler 1972). Numerous books and reviews of literature on this topic, in addition to the multitude of journal articles now published, make further review and analysis seem frivolous.[1] There has been comparatively little research, however, of the modification of children's academic behaviors. Apparently, there is growing interest in turning the methods of behavior modification or applied behavior analysis to the problems of academic learning, as evidenced by the recent publication of several volumes in which studies of teaching procedures and academic responses are highlighted (e.g., Haring and Hayden 1972; Ramp and Hopkins 1971; Semb 1972). The emergence of a body of literature concerned with the application of behavior principles to academic learning has particular significance for learning disabled children, in whom academic retardation is a primary problem. Consequently, this chapter will deal primarily with the modification of academic behavior.

THEORY AND METHODOLOGY IN BEHAVIOR MODIFICATION

Behavior modification methodology is based primarily on the work of B. F. Skinner, an individual who has tried to dissociate himself from the pursuit of theory (cf. Skinner 1953, 1971). Although behavior modifiers have maintained a visceral distrust of theory, Scriven (1973) has noted that "the whole movement is redolent of ideology, and that is usually the smoke from a small theoretical fire, or at least from the embers of immolated theory" (p. 422). The ideology of radical behaviorism in the field of learning disabilities has been articulated by Throne (1973):

> Radical behaviorists do not deny that the organism contributes to learning. They only put the organism in what they regard to be its rightful place: as the contingent medium through which the environment acts to cause learning to occur. Parents and teachers should look less (and less productively) *inside* learning disabled children (and children who are otherwise impaired) to account for the response failures of these children. They should be more disposed to look more diligently *outside,* at the environment in which children who are learning disabled (or mentally retarded, brain-damaged, dyslexic, aphasic, emotionally disturbed, cerebral palsied, epileptic, etc.) are not functioning *aside from* the environment, and therefore may potentially be made to function better *because* of the environment. *This is no mere semantic quibble. The first viewpoint emphasizes the hopelessness of the organism, the second the hopefullness of the environment.* . . . [Parents and teachers] should become more cognizant of the fact that these children respond more successfully under extraordinary environmental conditions; and that, responsively, at least, all that distinguishes them from children who are normal is the need for extraordinary,

[1]Among the many books of readings and reviews of the use of behavior modification in classroom management are Becker (1971); Fargo, Behrns, and Nolen (1970); Haring and Phillips (1972); Harris (1972); O'Leary and O'Leary (1972); Wallace and Kauffman (1973); and Worell and Nelson (1974).

> as opposed to merely ordinary, environments in which to function more successfully, whatever their organismic statuses. (p. 546)

Skinner denies neither the operation of organismic variables nor the existence of private events, and some of his avid followers (e.g., Cautela 1973; Homme 1965) have given a good deal of attention to the subjective life.

> Yet [Skinner's] *research activities,* if analyzed by a "cognitive functionalist," would certainly be described as evidencing a commitment to radical behaviorism. And his theoretical works, including this one [*Beyond Freedom and Dignity*], have always shown at least some strands of argument which make clear that he hankers after and wishes desperately for the truth of radical behaviorism. If he had come any closer, especially earlier in his career, to believing in the functionality of the conscious mind for psychological explanation and even manipulation, he might well have been caught in a swamp from which he would never have struggled ashore to do good things. (Scriven 1973, p. 433)

Criticism of both Skinner's methodology and his ideology has been, in a few cases, reasoned; in most cases, it has been illogical and hysterical. Among the more reasoned and coherent critics of Skinner is Scriven (1973), who sees the philosophy of behavior modification as no worse than that of any other twentieth-century movement in psychology or education: "In point of fact, the concept of 'being philosophically more confused than "humanistic psychology," ' for example, not only lacks instances but is probably beyond the reach of human comprehension" (p. 423). Scriven argues that while Skinner's philosophical position is untenable, his practical-social contributions are valuable; and that while his philosophical shortcomings may have been responsible for some of his contributions in the practical-social area, correction of his philosophical errors may make progress beyond those contributions possible.

The remainder of this chapter will follow the behavior modification proclivity to sidestep direct discussion of theory and philosophy and attend to matters of methodology and research—the valuable practical-social contributions. Discussion will center on Skinner's operant model, for other paradigms, such as Wolpe's (1958) systematic desensitization and similar approaches, have had but limited applications to *educational* behavior modification, usually in the study of school phobia.

A basic assumption underlying behavior modification is that behavior is a function of its consequences. Therefore, behavior modifiers typically manipulate the events following a response in order to bring about the wanted change. Positive reinforcers, negative reinforcers, or punishing events may be withheld, presented, or withdrawn systematically until the desired effect is achieved. However, behavior may also be changed by varying events which precede and set the occasion for it. Instructions, cues, prompts, or curriculum materials, for example, may have a controlling influence on behavior under certain circumstances, and their effects on responses may be analyzed. Various imitative stimuli may be presented and analyzed for their functional relationship to the imitative behaviors which follow, and the effects of observing someone else experience consequences for certain behaviors (i.e., vicarious consequences) can be assessed. Finally, the programs which determine the presentation of various types of antecedent events or stimuli and the schedules which arrange the delivery of consequences may be examined for their effects on behavior.

The principles of behavior modification have been described in considerable detail elsewhere and will not be reviewed here.[2] Rather, problems of measurement, research design, and evaluation will be discussed.

Measurement

Perhaps the greatest single contribution of behavior modification to psychology and education has been the development of procedures for direct, continuous, and precise measurement of behavior. "*Direct measurement* means automatically recording a time sample of behavior in a controlled and specified environment. With direct measurement, no problems of observer bias or test validity occur; everyone admits that the behavior of concern has been directly recorded" (Lindsley 1964, p. 62). This procedure does not, therefore, make use of interviews, rating scales, or standardized tests in which measurement of the behavior in question is only indirectly implied from the subject's performance or interpreted by the observer. Thus, the child's specific academic behaviors themselves, not abilities supposedly revealed by a sampling of related performances, are the concern of behavior modifiers. For example, "If the target behavior is reading, direct measurement on various reading components would be obtained instead of using a standardized reading or achievement test to determine skills" (Lovitt 1970*a*, p. 88).

Continuous measurement involves recording the behavior repeatedly (usually daily) in order to observe any changes that are associated with or attributable to the modification procedures. Occasional sampling of behavior or pretests and post-tests simply do not allow one to observe directly the function of environmental manipulations in producing or eliminating target responses. Behavior must be measured over a series of days to assess its current or baseline level; subsequently it must be measured over a series of days during which environmental variables are systematically altered if the functional relations among environmental events are to be observed. Therefore, behavior modification research is typified by data which: (*a*) are obtained from an extended series of observations, (*b*) are recorded during several distinct experimental periods in which environmental conditions are systematically varied, and (*c*) are plotted on a graph showing time (usually days or sessions) on the abscissa.

Direct, continuous measurement of reading behavior has been compared to traditional achievement testing by Eaton and Lovitt (1972). They illustrated well, with two case studies, the superiority of direct, daily

[2] Among numerous works detailing the principles of behavior modification are Bandura (1969); Ferster and Perrott (1968); Skinner (1953); and Whaley and Malott (1971).

measurement for placement decisions, communication (with parents, other teachers, and the child himself), and evaluation of learning. With direct, daily measurement, the child's problems can be identified quickly, precisely, and reliably, avoiding the great opportunity for error which accompanies a one-shot testing session using materials that will not be employed in instruction. Precisely what the child has accomplished and the child's present performance can be communicated to others at any time, and what has been taught may be evaluated directly. Johnson (1971) also has presented evidence that daily performance data give a more accurate picture than standardized tests of the child's academic skills.

Precise measurement demands that one control the conditions under which behavior is directly and continuously recorded so that the reliability of observation and recording is assured. In much of the experimental research from which current behavior modification procedures were derived, behavior was recorded electromechanically, eliminating nearly all questions of observer bias and reliability. Furthermore, the laboratory environment was easily controlled with great precision, allowing relatively straightforward, unambiguous interpretation of the results of environmental manipulations. The movement of operant research into educational and other applied settings has added complications to the problem of measurement. Understandably, controversy regarding the most precise and appropriate means for measuring behavior in natural settings has developed.

In contrast to the manipulanda and automatic recording devices characteristically employed in controlled laboratory settings (see Bijou and Baer 1966; Ferster and DeMyer 1962; Staats 1965), behavior modification research in natural or field settings makes use of human observers and manual tabulation of data (e.g., Bijou, Peterson, and Ault 1968; Bijou, Peterson, Harris, Allen, and Johnston 1969; and Lovaas, Freitag, Gold, and Kassorla 1965). Under these nonautomated conditions, adequate measurement depends on defining the child's behavior as an observable event, the occurrence of which can be agreed upon by two or more independent observers.

A number of different recording procedures have been developed to suit the demands of differing situations. At the stage of selecting a response for definition and modification it may be appropriate to keep a running account or anecdotal log of the child's behavior and related environmental events. Bijou *et al.* (1969) have suggested recording objectively the behavior of the child and events antecedent and subsequent to it in order to obtain a useful definition and to infer the probably functional relationships among these variables. In Bijou's method, antecedent events, the child's responses, and consequent social events are recorded in chronological order under separate column headings so that one may note the sequence in which the events occurred.

The behavior selected for continuous recording must be defined in such a way that its frequency, duration, intensity, or other dimensions can be measured. It is at the point of constructing a definition and selecting recording and graphing techniques that disagreement concerning measurement is sharpest among behavior modifiers (Kauffman and Vicente 1972; Lovitt 1970*a*). Some researchers (e.g., Bijou *et al.* 1968, 1969; Hall 1971) have described a variety of recording and graphing methods which they feel are particularly useful. In some cases a simple frequency count of the behavior is made, as when each instance of verbalization, hitting, crying, etc., is counted and plotted as frequency per session (e.g., Kauffman and Hallahan 1973; Kauffman, La Fleur, Hallahan, and Chanes in press; Medland and Stachnik 1972). In other situations duration is recorded and plotted because the investigator is interested primarily in how long the behavior persists or the elapsed time that it has been exhibited, as in the case of thumbsucking (e.g., Kauffman and Scranton 1974; Skiba, Pettigrew, and Alden 1971). The procedures and apparatus described by Lovaas *et al.* (1965) were used to record measures of frequency and duration concurrently.

In still other circumstances, the investigator may divide the observation session into brief time intervals, as short as ten seconds or as long as several minutes depending on the nature of the behavior and the individual doing the recording. At the end of each interval the observer records one of the following: (*a*) whether or not the behavior occurred during the interval, (*b*) whether or not the behavior is being exhibited at the *moment* of observation, or (*c*) how many children in a group are engaged in a specified activity at the moment of observation. The data are then plotted as percent of intervals containing the behavior or percent of children behaving in the prescribed manner, as in the case of attending or study behavior (e.g., Feritor, Buckholdt, Hamblin, and Smith 1972; Hall, Lund, and Jackson 1968; Quilitch and Risley 1973). Behaviors recorded on an interval basis or as frequencies may be defined by criteria which include the dimensions of intensity or duration or they may be coded and tallied as members of a large response class (Bijou *et al.* 1969).

Finally, one may measure the permanent products of individuals. Permanent products are tangible evidence of a child's performance (as distinguished from the performance itself), such as answers written on paper, pictures painted, or puzzles completed. It is possible to translate such products into numerical terms and plot them as rate or percent of performance, as in the case of academic responses (e.g., Brigham, Graubard, and Stans 1972; Lovitt and Esveldt 1972). Because nearly all academic responses can be measured as permanent products (even oral language behaviors, which may be recorded on audio or video tape), this type of measurement is particularly germane to research in learning disabilities. An important feature of behavior modification of academic responses is that behavior is measured in small, discrete units rather than in large "chunks" or amorphous bits. For example, a child's reading performance might be recorded in terms of words read correctly per minute from specified instructional material rather than as a grade equivalent on a standardized test or as subtest standard scores. Arithmetic performance may be described as problems or operations completed correctly per minute with the type of problem specified. In short, adequate measurement of academic responses for the purposes of behavioral research depends on precise, molecular description.

The recording and graphing procedures just described have found wide acceptance among behavior modification researchers. There are alternative views on certain questions of measurement, however. "Some argue that events should be defined in terms of movement cycles, that the beginning and ending points of behavior be precisely described" (Lovitt 1970*a,* p. 88). These individuals use the methods of *precision teaching,* a measurement technology developed by Ogden R. Lindsley and his colleagues and students at the University of Kansas. Rate of behavior (i.e., responses per unit time, specifically responses per minute) is the primary datum recorded in precision teaching, and the data are always plotted on special semi-logarithmic paper, the standard behavior chart (Bradfield 1970; Kunzelmann, Cohen, Hulten, Martin, and Mingo 1970; Lindsley 1971). The exclusive use of behavioral rates and standard semi-log charting paper appear to have certain advantages in displaying and analyzing educational performance (Cohen, Gentry, Hulten, and Martin 1972).[3] However, the limited availability, high cost, and relative complexity of the semi-log paper, as well as the argot of precision teaching, apparently inhibit its wider acceptance in behavior modification research. One must ask whether the use of precision teaching, particularly its recording and graphing conventions, yields more interpretable results or greater change in the behavior of children than the use of ordinary arithmetic graph paper and the recording procedures previously described (Kauffman 1973). At present, only authoritative opinion is available on this question. It is noteworthy that only a relatively small proportion of current behavior modification research employs the methods of precision teaching. Whether this is a result of inherent limitations in precision teaching methodology (e.g., the semi-log charting paper), a lack of regard among precision teaching proponents for scientific verification (e.g., observer reliability and experimental design), or other factors is a moot question.

A more vital question than what datum should be recorded and how data should be displayed graphically is how to ensure reliability and lack of bias in measurement. In a survey of behavior modification literature, MacDonough and McNamara (1973) reported that less than half of the studies adequately controlled for observer bias.

Reliability of nonautomated behavioral records has typically been ex-

[3]Skinner (1953) has suggested that *rate* is the basic datum of a sciencd of human behavior. It is argued by proponents of precision teaching that logarithmic or ratio chart paper best shows rate or percent of change. With the use of standard charting paper, one can make direct comparisons across individuals and behaviors. Communication and analysis are simplified because the axes of the graph always represent essentially the same variables (days and movements per minute). Computational procedures and graphing conventions have been developed for displaying and analyzing several dimensions of educational performance, all based on rate per minute: accuracy, endurance, improvement, and trend.

pressed as interobserver agreement. Two or more observers independently record the individual's behavior at the same time. Later, their records are compared and percentages of agreement are computed. When frequencies, permanent products, or duration are recorded, percent of agreement usually is found by dividing the lesser number or time by the greater and multiplying by 100. When data are recorded on an interval basis, the records of two observers are compared interval by interval. To obtain percent agreement for one day or session the number of intervals for which the two observers agreed is divided by the number of intervals for which they agreed plus the number of intervals for which they disagreed, and this quotient is then multiplied by 100 (Bijou *et al.* 1968, 1969; Hall 1971).

It is not sufficient to assume that because two observers agree on the number of behaviors or on the intervals in which they occurred, adequate reliability or validity of measurement has been demonstrated (although in many published studies this seems to be assumed). Wahler and Leske (1973) investigated the agreement and accuracy of trained and untrained observers in recording from video tape replays of staged behavior. As their findings showed, "one cannot glibly assume that a reliable observer is also an accurate observer" (p. 393). Their trained observers were more *accurate* than untrained observers, but the trained observers had more disagreements among themselves. Reliability, as estimated by interobserver agreement, certainly does not ensure accuracy or validity of observation, as Bolstad and Johnson (1973) also have made clear.

One must take care to construct a definition of the behavior to be recorded that is both specific and comprehensive enough to allow the observation system to be replicated by others trained solely on the basis of the written definition.[4] If the observation and recording system or the behavior observed are relatively complex it may be particularly important to train observers in the use of equipment (e.g., stopwatches, event recorders), data sheets, or procedures. Without careful training and periodic checks, the observers' behavior is especially susceptible to bias, habituation, and unreliability. Moreover, the method of computing observer agreement may result in an inaccurate picture of the actual reliability of measurement (Johnson and Bolstad 1973). As Bijou *et al.* (1968) have noted, when frequencies are large and total frequency *per se* is the basis for computing percent of agreement, there is a possibility that the resulting agreement is misleading, particularly when the observation session is long (i.e., large absolute differences in number do not have much effect on percent of agreement and it is quite possible that the observers recorded different behaviors at different times). To avoid this problem, at least partially, they suggest com-

[4]The reviewers' comments on the observer reliability data presented by Lovaas, Koegel, Simmons, and Long in *Journal of Applied Behavior Analysis* 6 (1973): 165–66 are particularly relevant to this point. These reviewers noted that when observers must work out privately the definition of the behavior to be recorded, the measurement system may not be replicable by other investigators.

paring frequencies over shorter observation intervals.[5] When behaviors are recorded on an interval basis and the response being observed occurs at either a very high or a very low rate, interval-by-interval comparisons may yield unrealistically high agreement because the behavior was coded in (or, in the case of low-rate behavior, absent from) nearly every interval. As a partial solution, Bijou *et al.* (1968) suggest computing two agreements: one for occurrence and one for nonoccurrence.

In many cases, if not in most instances, it is highly desirable to have a third observer make periodic records and check the data he obtains against that of the other two observers. Also, the use of audio or video tape recordings may be beneficial in training observers or establishing reliability of observation during the course of a study (cf. Hall, Fox, Willard, Goldsmith, Emerson, Owen, Davis, and Porcia 1971; Garcia, Guess, and Byrnes 1973; Lovaas, Koegel, Simmons, and Long 1973; Romanczyk, Kent, Diament, and O'Leary 1973).

Romanczyk *et al.* (1973) conducted one of the few experimental studies of interobserver agreement. Both overt and covert reliability checks were made by experienced "assessors" (who were in some cases identified and in others unidentified to the observers) of less experienced observers' interval recording of individual children's classroom behavior as defined by a nine-item code. The observers consistently recorded fewer disruptive behaviors during covert reliability checks than during overt checks, and the agreement between assessor and observer was lower during covert checks. Romanczyk *et al.* interpreted their results as indicating that observers will vary their recording behavior when they are aware that their reliability is being checked and that variation in their records will be in the direction of closer agreement with the criteria of the assessor. While the results of this study are interesting, they are neither surprising nor conclusive. As the authors state in their discussion of problems in observing behavior, "The solutions to such difficulties remain, to date, completely a matter of speculation" (p. 183).

Among the limitations of the study by Romanczyk *et al.* was the lack of agreement between the two assessors whose records were the criteria against which reliabilities were judged. The overall agreement between the two assessors was 0.72, lower than the average agreement between observers and overt identified assessors during the course of the study. Thus, their study is analogous to calibrating stopwatches against two standards which do not agree, and one can conclude little or nothing from their results

[5]The same basic problem is encountered in recording duration or permanent products, and an analogous solution is suggested: agreements should be computed over shorter time segments or on the basis of smaller segments of the product. If percent agreement remains high when it is computed for shorter intervals or segments of a product, one can have more confidence that the observers were actually recording the same behavior at the same time. However, this does not suggest that all problems of observer agreement and measurement of behavior in naturalistic settings are resolved (see Johnson and Bolstad 1973; Wahler and Leske 1973).

except that observers are influenced by irrelevant factors in their environment.

It seems probable that as long as human assessors are used as the standards against which other human observers are judged, vagaries will continue to hamper the search for truly reliable measurement. Increased sophistication in automated environments (cf., Strang and George 1973) offers some hope that human observation of a wider variety of behaviors can in the future be judged against the precision of electromechanical devices, although it seems clear that some behaviors of interest will never be recordable except by human observers. The need for greater reliability of measurement is most obvious when social or oral language behaviors are recorded in an unstructured setting. Nevertheless, as Romanczyk *et al.* (1968) and O'Leary and Kent (1973) have noted, even measures of permanent products may be inconsistent and must be evaluated for their reliability. Clearly, there is an urgent need for research on the factors which determine observer accuracy and reliability. The methods or suggested techniques of a number of writers (e.g., Bijou *et al.* 1968; Johnson and Bolstad 1973; Lovaas *et al.* 1973; Romanczyk *et al.* 1973; Skindrud 1973; and Wahler and Leske 1973) are indicative of possible areas of investigation (e.g., use of video tape replays in training, use of a single, highly trained observer as a single reliability criterion, repeated random comparisons among observers, etc.).

As behavior modification research increases in quantity and sophistication, its measurement standards will become an increasing cause for concern. Problems in the measurement of academic responses will have particular significance for children with learning disabilities. Furthermore, the behavior of the *teacher,* in addition to that of the pupil, will become a more crucial area of concern as the efficacy of various teaching procedures is investigated. The analysis of teacher behavior will require as careful scrutiny of the reliability of observational data as the analysis of pupil behavior.

Research Design

The purpose of behavior modification research is to discover what variables control the responses being measured. This implies an analysis of behavior in relation to environmental events. As Baer, Wolf, and Risley (1968) have put it: "The analysis of a behavior . . . requires a believable demonstration of the events that can be responsible for the occurrence or nonoccurrence of that behavior. An experimenter has achieved an analysis of a behavior when he can exercise control over it. By common laboratory standards, that has meant the ability of the experimenter to turn the behavior on and off, or up and down, at will" (pp. 93–94).

The demonstration of experimental control in behavior modification research has been achieved primarily through the use of single-subject designs in which the effects of successive experimental conditions on the performance of individuals are observed. The superiority of such designs for analysis of behavior change has been argued cogently (Baer, Wolf, and Risley 1968; Kazdin 1973; Kendall 1973; Leitenberg 1973; and Sidman 1960), but several writers have recently suggested the increased use of experimental between-groups comparisons, such as those described by Campbell and Stanley (1963) and Kerlinger (1964), in cases where mean differences between groups are of interest in supplementing or extending the findings of analyses of individual data (e.g., Kazdin 1973; O'Leary and Kent 1973; Ross 1972; and Staats 1970).[6] Some behavior modification researchers have begun reporting data from group designs and employing traditional statistical analyses appropriate for such investigations (e.g., Felixbrod and O'Leary 1973).

Several alternative single-subject designs have been developed for behavior analysis in applied settings. Each has advantages and limitations which make it suitable or inappropriate for certain research problems. In all cases the recommended procedure is to obtain baseline data before any environmental manipulations are carried out. Baseline observation should establish that the behavior has stabilized at an undesirable level or is clearly trending in the undesired direction before any intervention is begun.

In the reversal or withdrawal design, an experimental variable is alternately introduced and reversed or withdrawn. If the experimental variable is causally related to the behavior under observation, then the behavior should be alternately increased and diminished when the environmental variable is manipulated. For example, Lahey, McNees, and Brown (1973), after collecting baseline data on children's comprehension of oral reading, reinforced correct comprehension responses with praise and pennies, then withdrew the reinforcement procedure (i.e., returned to baseline conditions), and, finally, reinstated the reinforcement condition. Systematic changes in percent of comprehension were noted; children testing below grade level in reading increased their level of comprehension under both reinforcement conditions and decreased to baseline_1 level during baseline_2. Goetz and Baer (1973) investigated children's blockbuilding by using a reversal design. They first collected baseline data on form diversity, then provided social reinforcement for diversity, reversed the contingency (i.e., provided reinforcement only for the same forms), and again reinforced diversity of form. More diverse forms were produced when form diversity was reinforced, indicating that blockbuilding form was functionally related to social reinforcement for the type of construction produced.

As an alternative strategy to reversing or withdrawing contingencies, one may record several baselines and introduce the experimental variable in each baseline in succession. One would expect that if the experimental variable were in fact functionally related to the behavior, then each baseline

[6]See also "Methodological and Assessment Considerations in Applied Settings: Reviewers' Comments," *Journal of Applied Behavior Analysis* 6 (1973): 532–39.

would change in the same direction and only at the time when the variable was applied. Multiple baseline designs may involve (*a*) multiple schedules, in which the same behavior of an individual or group is recorded in several different settings or under different stimulus conditions; (*b*) multiple responses, in which several different behaviors of the same individual or group are recorded under the same conditions; and (*c*) multiple subjects, in which the same behavior of several individuals or groups is recorded under the same conditions and modified using the same procedure. Hall, Cristler, Cranston, and Tucker (1970) have provided examples of all three types of multiple baselines. In one experiment, they recorded how many pupils were late in returning to their classroom after morning, noon, and afternoon recess and applied consequences to "on time" and late behavior for each recess in succession; i.e., they employed a multiple schedule design. In another case they recorded and successively applied consequences to three different behaviors of a ten-year-old girl—clarinet practice, a campfire project, and reading—in a multiple response design. Finally, they recorded and changed in succession the grades of three high school students, demonstrating the use of multiple subject design. In each of their experiments, Hall *et al.* found that all three baselines (dependent variables) changed predictably when and only when the independent variables were applied, indicating a reliable, causal relationship.

Another type of design consists of setting a succession of behavioral criteria for obtaining a consequence and observing whether the behavior changes to meet those criteria in a systematic manner. Hall (1971) refers to this as a "changing criterion design." Dietz and Repp (1973) recently reported an experiment in which they established a series of behavioral criteria (a series of differential reinforcement of low-rate schedules) which resulted in an orderly decline in misbehavior, showing that the changing criterion for reinforcement was functionally related to the dependent variable. Similarly, one may employ a design in which one gives a series of instructions, each setting the occasion for a different or more complex response. Lovitt and Smith (1972) conducted a study in which they employed such a design to evaluate the effects of instructions on a learning disabled child's verbal behavior. The child's oral language responses changed systematically with changes in instructions, strongly suggesting that the instructions were causally related to the child's verbal behavior.

Each of these designs has limitations which make it inappropriate for use under some circumstances. The reversal and withdrawal designs are usable only when the behavior is reversible and when practical and ethical considerations allow a procedural withdrawal or reversal. These limitations restrict the use of these designs in investigations of academic behavior to the analysis of performances that are already in the child's repertoire but are not being emitted at the desired rate or under the appropriate stimulus conditions, and, possibly, to situations where rate of acquisition can be studied over a considerable length of time. Reversal and withdrawal procedures would ordinarily not be appropriate for the study of the acquisition of new behaviors. In some studies of acquisition of academic responses, the AB design, in which baseline conditions are not reinstated or intervention conditions are not reversed, is considered sufficient to establish the effects of the independent variable(s). Multiple baseline designs are usable only when the baselines are independent to the degree that a change in one does not automatically result in change in another. Thus, the conditions, behaviors, or individuals representing the baselines must be selected with care, and one must be able to intervene in the remaining baselines in succession only after a stable change has been produced in the other(s). The study of highly interdependent or interrelated academic skills or the lack of administrative or procedural flexibility may preclude the use of multiple baseline designs. Changing criterion designs are appropriate only when one can measure and provide consequences or instructions for successive levels of performance along some meaningful dimension and when events controlling the attainment of one criterion are not so potent that achievement of the final criterion is premature. When the desired behavioral goal is defined as an all-or-nothing performance, when performance criteria are not precisely stated, or when an immediate, dramatic change is desired, a changing criterion design is of no value. Changing criterion designs have been little used, but they may have particular relevance for research on academic behavior if one can specify successive criteria for performance in the acquisition of new responses or successive steps in the improvement of skills.

Combinations of the designs described here may, of course, be used in a single study (e.g., Hall, Cristler, Cranston, and Tucker 1970; Kauffman and Scranton 1974). Additionally, it has been suggested that many variations of these procedures as well as new paradigms for research are needed (Baer, Wolf, and Risley 1968; O'Leary and Kent 1973).

Evaluation

The evaluation of behavorial change in behavior modification research has rested primarily on the judgment by researchers themselves of the reliability and practical or social significance of their results. Reliability has been judged more on the basis of replicability assessed through design than on the basis of statistical inference. Baer, Wolf, and Risley (1968) state: "How many reversals, or how many baselines, make for believability is a problem for the audience. If statistical analysis is applied, the audience must then judge the suitability of the inferential statistic chosen and the propriety of these data for that test. Alternatively, the audience may inspect the data directly and relate them to past experience with similar data and similar procedures. In either case, the judgments required are highly qualitative, and rules cannot always be stated profitably" (pp. 94–95).

While qualitative, nonstatistical judgment is likely to remain the dominant mode of evaluation in behavior modification research, the budding interest of behavior modifiers in between-groups designs, mentioned earlier, will demand a parallel increase in attention to statistical inference.

Furthermore, serious efforts have been made recently to apply inferential statistical methods to the evaluation of data from single-subject designs (Gentile, Roden, and Klein 1972; Jones 1973).

An issue of special importance for research on academic behavior is whether the specific components of behavior modification methods (e.g., rules, praise, prompts, and/or extrinsic reinforcers) should be analyzed separately, as suggested by Baer, Wolf, and Risley (1968), or whether it is sufficient merely to analyze the function of a procedural "package." One view on this question is that component analysis is relatively more important in experimental than in clinical research. Another viewpoint is that component analyses are appropriate only when isolating the effects of each variable is of some practical or theoretical significance (see Kazdin 1973 and the comments of reviewers on his paper). Axelrod (1971) has suggested that applied researchers and teachers should use the same methodology and that "teachers who fail to isolate the variables which will improve their students' performance might be committing themselves to a career of ineffectiveness" (p. 340). In any case, additional methodologies for component analysis are needed. A new paradigm for evaluation of component effects has been suggested recently by Kauffman, Hallahan, Payne, and Ball (1973). (See also Kauffman and Hallahan's chapter on evaluation of teaching performance, Vol. I.)

Evaluation of the type of research which has characterized behavior modification in the past may not be as important in the future as the assessment of the long-term effects of behavioral intervention. The need for longitudinal research is critical in all areas of special education (Cruickshank 1974), and the lack of such research in behavior modification has also been noted (Baer 1971; Kauffman 1973; MacDonough and McNamara 1973; O'Leary and Kent 1973; Staats 1970). It is only through long-term follow-up research that the practical and social significance of behavior modification methodology can be adequately evaluated.

RECENT RESEARCH ON THE MODIFICATION OF ACADEMIC BEHAVIOR

Much of the pioneering work in the application of learning principles to academic behavior was done by Arthur W. Staats and his associates. In a recent publication Staats (1973) has outlined the development of behavior modification techniques in education, including his own early work in the Fernald Clinic at UCLA with children who had academic learning difficulties. The seminal work of Staats has provided impetus for a behavioral analysis of learning difficulties as well as of the ordinary course of learning in children (see Staats 1968*a*, 1971; Staats and Staats 1963).

The application of behavior modification techniques to the assessment and instruction of children with learning disabilities has been sketched by Lovitt (1967*a*, 1968*a*, 1973*a*). As he noted in 1968, "there are only a few studies referring to the modification of academic behaviors in such areas as reading or arithmetic, and even fewer citing the use of operant procedures in modifying complex social and verbal behaviors" (Lovitt 1968*a*, p. 284). Although the number of studies dealing with academic responses has increased since 1968, the literature on modifying the academic behaviors of children with learning disabilities is still not extensive. Consequently, the following review includes some studies involving normal children or children with handicaps other than specific learning disabilities. Studies are reviewed in each of the following areas: reading, arithmetic, written language, oral language, and other cognitive and motor skills. Finally, areas of needed research are noted.

Reading

The acquisition of cognitive skills, including reading behavior, has been intensively researched by Staats. Based on his research with his own children and other subjects, he has developed a theory of reading.[7] An exposition of his theory is beyond the scope of this chapter, but several of its features are especially important for understanding a behavior modification approach to reading.

One aspect of Staats's theory is that reading involves cumulative-hierarchical learning. That is, the acquisition of certain skills provides the basis for acquisition of more complex skills. Reading begins with the learning of attention and discrimination skills: "These basic behavioral skills form the basis for learning the alphabet discriminations; these form the basis for learning the elementary reading units (grapheme-phoneme correspondences); these form the basis for acquiring a large repertoire of word-reading responses; and so on" (Staats, Brewer, and Gross 1970, p. 76).

One must analyze precisely the skills in this hierarchy which the child has acquired and teach those behaviors in which the child is deficient. This is true regardless of the child's age or biological development. While traditional formulations of learning attribute much to biological unfolding, a behavioral analysis suggests that cognitive skills are acquired through explicit training. One need not (indeed *should* not) wait for the child with learning difficulties to mature to the point of readiness for learning to read—"it is *learning that makes the child ready!*" (Staats 1973, p. 213). Included in the studies of Staats and his colleagues were children with severe learning problems, but these children learned well with the teaching procedures employed. Staats, Brewer, and Gross (1970) suggested that "these and the general findings encourage the wider employment of [our] approach in treating children with problems *at an early age.* This should be done so that children do not develop deficits in behavior that will make appropriate later adjustment difficult or impossible" (p. 79).

One of Staats's observations was that children typically are presented with many learning trials in the acquisition of oral language but that in the acquisition of reading behavior the child is given far fewer and more poorly

[7] For presentation of this research and theory see Staats (1968*a*, 1971; Staats, Brewer, and Gross 1970; Staats and Staats 1963).

arranged opportunities to respond. Consequently, Staats developed simple procedures and an apparatus for presenting many explicit learning trials and providing reinforcement for correct responses. His token-reinforcer system, in which the child was given plastic disks as tokens (which could be exchanged for a wide variety of toys or other items) for correct responses, was the first use of such procedures in educational behavior modification.

> This reinforcer system was first tried on several children who were considered to be difficult problems in the traditional classroom and to be retarded in reading. The learning materials concerned reading and were designed to be simple to administer and to facilitate the recording of the child's progress. That is, the child first learned the new words to be presented in a story: the word was presented singly and the child was told its name and was reinforced for looking at the word and saying its name. When the child could spontaneously read all the words, they were presented in the paragraphs of the story and then the whole story. Better performance was reinforced with a higher value plastic disk (there were three values). The important result was the immediate change in the children's behavior. They became vigorous, attentive workers and they learned well. (Staats 1973, p. 201)

Similar procedures were later used in a large number of studies with a variety of children and instructors (e.g., Ryback and Staats 1970; Staats and Butterfield 1965; Staats, Finley, Minke, and Wolf 1964; Staats, Minke, and Butts 1970; Staats, Minke, Finley, Wolf, and Brooks 1964; Staats, Minke, Goodwin, and Landeen 1967). In a number of cases, the children were taught by parents, volunteer housewives, high school seniors, or other nonprofessional instructors, testifying to the simplicity, generality, and efficacy of the procedures Staats developed. In many of his laboratory studies, Staats used an apparatus which, in combination with his procedures, offers a wide variety of possibilities for research: "The apparatus and reinforcement procedure, with adaptations in terms of type and kind of stimulus presentation and recording and type and kind of behaviors and recording, appears to enable the collection of objective data over long periods of time dealing with repertoires of varying degrees of complexity. It has the same advantages for children, and the study of complex learning, as the Skinner box has for animals and the study of simple learning" (Staats 1968*b*, p. 50).

In summary, over a period of more than a decade, Staats and his colleagues have developed useful apparatus and procedures and employed these tools to obtain experimental evidence that reading behavior can be taught directly, at a very early age, in spite of learning problems, and by professionals or nonprofessionals using simple procedures. In reviewing his research, Staats (1973) questioned the appropriateness of attributing nonreading or reading difficulties to biological or central nervous system defects *as long as the child has normal language.* It appears that the same types of learning principles and the same types of tasks are involved in learning oral language and in learning reading, and that *if appropriate con-*

ditions are arranged the child who learns language can learn to read (Staats 1973; Staats and Staats 1962).

Ryback and Staats (1970) provide an example of the type of research conducted over the years by Staats and his group. Four mothers were trained to use the Staats Motivation-Activating Reading Technique (SMART) to teach their own children. These mothers were high school-educated nonprofessionals of about average economic status. Their IQs ranged from dull normal to bright normal and their academic achievement varied from extremely low to very superior. The four children ranged in age from 8.5 to 13 years: One was diagnosed as mentally retarded; one as having reading and emotional problems; one as having learning disabilities with minimal cerebral dysfunction; and one as having learning disabilities and a heart ailment. The parents were trained in the use of materials and prompting and reinforcement procedures. The materials were stories, words, and questions selected from the Science Research Associates Reading Laboratory. For each story the new words to be learned were printed on 5 x 8 inch cards. Each new word was presented as a stimulus, and the child was prompted if he could not read the word. When the child had read all of the new words for the story in one correct unprompted trial (each word was deleted from the list as soon as it was read correctly), he read the paragraphs of the story (printed on 8½ x 11 inch paper). If the child could not read a word in the paragraphs, he was prompted and each paragraph was reread until no errors were made. Following oral reading the child read the paragraphs silently. Subsequently, the child was given comprehension questions on the story, and, if necessary, he reread the relevant paragraph and corrected his error. No criticism or punishment of the child's behavior was administered. The child's efforts at reading were reinforced with praise and tokens (plastics disks which could be accumulated and used to purchase various back-up reinforcers), the more crucial behaviors (e.g., reading a word correctly on the *first* trial) receiving reinforcers of higher values. The parent-tutors kept detailed records of the stimuli presented, their children's responses, and tokens delivered.

The results of the Ryback and Staats project are very encouraging: All of the subjects made significant gains on standardized tests as well as on vocabulary tests constructed by the authors from the reading materials; initial training required only one hour per parent, and supervisory sessions required only about five hours per parent; during an average of 51.25 hours of instruction, the children made an average of 74,730 single word reading responses; an average of only $18.34 per child was required to purchase back-up reinforcers, and the ratio of the monetary value of tokens given to reading responses *decreased* over time; two of the subjects' untreated siblings, who also had reading difficulties, did not make gains comparable to those of the subjects (although one was receiving special tutoring by a retired remedial reading specialist); and the subjects retained a good proportion of what they had learned, as evidenced by follow-up measures.

Other researchers also have employed parents or other non-professionals as reinforcement agents and as instructional agents. The results of these studies confirm that individuals other than teachers can effectively reinforce reading behavior and, when properly trained, can use instructional procedures to further children's learning.

The use of parents as reinforcement agents for academic performance at school has been investigated by Hawkins, Sluyter, and Smith (1972) and Sluyter and Hawkins (1972) in their work with elementary children who have school problems. In their studies, the child received a note from the teacher stating that he had done well in school that day, contingent upon his having achieved a criterion level of performance. The child's parents were then prompted to provide reinforcers contingent on his receiving a note. Although some improvement resulted from merely giving the child contingent notes to take home, the most marked improvement occurred when the parents provided back-up contingent reinforcement. This improvement was noted in measures of reading behavior as well as in other academic subjects and classroom deportment. Kroth, Whelan, and Stables (1970) also found that when parents reinforced their junior-high-age emotionally disturbed children for academic performance (including reading), as communicated by notes from their teacher, academic performance improved. Knight, Hasazi, and McNeil (1971) reported the use of parents to instruct their preschool children in unit (word or phoneme) reading responses. Their report does not allow one to draw any firm conclusions, but it does suggest that parents can be trained to teach reading to young children (CA three to six) successfully.

Several studies have used other students to teach remedial reading to pupils with learning problems. Staats, Minke, Goodwin, and Landeen (1967) successfully employed both volunteer housewives and high school seniors as teachers of seventh and eighth graders who had reading deficits. In another study, Willis, Crowder, and Morris (1972) had eighth graders use behavioral methods to tutor children with reading disabilities thirty minutes daily. The tutors received five hours of training before they began instructing. Only pre- to post-test data were reported, but the results suggested that children taught by other students gained much more than others who were instructed by certified teachers in a regular remedial program. Drass and Jones (1971) also taught pupils—learning disabled children—to modify the academic behavior, including pre-reading behaviors, of other children with learning disabilities. Again, the reported results were positive, but lack of experimental rigor does not allow one to draw firm conclusions. In a methodologically more sophisticated study, Davis (1972) trained two sixth grade remedial students as tutors of third grade remedial reading students. The results indicated that the sixth graders could effectively use behavioral methods to teach other remedial students and that in the process the tutors' own reading behavior improved.

The use of token reinforcement to modify academic behavior has been studied by several researchers. Wolf, Giles, and Hall (1968) gave points contingent on the academic work of disadvantaged remedial students: work completed and/or corrected in regular school, homework and remedial work completed in the remedial class, and grades on six-weeks report cards. Points were exchangeable for a variety of back-up reinforcers. (Other contingencies for teachers, for attendance, for good behavior, etc., were also in effect.) The remedial group of children made significantly greater gains than a control group (which received no remedial program) on standardized tests. The total program was evaluated as a success. Additionally, individual data for two students showed that "it is clear that the token reinforcement system functioned as such" (p. 60). Students completed more assignments in a particular academic area when they were given a greater number of token reinforcers for working on those specific assignments (e.g., a pupil completed more work in arithmetic than in reading or vice-versa when the schedule of reinforcement was richer for that activity). In teaching retarded children, Bijou, Birnbrauer, Kidder, and Tague (1966) and Birnbrauer, Wolf, Kidder, and Tague (1965) also found tokens (marks) to facilitate the acquisition of reading and other academic responses in the classroom. Clark, Lachowicz, and Wolf (1968) reported increases in reading and other academic achievement in school dropouts (CA sixteen to twenty-one) when a token system (backed up by money) was employed. It was found by Fleming, Kauffman, and Wallace (1973) that points exchangeable for special activities effectively reduced specific reading errors in a first grader with reading problems. McKerracher (1967) used a form of token reinforcement to increase reading skills in an eight-year-old boy with multiple problems: low academic achievement, poor reading, stammering, high anxiety, and occasional enuresis. The major intervention procedure consisted of turning on one light in a group of six bulbs mounted on a box each time the subject read six words correctly. "Whenever all six lights were on together, a sweet was handed to the subject and a few words of praise and support given, whilst he masticated slowly in a relaxed position in his chair" (p. 53). The boy gained 1 year 2 months in reading achievement over a nine-month period, during which he received 17.5 hours of instruction. Stephens, Hartman, and Cooper (1973) found that nonprofessional tutors could be trained to use token and social reinforcement combined with programmed instruction to increase the reading achievement of primary level children with academic difficulties.

In addition to these assays, other researchers have attempted, not always successfully, to use token reinforcement to increase reading behavior in classroom settings. In the evaluation of his Santa Monica Project for educationally handicapped children, Hewett (1968) found no significant gains in reading achievement attributable to the point system employed in his experimental classrooms. However, Holt (1971) conducted a study in which token reinforcement of programmed reading responses increased the number of words read and frames completed by first grade children in a laboratory school. Likewise, in an experiment with fifth graders Sulzer, Hunt, Ashby, Koniarski, and Krams (1971) found that a token system with strong back-up reinforcers increased percent correct and rate of correct responses in reading. It is important to note that in each of these studies behavior was averaged for the group rather than analyzed for individual children, a practice which may obscure significant effects or noneffects for individual subjects.

In their review of token reinforcement in the classroom, O'Leary and Drabman (1971) noted the lack of research of changes in academic behaviors:

> It appears that behaviors such as getting out of one's seat, talking out of turn, and turning around in one's seat are most likely to change with the introduction of the token program, whereas academic behavior would be most difficult to change. In fact, the most obvious dramatic changes in token programs seem to have occurred in programs where nonacademic behaviors served as the dependent variable. If token programs serve as a priming or incentive function, one would certainly expect academic behaviors to be more difficult to change than social behaviors, since children in token programs frequently have the appropriate social behaviors in their repertoire but not the academic skills necessary to progress without considerable instruction. (p. 385).

Kazdin and Bootzin (1972) also noted that relatively little research has been done in which the effects of token reinforcement on complex behaviors or academic responses are studied and that more individual data should be provided. However, the available research does indicate that academic responses are modifiable by token reinforcement, particularly when strong backup reinforcers are provided and when needed academic instruction is given. Although investigations in which academic behaviors are the dependent variables (or at least are among the dependent variables) are increasing in number, there is a need for additional research of the effects of token reinforcement on an individual's academic behavior and of the conditions under which tokens are needed in addition to social reinforcers and feedback on correctness.

A series of well-designed experimental studies of reading behavior has been reported by Lovitt and his research group at the University of Washington. In one of these studies (Lovitt, Schaaf, and Sayre 1970), a comparison was made of an eight-year-old child's reading behavior (correct and incorrect reading rate) when he read from three different curriculum materials (two basal readers and a high-interest low-vocabulary book). Each day the subject read for five minutes from each of the three books. Instruction consisted only of telling the child a word he mispronounced or did not attempt and remained the same throughout the study for all materials. After twenty-nine days, the boy's reading performance in the three books was compared. His performance was virtually the same in all three materials, although these materials varied considerably in their grade-level designations and readability indexes. The results imply that although indexes of readability and difficulty may be based on empirical data and logical dimensions—such as sentence length, vocabulary, linguistic structure—the pupil's reading responses are in the final analysis the best index of difficulty and interest. Teachers would be well advised to select material based on pupil-response data gathered over a trial period rather than on the basis of rated difficulty or interest.

Lovitt and Hurlbut (1974) investigated the effects of phonics instruction on phonics skills, oral reading, and improvement in oral reading from a reader designed on a whole-word approach compared to improvement in a reader designed on a phonics approach. In their first experiment a ten-year-old "dyslexic" boy was the subject. Each day, measures were obtained of five specific phonics skills (by means of worksheet exercises) and of his oral reading (correct and error) rates in two different readers. During baseline, the child was provided with feedback on his performance on the phonics tasks but no instruction was given during oral reading. In the following experimental condition, instruction in the five phonics skills was given for ten minutes daily, but none of this instruction was directed at the oral reading sessions. The data showed that the child improved in phonics skills when given specific instruction, that oral reading improved as phonics skills improved, and that greater improvement was evidenced in the phonics than in the non-phonics reader. Similar results were obtained in a second experiment with four other subjects. The results are relevant to the debate and confusion over the phoneme-grapheme versus whole-word approach to reading instruction. The findings are consonant with Staat's theory of cumulative-hierarchical learning—acquisition of a more elementary skill resulted in improvement in a more complex one. However, Staats (1973) has stated that a variety of skills must be learned if one is to become a proficient reader, and that focusing on one skill to the exclusion of others is not prudent. The finding of Lovitt and Hurlbut that improvement was greater in the phonics reader, where it is likely that a greater proportion of the words were phonetically regular, than in the non-phonics book, where non-phonetic words likely occurred more frequently, seems to underscore this statement.

Several different reinforcement contingencies for oral reading rate were studied in four experiments by Lovitt, Eaton, Kirkwood, and Pelander (1971). Using four elementary children with learning disabilities as subjects, they observed the effects of contingent leisure time (for three subjects) and contingent points (not redeemable) on correct and error rates in reading daily from two books, one of which was a control book to which no contingencies were applied directly. Reading comprehension data also were obtained for three of the four subjects. The specific procedures and results of these experiments are too complex to be detailed here. In general, comprehension improved for experimental readers when contingencies were applied to reading from them but dropped from non-contingent to contingent phases for reading from the control books. The contingencies for oral reading tended to be quite specific in their effects: correct reading rate went up when correct rate was reinforced and error rate declined when a response cost contingency (loss of available leisure time for errors) was applied. Thus, one may need to be careful in selecting wisely and specifying precisely the contingencies to be applied to reading behavior; the effects seem likely to be specific rather than general. Support for this caution was found also in a study by Fleming, Kauffman, and Wallace (1973), in which specific reading errors responded independently to specific contingencies.

In a dissertation by M. Eaton (reported by Lovitt 1973*a*), the effects of noncontingent "previewing" on oral reading was studied. Previewing by the child meant that the child read the passage (orally or silently) and received assistance on difficult words before he read it for purposes of measurement; teacher previewing meant that the teacher read the passage to the child before the child read it orally. All three techniques (oral, silent, and teacher previewing) were effective in improving oral reading in learning disabled youngsters. Also investigated was the relationship of oral reading to comprehension. Contingencies were applied alternately to oral reading rate and oral reading comprehension. Improvement was noted for those specific performances to which contingencies were applied. Additionally, it was found that: (*a*) when contingencies were applied to oral reading rate, oral reading comprehension was unchanged but silent reading and silent reading comprehension improved, and (*b*) when contingencies were applied to oral reading comprehension, oral reading rate, silent reading, and silent reading comprehension improved.

Specific aspects of reading behavior have been studied by a number of other researchers. Modification of deficits in reading comprehension was investigated by Lahey, McNees, and Brown (1973). Two sixth graders, whose tested reading comprehension was two years below grade level, were reinforced with pennies and praise for correct answers to comprehension questions during experimental sessions. When reinforcement was given, the performance of the subjects was comparable to that of other children whose reading comprehension was at grade level. As the authors noted, there were differences in instructional materials and procedures between their study and others (e.g., Staats and Butterfield 1965; Staats *et al.* 1967), making direct comparisons inappropriate. Also, questions regarding the generalization of improved comprehension to other types of reading materials and situations were left unanswered.

Several investigators have examined aspects of the acquisition of reading or prereading skills in young children. Corey and Shamow (1972) compared the reading responses of nursery school children when the reading program involved superimposition of correlated printed stimuli and pictures, fading of the pictures, and overt observing (touching) responses to the words. In the superimposition procedure, words and pictures were paired over several "reading" trials and then the words were presented alone. In the fading procedure, the pictures paired with the words were gradually darkened (faded) over several trials. The observing procedure required the child to touch each word before giving his reading response in both fading and superimposition conditions. The results, evaluated using a factorial design, indicated that the fading procedure improved performance but that observing responses did not. The fading technique used in this study differed somewhat from the titration procedure used in other discrimination training experiments, and important individual differences may have been obscured by the analysis of group data. Nevertheless, the major result (improved performance with fading) is consonant with the findings of other research on learning (cf., Estes 1970; Stevenson 1972) and suggests the development of sound instructional procedures.

Tawney (1972) found that four-year-olds learned letter discriminations better when they were reinforced during training sessions for responding to critical features of letter-like stimuli than when they were reinforced for responding to non-critical features. He concluded.: "This experiment confirmed the utility of a behavioral approach to the problem of letter (visual/perceptual) confusion. When a task is analyzed, critical features identified, and immediate reinforcement provided, young children can be trained to discriminate among stimuli that they had previously confused. Further, this approach proved more successful than reinforcing responses to features of stimuli that are 'simple' but not critical to letter discrimination" (p. 464).

In two investigations of preschoolers' acquisition of phonetic sounds, Massad and Etzel (1972) assessed the relative importance of response and reinforcement frequency and compared the effects of different tactile responses to letter forms. The results of their first experiment showed that children learned letter-sounds with fewer errors and in fewer sessions during conditions of a high ratio of required responses than when relatively few responses were required. Furthermore, their results suggested that frequent responding was more critical for fast acquisition than frequent reinforcement. Their second experiment indicated that tactile responding to sandpaper letters resulted in fewer errors and required fewer trials to criterion than tactile responses to painted letters. The implication of their finding regarding the importance of frequency of response is that teachers should incorporate in their instruction procedures which ensure frequent responding. Their findings regarding tactile stimuli suggest that teachers should evaluate different or novel teaching materials for their effects on acquisition rate.

The use of programming techniques and teaching machines in reading instruction has received some research attention. Haring and Phillips (1972) have reviewed the use of cybernetics and programming in remedial education. Partially automated, programmed reading instruction of learning disabled children has been described by Haring and Hauck (1969). Gray, Baker, and Stancyk (1969) presented a methodological tactic for teaching remedial reading which included aspects of binary logic, operant conditioning, and programmed instruction and a partially automated system for implementing the program. The use of automated (machine) instruction to teach a variety of reading skills to reading-deficient elementary students from poverty backgrounds has been reported by Strang (1972*a*, 1972*b*) and Strang and Wolf (1971). Using relatively inexpensive equipment, Strang has developed, in effect, an automated tutoring system which can be programmed to perform precisely and reliably many of the teaching functions usually carried out by teachers, parents, or other therapy-technicians. With the use of extrinsic back-up reinforcers for correct responses, Strang's automated instruction has produced good results in reading rate, reading comprehension, and practical reading skills (e.g., reading want ads, extracting facts from an encyclopedia, use of a card catalog). As advances are made in finding the most effective procedures for teaching reading skills, it seems probable that more teaching functions can be successfully programmed and automated.

Arithmetic

In arithmetic, as in reading, significant contributions to research and theory have been made by Staats and his co-workers. The acquisition of initial arithmetic behaviors has been studied by Staats, Brewer, and Gross (1970). Development of quantitative concepts was found to follow an orderly progression: Discrimination of numerosity is learned first, followed by counting learning, which requires that the child learn to point to and say numbers for objects in succession and coordinate the two performances. Without learning the sensorimotor repertoire (pointing in succession), the verbal repertoire (saying numbers) is meaningless, but after a basic sensorimotor repertoire is established the verbal behavior may be extended meaningfully by rote training (see also Staats 1973; Staats and Staats 1963).

Only comparatively few studies of simple arithmetic behavior have been conducted by Staats *et al.*, although Staats and Staats (1963) have proposed a behavioral analysis of relatively complex operations, such as multiplication and division. Parsons (1972) has outlined a program for teaching counting, computation, and comprehension in the development of arithmetic behavior. Grimm, Bijou, and Parsons (1973) have applied an operant problem-solving model for teaching basic counting skills to the instruction of two handicapped young children. In essence, they taught their subjects to coordinate the verbal and visual-motor performances of counting by reinforcing explicit components of the required behavioral sequences.

Other investigators have researched the effects of environmental manipulations on arithmetic performance in the classroom. Some of the studies in which token reinforcement was used to influence reading included data regarding math performance also (e.g., Clark, Lachowicz, and Wolf 1968; Wolf, Giles, and Hall 1968). These studies and others (e.g., McLaughlin and Hamblin 1971; Jenkins and Gorrafa 1972) have shown that a properly designed token contingency can increase arithmetic achievement or performance. Predictably, studies showing that parents could serve as effective reinforcement agents for children's reading responses showed a similar effect for arithmetic (e.g., Hawkins, Sluyter, and Smith 1972; Kroth, Whelan, and Stables 1970; Sluyter and Hawkins 1972).

The use of peer influence to modify arithmetic performance has been investigated by Evans and Oswalt (1968) and by Conlon, Hall, and Hanley

(1972). Special activities for the entire class were made contingent on the academic performance of several fourth and sixth grade underachieving pupils by Evans and Oswalt. Under these conditions, the performance of the underachieving pupils improved. Conlon *et al.* arranged for a learning disabled child to correct the arithmetic responses of his learning disabled peers by marking a big red *C* beside correct answers and ignoring incorrect answers. This procedure resulted in improved math performance for both the "corrector" and the pupils whose work he corrected.

Self-management of academic behavior has recently been explored in several projects. Felixbrod and O'Leary (1973), in a well-designed group study, compared self-imposed and externally (experimenter) imposed performance contingencies on the arithmetic behavior of normal second grade children. Children were more productive when self-determined contingencies were in effect than when there were no performance standards, and contingent reinforcement was just as efficacious when self-imposed as when externally imposed. However, children did become more lenient in their self-imposed performance demands over time. Felixbrod and O'Leary's data are in apparent opposition to those of Lovitt and Curtiss (1969; see also Lovitt 1973*b*, and Lovitt and Esveldt 1972), who found self-imposed contingencies to be superior to teacher-imposed contingencies in increasing response rate.

An interesting case of behavior modification of incorrect arithmetic responses was reported by Hasazi and Hasazi (1972). An eight-year-old boy, otherwise a very capable student, was observed almost invariably to reverse the digits in two-digit sums. Because this behavior had persisted for nearly a year, the child had been referred for several neurological and visual examinations and was given "extra help" by his teachers. That his digit-reversal behavior was probably a function of teacher attention was suggested by several observations: "First, Bob was able to discriminate easily between numbers containing the same but reversely ordered digits, such as 12 and 21. Second, he often pointed out reversals on his own paper to the teacher when she failed to notice them. Finally, he was observed on several occasions erasing correctly ordered sums and reversing the order of the digits contained" (p. 158). When "extra help" by the teacher was withdrawn (all sums marked "correct" whether reversed or not) and correct digit-order was reinforced with attention, the child's digit reversals decreased to near zero. A reversal design of this study indicated that the child's digit reversals were indeed functionally related to teacher attention. The finding that inappropriate academic responses can, like many social behaviors, be maintained by teacher attention has important implications for research on instructions; instructions or corrections may sometimes maintain rather than remediate problems (see also Sajwaj and Knight 1971).

Lovitt and his co-experimenters at the University of Washington Experimental Education Unit have conducted a group of significant studies of arithmetic behavior. The first in the series (Lovitt and Curtiss 1968) involved the use of an antecedent event rather than a consequence for performance. The subject was an eleven-year-old learning disabled boy whose accuracy in arithmetic computation was erratic. During baseline sessions the subject merely wrote his answer to problems; during the experimental phase he was required to vocalize the problem (e.g., for ? – 2 = 6, "some number minus two equals six") before writing his answer. In three successive experiments, each involving a different type of computational problem, the subject's performance was greatly improved when he vocalized the problem before writing his answer—error rate dropped dramatically and correct rate increased. The improvement was sustained when oral reading of the problems was no longer required. In a subsequent study, Smith, Lovitt and Kidder (1972) measured the effects of teaching aids (e.g., paper clips, abacus) and instructions on the subtraction performance of a ten-year-old academically deficient boy. Although such instructional procedures and teaching aids have been employed for many years, Smith *et al.* provided experimental data supporting their efficacy and described measurement techniques which any teacher can use to monitor their effects.

More recently, Smith and Lovitt (in press) have used modeling techniques to influence the acquisition of arithmetic computation skills in learning disabled children. In baseline sessions, children were given problems to complete but were given no instruction, feedback, or reinforcement. During some intervention phases, the teacher demonstrated a solution for the child and then left the example on the child's desk for the child to refer to. In other experimental phases the teacher provided feedback on correctness (but provided no model or instruction), modeled the solution but then removed the example so the child could not consult it, or provided only an example of a correctly completed problem. When problem solutions were modeled and the example was left for the child to consult, acquisition of the subtraction or other computational skill was swift and later performance remained high. Feedback on correctness alone did not produce acquisition. When only part of the modeling procedure was used (i.e., when the solution was not demonstrated or when the example was removed) the effects were not consistent for all subjects. As Wallace and Kauffman (1973) have noted, "Modeling or demonstration of appropriate behavior is commonly used by teachers in presenting academic tasks. Teachers characteristically demonstrate the solution of an arithmetic problem before expecting the child to solve a similar problem" (p. 41). However, until the research of Smith and Lovitt (in press) there was little if any experimental evidence of the value of such procedures for classroom instruction. Cullinan, Kauffman, and LaFleur (in press) have called for additional research of the use of observational learning, including modeling and imitation of cognitive skills, in special education settings.

In her doctoral dissertation, D. D. Smith (cited by Lovitt 1973*a*) researched arithmetic proficiency deficits—deficits in rate of correct performance. Several different methods of helping a child reach a proficiency criterion were investigated: pupils were instructed to "go faster"; toy models were given contingent on the child's earning points by making correct responses; feedback of various kinds was given on the child's performance; a combination of the "go faster" instruction and the toy model contingency was used. The procedures resulted in the following: feedback produced small, unimpressive gains for a few children; all children's correct rates improved under the toy model contingency, and correct rates tended to be maintained when the contingency was removed; "go faster" instructions were more effective than the toy model contingency; a combination of the "go faster" instruction and the toy model contingency produced very impressive results—in every case the proficiency criterion was reached. These results have strong implications for classroom instruction and further research, as will be discussed later.

Lovitt and Esveldt (1970) and Smith *et al.* (1972) have also researched the use of various reinforcement and response cost contingencies in altering mathematics responses. Using a multiple baseline design, Smith and Lovitt (1972) found that an eleven-year-old girl, whose computation accuracy was erratic, would increase her accuracy on worksheets when a response cost contingency (loss of recess time for errors) was applied. Improvement was noted only on the worksheets to which the contingency was applied, but after the contingency had been in effect and later removed, accuracy was maintained.

Lovitt and Esveldt (1970) conducted a series of four experiments on the effects of different reinforcement schedules on arithmetic responses rates. The subject was a twelve-year-old boy with learning difficulties. The results indicated that multiple ratio contingencies (a series of ratio bands similar to differential reinforcement of high rate schedules), which provided richer payoffs for higher rates, resulted in higher performance rates. The effects of various reinforcement schedules have received little research attention in educational behavior modification, particularly in classroom settings. O'Leary and Drabman (1971) have pointed out some possible reasons: "The absence of any tightly controlled scheduling research in field-experimental settings may reflect not only methodological difficulties in meeting precise schedule execution but also the rationale that schedule control from token and backup reinforcement is mitigated by numerous other reinforcers provided by teachers and peers" (p. 393). It is hoped that this situation will change in the near future. The simple device described by Kauffman, Cullinan, Scranton, and Wallace (1972) offers potential solutions to some methodological problems in scheduling ratio contingencies in applied settings. Moreover, schedules of reinforcement may be evaluated as components of contingency "packages."

Besides computational skills, which have been the topic of all the arithmetic research discussed to this point, story problems (application skills) are of concern to teachers. Lovitt (1973*a*) has begun work on unraveling the variables which contribute to children's failure on such tasks. He has attempted to isolate some of the features of story problems which contribute to errors (e.g., misleading information, irrelevant lead sentence, numerals presented in two forms, etc.) and to devise teaching methods to increase skills in story problem solution. Future reports of his research should contribute valuable data in this area.

Written Language

Written language involves three distinct behavioral repertoires: forming letter symbols (handwriting), sequencing letters in words (spelling), and using the rules of grammar and syntax to express ideas (composition). The development of these repertoires appears to be cumulative and hierarchical—composition depends to a great extent on the acquisition of fundamental spelling skills, which in turn requires previous development of handwriting (or typing) behaviors, and each of these three repertoires itself depends on the sequential acquisition of component skills. Research pertaining to each of these repertoires will be discussed.

Handwriting

The acquisition of initial writing skills has been researched by Staats, Brewer, and Gross (1970). Their analysis indicated that handwriting involves learning a basic motor imitation repertoire which can be generalized to increase the individual's ability to copy new letter forms. They were able in their research to produce imitative letter-writing behavior in young (*M* CA = 4 yr. 4 mo.) culturally deprived children by beginning with instruction in holding a writing utensil and gradually introducing more complex models for imitation (tracing lines, tracing large letters, copying large letters, copying smaller letters, etc.). The cumulative-hierarchical learning and cognitive acceleration (fewer trials to criterion on successive tasks in a set) observed for other skills—alphabet reading, word reading, and counting—were observed also for writing learning.

Other educational behavior modifiers have also constructed programs for teaching handwriting. Rayek and Nesselroad (1972) have described an instructional program which includes prewriting behaviors, such as pencil holding, discrimination of letters, copying manuscript letters from a visual model, writing letters from dictation, naming letters and, finally, cursive writing. Lovitt (1973*a*) has noted the apparent nonexistence of sound research data to support the assertion by some educators that manuscript writing should be taught before cursive writing. He and his colleagues conducted a study in which learning disabled children were taught cursive writing from the beginning of the school year regardless of their previous penmanship experiences. The study was designed to investigate not only the effects of instruction exclusively in cursive writing, but also generalization of learning across letters and type of writing and the effects of instruction on certain difficult letter sequences. The results showed that the children could be taught cursive writing quickly and effectively, regardless of their previous writing experience. (Note that Cruickshank *et al.* 1961 have also suggested cursive writing for learning disabled children.) When instruction was individualized rather than directed to "word families," the results were positive. Finally, improvement in some instances generalized from lower case to upper case letters, from letters on which instruction was given to non-taught letters, and from cursive to manuscript writing.

Lovitt (1973*a*) has also initiated research into teaching typing skills to learning disabled children. As he has observed, learning to type is a highly reinforcing activity for most children. Typewriters are readily available, and typing has certain advantages over handwriting—it is faster, after basic skills are learned, and produces a consistent, legible script. Lovitt was able to teach several children with learning disabilities to type, some at a higher rate than they were able to write, in three academic quarters without coaxing them to perform or resorting to elaborate reinforcement contingencies., Additionally, Campbell (1973) has recently presented evidence that "hunt-and-peck" typing, in lieu of handwriting, increased the reading achievement of learning disabled children.

Procedures for improving the handwriting performance of groups of children have been researched. Token reinforcement was found to increase the percent of correct programmed writing responses of public school kindergarten children (Brigham, Finfrock, Breunig, and Bushell 1972). Hopkins, Schutte, and Garton (1971) found that the rate at which first and second grade children printed (for first graders) or wrote cursively (for second graders) was increased when access to a playroom was made contingent on completing a daily copying assignment and having it scored by the teacher. These investigators also found that the children's performance improved as time to complete the assignments and then play was reduced by stages from fifty to thirty-five minutes. In a subsequent study, Salzberg, Wheeler, Devar, and Hopkins (1971) replicated and extended these findings with kindergarteners. Their subjects did not improve their printing performance when intermittent feedback was given, but the children did improve their performance when intermittent contingent access to play was scheduled.

The work of Hopkins and his co-workers (1971) was extended by Lovitt and his group (1973*a*). Hopkins *et al.* had found that errors decreased as rate correct increased for their subjects. Lovitt, on the other hand, found that specific contingencies regarding errors were needed to reduce errors when contingent leisure time was scheduled for writing tasks. When Lovitt's pupils were required to correct all writing errors one or more times the following day, in addition to completing that day's assignment before taking their leisure, their writing improved. These discrepancies between the results of Hopkins' work and Lovitt's, plus differences between the studies in children's rate of performance (Lovitt's subjects worked much faster), may be due to teacher differences or differences in measurement and instructional procedures (Lovitt 1973*a*).

Studies of the modification of specific behavioral difficulties in writing are few. Fauke, Burnett, Powers, and Sulzer-Azaroff (1973) used social and food reinforcers and a combination of instructional procedures—such as labeling, tracing, touching, and copying letters—to improve the handwriting of a six-year-old boy with academic difficulties. One cannot ascertain from their study which reinforcer(s) or procedure(s) were effective, but the package of techniques was effective in changing the child's writing behavior.

Spelling

Letter reversals, such as *b* for *d,* may occur in writing tasks and be analyzed as writing behavior. When such reversals occur in the context of being asked to write a word from dictation (e.g., *dad*), however, they may be considered spelling errors. A study of *b-d* spelling errors was conducted by Smith and Lovitt (1973). The subject was a ten-year-old boy with reading disabilities. It was noted during baseline assessment that his reversal of *b* and *d* was not pervasive; he most often substituted *b* for *d,* rarely wrote *d* for *b,* and reversed *d* more often in the initial than in the final position. The major intervention procedure was as follows:

> Every day during [intervention] the experimenter showed Greg the word *dam* written on an index card, and asked him first to read the word, then to name the initial letter of the word. Greg was then instructed to write the word *dam.* The experimenter then showed Greg the word *bam* (written on another index card) and asked him to name the initial letter of that word. Then, pointing to the word *bam,* the experimenter told Greg that he often wrote the word dam like this word. Greg was again told to name the first letter of the word dam. After he had done so, he was then instructed to write the letter *d.* The experimenter told Greg to be certain to write the word *dam* with a *d* and not with a *b.* (p. 359)

The effects of this simple procedure were immediate. After five days, Greg made no more errors. His improvement generalized to other spelling and writing tasks. Although this child did not exhibit consistent, pervasive reversals in spelling, the authors noted other behaviors which may, one could speculate, be associated with neurological defects—reversal of *R* (the initial of his last name), placing a period *before* his initial, and producing the word *dark* for *bark* to imitate a dog. Nevertheless, the simple instructional procedures employed in this study effectively "cured" his "dysgraphia."

When stringent behavioral data are required for definition, *bona fide* cases of letter and digit reversal in children older than eight or nine years appear to be rather rare (J. O. Cooper, personal communication). Furthermore, when such cases are identified, behavior modification techniques appear to be very effective in remediating the problem. Cooper (1970) identified four such cases ranging in age from eight to sixteen years: one was learning disabled, one educable mentally retarded, one a third grader who also attended a university learning center, and one was institutionalized in a state hospital. After baseline assessment, the children were subjected to the following conditions: a repeat probe was administered, in which the child again responded to the reversal stimulus; a correct model of the letter or digit was given contingent on reversal; concurrent reinforcement was provided for non-reversal and the correct model shown contingent on reversal; a reversed model (e.g., *t* for *j*) was given contingent on non-reversal; follow-up data were obtained. All reversal errors were eliminated in one or two ten-minute treatment sessions. The behavioral change generalized for all subjects from trained letters and digits to untrained stimuli. Providing a correct model alone was sufficient treatment for one subject, but the model and concurrent reinforcement combination were required to produce initial change in three subjects. However, for two of these three, the model alone was sufficient to produce non-reversal behavior after they had first experienced the model plus reinforcement condition.

Using learning disabled children as subjects, Lovitt (1973*a*) conducted two studies of spelling performance. In the first, children were first taught to spell a list of words containing the *ea* digraph merely by having the teacher point out that the words contained the ē sound and that this sound was spelled *ea*. Appropriate generalization to other *ea* words and inappropriate generalization to *ee* words were observed; i.e., when *ee* words were taught, many *ea* words were misspelled. Later, pupils were taught to discriminate *ee* and *ea* words by providing feedback, having pupils write incorrectly spelled words several times, and reinforcing correct spelling. Lovitt (1973*a*) speculated that teaching would be more efficient if one taught certain discriminations before teaching generalization "rules" for phoneme-grapheme correspondence or, possibly, if one taught discrimination and generalization simultaneously. In his second study, Lovitt investigated differences in children's acquisition of regular and irregular spellings (e.g., *beg* and *example* for /*g*/) and easy and difficult words (as rated by spelling texts). Instruction consisted of a form of feedback, in which words spelled by the child were marked as correct or incorrect, no feedback, or feedback in which the corrected paper was returned with misspelled words spelled correctly, depending on the list being taught. Acquisition of all spelling lists was prompt for a sample pupil when instruction was given, but generalization to noninstructed lists was not observed, probably because similarities across lists were not pointed out by the teacher. The subject retained the spelling of irregular and regular words equally well, but took longer to acquire words rated as difficult and retained them less well than easy words.

The effects of peer tutoring on the spelling performance of elementary children were researched by Harris, Sherman, Henderson, and Harris (1972). The results of their study indicated that peer tutoring was an effective instructional tactic in a variety of classrooms, including some in which children tested low in spelling skills. Working in a regular fourth grade classroom, Lovitt, Guppy, and Blattner (1969) found that contingent free time, accompanied by a slight rearrangement of the spelling program, effectively increased spelling performance. Pupils were given the spelling list and assignments for the week on Monday. Whenever a pupil scored 100 percent on the test (given four days each week) and handed in his assignments, he could spend the rest of the spelling period in leisure pursuits.

Composition

Relatively few behavioral studies of written composition are available. It was shown by Maloney and Hopkins (1973) that token reinforcement (points exchangeable for candy or extra recess) influenced the use of different words and sentence beginnings in ten-sentence stories written by fourth, fifth, and sixth graders. The students' sentences were rated as more creative and contained more different adjectives, different action verbs, and different sentence beginnings when these variables were reinforced. In a fifth grade remedial classroom, Brigham, Graubard, and Stans (1972) found that they could increase the length and quality of written compositions by reinforcing (with tokens and praise) specific aspects of composition, such as number of different words and number of ideas. Their rather clear findings that "creativity" and other aspects of composition were open to direct modification by reinforcement prompted these writers to comment: "The analysis of composition, 'creativity,' and similar topics are particularly important today because of the growing influence of free schools and British Infant Schools. Many teachers in these schools fervently believe that there is a reservoir of 'creativity' within children—that if only teachers would leave children alone, original and scintillating stories would soon appear. Thus, rigorous study and analysis of such problems as creativity is essential" (p. 429).

Lovitt (1973*a*) has also engaged in research on children's composition. Like Brigham *et al.*, he found aspects of composition to be influenced by consequences, in this case feedback and opportunity to read compositions to the class. Both content and mechanics of composition were influenced by feedback, mechanics to a greater extent than content, but feedback on mechanics improved both mechanics *and* content, a finding in opposition to the suggestion of some that attention to mechanics inhibits expression. Lovitt's subjects improved but did not become proficient in composition, and he suggested that modeling or extrinsic reinforcement may be necessary if proficiency is the objective. Modeling may be a particularly viable approach to the acquisition of such complex skills.

Oral Language

The child who has severe deficits in oral language is ordinarily considered mentally retarded, psychotic, hearing impaired, or speech handicapped. Behavior modification of the language deficits of such children and of milder forms of speech and language pathology has been described elsewhere (see also Turton's chapter in Volume 1).[8] Consequently, attention will be given here to only one issue.

In a recent provocative study, Lovitt and Smith (1972) investigated the effects of instruction on the language responses of a nine-year-old boy with learning disabilities. They found that when given explicit instructions, the child changed his linguistic responses accordingly. No reinforcement was

[8]Important research of language training for the severely language handicapped, for example, has been reported by Bricker and Bricker (1970), Gray (1970), Hartung (1970), Lovaas (1966, 1967), and Risley and Wolf (1967). The work of Guess and his associates with institutionalized retardates (Garcia, Guess, and Byrnes 1973; Guess 1969; Guess and Baer 1973; Sailor, Guess, and Baer 1973) and of Risley and his group with disadvantaged preschoolers (Hart and Risley 1968; Reynolds and Risley 1968; Risley and Hart 1968) is also noteworthy.

given. During this experiment the subject was shown pictures and told to describe them. When directed to vary the beginnings of his descriptive sentences, he did so; when told to emit longer sentences, he complied. The results of this study and a handful of other investigations of instructions (e.g., Rosenthal and Whitebook 1970) have direct and important implications for both educational practice and behavior modification research. As Lovitt and Smith suggested, some children in schools may exhibit apparent academic disabilities because they are uncertain of what is expected of them—they are never told *explicitly* what to do. Furthermore, some experimental studies in which reinforcement contingencies are manipulated may yield results that should not be attributed to the consequent events:

> It could be in certain of those studies, particularly when a reinforcement contingency has been verbalized, that the modification effects resulted as much from instructions either stated or implied as from the contingencies of reinforcement. For example, in an experiment that followed contingency contracting techniques the following instructions could be given to the student: "If you read at a rate in excess of 75 words per minute for 5 minutes, you will be allowed 15 minutes of free time." The data from such an experiment could reveal that during the phase of contingency contracting the pupil's reading rates surpassed those during the no contingency phase. The investigator could conclude that the performance effects were due to the free time contingency when in fact the pupil's efforts may have been altered as much or more by the instruction to read faster as by the prospect of being able to earn leisure time. (Lovitt and Smith 1972, pp. 691–92)

A case in point of research in which the influence of instructions on language responses may have been confounded with other effects is the study of Zimmerman and Pike (1972). Their investigation was of the differential effects of modeling plus reinforcement and reinforcement alone on the question-asking behavior of disadvantaged Mexican-American second graders. During baseline conditions and for the reinforcement-only and control groups, the following instructions were used:

> Specifically, after reading each page, T1 . . . showed the group picture(s) in the book pertaining to the material read and attempted to elicit child questions by asking, "What questions can you ask about this picture?" "Who can ask a question about this picture?" (p. 897)

Apparently, somewhat different instructions were given to the modeling-plus-reinforcement groups:

> Thus, after reading a particular page, T1 would show the picture to the *S*s and say, "Now I am going to ask some questions about the picture. Listen carefully to what I say." (T1 then asked a question or two about the picture, e.g., "What is this?" "Why is the boy running?" etc.) The T1 then *directed the children to ask questions just like hers about the story.* (p. 897, italics added)

The teacher's saying, "What questions can you ask about this picture?" or "Who can ask me a question about this picture?" has quite different demand characteristics than, "Ask a question just like mine," the type of directive apparently given to the modeling-plus-reinforcement groups. Silence or "None" may be appropriate responses to the teacher's queries, but imitation of the teacher is the only appropriate response to the teacher's imperative. To further confuse the situation, Zimmerman and Pike (1972) apparently combined both vague and explicit instructions in post-testing sessions:

> The test session was introduced as a "question-asking game," and *S* was instructed to "Play the game well, and if you do you will get a surprise." The *E* then introduced 12 pictorial cards . . . and instructed *S* to "ask me a question about the picture. Ask any question you want to." If the child responded with a declarative statement, for example, "The apple is red," *E* would probe further only once as follows, "Yes, but ask me a question about it." (p. 898)

If instructions are as powerful an influence on behavior as they appear to be, based on the available research, then the results of Zimmerman and Pike's otherwise well-designed study seem to be uninterpretable.

The powerful effect of instructions was recently brought forcefully to the present author's attention in his capacity as an educational behavior modification consultant in a state hospital. A middle-aged female patient was referred to him in the hope that a language teaching program could be arranged for her. The ward staff presented the case: encephalitis during childhood; severe visual impairment and bizarre behavior in the post-encephalitic period; institutionalization in early adulthood; voluntary mutism during the course of her nearly quarter-century institutional stay. Questioning of the staff revealed that the patient had almost no self-help skills: she walked only with assistance, did not dress, undress, groom, or bathe herself, and she was a sloppy eater. Upon being introduced to this patient, the author gave her the following instructions: "Walk with me to the dining room without holding onto me; reach out, find the door knob, and open the door; here's a chair—sit down; take only a little food on your spoon and don't close your mouth until the food is inside; unbutton your sweater; take off your sweater; put on your sweater; button your sweater; untie your shoe; take off your shoe; turn this sock right-side out; put on your sock; put on your shoe; lace your shoe; tie your shoe; follow me to the lavatory; comb your hair; turn on the water; wash your hands; turn off the water; dry your hands; hang up the towel." The patient followed *every* instruction! Finally, when the author gave her pencil and paper and said, "Write your name on this paper," she replied clearly, "*I don't know how to write my name!*" For approximately twenty-five years this woman had not performed the simplest self-help behaviors, but it was obvious that she could and would do so if given explicit instructions. Additionally, she terminated a series of instructions with a functional verbal response.

"Rise, take up thy bed, and walk" may seldom be a functional approach to behavior modification, but instructional control is one of the most neglected areas of research in the field. Other antecedent events, too, are seldom studied closely. Nearly a decade ago, Bijou and Baer (1966) concluded a chapter on operant research with children: "A future chapter of operant methods in child research would be expected to have a large section on setting events. Variables such as social-class membership, histories of institutional deprivation, education, socialization, injury, medication, etc. will probably have been studied in relation to operant techniques. This section may be closed, then, with the characterization of such variables as one of the promising and interesting areas for future investigation" (p. 784). The specific effects of these variables remain largely unresearched.

Bijou and Baer (1966) made three recommendations for research of antecedent events: systematic variations of instructions and other statements to determine the nature and range of their effects; elimination of instructions when their effects are not separately evaluated; and separation of the effects of instructions in individual analyses. The call for systematic investigation of antecedent events was echoed in a recent paper by Berman (1973). He noted the need for research of the characteristics of instructions, instructors, instructees, and of factors related to the effects of instructions on instructees.

Yet, there have been differences of opinion among leading researchers of the necessity of researching instructions. Bijou and Baer (1966) commented, "Perhaps it is undesirable for *E* to emulate a deaf-mute when dealing with child *S*s; however, a close approximation to such a practice would seem to be the safest and most economical alternative to an extensive study of the effect of *E*'s statements" (p. 784). Lindsley (1966), on the other hand, has contributed other observations:

> Now the business of talking to your subject: I know four separate operant conditioners who started with animals and then worked full time, committed and dedicated, with people. After the second or third year, they are usually pretty much de-ratified. One of these de-ratification criteria that I observed was that they sidled up to me at a meeting and said, "Ogden, now what are you doing about instruction? I mean what do you tell your subjects when you bring them in the room?" I said, "Well, that all depends on the subjects."
>
> "But, I mean," he said, "you don't do it all without instructions, do you?"
>
> I said, "Well, no."
>
> He said, "Well, did you ever tell them what to do in the room? . . ."
>
> And I said, "Well sure, if I wanted a baseline of discrimination to measure a drug effect, I don't waste 50 hours of acquisition without instruction to make that."
>
> He said, "Well Skinner says that you don't end up with the same kind of behavior."
>
> But I said that I couldn't tell the difference; maybe not using instructions is just a superstition. . . . I am and I think probably some others are a little more realistic and a little more relaxed about how much instruction they have or have not given to subjects. Here again is an example of no longer being afraid of the control of our own behavior to the extent that we are frightened of the influence of our instructions on the control of another variable that is much larger. Although we could measure instruction effects at the level we are working, they are minimal. (pp. 41–42)

The controversy here is the *relative* contribution of antecedent and consequent stimuli to behavior control—Lindsley also recognizes the importance of antecedent events (see Lindsley 1964, 1971). Two points deserve consideration in addition to the call for more research on antecedent stimuli. First, it seems clear that instructions are not effective following a history of absence of consequences for compliance (e.g., Ayllon and Azrin 1964; Bucher 1973; Schutte and Hopkins 1970). The lack of interest in instructions may have followed in part from the observation of their ineffectiveness with problem learners who apparently had histories of nonreinforcement for compliance and reinforcement for noncompliance (e.g., Haring and Phillips 1962) and the exponentially greater power of consequences with these same individuals in early research. Second, instructions may be included as part of a procedural "package" in applied research; they need not *always* be eliminated or analyzed separately for their effects. Nevertheless, further research is needed if ineffective instructions and needless consequences are to be eliminated.

Other Cognitive and Motor Skills

In a few studies, the effects of various environmental manipulations on aggregate academic responses (e.g., spelling, arithmetic, and reading combined) have been investigated. For example, Chadwick and Day (1971) showed that combined tangible and social reinforcers could be used to increase underachieving students' aggregate academic responses, and Lovitt and Curtiss (1969) found that the aggregate academic response rate of a child with school difficulties increased when he was allowed to arrange his own contingencies of reinforcement. Lovitt (1973*b*) has presented several cases demonstrating that children with learning and behavioral disabilities can be taught self-management skills, findings that may have broad implications for the development of independence in handicapped individuals. In the area of productive thinking, Covington (1970) and Payne (1974) have suggested ways in which behavior modification techniques may be used to increase cognitive skills. Reinforcement techniques have, in fact, been used to develop new or creative responses of young children in activities such as painting (Goetz and Salmonson 1972) and block-building (Goetz and Baer 1973). Dmitriev (1974) has presented a number of cases in which she and her colleagues have used behavior modification methods to develop perceptual-motor and cognitive skills in young handicapped children. The application of reinforcement was reported by Sachs and Mayhall (1972) to be effective in improving the motor performance of an eighteen-year-old athetoid cerebral palsied girl. Lovitt (1967*b*, 1967*c*, 1968*b*, 1968*c*) and Mira (1968, 1969) have devised measurement techniques for assessing the preference of learning disabled and other handicapped children for certain visual and auditory stimuli. Their research may have important implications for the identification and scheduling of high probability behaviors as well as for the assessment of attention and preference.

Areas of Needed Research

It is quite obvious that one cannot at this juncture consider any area of the curriculum to have been thoroughly researched using behavior modification techniques; the methods of applied behavior analysis have only recently been turned toward the assay of academic learning. Application of these methods to the analysis and remediation of academic deficits should pay dividends at an increasing rate as research findings accumulate. The dividends from behavioral research will be greatest if such investigation is characterized by systematic replication, longitudinal studies, ecological management, and generalizable procedures.

Systematic replication demands that a researcher conduct a series of studies in which the findings of one investigation lead to the next experiment. An area of investigation is chosen, and important questions in the area are addressed in an organized, sequential set of probes. The alternative is direct replication, in which little or nothing is varied from experiment to experiment, or haphazard research in which data must be obtained from disparate sources and pieced together. The work of Lovitt and his research group has provided a particularly good model of systematic replication in the analysis of academic behavior. Lovitt and Esveldt (1972), in presenting several of their studies, provided the following analogy: "Direct replication can be likened to the repeated rereading of one chapter of a book. Presumably the reader increases his knowledge of the content of that particular chapter with each rereading. Systematic replication is analogous to reading an entire book in that the first chapter gives meaning to the second, the second to the third, and so on, until, finally, when the reader finishes all the chapters, a message comprised of many constituent elements emerges" (p. 311).

The need for longitudinal studies was mentioned earlier in this chapter. As Cruickshank (1974) has observed, past and current educational research funding priorities have worked against the conducting of longitudinal studies, but until such research is done, little will be known of the real value of special education programs. The behavioral theory of cognitive learning outlined by Staats and his associates can be completed only by studies in which the acquisition of cognitive skills is measured over a period of years. Comparative data regarding cognitive development in normal and learning disabled children over the course of childhood are needed if truly adequate remedial and preventive instructional procedures are to be developed.

Behavior modification research should not be directed only to the academic and social deficits of children—appropriate intervention should, ideally, be applied to each of the multifarious facets of the child's psychosocial ecology. Such talk of research of ecological management is nonsensical in the absence of effective means for changing individual variables—an absence that has been painfully obvious in much of education (Kauffman 1974). However, as empirical evidence accumulates that behavior can be changed, and as behavior modification techniques gain wider acceptance, research of ecological management will seem less to be a pipe dream of impotent theoreticians.

> The widespread acceptance of behavior modification procedures could result in a common assessment and training framework. A multidisciplinary diagnosis, then, could result in more than a pedantic debate. Perhaps if a social worker, for example, obtained direct information about a student by observing him in his home rather than acquiring indirect hints by a telephone conversation with his parents, and perhaps if a school psychologist collected data expressly related to a pupil's math [performance] or peer relationships instead of depending on standardized test results or questionnaires, the two professionals could by their common technique establish better rapport with one another and, more importantly, with the pupil's teacher. Were all therapeutic personnel to measure behavior in a like manner, the jargon and mystique currently associated with each discipline would be eliminated. (Lovitt 1970*b*, p. 158)

Teaching procedures which are generalizable to the regular class should be an outgrowth of behavior modification research in the laboratory or experimental classroom. This implies the development of more systematic and thorough research programs than those characterizing the field today, but the goal should be clinical and field testing operations which eventually will allow the prescription of teaching methods based on sufficient empirical data. Teachers should not be required to test every instructional technique as if it had never been researched. The nefariousness of the "medical model" in special education has often been commented upon, and its supposed pernicious influence in the present context has not escaped notice:

> An analogy could be drawn to the field of medicine in which there is a period of research preceding the popular use of a certain drug. Once the critical properties of the drug are clearly established, widespread dissemination occurs and research efforts diminish. A similar method of operating might then be proposed for education. The analogy, however, is not a valid one. The effects of a certain drug are subjected to ongoing scrutiny. If a drug fails to prevent or cure a particular disorder, the results often become obvious due to the increased incidence of a certain disease. In education, the failure of our procedures may be more subtle (as in the case of a gradual decrement in reading proficiency) and be undetected without adequate scientific methodology. . . . The blind assumption that some stimulus event will reinforce or will continue to reinforce a behavior will be unfounded, but possibly unnoticed in some cases, if experimental controls are not exercised. (Axelrod 1971, p. 339)

Axelrod's analogy is poorly drawn. He has failed to observe differences between research and practice. In both medicine and education, sound practice demands measurement of effects, but not necessarily experimental control. A competent teacher will detect decrements in a pupil's performance, just as a competent physician will detect his patients' responses to drugs. Experimentation is required only when the expected outcome of treatment is not obtained or when the efficacy of new or modified practices is under scrutiny. The idiosyncratic responses of individuals to certain interventions underscore the indispensability of measurement for the competent practitioner, but they are a cause for research only in experimental settings where treatment methods are devised and tested. Admittedly, much additional research will be required before educational prescriptions can be written with confidence, but a properly drawn medical analogy would serve education well:

> No competent physician fails to monitor the effects of his treatment procedures. In cases of serious illness or hospitalization data regarding the patient's status are recorded daily; and in cases where intensive care is necessary, data are recorded continuously. When attending a minor illness for which there is a predictable outcome with a treatment of proven effectiveness, the physician typically leaves assessment of the outcome to the patient himself (or his caretakers) or makes simple postchecks of the results.
>
> Special educators who employ the behavioral model emphasize daily recording of behavior, postchecks, and continuous observation, depending on the demands of the situation. However, techniques for modifying or recording behavior are certainly no more thoroughly tested than basic medical procedures, and many prescriptions for classroom intervention are now typically written with limited confidence. As the learning model develops, the criteria for using specific procedures for monitoring intervention effects should more closely approximate those of the medical model. (Kauffman and Hallahan 1974, p. 100)

Regarding the most appropriate topics for future research, the field can only be characterized at this time as in the beginning stages of development. Only the simplest behaviors in the core academic areas have received even cursory attention. Behavior modification research of complex academic responses such as creative writing, critical reading, and problem solving, and curriculum areas such as science, art, music, geography, physical education, and so on, is almost nil. More detailed analyses are needed in every curriculum area of the ways in which tasks are presented to children, of the ways in which errors are corrected, and of the contingencies arranged for correct responses. Research on instructions and other programmatic variables and setting events is still a promising but mostly ignored area of study.

References

Ayllon, T., and Azrin, N. "Reinforcement and Instructions with Mental Patients." *Journal of the Experimental Analysis of Behavior* 7 (1964): 327–31.

Baer, D. M. "Behavior Modification: You Shouldn't." In *A New Direction for Education: Behavior Analysis 1971,* edited by E. A. Ramp and B. L. Hopkins. Lawrence, Kan.: University of Kansas, Department of Human Development, 1971.

______; Wolf, M. M.; and Risley, T. R. "Some Current Dimensions of Applied Behavior Analysis." *Journal of Applied Behavior Analysis* 1 (1968):91–97.

Bandura, A. *Principles of Behavior Modification.* New York: Holt, Rinehart, & Winston, 1969.

Becker, W. C., ed. *An Empirical Basis for Change in Education: Selections on Behavioral Psychology for Teachers.* Chicago: Science Research Associates, 1971.

Berman, M. L. "Instructions and Behavior Change: A Taxonomy." *Exceptional Children* 39 (1973): 644–50.

Bijou, S. W., and Baer, D. M. "Operant Methods in Child Behavior and Development." In *Operant Behavior: Areas of Research and Application,* edited by W. K. Honig. New York: Appleton-Century-Crofts, 1966.

———; Birnbrauer, J. S.; Kidder, J. D.; and Tague, C. "Programmed Instruction as an Approach to Teaching of Reading, Writing, and Arithmetic to Retarded Children." *Psychological Record* 16 (1966): 505–22.

———; Peterson, R. F.; and Ault, M. H. "A Method to Integrate Descriptive and Experimental Field Studies at the Level of Data and Empirical Concepts." *Journal of Applied Behavior Analysis* 1 (1968): 175–91.

———; Peterson, R. F.; Harris, F. R.; Allen, K. E.; and Johnston, M. S. "Methodology for Experimental Studies of Young Children in Natural Settings." *Psychological Record* (1969): 177–210.

Birnbrauer, J. S.; Wolf, M. M.; Kidder, J. D.; and Tague, C. "Classroom Behavior of Retarded Pupils with Token Reinforcement." *Journal of Experimental Child Psychology* 2 (1965): 219–35.

Bradfield, R. H. "Precision Teaching: A Useful Technology for Special Education Teachers." *Educational Technology* 10(8) (1970): 22–26.

Bricker, W. A., and Bricker, D. D. "A Program of Language Training for the Severely Language Handicapped Child." *Exceptional Children* 37 (1970): 101–11.

Brigham, T. A.; Finfrock, S. R.; Breunig, M. K.; and Bushell D. "The Use of Programmed Materials in the Analysis of Academic Contingencies." *Journal of Applied Behavior Analysis* 5 (1972): 177–82.

———; Graubard, P. S.; and Stans, A. "Analysis of the Effects of Sequential Reinforcement Contingencies on Aspects of Composition." *Journal of Applied Behavior Analysis* 5 (1972): 421–29.

Bucher, B. "Some Variables Affecting Children's Compliance with Instructions." *Journal of Experimental Child Psychology* 15 (1973): 10–21.

Campbell, D. D. "Typewriting Contrasted with Handwriting: A Circumvention Study of Learning-Disabled Children." *Journal of Special Education* 7 (1973): 155–68.

Campbell, D. T., and Stanley, J. C. *Experimental and Quasi-Experimental Designs for Research.* Chicago: Rand McNally, 1963.

Cautela, J. R. "Covert Processes and Behavior Modification." *Journal of Nervous and Mental Disease* 157 (1973): 27–36.

Chadwick, B. A., and Day, R. C. "Systematic Reinforcement: Academic Performance of Under-Achieving Students." *Journal of Applied Behavior Analysis* 4 (1971): 211–19.

Clark, M.; Lachowicz, J.; and Wolf, M. M. "A Pilot Basic Education Program for School Dropouts Incorporating a Token Reinforcement System." *Behaviour Research and Therapy* 6 (1968): 183–88.

Cohen, M. A.; Gentry, N. D.; Hulten, W. J.; and Martin, G. L. "Measures of Classroom Performance." In *The Improvement of Instruction,* edited by N. G. Haring and A. H. Hayden. Seattle: Special Child, 1972.

Conlon, M. F.; Hall, C.; and Hanley, E. M. "The Effects of a Peer Correction Procedure on the Arithmetic Accuracy for Two Elementary School Children." In *Behavior Analysis and Education—1972,* edited by G. Semb. Lawrence, Kan.: University of Kansas, Department of Human Development, 1972.

Cooper, J. O. "Eliminating Letter and Number Reversal Errors with Modeling and Reinforcement Procedures." Doctoral dissertation, University of Kansas. Ann Arbor, Mich.: University Microfilms, 1970. No. 71-13, 390.

Corey, J. R., and Shamow, J. "The Effects of Fading on the Acquisition and Retention of Oral Reading." *Journal of Applied Behavior Analysis* 5 (1972): 311–15.

Covington, B. V. "Behavior Modification of Productive Thinking." In *Behavior Modification: The Human Effort,* edited by R. H. Bradfield. San Rafael, Calif.: Dimensions, 1970.

Cruickshank, W. M. Foreword. In *Teaching Children with Behavior Disorders: Personal Perspectives,* edited by J. M. Kauffman and C. D. Lewis. Columbus, Ohio: Merrill, 1974.

———; Bentzen, F. A.; Ratzeburg, F. H.; and Tannhauser, M. T. *A Teaching Method for Brain-Injured and Hyperactive Children.* Syracuse, N.Y.: Syracuse University Press, 1961.

Cullinan, D. A.; Kauffman, J. M.; and LaFleur, N. K. "Observational Learning: Research with Implications for Special Education." *Journal of Special Education,* in press.

Davis, M. "Effects of Having One Remedial Student Tutor Another Remedial Student." In *Behavior Analysis and Education—1972,* edited by G. Semb. Lawrence, Kan.: University of Kansas, Department of Human Development, 1972.

Dietz, S. M., and Repp, A. C. "Decreasing Classroom Misbehavior Through the Use of DRL Schedules of Reinforcement." *Journal of Applied Behavior Analysis* 6 (1973): 457–63.

Dmitriev, V. "Motor and Cognitive Development in Early Education." In *Behavior of Exceptional Children: An Introduction to Special Education,* edited by N. G. Haring. Columbus, Ohio: Merrill, 1974.

Drass, S. D., and Jones, R. L. "Learning Disabled Children as Behavior Modifiers." *Journal of Learning Disabilities* 4 (1971): 418–25.

Eaton, M. D., and Lovitt, T. C. "Achievement Tests vs. Direct and Daily Measurement." In *Behavior Analysis and Education—1972,* edited by G. Semb. Lawrence, Kan.: University of Kansas, Department of Human Development, 1972.

Estes, W. K. *Learning Theory and Mental Development.* New York: Academic Press, 1970.

Evans, G. W., and Oswalt, G. L. "Acceleration of Academic Progress Through the Manipulation of Peer Influence." *Behaviour Research and Therapy* 6 (1968): 189–95.

Fargo, G. A.; Behrns, C.; and Nolen, P., eds. *Behavior Modification in the Classroom.* Belmont, Calif.: Wadsworth, 1970.

Fauke, J.; Burnett, J.; Powers, M. A.; and Sulzer-Azaroff, B. "Improvement of Handwriting and Letter Recognition Skills: A Behavior Modification Procedure." *Journal of Learning Disabilities* 6(5) (1973): 25–29.

Felixbrod, J. J., and O'Leary, K. D. "Effects of Reinforcement on Children's Academic Behavior as a Function of Self-Determined and Externally Imposed Contingencies." *Journal of Applied Behavior Analysis* 6 (1973): 241–50.

Ferritor, D. E.; Buckholdt, D.; Hamblin, R. L.; and Smith, L. "The Noneffects of Contingent Reinforcement for Attending Behavior on Work Accomplished." *Journal of Applied Behavior Analysis* 5 (1972): 7–17.

Ferster, C. B., and DeMyer, M. K. " A Method for the Experimental Analysis of the Behavior of Autistic Children." *American Journal of Orthopsychiatry* 32 (1962): 89–98.

———, and Perrott, M. C. *Behavior Principles.* New York: New Century, 1968.

Fleming, D.; Kauffman, J. M.; and Wallace, G. "Reduction of Specific Reading Errors Using Token Reinforcement: Remediation of a Child's Learning Problem." Unpublished manuscript, University of Virginia, 1973.

Franklin, B. [B. F. Skinner]. "Operant Reinforcement of Prayer." *Journal of Applied Behavior Analysis* 2 (1969): 247.

Garcia, E.; Guess, D.; and Byrnes, J. "Development of Syntax in a Retarded Girl Using Procedures of Imitation, Reinforcement, and Modelling." *Journal of Applied Behavior Analysis* 6 (1973): 299–310.

Gentile, J. R.; Roden, A. H.; and Klein, R. D. "An Analysis-of-Variance Model for the Intrasubject Replication Design." *Journal of Applied Behavior Analysis* 5 (1972): 193–98.

Goetz, E. M., and Baer, D. M. "Social Control of Form Diversity and the Emergence of New Forms in Children's Blockbuilding." *Journal of Applied Behavior Analysis* 6 (1973): 209–17.

———, and Salmonson, M. M. "The Effect of General and Descriptive Reinforcement on 'Creativity' in Easel Painting." In *Behavior Analysis and Education—1972*, edited by G. Semb. Lawrence, Kan.: University of Kansas, Department of Human Development, 1972.

Gray, B. B. "Language Acquisition Through Programmed Conditioning." In *Behavior Modification: The Human Endeavor*, edited by R. H. Bradfield. San Rafael, Calif.: Dimensions, 1970.

———; Baker, R. D.; and Stancyk, S. E. "Performance Determined Instruction for Training in Remedial Reading." *Journal of Applied Behavior Analysis* 2 (1969): 255–63.

Grimm, J. A.; Bijou, S. W.; and Parsons, J. A. "A Problem-Solving Model for Teaching Remedial Arithmetic to Handicapped Young Children." *Journal of Abnormal Child Psychology* 1 (1973): 26–39.

Guess, D. "A Functional Analysis of Receptive Language and Productive Speech: Acquisition of the Plural Morpheme." *Journal of Applied Behavior Analysis* 2 (1969): 55–64.

———, and Baer, D. M. "An Analysis of Individual Differences in Generalization between Receptive and Productive Language in Retarded Children." *Journal of Applied Behavior Analysis* 6 (1973): 311–29.

Hall, R. V. *Managing Behavior. Part I, Behavior Modification: The Measurement of Behavior.* Lawrence, Kan.: H & H Enterprises, 1971.

———; Cristler, C.; Cranston, S. S.; and Tucker, B. "Teachers and Parents as Researchers Using Multiple Baseline Designs." *Journal of Applied Behavior Analysis* 3 (1970): 247–55.

———; Fox, R.; Willard, L.; Goldsmith, L.; Emerson, M.; Owen, M.; Davis, F.; and Porcia, E. "The Teacher as Observer and Experimenter in the Modification of Disputing and Talking-Out Behaviors." *Journal of Applied Behavior Analysis* 4 (1971): 141–49.

———; Lund, D.; and Jackson, D. "Effects of Teacher Attention on Study Behavior." *Journal of Applied Behavior Analysis* 1 (1968): 1–12.

Hallahan, D. P., and Cruickshank, W. M. *Psychoeducational Foundations of Learning Disabilities.* Englewood Cliffs, N.J.: Prentice-Hall, 1973.

Haring, N. G., and Hauck, M. A. "Improved Learning Conditions in the Establishment of Reading Skills with Disabled Readers." *Exceptional Children* 35 (1969): 341–52.

———, and Hayden, A. H., eds. *The Improvement of Instruction.* Seattle, Wash.: Special Child, 1972.

———, and Phillips, E. L. *Educating Emotionally Disturbed Children.* New York: McGraw-Hill, 1962.

———, and Phillips, E. L. *Analysis and Modification of Classroom Behavior.* Englewood Cliffs, N.J.: Prentice-Hall, 1972.

Harris, M. B., ed. *Classroom Uses of Behavior Modification.* Columbus, Ohio: Merrill, 1972.

Harris, V. W.; Sherman, J. A.; Henderson, D. G.; and Harris, M. S. "Effects of Peer Tutoring on the Spelling Performance of Elementary Classroom Students." In *Behavior Analysis and Education—1972*, edited by G. Semb. Lawrence, Kan.: University of Kansas, Department of Human Development, 1972.

Hart, B., and Risley, T. "Establishing Use of Descriptive Adjectives in the Spontaneous Speech of Disadvantaged Preschool Children." *Journal of Applied Behavior Analysis* 1 (1968): 109–20.

Hartung, J. R. "A Review of Procedures to Increase Verbal Imitation Skills and Functional Speech in Autistic Children." *Journal of Speech and Hearing Disorders* 5 (1970): 203–17.

Hasazi, J. E., and Hasazi, S. E. "Effects of Teacher Attention on Digit-Reversal Behavior in an Elementary School Child." *Journal of Applied Behavior Analysis* 5 (1972): 157–62.

Hawkins, R. P.; Sluyter, D. J.; and Smith, C. D. "Modification of Achievement by a Simple Technique Involving Parents and Teacher." In *Classroom Uses of Behavior Modification,* edited by M. B. Harris. Columbus, Ohio: Merrill, 1972.

Hewett, F. M. *The Emotionally Disturbed Child in the Classroom.* Boston: Allyn & Bacon, 1968.

Holt, G. L. "Effect of Reinforcement Contingencies in Increasing Programmed Reading and Mathematics Behaviors in First-Grade Children." *Journal of Experimental Child Psychology* 12 (1971): 362–69.

Homme, L. E. "Control of Coverants, the Operants of the Mind." *Psychological Record* 15 (1965): 501–11.

Hopkins, B. L.; Schutte, R. C.; and Garton, K. L. "The Effects of Access to a Playroom on the Rate and Quality of Printing and Writing of First and Second-Grade Students." *Journal of Applied Behavior Analysis* 4 (1971): 77–87.

Jenkins, J. R., and Gorrafa, S. "Superimposing Contracts upon a Token Economy." In *Behavior Analysis and Education—1972,* edited by G. Semb. Lawrence, Kan.: University of Kansas, Department of Human Development, 1972.

Johnson, N. J. A. "Daily Arithmetic Performance Compared with Teacher Ratings, I. Q., and Achievement Tests." In *Operant Conditioning in the Classroom,* edited by C. E. Pitts. New York: Crowell, 1971.

Johnson, S. M., and Bolstad, O. D. "Methodological Issues in Naturalistic Observations: Some Problems and Solutions for Field Research." In *Behavior Change: Methodology, Concepts, and Practice,* edited by L. A. Hamerlynck, L. C. Handy, and E. J. Mash. Champaign, Ill.: Research Press, 1973.

Jones, R. R. "Behavioral Observation and Frequency Data: Problems in Scoring, Analysis, and Interpretation." In *Behavior Change: Methodology, Concepts, and Practice,* edited by L. A. Hamerlynck, L. C. Handy, and E. J. Mash. Champaign, Ill.: Research Press, 1973.

Kauffman, J. M. "Psychoeducational Technology: Criteria for Assessment and Control in Special Education." *Focus on Exceptional Children* 5(3) (1973): 1–5.

———. "Issues." In *Teaching Children with Behavior Disorders: Personal Perspectives,* edited by J. M. Kauffman and C. D. Lewis. Columbus, Ohio: Merrill, 1974.

———; Cullinan, D. A.; Scranton, T. R.; and Wallace, G. "An Inexpensive Device for Programming Ratio Reinforcement." *Psychological Record* 22 (1972): 543–44.

———, and Hallahan, D. P. "Control of Rough Physical Behavior Using Novel Contingencies and Directive Teaching." *Perceptual and Motor Skills* 36 (1973): 1225–26.

———, and Hallahan, D. P. "The Medical Model and the Science of Special Education." *Exceptional Children* 41 (1974): 97–102.

———; Hallahan, D. P.; Payne, J. S.; and Ball, D. W. "Teaching/Learning: Quantitative and Functional Analysis of Educational Performance." *Journal of Special Education* 7 (1973): 261–68.

———; LaFleur, N. K.; Hallahan, D. P.; and Chanes, C. M. "Imitation as a Consequence for Children's Behavior: Two Experimental Case Studies." *Behavior Therapy,* in press.

———, and Scranton, T. R. "Parent Control of Thumb-Sucking in the Home." *Child Study Journal* 4 (1974): 1–10.

———, and Vicente, A. R. "Bringing in the Sheaves: Observations on Harvesting Behavioral Change in the Field." *Journal of School Psychology* 10 (1972): 263–68.

Kazdin, A. E. "Methodological and Assessment Considerations in Evaluating Reinforcement Programs in Applied Settings." *Journal of Applied Behavior Analysis* 6 (1973): 517–31.

———, and Bootzin, B. R. "The Token Economy: An Evaluative Review." *Journal of Applied Behavior Analysis* 5 (1972): 343–72.

Kendall, M. G. "Hiawatha Designs an Experiment." *Journal of Applied Behavior Analysis* 6 (1973): 331–32.

Kerlinger, F. N. *Fundamentals of Behavioral Research.* New York: Holt, Rinehart & Winston, 1964.

Knight, M. F.; Hasazi, S. E.; and McNeil, M. E. "A Home Based Program for the Development of Reading Skills for Preschoolers." In *A New Direction for Education: Behavior Analysis 1971,* edited by E. A. Ramp and B. L. Hopkins. Lawrence, Kan.: University of Kansas, Department of Human Development, 1971.

Krasner, L., and Ullmann, L. P., eds. *Research in Behavior Modification.* New York: Holt, Rinehart, & Winston, 1965.

Kroth, R.; Whelan, R. J.; and Stables, J. M. "Teacher Application of Behavior Principles in Home and Classroom Environments." *Focus on Exceptional Children* 2(1) (1970): 1–10.

Kunzelmann, H. P.; Cohen, M. A.; Hulten, W. J.; Martin, G. L.; and Mingo, A. R. *Precision Teaching—An Initial Training Sequence.* Seattle: Special Child, 1970.

Lahey, B. B.; McNees, M. P.; and Brown, C. C. "Modification of Deficits in Reading for Comprehension." *Journal of Applied Behavior Analysis* 6 (1973): 475–80.

Leitenberg, H. "The Use of Single-Case Methodology in Psychotherapy Research." *Journal of Abnormal Psychology* 82, (1973): 87–101.

Lindsley, O. R. "Direct Measurement and Prosthesis of Retarded Behavior." *Journal of Education* 147 (1964): 62–81.

______. "Discussion of Dr. Homme's Paper." In *The Learning Environment: Relationship to Behavior Modification and Implications for Special Education,* edited by N. G. Haring and R. J. Whelan. *Kansas Studies in Education* 16(2) (1966): 40–47.

______. "Precision Teaching in Perspective: An Interview with Ogden R. Lindsley." *Teaching Exceptional Children* 31 (1971): 114–19.

Lovaas, O. I. "A Program for the Establishment of Speech in Psychotic Children." In *Early Childhood Autism: Clinical, Educational, and Social Aspects,* edited by J. K. Wing. New York: Pergamon, 1966.

______. "A Behavior Therapy Approach to the Treatment of Childhood Schizophrenia." In *Minnesota Symposia on Child Psychology, Vol. I,* edited by J. P. Hill. Minneapolis: University of Minnesota Press, 1967.

______; Freitag, G.; Gold, V. J.; and Kassorla, I. C. "Recording Apparatus and Procedure for Observation of Behaviors of Children in Free Play Settings." *Journal of Experimental Child Psychology* 2 (1965): 108–20.

______; Koegel, R.; Simmons, J. Q.; and Long, J. S. "Some Generalization and Follow-Up Measures on Autistic Children in Behavior Therapy." *Journal of Applied Behavior Analysis* 6 (1973): 131–65.

Lovitt, T. C. "Assessment of Children with Learning Disabilities." *Exceptional Children* 34 (1967*a*): 233–39.

______. "Free-Operant Preference for One of Two Stories: A Methodological Note." *Journal of Educational Psychology* 58 (1967*b*): 84–87.

______. "Use of Conjugate Reinforcement to Evaluate the Relative Reinforcing Effects of Various Narrative Forms." *Journal of Experimental Child Psychology* 5 (1967*c*): 164–71.

______. "Operant Conditioning Techniques for Children with Learning Disabilities." *Journal of Special Education* 2 (1968*a*): 283–89.

______. "Relationship of Sequential and Simultaneous Preference as Assessed by Conjugate Reinforcement." *Behaviour Research and Therapy* 6 (1968*b*): 77–81.

______. "Operant Preference of Retarded and Normal Males for Rate of Narration." *Psychological Record* 18 (1968*c*): 205–14.

______. "Behavior Modification: The Current Scene." *Exceptional Children* 37 (1970*a*):85–91.

______. "Behavior Modification: Where Do We Go from Here?" *Exceptional Children* 37 (1970*b*):157–67.

———. "Applied Behavior Analysis Techniques and Curriculum Research. Report submitted to the National Institute of Education, 1973*a*.

———. "Self-Management Projects with Children with Behavioral Disabilities." *Journal of Learning Disabilities* 6 (1973*b*):138–50.

———, and Curtiss, K. A. "Effects of Manipulating an Antecedent Event on Mathematics Response Rate." *Journal of Applied Behavior Analysis* 1 (1968):329–33.

———, and Curtiss, K. A. "Academic Response Rate as a Function of Teacher- and Self-Imposed Contingencies." *Journal of Applied Behavior Analysis* 2 (1969):49–53.

———; Eaton, M.; Kirkwood, M.; and Pelander, J. "Effects of Various Reinforcement Contingencies on Oral Reading Rate." In *A New Direction for Education: Behavior Analysis 1971,* edited by E. A. Ramp and B. L. Hopkins. Lawrence, Kan.: University of Kansas, Department of Human Development, 1971.

———, and Esveldt, K. A. "The Relative Effects on Math Performance of Single- versus Multiple-Ratio Schedules: A Case Study." *Journal of Applied Behavior Analysis* 3 (1970):261–70.

———, and Esveldt, K. A. "A Contingency Management Classroom: Basis for Systematic Replication (Four Studies)." In *The Improvement of Instruction,* edited by N. G. Haring and A. H. Hayden. Seattle: Special Child, 1972.

———; Guppy, T. E.; and Blattner, J. E. "The Use of Free-Time Contingency with Fourth Graders to Increase Spelling Accuracy." *Behaviour Research and Therapy* 7 (1969):151–56.

———, and Hurlbut, M. "Using Behavioral Analysis Techniques to Assess the Relationship between Phonics Instruction and Oral Reading." *Journal of Special Education* 8 (1974): 57–72.

———; Schaaf, M. E.; and Sayre, E. "The Use of Direct and Continuous Measurement to Evaluate Reading Materials and Procedures." *Focus on Exceptional Children* 2 (1970): 1–11.

———, and Smith, J. O. "Effects of Instructions on an Individual's Verbal Behavior." *Exceptional Children* 38 (1972):685–93.

MacDonough, T. S., and McNamara, J. R. "Design-Criteria Relationships in Behavior Therapy Research with Children." *Journal of Child Psychology and Psychiatry and Allied Disciplines* 14 (1973): 271–82.

McKerracher, D. W. "Alleviation of Reading Difficulties by a Simple Operant Conditioning Technique." *Journal of Child Psychology and Psychiatry and Allied Disciplines* 8 (1967):51–56.

McLaughlin, T. F., and Malaby, J. E. "Development of Procedures for Classroom Token Economies." In *A New Direction for Education: Behavior Analysis 1971,* edited by E. A. Ramp and B. L. Hopkins. Lawrence, Kan.: University of Kansas, Department of Human Development, 1971.

Maloney, K. B., and Hopkins, B. L. "The Modification of Sentence Structure and its Relationship to Subjective Judgments of Creativity in Writing." *Journal of Applied Behavior Analysis* 6 (1973):425–33.

Massad, V. I., and Etzel, B. C. "Acquisition of Phonetic Sounds by Preschool Children." In *Behavior Analysis and Education—1972,* edited by G. Semb. Lawrence, Kan.: University of Kansas, Department of Human Development, 1972.

Medland, M. B., and Stachnik, T. J. "Good-Behavior Game: A Replication and Systematic Analysis." *Journal of Applied Behavior Analysis* 5 (1972):45–51.

Mira, M. P. "Individual Patterns of Looking and Listening Preferences among Learning Disabled and Normal Children." *Exceptional Children* 34 (1968):649–58.

———. Effects of Response Force on Conjugate Rates." *Behaviour Research and Therapy* 7 (1969):331–33.

O'Leary, K. D., and Drabman, R. S. "Token Reinforcement Programs in the Classroom: A Review." *Psychological Bulletin* 75 (1971): 379–98.

———, and Kent, R. "Behavior Modification for Social Action: Research Tactics and Problems." In *Behavior Change: Methodology, Concepts, and Practice,* edited by L. A. Hamerlynck, L. C. Handy, and E. J. Mash. Champaign, Ill.: Research Press, 1973.

———, and O'Leary, S. G., eds. *Classroom Management: The Successful Use of Behavior Modification.* New York: Pergamon, 1972.

Parsons, J. A. "The Reciprocal Modification of Arithmetic Behavior and Program Development." In *Behavior Analysis and Education—1972,* edited by G. Semb. Lawrence, Kan.: University of Kansas, Department of Human Development, 1972.

Payne, J. S. "The Gifted." In *Behavior of Exceptional Children: An Introduction to Special Education,* edited by N. G. Haring. Columbus, Ohio: Merrill, 1974.

Quilitch, H. R., and Risley, T. R. "The Effects of Play Materials on Social Play." *Journal of Applied Behavior Analysis* 6 (1973): 573–78.

Ramp, E., and Hopkins, B. L., eds. *A New Direction for Education: Behavior Analysis 1971.* Lawrence, Kan.: University of Kansas, Department of Human Development, 1971.

Rayek, E., and Nesselroad, E. "Application of Behavior Principles to the Teaching of Writing, Spelling, & Composition." In *Behavior Analysis and Education—1972,* edited by G. Semb. Lawrence, Kan.: University of Kansas, Department of Human Development, 1972.

Reynolds, N. J., and Risley, T. R. "The Role of Social and Material Reinforcers in Increasing Talking of a Disadvantaged Preschool Child." *Journal of Applied Behavior Analysis* 1 (1968):253–62.

Risley, T. R., and Hart, B. "Developing Correspondence between the Non-Verbal and Verbal Behavior of Preschool Children." *Journal of Applied Behavior Analysis* 1 (1968):267–81.

———, and Wolf, M. M. "Establishing Functional Speech in Echolalic Children." *Behaviour Research and Therapy* 5 (1967):73–88.

Romanczyk, R. G.; Kent, R. N.; Diament, C.; and O'Leary, K. D. "Measuring the Reliability of Observational Data: A Reactive Process." *Journal of Applied Behavior Analysis* 6 (1973):175–84.

Rosenthal, T. L., and Whitebook, J. S. "Incentives versus Instructions in Transmitting Grammatical Parameters with Experimenter as Model." *Behaviour Research and Therapy* 8 (1970):189–96.

Ross, A. O. "Behavior Therapy." In *Psychopathological Disorders of Childhood,* edited by H. C. Quay and J. S. Werry. New York: Wiley, 1972.

Ryback, D., and Staats, A. W. "Parents as Behavior Therapy-Technicians in Treating Reading Deficits (Dyslexia)." *Journal of Behavior Therapy and Experimental Psychiatry* 1 (1970):109–19.

Sachs, D. A., and Mayhall, B. "The Effects of Reinforcement Contingencies upon Pursuit Rotor Performance by a Cerebral-Palsied Adult." *Journal of Nervous and Mental Disease* 155 (1972):36–41.

Sailor, W.; Guess, D.; and Baer, D. M. "Functional Language for Verbally Deficient Children: An Experimental Program." *Mental Retardation* 11(3) (1973):27–35.

Sajwaj, T., and Knight, P. "The Detrimental Effects of a Correction Procedure for Errors in a Tutoring Program for a Young Retarded Boy." In *A New Direction for Education: Behavior Analysis 1971,* edited by E. A. Ramp and B. L. Hopkins. Lawrence, Kan.: University of Kansas, Department of Human Development, 1971.

Salzberg, B. H.; Wheeler, A. J.; Devar, L. T.; and Hopkins, B. L. "The Effect of Intermittent Feedback and Intermittent Contingent Access to Play on Printing of Kindergarten Children." *Journal of Applied Behavior Analysis* 4 (1971):163–71.

Schutte, R. D., and Hopkins, B. L. "The Effects of Teacher Attention on Following Instructions in a Kindergarten Class." *Journal of Applied Behavior Analysis* 3 (1970):117–22.

Scriven, M. "The Philosophy of Behavioral Modification." In *Behavior Modification in Education,* edited by C. Thoresen. Seventy-second yearbook of the National Society for the Study of Education, Part I. Chicago: University of Chicago Press, 1973.

Semb, G., ed. *Behavior Analysis and Education—1972.* Lawrence, Kan.: University of Kansas, Department of Human Development, 1972.

Sidman, M. *Tactics of Scientific Research.* New York: Basic Books, 1960.

Skiba, E. A.; Pettigrew, L. E.; and Alden, S. E. "A Behavioral Approach to the Control of Thumbsucking in the Classroom." *Journal of Applied Behavior Analysis* 4 (1971):121–25.

Skindrud, K. "Field Observation of Observer Bias under Overt and Covert Monitoring." In *Behavior Change: Methodology, Concepts, and Practice,* edited by L. A. Hamerlynck, L. C. Handy, and E. J. Mash. Champaign, Ill.: Research Press, 1973.

Skinner, B. F. *Science and Human Behavior.* New York: Free Press, 1953.

———. *Beyond Freedom and Dignity.* New York: Knopf, 1971.

Sluyter, D. J., and Hawkins, R. P. "Delayed Reinforcement of Classroom Behavior by Parents." *Journal of Learning Disabilities* 5 (1972):16–24.

Smith, D. D.; Lovitt, T. C.; and Kidder, J. D. "Using Reinforcement Contingencies & Teaching Aids to Alter Subtraction Performance of Children with Learning Disabilities." In *Behavior Analysis and Education—1972,* edited by G. Semb. Lawrence, Kan.: University of Kansas, Department of Human Development, 1972.

———, and Lovitt, T. C. "The Educational Diagnosis and Remediation of Written *b* and *d* Reversal Problems: A Case Study." *Journal of Learning Disabilities* 6 (1973):356–63.

———, and Lovitt, T. C. "The Use of Modeling Techniques to Influence the Acquisition of Computational Arithmetic Skills in Learning Disabled Children." In *Behavior Analysis and Education—1973,* edited by G. Semb. New York: Appleton-Century-Crofts, in press.

Staats, A. W. "A Case in and a Strategy for the Extension of Learning Principles to Problems of Human Behavior." In *Research in Behavior Modification,* edited by L. Krasner and L. P. Ullmann. New York: Holt, Rinehart, & Winston, 1965.

———. *Learning, Language, and Cognition.* New York: Holt, Rinehart, & Winston, 1968*a*.

———. "A General Apparatus for the Investigation of Complex Learning in Children. *Behaviour Research and Therapy* 6 (1968*b*): 45–50.

———. "Reinforcer Systems in the Solution of Human Problems." In *Behavior Modification in the Classroom.* edited by G. A. Fargo, C. Behrns, and P. Nolen. Belmont, Calif.: Wadsworth, 1970.

———. *Child Learning, Intelligence, and Personality.* New York: Harper & Row, 1971.

———. "Behavior Analysis and Token Reinforcement in Educational Behavior Modification and Curriculum Research." In *Behavior Modification in Education,* edited by C. Thoresen. Seventy-second yearbook of the National Society for the Study of Education, Part I. Chicago: University of Chicago Press, 1973.

———; Brewer, B. A.; and Gross, M. C. "Learning and Cognitive Development: Representative Samples, Cumulative-Hierarchical Learning, and Experimental-Longitudinal Methods." *Monographs of the Society for Research in Child Development* 35(8) (1970): serial no. 141.

———, and Butterfield, W. H. "Treatment of Nonreading in a Culturally Deprived Juvenile Delinquent: An Application of Learning Principles." *Child Development* 36 (1965):925–42.

———; Finley, J. R.; Minke, K. A.; and Wolf, M. M. "Reinforcement Variables in the Control of Unit Reading Responses." *Journal of the Experimental Analysis of Behavior* 7 (1964): 139–49.

———; Minke, K. A.; and Butts, P. "A Token-Reinforcement Remedial Reading Program Administered by Black Therapy-Technicians to Problem Black Children." *Behaviour Therapy* 1 (1970):331–53.

———; Minke, K. A.; Finley, J. R.; Wolf, M. M.; and Brooks, L. O. "A Reinforcer System and Experimental Procedure for the Laboratory Study of Reading Acquisition." *Child Development* 35 (1964):209–31.

———; Minke, K. A.; Goodwin, R. A.; and Landeen, J. "Cognitive Behaviour Modification: 'Motivated Learning' Reading Treatment with Sub-Professional Therapy-Technicians." *Behaviour Research and Therapy* 5 (1967):283–99.

———, and Staats, C. K. "A Comparison of the Development of Speech and Reading Behavior with Implications for Research." *Child Development* 33 (1962):831–46.

———, and Staats, C. K. *Complex Human Behavior.* New York: Holt, Rinehart, & Winston, 1963.

Stephens, T. M.; Hartman, A. C.; and Cooper, J. O. "Directive Teaching of Reading with Low-Achieving First- and Second-Year Students." *Journal of Special Education* 7 (1973):187–96.

Stevenson, H. W. *Children's Learning.* New York: Appleton-Century-Crofts, 1972.

Strang, H. R. "The Automated Instruction of Practical Reading Skills to Disadvantaged Sixth Grade Children" *University of Virginia Education Review* 10(1) (1972*a*):6–12.

———. "An Automated Approach to Remedial Reading." *Psychology in the Schools* 9 (1972*b*):434–39.

———, and George, J. R. "Instrumentation in Monitoring and Recording Human Behavior." In *Observational Methods in the Classroom,* edited by C. W. Beegle and R. M. Brandt. Washington, D. C.: Association for Supervision and Curriculum Development, 1973.

———, and Wolf, M. M. "Automated Reading Instruction in the Ghetto." *Child Study Journal* 1 (1971):187–201.

Sulzer, B.; Hunt, S.; Ashby, E.; Koniarski, C.; and Krams, M. "Increasing Rate and Percentage Correct in Reading and Spelling in a Fifth Grade Public School Class of Slow Readers by Means of a Token System." In *A New Direction for Education: Behavior Analysis 1971,* edited by E. A. Ramp and B. L. Hopkins. Lawrence, Kan.: University of Kansas, Department of Human Development, 1971.

Tawney, J. W. "Training Letter Discrimination in Four-Year-Old Children." *Journal of Applied Behavior Analysis* 5 (1972): 455–65.

Throne, J. M. "Learning Disabilities: A Radical Behaviorist Point of View." *Journal of Learning Disabilities* 6 (1973):543–46.

Ullmann, L. P., and Krasner, L., eds. *Case Studies in Behavior Modification.* New York: Holt, Rinehart, & Winston, 1965.

Wahler, R. G., and Leske, G. "Accurate and Inaccurate Observer Summary Reports." *Journal of Nervous and Mental Disease* 156 (1973):387–94.

Wallace, G., and Kauffman, J. M. *Teaching Children with Learning Problems.* Columbus, Ohio: Merrill, 1973.

Whaley, D. L., and Malott, R. W. *Elementary Principles of Behavior.* New York: Appleton-Century-Crofts, 1971.

Willis, J.; Crowder, J.; and Morris, B. "A Behavioral Approach to Remedial Reading Using Students as Behavioral Engineers." In *Behavior Analysis and Education*—1972, edited by G. Semb. Lawrence, Kan.: University of Kansas, Department of Human Development, 1972.

Winett, R. A., and Winkler, R. C. "Current Behavior Modification in the Classroom: Be Still, Be Quiet, Be Docile." *Journal of Applied Behavior Analysis* 5 (1972):499–504.

Wolf, M. M.; Giles, D. K.; and Hall, R. V. "Experiments with Token Reinforcement in a Remedial Classroom." *Behaviour Research and Therapy* 6 (1968):51–64.

Wolpe, J. *Psychotherapy by Reciprocal Inhibition.* Stanford, Calif.: Stanford University Press, 1958.

———, and Theriault, N. "Francois Leuret: A Progenitor of Behavior Therapy." *Journal of Behavior Therapy and Experimental Psychiatry* 2 (1971):19–21.

Worell, J., and Nelson, C. M. *Managing Instructional Problems: A Case Study Workbook.* New York: McGraw-Hill, 1974.

Zimmerman, B. J., and Pike, E. O. "Effects of Modeling and Reinforcement on the Acquisition and Generalization of Question-Asking Behavior." *Child Development* 43 (1972):892–907.

Zimmerman, E. H., and Zimmerman, J. "The Alteration of Behavior in a Special Classroom Situation." *Journal of the Experimental Analysis of Behavior* (1962):59–60.

Editors' Note: In Volumes 1 and 2 there have been presentations of various educational strategies for dealing with the child with learning problems. The thrust to educate the child with learning problems, however, must be an interdisciplinary effort. In recent years, the use of drugs has been advocated to combat learning problems of children. In particular, success has been claimed in the pharmaceutical treatment of distractible and hyperactive children. Accompanying the use of drugs, however, there has arisen a growing concern with a variety of social and medical issues associated with drug therapy. In this chapter, Dr. Kornetsky reviews research related to the use of drugs in the treatment of the learning problems of children.

Conan Kornetsky, Ph.D., is Professor of Psychiatry (Psychology) and Pharmacology at Boston University School of Medicine. Formerly, he was a Research Scientist at the National Institute on Mental Health, Bethesda, Maryland. He is a fellow of the American Psychological Association, the American College of Neuropsychopharmacology, a member of the American Society for Pharmacology and Experimental Therapeutics and the Collegium Internationale Neuro-psychopharmacologicum. His major research contributions have been in the field of drug addiction, schizophrenia, and the effects of drugs on behavior in both animals and man. In recent years, Dr. Kornetsky has been interested in the effects of drugs on immature organisms and has been involved in animal research on the prenatal effects of drugs on the behavior of the offspring.

11

Minimal Brain Dysfunction and Drugs

CONAN KORNETSKY

Most teachers find a certain joy and satisfaction in teaching most students. However, since the time of the first classroom there probably have always been a few children who seem to be unable to learn or do not seem to want to learn. This has been the special problem of the educator, and in recent years society has been turning to the use of various pharmacological agents as adjuncts to the educational process in some children. The use of drugs has not been without its problems. Its detractors have pointed out that drugs are being used as substitutes for good teaching practices, for keeping the difficult child "doped-up," that such drug use leads to drug abuse, and that it is part of a plan of the majority to enslave the minority.

The physician who is asked by parents to treat their child because of a behavior disorder is faced with a difficult problem. The putative pathological condition may not be pathological in the manner that physicians define *pathology*. The condition is not easily defined as when the presenting symptoms are fever and an inflamed throat. The physician is confronted with a pattern of behavior in which the degree of abnormality is relative to the total behavioral manifestations of a child who comes from a particular background and social class.

For many children in our society the first recognition of a behavior problem is by the teacher. As our social and educational programs improve the physician will be asked, if not compelled, to attend to children who have rarely been seen by a physician. These are children whose mothers did not seek out a physician from the moment of conception, whose prenatal care was not instituted until the mother was in labor, whose contact with physicians may have only been in a hospital emergency room, and whose mothers are not aware of the latest (not necessarily the best) child rearing practices. The fact that a child is hyperactive or withdrawn in the classroom

The author is a Research Scientist Awardee, MH 1759 from the National Institute of Mental Health. The writer would like to acknowledge and thank Ms. Marjorie O'Connell, Dr. Richard Marcus, and Mr. Robert Markowitz for their aid in the preparation of this chapter.

or does not learn may, in many instances, be more of a social problem than one of psychopathology or pathology or organic disease.

Despite the difficulties in diagnosis the point of view that will be presented in this chapter is that drugs are useful in some children with certain types of learning disabilities. They are not a panacea and they can *never* substitute for good teaching practices.

For the most part the drugs that have been employed in the treatment of the condition called minimal brain dysfunction (MBD) have been those classified as central nervous system (CNS) stimulants. The term "minimal brain dysfunction" (MDB) was adopted by a conference held under the auspices of the U.S. Department of Health, Education and Welfare and the National Easter Seal Society for Crippled Children and Adults (Public Health Service Publication 1966). See below for a detailed description for the use of the term MDB. The two most common CNS stimulants used are the amphetamines and methylphenidate (Ritalin). There have been some clinical reports of the usefulness of some of the phenothiazine drugs—drugs used in the treatment of schizophrenia—as well as some of the drugs used in the treatment of depression. The latter two classes of drugs are not classified as CNS stimulants, though the antidepressant drugs do have some similarity in mechanism of action with the amphetamines.

The present chapter will discuss the syndrome called minimal brain dysfunction, the pharmacology of the drugs used in treating MBD, the effects of the drugs on the MBD child, and finally the socio-political implications of drug therapy. No attempt is made to be all-inclusive. The reader is referred to the following reviews for further reading on the use of drugs in children—Grant (1962); Eisenberg (1966); Millichap and Fowler (1967); Millichap (1968); Werry (1968); Fish (1968); Cole (1969); Conners (1971); and Millichap (1973) —and to a recent book by Wender (1971) and a report of the New York Academy of Sciences (De La Cruz, Fox, and Roberts 1973) for detailed reviews of the various aspects of MBD.

THE PHARMACOLOGY

Amphetamines

The amphetamines belong to the general class of compounds called sympathomimetic amines. Drugs of this group have actions, more or less, in the peripheral nervous system that are similar to those seen when the sympathetic branch of the autonomic nervous system is stimulated (see below).

There is evidence that sympathomimetic drugs were used in China five thousand years ago. The herb *ma huang* (Ephedra vulgaris) has been continually used for many medicinal purposes including the treatment of respiratory diseases (Leake 1958). Approximately seventy-five years ago ephedrine was isolated from *ma huang*. At that time it was believed to be too toxic a compound and was not used for clinical purposes. It was not until 1925 that ephedrine was rediscovered by Chen and Schmidt who introduced the compound into Western medicine (Levy and Ahlquist 1965).

Ephedrine was quickly accepted as the drug of choice for the symptomatic relief of bronchial asthma. It was far superior to epinephrine, the prototype of the sympathomimetic amines, which has many more centrally stimulating effects as well as having a much shorter duration of action than ephedrine.

Attempts to make a synthetic substitute for ephedrine resulted in the synthesis of amphetamine in 1927. Amphetamine was given the trade name of Benzedrine by Smith, Kline and French Laboratories, and in 1932 the Benzedrine inhaler was introduced for the symptomatic relief of respiratory infections.

The stimulating effects of amphetamine on the central nervous system were first described by Alles (1933). He observed that it antagonized the hypnotic effects of anesthetics in animals and that it caused insomnia in man. Prinzmetal and Bloomberg (1935) described the clinical use of the drug in the treatment of narcolepsy.

There are three amphetamines currently used: the racemic form which is known as amphetamine, dextroamphetamine (*d*-amphetamine), and methamphetamine. Of the three the dextro form has the greatest amount of central nervous system stimulating properties, with methamphetamine falling somewhere between amphetamine and *d*-amphetamine in central stimulating properties. The racemic form (amphetamine) has the most potent peripheral actions. Most abuse of amphetamines is with methamphetamine. The dextro form is the amphetamine of choice for the treatment of the MBD child. Although the drug is usually given by the oral route it is available in injectable form, with methamphetamine more commonly administered parenterally (by injections).

As mentioned earlier, the amphetamines fall into the broad class of compounds called sympathomimetic amines and share many of their classic effects (for a detailed discussion of sympathomimetic drugs and their actions see Innes and Nickerson 1970). In general, when the sympathetic branch of the autonomic nervous system is stimulated there is dilatation of the pupils, rise in blood pressure, increase in heart rate, constriction of blood vessels, variability in cardiac output, and the relaxation of intestinal muscles. Amphetamines will cause many but not necessarily all the effects of sympathetic nervous system stimulation. It is important to recognize that the effects of amphetamine are dose-related, and many actions seen at high doses are not manifested at low or moderate doses.

The amphetamines cause an increase in blood pressure. Although heart rate is often increased, the opposite effect has been observed. Large doses may cause cardiac arrhythmias as well as an increase in respiratory rate.

One of the characteristic actions of the sympathomimetic amines is relaxation of smooth muscle (involuntary muscle). Although the bronchial muscles are relaxed after amphetamine, the effect is not sufficient to be of therapeutic value. There is a contractile effect on the urinary bladder sphincter which can be sufficient to cause pain and difficulty in micturation. This action has led to the occasional use of amphetamines in the treatment of enuresis. The action on the gastrointestinal tract will vary with the state of motility of the gut. If the activity is high, amphetamines may cause relaxation and reduction in enteric motility. If there is already relaxation of the gut, the opposite effect may result.

The main effects of the amphetamines are on the central nervous system. They will counteract the depressant effects of barbiturates and anesthetics. They cause an increase in motor activity, hypersensitivity to stimuli, and insomnia. They counteract feelings of fatigue, increase alertness, and often give the drug taker a feeling of well-being.

One of the primary clinical uses of amphetamine is to decrease appetite. The appetite-depressant effects of amphetamine were first described by Nathanson in 1939. The weight loss caused by the use of amphetamine is almost completely the result of a reduction in food intake. Changes in basal metabolism, digestive processes, or water balance are not significant enough to cause the loss of weight seen after chronic use. It is believed that these anorectic effects are due to the action of the amphetamines on those centers of the brain directly involved with appetite control. Although the exact mechanism for this action is not known, a great deal of research has implicated portions of the hypothalamus.

A question that is often asked concerning the CNS stimulants is whether or not they will enhance performance. Although it is clear that the amphetamines will improve all types of performance that are impaired for such reasons as boredom or fatigue, it is not clear that they can enhance performance above that seen in the interested, motivated, unfatigued subject. Smith and Beecher (1959, 1960) studied the performance of trained athletes and found enhancement in both swimming and running speed. Although it could be argued that these are fatiguing athletic events and the drug simply counteracted the effects of fatigue, these investigators found that performance in field events was improved after amphetamine. Although a weight thrower expends a great deal of energy, the expenditure is brief. In all of these experiments the facilatory effect was slight but statistically significant. The mean percent improvement in swimming time was only 1 percent. For a competitive athlete a 1 percent improvement is enough to break a world record. These investigators did not find consistent improvement in similar studies in untrained volunteers.

Amphetamines will often impair the performance of well-functioning motivated subjects (Kornetsky 1958). This impairment may be a function of a lowering of the threshold for sensory input so that instead of the drug focusing attention, it causes an increase in sensory input that is not relevant to the task. It is clear that the amphetamines will enhance performance that is impaired due to sleep loss. In all the experiments in which there is enhancement of performance, the facilitation is slight. Laties and Weiss (1967), in reviewing the literature on performance enhancement after amphetamines, point out that if performance can be improved by amphetamine, independent of simple fatigue and boredom, performance can also be improved by careful manipulation of the variables that control behavior.

Acute toxic effects of amphetamine usually consist of a greater magnitude of its usual pharmacologic actions. Except in highly amphetamine-sensitive individuals, toxic actions are usually the result of excessive dose. An overdose will result in restlessness, tremor, hyperactive reflexes, irritability, insomnia, confusion, anxiety, and occasionally hallucinations and delirium. Cardiovascular effects may include marked increases in blood pressure, though hypotension is not unknown, arrhythmias, anginal pain, dry mouth, nausea, vomiting, and diarrhea. Death from an overdose is preceded by convulsions and coma. The chronic toxic effects are similar to those seen after acute toxic doses except that the manifestation of psychotic-like behavior is much more common. The psychosis resembles an acute paranoid schizophrenic state.

Tolerance to the central stimulating effects of amphetamine develops with chronic use. Chronic nonclinical use of the drug is characterized by the taking of larger and larger doses in order to overcome the decrease in effects due to the developing tolerance.

In addition to the use of the amphetamines in treating the MBD child, amphetamines are used in the treatment of obesity, depressive states, fatigue, and narcolepsy. For a review of the use of amphetamines the reader is referred to Cole (1969).

Methylphenidate Hydrochloride (Ritalin)

Methylphenidate is considered the drug of choice in the treatment of the MBD child by many clinicians (Millichap 1973) because of its putative lesser tendency to cause anorexia. Methylphenidate is a mild CNS stimulant. It has many of the same sympathomimetic actions of the amphetamines. However, respiration and blood pressure seem to be affected less than with amphetamines at doses that cause central stimulation.

Magnesium Pemoline (Cylert)

Pemoline is a CNS stimulant that is structurally distinguishable from amphetamine and methylphenidate. Despite this difference it does cause many of the same side effects seen with the other CNS stimulants used in the treatment of MBD. The most common side effects are anorexia and insomnia. As of this writing, it has only been approved for investigational use for the treatment of the hyperkinetic syndrome in the United States. It is very likely that it will soon receive approval by the FDA for clinical use. It has received approval for clinical use in the United Kingdom in the treatment of the MBD child.

Phenothiazines

The phenothiazines are a class of compounds used mostly in the treatment of schizophrenic patients. Although some success has been reported with these compounds in the treatment of the MBD child, they have proved to be significantly poorer as therapeutic agents in the treatment of the hyperkinetic child.

The two most commonly used drugs of this class have been chlorpromazine (Thorazine) and thioridazine (Mellaril). These drugs are not CNS stimulants and seem to make use of their central depressant effects in decreasing hyperkinesis. The most common side effect seen in the MBD child treated with phenothiazines is drowsiness; however, these drugs are capable of causing a number of other side effects—some of which are only bothersome, such as dry mouth and nasal stuffiness, while others such as skin rash, jaundice, extrapyramidal effects, and blood dyscrasias may be dangerous to life. As far as this writer is aware these more severe effects have not been reported in the MBD child treated with phenothiazines. The lack of serious side effects may be due to the relatively low doses of phenothiazines used as compared to doses used in the treatment of the schizophrenic patient and/or the fact that relatively few MBD children have been treated with these drugs and the incidence of serious complications is rare.

Chlordiazepoxide (Librium)

Chlordiazepoxide is a minor tranquilizer used primarily for the treatment of anxiety. It is a member of a class of drugs called benzodiazepines. Two other drugs of this class are extensively used in the treatment of the anxious patient. These are diazepam (Valium) and oxazepam (Serax). In addition to their putative anti-anxiety properties the benzodiazepines have skeletal muscle relaxing properties. The major side effects are drowsiness and ataxia. More severe but less frequent side effects are nausea and skin rash.

Antidepressants

The antidepressant that has been most commonly used in the treatment of MBD is imipramine (Tofranil). Among the side effects of imipramine are dry mouth, nasal stuffiness, hypotension, constipation, and urine retention. The latter effect led to its use in the treatment of enuretic children. The incidence of side effects is relatively high with this drug. In one study reviewed by Millichap (1973) side effects were observed in nineteen of fifty-two children given the drug.

Summary

In a number of studies reviewed by Millichap (1973) it was clear that methylphenidate or amphetamine were superior, both in therapeutic outcome and in many cases in terms of fewer side effects than the other drugs used. It must be remembered that drug effects are dose related—that is, the larger the dose the greater the effect. This is true for the therapeutic action of the drug as well as the unwanted side effects. The ideal medication will produce the wanted therapeutic action with no or a minimum of side effects. Some side effects are not dose related but are due to the idiosyncratic responses of an individual to a drug. Also, it must be remembered that not all individuals show the same sensitivity to drugs. Some patients will respond therapeutically at relatively low doses while others require larger doses. This holds true not only for the therapeutic action but also for the side effects of a drug. Often a patient will not respond to one drug or will have excessive side effects but will respond very favorably to another drug that is quite similar in action.

MINIMAL BRAIN DYSFUNCTION

Behavior

The MBD syndrome has come to be used synonymously with the constellation of symptoms and signs that has been called hyperkinesis. The term hyperkinesis (also hyperkinesia) literally means pathological excessive motion. Clinically MBD refers to children who are characterized by restlessness and hyperactivity, distractibility and poor attention span, low frustration tolerance and emotional lability, as well as aggressive behavior. MBD is not associated with low intelligence; however, there are learning or behavioral impairments. These deviations will manifest themselves by various combinations of perceptual, conceptual, language, or memory problems.

The difficulty with the above description of the MBD syndrome is that the terms used to define the characteristics are terms used to describe, to a lesser or greater degree, the behavior of all children at some time. That is, the normal child will not manifest all of these characteristics at the same time, but the normal child shows some hyperactivity or distractibility, exhibits emotional lability, or may have had difficulty with learning. This use of terms that describe most children at some time probably has led to a great deal of confusion, the overdiagnosing of MBD, as well as the failure to recognize it in many cases.

The syndrome may be organized as dysfunction in the following areas of behavior: motor activity and coordination, attention and cognitive function, impulse control, interpersonal relations, and emotionality. The child may not show equal dysfunction in all of these areas of behavior, but the extent of dysfunctioning will be consistent and severe so that parents usually report a long history of disturbed behavior. Parents report that the child was active and restless during infancy, stood and walked early, "and then, like an infant King Kong, burst the bars of his crib asunder and sallied forth to destroy his parents' house" (Wender 1971, p. 12). He would often break his toys, and it was often a struggle for the parents to preserve the physical integrity of the household from the inadvertent assault of the child. Colic during infancy as well as sleep disturbances and feeding problems have been reported (Stewart *et al.* 1966). Increase in motor activity is often accompanied by increase in verbal activity that lacks a focus. Many of the children exhibit significant incoordination, the two left hands and two left feet syndrome. However, there are many reported histories of MBD children with good athletic ability. Although many walk at an early age, they have a history of being described as clumsy. The child is slow to learn to tie his shoelaces or ride a two-wheeled bicycle, and buttons are a challenge. The child's handwriting is usually poor.

The MBD child seems unable to concentrate and maintain attention. The child does not engage in the same activity for any length of time and quickly moves from one thing to another. Failure to attend in the classroom situations is often labeled "daydreaming" by teachers. The "daydreaming" is not characterized by a richness of fantasy but is more often the anticipation of activities once released from the confines of the school. Poor performance in school may be a function of this seeming inability to focus attention or concentrate; however, these may be learning difficulties associated with dyslexia among the MBD children.

Although learning difficulties are one of the most common difficulties of MBD children, poor performance in school is not diagnostic of MBD. Unfortunately, there are many reasons "why Johnny won't learn" besides the possibility of MBD. Wender (1971, p. 16) states, without documentation, that one-half to two-thirds of MBD children manifest learning difficulties in school and "that among children with normal intelligence and with good school experience MBD is a very frequent source of academic difficulty." Among children diagnosed as dyslexic, a heterogeneous group, the single most common subgroup consists of children with MBD. Unfortunately, the specific data to confirm this statement of Wender is not available, except that repeated studies have shown that poor school performance is one of the most characteristic behaviors of the MBD child.

MBD children often show marked differences in emotionality and impulse control as compared to normal children. They are often reckless and seem to show no concern for their own safety. This leads to frequent injuries and reports that the children are accident prone. They show a low level of tolerance to frustration, often responding violently to small frustrations. They often show evidence of emotional problems as manifested in irritability, acute anxiety, aggressiveness, depression, and a lack of responsiveness to external controls. Whether or not these symptoms are primary is unknown. However, it is more likely that the lack of impulse control may be primary, and this, plus many of the other factors, certainly could lead to some of the emotional symptoms seen.

Neurological Signs

Benton (1973) has characterized MBD as "a behavioral concept with neurological implications." Benton points out that a patient can have clear evidence of a disease of the brain without any observable evidence of functional abnormality. However, a child cannot have MBD without behavioral manifestations. Furthermore, the term MBD implies that there is a cerebral abnormality that is the primary basis for the behavior. In this section some of the evidence for central nervous system bases will be discussed for at least some of the children that are called hyperkinetic or MBD.

Many investigators have investigated the possibility of central nervous system pathology. It is generally agreed that there is an increased prevalence of soft neurological signs in the MBD child. One or more of the following soft signs will be revealed in neurological examination of the MBD child: abnormalities of resting muscle tone, some clumsiness of either gross or fine motor movements, hyperactive deep tendon reflexes, extensor plantar responses, abnormal extraocular movements, frequent tics and grimaces, disturbed position sense, choreiform movements, dyskinesias, mild ataxia, minimal gait abnormalities with asymmetries of associated movement, left-right confusion, poor visual motor skills, dysphasia, finger agnosia, and dyslexia. There does not seem to be any relationship between hard neurological signs and the MBD syndrome. Soft neurological signs are slight and often inconsistently present. They are not associated with specific neural pathology. For a more detailed listing of neurological signs see Clements (1966, p. 12).

Soft neurological signs are not diagnostic of MBD. They occur in a relatively high percentage of normal children; however, it is believed that 50 percent of MBD children have such soft signs (Wender 1971, p. 27). Wikler, Dixon and Parker (1970), in a study of twenty-four patient children with twenty-four matched controls, found that twenty of their control children had one or more soft neurological signs. In the patient group soft neurological signs were found in twenty-two of the twenty-four subjects. However, there was a total of ninety-two soft signs in the patients as compared to thirty in the normal group. In the Wikler, Dixon, and Parker study twenty-four children who had no evidence of classical neurological disease and who were referred to a psychiatric outpatient clinic because of a variety of scholastic and behavioral problems were compared to twenty-four matched control children. The age range of the children was five to fifteen years. The control children were matched with the experimental children for age, race, sex, IQ, and socioeconomic class. Of the twenty-four experimental children eleven were definitely considered hyperactive and nine definitely hypoactive. Table 11.1 summarizes the total neurological soft signs reported by this group of investigators. Of interest is that even those children that were non-hyperactive showed a greater incidence of soft neurological signs than did the appropriate matched controls.

Table 11.1
Total Neurological Soft Signs

	Total Soft Signs	
All patients (N = 24)	92	p < .01
All controls (N = 24)	39	
Hyperactive patients (N = 11)	43	p < .01
Matched controls (N = 11)	21	
Non-hyperactive patients (N = 9)	33	p < .01
Matched controls (N = 9)	14	
Hyperactive patients (N = 11)	43	N.S.
Non-hyperactive patients (N = 9)	33	

Abstracted from Wikler, Dixon, and Parker (1970).

EEG Findings

Stevens, Sachdev, and Milstein (1968) and Wikler, Dixon, and Parker (1970), in reviewing the literature going back to 1938, report that there is a repeated finding of EEG abnormality in children with behavior disorders. Most of the children sampled in these studies would meet the criterion of the MBD syndrome. In the studies reported by Stevens *et al.* the range of the mean percent of control children with abnormalities in the EEG went from 5 to 27 percent, while in the experimental series the range of mean percent of behavior disordered children went from 35 to 73 percent. In the actual experimental study of Stevens *et al.* a total of ninety-seven children ages six to sixteen years, all referred to the clinic for behavioral abnormalities, the referring symptoms were, for the most part, compatible with the diagnosis of MBD, though the authors do not make such a diagnosis. The control group consisted of eighty-eight children matched to the experimental group with respect to age and sex, and as closely as possible they were matched for socioeconomic background. Control subjects were obtained from pediatric, medical, and orthopedic outpatient clinics of the hospital as well as from the schools. As in previously reported studies there was a significantly higher incidence of EEG abnormality in the experimental group than in the control group.

The study by Stevens *et al.* (1968) is of interest because of the detailed analysis of the EEG that was made as well as the investigators' search for EEG correlates of specific behavioral patterns. The authors comment that the presence or absence of abnormality in the EEG by itself is of little value in predicting clinical or etiological factors. However, their results suggest that there are relationships between specific behavioral traits, predisposing factors, and specific abnormalities in the EEG. For example, they found slowing of EEG frequencies was associated with hyperactivity, while EEG spike activity was associated with disturbances in attention, time sense, ideation, and finger agnosia.

The Wikler *et al.* (1970) study is somewhat unusual, for not only did it compare behavior problem children with matched controls but it compared hyperactive behavior problem children with non-hyperactive behavior problem children. In addition, this study compared these groups to matched controls. Also unique in the Wikler *et al.* study was that their analyses of the EEG took into account the age differences between the subjects. The primary finding of the study was the emergence of two relatively distinct syndromes. The first is characterized by hyperactive behavior, perceptual motor deficits, high incidence of soft neurological signs, and an EEG with excessive slow activity and abnormal transient discharges. The EEG changes were not age dependent. The second syndrome was similar in terms of soft neurological signs and excessive slow activity in the EEG; however, the latter was age dependent—that is, the amount of slow activity decreased with age. The group was different from the hyperactive group in their lack of hyperactivity and lack of perceptual motor deficits.

Satterfield, Cantwell, Lesser, and Podosin (1972) studied a group of thirty-one children diagnosed as hyperkinetic with a control group of twenty-one children matched for age. The mean age for both groups was 7.75 years with a range of six to nine years. However, the groups differed significantly in IQ, with a WISC score of 104 and 118 for the hyperkinetic children and control children, respectively. They did not match each patient subject with a paired control subject as in the Wikler *et al.* study, and unfortunately they do not describe the method used for obtaining the control group, though they go into a great deal of detail describing the criterion of selection of the hyperkinetic children. Although the method of EEG analysis was different than in the Wikler *et al.* study the results were similar in that there was more slow wave activity in the hyperkinetic children than in the control group.

From the results of various neurological studies of behavior problem children it would seem that it is difficult to accept the view that these children are not suffering from some CNS abnormality. In general, most EEG studies report slowing of the EEG as one of the most characteristic effects, and in the study by Stevens *et al.* (1968) there is strong evidence that specific behavior patterns are correlated with specific abnormalities of the EEG.

One of the clearest experimental demonstrations that the MBD child has a CNS that is abnormally sensitive to stimulation is an experiment by Laufer, Denhoff, and Solomons (1957). Neither they nor, as far as this writer knows, has anyone ever replicated this experiment. Considering the procedure used, the failure to replicate this study is understandable. The thesis was that a dysfunction of the diencephalon is related to the hyperkinetic syndrome. The procedure that was used was the photo-Metrazol technique of Gastant (1950) and Gastant and Hunter (1950). This procedure consists of determining the threshold dose of pentylenetetrazol (Metrazol) per mg/body weight necessary to cause EEG spike-wave bursts and myoclonic jerking of the forearms when the patient was subjected to stroboscopic stimulation. In human and animal subjects the threshold was lower in those subjects in which there was some dysfunction of subcortical areas.

Laufer and his co-workers studied thirty-two children who were diagnosed as hyperkinetic impulse disordered, with eleven of the thirty-two having an unequivocal history of brain organicity. The remaining eighteen children had a diagnosis of behavior disorders other than the hyperkinetic syndrome. The results of this study are of considerable interest, for it is the only study that has come to this writer's attention where there was direct experimental manipulation of the CNS. These investigators found a significant separation between the hyperkinetic and non-hyperkinetic groups (see Table 11.2). Although it was possible to identify the hyperkinetic children with a history of organic brain damage from those without such a history, both groups together differed from the non-hyperkinetic group. Of further interest is that these investigators selected thirteen of the hyperkinetic children who had a low pentylenetetrazol threshold to the

Table 11.2
Comparison of the Number of Hyperkinetic and Non-Hyperkinetic Children That Were Above and Below the Median of the Photo-Metrazol Threshold Dose

	>Median	<Median	
Number of hyperkinetic children	9	23	32
Number of non-hyperkinetic children	16	2	18

Abstracted from Laufer, Denhoff, and Solomons (1957).

photic stimulation and repeated the procedure with and without *d*-amphetamine. The control threshold value in this group was 4.8 mg/kg of pentylenetetrazol, while after *d*-amphetamine the threshold mean was 6.7 mg/kg. This difference was statistically significant. It is unfortunate that these investigators did not do the same *d*-amphetamine experiment with some of their non-hyperkinetic subjects. This additional experiment would have allowed them to determine whether or not a real paradoxical effect exists, at least as far as the excitability of the CNS is concerned.

Etiology

Wender (1971, pp. 37–43; 1972) reviewed the evidence suggesting that the MBD syndrome was due to organic brain damage and/or a genetic factor. He concluded that there are well-documented associations between complications in pregnancy and during birth and the later manifestation of the MBD syndrome. Wender points out that despite this association of the MBD syndrome (as well as other behavior pathology) with complications of pregnancy, most children who could be described as at risk escape such pathology. Why some children seem to escape the possible consequences of this early insult is not presently known. The failure of many children who are at risk due to complicated pregnancy or birth to manifest subsequent behavioral disorders speaks well for the resiliency of the biological system. However, there may be sequelae of this early assault that are either subtle enough that they are not noticed, or it may be that our instruments for measuring human behavior are not sensitive enough to measure these slight impairments. Another possibility is that the early prenatal and perinatal assault may cause specific organic alteration in the CNS, but due to the tremendous redundancy of the biological system, these "lesions" of the CNS are of no significant consequence.

There is reason to believe that specific toxic substances ingested during pregnancy or during early infancy could be responsible for some of the later behavioral manifestations. Two recent reports of studies in rats and mice in which varying concentrations of lead were given to nursing mothers yielded significant changes in the chemistry of the brains (Sauerhoff and Michaelson 1973) and alteration in the behavior (Silbergeld and Goldberg 1973) of the offspring. In the Silbergeld and Goldberg study there was an increase in the motor behavior of the mice who had a high lead content in the diet that could be reversed by the administration to the animal of appropriate doses of *d*-amphetamine, *l*-amphetamine, or methylphenidate (Silbergeld and Goldberg 1974). Phenobarbital not only did not attenuate this hyperactivity of the mice but caused an increase in their activity.

Only a relatively few experiments have studied the effects of prenatal drug administration on the behavior of the developing offspring, but within the past few years there has been increased interest and concomitant increase in research in this area. For the most part, studies of the effects of chemical insult to the gravid animal have been concerned with the incidence of fetal death and the teratogenic effects of drugs. However, in recent years there have been more experiments demonstrating the effects of prenatal drug administration to animals on the later physiology and behavior of the offspring (Kornetsky 1970; Dancis and Hwang 1974) as well as studies demonstrating alterations in the behavior of offspring in which the mothers were fed a diet deficient in some essential nutrient (Shoemaker and Wurtman 1973). The effects on the offspring of gravid animals given drugs are often quite subtle—that is, simple observation of the animal gives no clue as to the presence of some alteration in the behavior. Sometimes the changes in behavior can be seen by the use of a simple activity chamber that objectively measures the amount of movement of the animal, as in the experiments on nursing mice in which the mothers were fed a diet containing lead (Silbergeld and Goldberg 1973). Experiments have made use of more complex behavior than activity, and these have included maze learning as well as other conditioned behavior (Werboff and Kesner 1963; Hoffeld and Webster 1965; Ordy *et al.* 1966; and Golub and Kornetsky 1973). In a series of experiments by Golub and Kornetsky (1973), convulsive thresholds were determined in the offspring by means of the administration of flurothyl. In one experiment, prenatal administration of chlorpromazine resulted in a lower convulsive threshold in the offspring. In another experiment in which the gravid female received low-level electrical stimulation to the reticular formation (that part of the brain concerned with sleep and wakefulness) by means of an electrode surgically implanted prior to mating there was a raising of the convulsive threshold (unpublished data). These experiments indicate that subtle changes in the excitability of the CNS can be achieved by, in some cases, slight interventions in the pregnant animal.

Despite these provocative experiments in animals, it is far from proven that these are models for the MBD syndrome or, for that matter, for any behavioral disturbance seen in man. It may very well be that a variety of childhood behavioral disturbances including MBD can be caused by a variety of prenatal, perinatal, or early dietary deficiencies, but as yet there is no specific type of insult that can be clearly associated with any of the childhood behavioral disorders except those in which there are gross and obvious organic sequelae accompanying the behavioral disorder.

Wender (1971, pp. 40–43) suggests a possible genetic etiology in some instances of MBD. However, he bases this possibility on three clinical observations not documented by published studies. He has observed (1) a "pronounced clustering" within the same family, and (2) an apparent higher incidence of severe psychopathology in the parents of MBD children, (3) a few instances of the syndrome in adopted children whose biological parents had severe psychopathological disturbances. Wender does point out that there seems to be a familial clustering of dyslexia, a specific reading disorder that is often associated with MBD. There are two studies demonstrating such a familial relationship of dyslexia, the most recent published in 1967 (Hallgren 1950, and Frisk *et al.* 1967). Considering the recent increase in the identification and interest in the dyslexic child, it is somewhat surprising that there have not been additional studies on the familial aspects of dyslexia. Dyslexia is a specific reading disability that indicates some failure in cerebral organization, so if there are familial factors it might be relatively easy to identify them. However, MBD is a constellation of symptoms, and what we call MBD may be a number of diseases each with its own etiology. Also, some of those children diagnosed as MBD may not be suffering from anything more than misdiagnosis.

The fact that at least many MBD children respond favorably to stimulant drugs has led some to give this as qualified support for the concept that the disease is due to some biochemical abnormality that is reversed by the drug (Wender 1972). Wender does point out that response to treatment is not proof of etiology since the treatment may reverse abnormalities anywhere "from the primary abnormality through its causal chain." However, despite that qualification he does state that "the drug responsiveness of MBD children does suggest a fairly specific biochemical lesion." If we could then know how amphetamines or other stimulants work in the MBD child we would know the cause of the disorder. However, the specific mechanism of action of amphetamine or other CNS stimulants in decreasing hyperkinetic behavior is not known. Common sense would suggest that a CNS stimulant, if anything, would make the hyperkinetic child worse and the drug of choice would be one of the CNS depressants, i.e., a barbiturate. Laufer and Denhoff (1957), in reviewing the literature on drug treatment of the MBD child, reported that not only are barbiturates ineffective, but they often result in an increase of the behavior problems of the child—the "reaction is so marked as almost to provide a specific diagnostic test itself." Eisenberg (1966), in reviewing the pharmacotherapy of the MBD child, states that barbiturates are contraindicated because of the frequency of paradoxical excitement they may cause in these children.

One of the central clinical characteristics of the MBD child is increased activity. Wender (1972) reports, without giving any data, that many MBD children have difficulty in falling asleep, awake frequently, and sleep for short durations. Despite this apparent hyperarousal, there is some evidence suggesting that they may really be centrally hypoaroused. Stevens, Sachdev, and Milstein (1968) found a relationship between hyperactivity and inattentiveness and the slowing of cortical EEG frequencies recorded from the occipital area. Wikler, Dixon, and Parker (1970) reported that the MBD child showed an increase in low-frequency waves when compared to a control group. Slow waves in the EEG are usually associated with hypoarousal. The impairment on various psychological tests, especially those that putatively measure attention (Conners and Rothchild 1968; Sprague, Barnes, and Werry 1970) could be interpreted as either hypo- or hyperarousal; thus the psychological test data by itself gives us no clue as to the central arousal state of the child.

Further evidence supporting the hypoarousal theory can be found in the results of experiments by Satterfield and Dawson (1971). These investigators studied the galvanic skin response (GSR) in twenty-four hyperkinetic children. The GSR is a measure of the skin's electrical resistance. During periods of excitement the resistance is low, and during periods of calm the resistance is usually high. The GSR gives two resistance measures, the basal resistance level and the change in resistance to a specific stimulus (this is the actual GSR). Satterfield and Dawson found that basal resistance levels were higher than that in a normal control group. A higher basal level is considered a measure of low arousal. They also found that the response to specific stimuli was less than in the controls and that there were fewer spontaneous GSRs than in the normal child. These results showing hypoarousal in the MBD child are surprising, for the basal skin resistance usually correlates negatively with increased motor activity. The lower GSR response to stimuli could be a function of the failure of the MBD child to attend to the specific stimuli used. Another problem in the interpretation of the results of the Satterfield and Dawson study is the use of electrical resistance as their GSR measure. This measure correlates with basal level. More appropriate measures have been used which do not or correlate less with basal levels; however, the study is of interest and it will be important for someone to replicate it.

The question of hypo- versus hyperarousal is important because it does suggest that if the majority of hyperkinetic children are hypoaroused, at least in terms of what is going on in the central nervous system, then there is a dissociation between central arousal and behavioral arousal. This type of phenomenon has been reported with regard to schizophrenic patients (Kornetsky and Mirsky 1966). However, in the case of schizophrenia, it is believed that patients are centrally hyperaroused despite obvious behavioral hypoarousal in many of the patients. The question of hypo- versus hyperarousal has meaning in terms of the response of the child to the therapeutic drugs since most of these are CNS stimulants. It has been generally believed that the therapeutic response to these CNS stimulants is a paradoxical response. However, if the hyperkinetic child is hypoaroused it would suggest that the effect was really not paradoxical. The research data are not completely clear. As previously mentioned, the photo-Metrazol test employed by Laufer *et al.* (1957) suggests that the MBD child is centrally hyperaroused.

The hyperkinetic child may be doing poorly in school, may show the inability to sit still, may show many of the symptoms of the syndrome because the child is continually responding to all types of stimuli, both internal and external. The previously mentioned EEG studies and GSR studies would suggest that this is due to hypoarousal, especially the decrease in spontaneous GSRs of the hyperkinetic child that was reported by Satterfield and Dawson. However, as also mentioned, the latter result may be due to the use of an inappropriate GSR measure. If the hyperkinetic child continually responded to all types of sensory input, attending to a specific task would be precluded. The notion of hyperarousal could be compatible with the effects of CNS stimulants with no paradoxical effect. Thus the paradoxical effect could be considered more apparent than real.

Conners (1966) and Conners and Rothchild (1968) suggest that the action of the CNS stimulants in the hyperkinetic child is not a true paradoxical effect, but merely one of the characteristics of this class of compounds. The CNS stimulants, in addition to their general exciting action, also cause an increase in focused attention. If the drug does have as its major action the ability to focus attention, then responses to interfering stimuli would be decreased and this could result in the child being more amenable to positive reinforcement by both parents and teachers.

Drug Treatment

In this section a review will be made of some of the findings of studies in which drugs have been used in the treatment of the MBD child. Since 1962 there have been a number of reviews of the use of drugs in children (Grant 1962; Eisenberg 1966; Millichap and Fowler 1967; Millichap 1968; Werry 1968; Fish 1968; Cole 1969; Conners 1971; and Millichap 1973).

Although there are probably reports in the literature prior to 1937 in which children with behavior disorders were treated with drugs, most reviews of the field take as their starting point a report by Charles Bradley (1937) on the effects of amphetamine. It is of some historical interest that Matthew Molitch and August Eccles (1937) published a report on the effects of amphetamine on intelligence test scores in behavior problem children the same month and in the same journal in which Bradley's paper appeared. Molitch published another paper on the same subject the same year (Molitch and Sullivan 1937). Despite the apparent simultaneous reports of Bradley and Molitch and his co-workers, Bradley is usually given credit for the discovery of the use of amphetamines in the treatment of behavior problems in children.

Bradley reported in his 1937 paper that Benzedrine (amphetamine) caused a "spectacular" improvement in school performance in fifteen out of thirty children studied. He stated that "a large proportion became subdued without losing interest in their surroundings." This paper was followed a few years later by a report by Bradley and Bowen (1940) on the effects of amphetamine on schoolroom performance. They reported that the drug improved performance in arithmetic, but the drug had only variable effects on spelling performance. The 1940 paper was quickly followed by a report of the use of amphetamine in the treatment of one hundred hospitalized problem children by Bradley and Bowen (1941). The drug caused a subdued type of behavior in fifty-four of the children, failed to have any effect in twenty-one of the children, caused behavioral stimulation in nineteen of the children, and improved school performance in six of the children with no evidence of side effects. Bradley and Bowen suggested that the drug altered the emotional reaction of the children to irritating situations rather than causing any direct effect on the specific behavior problem.

In the two 1937 studies by Molitch and collaborators one of the reports dealt with ninety-three males, aged eleven to seventeen, while the other reported results in which ninety-six males of the same age range were studied. It is not clear from the reports whether or not the subjects used in the first study were included in the second. In these studies, a placebo was used as a control for the medication. Molitch and his co-workers found that more of the subjects showed an improvement in their performance on an intelligence test after receiving amphetamine than after receiving a placebo. No statistical analyses of the data were done in these early studies. This could be considered fortunate or unfortunate, depending on whether or not the reader believes that amphetamines are useful in treating behavior problems.

Also among the early workers with amphetamine in children was Lauretta Bender (Bender and Collington 1942). Although she used no objective measures in her studies, she was impressed with the results achieved with amphetamine and wrote, "Benzedrine is a useful adjunct to the treatment of the neurotic child in that it gives him a feeling of well being and temporarily allows him to feel secure and loved."

Lindsley and Henry (1942) reported the effects of amphetamine, diphylhydantoin (Dilantin), and phenobarbital on the behavior and EEG in thirteen subjects, eight to twelve years of age, with behavior problems. The behavior problems included negativism, hyperactivity, impulsiveness, destructiveness, aggression, and distractibility (all symptoms used to describe the MBD child). Only amphetamine and diphylhydantoin were effective in ameliorating the symptoms, with amphetamine the more effective drug of the two. The EEGs of the children which were considered abnormal prior to treatment did not reflect the improvement in behavior. These early studies did not have all the appropriate controls that are considered a necessary part of a modern clinical study of a drug. Statistical analyses yielding an unacceptable probability level could have precluded work with amphetamines as a pharmacotherapy of behavior problems for many years.

Fisher (1959, p. 202), in reviewing research published in the English language up to that time, reported that out of 159 studies only thirty-three contained "some aspect of experimental design." Among these thirty-three reports, thirteen were primarily studies of adults or of neurological disorders. Of the remaining studies all were flawed to some degree except for three which could be considered acceptable by present standards (Fish 1968). Freeman (1966), in reviewing drug studies on learning in children, concluded that "it remains difficult to draw firm conclusions about the influence of drugs on learning behavior."

Millichap and Fowler (1967) took a more sanguine attitude. They felt that despite the lack of scientific acceptability in many of the studies, some drugs consistently proved to be useful. During the past ten years there have been a number of studies that have met the criteria of the more rigorous clinical pharmacologists and that have demonstrated the effectiveness of these drugs in improving performance on a variety of cognitive, perceptual, and psychomotor tests.

Conners (1971), reviewing some of the problems inherent in research with drugs in children, states that there are special problems that are not found in research with adults plus there are all the difficulties that are found in all drug experimentation in man. Since the research is always within a clinical treatment context, it may not be feasible to meet all the criteria needed for good experimental design. The heterogenicity of the diagnostic characteristics of the children under study may be impossible to control. This leads to a large diagnostic variability, or the experimenter is forced to study very small samples. Conners goes on to state that treatment studies of children are influenced to a greater degree than are such studies of adults by the immediate family as well as the school.

Many of the studies of the MBD child, including some of the earlier ones, looked for organic etiology as well as for the presence of some signs of organicity. As already mentioned, the incidence of soft neurological signs is higher in the MBD child than in comparable control groups. The later studies attempted in a systematic manner to look for specific behavioral deficits in this group of children as well as which specific deficits would be most likely to respond to pharmacotherapy. The MBD syndrome is seen in children with a history of possible organic etiology, including birth trauma, encephalitis, and head injury. However, the syndrome is also seen in children who present no clear cut history of organic factors. It was suggested as early as 1942 that only the more "organic" group responds to pharmacotherapy (Lindsley and Henry 1942, and later by Lytton and Knobel 1959). Subsequent studies have indicated that MBD children with and without organic signs respond to drug treatment; however, there does seem to be a better response to drug therapy in the "organic" than the "nonorganic" MBD children (Epstein *et al.* 1968).

The study by Satterfield *et al.* (1972), previously mentioned with regard to other EEG findings, found that those children diagnosed as hyperkinetic showed a differential response to methylphenidate that was dependent upon their degree of pretreatment arousal as measured by the EEG, skin conductance level, and evoked cortical response. Although their "worst" responders to methylphenidate differed on the various physiological measures as compared to a control group, they also differed in the level of pretreatment arousal.

Although some of the actions of drugs in the hyperkinetic child have already been mentioned, the following section will attempt a more systematic review of the specific effects of drugs in the MBD child. One of the difficulties in a field such as this is that there is the problem of molar versus molecular measurement of change. Conners (1971) points out that the clinican is most interested in the total impact of a drug on the patient. This is a characteristic in those areas of medicine that are most subjective with a less well-defined description of the disease. Although the internist is interested in the total impact of a medication on the subjective feeling of the patient, the internist is most interested in what the drug does to, for example, blood pressure in the hypertense patient. If we are to obtain a real understanding of the therapeutic actions of drugs in the hyperkinetic child it is necessary that we define as objectively as possible the behavior under study and that we know something about the reliability and validity of the behavior measure. Reliability is usually not difficult to determine, nor is it a difficult concept. On the other hand, validity is a most difficult concept in the behavioral and social sciences. The usual definition of *validity* is the degree to which a test is in fact measuring what it is supposed to measure. The difficulty is that the measure is often defined by the test or poorly defined correlates of the test. Thus we can determine reliability but we falter in the area of validity and this is what leads to a great deal of the confusion in social science. Conners (1971) pinpoints another problem that is not unique for those who study the hyperkinetic child—the problem of the relevant behavior to study. Relevance is also related to validity. If, for example, a critical skill for a child is the ability to throw a ball so that it crosses a "plate" within a circumscribed area, and if we find that the ability to accurately throw marbles into a small hole correlates with the ball-throwing behavior, we have a both valid and relevant test. However, if ball throwing is not a necessary skill, we may still have a valid test of ball throwing, but the behavior itself is not particularly relevant. Most of the procedures that deal with the molecular level of behavior are believed to be relevant for the more global behavior that is necessary for successful functioning.

Psychopharmacological studies that have attempted to delineate the action of drugs in the hyperkinetic child or the child with learning disabilities have focused on those actions usually associated with learning skills. In order for anyone to learn or perform any task the first factor that is necessary, but certainly not sufficient, is the ability to attend to the task. Unless attention is maintained in the task at hand no learning or successful performance can take place. Sprague and Sleator (1973), summarizing their own work as well as the work of others, point out that sustained attention is a particular impairment of the hyperkinetic child and that the central stimulants either reverse or ameliorate this deficit. Conners and Rothschild (1968) used a modified form of the Continuous Performance Test (CPT) (Rosvold *et al.* 1956) to study the effects of *d*-amphetamine or methylphenidate on vigilance. The test that he used consisted of a panel with four display buttons arranged in a square with a response button in the center. The corner display buttons presented to the subject color-form patterns (red-blue and horizontal-vertical stripes) at the rate of one every 1.6 seconds.

When the critical stimulus appeared (vertical red pattern) on any of the four corner displays the subject was required to press the center button as quickly as possible. On the average, one out of every six presentations of the four stimuli would have a critical stimulus. Subjects could make omission errors (failure to respond when the critical stimulus was presented) or commission errors (a response to a noncritical stimulus). In addition to errors, latency of response was recorded. A second vigilance task was used in which the child was required to view a series of alphabetic characters passing by a viewing window. In this procedure the critical stimulus was the letter *A*. Each letter was visible for approximately 0.8 seconds. Both *d*-amphetamine and methylphenidate decreased errors of omission and commission on these tasks (Conners 1970; and Conners and Rothschild 1968).

Two more recent studies have made use of the Continuous Performance Test (Sykes, Douglas, and Weiss 1971; and Sykes, Douglas, and Morgenstern 1972). In the first study the performances of hyperactive and control children on the CPT were compared. These investigators found significant relative impairment in the hyperkinetic children which was reversed by methylphenidate. In one of the studies the researchers compared the performance of the children on an experimenter-paced task, the CPT, with a similar task in which the subject had control of the presentation of stimuli. On the experimenter-paced task the hyperkinetic children showed greater impairment relative to the control subjects than on the subject-paced task. This finding further supports the notion that there is a specific attentional dysfunction in the hyperkinetic child that is reversed by the central stimulants. Sprague, Barnes, and Werry (1970) studied the effects on a vigilance task, of methylphenidate or thioridazine in twelve boys with a history of poor school performance. In this study classroom observation was made and performance data on the attention task was obtained. The investigators were interested in whether or not the objective performance data was predictive of what happens in the classroom. The task for the child was to look at a number of pictures presented simultaneously for a brief exposure and then, after a lapse of a few seconds, indicate whether or not a particular picture was among those presented. This is a modification of the Continuous Performance Test. Methylphenidate significantly increased correct responding as well as speed of responding in the hyperkinetic children. In this study methylphenidate was compared to thioridazine (a phenothiazine drug). The latter drug caused the opposite effect, greater numbers of errors and slower response time. In these same children methylphenidate increased the hyperkinetic child's attention in the school situation as measured by a standard observational scale. In addition, appropriate social behavior increased in the classroom.

One of the most commonly reported behaviors of the MBD child is hyperactivity. A study reported by Millichap (1973) in which motor activity was measured before and after treatment with methylphenidate showed a marked reduction in activity following drug administration. However, this reduction in motor activity was most pronounced in those children who prior to treatment had the highest level of motor activity, and some of the children with the lowest activity level even showed an increase in activity when treated with methylphenidate.

Conners (1971) states that impulsive behavior is characteristic of many poor learners and that the drugs may enhance the child's ability to "delay, plan, and respond in a more controlled, integrated manner." He goes on to state that this general "inhibitory" quality of medication "is perhaps the single most important effect on behavior in children." This only slightly qualified unequivocal statement is based on the results that Conners and his colleagues obtained in studies in which the performance of children on the Porteus Maze was enhanced by amphetamine or methylphenidate (Conners, Eisenberg, and Barcai 1967; Conners, Eisenberg, and Sharpe 1964; Conners and Eisenberg 1963; Conners *et al.* 1969; and Conners and Rothschild 1968).

The Porteus Maze requires the subject to find his or her way with a pencil through a maze. Successful performance on the task seems to require some ability to plan ahead, and performance is correlated with other types of intelligence tests. Although the results of these studies are clear, what is not clear is the interpretation. Failure on the test could certainly be attributed to lack of attention, and improvement caused by the drug could be attributed to the drug's ability to focus attention. This seems like a more parsimonious explanation than evoking some "inhibitory" action of the drug.

The CNS stimulants also enhance performance on a variety of motor skill tests. These studies have measured hand steadiness and tapping speed (Conners 1971). Conners suggests that the drugs may allow the child to exert greater control of his motor behavior or possibly increase the motivation of the child to perform well. The best evidence that Conners (1971) gives for the disinhibitory-inhibitory action of stimulants is in the study in which the CPT was used (Conners and Rothschild 1968). The latency of responses to the critical stimulus was longer in the stimulant-treated children than in the placebo-treated children, while errors were greater in the latter group. Thus it was believed that the stimulant drugs reduced impulsive behavior which seems to be one of the characteristics of the MBD child.

There have been few studies, starting with the one of Molitch and Eccles (1937), demonstrating that intelligence test scores of behavior or learning problem children are improved by treatment with CNS stimulants. Zimmerman and Burgermeister (1958) and Knights and Hinton (1968) reported improvement on the WISC performance IQ in children treated with methylphenidate and Epstein, Lasagna, Conners, and Rodriguez (1968) obtained similar results with *d*-amphetamine. Since an intelligence tests taps many functions it is not clear what exactly is being improved with stimulant drugs. In the studies cited above improvement was found only on the performance scale of the WISC. Bradley and Green (1940) stated that in their results there were no striking IQ changes that could be attributed to stimulant drugs. This apparent contradiction in findings could be accounted for by a number of variables that include the sample of subjects used, the IQ test employed, and what is meant by "striking" or "significant" improvement. The early study by Molitch and Eccles (1937), in which a placebo was used, reported an increase in IQ of approximately 18 percent. In the more recent study by Epstein *et al.* (1968), ten hyperkinetic children were tested on the WISC. A cross-over design was used so that subjects were tested after both *d*-amphetamine treatment and placebo treatment. The subjects were divided into two groups—organic and nonorganic—on the basis of the presence or absence of gross neurological abnormalities. Although the organic group showed greater clinical improvement with drug treatment than did the nonorganic group, the organic group had a drop of 13 IQ points on the verbal scale. The nonorganic group showed no change. However, both groups showed an increase in performance IQ (7 points for the organic versus 8 points for the nonorganic). The performance IQ improvement with drug as compared to placebo was statistically significant.

One of the major problems concerning the use of drugs in learning disabilities is the question of whether or not we are dealing with a homogeneous group. The evidence certainly suggests that we are not dealing with a homogeneous group and that many children not specifically diagnosed as MBD children, but who seem to have learning disabilities and/or school behavior problems, seem to respond to the CNS stimulants. Conners, Eisenberg, and Barcai (1967) conducted a systematic study specifically designed to determine whether or not a sample of children with learning problems and who were not specifically selected because of psychiatric and neurological diagnoses would show improvement in school behavior (as determined by the teachers) when given *d*-amphetamine. The study was conducted in two elementary schools in the Baltimore area. The schools were in low-income areas of Baltimore, and all of the fifty-two children studied were black. The authors state that many of the problems reported by the teachers would be related to the "condition of economic and cultural deprivation."

Table 11.3 lists the teacher's referral complaints of the children used in this study. As can be seen, they cover most if not all of the complaints that teachers have with difficult children. Also, many of the behaviors listed have been used to describe the MBD child. The authors used two dependent measures in their study of these children: teacher ratings and a number of objective situational tests. The teachers used a check list divided into three areas: classroom behavior, group participation, and attitude toward authority.

The experimental design called for a crossover treatment of 10 mg *d*-amphetamine or placebo. The study made use of a double-blind procedure. Duration of the study was two months, with active medication for one month and a placebo for one month. The results clearly showed improvement in classroom behavior, group participation, and attitude toward authority that could be attributed to the drug. Although there was improve-

Table 11.3
Examples of Teacher Referral Complaints for Children in the Conners, Eisenberg, and Barcai (1967) Study

1. Poor study habits and always fails written tests. Is shy and slow when called upon for oral recitation but does not seem embarrassed when he cannot respond. Very defiant.
2. Very slow child. Does not respond to stimulation. Not an active member of the class.
3. Very restless and inattentive. Disturbs others most of the time.
4. Very inattentive; has difficulty in concentrating. Is failing in all subjects.
5. Sullen and sulky, frequent behavior problem. Not emotionally or physically adjusted to his class.
6. Has outbursts of temper and laughter. Below average skills in reading and language arts.
7. Very nervous and fidgety child. Below average in reading. Frequently does not participate orally. Stutters a little.
8. Aggressive, bullying, fights constantly. Seeks attention.
9. Inattentive, compulsive, talkative, aggressive, and stubborn.
10. Appears nervous but can keep still long. Quite fidgety, quite talkative. Likes to play with small objects.
11. Very arrogant and defiant. Has little respect for authority. Shows little effort, exhibits very little self-control.
12. Very shy, withdrawn, does not socialize, and is very submissive. Does not engage in classroom activities.
13. Frequently daydreams. Very short attention span.
14. Poor reader. Is restless, playful, often uncooperative. Has very poor work and social habits. Is a disturbing element in classroom. A poor achiever.

ment over time, regardless of the treatment, the improvement seen after drug was significant, independent of the order of the treatments. This study was most carefully designed to rule out teacher expectation of benefits to be derived from drug treatment. The children selected exhibited behavior prior to treatment that teachers could not help but respond to negatively so that the mere presence of a research project in the school in which the teachers were active participants could lead to improvement independent of the drug. This is reflected in the significant order effect. That is, subjects were rated as improved even when receiving a placebo. However, the degree of improvement under placebo conditions was significantly less than that seen under drug treatment. Unfortunately, the authors did not directly compare the behavior scores prior to treatment to those scores after treatment. In addition, there were mean differences in the pretreatment scores between those subjects who received the drug first and those receiving the placebo first. No statistical results are presented to enable the reader to determine if these pretest differences were significant. The authors did make use of a covariance analysis using the pretest scores as the covariate so that their statistical analysis did control for pretest behavior scores.

The crossover design controlled for the possible teacher bias. Conners *et al.* (1967) added one additional important control that is often lacking in crossover design experiments. They did not inform the teachers that such a crossover of treatments would take place. There are various levels of double blindness in drug studies, and if the observers know exactly when critical periods of the experiment occur they cannot be considered blind, unbiased observers.

The authors confront another possible area of influence on the teacher ratings. There is the possibility that side effects caused by *d*-amphetamine would let the teacher know that a child was receiving the active medication and not the placebo. They point out that this type of bias is controlled by the unannounced drug crossover. Furthermore, they indicate that the dosage of *d*-amphetamine used leads to few observable side effects, and that teachers did not report any cues that might have influenced their ratings. This latter point could be argued, because 10 mg of *d*-amphetamine can cause side effects that could be observed by the teachers. The failure of the teachers to report side effects or cues may not necessarily be because they were not observed but could be because they were not specifically asked to report such changes.

Despite some of the minor points of difficulty that could preclude an unequivocal interpretation of the results, this study is a very good example of a well-controlled study of the action of stimulants on school behavior, and it clearly indicates that a student's behavior problems in school can be ameliorated to some degree by a CNS stimulant.

As mentioned previously, many of the referral complaints of the teachers are characteristics of the MBD child. These children, at least in the Conners study, were not diagnosed as MBD children. The sample used consisted of fifty-one out of sixty-one children originally referred by the principals and faculty of two schools. All the children were in the fifth and sixth grades of these two schools. It would have been of interest to know the total number of children in the fifth and sixth grades of these schools. If sixty-one children is a large percentage of the children suffering from MBD in these grades the issue of whether or not society wishes to treat such a large percentage of children in a school with drugs must be considered. The prevalence of behavior problems in the schools as defined by the Conners *et al.* study is probably not as high in our suburban communities as it is in our core cities. Eisenberg (1966), in a study of the epidemiology of reading retardation in the entire sixth grade of a large urban area, found that 28 percent of the children were two or more grades below expected levels and that there was a decrease in the amount of retardation in reading the farther away the child lived from the central city. If reading disabilities and behavior problems decrease the farther one lives from the core city and if we can correctly assume that socioeconomic level correlates with the distance one lives from the core city, then it would strongly indicate a relationship between behavior, learning problems, and socioeconomic level of the family. This by itself does not explain the behavioral problems. Although it is not the scope of this chapter to analyze the manner in which social class or disorganization of the community contribute to the problem, it is important that we confront the fact that at least for the children who come from the same social class as in the Conners *et al.* study, drugs will produce effects that we might prefer to see produced by social change. However, as previously mentioned, the hyperkinetic child is not simply a manifestation of the disorganization of community or family.

Although the treatment of the MBD child with central stimulant drugs decreases attentional and motor disorders that interfere with the child's school performance, they do not directly improve learning. They allow the child to function more adequately in the school situation and thus become more likely to learn. Eisenberg (1972) strongly states that the central stimulants are far superior to other drugs in the treatment of the MBD child. Millichap (1973), in reviewing drug therapy, states that methylphenidate is the treatment of choice. Although the central actions of these two drugs are similar, methylphenidate seems to cause less anorexia. Eisenberg (1972) does point out that a given child will sometimes respond to one and not to the other.

Eisenberg, who was instrumental in stimulating as well as conducting research on the effects of drugs in the MBD child during the 1960s, believes that too many clinicians abandon treatment after only a brief and inadequate trial of medication. He states (1972) that the strategy is to begin with a small dose of 5 mg of *d*-amphetamine or 10 mg of methylphenidate. The drug should be given once each morning with breakfast at two to three-day intervals. If improvement in behavior does not result, the dosage should be increased in like increments. The suggested maximum daily dose is 40 mg for *d*-amphetamine or 80 mg for methylphenidate.

Long-term Effects of Drug Treatment

One of the major concerns of drug treatment of the MBD child is the effect of long-term therapy. Before we can intelligently answer that question we must first ask the question, what happens to the MBD child who is not treated or at least is not treated by means of pharmacotherapy?

Menkes, Rowe, and Menkes (1967) evaluated fourteen of eighteen cases that were previously seen on one or more occasions during the years 1937 and 1946 at The Johns Hopkins Hospital Child Psychiatry Out Patient Clinic. All were originally seen because of hyperactivity and learning difficulties. The selected subjects had exhibited the following behavior that is characteristic of the MBD child: distractibility, short attention span, emotional lability, impulsivity, and a low frustration threshold. In addition the subjects selected presented with hyperactivity and learning difficulties and had one or more of the following neurological signs: poor coordination of fine motor movements, visual-motor deficits, and impaired or delayed development of speech.

At the time of follow-up, the patients ranged from twenty-two to forty years of age. Table 11.4 summarizes some of the presenting factors and

Table 11.4
Summary of the Follow-up Data on 14 Patients
Previously Diagnosed as Hyperkinetic Children

	Neurological Abnormalities					
$\bar{x}$ age	Definite	Probable	None	Not Seen	Institutionalized	Past History of Institutionalization
30.9	8	1	2	3	4	4

Abstracted from Menkes, Rowe, and Menkes (1967).

statuses of the patients at the time of follow-up. For most of the patients, it was reported that "restlessness" had disappeared at about the time of adolescence. However, three subjects reported that they still felt "restlessness." They said that they found it difficult to settle down to anything, including watching television; they changed jobs frequently. Four subjects were institutionalized with a reported diagnosis of psychosis at the time of the follow-up, two others were diagnosed as retarded and supported by their families. Although eight subjects were self-supporting, four of these had spent time in institutions.

There is much wrong with this follow-up study. It would have been a much better study if a matched group of children were also followed up and if the follow-up examinations and testings were done in a double-blind fashion. Despite these major shortcomings, the study strongly suggests that the MBD child who is untreated or treated with non-drug therapies has a poor prognosis.

Other follow-up studies of the hyperkinetic child showed that these problems continue and that the prognosis for good outcome without treatment is poor, though not as bad as in the Menkes *et al.* (1967) study.

Weiss, Minde, Werry, Douglas, and Nemeth (1971) did a five-year follow-up study of sixty-four hyperkinetic children. They found that despite the diminished hyperactivity in adolescence of this group, social, psychological, attentional, and learning disorders persisted. All of the children in the follow-up study had been initially treated with chlorpromazine. At the time of follow-up only five were still taking medication. Most had taken chlorpromazine for one to two years (it should be noted that chlorpromazine is not presently believed to be the drug of choice with the MBD child). Some of the children were treated with other medications, and 20 percent had remained on these for "varying periods." It is of interest that despite a high incidence of academic difficulty at referral only 15 percent of the children received remedial education. The authors point out that "this small percentage reflects the dearth of, rather than any lack of, need for remedial educational facilities."

The findings of this study are interesting, for they certainly suggest long-term persistence of various components of the syndrome despite a decrease in hyperactivity at adolescence. Unfortunately, the results are not unequivocal, since no control group was used, and, though it is unlikely, it could be concluded from this study that treatment for one to two years with chlorpromazine could lead to the long-term poor outcomes. The authors' findings of persistent disability do agree with other observations of the long to persistent sequelae of the syndrome (Mendelson, Johnson, and Stewart 1971). Further evaluation of the data from this group (Minde, Weiss, and Mendelson 1972) considered duration of treatment with chlorpromazine as it related to good or poor outcome. No significant relationship was observed. They did comment on a trend that was far from significant that those who took the drug more than three years were the more poorly adjusted. They state that this confirmed their impression that families who relied on medication alone as therapy were "often dissappointed."

This report, like many in the follow-up area, lacks certain information that would allow at least an approach to unequivocal answers. Some of the subjects received *d*-amphetamine at some time, but the details concerning the number receiving drug and duration of treatment are not given. The study lacks a control group of children matched for significant variables but not diagnosed as hyperkinetic.

The study by Mendelson, Johnson, and Stewart (1971) of eighty-three children between the ages of twelve and sixteen who had been diagnosed as being hyperkinetic two to five years earlier found that about 50 percent of the children were markedly impaired, 25 percent remained unchanged, and the remaining 25 percent fell somewhere in between. Although the authors state that 92 percent of the children had been treated with either *d*-amphetamine or methylphenidate, they do not relate length of therapy with eventual outcome.

Laufer (1973), by means of a questionnaire sent to one hundred former hyperkinetic children treated with amphetamine or methylphenidate, obtained responses to his questionnaire from sixty-six of the subjects. At the onset of drug therapy the children ranged in age from three to thirteen years and at the time of the written inquiry they ranged from fifteen to twenty-six. Although this study is based only on questionnaire material, the responses received do not suggest any dire outcome from long-term use of the central stimulants in the hyperkinetic child. Out of thirty-seven who were nineteen years of age or older, eighteen were employed and 14 were attending college or graduate school. Of fifty-seven subjects who responded to the question regarding experimentation with drugs such as marijuana or LSD only five subjects responded that they had tried these drugs. None reported that they were "hooked." None reported habitual use of stimulants to produce a "high," and only three subjects reported some "experimentation with Dexedrine, Benzedrine, 'Speed,' etc." Twenty of fifty-six respondents reported need of psychiatric help, mostly in early adolescence. However, only five were in psychiatric treatment at the time of the questionnaire. Overall the group was much better adjusted than untreated groups. However, unequivocal answers cannot be given because of the lack of an appropriate control group, the failure to receive responses from thirty-four of the subjects, the failure of subjects to answer all questions, and the failure of the experimenters to see the subjects for verification of the validity of the responses.

Sleator, von Neumann, and Sprague (1974) followed up forty-two hyperkinetic children who had previously been used as subjects in a double-blind study of the effects of methylphenidate on behavior and school performance. Thirteen were followed for two years and twenty-four for one year. During one month of the school year, with teachers and subjects "blind," placebos were given. Seventeen of the forty-two subjects showed deterioration in behavior and school performance during the placebo month. Five of the subjects could not be kept on placebos because of the extreme regression in their behavior. Sleator *et al.* found that eleven of the subjects showed no deterioration when placed on placebos. These investigators state that their findings indicate that physicians treating the hyperkinetic child with stimulants "should periodically try drug-free periods during the school year."

Denhoff (1973), in reviewing the available evidence from the few follow-up studies, concluded that there was no evidence to suggest that properly prescribed stimulant drugs have any long-term harmful effects. Despite the lack of real evidence that the drugs are causing any long-term problems in the children as they mature there is also a paucity of evidence that the drugs cause a real long-term gain in these children. Although there is a wealth of experimental evidence indicating the effectiveness of the medication in some children, we do not know with certainty if ten years after treatment the child who received pharmacotherapy is any better off than the child who did not.

There is one published paper that strongly suggests a negative effect from long-term use of central stimulants in the treatment of the hyperkinetic child (Safer and Allen 1973). In this study the effects of two or more years of treatment were evaluated in forty-nine children (twenty-nine received *d*-amphetamine and twenty received methylphenidate) and compared to fourteen hyperkinetic children who received no medication. These investigators found a significant reduction in growth in weight and height in the drug-treated group when compared to the non–drug-treated group. This suppression of growth was most pronounced in the *d*-amhetamine group and the high dose of methylphenidate group (> 20 mg/day). This study is a replication of an earlier study by these same investigators in which the differences were less but a small sample size was used. Considering the number of children currently receiving central stimulants, it would be most important to have this study repeated. Unfortunately, the subjects in the study were not preselected. The controls were hyperkinetic children whose parents refused to permit the use of medication. Data was presented in terms of percentile changes based upon age and sex norms for a normal population rather than actual weight and height changes. Another point in the paper that makes evaluation difficult is that the number of years between the first and last weights used in the study was significantly larger for the control group than for the drug groups. Despite these shortcomings, this is an important finding, and as mentioned, the study should be repeated.

SOCIAL AND POLITICAL IMPLICATIONS

There has been a great deal of criticism of the use of drugs in the MBD syndrome. Some of the criticism seems well founded in that MBD diagnosis can be abused and that there is a tendency to treat with drugs every child who is difficult to manage in school (Divoky 1973). An article by Charles Witter (1971) summarized the position of those who are against the use of drugs in the treating of MBD children. Witter was staff director for Congressman Cornelius E. Gallagher who was chairman of the House Privacy Subcommittee that held hearings in the fall of 1970 on the use of stimulant drugs in children (see Gallagher 1970). The fears of those who are against the use of drugs in children is succinctly stated by Witter (1971, p. 31): "it must be recognized that drugs are a cheap alternative to the massive spending so obviously necessary to revitalize the public school system." There is the expressed fear of many that the drugs will be used to control black children and the drugs will be a substitute for social change. These fears have led the Black Caucus of the legislative body of the Commonwealth of Massachusetts to sponsor and have passed a law that makes it unlawful to use children in any of the public schools in Massachusetts as research subjects in studies involving the use of drugs. As one worker in the field stated: "The use of drugs in children will not be stopped, the only thing that will be stopped is our finding out how they work" (Cole, personal communication). I do not wish to indulge in a polemic, but it is clear that there is tremendous fear by some that the drugs will be used for control. There may be some who feel that we can substitute drugs for good schools, but the danger that we face is that we overcontrol in the other direction. The evidence is strong that the CNS drugs do work in many of the children with a diagnosis of MBD. What is needed is not a decrease in the research or controls that will not allow the researcher access to the subject, but safeguards for the subjects and more research that will delineate the syndrome. We must know if the drugs are working specifically on some organic bases or the disease of if we are merely suppressing behavior because the CNS stimulants are really not acting as stimulants. We could, for example, control all acting-out behavior by giving large enough doses of depressant drugs such that we would suppress all behavior. The CNS stimulant drugs do not seem to cause a general depression in behavior but seem to allow the child to take better advantage of those factors in the environment that will allow a fuller and more useful life for the child and for society.

Statements such as the following are attributed to Congressman Gallagher by Witter (1971, p. 34): "the suspicion still exists that these programs will be used to modify the behavior of black children to have them conform to white society's norm." If learning to read, if exploiting available educational resources, if allowing the child to become a more adequate person is conforming to "white society's norm," then I would think it would also be the norm of the black community or at least a goal of that community.

Eisenberg (1972) asks the question: "Are these drugs mind control agents to suppress rebellion against excessively rigid teachers and school?" Eisenberg answers his own question by indicating that the answer could only be forthcoming if the drugs were administered to normal children. The implication is that only by the study of the effects of these drugs in the normal child could we determine if the drugs are "mind control agents." If the normal child is stimulated rather than "controlled" by the drug, it would certainly indicate that stimulant drugs cannot be used indiscriminately to control classroom behavior. Eisenberg appropriately points out that giving drugs to the normal child would be a breach of ethics. However, the answer that he gives to the question of "mind control" would not answer the question. The problem is that the question is a political one rather than a scientific or medical one. Certainly large numbers of MBD children improve when given central stimulant drugs. The improvement is not only seen in poor schools in the large urban areas but the improvement is also seen in what could popularly be considered good schools. The improvement in behavior is not only in the school but in the home. Eisenberg states that there is schoolroom behavior that could be classified as overactivity and distractibility in which drugs would be "grossly inappropriate." The first point that he makes is that it is important to make the proper diagnosis. Many of the behavioral symptoms of MBD could be caused by intense anxiety in the presence of a grossly disorganized family situation. The second condition that he lists is that inability to concentrate can be caused by hypoglycemia in a malnourished child who often does not eat breakfast. As mentioned previously, there is the strong possibility that lead poisoning could lead to many of the symptoms seen in MBD. Other factors not mentioned by Eisenberg but ones that should not be overlooked are the possibility of physical illness not caused by malnourishment or physical disabilities, poor hearing, or poor eyesight. As mentioned in the introduction to this chapter, there are many children whose only contact with a physician is in the emergency room of a hospital.

The third point that Eisenberg makes is one concerning the state of the environment in which the child is required to do his learning. Is the classroom inadequate and crowded? Is the teacher competent? It is this writer's opinion that the question of classroom adequacy or inadequacy is not the problem in the case of the MBD child. Certainly an inadequate school will contribute to the problem, but an adequate school will not solve the problem.

The stimulant drugs, as previously mentioned, do not sedate, and, as Eisenberg states, "the myth that stimulants make hyperkinetic children into conforming robots is arrant nonsense." If they do not make "conforming robots" out of the diagnostically confirmed MBD child there is no reason to assume that the stimulants will make "conforming robots" of the non-MBD child who unfortunately goes to a school in which the environment is not conducive to good learning. If we want to make our classrooms quiet, if we want children to lock-step, I would not recommend a stimulant drug. Even if one used depressant drugs such as barbiturates, there would be a significant number of students in the classroom who would manifest excitement unless the dose was sufficiently large to guarantee suppression of behavior.

The answer to the problem of the non-hyperkinetic child who does not learn in school is not with medicine. Learning problems are for the educators to solve. However, for those children who clearly fit the definition of the MBD child—and this usually includes a history of MBD prior to entering school—the answer may not simply be that the teaching is inadequate. That child may be helped with medication, and the failure to adequately diagnose and treat the MBD child is just as criminal as treating the difficult child with drugs rather than good teaching. Just because the hyperkinesis of the MBD child seems to disappear in adolescence is no reason to ignore and fail to treat the syndrome. Maladaptive behavior in the early school years that is not properly handled leads to continued maladaptive behavior in subsequent years. Failure in the second grade, no matter the cause, is much more amenable to remedial help in the second grade than failure in the second grade that is treated in the sixth grade. The teacher with the parent and, if there is suspicion of MBD, with the physician must vigorously not allow the second grade problem to become the third, fourth, or fifth grade problem.

REFERENCES

Alles, G. A. "The Comparative Physiological Actions of d,l-beta-Phenylisopropylamines." *Journal of Pharmacology and Experimental Therapeutics* 47 (1933): 339–54.

Bender, L., and Collington, F. "The Use of Amphetamine Sulfate (Benzedrine) in Child Psychiatry." *American Journal of Psychiatry* 99 (1942): 116–21.

Benton, A. L. "Minimal Brain Dysfunction from a Neuropsychological Point of View." In *Minimal Brain Dysfunction*, edited by F. F. De La Cruz, B. H. Fox, and R. H. Roberts. *Annals of the New York Academy of Sciences* 205 (1973): 29–37.

Bradley, C. "The Behavior of Children Receiving Benzedrine." *American Journal of Psychiatry* 94 (1937): 577–85.

———, and Bowen, M. "School Performance of Children Receiving Amphetamine (Benzedrine) Sulfate." *American Journal of Orthopsychiatry* 10 (1940): 782–88.

———, and Bowen, M. "Amphetamine (Benzedrine) Therapy of Children's Behavior Disorder." *American Journal of Orthopsychiatry* 11 (1941): 92–103.

———, and Green, E. "Psychometric Performance of Children Receiving Amphetamine (Benzedrine) Sulfate." *American Journal of Psychiatry* 97 (1940): 388–94.

Clements, S. D. "Minimal Brain Dysfunction in Children: Terminology and Identification Phase One of a Three Phase Project." NINDB Monograph No. 3, U.S. Department of Health, Education and Welfare, 1966.

Cole, J. O. "The Amphetamines in Child Psychiatry: A Review." *Seminars in Psychiatry* 1 (1969): 174–78.

Conners, C. K. "The Effect of Dexedrine on Rapid Discrimination and Motor Control of Hyperkinetic Children Under Mild Stress." *Journal of Nervous and Mental Disease* 142 (1966): 429–33.

———. "Symptom Patterns in Hyperkinetic, Neurotic and Normal Children." *Child Development* 41 (1970): 667–82.

———. "Drugs in the Management of Children with Learning Disabilities." In *Learning Disorders in Children: Diagnosis, Medication, Education,* edited by L. Tarnopol. Boston: Little Brown, 1971.

———, and Eisenberg, L. "The Effects of Methylphenidate on Symptomatology and Learning in Disturbed Children." *American Journal of Psychiatry* 120 (1963): 458–64.

———; Eisenberg, L.; and Barcai, A. "Effect of Dextroamphetamine on Children: Studies on Subjects with Learning Disabilities and School Behavior Problems." *Archives of General Psychiatry* 17 (1967): 478–85.

———; Eisenberg, L.; and Sharpe, L. "Effects of Methylphenidate (Ritalin) on Paired-Associate Learning and Porteus Maze Performance in Emotionally Disturbed Children." *Journal of Consulting Psychology* 28 (1964): 14–22.

———, and Rothschild, G. H. "Drugs and Learning in Children." *Learning Disorders* 3 (1968): 195–223.

———; Rothschild, G. H.; Eisenberg, L.; Shwartz, L.; and Robinson, E. "Dextroamphetamine Sulfate in Children with Learning Disorders: Effects on Perception, Learning and Achievement." *Archives of General Psychiatry* 21 (1969): 182–90.

Dancis, J., and Hwang, J. C., eds. *Perinatal Pharmacology: Problems and Priorities.* New York: Raven Press, 1974.

De La Cruz, F. F.; Fox, B. H.; and Roberts, R. H., eds. *Minimal Brain Dysfunction. Annals of the New York Academy of Sciences* 205 (1973).

Denhoff, E. "The Natural Life History of Children with Minimal Brain Dysfunction." In *Minimal Brain Dysfunction,* edited by F. F. De La Cruz, B. H. Fox, and R. H. Roberts. *Annals of the New York Academy of Sciences* 205 (1973): 188–205.

Divoky, D. "Toward a Nation of Sedated Children." *Learning* 1 (1973): 6–12.

Eisenberg, L. "The Management of the Hyperkinetic Child." *Developmental Medicine and Child Neurology* 8 (1966): 593–98.

———. "Symposium: Behavior Modification by Drugs. III. The Clinical Use of Stimulant Drugs in Children." *Pediatrics* 49 (1972): 709–15.

Epstein, L. C.; Lasagna, L.; Conners, C. K.; and Rodriguez, A. "Correlation of Dextroamphetamine Excretion and Drug Response in Hyperkinetic Children." *Journal of Nervous and Mental Disease* 146 (1968): 136–46.

Fish, B. "Methodology in Child Psychopharmacology." In *Psychopharmacology, A Review of Progress 1957–1967,* edited by D. H. Efron. Washington, D.C.: USGPO, 1968. Public Health Service Publication No. 1836, pp. 989–1001.

———. "Drug Use in Psychiatric Disorders of Children." *American Journal of Psychiatry* 124 (1968): 31–36.

Fisher, S., ed. *Child Research in Psychopharmacology.* Springfield, Ill.: Thomas, 1959.

Freeman, R. D. "Drug Effects on Learning in Children: A Selective Review of the Past Thirty Years." *Journal of Special Education* 1 (1966): 17–44.

Frisk, M.; Wegelius, B.; Tenhunen, T.; Windholm, O.; and Hortling, H. The Problem of Dyslexia in Teenage." *Acta Paediatrica Scandinavica* 56 (1967): 333–43.

Gallagher, C. E., presiding. "Federal Involvement in the Use of Behavior Modification Drugs on Grammar School Children of the Right to Privacy Inquiry." Hearing before a *Subcommittee of the Committee on Government Operations House of Representatives* 91 Congress, Second Session, Sept. 29, 1970. USGPO.

Gastant, H. "Combined Photic and Metrazol Activation of the Brain." *Electroencephalography and Clinical Neurophysiology* 2 (1950): 249–61.

———, and Hunter, J. "An Experimental Study of the Mechanism of Photic Activation in

Ideopathic Epilepsy." *Electroencephalography and Clinical Neurophysiology* 2 (1950): 263–87.

Golub, M., and Kornetsky, C. "Seizure Susceptibility and Avoidance Conditioning in Adult Rats Treated Prenatally with Chlorpromazine." *Developmental Psychobiology* 7 (1974): 79–88.

Grant, G. R. "Psychopharmacology in Childhood Emotional and Mental Disorders." *Journal of Pediatrics* 61 (1962): 626–37.

Hallgren, B. "Specific Dyslexia ('Congenital Word Blindness'): A Clinical and Genetic Study." *Acta Psychiatrica Scandinavica, Supplement* 65 (1950): 1–287.

Hoffeld, D. R., and Webster, R. L. "Effect of Injection of Tranquilizing Drugs During Pregnancy on Offspring." *Nature* 205 (1965): 1070–72.

Innes, I. R., and Nickerson, M. "Drugs Acting on Postganglionic Nerve Endings and Structures Innervated by Them (Sympathomimetic Drugs)." In *The Pharmacological Basis of Therapeutics,* edited by L. S. Goodman and A. Gilman. New York: Macmillan, 1970.

Knights, R. M., and Hinton, G. "The Effects of Methylphenidate (Ritalin) on the Motor Skills and Behavior of Children with Learning Problems." *Research Bulletin* No. 102, University of Western Ontario, 1968 (as reviewed in Conners 1971).

Kornetsky, C. "Effects of Meprobamate, Phenobarbital and Dextroamphetamine on Reaction Time and Learning in Man." *Journal of Pharmacology and Experimental Therapeutics* 123 (1958): 216–19.

———. "Psychoactive Drugs in the Immature Organism." *Psychopharmacologia* 17 (1970): 105–36.

———, and Mirsky, A. F. "On Certain Psychopharmacological and Physiological Differences between Schizophrenics and Normal Persons." *Psychopharmacologia* 8 (1966): 309–18.

Laties, V. G., and Weiss, B. "Performance Enhancement by the Amphetamines: A New Approach." In Proceedings of the Fifth International Congress of Neuropsychopharmacology, edited by H. Brill, J. O. Cole, P. Deniker, H. Hippius, and P. B. Bradley. Amsterdam, *Exerpta Medica Foundation* (1967): 800–808.

Laufer, M. W. "Long-term Management and Some Follow-up Findings on the Use of Drugs with Minimal Cerebral Syndromes." *Journal of Learning Disabilities* 4 (1971): 518–22.

———, and Denhoff, E. "Hyperkinetic Behavior Syndrome in Children." *Journal of Pediatrics* 50 (1957): 463–74.

———; Denhoff, E.;and Solomons, G. "Hyperkinetic Impulse Disorder in Children's Behavior Problems." *Psychosomatic Medicine* 19 (1957): 38–49.

Leake, C. D., ed. *The Amphetamines.* Springfield, Ill: Thomas, 1958.

Levy, B., and Ahlquist, R. P. "Adrenergic Drugs." In *Drill's Pharmacology in Medicine,* edited by J. R. DiPalma. New York: McGraw-Hill, 1965.

Lindsley, D. B., and Henry, C. E. "Effects of Drugs on Behavior and the Electroencephalograms of Children with Behavior Disorders." *Psychosomatic Medicine* 4 (1942): 140–49.

Lytton, G. V., and Knobel, M. "Diagnosis and Treatment of Behavior Disorders in Children." *Diseases of the Nervous System* 20 (1959): 334–40.

Mendelson, W.; Johnson, N.; and Stewart, M. A. "Hyperactive Children as Teenagers: A Follow-up Study." *Journal of Nervous and Mental Disease* 153 (1971): 273–79.

Menkes, M. M.; Rowe, J. S.; and Menkes, J. H. "A Twenty-five Year Follow-up Study of the Hyperkinetic Child with Minimal Brain Dysfunction." *Pediatrics* 39 (1967): 393–99.

Millichap, J. G. "Drugs in Management of Hyperkinetic and Perceptually Handicapped Children." *Journal of the American Medical Association* 206 (1968): 1527–30.

———. "Drugs in Management of Minimal Brain Dysfunction." In *Minimal Brain Dys-*

function, edited by F. F. De La Cruz, B. H. Fox, and R. H. Roberts. *Annals of the New York Academy of Sciences* 205 (1973): 321–34.

———, and Fowler, G. "Treatment of 'Minimal Brain Dysfunction' Syndromes: Selection of Drugs for Children with Hyperactivity and Learning Disabilities." *Pediatric Clinics of North America* 14 (1967): 767–77.

Minde, K.; Weiss, G.; and Mendelson, N. "A 5-Year Follow-up Study of 91 Hyperactive School Children." *Journal of the American Academy of Child Psychiatry* 11 (1972): 595–610.

Molitch, M., and Eccles, A. K. "Effect of Benzedrine Sulfate on Intelligence Scores of Children." *American Journal of Psychiatry* 94 (1937): 587–90.

———, and Sullivan, J. P. "Effects of Benzedrine Sulfate on Children Taking the New Stanford Achievement Test." *American Journal of Orthopsychiatry* 7 (1937): 519–22.

Nathanson, M. H. "The Central Actions of Beta-amino-amino-propylbenzine (Benzedrine): Clinical Observations." *Journal of the American Medical Association* 108 (1939): 528–31.

Ordy, J. M.; Samorajski, T.; Collins, R. L.; and Rolsten, C. "Prenatal Chlorpromazine Effects on Liver, Survival and Behavior of Mice Offspring." *Journal of Pharmacology and Experimental Therapeutics* 151 (1966): 110–25.

Prinzmetal, M., and Bloomberg, W. "The Use of Benzedrine for the Treatment of Narcolepsy." *Journal of the American Medical Association* 105 (1935): 2051–55.

Public Health Service Publication No. 1415. "Minimal Brain Dysfunction in Children." Washington, D.C.: U.S. Department of Health, Education and Welfare, 1966.

Rosvold, H. E.; Mirsky, A. F.; Sarason, S. B.; Bransome, E. B. Jr.; and Beck, L. H. "A Continuous Performance Test of Brain Damage." *Journal of Consulting Psychology* 20 (1956): 343–50.

Safer, D. V., and Allen, R. P. "Factors Influencing the Suppressant Effects of Two Stimulant Drugs on the Growth of Hyperactive Children." *Pediatrics* 51 (1973): 660–67.

Satterfield, J. H.; Cantwell, D. P.; Lesser, L. I.; and Podosin, R. L. "Physiological Studies of the Hyperkinetic Child: I." *American Journal of Psychiatry* 128 (1972): 1418–25.

———, and Dawson, M. E. "Electrodermal Correlates of Hyperactivity in Children." *Psychophysiology* 8 (1971): 191–97.

Sauerhoff, M. W., and Michaelson, I. A. "Hyperactivity and Brain Catecholamines in Lead-Exposed Developing Rats." *Science* 182 (1973): 1022–24.

Shoemaker, W. J., and Wurtman, R. J. "Effect of Undernutrition on the Metabolism of Catecholamines in the Rat Brain." *Journal of Nutrition* 103 (1973): 1537–47.

Silbergeld, E. K., and Goldberg, A. M. "A Lead-Induced Behavioral Disorder." *Life Sciences* 13 (1973): 1275–83.

———, and Goldberg, A. M. "Lead-Induced Behavioral Dysfunction: An Animal Model of Hyperactivity." *Experimental Neurology* 42 (1974): 146–57.

Sleator, E. K.; von Neumann, A.; and Sprague, R. L. "Hyperactive Children: A Continuous Long-term Placebo-Controlled Follow-up." *Journal of the American Medical Association* 229 (1974): 316–17.

Smith, G. M., and Beecher, H. K. "Amphetamine Sulfate and Athletic Performance. I. Objective Effects." *Journal of the American Medical Association* 170 (1959): 542–57.

———, and Beecher, H. K. "Amphetamine, Secobarbital and Athletic Performance. II. Subjective Evaluation of Performance, Mood, and Physical States." *Journal of the American Medical Association* 172 (1960): 1502–14.

Sprague, R. L.; Barnes, K. R.; and Werry, J. S. "Methylphenidate and Thioridazine: Learning, Reaction Time, Activity and Classroom Behavior in Emotionally Disturbed Children." *American Journal of Orthopsychiatry* 40 (1970): 615–28.

———, and Sleator, E. K. "Effects of Psychopharmacologic Agents on Learning Disorders." *Pediatric Clinics of North America* 20 (1973): 719–35.

Stevens, J. R.; Sachdev, K.; and Milstein, V. "Behavior Disorders of Childhood and the Electroencephalogram." *Archives of Neurology* 18 (1968): 160–77.

Stewart, M. A.; Pitts, F. N. Jr.; Craig, A. G.; and Dieruf, W. "The Hyperactive Child Syndrome." *American Journal of Orthopsychiatry* 36 (1966): 861–67.

Sykes, D. H.; Douglas, V. I.; and Morgenstern, G. "The Effects of Methylphenidate (Ritalin) on Sustained Attention in Hyperactive Children." *Psychopharmacologia* 25 (1972): 262–74.

———; Douglas, V. I.; and Weiss, G. "Attention in Hyperactive Children and the Effects of Methylphenidate (Ritalin)." *Journal of Child Psychology and Psychiatry* 12 (1971): 129–39.

Weiss, G.; Minde, K.; Werry, J. S.; Douglas, V.; and Nemeth, E. "Studies on the Hyperactive Child: VIII. Five Year Follow-up." *Archives of General Psychiatry* 24 (1971): 409–14.

Wender, P. H. *Minimal Brain Dysfunction in Children.* New York: Wiley, 1971.

———. "The Minimal Brain Dysfunction Syndrome in Children." *Journal of Nervous and Mental Disease* 165 (1972): 55–71.

Werboff, J., and Kesner, R. "Learning Deficits of Offspring after Administration of Tranquilizing Drugs to the Mother." *Nature* 197 (1963): 106–107.

Werry, J. S. "Developmental Hyperactivity." *Pediatric Clinics of North America* 15 (1968): 581–99.

Wikler, A.; Dixon, J. F.; and Parker, J. B. Jr. "Brain Function in Problem Children and Controls: Psychometric, Neurological, and Electroencephalographic Comparisons." *American Journal of Psychiatry* 127 (1970): 634–45.

Witter, C. "Drugging and Schooling." *Trans-Action* (July/August 1971): 31–34.

Zimmerman, F. T., and Burgermeister, B. B. "Action of Methylphenidylacetate (Ritalin) and Reserpine in Behavior Disorders in Children and Adults." *American Journal of Psychiatry* 115 (1958): 323–28.

Index

PERCEPTUAL AND LEARNING DISABILITIES IN CHILDREN

VOLUME 2

Research and Theory

was composed in 10-point Datapoint Times Roman and leaded one point with display type in Photon 200 Times New Roman and Univers by Science Press. It was printed offset on 60-pound Old Forge Velvelith by Science Press; Smyth-sewn and bound in Columbia's Bayside Chambray over boards by Vail-Ballou Press; and published by

SYRACUSE UNIVERSITY PRESS
Syracuse, New York 13210